FORENSIC USES OF CLINICAL ASSESSMENT INSTRUMENTS

FORENSIC USES OF CLINICAL ASSESSMENT INSTRUMENTS

EDITED BY

ROBERT P. ARCHER
EASTERN VIRGINIA MEDICAL SCHOOL

Psychology Press
Taylor & Francis Group

New York   London

This book was typeset in 10.5/12 pt. Times, Italic, Bold, and Bold Italic.
The heads were typeset in Engravers Gothic, Zapf Humanist and Revival.

First published by Lawrence Erlbaum Associates, Inc., Publishers
10 Industrial Avenue
Mahwah, New Jersey 07430

Reprinted 2008 by Psychology Press

Psychology Press
Taylor & Francis Group
27 Church Road
Hove, East Sussex BN3 2FA

Library of Congress Cataloging-in-Publication Data

Forensic uses of clinical assessment instruments / edited by Robert P. Archer.
   p. cm.
  Includes bibliographical references and index.
  ISBN 0-8058-5519-X (casebound : alk. paper)
  1. Forensic psychology. 2. Psychological tests.   I. Archer, Robert P.   II. Title.

  RA1148.F559   2006
  614'.15—dc22   2005036676

Printed in the United States of America
10 9 8 7 6 5 4 3 2 1

To Linda R. Archer, Ph.D.,
for her constant encouragement and support

CONTENTS

PREFACE

Forensic psychology is one of the fastest growing areas in the field of psychology, and an increasing number of psychologists are presenting evaluation findings in courtroom settings. For example, psychologists are providing crucial data to the "trier of fact" in the determination of damages in personal injury cases, in the evaluation of parents and children custody cases, and in the assessment of competency to stand trial or of insanity at the time of the commission of an offense in criminal cases. As psychologists and neuropsychologists have made this transition into the courtroom, they have taken with them many of the clinical assessment instruments traditionally used in clinical practice. Although these clinical instruments have proven their value for psychological diagnosis and treatment planning, the utilization of these instruments is often more challenging and complex when applied to such forensic issues as competency to stand trial, competency to waive Miranda rights, and proximate causation in personal injury cases. The purpose of this book is to provide in-depth research-based evaluations of 10 of the most commonly used psychological assessment instruments (or classes or families of instruments) in clinical practice in terms of their uses and limitations when applied in forensic settings.

There is considerable need for a book that can summarize, in a single volume, the extensive research on the use of various popular clinical assessment tools as applied in forensic settings. Although a number of excellent volumes on forensic mental health assessment are available, these focus largely on the legal standards or principles involved in various types of forensic evaluations or on instruments that have been developed specifically for forensic purposes. However, many popular assessment tools originally developed for clinical use are also frequently used in forensic evaluations, and most have received research attention regarding their use for these purposes. These clinical instruments may, however, require some modification in administrative and interpretive techniques when used for forensic purposes. There are currently no texts that explore and summarize these issues, and thus this book meets an important need for the growing number of psychologists engaged in forensic work. Its anticipated audience includes clinical psychologists who may perform forensic evaluations on an occasional basis as well as forensic psychologists who frequently perform civil and/or criminal forensic evaluations in a wide variety of forensic settings. The information in this book should also be appropriate for graduate-level forensic psychology courses.

Despite the increasing body of tests designed to address specific forensic issues, survey findings consistently show that the most frequently used instruments in forensic evaluation are traditional clinical assessment measures. What is the empirical basis for utilizing these instruments to address specific forensic questions? What are the best methods of utilizing these instruments to address such issues? What are the strengths and weaknesses of these instruments for forensic purposes, including their application with various racial or ethnic populations? Because of its rapid and dramatic recent growth, forensic psychology is now a broad and complex field, and it is clear that no single test or testing approach can be used to address adequately the numerous important topics encompassed within this emerging specialty area. Therefore, the current text examines a variety of popular clinical assessment measures that have been used to address psychological and neuropsychological issues with children, adolescents, and adults. Each chapter begins with a short summary of the development of the assessment instrument in its more traditional applications in clinical settings. The remainder of the chapter then provides a summary of the literature on the utilization of the instrument in forensic settings and discusses the types of forensic issues for which that instrument is typically utilized. Each chapter also describes the uses and limitations of the assessment techniques in addressing a variety of forensic issues and presents an illustrative case example.

In the creation of a textbook dedicated to providing an authoritative review of the forensic uses of clinical assessment measures, one critical issue concerns the qualifications of the contributing authors. The authors of the chapters in this book include senior figures in psychological assessment who are uniquely qualified to discuss specific tests covered. They possess a high degree of expertise on the instruments and either have been central in their original development or have made critical contributions to the research base. If an edited textbook is only as strong as the contributors selected to participate in the project, then this book is indeed a robust summary of the current state of traditional psychological instruments as utilized in forensic applications. It is our hope that it will be a useful and practical source of information for psychologists utilizing these instruments in applied forensic assessment work as well as provide sufficiently detailed information to stimulate future research efforts to further clarify the boundaries and characteristics of their application in forensic evaluations.

I would like to specifically acknowledge several individuals who played an invaluable role in the creation of this text. Dr. Eric Zillmer at Drexel University was invaluable in sparking much of the original discussion about the need for this textbook as well as providing me with consistent encouragement during the undertaking of this task. In addition, it was my privilege to work with Dr. Rebecca V. Stredny, the Post-Doctoral Fellow in Forensic Psychology at Eastern Virginia Medical School, whose hard work and diligence in reviewing and preparing chapter materials made the development of this text an enjoyable and collaborative work process. Dr. Meredith Zoby, who recently completed her Clinical Psychology Internship training at the Eastern Virginia Medical School, also played a crucial role in providing the resources necessary to successfully coordinate and facilitate the collection of the chapters. Susan Milmoe was the editor at Lawrence Erlbaum Associates (LEA) who originally encouraged me to submit a proposal for this text and made that submission and the review process exciting and enlightening. Steve Rutter subsequently took on this project in his role as senior editor at LEA and has done an outstanding job of providing me with excellent feedback and encouragement. Steve's detailed and constructive suggestions have greatly improved this work. Finally,

I would like to express my deepest gratitude to my wife, Dr. Linda R. Archer, and my daughter, Elizabeth M. Archer, for their patience and tolerance while I took time away from my family to work on this project.

I conclude this preface with the observation that traditional clinical assessment instruments will continue to play a vital role in forensic psychology in the foreseeable future. This assertion in no way attempts to minimize the important role of specialized forensic instruments; rather, it merely acknowledges that the broader scope of more traditional clinical assessment instruments, combined with the extensive research base typically available for these tests, permits reliable and relevant information to be provided to the "trier of fact." It is the hope of all the contributors to this book that the following eleven chapters will also provide valuable assistance to clinical and forensic psychologists who utilize such assessment instruments in forensic evaluations.

Contributors

Thomas M. Achenbach, Ph.D., is professor of Psychiatry and Psychology and Director of the Center for children, Youth and Families at the University of Vermont. His honors include APA Distinguished Contribution Award for Clinical Child Psychology and the Institute for Scientific Information's Most Highly Cited in the World Psychiatry and Psychology Literature. He developed the Achenbach System of Empirically Based Assessment (ASEBA).

Richard R. Abidin, Ed.D., ABPP clin, Professor emeritus, founder of the Clinical and School of Psychology Ph.D. program, University of Virginia. Founding Editor of Early Education and Development, President of APA Div Children Youth and Families Services, the Society for Clinical Child and Adolescent Psychology, Society for the Study of School psychology.

Robert P. Archer, Ph.D. ABPP, is the Frank Harrell Redwood Distinguished Professor of Psychiatry and Behavioral Sciences, Eastern Virginia Medical School. He was co-author of the MMPI-A manual, Founding Editor of *Assessment* and former Associate Editor of the *Journal of Personality Assessment*. His forensic practice includes psychological evaluation, attorney consultation, and expert testimony.

William G. Austin, Ph.D., is a practicing clinical and forensic psychologist in Northwest Colorado. He is the author of numerous articles on forensic methodology for conducting child custody evaluations that are research-based with practical applications.

Yossef S. Ben-Porath, Ph.D., is a Professor of Psychology at Kent State University. He is the current editor of the journal *Assessment* and former Associate Editor of *Psychological Assessment*. He is the Co-director of the MMPI-2 Workshops and Symposia series, a co-author of the MMPI-2 and MMPI-A manuals, and has an active practice in forensic psychological assessment.

Angela S. Book, Ph.D., completed her Ph.D. in Forensic Psychology at Queen's University in 2004. She went on to postdoctoral research at Carleton University investigating the relationship between psychopathy and deception in interpersonal contexts. She is currently on the faculty of Brock University.

Heather J. Clark, B.A., is a second year M.A. student in Forensic Psychology at Carleton University. Her research interests include assessing psychopathic subtypes in youth and psychopathy in the criminal justice system.

Robert J. Craig, Ph.D., ABPP, Director, Drug Abuse Program, Jesse Brown VA Medical Center, Chicago; Fellow in APA and in the Society of Personality Assessment, Professor, Roosevelt University, Chicago.

James R. Flens, Psy.D., is a clinical and forensic psychologist in private practice in Brandon, Florida, and a principal with Child Custody Consultants a national consulting group. His practice is devoted to child custody related issues, including evaluations, expert testimony and consultation with attorneys.

Adelle E. Forth, Ph.D., is an Associate Professor of Forensic Psychology at Carleton University. She is the senior author of the *Psychopathy Checklist: Youth Version,* co-author of the *Structured Assessment of Violence Risk in Youth,* and co-author of the textbook *Forensic Psychology.* Her research focuses on the assessment of psychopathy, the relation between emotional and cognitive processes and psychopathy, and violence risk assessment.

Heather Green, M.S., is currently enrolled in Drexel University's Clinical Psychology Doctoral Program. Prior to coming to Drexel, Heather earned her Masters Degree in Psychological Services from the University of Pennsylvania and completed her undergraduate study at Amherst College.

Byron A. Hammer, M.D., Medical Director of Child and Family Services, Jefferson Parish Human Services Authority, Medical Director of Juvenile Drug Court, Jefferson Parish, and Medical Director of the Center for Advancement of Early Relationships, Jefferson Parish. Dr. Hammer is also Adjunct Professor, Louisiana State University Health Services Center.

Jill Hayes Hammer, Ph.D., Associate Professor of Clinical Psychiatry, Louisiana State University Health Sciences Center, Department of Psychiatry. Dr. Hammer is the Director of Training for the LSUHSC Clinical Psychology Internship, the neuropsychologist for the HIV Outpatient Clinic in New Orleans, and a forensic psychologist specializing in criminal civil assessment.

Robert Hare, Ph.D., is Emeritus Professor of Psychology, University of British Columbia, and President of Darkstone Research group, Ltd., a forensic research and consulting firm. He has published extensively on psychopathy, its nature, assessment, and implications for mental health and criminal justice. He consults with several agencies, including the FBI and the RCMP.

Christopher J. Hopwood, M.S., is a clinical psychology doctoral student at Texas A&M University, having completed his master's degree at Eastern Michigan University.

His research interest involves personality assessment, psychopathology, and interpersonal process.

David Lachar, Ph.D., Professor, Department of Psychiatry and Behavioral Sciences, University of Texas-Houston Health Science Center, and Director, Psychological Assessment Clinic, University of Texas Mental Sciences Institute. He is the senior author of the *Personality Inventory for Youth,* the *Personality Inventory for Children, Second Edition,* and the *Student Behavior Survey* and fellow, American Psychological Association (Divisions 5,12,37, and 53) and Society of Personality Assessment.

Leslie C. Morey, Ph.D., is a Professor of Psychology at Texas A&M University. He is Associate Editor of *Journal of Personality Assessment,* and past Associate Editor of *Assessment* (1994–2003). He is the author of the Personality Assessment Inventory and the Personality Assessment Screener, and has published over 130 other articles, books, and chapters on the assessment and diagnosis of mental disorders.

Leslie Rescorla, Ph.D., is a Professor in the Psychology Department and Director of the Child Study Institute at Bryn Mawr College. She is a licensed clinical psychologist and a certified school psychologist with a practice serving children and adults. She is a co-author of ASEBA forms and profiles for children and adults and of numerous publications in the area of empirically based assessment of children, adolescents, and adults.

Martin Sellbom, M.A., is a clinical psychology doctoral student at Kent State University. His research interests primarily concern personality conceptualizations and assessment of psychopathy and affective disorders, the construct validity and clinical utility of the MMPI-2 Restructured Clinical Scales, and forensic applications of the MMPI-2. He has won awards at the university and national level for his research accomplishments.

Rebecca Vauter Stredny, Psy.D., completed her pre-doctoral internship and a post-doctoral fellowship in Forensic Psychology at the Eastern Virginia Medical School (EVMS). Her primary clinical and research interests are in personality and forensic assessment.

Irving B. Weiner, Ph.D., ABPP, Professor of Psychiatry and behavioral Medicine, University of South Florida. He has served as Editor of the *Journal of Personality Assessment* (1985–1993) and President of the International Rorschach Society (1999–2005), and is the current President of the Society for Personality Assessment (2005–2007).

Eric A. Zillmer, Psy.D., is the Carl R. Pacifico Professor of Neuropsychology at Drexel University and past President of the National Academy of Neuropsychology (2003). He is the co-author of the popular textbook *Principles of Neuropsychology,* and the neuropsychological assessment procedures the Tower of London-DX and the d2 Test of Attention. He currently serves as Drexel University's Director of Athletics.

Meredith M. Zoby, Psy.D., is currently a Post-Doctoral Fellow at Eastern Virginia Medical School where she has also completed her Pre-Doctoral Internship. She is actively pursuing a career aimed toward the provision of patient care, assessment, and research regarding the delivery of psychological services in medical and legal arenas.

1

INTRODUCTION TO FORENSIC USES OF CLINICAL ASSESSMENT INSTRUMENTS

ROBERT P. ARCHER
REBECCA VAUTER STREDNY
MEREDITH ZOBY

EASTERN VIRGINIA MEDICAL SCHOOL

THE RAPIDLY DEVELOPING FIELD OF FORENSIC PSYCHOLOGY

Although still relatively young, the field of forensic psychology has developed rapidly since the landmark 1962 ruling in *Jenkins v. United States* that facilitated the ability of psychologists to testify as expert witnesses in the courtroom. The origins of forensic psychology, however, can be dated back at least to the early 20th century, when psychological science began contributing to an understanding of the limitations of eyewitness testimony. The scope of psychology's role in the courtroom has expanded significantly since that time, and a number of court rulings have helped define and clarify what is considered admissible testimony from a psychological expert. Psychologists now provide expert testimony to the courts on a wide range of issues, including competency issues in both civil and criminal cases, issues concerning personal injury, and child custody issues. Furthermore, the growth of forensic psychology as a field has fueled the formation of professional societies, specialized journals, and advanced certifications. Based on these developments, forensic psychology has clearly emerged as a defined and well-established specialty practice area for psychologists.

Most of the development of forensic psychology as a field of practice occurred during the latter half of the 20th century. However, Hugo Münsterberg, a German immigrant to the United States in the early 20th century was the first person to promulgate research into forensic psychology in this country and to call for an increased role for psychologists in the legal system (Vaccaro & Hogan, 2004). Münsterberg was an applied psychologist with wide-ranging interests in the areas of memory, fatigue, social influence, and the effects of advertising. He also provided clinical treatment to individuals with mental illness, primarily through the mechanism of autosuggestion. Münsterberg's primary interest in forensic psychology was the reliability of eyewitness testimony, and his research demonstrated the malleability of memory as well as individual differences in the perception of events.

Münsterberg believed that individual experiences and biases played a role in recollection of events, and in 1908 he authored a book, *On the Witness Stand*, that called for increased research into the reliability of eyewitness testimony. The book also explored the phenomenon of false confessions, suggesting that people with strong needs for punishment or compliance were especially likely to admit to crimes they did not commit. Münsterberg called for an increased use of applied psychological knowledge in the courtroom and decried judges and lawyers for relying solely on "common sense." However, his book had minimal immediate impact (Vaccaro & Hogan, 2004). Research on psychological aspects of the legal process continued to be limited and tended to have little effect on the justice system. Moreover, psychologists did not begin to serve widely as expert witnesses until the 1960s. Prior to that time, expert testimony regarding mental disorders was typically provided by physicians, predominantly psychiatrists.

Psychologists began to be qualified as expert witnesses as the direct result of a U.S. Court of Appeals decision in the Washington, D.C., Circuit Court in 1962. In *Jenkins v. United States*, the defense of an individual on trial for housebreaking, assault, and intent to commit rape had originally involved the testimony of three psychologists in support of an insanity defense. At the trial's end, the judge instructed the jury to disregard the psychologists' opinions, ruling that psychologists were not qualified to provide expert opinions regarding mental functioning and disease. When the case was appealed, the circuit court reversed this instruction, stating specifically that individuals with training and expertise in mental disorders, including psychologists, were qualified to provide expert testimony on questions including a defendant's mental condition. This decision provided a basis for allowing psychologists to act as expert witnesses, and since 1962 there has been an exponential rate of growth in the role of psychological science within the justice system, resulting in psychologists' providing expert opinions across a wide and varying spectrum of legal matters.

At the time of the *Jenkins v. United States* decision, the operable federal standard for the admission of scientific knowledge as evidence during legal proceedings (as well as the standard in many states) was the *Frye* standard, determined in the case of *Frye v. United States* in 1923. The standard specified in that case is that testimony is admissible only if "the principle it is based on is sufficiently established to have a general acceptance to the field in which it belongs." This was a fairly restrictive standard that tended to limit the admission into evidence of new or emerging knowledge in a field of study, and efforts to revise or expand this standard occurred with increasing frequency in the 1980s and early 1990s. In the case of *Daubert v. Merrell Dow Pharmaceuticals* (1993), the U.S. Supreme Court stated that the federal rules of evidence were applicable to scientific testimony and laid out several factors that could be used by the courts in making determinations about the admissibility of such testimony. These factors involved the extent to which:

- The theory or technique has been scientifically tested.
- The theory or technique has been subjected to peer review and publication.

- The technique has a known or quantified error rate.
- The theory or technique has found acceptance in the relevant scientific community.

The identification of these factors was intended to create a more flexible test than the *Frye* standard afforded while still allowing the court to exclude testimony in those cases where the methodology underlying the opinion did not meet basic criteria for sound science. The *Daubert* test is now the standard in federal courts, although individual states are not required to apply it. However, many states have begun to employ this standard, although some continue to rely on the *Frye* standard or on other standards in making decisions about the admissibility of expert testimony. The *Daubert* criteria have been further defined by a number of subsequent decisions. These include *General Electric Company v. Joiner* (1997), which permits the court to consider whether an expert has extrapolated inappropriately from an accepted premise to an unfounded conclusion. In *Kumho Tire Co. v. Carmichael* (1999), the U.S. Supreme Court further expanded the *Daubert* factors beyond "scientific" expert testimony to include expert testimony based on "technical" or "other specialized" knowledge, and it also stated that the criteria specified in *Daubert* are not required or exclusive in qualifying experts for testimony. Although the *Daubert* decision expanded the criteria so as to allow expert opinions to rely on new or evolving science, the specific factors identified, in conjunction with the *Kumho Tire* and *Joiner* decisions, directly imply that expert opinions must be based on sound science, thereby requiring forensic experts to be very familiar with the scientific underpinnings of their methods and testimony (Medoff, 2003).

For forensic psychologists, the potential admissibility and usefulness of their conclusions are crucially related to the scientific basis of their testimony. Furthermore, the Ethical Principles of Psychologists and Code of Conduct, published by the American Psychological Association (APA, 2002), underscore the central role of empirical knowledge in formulating professional judgments and the importance of interpreting psychological assessment results within the context of research on the instrument's psychometric properties. The Specialty Guidelines for Forensic Psychologists (Committee on Ethical Guidelines for Forensic Psychologists, 1991) similarly emphasizes scientific knowledge in the selection and utilization of methods and procedures in forensic evaluations. Given these ethical standards, and in order to maximize the likelihood that data and opinions will be both accurate and admissible in court, it is especially important that forensic psychologists choose and utilize test instruments in a manner that is consistent with available scientific evidence and the instruments' intended use.

Currently, forensic psychologists provide expert knowledge to the courts on a wide variety of criminal issues, such as competence to stand trial, and criminal law constitutes a large area of forensic psychology practice. A number of other competencies are relevant to criminal questions as well, such as competence to waive Miranda rights, competence to waive counsel and act as one's own attorney, and competence to be executed. Beyond these competency issues, forensic psychologists working in the criminal arena may also conduct evaluations to assess potential mitigating factors in capital sentencing, offer recommendations for disposition in juvenile delinquency cases, determine mental status or diminished capacity at the time of offense, and provide risk assessments for sex offenders and other potentially violent offenders. The assessment of malingering is an additional significant concern in criminal forensic psychology as well as in most other areas of forensic practice (e.g., personal injury litigation and workers' compensation).

There are a number of civil questions that forensic psychologists may also address. These include competency to release information, consent to medication treatment, refuse hospitalization, and manage one's financial affairs. Other civil matters may involve personal injury or workers' compensation cases, in which a psychologist may address such questions as the extent and proximate cause of psychological or neuropsychological deficits, including conditions like posttraumatic stress disorder. As in criminal forensic practice, personal injury and workers' compensation cases usually involve individuals who are submitting claims that may involve opportunities for external gain, and thus the assessment of the accuracy of an individual's self-report is often of critical importance. Instruments such as the Structured Interview of Reported Symptoms (SIRS; Rogers, Bagby, & Dickens, 1992) and the Test of Memory Malingering (TOMM; Tombaugh, 1996) are used frequently to discern the presence of overreported or malingered symptoms, and the validity scales of the MMPI–2 are relevant to the detection of symptom underreporting and overreporting as well as response patterns that are random or inconsistently accurate.

Another major area of forensic practice is child custody and protection. The court may often turn to psychologists to help determine what is in the best interests of the child in cases where the parents' separation or divorce leads to custody disputes or where there are parenting capacity issues resulting from allegations of child abuse or neglect. Grounds for termination of parental rights can include abuse, neglect, abandonment, or the presence of parental conditions that cause incapacity to care for a child (such as mental illness or substance abuse). Because of the enormous difficulty and consequences of decisions related to parental custody, courts often tend to weight expert opinion in child protection proceedings to a greater extent than in many other areas of law (Goodman, Emery, & Haugaard, 1998).

The areas mentioned above represent a mere sampling of the kinds of issues addressed by forensic psychologists. These and the many other issues (e.g., risk assessment, sexual harassment, and jury selection) require a very broad range of forensic applications of psychological science. The expansion of the field of forensic psychology directly contributed to the formation of Division 41 of the American Psychological Association (the American Psychology-Law Society) in 1985 as well as the development of specialty guidelines for the practice of forensic psychology (Committee on Ethical Guidelines for Forensic Psychologists, 1991). There are currently several academic journals focusing on research and practice issues relevant to forensic psychology, including *Behavioral Sciences and the Law, Criminal Justice and Behavior, Journal of the American Academy of Psychiatry and Law, Law and Human Behavior*, and *Psychology, Public Policy, and Law*. The American Board of Forensic Psychology began awarding a diplomate in forensic psychology in 1979, providing a way of obtaining advanced credentials in the field. In August 2001, the American Psychological Association's Council of Representatives voted to recognize forensic psychology as an officially designated specialty area (Otto & Heilbrun, 2002). All of these developments have occurred within the last 25 years, indicating the rapid rate of growth of forensic psychology.

The use of traditional clinical assessment instruments in forensic settings holds tremendous promise for assisting the psychologist in reaching useful conclusions and recommendations as well as substantial potential for the misuse or misapplication of these tests. Melton, Petrila, Poythress, and Slobogin (1997) highlight the important differences between therapeutic assessment and forensic assessment, including the following:

- The scope of the evaluation.   Evaluations for the court may be centered on whether impairment of a specific type is present but do not usually address treatment concerns.
- The client's perspective.   The client's point of view is the primary concern in psychotherapy, while in forensic evaluations extensive collateral information is sought, and the examinee's perspective tends to be secondary.

- The voluntariness of the subject's participation. Most therapeutic clients embark on assessment voluntarily, while forensic examinees are often reluctant, extremely guarded, or overtly uncooperative.

- Threats to validity. Forensic examinees (and the collateral sources required) may have a wide variety of reasons to be dishonest during the evaluation, including avoidance of criminal consequences or the possibility of material gain. Deliberate or intentional dishonesty in clinical evaluations is rarer, and threats to validity are more likely to come from low self-awareness.

- Relationship dynamics. Treating clinicians generally focus on demonstrating empathy and achieving an interpersonal bond with their clients, whereas forensic evaluators, whose primary responsibility is to the court and not the client, are usually more detached and at times even confrontational. The presentation of oneself as an empathic and supportive examiner is, in fact, considered misleading and unethical by some forensic evaluators.

- The pace and setting of the evaluation. In forensic evaluations, access to the subject may be limited, time may be very short because of the constraints of court orders and schedules, and the physical realities of conducting evaluations in prisons and hospitals may be quite challenging. Additionally, forensic work products are time limited and not generally subject to change after being submitted to the court.

Forensic evaluations do not have a therapeutic objective but are typically performed solely to assist the trier of fact. There is an obvious implication, therefore, that the chosen assessment tools are selected to provide maximum benefit to the court and not necessarily to benefit the examinee. This forensic perspective represents a quite significant conceptual shift for clinicians new to this work.

SPECIALIZED FORENSIC INSTRUMENTS VERSUS TRADITIONAL CLINICAL TESTS

Standardized assessment measures employed in forensic evaluations include instruments expressly designed to be used in a forensic setting, often for a specific population or purpose, and traditional clinical assessment tools applied to answer forensic questions. One example of an instrument designed specifically for use in a forensic setting is the Massachusetts Youth Screening Instrument–Version 2 (MAYSI–2; Grisso & Barnum, 2003). This test is a brief, easy-to-read symptom self-report measure that can be administered to youths entering detention or correctional programs. It is used to identify significant levels of a variety of psychiatric symptoms and in particular to identify youths in psychological crisis who might require immediate intervention. While many of the MAYSI–2 items relate to a broad array of psychiatric symptoms, the test was designed specifically for use in detention and correctional settings, and norms are provided only for delinquent youths in these settings.

A series of tests developed for the assessment of competency to waive Miranda rights also provide an excellent illustration of instruments designed solely to address a specific forensic issue. These tests include the Comprehension of Miranda Rights (CMR), and related instruments, including the Comprehension of Miranda Rights–Recognition (CMR–R), the Comprehension of Miranda Rights–Vocabulary (CMR–V), and the Function of Rights in Interrogation (FRI; Grisso 1981, 1986). These four instruments are designed to assess the competency of both adult and juvenile defendants to meaningfully waive their Miranda rights. The CMR uses a semistructured interview format in which each of the four parts of the standard Miranda warning are presented to a subject with a request that the subject describe in his or her own words the meaning of each sentence. The CMR is also available in a true-false format that assesses the individual's ability to recognize accurately (rather than verbally express) the meaning of the content of Miranda warnings (CMR–R) and in a version that focuses on the vocabulary of the Miranda language (CMR–V) to help determine whether the individual has sufficient vocabulary knowledge to understand the Miranda warnings. The FRI consists of pictures and vignettes that serve to assess a subject's understanding of the functions of his or her right to remain silent and right to an attorney during interrogation. For example, one picture shows an individual seated at the defense table before a judge, and the subject is asked specific questions about critical aspects of the right to remain silent during court proceedings.

Otto and Heilbrun (2002) discussed what they described as an "explosion" in the development and publication of forensic assessment instruments and forensically relevant instruments. Forensically relevant instruments can be distinguished from forensic assessment instruments in that the former do not focus on specific legal standards (or specific functional capacities associated with the standard) but rather address clinical constructs that are often directly pertinent to evaluations conducted within the legal system (e.g., evaluations of malingering, violence risk, and psychopathy). Otto and Heilbrun noted that more forensic assessment instruments and forensically relevant instruments have been published in the past decade than in the preceding 40 years, and they placed the current number of such instruments at between 40 and 50.

Instruments designed specifically for forensic use have both advantages and disadvantages (see Table 1.1 for a summary). One obvious advantage is that they allow for a more precise focus on a legal issue or standard. For example, in the case of the CMR, the test quickly (in 10–15 minutes) provides a circumscribed evaluation of whether an individual is capable of understanding his or her Miranda rights, a salient legal concern. Relatively less extrapolation or inference beyond the subject's direct responses may be necessary, because the test itself employs the exact language used in the Miranda warnings. Such tests often have the additional advantage of providing normative data based on forensic populations, allowing individual results to be compared with overall results for the specific population of interest.

TABLE 1.1

Advantages and Disadvantages of Specialized Forensic Assessment Instruments

Advantages	Disadvantages
Specialized tests may offer a specific focus on the legal issue at hand.	Specialized tests often have a limited research literature, and have been the subject of minimal independent research.
Specialized tests typically require less reliance on extrapolation and inference to address a given legal issue.	The applicability of specialized tests may be limited by their specificity (e.g., state-specific language for Miranda warnings).
Specialized tests often provide normative data based on forensic populations, allowing for direct comparison of individual findings to the population of interest.	There are numerous specific legal issues for which there are no specialized forensic assessment measures.
	Specialized tests generally do not provide a broad understanding of overall psychological functioning.

Many specialized forensic tests, however, possess the disadvantage of having a very limited research literature, and thus of having reliability and validity characteristics that are not fully understood. Indeed, Otto and Heilbrun (2002) observed that a number of forensic instruments have been published and distributed following only preliminary research, sometimes in the absence of a comprehensive test manual. Some instruments designed to assess competence to stand trial, for example, have generally demonstrated inconsistent research results regarding their factor structure and, more broadly, their construct validity (Rogers, Jackson, Sewell, Tillbrook, & Martin, 2003). In addition, there is often little independent research on forensic assessment instruments beyond the group of researchers directly involved in their development. Another potential disadvantage is that tests focused on specific forensic issues offer, by design, a very restricted assessment range, providing information on only one area of interest and thus possibly requiring the use of one or more additional instruments to address other important issues. The major benefit of specialized tests, therefore, simultaneously acts as a significant limitation. To illustrate this issue, the specific wording of Miranda rights varies slightly among the states, thus potentially limiting the generalizability of the CMR to those states that employ the exact language used in the test. There are also many specific legal issues, such as competence to manage one's financial affairs and competence to consent to treatment, for which no specialized assessment instruments have been developed. Finally, because specialized forensic assessment instruments focus strictly on legal standards, they do not provide sufficient data to permit a broader and contextual understanding of the individual's overall psychological functioning. Many forensic psychologists frequently use traditional clinical assessment instruments to address this latter assessment issue.

THE ROLE OF TRADITIONAL CLINICAL TESTS IN FORENSIC PSYCHOLOGY

Despite the existence of a rapidly growing body of specialized forensic instruments, traditional clinical assessment tools continue to play a crucial role in forensic evaluations. Research surveys report that instruments such as the Wechsler intelligence scales, the Minnesota Multiphasic Personality Inventory–2 (MMPI–2; Butcher, Graham, Ben-Porath, Tellegen, Dahlstrom, & Kaemmer, 2001), and the Millon Clinical Multiaxial Inventory–Third Edition (MCMI–III; Millon, Davis, & Millon, 1997) are commonly used in forensic assessment, and a growing body of research literature is providing guidance and support for using clinical instruments in a forensic context. Although some cautions have been raised regarding the use of traditional clinical measures in forensic assessment (e.g., Melton et al., 1997), such tests have become widely accepted for forensic evaluation (e.g., Borum & Grisso, 1995; Gould & Stahl, 2000; Greenberg, Otto, & Long, 2003; Otto, Edens, & Barcus, 2000). There are some distinct challenges and difficulties, however, associated with "retrofitting" clinical instruments to address a forensic issue or standard. Clinicians who routinely perform forensic evaluations must be aware of these limitations and the appropriate uses of tests as identified by the research literature.

Surveys of clinicians who perform forensic evaluations on a regular basis indicate that a number of traditional clinical assessment tools are commonly employed. In a survey of psychologists who had been awarded a diploma in forensic psychology by the American Board of Forensic Psychology (Table 1.2), Lally (2003) found that the Wechsler Adult Intelligence Scale–Third Edition (WAIS–III; Wechsler, 1997) and the MMPI–2 were rated as "Recommended" for sanity evaluations by 60% and 54% of experts, respectively. Additional instruments considered "Acceptable" for such evaluations included the Halstead–Reitan Neuropsychological Battery (Reitan, 1979; 71%), the Personality

TABLE 1.2

Tests Rated by Diplomates in Forensic Psychology as Recommended, Acceptable, or Unacceptable
for Forensic Evaluations

Type of Evaluation and Tests	Recommended	Acceptable	Unacceptable
Mental status at the time of offense			
WAIS–III	60%	96%	—
MMPI–2	54%	94%	—
R–CRAS	—	94%	—
Halstead–Reitan	—	71%	—
PAI	—	69%	—
Luria–Nebraska	—	58%	—
MCMI–III	—	54%	—
S-B-R	—	52%	—
Projective drawings	—	—	81%
TAT	—	—	65%
Sentence completion	—	—	60%
Risk for violence			
PCL–R	63%	88%	—
MMPI–2	—	88%	—
PCL–SV	—	73%	—
VRAG	—	73%	—
WAIS–III	—	67%	—
PAI	—	61%	—
Projective drawings	—	—	90%
TAT	—	—	82%
Sentence completion	—	—	71%
Rorschach	—	—	53%
16PF	—	—	53%
Risk for sexual violence			
PCL–R	62%	91%	—
MMPI–2	—	81%	—
PCL–SV	—	71%	—
WAIS–III	—	71%	—
VRAG	—	67%	—
SORAG	—	62%	—
Plethysmograph	—	60%	—
SVR–20	—	57%	—
PAI	—	55%	—
Projective drawings	—	—	95%
Sentence completion	—	—	76%
TAT	—	—	76%
16PF	—	—	60%
Rorschach	—	—	52%
MCMI–III	—	—	50%
Competence to stand trial			
WAIS–III	62%	90%	—
MacCAT–CA	56%	90%	—
CAI	—	85%	—
CST	—	77%	—
MMPI–2	—	73%	—
GCCT	—	65%	—
Halstead–Reitan	—	64%	—
IFI–R	—	62%	—
S-B-R	—	54%	—

TABLE 1.2

(Continued)

PAI	—	52%	—
Luria–Nebraska	—	50%	—
Projective drawings	—	—	87%
TAT	—	—	77%
Sentence completion	—	—	60%
Rorschach	—	—	60%
16PF	—	—	58%
MCMI–III	—	—	50%
Competence to waive			
Miranda rights			
WAIS–III	83%	100%	—
Grisso instruments	55%	88%	—
MMPI–2	—	70%	—
Halstead-Reitan	—	68%	—
S-B-R	—	63%	—
Luria–Nebraska	—	55%	—
Projective drawings	—	—	95%
TAT	—	—	78%
Sentence completion	—	—	70%
Rorschach	—	—	63%
16PF	—	—	63%
MCMI–III	—	—	55%
Malingering			
MMPI 2	64%	92%	—
SIRS	58%	89%	—
WAIS–III	—	75%	—
Rey	—	68%	—
PAI	—	53%	—
VIP	—	53%	—
TOMM	—	64%	—
Halstead–Reitan	—	51%	—
Projective drawings	—	—	89%
Sentence completion	—	—	72%
TAT	—	—	72%
16PF	—	—	66%
Rorschach	—	—	55%

Note: Percentages across columns may total in excess of 100% because respondents could rate tests as "Recommended" and "Acceptable." Results for tests reported by Lally as producing only "No Opinion" ratings are omitted from this table. WAIS–III = Wechsler Adult Intelligence Scale–Third Edition; MMPI–2 = Minnesota Multiphasic Intelligence Scale–2; R–CRAS = Rogers Criminal Responsibility Assessment Scales; PAI = Personality Assessment Inventory; MCMI–III = Millon Clinical Multiaxial Inventory–Third Edition; S-B-R = Stanford-Binet Revised; TAT = Thematic Apperception Test; PCL–R = Psychopthy Checklist Revised; PCL–SV = Psychopathy Checklist Short Version; VRAG = Violence Risk Appraisal Guide; 16PF = 16 Personality Factors; SORAG = Sex Offender Risk Appraisal Guide; SVR–20 = Sexual Violence Risk–20; MacCAT–CA = MacArthur Competency Assessment Tool–Criminal Adjudication; CAI = Competency to Stand Trial Assessment Instrument; CST = Competency Screening Test; GCCT = Georgia Court Competency Test; IFI–R = Interdisciplinary Fitness Interview–Revised; SIRS = Structured Interview of Reported Symptoms; Rey = Rey 15-Item Visual Memory Test; VIP = Validity Indicator Profile; TOMM = Test of Memory Malingering; VSVT = Victoria Symptom Validity Test; PDRT = Portland Digit Recognition Test; MPS = Malingering Probability Scale. Adapted from "What Tests Are Acceptable for use in Forensic Evaluations? A Survey of Experts," by S.J. Lally, 2003, *Professional Psychology: Research and Practice, 34,* pp. 491–498. Copyright 2003 by the American Psychological Association. Adapted with permission of the American Psychological Association.

Assessment Inventory (PAI; Morey, 1991; 69%), the Luria–Nebraska Neuropsycholog-ical Battery (Golden, Hammeke, & Purisch, 1978; 58%), the MCMI–III (54%), and the Stanford-Binet–Revised (Thorndike, Hagen, & Sattler, 1986; 52%). In conducting risk-for-violence assessments, 63% of the clinicians in the survey rated the Psychopathy Checklist–Revised (PCL–R; Hare, 1991) as "Recommended." Instruments additionally named as "Acceptable" for such evaluations included the MMPI–2 (82%), the Psychopathy Checklist–Screening Version (PCL:SV; Hart, Cox, & Hare, 1995; 73%), the Violence Risk Appraisal Guide (VRAG; Harris, Rice, & Quinsey, 1993; 73%), the WAIS–III (67%), and the PAI (61%). The latter survey covered several other types of evaluations, including risk for sexual violence, competency to stand trial, competency to waive Miranda rights, and malingering. In all cases, traditional clinical assessment tools are prominently named as the instruments most frequently recommended for nearly all forms of forensic evalu-ation, whereas more specialized forensic instruments were identified more rarely and for much more restrictive uses.

Table 1.3 provides a summary of testing reported in surveys of evaluations conducted for child custody, competency to stand trial, determinations of criminal responsibility, and personal injury. When completing child custody evaluations, intelligence tests, projective tasks, and broad personality measures are most frequently used by evaluators. Ackerman and Ackerman (1997), for example, found that most custody evaluators (58%) reported using some type of intelligence test when assessing children. A projective task, typically either the Children's Apperception Test (Bellak & Bellak, 1949) or the Thematic Apper-ception Test (Murray, 1943), was identified as the next most popular (37%). Results from the same survey also showed that when assessing adults in custody evaluations, 92% of survey respondents used either the MMPI or the MMPI–2, 48% used the Rorschach (the scoring system used was not specified), and 43% used the Wechsler Adult Intelligence Scale–Revised (WAIS–R; Wechsler, 1981). A similar pattern of test usage in child custody evaluations has been noted by Hagen and Castagna (2001), who found that the MMPI–2 and the Rorschach remained the most popular tools for assessing adults (used in 84% and 31% of evaluations, respectively) and that either intelligence tests (26%) or the Bricklin Perceptual Scales (Bricklin, 1984; 26%) were most popular for assessing children.

In evaluations of juveniles' competence to stand trial, Ryba, Cooper, and Zapf (2003) reported that 82% of clinicians used the Wechsler Intelligence Scales for Children–Third Edition (WISC–III; Wechsler, 1991) and that 56% used either the MMPI–2 (presum-ably with 18-year-olds) or the Minnesota Multiphasic Personality Inventory–Adolescent (MMPI–A; Butcher et al., 1992). Although evaluators in this survey reported occasional use of specific forensic assessment instruments, general clinical instruments were used much more frequently.

Borum and Grisso (1995) conducted a survey of highly experienced forensic psycholo-gists and psychiatrists, predominantly board certified for forensic practice, regarding their usage of psychological tests in evaluations for competence to stand trial and criminal re-sponsibility. Among forensic psychologists, the use of psychological testing was rated as either essential or recommended by 68% of evaluators for criminal responsibility evalua-tions and by 51% for evaluations of competence to stand trial. In criminal responsibility evaluations, the most frequently used type of test was an objective personality instrument, with the MMPI or MMPI–2 reported as commonly used by 94% of these survey respon-dents. Next most frequently used were measures of intellectual functioning (mentioned by 80% of respondents), neuropsychological tests (50%), and projective tests (42%). In contrast, forensic instruments were reported as being used less frequently than clinical instruments, with 46% of forensic psychologists reporting that they never used such tests

TABLE 1.3

Percentage of Practitioners Reporting Use of Some Popular Clinical Assessment Instruments in Forensic Evaluations

Study	Type of Evaluation	MMPI, MMPI–2, or MMPI–A	WAIS–R or WAIS–III	MCMI–I or MCMI–II	Rorschach	Beck Depression Inventory	Non-Wechsler Intellectual Assessment Instruments	TAT, Projective Drawings, and Other Projective Tasks
Ackerman and Ackerman, 1997	CC	92%	43%	—	48%	—	58%	37%
Hagen and Castagna, 2001	CC	84%	—	—	31%	—	26%	—
Ryba, Cooper, and Zapf, 2003	CST (juvenile)	56%	82%	—	—	—	—	—
Borum and Grisso, 1995	CST	94%	78%	32%	32%	2%	—	—
Borum and Grisso, 1995	CR	86%	83%	18%	30%	4%	—	—
Boccaccini and Brodsky, 1999	PI	94%	54%	50%	41%	33%	—	—
Lees-Haley, Smith, Williams, and Dunn, 1995	PI	68%	76%	9%	14%	25%	—	6%

Note: CC = child custody; CR = criminal responsibility; CST = competence to stand trial. PI = personal injury. Data from Borum and Grisso (1995) are presented separately for two types of evaluations, but these data are from the same study.

in criminal responsibility evaluations and 20% reporting that they rarely used them. Regarding test usage in assessments of competence to stand trial, similar results were found overall. Psychological testing was rated as essential or recommended by 51% of respondents, and objective personality inventories or intellectual testing were mentioned by 90% for this type of assessment. Neuropsychological tests were also frequently mentioned (42%), as were projective tasks (33%). Forensic psychiatrists generally rated psychological testing as essential or recommended for assessing criminal responsibility and competence to stand trial at frequencies similar to those for forensic psychologists, although psychiatrists reported less actual use of such testing.

In a survey focused on personal injury evaluations related to emotional damage (Boccaccini & Brodsky, 1999), forensic psychologists reported most commonly using the MMPI or MMPI–2 (94%), the WAIS–R or WAIS–III (54%), and the MCMI–II or MCMI–III (50%), with the Rorschach and the Beck Depression Inventory (Beck, Ward, Mendelson, Mock, & Erbaugh, 1961) being used somewhat less often (41% and 33%, respectively). In a survey of forensic neuropsychological evaluations (Lees-Haley, Smith, Williams, & Dunn, 1996), the WAIS–R and the MMPI or MMPI–2 were found to be the two most popular tests, followed by the Wechsler Memory Scale (Wechsler, 1987), Trailmaking Tests A and B (Army Individual Test Battery, 1944), the Finger Oscillation Test (Halstead, 1947), the Bender-Gestalt Visual Motor Test (Bender, 1946), the Category Test (Halstead, 1947), and the Wisconsin Card Sorting Test (Berg, 1948). The differences seen in the results reported by Boccaccini and Brodsky (1999) and Lees-Haley et al. (1996) reflect differences in the focus of the evaluations in these surveys (i.e., psychological/emotional injury versus neuropsychological/brain injury). See Table 1.4 for a listing of the most popular neuropsychological instruments in forensic evaluations as reported by Lees-Haley and his colleagues. Regarding the assessment of malingering, Slick, Tan, Strauss, and Hultsch (2004) surveyed forensic neuropsychologists and found that 79% of respondents used specialized forensic tests to assess malingering, with 50% reporting that they routinely gave such tests at the outset of each evaluation. The most commonly reported tests in this survey were the Rey 15-Item Test (Rey, 1964) and the Test of Memory Malingering (TOMM; Tombaugh, 1996).

In addition to the consistent evidence of the marked popularity of clinical instruments in forensic evaluations, there is a growing body of research literature that supports the forensic use of these instruments. Some of the most popular instruments, as indicated by survey research, have also garnered the most extensive research regarding their use in forensic evaluations. For example, as summarized by Pope, Butcher, and Seelen (2000), there is considerable research on the forensic applications of the MMPI–2 and, to a lesser extent, the MMPI–A. Neuropsychological tests commonly used in forensic evaluations have also gained substantial research attention (e.g., Horton & Hartlage, 2003; Sweet, 1999; Sweet & King, 2002). Further, McCann and Dyer (1996) have summarized the research literature on forensic uses of the MCMI–III, and there are several reviews available on the use of the Rorschach in forensic evaluation (e.g., McCann, 1998; Weiner, 2003). Other tests featured in this book have generated less forensic research but appear likely to be thoroughly investigated in the coming years. Therefore, an ample research base is rapidly developing to provide the psychologist with critical information concerning the strengths and limitations of several clinical assessment instruments for various forensic applications.

However, there are also inherent difficulties associated with using tests developed for clinical purposes to address forensic issues that involve clinical constructs. One concern is that the original development of these instruments typically focused not on forensic

TABLE 1.4

Instruments Used in 20% or More of Forensic Neuropsychological Evaluations

Rank	Test
1	WAIS and WAIS–R (76%)
2	MMPI and MMPI–2 (68%)
3	WMS and WMS–R (51%)
4	Trails A (48%)
5	Trails B (47%)
6	Finger Oscillation Test, Finger Tapping Test (38%)
7	Bender Gestalt (34%)
8	Category Test—all forms (32%)
9	Wisconsin Card Sorting Test (29%)
10	Sentence Completion Test—various forms (28%)
11	Tactual Performance Test (26%)
12	WRAT and WRAT–R (25%)
13	Beck Depression Inventory (25%)
14	Reitan-Klove Sensory Perceptual Examination (23%)
15	Grooved Pegboard (23%)
16	Seashore Rhythm (23%)
17	Speech Sounds Perception Test (21%)
18	Boston Naming Test, Boston Naming Test–Revised (21%)
19	Hooper Visual Organization Test (20%)

Note: From "Forensic Neuropsychological Test Usage: An Empirical Survey," by P.R. Lees-Haley, H.H. Smith, C.W. Williams, and J.T. Dunn," 1996, *Archives of Clinical Neuropsychology, 11*, p. 48. Copyright 1996 by Elsevier. Adapted with permission by Elservier.

applications, but on diagnostic and treatment planning issues. The MMPI–2 basic scales, for example, are named for diagnostic categories, not for legal issues or standards (e.g., there is no "competency to stand trial" scale in the MMPI–2). Podboy and Kastl (1993) pointed out that the potential forensic applications of traditional psychological tests were generally never considered during their development, and such tests have been subjected to notable misuse in the courtroom setting. To illustrate this latter point, Podboy and Kastl observed that attorneys have employed such tactics as presenting highly selective quotations from computerized interpretations and drawing overly broad conclusions based on a single narrowly focused instrument designed to assess traits such as anxiety or depression. Although there have been some attempts to devise new scales for traditional clinical instruments that would be relevant to forensic evaluation, such as the Malingered Depression scale for the MMPI–2 (Steffan, Clopton, & Morgan, 2003), these efforts have generally been limited, and the effectiveness of these measures is not yet established by systematic research findings.

Another concern regarding the use of clinical instruments for forensic purposes is that the research base for forensic applications varies quite widely depending on the individual instrument. As previously pointed out, many of the most popular clinical tests used in forensic evaluations have extensive research to support their use in this context. However,

TABLE 1.5

Uses and Limitations of Clinical Assessment Instruments in Forensic Applications

Uses	Limitations
Traditional clinical tests can provide a broad understanding of an individual's intellectual, emotional, and personality functioning.	The original development of most traditional clinical tests focused on diagnosis and treatment planning, not on forensic applications.
Instruments such as the MMPI–2 contain validity indicators that are an important source for evaluating defensiveness and/or malingering.	Few clinical assessment instruments have developed appropriate forensic norms.
The broader scope of these instruments helps to generate hypotheses for further evaluation.	The research base for forensic applications varies widely by individual instrument.
Many traditional tests have extensive research bases and well-established psychometric properties, which can enhance the conclusions in court testimony.	Results from traditional tests often cannot be used to directly address specific legal issues.

other tests that evaluators may be accustomed to using in their clinical practices may have more limited research support for their use in forensic evaluations. Some clinical tests that are employed in forensic settings may lack research-based correlates for forensic use, and few clinical instruments have developed appropriate forensic norms. One rare exception to the former limitation is the Megargee classification system for the MMPI and MMPI–2, which does provide forensic correlates for these instruments as well as a profile classification system designed specifically for adult offender populations (e.g., Megargee, 1994; Megargee & Carbonell, 1985). See Table 1.5 for a summary of the uses and limitations of clinical assessment instruments in forensic applications.

Clinical assessment tools may be employed for forensic purposes when they are appropriate and relevant to the specific legal question, but evaluators must maintain an awareness of how their methods will be received by the trier of fact (Medoff, 2003). Similarly, clinical assessment tools should not be used to address forensic questions beyond the scope of the instrument. For example, forensic evaluators are sometimes asked to reconstruct an individual's mental state at a prior point in time; however, traditional clinical tests are typically of very limited value for such reconstructions (Melton et al., 1997). Moreover, Greenberg et al. (2003) suggested that because standard clinical assessment instruments may be limited in their ability to directly answer legal questions, they should instead be used only to generate hypotheses to be addressed by means of further evaluation. Rogers (2003) also cautions that when using multiscale inventories such as the MMPI–2 in forensic evaluations, clinicians should be especially wary of exercising a "confirmatory bias" through highly selective interpretation of test results. To illustrate this latter point, the MMPI–2 contains 567 items and in excess of 100 scales and subscales: it is quite likely that some isolated result can be found to support almost any point or contention regarding an individual's psychological functioning. Fortunately, knowledgeable interpreters understand and can explain to the trier of fact that MMPI–2 results are not interpreted in isolation but within the context of overall test findings.

Formal psychological assessment may provide an important additional source of information, in combination with interviews and collateral data, that sets psychological evaluations apart from psychiatric evaluations (Heilbrun, Marczyk, & DeMatteo, 2002). Instruments designed to assess specific legal issues, such as various competencies, serve a valuable function in many types of evaluations. Nonetheless, many forensic evaluations call for a broad understanding of personality, emotional, and cognitive functioning that may best be achieved through the use of existing, well-validated measures that illuminate multiple aspects of individual functioning.

Clinical tests must be used wisely and appropriately in the forensic setting, and it is critically important that forensic psychologists recognize the appropriate and inappropriate application of clinical instruments in forensic evaluations. Child custody, personal injury litigation, and sentencing in capital punishment cases, for example, represent highly sensitive areas in which the opinion of a psychological expert can have enormous life-altering consequences. Psychologists evaluating the competency of defendants to stand trial or waive Miranda rights are charged with tasks that contribute to upholding the integrity of judicial proceedings and protecting individual rights. Providing an expert opinion in legal proceedings comes with a weighty responsibility to serve the court, and the public good, to the greatest degree possible. Therefore, it is incumbent upon clinicians who perform forensic evaluations to use psychological tests appropriately and only for purposes for which their use is empirically supported. If psychological testing was to be regularly misapplied in the forensic arena, it could undermine the integrity of the justice system, harm the individuals who rely upon it, and diminish psychological science in the eyes of the public. Furthermore, the work of forensic psychologists is often subject to intense scrutiny and cross-examination in the courtroom, and the evaluator must frequently justify his or her choice of methods (as well as test findings and conclusions) in much greater detail than is generally necessary in the case of clinical evaluations (Heilbrun et al., 2003). In general, the most persuasive basis for the successful defense of one's assessment procedures is to be familiar with the research on the measures that were used in the evaluation (Hilsenroth & Stricker, 2004). Given the potential benefit of using psychological tests in forensic evaluations, as well as the potential pitfalls of their improper use, knowledge of the appropriate and inappropriate forensic uses of traditional clinical assessment instruments is vital for forensic psychologists.

The purpose of this text is to provide a firm basis for psychologists to understand the appropriate uses and limitations of popular clinical assessment measures when used to assess clinical constructs relevant to forensic issues. The instruments were selected because of their wide utilization and their importance in both clinical and forensic settings. The first four instruments discussed are broad-spectrum, multidimensional personality instruments used in a variety of forensic evaluations and settings. These include the MMPI–2 (chapter 2, by Martin Sellbom and Yossef Ben-Porath); the MMPI–A (chapter 3, by Robert Archer, Meredith Zoby, and Rebecca Stredny), the PAI (chapter 4, by Lesley Morey), and the MCMI–II (chapter 5, by Robert Craig). Chapter 6, by Angela Book, Heather Clark, Adelle Forth, and Robert Hare, presents the PCL–R, a forensically relevant clinical instrument typically used in forensic settings. In the following chapter, Irving Weiner describes the Rorschach, the most frequently used projective instrument in forensic evaluations. Chapter 8, by Eric Zillmer and Heather Green, is on neuropsychological assessment instruments, a diverse group of clinical tests that are frequently associated with personal injury evaluation, but are also used in criminal forensic evaluations. The final three chapters cover the families of tests most often used in child custody, child protection, and juvenile evaluations. These include the Achenbach System of Empirical Assessment (ASEBA; Achenbach, 1991), discussed by Thomas Achenbach and Leslie Rescorla in chapter 9; the Personality Inventory for Children–Second Edition and related measures (PIC–2; Lachar & Gruber, 2001), discussed by David Lachar, Byron Hammer, and Jill Hammer in chapter 10; and the Parenting Stress Index (PSI; Abidin, 1995), discussed by Richard Abidin, Jay Flens, and William Austin in chapter 11.

The chapter authors were selected because of their unique expertise regarding each instrument—an expertise resulting from their role in its development, and/or their crucial contributions to its research base. These authors were given the task of presenting and discussing both the strengths and weaknesses of the clinical assessment instrument in the forensic domain. Each chapter specifically details appropriate uses and inappropriate applications or extensions of the instrument. The main purpose is to describe the most responsible and appropriate manner of applying the instrument in forensic settings. The overall goal of the contributing authors' efforts was the creation of a comprehensive overview, within a single text, of prominent clinical assessment instruments widely used for forensic purposes. This text is not intended to provide sufficient training to allow clinical psychologists to develop the expertise necessary to present themselves as forensic psychologists; rather, it is designed to facilitate the optimal use of clinical assessment instruments by psychologists who have undertaken the training necessary to understand and apply psychological principles and test findings to salient legal standards or issues.

REFERENCES

Abidin. R.R. (1995). *Manual for the Parenting Stress Index*. Charlottesville. VA: Pediatric Psychology Press.

Achenbach. T.M. (1991). *Manual for the Child Behavior Checklist/4–18 and 1991 Profile*. Burlington: University of Vermont.

Ackerman. M.J., & Ackerman. M.C. (1997). Custody evaluations practices: A survey of experienced professionals (revisited). *Professional Psychology: Research and Practice, 28*. 137–145.

American Psychological Association. (2002). Ethical principles of psychologists and code of conduct. *American Psychologist, 57*. 1060–1073.

Army Individual Test Battery. (1944). *Manual of directions and scoring*. Washington, DC: War Department. Adjutant General's Office.

Beck. A.T., Ward, C.H., Mendelson. M., Mock. J.E., & Erbaugh. J.K. (1961). An inventory for measuring depression. *Archives of General Psychiatry, 4*. 53–63.

Bellak. L., & Bellak. S.S. (1949). *Children's Apperception Test (CAT)*. Larchmont. NY: CPS Inc.

Bender. L. (1946). *Instructions for the use of the Visual Motor Gestalt Test*. New York:American Orthopsychiatric Association.

Berg. E.A. (1948). A simple objective treatment for measuring flexibility in thinking. *Journal of General Psychology, 39*. 15–22.

Boccaccini. M.T., & Brodsky. S.L. (1999). Diagnostic test use by forensic psychologists in emotional injury cases. *Professional Psychology: Research and Practice, 30*. 253–259.

Borum. R., & Grisso. T. (1995). Psychological test use in criminal forensic evaluations. *Professional Psychology: Research and Practice, 26*. 465–473.

Bricklin. B. (1984). *Bricklin Perceptual Scales*. Furlong. PA: Village.

Butcher. J.N., Graham. J.R., Ben-Porath. Y.S., Tellegen. A., Dahlstrom, W.G., & Kaemmer. B. (2001). *Minnesota Multiphasic Personality Inventory–2 (MMPI–2): Manual for administration and scoring*. Minneapolis: University of Minnesota.

Butcher. J.N., Williams, C.L., Graham, J.R., Archer. R.P., Tellegen. A., Ben-Porath. Y.S., et al. (1992). *MMPI–A (Minnesota Multiphasic Personality Inventory–Adolescent): Manual for administration, scoring, and interpretation*. Minneapolis: University of Minnesota Press.

Committee on Ethical Guidelines for Forensic Psychologists. (1991). Specialty guidelines for forensic psychologists. *Law and Human Behavior, 15*. 655–665.

Daubert v. Merrell Dow Pharmaceuticals. Inc., 113 S.Ct. 2786 (1993).

Frye v. United States, 408 A.2d 364 (1979).

General Electric v. Joiner. 118 S.Ct. 512 (1997).

Golden, C.J., Hammeke, T.A., & Purisch, A.O. (1978). Diagnostic validity of a standardized neuropsychological battery derived from Luria's neuropsychological tests. *Journal of Consulting and Clinical Psychology, 46,* 1258–1265.

Goodman, G.S., Emery, R.E., & Haugaard, J.J. (1998). Developmental psychology and law: Divorce, child maltreatment, foster care, and adoption. In W. Damon (Ed.), *Handbook of child psychology* (Vol. 4, pp. 775–874). New York: Wiley.

Gould, J.W., & Stahl, P.M. (2000). The art and science of child custody evaluations: Integrating clinical and forensic mental health models. *Family and Conciliation Courts Review, 38,* 392–414.

Greenberg, S.A., Otto, R.L., & Long, A.C. (2003). The utility of psychological testing in assessing emotional damages in personal injury litigation. *Assessment, 10,* 411–419.

Grisso, T. (1981). *Juveniles' waiver of rights: Legal and psychological competence.* New York: Plenum.

Grisso, T. (1986). *Evaluating competencies: Forensic assessments and instruments.* New York: Plenum.

Grisso, T., & Barnum, R. (2003). *Massachusetts Youth Screening Instrument – Version 2: User's manual and technical report.* Sarasota, FL: Professional Resource Press.

Hagen, M.A., & Castagna, N. (2001). The real numbers: Psychological testing in custody evaluations. *Professional Psychology: Research and Practice, 32,* 269–271.

Halstead, W.C. (1947). *Brain and intelligence.* Chicago: University of Chicago Press.

Hare, R.D. (1991). *The Hare Psychopathy Checklist—Revised.* Toronto, Ontario, Canada: Multi-Health Systems.

Harris, G.T., Rice, M.E., & Quinsey, V.L. (1993). Violent recidivism of mentally disordered offenders: The development of a statistical prediction instrument. *Criminal Justice and Behavior, 20,* 315–335.

Hart, S.D., Cox, D.N., & Hare, R.D. (1995). *The Hare Psychopathy Checklist—Screening Version (PCL:SV).* Toronto, Ontario, Canada: Multi-Health Systems.

Heilbrun, K., Marczyk, G.R., & DeMatteo, D. (2002). *Forensic mental health assessment: A casebook.* New York: Oxford University Press.

Heilbrun, K., Marczyk, G.R., DeMatteo, D., Zillmer, E.A., Harris, J., & Jennings, T. (2003). Principles of forensic mental health assessment: Implications for neuropsychological assessment in forensic contexts. *Assessment, 10,* 329–343.

Hilsenroth, M.J., & Stricker, G. (2004). A consideration of challenges to psychological assessment instruments used in forensic settings: Rorschach as exemplar. *Journal of Personality Assessment, 83,* 141–152.

Horton, A.M., Jr., & Hartlage, L.C. (Eds). (2003). *Handbook of forensic neuropsychology.* New York: Springer.

Jenkins v. United States, 307 F. 2d 637 (1962).

Kumho Tire Co. v. Carmichael, 526 U.S. 137 (1999).

Lachar, D., & Gruber, C.P. (2001). *Personality Inventory for Children, Second Edition.* Los Angeles: Western Psychological Services.

Lally, S.J. (2003). What tests are acceptable for use in forensic evaluations? A survey of experts. *Professional Psychology: Research and Practice, 34,* 491–498.

Lees-Haley, P. (1992). Psychodiagnostic test usage by forensic psychologists. *American Journal of Forensic Psychology, 10,* 25–30.

Lees-Haley, P.R., Smith, H.H., Williams, C.W., & Dunn, J.T. (1996). Forensic neuropsychological test usage: An empirical survey. *Archives of Clinical Neuropsychology, 11,* 45–51.

McCann, J.T., (1998). Defending the Rorschach in court: An analysis of admissibility using legal and professional standards. *Journal of Personality Assessment, 70,* 125–144.

McCann, J.T., & Dyer, F.J. (1996). *Forensic assessment with the Millon inventories.* New York: Guilford Press.

Medoff, D. (2003). The scientific basis of psychological testing: Considerations following Daubert, Kumho, and Joiner. *Family Court Review, 41,* 199–213.

Megargee, E.I. (1994). Using the Megargee MMPI-based classification system with MMPI-2s of male prison inmates. *Psychological Assessment, 6,* 337–344.

Megargee, E.I., & Carbonell, J.L. (1985). Predicting prison adjustment with MMPI correctional scales. *Journal of Consulting and Clinical Psychology, 53,* 874–883.

Melton, G.B., Petrila, J., Poythress, N.G., & Slobogin, C. (1997). *Psychological evaluations for the courts.* New York: Guilford Press.

Millon, T., Davis, R.D., & Millon, C. (1997). *Manual for the Millon Clinical Multiaxial Inventory–III (MCMI–III)*. Minneapolis, MN: National Computer Systems.

Morey, L.C. (1991). *Personality Assessment Inventory: Professional manual*. Odessa, FL: Psychological Assessment Resources.

Murray, H.A. (1943). *Thematic Apperception Test*. New York: Oxford University Press.

Otto, R.K., Edens, J.F., & Barcus, E.H. (2000). The use of psychological testing in child custody evaluations. *Family and Conciliation Courts Review, 38*, 312–340.

Otto, R.K., & Heilbrun, K. (2002). The practice of forensic psychology: A look toward the future in the light of the past. *American Psychologist, 57*, 5–18.

Podboy, J.W., & Kastl, A.J. (1993). The intentional misuse of standard psychological tests in complex trials. *American Journal of Forensic Psychology, 11*, 47–54.

Pope, K.S., Butcher, J.N., & Seelen, J. (2000). *The MMPI, MMPI–2 and MMPI–A in court: A practical guide for expert witnesses and attorneys* (2nd ed.). Washington, DC: American Psychological Association.

Reitan, R.M. (1979). *Manual for administration of neuropsychological test batteries for adults and children*. Tucson, AZ: Author.

Rey, A. (1964). *L'examen clinique en psychologie*. Paris: Presses Universitaires de France.

Rogers, R. (2003). Forensic use and abuse of psychological tests: Multiscale inventories. *Journal of Psychiatric Practice, 9*, 316–320.

Rogers, R., Bagby, R.M., & Dickens, S.E. (1992). *Structured Interview of Reported Symptoms (SIRS) and professional manual*. Odessa, FL: Psychological Assessment Resources.

Rogers, R., Jackson, R.L., Sewell, K.W., Tillbrook, C.E., & Martin, M.A. (2003). Assessing the dimensions of competency to stand trial: Construct validation of the ECST-R. *Assessment, 10*, 344–351.

Ryba, N.L., Cooper, V.G., & Zapf, P.A. (2003). Juvenile competence to stand trial evaluations: A survey of current practices and test usage among psychologists. *Professional Psychology: Research and Practice, 34*, 499–507.

Slick, D.J., Tan, J.E., Strauss, E.H., & Hultsch, D.F. (2004). Detecting malingering: A survey of experts' practices. *Archives of Clinical Neuropsychology, 19*, 465–473.

Steffan, J.S., Clopton, J.R., & Morgan, R.D. (2003). An MMPI-2 scale to detect malingered depression (Md scale). *Assessment, 10*, 382–392.

Sweet, J.J. (1999). *Forensic neuropsychology: Fundamentals and practice*. Lisse, Netherlands: Swets & Zeitlinger.

Sweet, J.J., & King, J.H. (2002). Category test validity indicators: Overview and practice recommendations. *Journal of Forensic Neuropsychology, 3*, 241–274.

Thorndike, R.L., Hagen, E.P., & Sattler, J.M. (1986). *Stanford-Binet Intelligence Scale: Guide for administering and scoring the fourth edition*. Chicago: Riverside Publishing.

Tombaugh, T.N. (1996). *Test of Memory Malingering (TOMM)*. New York: Multi-Health Symptoms.

Vaccaro, T.P., & Hogan, J.D. (2004). The origins of forensic psychology in America: Hugo Munsterberg on the witness stand. *New York State Psychologist, 16*, 14–17.

Wechsler, D. (1981). *Wechsler Adult Intelligence Scale—Revised manual*. New York: The Psychological Corporation.

Wechsler, D. (1987). *Wechsler Memory Scale—Revised*. New York: The Psychological Corporation.

Wechsler, D. (1991). *Wechsler Intelligence Scale for Children—Third Edition*. San Antonio, TX: The Psychological Corporation.

Wechsler, D. (1997). *Wechsler Adult Intelligence Scale—Third Edition*. San Antonio, TX: The Psychological Corporation.

Weiner, I.B. (2003). *Principles of Rorschach interpretation* (2nd ed.). Mahwah, NJ: Lawrence Erlbaum Associates.

2

THE MINNESOTA MULTIPHASIC PERSONALITY INVENTORY–2

MARTIN SELLBOM
YOSSEF S. BEN-PORATH

KENT STATE UNIVERSITY

BASIC DESCRIPTION OF THE MMPI–2

Before being replaced by an updated version, the original Minnesota Multiphasic Personality Inventory (MMPI; Hathaway & McKinley, 1943) was the most frequently used self-report inventory measuring personality and psychopathology (Lubin, Larsen, & Matarazzo, 1984; Piotrowski & Keller, 1989) as well as the most researched (Reynolds & Sundberg, 1976). This pattern has continued with the MMPI–2 (Butcher et al., 2001), which is used in a variety of settings (Camara, Nathan, & Puente, 2000) and remains the most frequently investigated psychological test (Butcher & Rouse, 1996).

Administration of the MMPI–2

The MMPI–2 should only be administered to those who are 18 years of age or older. Younger individuals should be administered the adolescent version of the test, the MMPI–A (Butcher et al., 1992). Moreover, there are certain test conditions that may preclude an individual from taking the MMPI–2. The manual authors (Butcher et al., 2001) recommend that individuals who have less than a sixth-grade reading level not be administered the MMPI–2 in the standard format; however, some persons with limited reading ability can complete the test if it is presented using a standard audio version available on cassette or CD. Other conditions that might preclude MMPI–2 administration include altered cognitive states or confusion stemming from brain impairment as well as severe psychopathology.

The MMPI–2 should be administered in a quiet and comfortable place for the test taker. About one to one and a half hours is needed to complete the test in standard booklet and answer sheet form for individuals of normal intellectual functioning (Graham, 2006). Complicating factors such as disabling psychopathology, low reading level, or lower intellectual functioning may require a longer time, such as 2 hours or more. Administration by computer using standard software available through Pearson Assessments reduces the amount of time needed to complete the inventory.

MMPI–2 Scales

The standard scales of the MMPI–2 currently include 9 Validity Scales, 10 Clinical Scales (and 31 subscales), 9 Restructured Clinical (RC) Scales, 15 Content Scales (and 28 Content Component Scales), 15 Supplementary Scales, and 5 Personality Psychopathology Five (PSY-5) Scales. Many other scales have been developed or proposed for the test; however, only the standard scales just mentioned are recommended for use by the publisher.

The MMPI–2 *Validity Scales* constitute an essential component of the test. Some Validity Scales were first introduced when the original MMPI was published to address a challenge inherent in self-report inventories: their susceptibility to misleading responding and scoring error. The scales are discussed in the order in which they appear on the MMPI–2 profile, which is also the order recommended for interpretation (see Butcher et al., 2001).

The Cannot Say count measures nonresponding. This index should always be consulted first, as item omissions affect all remaining scales, including the other Validity Scales. A protocol where 30 or more items cannot be scored may be of questionable validity. Automated scoring systems indicate the percentage of items answered on each MMPI–2 scale, allowing for a more refined interpretation of the effects of item omissions. The absence of elevation on a scale with less than 90% of its items answered should generally not be interpreted.

The Variable Response Inconsistency (*VRIN*) and True Response Inconsistency (*TRIN*) scales measure inconsistent responding. *VRIN* assesses random responding, whereas *TRIN* measures fixed responding in either the true or false directions. The scales are scored by comparing the test taker's responses to pairs of items. A T-score greater than 79 on either of these scales indicates that the MMPI–2 protocol is invalid and uninterpretable (Butcher et al., 2001).

The Infrequency (F) scale was originally developed to detect random responding and clerical scoring error but is currently used primarily to identify overreporting of psychopathology. The manual authors state that T-scores greater than 100 *may* indicate an invalid protocol; however, this possibility needs to be evaluated by considering scores on the *VRIN, TRIN,* and F_P (discussed later) scales (Butcher et al., 2001). Because all the F scale items appear within the first 361 items on the test, a scale to measure infrequent responding to items in the second half of the test booklet was developed. The Back-Infrequency (F_B) scale has been found to successfully detect shifts in response sets across the inventory (Berry, Baer, & Harris, 1991; Clark, Gironda, & Young, 2003).

Arbisi and Ben-Porath (1995) developed the Infrequency-Psychopathology (F_P) scale to address a problem posed by the confounding of severe psychopathology and distress with overreporting as sources of elevation of the F scale. The F_P scale consists of items that are infrequently endorsed in both normal and abnormal populations; thus, individuals scoring high on this scale report symptoms that even individuals experiencing severe symptoms of psychopathology are unlikely to endorse. The manual authors state that T-scores greater than 99 on Fp indicate that the protocol is likely invalid.

The Lie (L) scale was developed to detect underreporting. High scorers present in an unusually virtuous manner and deny personal flaws that most people would be willing to admit. The manual authors indicate that a T-score greater than 79 on L identifies a protocol as being likely invalid. The Correction (K) scale is a more subtle indicator of underreporting. T-scores greater than 74 may indicate an invalid profile (Butcher et al., 2001) in nonclinical settings. Finally, the Superlative (S) scale is also designed to assess underreporting. T-scores greater than 69 on this scale raise the possibility that the profile may be invalid.

The *Clinical Scales* were developed using an empirical keying method that identified items that discriminate between a specific diagnostic group and a normal group. The MMPI-2 Clinical Scales include Scales 1 (Hypochondriasis [Hs]), 2 (Depression [D]), 3 (Hysteria [Hy]), 4 (Psychopathic Deviate [Pd]), 5 (Masculinity [Mf]), 6 (Paranoia [Pa]), 7 (Psychasthenia [Pt]), 8 (Schizophrenia [Sc]), 9 (Hypomania [Ma]), and 0 (Social Introversion [Si]). Because of the methodology used in their development, the Clinical Scales are very heterogeneous, making their interpretation difficult. As a result, Harris and Lingoes (1955) developed subscales for the Clinical Scales that focused on grouping items of specific content domains together to facilitate interpretation.

Another method to tease out the overlapping variance among the Clinical Scales involves classifying protocols into codetypes based on the two or three most elevated scales in the profile. The manual authors recommend interpreting only well-defined codetypes (i.e., the lowest scale in the codetype is at least 5 T-score points greater than the highest scale outside the codetype).

The MMPI-2 *Restructured Clinical (RC) Scales* (Tellegen et al., 2003) are the most recent addition to the MMPI-2. The RC Scales were developed to remove a common Demoralization factor that saturates the original Clinical Scales and improve their discriminant and convergent validity (Tellegen et al., 2003). Demoralization was conceptualized through the Tellegen's (1985) framework of positive and negative emotionality as corresponding to the pleasantness-unpleasantness vector between these two orthogonal affective dimensions. Tellegen's (1985) model links depression to low positive emotionality and anxiety to high negative emotionality. Therefore, as a first step in RC Scale construction, Demoralization markers were identified based on factor analyses of Clinical Scales 2 and 7.

The next step in developing the RC Scales involved identifying the unique core components of each Clinical Scale after Demoralization items had been removed. This was followed by analyses designed to maximize the distinctiveness of each core component and identify items throughout the MMPI-2 pool that are related uniquely to this core. The final set of RC scales includes 192 nonoverlapping items scored in scales labeled Demoralization (*RCd*), Somatic Complaints (*RC1*), Low Positive Emotions (*RC2*), Cynicism (*RC3*), Antisocial Behavior (*RC4*), Ideas of Persecution (*RC6*), Dysfunctional Negative Emotions (*RC7*), Aberrant Experiences (*RC8*), and Hypomanic Activation (*RC9*). In comparison with the Clinical Scales, the RC Scales are more homogeneous and less intercorrelated, resulting in improved convergent and discriminant validity (Sellbom & Ben-Porath, in press; Sellbom, Ben-Porath, & Graham, 2004; Tellegen et al., 2003).

The MMPI-2 *Content Scales* (Butcher, Graham, Williams, & Ben-Porath, 1990) were developed through a series of rational-conceptual and empirical analyses modeled after Wiggins's (1969) original set of Content Scales for the MMPI. They are designed to facilitate test interpretation by providing a reliable indication of the individual's self-presentation and expanding the content domains represented by the original Clinical Scales. The 15 Content Scales include Anxiety (*ANX*), Fears (*FRS*), Obsessiveness (*OBS*), Depression (*DEP*), Health Concerns (*HEA*), Bizarre Mentation (*BIZ*), Anger (*ANG*), Cynicism (*CYN*), Antisocial Practices (*ASP*), Type A Behavior (*TPA*), Low Self-Esteem (*LSE*), Social Discomfort (*SOD*), Family Problems (*FAM*), Work Interference (*WRK*), and Negative Treatment Indicators (*TRT*) scales. Twelve of the scales also have Content Component Scales (Ben-Porath & Sherwood, 1993) that were developed through principal components analyses and are designed to further focus Content Scale interpretation.

The *Supplementary Scales* are a collection of MMPI–2 measures developed over the test's history. They include Welsh's (1956) Anxiety (*A*) and Repression (*R*) scales, which measure the two factors that are commonly derived when the Clinical Scales are factor analyzed. The *A* scale is a measure of general emotional distress. Other Supplementary Scales include broad personality measures (Ego Strength [*Es*], Dominance [*Do*], and Social Responsibility [*Re*]); general maladjustment scales, such as the College Maladjustment and Martial Distress Scale (MDS; Hjemboe, Almagor, & Butcher, 1992); and behavioral dyscontrol scales (Hostility [*Ho*] and Over-controlled Hostility [*O-H*]). The substance abuse scales include the MacAndrews Alcoholism Scale–Revised (*MAC–R*; MacAndrew, 1965), the Addiction Admission Scale (*AAS*; Weed, Butcher, McKenna, & Ben-Porath, 1992), and the Addiction Potential Scale (*APS*; Weed et al., 1992).

The *Personality Psychopathology Five* (PSY-5; Harkness, McNulty, & Ben-Porath, 1995) Scales were designed to measure five dimensional personality constructs that describe normal-to abnormal-range personality traits. The PSY-5 dimensions were identified by Harkness and McNulty (1994) as major dimensions of personality pathology. The PSY-5 scales were developed to assist in assessing personality pathology from a dimensional perspective. The scales include Aggressiveness (*AGGR*), Psychoticism (*PSYC*), Disconstraint (*DISC*), Neuroticism/Negative Emotionality (*NEGE*), and Introversion/Low Positive Emotionality (*INTR*).

HISTORY OF THE DEVELOPMENT OF THE MMPI AND MMPI–2

The MMPI was developed by Hathaway and McKinley (1943) to facilitate psychodiagnosis. Although the MMPI has often been described as having been constructed in an atheoretical vaccum, this was actually not the case. The then contemporary descriptive nosological system and a combination of psychodynamic and behavioral theory played a role in generating the test's items and scale construction (Ben-Porath, in press). In developing the instrument, Hathaway and McKinley gathered an item pool by examining the literature concerning the major psychiatric diagnoses of the time complemented by their own extensive clinical experience. This procedure generated close to 1,000 test items. The authors employed an empirical keying method to assign items to a particular scale without consideration of their content. By ignoring item content in the construction process, Hathaway and McKinley believed that the resulting scales would be less susceptible to distortion because items were statistically but not necessarily manifestly related to the target constructs. Moreover, in the case of the instrument as expanded by Meehl (1945), because the scales were constructed and to be interpreted empirically, there was no need to assume that the items had similar meaning to different individuals.

Hathaway and McKinley administered the candidate items to various groups of psychiatric patients as well as a normative group consisting on approximately 750 individuals, primarily skilled laborers and farmers, many of whom were visitors to the University of Minnesota Hospital. Items were selected for a particular diagnostic scale if they discriminated sufficiently between members of a specific diagnostic group (e.g., individuals with depression) and members of the normal group. This procedure yielded the eight original MMPI Clinical Scales.

Although initially insufficiently effective in predicting membership in specific diagnostic categories (Hathaway, 1960), the MMPI underwent a transformation from an instrument designed to predict diagnostic taxonomies to one that relies on empirically derived correlates in assessing symptomotology and personality patterns. The call for establishing empirical correlates for the MMPI was made by Meehl (1945, 1954), who suggested that the test would be optimally used if such correlates were established. These recommendations were subsequently followed by Meehl's (1956) call for a "good cookbook" that would inform clinicians about the empirical correlates of the MMPI scales.

Several large-scale studies establishing the empirical correlates of MMPI codetypes were conducted after Meehl issued his call. Marks and Seeman (1963) published an empirical codebook that provided correlates of codetypes for psychiatric inpatients. Gilberstadt and Duker (1965) published empirical correlates of codetypes for 360 male VA inpatients. These and other source books serve as the foundation for contemporary interpretation texts such as those written by Graham (2006) and Greene (2000).

In the 1970s, it was becoming increasingly apparent that some changes were in order for the MMPI. One of the greatest needs was to update the tests norms. As mentioned earlier, the original normative data were collected in the late 1930s and consisted primarily of Caucasian, working-class, rural Minnesotans possessing an average of 8 years of education. Although this sample was appropriate during the MMPI's initial conception, it was no longer adequate given its widespread use across the United States and the world. The second need was to revise some MMPI items that were outdated or phrased awkwardly. Some items had content that was no longer clear, relevant, or appropriate based on modern language use, cultural practices, and social norms. Other items contained sexist language or controversial religious statements. A final issue concerned the need to encompass a broader range of content domains, including domains that were not necessarily salient in the 1930s but had grown very relevant in contemporary assessment (e.g., suicidal ideation, Type A behavior, substance abuse, low self-esteem, and treatment indicators).

In order to deal with the problems just noted, the University of Minnesota Press, the test's publisher, formed a restandardization committee to coordinate the revision of the MMPI. This committee had two major goals: to improve the test and at the same time to maintain continuity with the original version to the extent possible. The second goal was necessary to ensure that the large amount of research generated on the original MMPI could still be applied with the revision.

The restandardization project produced the MMPI-2 (Butcher, Dahlstrom, Graham, Tellegen, & Kaemmer, 1989), including a new normative sample (described in greater detail next) consisting of 1,138 men and 1,462 women of diverse ethnic backgrounds and from different regions of the United States. The MMPI-2 consists of 567 items. Of the 383 items on the basic Validity and Clincial Scales, 372 were retained in the MMPI-2. Eleven items were deleted, and a total of 64 items were slightly revised. Ben-Porath and Butcher (1989a, 1989b) found that these changed did not alter the psychometric functioning of the Validity or Clinical Scales.

PSYCHOMETRIC CHARACTERSTICS OF THE MMPI-2

Standardization and Norms

The MMPI-2 normative sample consists of 1,138 male and 1,462 female community volunteers who were tested in seven states (California, Minnesota, North Carolina, Ohio,

Pennsylvania, Virginia, and Washington) and their demographic makeup was designed to match the 1980 U.S. census. A comparison with the 1997 annual census information reveals even closer similarities (Butcher et al., 2001), except that Hispanics are underrepresented in the normative sample.

The racial distribution of the MMPI–2 normative sample is 82% Caucasian, 11% African American, 3% Hispanic, 3% Native American, and less than 1% Asian American for the men, and 81% Caucasian, 13% African American, 3% Hispanic, 3% Native American, and 1% Asian American for the women. Individuals in the normative sample have an average of 14.72 years of education, which is slightly higher than for the general adult U.S. population (according to 1997 census information). Normative sample members range in age from 18 to 85 years old. Analyses were conducted for various age subgroupings, and it was determined that separate norms were not needed.

Several studies have examined the associations between demographic variables and scores on MMPI–2 scales. Schinka, LaLone, and Greene (1998) concluded that demographics contributed little to the ability of the majority of MMPI–2 scales to discriminate between psychiatric inpatients and the normative sample, with the exception of gender, which added significantly to the discrimination for *ASP, FRS,* and *MAC–R* but also gender-based scales such as scale 5 and the two Gender Roles Supplementary Scales. Moreover, Long, Graham, and Timbrook (1994) concluded that educational and family income levels likely have little association with MMPI–2 scores. Some researchers have criticized the MMPI–2 normative sample for its high educational level. Schinka and LaLone (1997) examined this issue and concluded that the higher-than-average education level of the MMPI–2 normative sample has no meaningful impact on test scores.

Because of concerns that there may be confounding gender differences in test-taking approaches to the MMPI/MMPI–2, the instrument has traditionally had separate norms for men and women. This approach reflected concerns that women might be more willing to endorse symptoms of psychopathology than men (Graham, 2006). More recently, Ben-Porath and Forbey (2003) developed non-gender-based norms for MMPI–2 scores. These norms were necessary to create in order to comply with the congressional Civil Rights Act of 1991, which prohibits gender-based norming in preemployment evaluations. Ben-Porath and Forbey (2003) reported that moving from gendered to nongendered norms had negligible impact on MMPI–2 *T*-scores, indicating that concerns about a possible gender-based confounding are unwarranted.

MMPI–2 raw scores are converted to *T*-scores to facilitate standardized interpretation. For MMPI–2 psychopathology measures, uniform *T*-scores are used to ensure percentile comparability across scales (Tellegen & Ben-Porath, 1992). Uniform *T*-scores are used for the Clinical, RC, Content, and PSY-5 scales.

Reliability

The MMPI–2 manual (Butcher et al., 2001), the PSY-5 test report (Harkness, McNulty, Ben-Porath, & Graham, 2002), and the RC Scale monograph (Tellegen et al., 2003) provide detailed information concerning the reliability of the various MMPI–2 scales. Thus, only a concise summary is provided here.

In terms of internal consistency, the Clinical Scales are the least internally consistent, which would be expected, as they were not designed to be homogeneous scales. The Content, PSY-5, and RC Scales were all constructed with an emphasis on internal consistency. In the normative sample, the internal consistencies for the Clinical Scales range from .34 to .85 for men and from .37 to .87 for women, the RC Scales from .63 to .87 for men and from .62 to .89 for women, and the Content Scales from .72 to .86 for men and from .68 to .86 for women. The internal consistencies for the Supplementary Scales range from .34 to .89 for men and from .24 to .90 for women, whereas those for the PSY-5 Scales range from .65 to .84 for both men and women.

In the normative sample, the test-retest correlations for the Clinical Scales range from .67 to .93 for men and from .54 to .92 for women, those for the RC Scales range from .62 to .88 for the combined sample, and those for the Content Scales range from .77 to .91 for men and from .78 to .91 for women. The Supplementary Scales had test-retest correlations that range from .63 to .91 for men and from .69 to .91 for women. Harkness et al. (2002) reported PSY-5 Scale test-retest coefficients for the overall sample that range from .78 to .88.

Validity

The MMPI–2 is unparalleled in terms of the number of validity studies that it has generated (e.g., Butcher & Rouse, 1996). Dahlstrom, Welsh, and Dahlstrom (1975) referenced over 6,000 research studies conducted with the original MMPI. Many of these studies followed Meehl's (1956) call for a "good cookbook" and for researchers to identify empirical correlates for the test's scales and codetypes. Numerous studies were conducted with psychiatric inpatients (e.g., Marks and Seeman, 1963; Gilberstadt and Duker, 1965), medical patients (Guthrie, 1949), adolescents (Archer, Gordon, Giannetti, & Singles, 1988; Hathaway & Monachesi, 1963), and normal college students (e.g., Black, 1953).

The research with the MMPI–2 has continued in the same vein. Graham (2006) indicated that since the MMPI–2 was published, 2,800 journal articles, book chapters, and textbooks about the test have been published. Although it is well beyond the score of this chapter to summarize these studies, we provide some overall conclusions regarding the validity of the various MMPI–2 scales.

Many research studies have supported the use of the Validity Scales in detecting both over- and underreporting (e.g., Graham, Watts, & Timbrook, 1991). Rogers, Sewell, Martin, and Vitacco (2003) conducted a meta-analysis of the MMPI–2 overreporting scales and found that the infrequency scales (F, F_B, and F_P) were effective in detecting malingering. They also noted that F_P consistently had the largest effect size in differentiating individuals asked to malinger from those who took the test under standard instructions. Arbisi and Ben-Porath (1998) found that F_P added incrementally to F in differentiating psychiatric inpatients asked to overreport from those who took the test honestly. Another meta-analysis by Baer and Miller (2002) indicated that the L scale was consistently the best predictor of underreporting but noted effectiveness for K as well.

The convergent validity of the Clinical, Content, Supplementary, and PSY-5 Scales and codetypes has been established in outpatient (Graham, Ben-Porath, & McNulty, 1999; Harkness et al., 2002), inpatient (Arbisi, Ben-Porath, & McNulty, 2003; Archer, Aiduk, Griffin, & Elkins, 1996; Archer, Griffin, & Aiduk, 1995), forensic (Petroskey, Ben-Porath, & Stafford, 2003), college student (Ben-Porath, McCully, & Almagor, 1993), and private practice samples (Sellbom, Graham, & Schenk, 2005). These correlates have been remarkably similar across studies and also congruent with those of the original MMPI (Graham, 2006), indicating that the correlates of the MMPI–2 generalize well across settings.

However, the discriminant validity for several MMPI–2 scales has been problematic. Many of the correlate studies just mentioned show that MMPI–2 scales, most so the Clinical Scales, are significantly correlated with affective-laden (i.e., depression, anxiety) criteria, including scales where this would not be expected. Welsh (1956) indicated early through factor analysis that a common higher order factor labeled "Anxiety" saturates the Clinical Scales. Tellegen et al. (2003) more recently labeled this component "Demoralization." In restructuring the Clinical Scales, they sought to minimize its impact to the extent theoretically indicated and empirically feasible. Research on the RC Scales has demonstrated comparable to improved convergent and significantly improved discriminant validity compared with the Clinical Scales (Sellbom & Ben-Porath, in press; Sellbom, Ben-Porath, & Graham, 2004; Tellegen et al., 2003).

Psychometric Strengths and Weaknesses

The strengths of the MMPI–2 include the vast research literature on the scales supporting their convergent validity as well as effectiveness in detecting a variety of clinically relevant problems, such as substance abuse difficulties and malingering. However, limitations of the test include the just discussed excessive intercorrelations among the Clinical Scales. This challenge requires test interpreters to rely on other MMPI–2 sources (e.g., codetypes, Content Scales). Moreover, the inclusion of "subtle items" and the use of the K correction may attenuate the convergent validity of the Clinical Scales (Barthlow, Graham, Ben-Porath, Tellegen, & McNulty, 2002; Detrick, Chibnall, & Rosso, 2001; Weed, Ben-Porath, & Butcher, 1990). Most of these challenges have been remedied through the development of the RC Scales, but more research is needed to establish their validity in a variety of settings.

CLINICAL USES AND LIMITATIONS

The original purpose of the MMPI was to assist in psychodiagnosis, but it was quickly determined that this could not be accomplished with sufficient accuracy. Instead, MMPI–2 information now focuses on assessing the test taker's level of adjustment, specific symptoms of psychopathology, personality characteristics, and interpersonal functioning. This information can, of course, be considered in generating diagnostic impressions as well as in treatment planning and to form opinions for various decisions, including those regarding psychological functioning.

Mental Health Settings

Not surprisingly, the MMPI–2 is most commonly used in mental health assessment and treatment centers (Graham, 2006). Several researchers have provided detailed information on the correlates of the MMPI and MMPI–2 in these settings as well as recommendations for interpretation (Archer et al., 1995; Gilberstadt & Duker, 1965; Graham et al., 1999; Harkness et al., 2002; Marks & Seeman, 1963; Tellegen et al., 2003). Relatedly, Sellbom, Graham et al. (2005) reported the correlates of MMPI–2 scales and codetypes for clients in private practice and found that the correlational patterns were virtually identical to those obtained in other outpatient studies (e.g., Graham et al., 1999).

The MMPI–2 is generally used to identify clinical conditions in these settings. The test can generate inferences regarding general maladjustment and psychopathology symptoms (e.g., depression, anxiety, hallucinations) to aid in diagnosis and case conceptualization. The MMPI–2 can also be used to screen for substance abuse problems, as indicated by scores on *MAC–R, AAS,* and *APS* (Graham & Strenger, 1988; Weed, Butcher, McKenna, & Ben-Porath, 1992). Finally, the MMPI–2 can produce information about personality traits that should be considered in case conceptualization and treatment planning.

Medical Settings

The MMPI–2 is frequently used is medical settings. Arbisi and Butcher (2004) provide a detailed review of the instrument's use in these settings. One important use of the MMPI–2 with medical patients has been to screen for serious psychopathology that may not have been detected (Graham, 2006). The MMPI–2 can further be used to understand how persons with medical problems are affected by them psychologically by consulting the variety of scales that give indications of general emotional distress (e.g., RC Demoralization, Mean 8 Clinical Scales). Conversely, the role of psychological factors in physical health complaints can also be examined with the MMPI–2.

Substance abuse problems are quite common among persons being treated primarily for medical conditions. The MMPI–2 can be useful in alerting clinicians to the possibility of substance abuse. Fordyce (1979) suggested that the MMPI could be helpful in identifying individuals who misuse prescribed medication. He argued that high scores on Clinical Scales 2 and 9 were particularly helpful. The Supplementary Scales *MAC–R, AAS*, and *APS* are helpful in indicating increased risk for or actual substance abuse.

The MMPI–2 can also provide important information concerning how medical patients are likely to respond psychologically to medical interventions, including the prediction of pre- and postoperative adjustment (Henrichs & Waters, 1972), psychosocial adjustment of cancer patients (Sobel & Worden, 1979), gastric bypass surgery (Barrash, Rodriguez, Scott, Mason, & Sines, 1987; Tsushima, Bridenstine, & Balfour, 2004), and response to chronic pain treatment programs (Akerlind, Hornquist, & Bjurulf, 1992; Vendrig, Derksen, & de Mey, 1999). The MMPI/MMPI–2 has also demonstrated some success in identifying individuals at higher risk for coronary heart disease (Barefoot, Dahlstrom, & Williams, 1983; Kawachi et al., 1998; Williams et al., 1980).

Preemployment Screening

The MMPI/MMPI–2 is frequently used in selecting employees for sensitive occupations (e.g., law enforcement, commercial piloting, nuclear power plant operation) (Butcher, 1979, 1985). Preemployment screening is particularly justified when the presence of psychological dysfunction may jeopardize the safety of the community. Consider, for example, an airline pilot with a substance abuse problem or a law enforcement officer with an impulsive disposition. Several research studies have demonstrated that the MMPI can be useful in screening for psychopathology in nonclinical settings (e.g., Lachar, 1974). These studies cover individuals in a wide range of occupations, including police applicants (e.g., Bernstein, 1980; Beutler, Storm, Kirkish, Scogin, & Gaines, 1985; Costello, Schoenfeld, & Kobos, 1982; Hartman, 1987; Inwald, 1988), physician's assistants (Crovitz, Huse, & Lewis, 1973), medical assistants (Stone, Bassett, Brousseau, Demers, & Stiening, 1972), psychiatric residents (Garetz & Anderson, 1973), clinical psychology graduate students (Butcher, 1979), nurses (Kelly, 1974), firefighters (Avery, Mussio, & Payne, 1972; Liao, Arvey, Butler, & Nutting, 2000), probation officers (Solway, Hays, & Zieben, 1976), and nuclear power plant personnel (Dunnette, Bownas, & Bosshardt, 1981). Most of these studies have focused primarily on the ability of the Clinical Scales to identify potential problems in applicants.

Detrick et al. (2001) found that MMPI–2 scores correlated moderately with scores on the Inwald Personality Inventory (IPI), which was designed to identify problem areas specific to law enforcement candidates. Other studies found that Clinical Scales 4 and 9 were particularly (but modestly) related to worse job outcomes (Bartol, 1991; Costello,

Schneider, & Schoenfeld, 1996). More recently, Fischler (2005) reported that MMPI–2 scores can predict negative outcomes (e.g., sustained Internal Affairs complaints) for police officers, with the RC Scales showing particular promise in this area.

Strengths and Limitations

The major strength of the MMPI–2 is the vast amount of research that has been conducted with the instrument, which has established its utility for many purposes. This research has focused on symptom and personality correlates, the instrument's accuracy in classifying various conditions, and its predictive validity, to mention a few areas. Moreover, the MMPI–2 validity scales are unparalleled in terms of research support for effectively identifying misleading response styles. This makes the instrument very appealing for most types of evaluations, including those in which individuals might have a strong incentive to distort their self-report.

As discussed earlier, in spite of the broad literature available to guide their interpretation, there exist significant challenges to the interpretation of the Clinical Scales stemming from the methods used to construct them. These have been addressed previously through the development of a variety of strategies to augment their interpretation, including reliance on codetypes, subscales, and a variety of supplementary sources of information. As a result, MMPI–2 interpretation can be rather complex. The recently introduced RC Scales were designed to provide a more parsimonious solution to these challenges. Initial findings are promising; however, further research is needed to identify and replicate their correlates in a variety of settings.

Another limitation concerns the generation of diagnostic impressions. Although the MMPI–2 provides information regarding symptomotology associated with various forms of psychopathology, the MMPI–2 in itself cannot be relied upon to generate diagnostic impressions. Efforts to generate MMPI–2 profiles that are consistent with specific types of psychopathology have failed. Examples include so-called "floating" profiles for borderline personality disorder (e.g., Gartner, Hurt, & Gartner, 1989) and posttraumatic stress disorder (PTSD; see Keane, Malloy, & Fairbank, 1984).

FORENSIC USES AND LIMITATIONS

Early use of the MMPI focused primarily on the characterization and explanation of criminal behavior (see Dahlstrom et al., 1975). Studies by Capwell (1945a, 1945b) and Hathaway and Monachesi (1953, 1957) examined the personality patterns of juvenile delinquents. Hatahway and Monachesi found that certain Clinical Scales were of an "excitatory" nature (4, 8, and 9), meaning that they predicted greater likelihood for acting out, whereas other scales were of an "inhibitory" nature (2, 5, and 0). Delinquents were found to score higher on the excitatory scales than nondelinquents. A number of early researchers focused on the etiology of criminal behavior, using the MMPI as a proxy for underlying personological explanations for various crimes, including heroin dependency (Sutker & Allain, 1973) and aggressiveness (e.g., Megargee & Mendelsohn, 1962). For instance, Pothast (1956) conducted an early study in which he examined personological differences between instrumental murderers and affective/reactive murderers. He found that the psychoticism scales were higher among the instrumental murderers, whereas the neuroticism scales were higher among the affective murderers.

Present forensic applications of the MMPI–2 are extensive. Several surveys have indicated that the MMPI–2 is more frequently used in forensic settings than any other test

(Lees-Haley, 1992) and is considered appropriate for most forensic questions (Lally, 2003). The MMPI–2 is second only to the Wechsler Intelligence Scales in forensic neuropsychological evaluations (Lees-Haley, Smith, Williams, & Dunn, 1996). The test is also used quite frequently in other countries, such as Australia (Martin, Allan, & Allan, 2001), for forensic purposes. Given the instrument's widespread use in forensic assessments, Otto (2002) indicates that the question is not whether it is appropriate to use the MMPI–2 in forensic settings but rather for what purposes. We concur and address this question later. However, we first discuss some general issues concerning using the MMPI–2 in forensic assessment.

Issues Concerning MMPI–2 Use in Forensic Assessment

Admissibility of MMPI–2 Testimony

If an expert relies on the MMPI–2 to form an opinion to be offered in testimony, the basis for this opinion may be scrutinized and admissibility denied if the testimony fails to meet certain standards. In federal courts and most state courts, the applicable standards are outlined in the U.S. Supreme Court decision in *Daubert v. Merrell Dow Pharmaceuticals, Inc.* (1993). In its ruling on *Daubert*, the Supreme Court established that trial judges must determine the validity of inferences based on a scientific technique by considering whether (1) the technique can be and has been tested empirically, (2) the technique has been subjected to peer review, (3) the error rates of the technique are known, (4) there are standards for applying the technique, and (5) the technique is generally accepted in the relevant scientific discipline. The last criterion refers back to the *Frye v. U.S.* (1923) ruling regarding expert testimony, which still applies in several states.

In general, the MMPI–2 meets these criteria. It was developed through an empirical method, and much of its interpretation is based on empirical correlates derived for the scales. Moreover, the applications of the test are inheritably testable. The MMPI/MMPI–2 has been studied in over 8,800 publications that have appeared in peer-reviewed journals. Psychometric techniques lend themselves well to analyses of error rates (by considering test score reliability), and numerous research studies have examined the false-positive and -negative rates of the test's scales in predicting a variety of phenomena. The MMPI–2 test manual provides direct guidelines for standardized administration and scoring. Finally, as mentioned earlier, the MMPI–2 is one of the most used psychological tests in both clinical practice (Camara et al., 2000) and forensic settings (Lees-Haley, 1992).

However, these general statements alone do not justify using the MMPI–2 in forensic evaluations. In any given case, the question is whether a specific conclusion reached by an expert on the basis of MMPI–2 findings can meet the standards for admissibility. Thus, when faced with a *Daubert* challenge, the expert must be prepared to cite original peer-reviewed research to support his or her conclusions as well as to answer any other *Daubert*-relevant questions. For example, in *U.S. v. Huberty* (2000), Lt. Col. Huberty was facing criminal charges of indecent exposure. An expert witness testifying for the defense argued that Huberty could not be guilty of the crime because his MMPI–2 profile was not indicative of exhibitionism. The testimony was not admitted, however, because no empirical research has demonstrated that exhibitionists produce specific MMPI–2 profiles.

Of specific concern to those who use the MMPI–2 in forensic assessments is how to incorporate innovations in their interpretations. As described earlier, the MMPI/MMPI–2 is an empirically grounded instrument that is constantly undergoing scrutiny, change, and improvement as a result of ongoing research and development. Thus, for example, the recently introduced RC Scales offer significant improvements over the original Clinical Scales; however, they do not at this time have as broad and extensive a research base as the original Clinical Scales to guide their interpretation. Fortunately, forensic examiners need not choose between interpreting one or another of these sets of scales. Rather the current recommendation is to use the RC Scales to help refine Clinical Scale interpretation (Tellegen et al., 2003) in the same way that codetypes, subscales, and Supplementary Scales are relied upon. Indeed, integration of RC Scale results with the results from other MMPI–2 sources often shows consistency. Thus, at this time, the RC Scales are best viewed as a parsimonious set of scales that can help guide MMPI–2 interpretation by disentangling some of the complexities involved in its interpretation in a manner that can then be corroborated by consulting additional MMPI–2 sources (codetypes, subscales, and various Supplementary Scales). This approach is illustrated in the case example at the end of the chapter. As the empirical research base on the RC Scales accumulates over the next few years, it will become increasingly less necessary to corroborate RC Scale findings with longer-established supplementary MMPI–2 sources.

Malingering and Defensiveness

The incentive to distort one's responses on the MMPI–2 is high in both criminal and civil evaluations. The *Diagnostic and Statistical Manual of Mental Disorders* (*DSM–IV–TR*; American Psychiatric Association, 2000) defines malingering as the exaggeration or fabrication of physical and psychological symptoms for external incentives. For instance, an individual faced with criminal charges might want to appear more psychologically disturbed than he or she really is in order to be found not guilty by reason of insanity. Several research studies have suggested that malingering is in fact common in forensic evaluations. Grossman and Wasyliw (1988) estimated that almost 41% of all insanity defendants malinger during psychological evaluations. In personal injury settings, it has been estimated that 18–33% of clients intentionally distort their responses (Binder, 1993; Mittenburg, Patton, Canyock, & Condit, 2002).

As mentioned earlier, several MMPI–2 scales have been designed to measure over-reporting. The F scales (F, F_B, F_P) are quite useful for this purpose. The F_P scale is the most effective indicator when the base rate for psychopathology is high (Arbisi & Ben-Porath, 1998), and a recent meta-analysis (Rogers et al., 2003) indicates that it has the highest effect size of all MMPI–2 overreporting indicators in identifying malingering protocols. Although relatively few research studies have examined the utility of the F scales in forensic settings specifically, some studies have shown that the scales can differentiate individuals who have been asked to malinger on the MMPI–2 from forensic inpatients and criminal defendants (Bagby, Buis, & Nicholson, 1995; Bagby, Rogers, & Buis, 1994; Hawk & Cornell, 1989; Roman, Tuley, Villanueva, & Mitchell, 1990). In a more recent study, Gallagher (1997) showed that the F_P scale added incrementally to F in differentiating correctional inpatients asked to malinger from those who took the test under standard instructions. Moreover, there is no reason to expect that the F scales would function any differently in forensic settings than they do in the multitude of other settings in which they have been studied.

A frequently studied scale in personal injury contexts is the Fake Bad Scale (FBS; Lees-Haley, English, & Glenn, 1991). It was proposed as an alternative to the F Scales as the latter set are sensitive to "acting crazy" exaggeration, which presumably does not frequently occur in personal injury settings in which the individual "acts hurt" (Larrabee, 2003a). Thus, the FBS focuses primarily on somatic embellishment. This scale has gained some empirical support, particularly for identifying individuals who perform sub-optimally on cognitive tasks (Greiffenstein, Baker, Gola, Donders, & Miller, 2002; Larrabee, 2003b, 2003c; Slick, Hopp, Strauss, & Spellacy, 1996). Some researchers have questioned its construct validity (Bury & Bagby, 2002; Butcher, Arbisi, Atlis, & McNulty, 2003; Dearth et al., 2005; Rogers et al., 2003), as scores on the FBS have been found to be potentially confounded with genuine somatic problems, possibly limiting its ability to differentiate between litigants who have suffered genuine physical injuries and those attempting to malinger such conditions (Butcher et al., 2003). Some questions have also been raised regarding its utility in detecting spurious PTSD complaints (Bury & Bagby, 2002; Elhai, Gold, Frueh, & Gold, 2000). Greiffenstein, Fox, and Lees-Haley (2006) address these concerns and offer recommendations for adjusting cutoffs on the FBS that should alleviate the potential for false positive findings.

Some individuals undergoing forensic assessments may minimize or deny psychological problems. Examples include parents undergoing a child custody evaluation or patients seeking early release from a forensic hospital. Several MMPI–2 scales mentioned earlier (L and K) can be useful in identifying underreporting. Many studies have supported their clinical use in general (see Baer & Miller, 2002, for a meta-analysis), but few studies have examined their ability to detect defensiveness in forensic settings per se. Although there is no a priori reason to assume that findings from other settings would not generalize to test takers in forensic settings, future research should nonetheless explore the utility of the L and K scales in forensic evaluations specifically.

Another issue concerning the assessment of malingering and defensiveness involves coaching. Wetter and Corrigan (1995) found that almost 50% of attorneys and 33% of law students felt that it was their responsibility to inform their clients about the test's Validity Scales and their operation. Such information certainly could reduce the MMPI–2's ability to detect response distortion. Mere knowledge and professional understanding of clinical syndromes does not appear to aid in avoiding detection by the Validity Scales (Bagby et al., 1997; Rogers, Bagby, & Chakraborty, 1993; Wetter, Baer, Berry, & Reynolds, 1994); however, instruction about how the Validity Scales function does have an effect (Rogers et al., 1993, 2003; Storm & Graham, 2000). Despite this effect, a large portion of coached malingerers were still correctly identified in these studies.

The Utility of K Correction

Although K correction, a procedure that involves adding a certain proportion of the K raw score to five of the Clinical Scales, has an extensive history, its utility has long been questioned (Graham, 2006; Greene, 2000; see also Dahlstrom & Welsh, 1960). The MMPI–2 publisher recommends that in cases where a test taker produces deviant scores on K (i.e., where K correction is likely to significantly alter Clinical Scale scores), the non-K-corrected profile be reviewed in order to determine the impact of the K correction. Moreover, none of the supplementary sources used to refine Clinical Scale interpretation (e.g., Harris-Lingoes subscales and RC, Content, and PSY-5 Scales) are K corrected, confounding differences between the Clinical Scales and these supplementary sources.

Norms for non-K-corrected Clinical Scale scores have been available since the MMPI–2 was first published in 1989. The Extended Score Report, an automated scoring system for the MMPI–2 distributed by Pearson Assessments, provides scores on both K-corrected and non-K-corrected profiles. As early as 1960, Dahlstrom and Welsh raised questions about the applicability of K correction in a correctional setting, but it has nonetheless been used routinely because of concerns that the correlate literature is based on K-corrected scales (Dahlstrom et al., 1975). Recent research indicates that in clinical settings K-corrected scores are no more valid than non-K-corrected scores (Barthlow et al., 2002), and in nonclinical settings characterized by a significant incentive to underreport, K correction may substantially attenuate if not altogether obliterate the validity of Clinical Scale scores. Following up on this research, Ben-Porath and Forbey (2004) examined the impact of K correction in three clinical and three nonclinical archival samples. They concluded that K correction did not improve the validity of Clinical Scale scores in any setting and significantly attenuated their validity in some instances. They also reported that correlates of codetypes classified based on non-K-corrected scores of the clinical scales are similar in content to but tend to be stronger in magnitude than those based on K-corrected scores. Thus, MMPI–2 codetypes based on non-K-corrected Clinical Scales can be interpreted on the basis of the existing research literature, but with greater confidence. Therefore, it is our recommendation that forensic examiners consider the non-K-corrected profile in their MMPI–2 interpretation. If it points to a different inference than does the K-corrected profile, interpreters should rely on other MMPI–2 sources and the just described research findings in determining which inference is most likely to be correct. This procedure is illustrated by means of the case example at the end of the chapter.

Ethnic Minority Considerations

The original MMPI was developed and normed primarily with Caucasians. As a result, it was questioned whether the test would be appropriate for use with members of ethnic minorities, which sparked a plethora of studies examining differences in MMPI scores among various ethnic groups. A review by Greene (1987) concluded that there were no systematic MMPI score differences between Caucasians and any of the ethnic minorities studied, and the few differences that were found were not clinically meaningful.

The MMPI–2 normative sample was more racially diverse and more closely matched the U.S. population as determined by most recent U.S. census. However, studies have continued to examine potential differences between the scores of Caucasians and ethnic minorities on the MMPI–2. Hall, Bansal, and Lopez (1999) conducted a meta-analysis that revealed no systematic mean group differences between Caucasians and African Americans, Latinos, and Asian Americans. However, to study test bias, it is not sufficient to examine group differences, as these differences may actually reflect real differences and not bias. Conversely, test bias may still exist in the absence of group differences. Therefore, researchers have begun to examine differential predictive validity for Caucasians and ethnic minority groups tested using the MMPI–2. Timbrook and Graham (1994) found that MMPI–2 scale scores predicted extra test criteria equally well for Caucasian and African-American individuals in the MMPI–2 normative sample. This finding has been replicated in a community mental health center (McNulty, Graham, Ben-Porath, & Stein, 1997). A more recent study (Arbisi, Ben-Porath, & McNulty, 2002) examined the differential predictive validity of MMPI–2 scores for Caucasian and African-American inpatients using hierarchical regression analyses. They found very few differences across the Clinical and Content Scales, and where there were differences, the MMPI–2 scores appeared to unexpectedly underpredict psychopathology for Caucasians rather than African Americans. These differences, however, were not clinically meaningful.

A recent study comparing Native Americans with the MMPI–2 normative sample revealed few systematic group differences (Robin, Greene, Albaugh, Caldwell, & Goldman,

2003). The differences that did emerge were expected and likely indicated real differences in psychopathology (e.g., scales 4, 8, 9, *CYN, MAC–R*, and *AAS*). Greene, Robin, Albaugh, Caldwell, and Goldman (2003) conducted a follow-up study in which they examined the correlations for MMPI–2 scores with extra test criteria for the Native-American samples. They generally found expected correlates, with a few exceptions (e.g., *MAC–R*).

Recent studies with Asian Americans have focused on the effect of acculturation (the degree to which an individual has assimilated the values and behaviors of the majority culture) on MMPI–2 scores (Tsai & Pike, 2000). The authors found that the less acculturated students had higher scores than Caucasian students on most MMPI–2 scales, with the greatest differences on the *F* Scale and Scale 8. Highly acculturated students did not differ meaningfully from the Caucasian students. Okazaki and Sue (1995) have stressed the importance of considering the acculturation levels of Asian Americans when conducting psychological evaluations. No studies have examined the differential predictive validity of MMPI–2 scores for Caucasian and Asian-American individuals. Such research is needed, as the acculturation-related differences just noted may also reflect adjustment difficulties that are accurately captured by the MMPI–2 scale elevations found in less acculturated individuals.

Although several research studies have focused on mean group differences between Caucasians and Hispanics (see Greene, 1987, and Hall et al., 1999), no studies have examined the differential predictive validity of MMPI–2 scores for Hispanic individuals. Such research is also very much needed, especially given the large growth of the Hispanic population in the United States.

A few research studies have examined MMPI and MMPI–2 differences between Caucasians and ethnic minorities in forensic settings. These studies have primarily focused on mean group differences. African Americans tend to score higher on Scale 9, lower on Scale 0 (Holcomb & Adams, 1982), and higher on Scale 4 (Elion & Megargee, 1975). Ben-Porath, Shondrick, and Stafford (1995) compared the MMPI–2 scores of African-American and Caucasian men who underwent court-ordered psychological evaluations. The African-American group scored higher on the Antisocial Practices and Cynicism Content Scales. Gironda (1999) has found in the same court-ordered sample that MMPI–2 scale scores predicted external criteria equally well for both Caucasian and African-American men.

Finally, it is worth noting that the MMPI–2 has been translated into dozens of languages and adopted successfully in many diverse countries and cultures (e.g., Butcher, 1996). This indicates that the instrument is quite robust to cultural differences and can be applied appropriately with a broad range of individuals undergoing forensic examinations.

In conclusion, additional research is needed to examine the differential predictive validity for MMPI–2 scales across ethnic minority groups, especially in forensic settings. However, the empirical findings to date to suggest that the MMPI–2 scales will be equally valid for Caucasian and African-American test takers, including those undergoing forensic evaluations.

Administrative and Interpretative Issues

Graham (2006) offered several recommendations concerning the administration and interpretation of the MMPI–2 in forensic settings. It is very important that individuals taking the MMPI–2 in a forensic setting be monitored by trained professionals or technicians. This issue becomes especially salient when the forensic examiner is faced with the task of testifying as to whether the defendant took the MMPI–2 under supervised conditions to ensure that no external influences contaminated the responses.

The standard administration requires a test booklet or computer, but if the defendant cannot read at a sixth-grade level, there are audio versions of the MMPI–2 available on cassette or CD. It is not appropriate to read MMPI–2 items to the test taker, as a variety of nonverbal behaviors might influence the answers.

Short forms of the MMPI–2 should be avoided. Research has generally indicated that most short forms of the MMPI/MMPI–2 are not as valid as the full-length version (Graham, 2006). One potential short form would be to administer only the first 370 items of the test, which include the basic validity (L, F, K) and Clinical Scales. We recommend against this practice because a number of standard components of the test (e.g., the $VRIN$, $TRIN$, F_P, Content, PSY-5, and RC Scales) cannot be scored based on the abbreviated administration.

Scoring the MMPI–2 in a forensic assessment can be accomplished using any of the standard techniques described earlier. These include hand scoring with templates or automatic scoring with a number of available systems. Because of the possibility of error and the tendency to score fewer scales when hand scoring, this approach, though possible, is not recommended for forensic practice. Automated scoring is more time efficient and less error prone, provided that the forensic examiner use only officially licensed and approved software. In addition to raising questions about the knowledge and credibility of the examiner, reliance on unlicensed (i.e., bootleg) software to score an MMPI–2 test often results in scoring errors that could significantly skew the results.

As indicated, MMPI–2 interpretation can be informed by an extensive empirical literature. Implications of this literature are reflected in standard interpretative texts such as Graham (2006) and Greene (2000). However, in the adversarial forensic environment, it behooves the forensic examiner to be able to cite original empirical research, not just secondary sources, to support his or her opinions and conclusions.

Specific Forensic Applications

Competency to Stand Trial

Psychologists are often asked to provide opinions regarding a defendant's competency to stand trial. The current criteria for competency were first outlined in *Dusky v. United States* (1960), which established that to be considered competent to stand trial defendants must (a) reasonably understand the legal proceedings they face, including the roles of various participants in this process, and (b) have the ability to meaningfully assist in own defense. These criteria are of a functional nature, and Ogloff (1995) stated that the MMPI–2 may have little to offer in this regard. However, a threshold question in conducting a competency-to-stand-trial evaluation is whether the defendant has a mental condition that could impair these functions. Moreover, the possibility of malingering must always be considered in conducting such an evaluations. Thus, although the MMPI–2 cannot directly answer the questions of competency (other information is needed for that purpose), there are several ways in which MMPI–2 data can add to the information upon which a competency opinion is based. The Validity Scales can provide relevant information regarding the possibility of malingering, or the lack thereof, and the MMPI–2 substantive scales (Clinical, RC, Content, etc.) can provide information regarding the likelihood that the individual has a mental condition that could impair his or her competency to stand trial. For example, Stafford and Wygant (2005) reported that psychotic symptoms are frequently found in defendants who are incompetent to stand trial. The MMPI–2 has a number of valid scales to predict psychotic symptomotology.

Criminal Responsibility

In order to be found guilty of a crime, a defendant must have the capacity to form criminal intent. Otherwise, the defendant is determined to be not guilty by reason of insanity (NGRI). Over the past 2 decades, several definitions have been employed concerning the determination of sanity. These generally require a mental incapacity that affects behavior. Most standards also include cognitive incapacity that influences the defendant's ability to appreciate the nature or wrongfulness of his or her actions and/or volitional incapacity that encompasses the inability to control behavior (Melton, Petrila, Poythress, & Slobogin, 1997).

The assessment of criminal responsibility is retrospective in nature. The forensic examiner will evaluate the defendant weeks, months, or (on rare occasions) years after the alleged criminal act. Because the determination of legal sanity requires answering specific questions regarding an individual's mental state at the time of the offense, the MMPI–2 and similar tests have more limited utility in NGRI evaluations than in competency-to-stand-trial evaluations. Moreover, there is little research to support the use of the MMPI–2 in answering legal questions directly related to insanity. For example, Rogers and McKee (1995) found that there is no research to suggest that insane defendants score differently than sane defendants on the MMPI–2, with the exception of the antisocial behavior scales (e.g., Scale 4, ASP) on which insane defendants score lower.

Nevertheless, Lally (2003) reported that the majority of the diplomate forensic examiners in his study recommended using the MMPI–2 for criminal responsibility evaluations. This finding is likely because the MMPI–2 generates information that is relevant to the evaluation even though it does not directly address the psycholegal questions. The MMPI–2 Validity Scales can assist in the identification of current attempts to malinger. This is noteworthy because if a defendant attempts to fake psychopathology in the course of an NGRI evaluation, it occurs at the time of the evaluation, not for the alleged crime. In addition, individuals who were found NGRI are likely to have chronic and severe disorders that would be reflected in a current MMPI–2 protocol. Finally, such defendants have sometimes had prior contact with the mental health system, and preoffense MMPI–2 protocols may exist that can be compared with a current protocol to help establish the presence or absence of a severe disorder prior to an alleged offense.

Risk Assessment

Risk assessment is generally defined as the prediction of future dangerousness toward oneself or others. Researchers (e.g., Heilbrun & Heilbrun, 1995; Monahan, 2003) have indicated that a variety of factors should be considered when making a dangerousness prediction. These include historical factors (e.g., arrest history, juvenile delinquency), demographic/dispositional factors (e.g., psychopathic personality, age, gender), contextual factors (e.g., availability of weapons, social support), and clinical factors (e.g., psychosis, substance abuse), which may interact and produce a potentially violent individual.

Although the MMPI–2 cannot directly predict who will be violent in the future, it may provide some information that can aid in such prediction. For instance, Swanson, Holzer, Ganju, and Jono (1990) found that individuals exhibiting certain forms of psychopathology (e.g., schizophrenia, bipolar disorder, substance abuse) were more likely (12%) to have acted violently within the past year than individuals who were not diagnosed with mental disorders (2%). The ability of the MMPI–2 to identify symptoms associated with various forms of psychopathology is well documented.

Heibrun and Heilbrun (1995) have made some recommendations as to how the MMPI–2 can aid in risk assessment. For example, it can aid in the assessment of psychopathy, which is the single best predictor of violence risk (Harris, Rice, & Cormier, 1991). Heilbrun (1979) recommended high scores on Scale 4 coupled with low intelligence as a marker for high risk. We would caution against this approach. Scale 4 is too heterogeneous and does not correlate strongly with other measures of psychopathy (Hare, 1985; Harpur, Hare, & Hakstian, 1989). On the other hand, the MMPI–2 RC Scales do provide valid information for psychopathy assessment, especially in cases where high scores on *RC4* and *RC9* are coupled with low scores on *RC2* and *RC7* (Sellbom, Ben-Porath, Lilienfeld, Patrick, & Graham, in press).

In correctional settings, Megargee and colleagues developed a configural classification system for use with the MMPI (Megargee, Bohn, Meyer, & Sink, 1979) and, more recently, the MMPI–2 Clinical Scales. They found that certain groups were more likely to recidivate after release (Group Foxtrot, 64%) and act more aggressively in prison (Group Jupiter).

Sellbom, Ben-Porath, Baum, Erez, and Gregory (2005) reported preliminary results with the MMPI–2 and the prediction of violent recidivism among offenders undergoing treatment in a batterers intervention program. They found that individual MMPI–2 Scales (especially *RC4* and *RC9*) were able to predict recidivism. For example, offenders who produced elevated scores on *RC9* were 2.5 times more likely to reoffend. The RC Scales predicted recidivism even after historical variables (e.g., arrest history) and demographic variables (e.g., age, income) had been accounted for.

Finally, much more research on predicting the risk of violence with the MMPI–2, especially in conjunction with other important variables, is needed. The strongest studies will include a clear definition of dangerousness and data on violent reoffending, and will examine predictive abilities of in the MMPI–2 scales conjunction with historical, dispositional, contextual, and clinical factors.

Child Custody

The Uniform Marriage and Divorce Act (UMDA, 1979) states that child custody arrangements should be made in the "best interest of the child." Consideration of a child's best interest typically includes the mental health of all parties involved. As is the case with all other forensic assessments, psychological testing is not sufficient for making such decisions. Interviews with parents and children, the review of relevant records, and interviews with less subjective third parties (e.g., neighbors, teachers) provide important information as well. In terms of testing, Hagen and Castagna (2001) found that the MMPI–2 is the most frequently used psychological test in child custody evaluations.

As might be expected, most individuals undergoing child custody evaluations approach the examination defensively and attempt to make a favorable impression (Bagby, Nicholson, Buis, Radovanovic, & Fidler, 1999). Four general types of MMPI–2 protocols are often obtained in child custody evaluations: (1) a defensive protocol with no elevations on the substantive scales, (2) a nondefensive protocol with no elevations on the substantive scales, (3) a defensive profile with substantive scale elevations, and (4) a nondefensive protocol with substantive scale elevations. In cases 3 and 4, the substantive elevations may be relied upon in describing characteristics associated with the elevated indicators. As discussed earlier, caution should be exercised in relying on elevations on *K*-corrected Clinical Scale scores when the non-*K*-corrected scores are not elevated. Of course, in case 3, the possibility remains that the test taker is only admitting part of his or her maladaptive functioning. In case 2, cautious inferences about the absence of significant maladjustment may be reached. Caution is indicated because, generally speaking, MMPI–2 scale scores are more informative when they are elevated rather than nonelevated. Finally, in case 1, no information can be reached about the test taker's adjustment because it is impossible to determine whether the absence of elevation is a product of defensiveness, good adjustment, or some combination of both.

Only limited research has been conducted with the MMPI–2 in child custody settings. Although it is unlikely that MMPI–2 research will yield any profiles indicative of a bad parent (Otto & Collins, 1995), it would nonetheless be important to examine whether individual scales might be more effective in highlighting characteristics associated with poor outcomes after custody decisions have been made.

Personal Injury

Psychologists are often asked to conduct psychological evaluations with individuals who have been exposed to a traumatic event and who alleged to have suffered psychological or emotional difficulties as a result. Pope, Butcher, & Seelen (2000) raise three important questions that need to be addressed in personal injury evaluations: (1) the actual presence of psychological or emotional problems, (2) whether the trauma caused the psychological problems as opposed to a pre-existing condition or subsequent events, and (3) the likely course of recovery.

The MMPI–2 can aid to some degree in answering these questions. The Validity Scales can help determine whether the individual is malingering. Berry et al. (1995) found that individuals who malinger brain injury are accurately detected by the MMPI–2 Validity Scales. As mentioned earlier, the FBS was designed to detect malingering in these evaluations. Greiffenstein, Fox, and Lees-Haley (2006) provided specific recommendations for use of this scale in such evaluations.

The MMPI–2 can provide useful information about psychological and emotional difficulties once the profile has been determined to be interpretable. Many personal injury claimants specifically indicate that they may suffer from PTSD. Although individuals with PTSD often produce multiple Clinical Scale elevations (Graham, 2006), especially in Scales 2, 4, 7, and 8, these profiles do not discriminate PTSD individuals from others with extensive psychopathology (Keane et al., 1984). Other researchers have found that there is no prototypical PTSD profile for personal injury litigants (Platt & Husband, 1987). Keane et al. (1984) developed a PTSD scale (PK), but its utility presently is limited to combat veterans. Thus, as is the case with other disorders, the MMPI–2 is best relied upon to generate information about possible symptoms associated with PTSD rather than to predict the presence or absence of the disorder.

MMPI–2 data provide very limited information on the association between traumatic events and any psychopathology reflected in the test protocol. As is the case with NGRI evaluations, occasionally a pre-event MMPI–2 profile may exist that can shed some light on the individual's psychological functioning prior to the trauma. In such cases, limited inferences about the relation between a traumatic event and current psychopathology may be indicated, but these would need to be corroborated by collateral information.

Correctional Settings

In a landmark prospective study, Hathaway and Monachesi (1953, 1957) found that Scale 4 was particularly valid for predicting juvenile delinquency in both boys and girls. More recent research concerning the use of MMPI–2 in correctional settings has been directed by Megargee and Carbonell (1995), who have emphasized the importance of efficient classification within the correctional system, primarily because of lack of resources.

This research focused initially on aggression and conduct problems among prison inmates and eventually led to the classification system mentioned earlier. Megargee and colleagues (1979) developed a configural system through cluster analysis of the Clinical Scales, yielding 10 profile types. They were able to classify 85–95% of MMPI profiles into 1 of 10 groups. This classification system has also been adapted for the MMPI–2 (see Megargee, 1994). The classification system had originally been developed for male prisoners; Megargee (1997) adapted the classification rules for women as well. Almost 98% of women offenders could be classified. Extra test correlates—such as institutional infractions; psychological adjustment; educational, work, and health histories; prison adjustment; and recidivism—were generated for each of the 10 types. Megargee, Carbonell, Bohn, and Sliger (2001) summarized these for the MMPI–2.

CASE EXAMPLE

The following case study is designed to illustrate a number of the points made in this chapter about forensic applications of the MMPI–2. In order to mask the identity of the forensic examinee whose MMPI–2 protocol is analyzed, the background information presented is based on a composite of several actual forensic evaluations conducted by one of the authors of this chapter (Ben-Porath).

Background

J.R. is a 25-year-old Caucasian male referred for a competency-to-stand-trial and NGRI evaluation. J.R. is facing charges of vehicular homicide, aggravated assault, willful fleeing, and hit and run. He was observed by a police officer to be swerving dangerously and failed to pull over when the officer signaled him to do so. A high-speed chase ensued, and in the course of the chase the defendant struck a pedestrian, who died as a result of the injuries she sustained. The defendant eventually ran out of gas and was arrested following a brief struggle. He refused to undergo a breathalyzer exam, but the arresting officer indicated that he detected alcohol on the defendant's breath and that he was slurring his speech. The defendant subsequently told his attorney that at the time of the alleged offenses he was hearing voices telling him that the police officer chasing him was an imposter who wanted to kill him. He maintained that he still believed he was the victim of a conspiracy. Based on these assertions, the attorney requested a competency-to-stand-trial evaluation and entered a plea of not guilty by reason of insanity on behalf of the defendant.

A review of J.R.'s history indicated that he had one prior felony conviction for assault, stemming from a bar fight. He was placed on probation and as a condition of his sentence had to complete an anger management program. At intake to the program, approximately 1 year prior to the alleged offenses, a mental health counselor described the defendant as angry and defiant but free of any signs of thought disturbance. He attended all of the mandatory sessions but was described at discharge as having failed to benefit from the program. J.R. had no other history of involvement with the mental health or criminal justice systems.

MMPI–2 Results and Interpretation

As part of the court-ordered evaluation J.R. was administered the MMPI–2 and produced the protocol that appears in Fig. 2.1. The protocol was scored using the MMPI–2 Extended Score Report (ESR) distributed by Pearson Assessments. The first page of the figure

MMPI-2 VALIDITY AND CLINICAL SCALES PROFILE

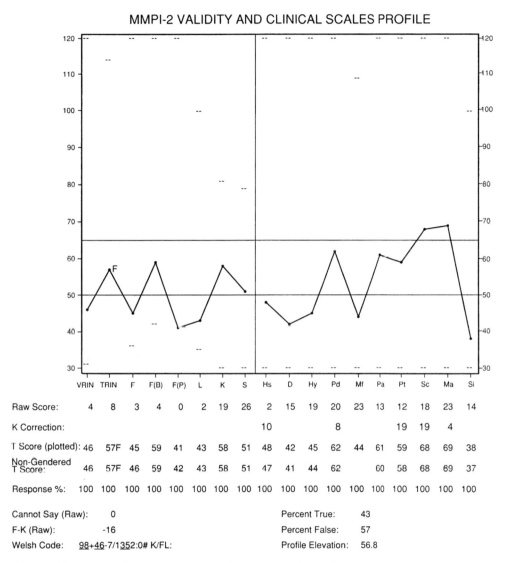

	VRIN	TRIN	F	F(B)	F(P)	L	K	S	Hs	D	Hy	Pd	Mf	Pa	Pt	Sc	Ma	Si
Raw Score:	4	8	3	4	0	2	19	26	2	15	19	20	23	13	12	18	23	14
K Correction:									10			8			19	19	4	
T Score (plotted):	46	57F	45	59	41	43	58	51	48	42	45	62	44	61	59	68	69	38
Non-Gendered T Score:	46	57F	46	59	42	43	58	51	47	41	44	62		60	58	68	69	37
Response %:	100	100	100	100	100	100	100	100	100	100	100	100	100	100	100	100	100	100

Cannot Say (Raw):	0		Percent True:	43
F-K (Raw):	-16		Percent False:	57
Welsh Code:	98+46-7/1352:0# K/FL:		Profile Elevation:	56.8

Note: The highest and lowest T scores possible on each scale are indicated by a "--".

FIG. 2.1. MMPI-2 Extended Score Report for Case Example

MMPI-2 **NON-K-CORRECTED** VALIDITY/CLINICAL SCALES PROFILE

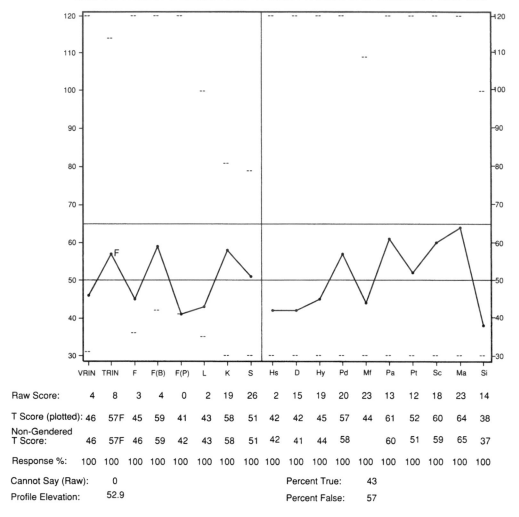

	VRIN	TRIN	F	F(B)	F(P)	L	K	S	Hs	D	Hy	Pd	Mf	Pa	Pt	Sc	Ma	Si
Raw Score:	4	8	3	4	0	2	19	26	2	15	19	20	23	13	12	18	23	14
T Score (plotted):	46	57F	45	59	41	43	58	51	42	42	45	57	44	61	52	60	64	38
Non-Gendered T Score:	46	57F	46	59	42	43	58	51	42	41	44	58		60	51	59	65	37
Response %:	100	100	100	100	100	100	100	100	100	100	100	100	100	100	100	100	100	100

Cannot Say (Raw):   0   Percent True: 43

Profile Elevation: 52.9   Percent False: 57

Notes: The highest and lowest T scores possible on each scale are indicated by a "--".

Non-K-corrected T scores allow interpreters to examine the relative contributions of the Clinical Scale raw score and the K correction to K-corrected Clinical Scale T scores. Because all other MMPI-2 scores that aid in the interpretation of the Clinical Scales (the Harris-Lingoes subscales, Restructured Clinical Scales, Content and Content Component Scales, PSY-5 Scales, and Supplementary Scales) are not K-corrected, they can be compared most directly with non-K-corrected T scores.

MMPI-2 RESTRUCTURED CLINICAL SCALES PROFILE

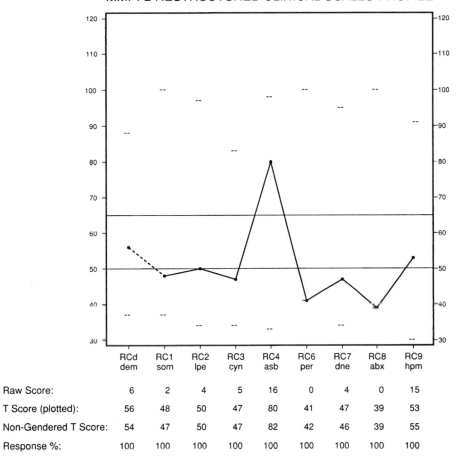

	RCd dem	RC1 som	RC2 lpe	RC3 cyn	RC4 asb	RC6 per	RC7 dne	RC8 abx	RC9 hpm
Raw Score:	6	2	4	5	16	0	4	0	15
T Score (plotted):	56	48	50	47	80	41	47	39	53
Non-Gendered T Score:	54	47	50	47	82	42	46	39	55
Response %:	100	100	100	100	100	100	100	100	100

Note: The highest and lowest Uniform T scores possible on each scale are indicated by a "--".

LEGEND

dem= Demoralization   **cyn** = Cynicism   **dne** = Dysfunctional Negative Emotions
som= Somatic Complaints   **asb** = Antisocial Behavior   **abx** = Aberrant Experiences
lpe = Low Positive Emotions **per** = Ideas of Persecution **hpm**= Hypomanic Activation

---

For information on the RC scales, see Tellegen, A., Ben-Porath, Y.S., McNulty, J.L., Arbisi, P.A., Graham, J.R., & Kaemmer, B. (2003). *The MMPI-2 Restructured Clinical (RC) Scales: Development, validation, and interpretation.* Minneapolis: University of Minnesota Press.

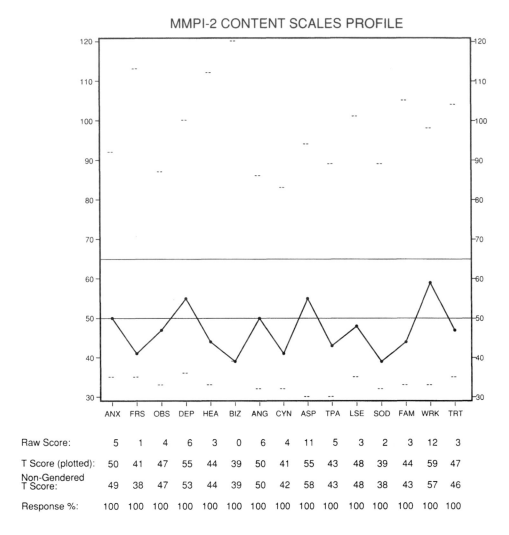

MMPI-2 CONTENT SCALES PROFILE

	ANX	FRS	OBS	DEP	HEA	BIZ	ANG	CYN	ASP	TPA	LSE	SOD	FAM	WRK	TRT
Raw Score:	5	1	4	6	3	0	6	4	11	5	3	2	3	12	3
T Score (plotted):	50	41	47	55	44	39	50	41	55	43	48	39	44	59	47
Non-Gendered T Score:	49	38	47	53	44	39	50	42	58	43	48	38	43	57	46
Response %:	100	100	100	100	100	100	100	100	100	100	100	100	100	100	100

Note: The highest and lowest Uniform T scores possible on each scale are indicated by a "--".

MMPI-2 SUPPLEMENTARY SCALES PROFILE

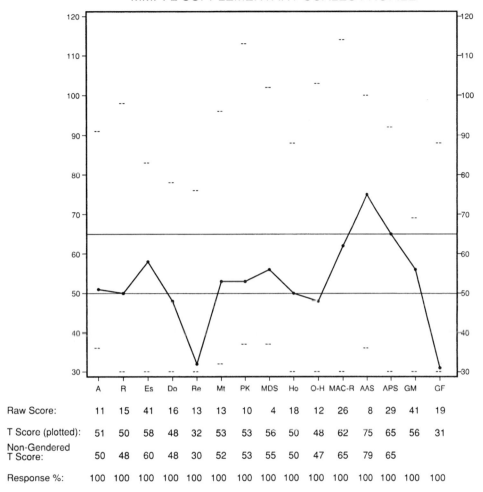

	A	R	Es	Do	Re	Mt	PK	MDS	Ho	O-H	MAC-R	AAS	APS	GM	GF
Raw Score:	11	15	41	16	13	13	10	4	18	12	26	8	29	41	19
T Score (plotted):	51	50	58	48	32	53	53	56	50	48	62	75	65	56	31
Non-Gendered T Score:	50	48	60	48	30	52	53	55	50	47	65	79	65		
Response %:	100	100	100	100	100	100	100	100	100	100	100	100	100	100	100

Note: The highest and lowest T scores possible on each scale are indicated by a "--".

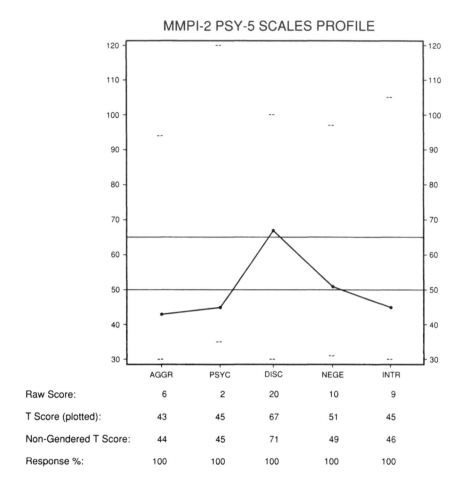

MMPI-2 PSY-5 SCALES PROFILE

	AGGR	PSYC	DISC	NEGE	INTR
Raw Score:	6	2	20	10	9
T Score (plotted):	43	45	67	51	45
Non-Gendered T Score:	44	45	71	49	46
Response %:	100	100	100	100	100

Note: The highest and lowest Uniform T scores possible on each scale are indicated by a "--".

CLINICAL SUBSCALES

HARRIS-LINGOES SUBSCALES
(to be used as an aid in interpreting the parent scale)

	Raw Score	T Score	Non-Gendered T Score	Resp %
Depression Subscales				
Subjective Depression (D1)	8	53	52	100
Psychomotor Retardation (D2)	6	54	53	100
Physical Malfunctioning (D3)	3	51	50	100
Mental Dullness (D4)	5	62	62	100
Brooding (D5)	1	45	44	100
Hysteria Subscales				
Denial of Social Anxiety (Hy1)	4	51	51	100
Need for Affection (Hy2)	6	47	47	100
Lassitude-Malaise (Hy3)	4	57	56	100
Somatic Complaints (Hy4)	1	43	42	100
Inhibition of Aggression (Hy5)	2	40	39	100
Psychopathic Deviate Subscales				
Familial Discord (Pd1)	2	51	51	100
Authority Problems (Pd2)	5	60	64	100
Social Imperturbability (Pd3)	5	57	58	100
Social Alienation (Pd4)	4	50	50	100
Self-Alienation (Pd5)	7	67	68	100
Paranoia Subscales				
Persecutory Ideas (Pa1)	3	58	58	100
Poignancy (Pa2)	4	62	60	100
Naivete (Pa3)	6	56	55	100
Schizophrenia Subscales				
Social Alienation (Sc1)	3	51	50	100
Emotional Alienation (Sc2)	2	59	59	100
Lack of Ego Mastery, Cognitive (Sc3)	4	66	67	100
Lack of Ego Mastery, Conative (Sc4)	7	76	76	100
Lack of Ego Mastery, Defective Inhibition (Sc5)	1	47	47	100
Bizarre Sensory Experiences (Sc6)	1	46	45	100
Hypomania Subscales				
Amorality (Ma1)	3	58	60	100
Psychomotor Acceleration (Ma2)	7	58	59	100
Imperturbability (Ma3)	4	53	54	100
Ego Inflation (Ma4)	4	56	56	100
SOCIAL INTROVERSION SUBSCALES				
Shyness/Self-Consciousness (Si1)	1	39	39	100
Social Avoidance (Si2)	1	41	42	100
Alienation–Self and Others (Si3)	5	50	50	100

Uniform T scores are used for Hs, D, Hy, Pd, Pa, Pt, Sc, Ma, and the content scales; all other MMPI-2 scales use linear T scores.

CONTENT COMPONENT SCALES

	Raw Score	T Score	Non-Gendered T Score	Resp %
Fears Subscales				
Generalized Fearfulness (FRS1)	1	53	51	100
Multiple Fears (FRS2)	0	37	34	100
Depression Subscales				
Lack of Drive (DEP1)	2	51	51	100
Dysphoria (DEP2)	1	50	48	100
Self-Depreciation (DEP3)	3	62	62	100
Suicidal Ideation (DEP4)	0	45	46	100
Health Concerns Subscales				
Gastrointestinal Symptoms (HEA1)	0	44	44	100
Neurological Symptoms (HEA2)	1	47	46	100
General Health Concerns (HEA3)	0	40	41	100
Bizarre Mentation Subscales				
Psychotic Symptomatology (BIZ1)	0	44	44	100
Schizotypal Characteristics (BIZ2)	0	41	41	100
Anger Subscales				
Explosive Behavior (ANG1)	2	52	53	100
Irritability (ANG2)	3	51	51	100
Cynicism Subscales				
Misanthropic Beliefs (CYN1)	4	44	45	100
Interpersonal Suspiciousness (CYN2)	0	34	35	100
Antisocial Practices Subscales				
Antisocial Attitudes (ASP1)	6	49	51	100
Antisocial Behavior (ASP2)	5	74	79	100
Type A Subscales				
Impatience (TPA1)	2	45	46	100
Competitive Drive (TPA2)	3	50	51	100
Low Self-Esteem Subscales				
Self-Doubt (LSE1)	1	44	44	100
Submissiveness (LSE2)	1	48	47	100
Social Discomfort Subscales				
Introversion (SOD1)	2	42	43	100
Shyness (SOD2)	0	36	36	100
Family Problems Subscales				
Family Discord (FAM1)	3	50	49	100
Familial Alienation (FAM2)	0	40	41	100
Negative Treatment Indicators Subscales				
Low Motivation (TRT1)	0	42	42	100
Inability to Disclose (TRT2)	1	45	46	100

provides scores on the standard MMPI–2 Validity Scales and the K-corrected clinical scale profile. Examination of the Cannot Say score indicates that the test taker responded to all of the test items, and thus the last row of numbers under the profile (labeled "Response %") shows that 100% of the items were answered on all of the scales. Both gendered and nongendered T-scores (discussed earlier) are provided for all of the MMPI–2 scales, and as reported by Ben-Porath and Forbey (2003), differences between the two sets of scores are negligible. Therefore, the focus of this interpretation will be on the gender-based T-scores, which are also the ones plotted throughout the protocol.

Examination of scores on the consistency scales (*VRIN* and *TRIN*) indicates that J.R. responded consistently to the MMPI–2 items and showed no signs of random or fixed responding. Scores on the infrequency scales (F, F_B, and F_P) do not show any indications of overreporting, and scores on the defensiveness indicators (L, K, and S) do not show any signs of underreporting. Overall, J.R. produced a valid and interpretable profile that should provide an accurate indication of his psychological functioning.

J.R.'s scores on the K-corrected Clinical Scale profile form a well-defined and elevated 89/98 codetype, as Clinical Scales 8 and 9 are both elevated above 65 and at least 5 points higher than the remaining Clinical Scales in the profile. Considered in isolation, this finding could be interpreted as indicating the possible presence of symptoms of a thought and/or mood disorder that may be consistent with J.R.'s explanation of his behavior at the time of the alleged offenses. However, examination of the non-K-corrected profile (page 40) indicates that, with the removal of the K correction, neither Scale 8 nor 9 remains elevated, and the codetype is no longer well defined. In considering which of the two Clinical Scale profiles to give more weight to in the interpretation, the user should examine other MMPI–2 scales. The RC Scales (page 41) point to a very different interpretation. Only *RC4* (Antisocial Behavior) is substantially elevated, and the restructured versions of Clinical Scales 8 and 9 are well within normal limits. Indeed, there is no evidence of symptoms associated with a thought or mood disorder on the RC Scale profile.

Tellegen et al., (2003) indicate that individuals who produce elevated scores on *RC4* "are likely to engage in various antisocial behaviors, tend to behave aggressively toward others, and are viewed as being antagonistic, angry, and argumentative. [They] find it difficult to conform to societal norms and expectations and may, as a result, experience legal difficulties. They are at increased risk for engaging in substance abuse and sexual acting out" (p. 56).

The MMPI–2 Content Scales (page 42) show no clinically significant elevations. The absence of elevation on Bizarre Mentation (*BIZ*) is consistent with the RC Scales and more consistent with the non-K-corrected Clinical Scale profile. The absence of elevation on Antisocial Practices (*ASP*), however, appears to be at odds with the RC Scale findings. A primary difference between *RC4* and *ASP* is that the latter confounds antisocial behavior and cynicism, whereas on the RC Scales these two constructs are measured separately, by *RC4* and *RC3*, respectively. The Content Component Scales for *ASP* (page 46) separate these two constructs. *ASP1* (Antisocial Attitudes) includes the cynicism-measuring items of *ASP*, whereas *ASP2* (Antisocial Behavior) incorporates the *ASP* items that tap the same construct as *RC4*. As seen in this case, the results on *ASP2* are consistent with *RC4* in identifying J.R. as likely to engage in antisocial behavior.

The MMPI–2 Supplementary Scales (page 43) show elevations on two scales: Addiction Acknowledgement (*AAS*) and Addiction Potential (*APS*). These results are consistent with *RC4* in indicating that J.R. has personality characteristics that place him at increased risk for substance abuse and that he acknowledges engaging in such behavior.

Finally, the PSY-5 Scales (page 44) show an elevation on Disconstraint (*DISC*). Harkness et al. (2002) describe individuals who produce elevated scores on this scale as impulsive risk takers who are likely to be aggressive and antisocial and are at increased risk for having a history of being arrested and engaging in substance abuse. The absence of elevation on the PSY-5 Psychoticism (*PSYC*) Scale is consistent with the non-*K*-corrected Clinical Scales, RC Scale, and Content Scale results in indicating that symptoms of a thought disorder of the type described by J.R. are unlikely.

Considered in their totality, the MMPI–2 substantive scale results are not consistent with the presence of symptoms of either a thought or mood disorder. Rather, they point to a likely pattern of externalizing behavior marked by impulsive acting out, rule breaking, and substance abuse. Diagnostically, they suggest the possibility of a substance-related and/or antisocial personality disorder. As a result, it should be determined whether J.R. meets *DSM–IV* diagnostic criteria for these or other disorders.

The MMPI–2 results do not point to the presence of a mental disorder that would impair J.R.'s ability to participate meaningfully in the legal proceedings he faces, nor do they point to a severe and chronic disorder that would have impaired his ability to know the wrongfulness of his alleged acts. As mentioned earlier, MMPI–2 data cannot be relied on to generate an ultimate psycholegal opinion, directly but these results are inconsistent with J.R.'s claim to have been experiencing psychotic symptoms at the time of the evaluation and at the time of the alleged offenses.

This case illustrates several MMPI–2 interpretive issues addressed in this chapter. First, the *K*-corrected Clinical Scale profile should be interpreted only after considering the non-*K*-corrected profile, the RC Scales, and all other MMPI–2 interpretive sources. In this case, the *K*-corrected profile was at odds with the remaining MMPI–2 sources and the defendant's history. The RC Scales identified a significant proclivity toward antisocial behavior that was not captured by the Clinical Scales but was reflected by elevations on the *ASP2* Content Component Scale, the *AAS* and *APS* Supplementary Scales, and the PSY-5 *DISC* Scale.

REFERENCES

Akerlind, I., Hornquist, J.O., & Bjurulf, P. (1992). Psychological factors in the long-term prognosis of chronic low back pain patients. *Journal of Clinical Psychology, 48,* 596–606.

American Psychiatric Association. (2000). *Diagnostic and statistical manual of mental disorders* (4th ed., rev.). Washington, DC: Author.

Arbisi, P.A., & Ben-Porath, Y.S. (1995). An MMPI-2 infrequent response scale for use with psychopathological populations: The Infrequency Psychopathology scale, F(p). *Psychological Assessment, 7,* 424–431.

Arbisi, P.A., & Ben-Porath, Y.S. (1998). The ability of Minnesota Multiphasic Personality Inventory–2 validity scales to detect fake-bad responses in psychiatric inpatients. *Psychological Assessment, 10,* 221–228.

Arbisi, P.A., Ben-Porath, Y.S., & McNulty, J. (2002). A comparison of MMPI-2 validity in African American and Caucasian psychiatric inpatients. *Psychological Assessment, 14,* 3–15.

Arbisi, P.A., Ben-Porath, Y.S., & McNulty, J. (2003). Empirical correlates of common MMPI-2 two-point codes in male psychiatric inpatients. *Assessment, 10,* 237–247.

Arbisi, P.A., & Butcher, J.N. (2004). Relationship between personality and health symptoms: Use of the MMPI-2 in medical assessments. *International Journal of Clinical and Health Psychology, 4,* 571–595.

Archer, R.P., Aiduk, R., Griffin, R., & Elkins, D.E. (1996). Incremental validity of the MMPI-2 content scales in a psychiatric sample. *Assessment, 3,* 79–90.

Archer, R.P., Gordon, R.A., Giannetti, R., & Singles, J.M. (1988). MMPI scale clinical correlates for adolescent inpatients. *Journal of Personality Assessment, 52,* 707–721.

Archer, R.P., Griffin, R., & Aiduk, R. (1995). MMPI-2 clinical correlates for the common codes. *Journal of Personality Assessment, 65*, 391–407.

Avery, R.D., Mussio, S.J., & Payne, G. (1972). Relationships between MMPI scores and job performance measures of fire fighters. *Psychological Reports, 31*, 199–202.

Baer, R.A., & Miller, J. (2002). Underreporting of psychopathology on the MMPI-2: A meta-analytic review. *Psychological Assessment, 14*, 16–26.

Bagby, R.M., Buis, T., & Nicholson, R.A. (1995). Relative effectiveness of the standard validity scales in detecting fake-bad and fake-good responding: Replication and extension. *Psychological Assessment, 7*, 84–92.

Bagby, R.M., Nicholson, R.A., Buis, T., Radovanovic, H., & Fidler, B.J. (1999). Defensive responding on the MMPI-2 in family custody and access evaluations. *Psychological Assessment, 11*, 24–28.

Bagby, R.M., Rogers, R., & Buis, T. (1994). Detecting malingered and defensive responding on the MMPI-2 in a forensic inpatient sample. *Journal of Personality Assessment, 62*, 191–203.

Bagby, R.M., Rogers, R., Nicholson, R.A., Buis, T., Seeman, M.V., & Rector, N.A. (1997). Effectiveness of the MMPI-2 validity indicators in the detection of defensive responding in clinical and non-clinical samples. *Journal of Personality Assessment, 68*, 650–664.

Barefoot, J.C., Dahlstrom, W.G., & Williams, R.B. (1983). Hostility, CHD incidence, and total mortality: A 25-year follow-up study of 255 physicians. *Psychosomatic Medicine, 45*, 59–63.

Barrash, J., Rodriguez, E.M., Scott, D.H., Mason, E.E., & Sines, J.O. (1987). The utility of MMPI subtypes for the prediction of weight loss after bariatric surgery. *International Journal of Obesity, 11*, 115–128.

Barthlow, D.L., Graham, J.R., Ben-Porath, Y.S., Tellegen, A., & McNulty, J.L. (2002). The appropriateness of the MMPI-2 K correction. *Assessment, 9*, 219–229.

Bartol, C.R. (1991). Predictive validation of the MMPI for small-town police officers who fail. *Professional Psychology: Research and Practice, 22*, 127–132.

Ben-Porath, Y.S. (in press). Differentiating normal from abnormal personality with the MMPI-2. In S. Strack & M. Lorr (Eds.), *Differentiating normal and abnormal personality* (2nd ed., pp. 361–401). New York: Springer.

Ben-Porath, Y.S., & Butcher, J.N. (1989a). Psychometric stability of rewritten MMPI items. *Journal of Personality Assessment, 53*, 645–653.

Ben-Porath, Y.S., & Butcher, J.N. (1989b). The comparability of MMPI and MMPI-2 scales and profiles. *Psychological Assessment: A Journal of Consulting and Clinical Psychology, 1*, 345–347.

Ben-Porath, Y.S., & Forbey, J.D. (2003). *Non-gendered norms for the MMPI-2*. Minneapolis: University of Minnesota Press.

Ben-Porath, Y.S., & Forbey, J.D. (2004, May). *Detrimental effects of the K correction on Clinical Scale valdiity.* Paper presented at the 39th Annual Symposium on Recent Developments of the MMPI-2/MMPI-A, Minneapolis, MN.

Ben-Porath, Y.S., McCully, E., & Almagor, M. (1993). Incremental validity of the MMPI-2 content scales in the assessment of personality and psychopathology by self-report. *Journal of Personality Assessment, 61*, 557–575.

Ben-Porath, Y.S., & Sherwood, N.E. (1993). *The MMPI-2 content component scales*. Minneapolis: University of Minnesota Press.

Ben-Porath, Y.S., Shondrick, D.D., & Stafford, K.P. (1995). MMPI-2 and race in a forensic diagnostic sample. *Criminal Justice and Behavior, 22*, 19–32.

Bernstein, I.H. (1980). Security guards' MMPI profiles: Some normative data. *Journal of Personality Assessment, 44*, 377–380.

Berry, D.T.R., Baer, R.A., & Harris, M.J. (1991). Detection of malingering on the MMPI: A meta-analysis. *Clinical Psychology Review, 11*, 585–598.

Berry, D.T.R., Wetter, M.W., Baer, R.A., Youngjohn, J.R., Gass, C.S., Lamb, D.G., et al. (1995). Overreporting of closed-head injury symptoms on the MMPI-2. *Psychological Assessment, 7*, 517–523.

Beutler, L.E., Storm, A., Kirkish, P., Scogin, F., & Gaines, J.A. (1985). Parameters in the prediction of police officer performance. *Professional Psychology: Research and Practice, 16*, 324–335.

Binder, L.M. (1993). "Assessment of malingering after mild head trauma with the Portland Digit Recognition Test": Erratum. *Journal of Clinical and Experimental Neuropsychology, 15*, 852.

Black, J.D. (1953). *The interpretation of MMPI profiles of college women.* Unpublished doctoral dissertation, University of Minnesota, Minneapolis.

Bury, A.S., & Bagby, R. (2002). The detection of feigned uncoached and coached posttraumatic stress disorder with the MMPI-2 in a sample of workplace accident victims. *Psychological Assessment, 14,* 472–484.

Butcher, J.N. (1979). Use of the MMPI in personnel selection. In J.N. Butcher (Ed.), *New developments in the use of the MMPI* (pp. 165–201). Minneapolis: University of Minnesota Press.

Butcher, J.N. (1985). Personality assessment in industry: Theoretical issues and illustrations. In H.J. Bernardin (Ed.), *Personality assessment in organizations* (pp. 277–310). New York: Praeger.

Butcher, J.N. (1996). Translation and adaptation of the MMPI-2 for international use. In J.N. Butcher (Ed.), *International adaptations of the MMPI-2: Research and clinical applications* (pp. 26–43). Minneapolis: University of Minnesota Press.

Butcher, J.N., Arbisi, P.A., Atlis, M.M., & McNulty, J.L. (2003). The construct validity of the Lees-Haley Fake Bad Scale: Does this measure somatic malingering and feigned emotional distress? *Archives of Clinical Neuropsychology, 18,* 473–485.

Butcher, J.N., Dahlstrom, W.G., Graham, J.R., Tellegen, A., & Kaemmer, B. (1989). *Minnesota Multiphasic Personality Inventory-2 (MMPI-2): Manual for administration and scoring.* Minneapolis: University of Minnesota Press.

Butcher, J.N., Graham, J.R., Ben-Porath, Y.S., Tellegen, A., Dahlstrom, W.G., & Kaemmer, B. (2001). *MMPI-2 (Minnesota Multiphasic Personality Inventory-2): Manual for administration, scoring, and interpretation, revised edition.* Minneapolis: University of Minnesota Press.

Butcher, J.N., Graham, J.R., Williams, C.L., & Ben-Porath, Y.S. (1990). *Development and use of the MMPI-2 content scales.* Minneapolis: University of Minnesota Press.

Butcher, J.N., & Rouse, S.V. (1996). Personality: Individual differences and clinical assessment. *Annual Review of Psychology, 47,* 87–111.

Butcher, J.N., Williams, C.L., Graham, J.R., Archer, R.P., Tellegen, A., Ben-Porath, Y.S., et al. (1992). *Minnesota Multiphasic Personality Inventory–Adolescent (MMPI-A): Manual for administration, scoring, and interpretation.* Minneapolis: University of Minnesota Press.

Camara, W.J., Nathan, J.S., & Puente, A.E. (2000). Psychological test usage: Implications in professional psychology. *Professional Psychology: Research and Practice, 31,* 141–154.

Capwell, D. F. (1945a). Personality patterns of adolescent girls: I. Girls who show improvement in IQ. *Journal of Applied Psychology, 29,* 212–228.

Capwell, D. F. (1945b). Personality patterns of adolescent girls: II. Delinquents and non- delinquents. *Journal of Applied Psychology,* 29, 289–297.

Clark, M.E., Gironda, R.J., & Young, R.W. (2003). Detection of back random responding: Effectiveness of MMPI-2 and Personality Assessment validity indices. *Psychological Assessment, 15,* 223–234.

Costello, R.M., Schneider, S.L., & Schoenfeld, L.S. (1996). Validation of a preemployment MMPI index correlated with interdisciplinary suspension days of police officers. *Psychology: Crime and Law, 2,* 299–306.

Costello, R.M., Schoenfeld, L.S., & Kobos, J. (1982). Police applicant screening: An analogue study. *Journal of Clinical Psychology, 38,* 216–221.

Crovitz, E., Huse, M.N., & Lewis, D.E. (1973). Selection of physicians' assistants. *Journal of Medical Education, 48,* 551–555.

Dahlstrom, W.G., & Welsh, G.S. (1960). *An MMPI handbook: A guide to use in clinical practice and research.* Minneapolis: University of Minnesota Press.

Dahlstrom, W.G., Welsh, G.S., & Dahlstrom, L.E. (1975). *An MMPI handbook: Vol. II. Research applications.* Minneapolis: University of Minnesota Press.

Daubert v. Merrell Dow Pharmaceuticals, 727 F. Supp. 570 (S.D.Cal. 1989), aff'd, 951F.2d 1128 (9th Cir. 1990), vacated, 1123 S.Ct. 2786 (1993).

Dearth, C.S., Berry, D.T.R., Vickery, C.D., Vagnini, V.L., Baser, R.E., Orey, S.A., et al. (2005). Detection of feigned head injury symptoms on the MMPI-2 in head injured patients and community controls. *Archives of Clinical Neuropsychology, 20,* 95–110.

Detrick, P., Chibnall, J.T., & Rosso, M. (2001). Minnesota Multiphasic Personality Inventory-2 in police officer selection: Normative data and relation to the Inwald Personality Inventory. *Professional Psychology: Research and Practice, 32,* 484–490.

Dunnette, M.D., Bownas, D.A., & Bosshardt, M.J. (1981). *Electric power plant study: Prediction of inappropriate, unreliable or aberrant job behavior in nuclear power plant settings.* Minneapolis, MN: Personnel Decisions Research Institute.

Dusky v. United Sates, 362 U.S. 402 (1960).

Elhai, J.D., Gold, P.B., Frueh, B.C., & Gold, S.N. (2000). Cross-validation of the MMPI-2 in detecting malingered posttraumatic stress disorder. *Journal of Personality Assessment, 75*, 449–463.

Elion, V.H., & Megargee, E.I. (1975). Validity of the MMPI Pd scale among black males. *Journal of Consulting and Clinical Psychology, 43*, 166–172.

Fischler, G.L. (2005, April). *MMPI-2 predictors of police officer integrity problems.* Paper presented at the 40th Annual Symposium on Recent Research with the MMPI-2/MMPI-A, Ft. Lauderdale, FL.

Fordyce, W.E. (1979). *Use of the MMPI in the assessment of chronic pain* (Clinical Notes on the MMPI No. 3). Minneapolis, MN: National Computer Systems.

Frye v. United States, 293 F.1012 (D.C.Cir. 1923).

Gallagher, R.W. (1997). *Detection of malingering at the time of intake in a correctional setting with the MMPI-2 validity scales.* Unpublished doctoral dissertation, Kent State University, Kent, OH.

Garetz, F.K., & Anderson, R.W. (1973). Patterns of professional activities of psychiatrists: A follow-up of 100 psychiatric residents. *American Journal of Psychiatry, 130*, 981–984.

Gartner, J., Hurt, S.W., & Gartner, A. (1989). Psychological test signs of borderline personality disorder: A review of the empirical literature. *Journal of Personality Assessment, 53*, 423–441.

Gilberstadt, H., & Duker, J. (1965). *A handbook for clinical and actuarial MMPI interpretation.* Philadelphia: Saunders.

Gironda, R.J. (1999). *Comparative validity of MMPI-2 scores of African-Americans and Caucasians in a forensic diagnostic sample.* Unpublished doctoral dissertation, Kent State University, Kent, OH.

Graham, J.R. (2006). *The MMPI-2: Assessing personality and psychopathology* (4th ed.). New York: Oxford University Press.

Graham, J.R., Ben-Porath, Y.S., & McNulty, J.L. (1999). *MMPI-2 correlates for outpatient mental health settings.* Minneapolis: University of Minnesota Press.

Graham, J.R., & Strenger, V.E. (1988). MMPI characteristics of alcoholics: A review. *Journal of Consulting and Clinical Psychology, 56*, 197–205.

Graham, J.R., Watts, D., & Timbrook, R.E. (1991). Detecting fake-good and fake-bad MMPI-2 profiles. *Journal of Personality Assessment, 57*, 264–277.

Greene, R.L. (1987). Ethnicity and MMPI performance: A review. *Journal of Consulting and Clinical Psychology, 55*, 497–512.

Greene, R.L. (2000). *The MMPI-2: An interpretive manual* (2nd ed.). Boston: Allyn & Bacon.

Greene, R.L., Robin, R.W., Albaugh, B., Caldwell, A., & Goldman, D. (2003). Use of the MMPI-2 in American Indians: II. Empirical correlates. *Psychological Assessment, 15*, 360–369.

Greiffenstein, M.F., Baker, W.J., Gola, T. Donders, J., & Miller, L. (2002). The Fake Bad Scale in atypical and severe closed head injury litigants. *Journal of Clinical Psychology, 58*, 1591–1600.

Greiffenstein, M.F., Fox, D., & Lees-Haley, P.R. (2006). The MMPI-2 Fake Bad Scale in detection of noncredible brain injury claims. In K. Boone (Ed.) *Detection of noncredible cogntive performance.* New York: Guilford Press.

Grossman, L.S., & Wasyliw, O.E. (1988). A psychometric study of stereotypes: Assessment of malingering in a criminal forensic group. *Journal of Personality Assessment, 52*, 549–563.

Guthrie, G.M. (1949). *A study of the personality characteristics associated with the disorders encountered by an internist.* Unpublished doctoral dissertation, University of Minnesota, Minneapolis.

Hagen, M.A., & Castagna, N. (2001). The real numbers: Psychological testing in custody evaluations. *Professional Psychology: Research and Practice, 32*, 269–271.

Hall, G.N.C., Bansal, A., & Lopez, I.R. (1999). Ethnicity and psychopathology: A meta-analytic review of 31 years of comparative MMPI/MMPI-2 research. *Psychological Assessment, 11*, 186–197.

Hare, R.D. (1985). Comparison of the procedures for the assessment of psychopathy. *Journal of Clinical and Consulting Psychology, 53*, 111–119.

Harkness, A.R., & McNulty, J.L. (1994). The Personality Psychopathology Five (PSY-5): Issues from the pages of a diagnostic manual instead of a dictionary. In S. Strack & M. Lorr (Eds.), *Differentiating normal and abnormal personality* (pp. 291–315). New York: Springer.

Harkness, A.R., McNulty, J.L., & Ben-Porath, Y.S. (1995). The Personality Psychopathology Five (PSY-5): Constructs and MMPI-2 scales. *Psychological Assessment, 7*, 104–114.

Harkness, A.R., McNulty, J.L., Ben-Porath, Y.S., & Graham, J.R. (2002). *MMPI-2 Personality Psychopathology Five (PSY-5) Scales: Gaining an overview for case conceptualization and treatment planning.* Minneapolis: University of Minnesota Press.

Harpur, T.J., Hare, R.D., & Hakstian, A.R. (1989). Two-factor conceptualization of psychopathy: Construct validity and assessment implications. *Psychological Assessment, 1*, 6–17.

Harris, G.T., Rice, M.E., & Cormier, C.A. (1991). Psychopathy and violent recidivism. *Law and Human Behavior, 15*, 625–637.

Harris, R., & Lingoes, J. (1955). *Subscales for the Minnesota Multiphasic Personality Inventory.* Mimeographed materials. San Francisco, CA: Langley Porter Clinic.

Hartman, B.J. (1987). Psychological screening of law enforcement candidates. *American Journal of Forensic Psychology, 1*, 5–10.

Hathaway, S.R. (1960). Foreword to the first edition. In W.G. Dahlstrom & G.S. Welsch (Eds.), *An MMPI handbook: A guide to use in clinical practice and research* (pp. vii–xi). Minneapolis: University of Minnesota Press.

Hathaway, S.R., & McKinley, J.C. (1943). *The Minnesota Multiphasic Personality Inventory manual.* New York: Psychological Corporation.

Hathaway, S.R., & Monachesi, E.D. (1953). *Analyzing and predicting juvenile delinquency with the MMPI.* Minneapolis: University of Minnesota Press.

Hathaway, S.R., & Monachesi, E.D. (1957). The personalities of predelinquent boys. *Journal of Criminal Law, Criminology, and Political Science, 48*, 149–163.

Hathaway, S.R., & Monachesi, E.D. (1963). *Adolescent personality and behavior: MMPI patterns of normal, delinquent, dropout, and other outcomes.* Minneapolis: University of Minnesota Press.

Hawk, G.L., & Cornell, D.G. (1989). MMPI profiles of malingerers diagnosed in pretrial forensic evaluations. *Journal of Clinical Psychology, 45*, 673–678.

Heilbrun, A.B. (1979). Psychopathy and violent crime. *Journal of Consulting and Clinical Psychology, 47*, 509–516.

Heilbrun, K., & Heilbrun, A.B. (1995). Risk assessment with the MMPI-2 in forensic evaluations. In Y.S. Ben-Porath, J.R. Graham, G.C.N. Hall, R.D. Hirshman, & M.S. Zaragoza (Eds.), *Forensic applications of the MMPI-2* (pp. 160–178). Thousand Oaks, CA: Sage.

Henrichs, T.F., & Waters, W.F. (1972). Psychological adjustment and responses to open- heart surgery: Some methodological considerations. *British Journal of Psychiatry, 120*, 491–496.

Hjemboe, S., Almagor, M., & Butcher, J.N. (1992). Empirical assessment of marital distress: The Marital Distress Scale (MDS) for the MMPI-2. In J.N. Butcher & C.D. Spielberger (Eds.), *Advances in personality assessment* (Vol. 9, pp. 141–152). Hillsdale, NJ: Lawrence Erlbaum Associates.

Holcomb, W.R., & Adams, N. (1982). Racial influences on intelligence and personality measures of people who commit murder. *Journal of Clinical Psychology, 38*, 793–796.

Inwald, R.E. (1988). Five-year follow-up study of departmental terminations as predicted by 16 preemployment psychological indicators. *Journal of Applied Psychology, 4*, 703–710.

Kawachi, I., Sparrow, D., Kubazansky, L.D., Spiro, A., Vokonas, P.S., & Weiss, S.T. (1998). Prospective study of a self-report Type A scale and risk of coronary heart disease: Test of the MMPI-2 Type A scale. *Circulation, 98*, 405–412.

Keane, T.M., Malloy, P.F., & Fairbank, J.A. (1984). Empirical development of an MMPI subscale for the assessment of combat-related post-traumatic stress disorder. *Journal of Consulting and Clinical Psychology, 52*, 888–891.

Kelly, W.L. (1974). Psychological prediction of leadership in nursing. *Nursing Research, 23*, 38–42.

Lachar, D. (1974). Prediction of early U.S. Air Force cadet adaptation with the MMPI. *Journal of Counseling Psychology, 21*, 404–408.

Lally, S.J. (2003). What tests are acceptable for use in forensic evaluations? A survey of experts. *Professional Psychology: Research and Practice, 34*, 491–498.

Larrabee, G.J. (2003a). Detection of symptom exaggeration with the MMPI-2 in litigants with malingered neurocognitive dysfunction. *The Clinical Neuropsychologist, 17*, 54–68.

Larrabee, G.J. (2003b). Detection of malingering using atypical performance patterns on standard neuropsychological tests. *The Clinical Neuropsychologist, 17,* 410–425.

Larabee, G.J. (2003c). Exaggerated MMPI-2 symptoms report in personal injury litigants with malingered neurocognitive deficit. *Archives of Clinical Neuropsychology, 18,* 673–686.

Lees-Haley, P.R. (1992). Psychodiagnostic test usage by forensic psychologists. *American Journal of Forensic Psychology, 10,* 25–30.

Lees-Haley, P.R., English, L.T., & Glenn, W.J. (1991). A fake-bad scale on the MMPI-2 for personal injury claimants. *Psychological Reports, 68,* 203–210.

Lees-Haley, P.R., Smith, H.H., Williams, C.W., & Dunn, J.T. (1996). Forensic neuropsychological test usage: An empirical survey. *Archives of Clinical Neuropsychology, 11,* 45–51.

Liao, H., Arvey, R.D., Butler, R.J., & Nutting, S.M. (2000). Correlates of work injury frequency and duration among firefighters. *Journal of Occupational Health Psychology, 6,* 229–242.

Long, K.A., Graham, J.R., & Timbrook, R.E. (1994). Socioeconomic status and MMPI-2 interpretation. *Measurement and Evaluation in Counseling and Development, 27,* 158–177.

Lubin, B., Larsen, R.M., & Matarazzo, J.D. (1984). Patterns of psychological test usage in the United States: 1935–1982. *American Psychologist, 39,* 451–454.

MacAndrew, C. (1965). The differentiation of male alcoholic out-patients from nonalcoholic psychiatric patients by means of the MMPI. *Quarterly Journal of the Studies on Alcohol, 26,* 238–246.

Marks, P.A., & Seeman, W. (1963). *Actuarial description of abnormal personality.* Baltimore: Williams & Wilkins.

Martin, M.A., Allan, A., & Allan, M.M. (2001). The use of psychological tests by Australian psychologists who do assessments for the courts. *Australian Journal of Psychology, 53,* 77–82.

McNulty, J.L., Graham, J.R., Ben-Porath, Y.S., & Stein, L.A.R. (1997). Comparative validity of MMPI-2 scores of African American and Caucasian mental health center clients. *Psychological Assessment, 9,* 464–470.

Meehl, P.E. (1945). The dynamics of "structured" personality tests. *Journal of Clinical Psychology, 1,* 296–303.

Meehl, P.E. (1954). *Clinical versus statistical prediction: A theoretical analysis and a review of the evidence.* Minneapolis: University of Minnesota Press.

Meehl, P.E. (1956). Wanted—a good cookbook. *American Psychologist, 11,* 263–272.

Megargee, E.I. (1994). Using the Megargee MMPI-based classification system with MMPI-2's of male prison inmates. *Psychological Assessment, 6,* 337–344.

Megargee, E.I. (1997). Using the Megargee MMPI-based classification system with the MMPI-2's of female prison inmates. *Psychological Assessment, 9,* 75–82.

Megargee, E.I., Bohn, M.J., Meyer, J.E., Jr., & Sink, F. (1979). *Classifying criminal offenders: A new system based on the MMPI.* Beverly Hills, CA: Sage.

Megargee, E.I., & Carbonell, J.L. (1995). Use of the MMPI-2 in correctional settings. In Y.S. Ben-Porath, J.R. Graham, G.C.N. Hall, R.D. Hirshman, & M.S. Zaragoza (Eds.), *Forensic applications of the MMPI-2* (pp. 127–159). Thousand Oaks, CA: Sage.

Megargee, E.I., Carbonell, J.L., Bohn, M.J., & Sliger, G.L. (2001). *Classifying criminal offenders with the MMPI-2: The Megargee System.* Minneapolis: University of Minnesota Press.

Megargee, E.I., & Mendelsohn, A. (1962). A cross-validation of twelve MMPI indices of hostility and control. *Journal of Abnormal and Social Psychology, 65,* 431–438.

Melton, G.B., Petrila, J., Poythress, N., & Slobogin, C. (1997). *Psychological evaluations for the courts: A handbook for mental health professionals and lawyers.* New York: Guilford.

Mittenburg, W., Patton, C., Canyock, E.M., & Condit, D.C. (2002). Base rates of malingering and symptom exaggeration. *Journal of Clinical and Experimental Neuropsychology, 24,* 1094–1102.

Monahan, J. (2003). Violence risk assessment. In A.M. Goldstein (Ed.), *Handbook of forensic psychology: Vol. 11. Forensic psychology* (pp. 527–540). New York: Wiley.

Ogloff, J.R.P. (1995). The legal basis of forensic applications of the MMPI-2. In Y.S. Ben-Porath, J.R. Graham, G.C.N. Hall, R.D. Hirshman, & M.S. Zaragoza (Eds.), *Forensic applications of the MMPI-2* (pp. 18–47). Thousand Oaks, CA: Sage.

Okazaki, S., & Sue, S. (1995). Cultural considerations in psychological assessment of Asian-Americans. In J.N. Butcher (Ed.), *Clinical personality assessment: Practical approaches* (pp. 107–119). New York: Oxford University Press.

Otto, R.K. (2002). Use of the MMPI-2 in forensic settings. *Journal of Forensic Psychology Practice, 2,* 71–92.

Otto, R.K., & Collins, R.P. (1995). Use of the MMPI-2/MMPI-A in child custody evaluations. In Y.S. Ben-Porath, J.R. Graham, G.C.N. Hall, R.D. Hirshman, & M.S. Zaragoza (Eds.), *Forensic applications of the MMPI-2* (pp. 222–252). Thousand Oaks, CA: Sage.

Petroskey, L.J., Ben-Porath, Y.S., & Stafford, K.P. (2003). Correlates of the Minnesota Multiphasic Personality Inventory–2 (MMPI-2) Personality Psychopathology–Five (PSY-5) scales in a forensic assessment setting. *Assessment, 10,* 393–399.

Piotrowski, C., & Keller, J.W. (1989). Psychological testing in outpatient mental health facilities: A national survey. *Professional Psychology: Research and Practice, 20,* 423–425.

Platt, J.R., & Husband, S.D. (1987). Posttraumatic stress disorder and motor vehicle accident victims. *American Journal of Forensic Psychology, 5,* 35–42.

Pope, K.S., Butcher, J.N., & Seelen, J. (2000). *The MMPI, MMPI-2, and MMPI-A in court: A practical guide for expert witnesses and attorneys* (2nd ed.). Washington, DC: American Psychological Association.

Pothast, M.D. (1956). *A personality study of two types of murderers.* Unpublished doctoral dissertation. University of Minnesota, Minneapolis.

Reynolds, W.M., & Sundberg, D. (1976). Recent research trends in testing. *Journal of Personality Assessment, 40,* 228–233.

Robin, R.W., Greene, R.L., Albaugh, B., Caldwell, A., & Goldman, D. (2003). Use of the MMPI-2 in American Indians: I. Comparability of the MMPI-2 between two tribes and with the MMPI-2 normative group. *Psychological Assessment, 15,* 351–359.

Rogers, R., Bagby, R.M., & Chakraborty, D. (1993). Feigning schizophrenic disorders on the MMPI-2: Detection of coached simulators. *Journal of Personality Assessment, 60,* 215–226.

Rogers, R., & McKee, G.R. (1995). Use of the MMPI-2 in the assessment of criminal responsibility. In Y.S. Ben-Porath, J.R. Graham, G.C.N. Hall, R.D. Hirshman, & M.S. Zaragoza (Eds.), *Forensic applications of the MMPI-2* (pp. 103–126). Thousand Oaks, CA: Sage.

Rogers, R., Sewell, K.W., Martin, M.A., & Vitacco, M.J. (2003). Detection of feigned mental disorders: A meta-analysis of the MMPI-2 and malingering. *Assessment, 10,* 160–177.

Roman, D.D., Tuley, M.R., Villanueva M.R., & Mitchell, W.E. (1990). Evaluating MMPI validity in a forensic psychiatric population: Distinguishing between malingering and genuine psychopathology. *Criminal Justice and Behavior, 17,* 186–198.

Schinka, J.A., & LaLone, L. (1997). MMPI-2: Comparisons with a census-matched subsample. *Psychological Assessment, 9,* 307–311.

Schinka, J.A., LaLone, L., & Greene, G.L. (1998). Effects of psychopathology and demographic characteristics on MMPI-2 scale scores. *Journal of Personality Assessment, 70,* 197–211.

Sellbom, M., & Ben-Porath, Y.S. (in press). Mapping the MMPI-2 Restructured Clinical (RC) Scales onto normal personality traits: Evidence of construct validity. *Journal of Personality Assessment.*

Sellbom, M., Ben-Porath, Y.S., Baum, L.J., Erez, E., & Gregory, C. (2005). *Empirical correlates of the MMPI-2 Restructured Clinical (RC) Scales in a forensic setting.* Paper presented at the 2005 Annual Meeting of the Society for Personality Assessment, Chicago.

Sellbom, M., Ben-Porath, Y.S., & Graham, J.R. (2004, May). *Correlates of the MMPI-2 Restructured Clinical (RC) Scales in a college counseling setting.* Paper presented at the 39th Annual Symposium on Recent Developments in the Use of the MMPI-2 and MMPI-A, Minneapolis, MN.

Sellbom, M., Ben-Porath, Y.S., Lilienfeld, S.O., Patrick, C.J., & Graham, J.R. (in press). Assessing psychopathic personality traits with the MMPI-2. *Journal of Personality Assessment.*

Sellbom, M., Graham, J.R., & Schenk, P.W. (2005). Symptom correlates of MMPI-2 scales and code types in a private practice setting. *Journal of Personality Assessment, 84,* 163–171.

Slick, D.J., Hopp, G.A., Strauss, E.H., & Spellacy, F.J. (1996). Victoria Symptom Validity Test: Efficiency for detecting feigned memory impairment and relationship to neuropsychological tests and MMPI-2 validity scales. *Journal of Clinical and Experimental Neuropsychology, 18,* 911–922.

Sobel, H.J., & Worden, W. (1979). The MMPI as a predictor of psychosocial adaptation to cancer. *Journal of Consulting and Clinical Psychology, 47,* 716–724.

Solway, K.S., Hays, J.R., & Zieben, M. (1976). Personality characteristics of juvenile probation officers. *Journal of Community Psychology, 4*, 152–156.

Stafford, K.P., & Wygant, D.B. (2005). The role of competency to stand trial in mental health courts. *Behavioral Sciences and the Law, 23*, 245–258.

Stone, L.A., Bassett, G.R., Brousseau, J.D., Demers, J., & Stiening, J.A. (1972). Psychological test scores for a group of MEDEX trainees. *Psychological Reports, 31*, 827–831.

Storm, J., & Graham, J.R. (2000). Detection of coached general malingering on the MMPI-2. *Psychological Assessment, 12*, 158–165.

Sutker, P.B., & Allain, N. (1973). Incarcerated and street heroin addicts: A personality comparison. *Psychological Reports, 32*, 243–246.

Swanson, J., Holzer, C., Ganju, V., & Jono, R. (1990). Violence and psychiatric disorder in the community: Evidence from the Epidemiologic Catchment Area Surveys. *Hospital and Community Psychiatry, 41*, 761–770.

Tellegen, A. (1985). Structures of mood and personality and their relevance to assessing anxiety, with an emphasis on self-report. In A.H. Tuma & J.D. Maser (Eds.), *Anxiety and the anxiety disorders* (pp. 681–706). Hillsdale, NJ: Lawrence Erlbaum Associates.

Tellegen, A., & Ben-Porath, Y.S. (1992). The new uniform T scores for the MMPI-2: Rationale, derivation, and appraisal. *Psychological Assessment, 4*, 145–155.

Tellegen, A., Ben-Porath, Y.S., McNulty, J.L., Arbisi, P.A., Graham, J.R., & Kaemmer, B. (2003). *MMPI-2 Restructured Clinical (RC) Scales: Development, validation, and interpretation.* Minneapolis: University of Minnesota Press.

Timbrook, R.E., & Graham, J.R. (1994). Ethnic differences on the MMPI-2? *Psychological Assessment, 6*, 212–217.

Tsai, D.C., & Pike, P.L. (2000). Effects of acculturation on the MMPI-2 scores of Asian American students. *Journal of Personality Assessment, 74*, 216–230.

Tsushima, W.T., Bridenstine, M.P., & Balfour, J.F. (2004). MMPI-2 scores in the outcome prediction of gastric bypass surgery. *Obesity Surgery, 14*, 528–532. United States v. Huberty, 53 MJ 369 (2000).

Vendrig, A.A., Derksen, J.J.L., & de Mey, H.R. (1999). Utility of selected MMPI-2 scales in the outcome prediction for patients with chronic back pain. *Psychological Assessment, 11*, 381–385.

Weed, N.C., Ben-Porath, Y.S., & Butcher, J.N. (1990). Failure of Wiener and Harmon Minnesota Multiphasic Personality Inventory (MMPI) subtle scales as personality descriptors and as validity indicators. *Psychological Assessment: A Journal of Consulting and Clinical Psychology, 2*, 281–285.

Weed, N.C., Butcher, J.N., McKenna, T., & Ben-Porath, Y.S. (1992). New measures for assessing alcohol and drug abuse with the MMPI-2: The APS and AAS. *Journal of Personality Assessment, 58*, 389–404.

Welsh, G.S. (1956). Factor dimensions A and R. In G.S. Welsh & W.G. Dahlstrom (Eds.), *Basic readings on the MMPI in psychology and medicine* (pp. 264–281). Minneapolis: University of Minnesota Press.

Wetter, M.W., Baer, R.A., Berry, D.T.R., & Reynolds, S.K. (1994). The effect of symptom information on faking on the MMPI-2. *Assessment, 1*, 199–207.

Wetter, M.W., & Corrigan, S.K. (1995). Providing information to clients about psychological tests: A survey of attorneys' and law students' attitudes. *Professional Psychology: Research and Practice, 26*, 1–4.

Wiggins, J.S. (1969). Content dimensions in the MMPI. In J.N. Butcher (Ed.), *MMPI: Research developments and clinical applications* (pp. 127–180). New York: McGraw-Hill.

Williams, R.B., Haney, T.L., Lee, K.L., Kong, Y.H., Blumenthal, J.A., & Whalen, R.E. (1980). Type A behavior, hostility, and coronary atherosclerosis. *Psychosomatic Medicine, 42*, 539–549.

3

THE MINNESOTA MULTIPHASIC PERSONALITY INVENTORY—ADOLESCENT

ROBERT P. ARCHER

MEREDITH ZOBY

REBECCA VAUTER STREDNY

EASTERN VIRGINIA MEDICAL SCHOOL

HISTORY AND DEVELOPMENT

The Minnesota Multiphasic Personality Inventory–Adolescent (MMPI–A) is a 478-item objective personality assessment instrument designed for use with adolescents. It provides an array of validity and clinical scales, and interpretation is facilitated by a substantial research literature. The MMPI–A is an adaptation of the Minnesota Multiphasic Personality Inventory (MMPI), and therefore an understanding of its development, psychometric characteristics, and research base necessarily begins with a history and description of the MMPI.

In 1937, Starke R. Hathaway and J.C. McKinley began construction on what eventually became the Minnesota Multiphasic Personality Inventory. Their work was stimulated, in part, by their observation that many patients in medical settings displayed symptoms that were psychological or "psychoneurotic in nature" (McKinley & Hathaway, 1943, p. 161). Furthermore, they believed that an objective self-report instrument could identify and describe the psychological features of patients more accurately than the traditional psychiatric interview used as the primary diagnostic procedure in the 1930s. The MMPI was also designed to provide a standard diagnostic tool for researchers evaluating the effectiveness of newly developed interventions. An additional goal was the creation of a personality measure that would be sensitive to psychological changes over time, allowing for a longitudinal view of psychological functioning through repeat administrations. Although Hathaway and McKinley originally sought to develop their instrument for use at the University of Minnesota Hospitals, the MMPI was published in 1942 and rapidly became established as the most commonly utilized objective personality assessment instrument in the United States across a variety of clinical settings (e.g., Lubin, Larsen, & Matarazzo, 1984; Lubin, Larsen, Matarazzo, & Seever, 1985; Lubin, Wallis, & Paine, 1971; Piotrowski & Keller, 1989).

Hathaway and McKinley developed the scales of the MMPI using a method known as empirical or criterion keying, and its application in the development of a personality assessment instrument was revolutionary. Previous personality test development methods had often relied on the rational selection of items using face validity as the primary criterion; that is, items were selected based on the degree to which they appeared to the test developer to be related to a given construct. In contrast, the empirical keying approach identifies test items based solely on the results of statistical procedures. Potential test items were administered to a normal sample and a variety of criterion samples, the latter containing individuals who appeared to display clear and unambiguous symptoms related to a specific diagnosis. Items were then selected for scale membership based on their ability to differentiate effectively between normal and criterion groups.

Prior to its release in 1942, preliminary versions of the MMPI were termed the "Medical and Psychiatric Inventory" and the "Minnesota Personality Schedule" (Colligan & Offord, 1992). The initial item pool was created by reviewing prominent psychiatric textbooks as well as previously established scales of social attitude, temperament, and psychological functioning. Indeed, the Humm-Wadsworth Temperament Scale (1933) appears to have served as a source for approximately 150 items eventually selected for the MMPI (Colligan & Offord, 1992). The early item pool comprised over 1,000 items and then was reduced to 504 by eliminating redundant items as well as items that appeared to hold little utility for a personality inventory. The potential items were then administered to 724 visitors of patients at the University of Minnesota Hospital, and to this core group Hathaway and McKinley eventually added smaller normative samples consisting of students receiving precollege counseling, individuals employed through the Federal Works Progress Administration (WPA), and a limited number of medical patients who did not display psychiatric disorders. The criterion groups used for scale development were relatively small subgroups of clinical patients divided into discrete diagnostic categories, including Hypochondriasis (Hs), Depression (D), Hysteria (Hy), Psychopathic Deviancy (Pd), Paranoia (Pa), Psychasthenia (Pt), Schizophrenia (Sc), and Mania (Ma). Eventually the Masculinity-Femininity (Mf) and Social Introversion (Si) scales were also added, although these were considered nonclinical scales and were often omitted by early test users.

Hathaway and McKinley recognized that test takers did not always respond in an open and candid manner to psychological tests, and therefore they created several validity scales in addition to the MMPI basic clinical scales. These scales were developed to provide a standardized assessment of the individual's test-taking attitude or response style. The Cannot Say or (?) scale is the total of the items omitted by the test taker or endorsed in both the true and false direction. The *Lie* or *L* scale comprises 15 items that were rationally derived to evaluate a defensive test-taking attitude involving the denial of common human failings or faults. A 64-item *Infrequency* or *F* scale was also developed containing statements that were endorsed in the deviant direction by 10% or fewer of the normative sample. The content of the *F* scale varies widely, but elevations on this scale may be the result of carelessness, problems in literacy, and conscious or unconscious efforts to overreport or exaggerate symptomatology, as well as more severe forms of genuine psychopathology. Finally, the Defensiveness or K scale was added to identify more subtle efforts to deny symptomatology or psychopathology as part of a defensive response style. In addition to serving as a measure of psychological defensiveness, the *K* scale was proposed by McKinley, Hathaway, and Meehl (1948) as a correction factor for five of the MMPI–A basic scales. Thus, the *K* scale also serves as a correction adjustment to basic scales *Hs, Pd, Pt, Sc,* and *Ma* to compensate for suppression of scores due to psychological defensiveness.

History of the Original MMPI With Adolescents

Dora Capwell undertook the first research investigation of the MMPI with adolescents in 1941, prior to the actual publication of the test. Capwell (1945a) demonstrated the ability of the MMPI to accurately discriminate between groups of delinquent and nondelinquent girls based on Pd scale elevations, and a further investigation showed that these differences were maintained in follow-up studies conducted 4 to 15 months following the initial administration (Capwell, 1945b). In the largest MMPI data set ever collected with adolescents, Hathaway and Monachesi (1953, 1963) conducted a large-scale longitudinal study of the relationship between the MMPI findings from 15,000 high school students in the late 1940s and early 1950s and subsequent delinquent behaviors as reflected in school, police, and court records. Hathaway and Monachesi (1963) and Monachesi and Hathaway (1969) summarized their findings by proposing that elevations on MMPI scales *Pd, Sc,* and *Ma,* (the excitatory scales) were associated with higher delinquency rates, whereas elevations on scales *D, Mf,* and *Si* (the inhibitory scales) were related to reduced risk of delinquent or antisocial behaviors.

Marks and Briggs (1972) generated the most frequently used set of adolescent norms for the original MMPI based on 1,766 normal adolescents. Their norms were grouped separately for girls and boys and were provided for ages 17, 16, 15, and a category of 14 and below. Marks, Seeman, and Haller (1974) reported the first actuarially based personality descriptors for a series of 29 MMPI codetypes. Their codetype study was based on the responses of approximately 1,250 adolescents aged 12 though 18 who had undergone at least 10 hours of psychotherapy between 1965 and 1973. This study also employed 172 therapists from 30 states who provided descriptive ratings for these adolescents from a correlate pool of 1,265 descriptors that appeared relevant to both male and female adolescents. The Marks et al. (1974) study was critical in providing clinicians with the first correlate information necessary to interpret adolescent codetype patterns. In 1987, Archer produced a comprehensive guide to using the MMPI with adolescents, and in 1991, a survey conducted by Archer, Maruish, Imhof, and Piotrowski found that the original form of the MMPI was the most frequently utilized objective personality assessment instrument in evaluations of adolescents in the United States.

History of the Development of the MMPI–A

Several areas of concern in regard to the use of the MMPI with adolescents emerged in the 1991 survey conducted by Archer and his colleagues. Disadvantages cited included the length of the test, the lack of contemporary norms, the demanding reading level associated with the instrument, and the presence of inappropriate or outdated items (e.g., "I used to play drop-the-handkerchief"). In addition, because the MMPI was primarily developed as an adult assessment instrument, questions designed to assess important aspects of adolescent experience were not included in the original inventory. These content areas included adolescent substance abuse, eating disorders, and school problems.

Regarding the lack of contemporary norms cited as a problem by respondents in the 1991 survey, the Marks and Briggs (1972) norms commonly employed with adolescents had been collected from the mid-1940s to the mid-1960s in a sample that contained very few non-Caucasian adolescents (Archer, 2005). Pancoast and Archer (1988) examined the adequacy of the Marks and Briggs norms in an analysis of MMPI results for normal adolescent samples collected between 1965 and 1974, contrasted with samples of more contemporary adolescents collected following 1975. Their findings indicated that the Marks and Briggs adolescent norms were not providing an adequate normative baseline for evaluations of more contemporary samples of adolescents.

DESCRIPTION OF THE MMPI–A

In July 1989, an advisory committee was appointed by the University of Minnesota Press to develop an adolescent form of the MMPI. An overarching goal was to maintain substantive continuity with the original MMPI, including the preservation of the basic validity and clinical scales. Therefore, an effort was made to minimize the changes to most MMPI basic scales while recognizing that more extensive changes would be needed for scales *F*, *Mf*, and *Si*. Although it understood the need for continuity with the original MMPI, the committee also perceived the revision as an opportunity to improve the item pool for adolescents and to provide several new scales directly relevant to adolescent development and psychopathology. A final goal of the project was the collection of a new normative sample representative of a diverse and contemporary population of adolescents.

Data were initially collected from about 2,500 adolescents in Minnesota, Ohio, California, Virginia, Pennsylvania, New York, North Carolina, and Washington. Participants were excluded if they produced incomplete data, their *F* raw score value exceed 25, their Carelessness scale value exceeded 35, or their age was above 18 or below 14. The resulting normative sample of 1,620 adolescents included 805 boys and 815 girls. The mean age was 15.5 ($SD = 1.7$) for boys and 15.6 ($SD = 1.18$) for girls. The ethnic makeup of the sample was 76% Caucasian, 12% African American, and 12% from other ethnic groups. Although the MMPI–A normative data set was a clear improvement over the Marks and Briggs (1972) normative sample in terms of geographic and ethnic diversity, the contemporary norms also have some less desirable characteristics. As noted by Archer (2005) and Black (1994), many adolescents included in the MMPI–A normative set were children of highly educated parents. For example, about 50% of the adolescents' fathers and about 40% of their mothers reported obtaining a bachelor's degree or higher; in contrast, according U.S. census data from 1980, only about 20% of men and 13% of women held college degrees. Butcher et al. (1992) also noted that the MMPI–A norms were less representative of adolescents who had a history of truancy or delinquency or who had dropped out of school, particularly important issues for adolescents evaluated in juvenile justice detention or correctional facilities.

Despite efforts to minimize the length of the MMPI–A, the final form continues to be time consuming in comparison with other similar tests. The adolescent version of the Personality Assessment Inventory (PAI–A) is expected to contain 264 items, or a little over half of the number of items on the MMPI–A (Morey, 2000). The Millon Adolescent Clinical Inventory (MACI) is a 160-item test that typically requires only about 30 minutes to administer (Millon, 1993). In contrast, the 478 items of the MMPI–A typically require 60–90 minutes for completion (Archer & Krishnamurthy, 2002). Although it is possible to administer an abbreviated version of the MMPI–A limited to the first 350 items, this format should be considered only as a last resort, because the validity scales *VRIN, TRIN, F*, and *F*2 and the content and supplementary scales cannot be scored.

The MMPI–A is designed to be used with adolescents aged 14–18 and should never be given to an individual older than 18 (Butcher et al., 1992). At the other end of the age continuum, the MMPI–A can be used selectively with 12- and 13-year-old examinees if they are developmentally advanced and have sufficient cognitive and reading skills (Butcher et al., 1992). It is important to note, however, that many younger adolescents assessed in juvenile justice settings will lack the sixth- to seventh-grade reading ability necessary to respond successfully to the MMPI–A (Archer & Krishnamurthy, 2002). An audiotaped version of the MMPI–A is available for reading-disabled adolescents who otherwise have the cognitive skills necessary to understand the MMPI–A item pool, and this administration form typically requires about 1 hour and 40 minutes.

MMPI–A Scale Structures

The MMPI–A consists of 478 items, and an abbreviated administration may be conducted using the first 350 items, which permits scoring of validity scales *L, F1*, and *K*, as well as the 10 basic clinical scales. However, all 478 items of the MMPI–A must be administered in order to obtain the content scale results. The MMPI–A was adapted from the original MMPI form with the following changes: 58 standard scale items were deleted from the basic scales, with 88% of these items coming from the *F, Mf*, and *Si* scales. Items eliminated from the original form of the MMPI in the development of the MMPI–A typically pertained to religious attitudes and practices, sexual preferences, bowel and bladder functioning, or topics deemed inappropriate in evaluating adolescents (e.g., voting in elections). The resulting MMPI–A includes the original 10 basic clinical scales and 3 basic validity scales, 4 newly developed validity scales, 15 content scales, 6 supplementary scales, and 28 Harris-Lingoes and 3 *Si* subscales. The new validity scales included in the MMPI–A are the *F1* and *F2* subscales, the True Response Inconsistency (TRIN) scale, and the Variable Response Inconsistency (VRIN) scale. Table 3.1 provides an overview of the MMPI–A scale structure.

There is a considerable degree of overlap between the 15 content scales on the MMPI-2 and the MMPI–A. A thorough discussion of the development of the MMPI–A content scales is provided in Williams, Butcher, Ben-Porath, and Graham (1992). After the identification of items in the MMPI-2 content scales deemed appropriate for the assessment of adolescents, the MMPI–A content scales were refined by adding or deleting items based on their relative contributions to the overall reliability of the scale. A rational review of scale item content was then completed to ensure that items appeared appropriate for measuring underlying scale constructs. Finally, items correlating more strongly with scales other than the content scale to which they were originally assigned were deleted. The development process for the MMPI–A content scales rendered the scales face valid and thereby easily influenced by response style in terms of overreporting or underreporting symptoms. When interpreting the MMPI–A content scales, it is important to carefully consider the validity indicators, particularly scores on the Defensiveness or *K* scale. Furthermore, although the MMPI–A content scales have relatively high alpha coefficient values, most of the scales also possess one or more subcomponents. Sherwood, Ben-Porath, and Williams (1997) have recently developed a set of content component scales for 13 of the 15 MMPI–A content scales to facilitate the evaluation of specific areas of content endorsement. A profile sheet for the content component scales is not yet available.

TABLE 3.1
Overview of the MMPI–A Scales and Subscales

Basic Profile Scales (17 scales)

Standard Scales (13)
  L through *Si*

Additional Validity Scales (4)
  F1/F2 (Subscales of *F* Scale)
  VRIN (Variable Response Inconsistency)
  TRIN (True Response Inconsistency)

Content and Supplementary Scales (21 scales)

Content Scales (15)
  A-anx (Anxiety)
  A-obs (Obsessiveness)
  A-dep (Depression)
  A-hea (Health Concerns)
  A-aln (Alienation)
  A-biz (Bizarre Mentation)
  A-ang (Anger)
  A-cyn (Cynicism)
  A-con (Conduct Problems)
  A-lse (Low Self-Esteem)
  A-las (Low Aspirations)
  A-sod (Social Discomfort)
  A-fam (Family Problems)
  A-sch (School Problems)
  A-trt (Negative Treatment Indicators)

Supplementary Scales (6)

  MAC-R (MacAndrew Alcoholism–Revised)
  ACK (Alcohol/Drug Problem Acknowledgment)
  PRO (Alcohol/Drug Problem Proneness)
  IMM (Immaturity)
  A (Anxiety)
  R (Repression)

Harris-Lingoes and Si Subscales (31 scales)

Harris-Lingoes Subscales (28)
  D1 (Subjective Depression)
  D2 (Psychomotor Retardation)
  D3 (Physical Malfunctioning)
  D4 (Mental Dullness)
  D5 (Brooding)
  Hy1 (Denial of Social Anxiety)
  Hy2 (Need for Affection)
  Hy3 (Lassitude-Malaise)
  Hy4 (Somatic Complaints)
  Hy5 (Inhibition of Aggression)
  Pd1 (Familial Discord)
  Pd2 (Authority Problems)
  Pd3 (Social Imperturbability)

TABLE 3.1

(Continued)

    Pd4 (Social Alienation)
    Pd5 (Self-Alienation)
    Pa1 (Persecutory)
    Pa2 (Poignancy)
    Pa3 (Naiveté)
    Sc1 (Social Alienation)
    Sc2 (Emotional Alienation)
    Sc3 (Lack of Ego Mastery, Cognitive)
    Sc4 (Lack of Ego Mastery, Conative)
    Sc5 (Lack of Ego Mastery, Defective Inhibition)
    Sc6 (Bizarre Sensory Experiences)
    Ma1 (Amorality)
    Ma2 (Psychomotor Acceleration)
    Ma3 (Imperturbability)
    Ma4 (Ego Inflation)
Si Subscales (3)
    Si1 (Shyness/Self-Consciousness)
    Si2 (Social Avoidance)
    Si3 (Alienation–Self and Others)

Note: From Archer, R.P. (2005). *MMPI–A: Assessing adolescent psychopathology* (3rd ed.). Lawrence Erlbaum Associates. Reprinted with permission.

The Supplementary scales of the MMPI–A include three scales developed for the original MMPI: Anxiety *(A)*, Repression *(R)*, and the MacAndrew Alcoholism Revised *(MAC–R)*. Additional Supplementary scales include the Immaturity *(IMM)* scale developed by Archer, Pancoast, and Gordon (1994), the Alcohol Drug Acknowledgment *(ACK)* scale, and the Alcohol/Drug Problem Proneness *(PRO)* scale developed by Weed, Butcher, and Williams (1994). The relatively low number of item deletions made to the MMPI–A clinical scales made it possible to retain the Harris-Lingoes Content subscales and extend these subscales to the MMPI–A content scales. Additionally, the *Si* subscales developed for the MMPI-2 by Ben-Porath, Hostetler, Butcher, and Graham (1989) were also included on the MMPI–A Subscale Profile Sheet. Thus, a review of MMPI–A scale and subscale features reveals numerous similarities between the MMPI–A and both the original MMPI and the MMPI-2.

PSYCHOMETRIC CHARACTERISTICS

Information on the test-retest reliability, internal consistency, and factor structure of the MMPI–A, as well as correlate information for normal and clinical samples, is provided in the MMPI–A manual (Butcher et al., 1992) and was recently updated in Archer (2005). The MMPI–A is a psychometrically sound instrument that exhibits test-retest correlates for basic scales ranging from $r = .19$ for the $F1$ subscale to $r = .84$ for the Si scale. Stein, McClinton, and Graham (1998) evaluated the one-year test-retest reliability of the basic MMPI–A scales and reported values ranging from $r = .51$ for the Pa scale to $r = .75$ for the Si scale. Similarly, test-retest correlations for the content scales ranged from $r = .40$ for the *A-trt* to $r = .73$ for the *A-sch* content scale. The standard error of measurement for the basic scales on the MMPI–A is typically estimated to fall between 2 and 3 raw score points (Butcher et al., 1992). The internal consistency (coefficient alpha) values for the MMPI–A scales range from lower values on scales Mf ($r = .43$), and Pa ($r = .57$) to relatively higher values ($r \geq .80$) on many of the content scales and the IMM scale. A major advantage of using the MMPI–A in forensic settings is certainly its array of validity scales capable of accurately identifying problems in test-taking attitudes or response patterns.

Forbey (2003) has estimated that approximately 120 studies have been completed on the MMPI–A from the time of its initial publication in 1992 through 2002. In addition, Archer and Krishnamurthy (2002) note that the MMPI–A has been the subject of numerous master's thesis studies and doctoral dissertations, further reflecting the strong research interest in the MMPI–A. Because the MMPI–A retains many features of the MMPI, particularly regarding the basic validity and clinical scales, the research done with adolescents on the original MMPI is largely generalizable to the MMPI–A (Archer, 2005). Furthermore, research has found that correlates for the basic scales and for several supplementary scales appear similar for adolescents and adults. (Archer, Gordon, Anderson, & Giannetti, 1989; Archer, Gordon, Giannetti, & Singles, 1988; Williams & Butcher, 1989).

Independent research pertaining to the MMPI–A content and supplementary scales, including scales such as $ACK, PRO,$ and IMM, has also begun to accumulate. For example, Krishnamurthy, Archer, and House (1996) reported a hit rate of .68 using either the MMPI–A scale 2 or the A-Dep scale for identifying adolescents given depression diagnoses. For conduct disorder, scales A-Con and A-Cyn yielded hit rates of .61 and .66, respectively, using the T-score cutoff of $T \geq 65$. Further, Imhof and Archer (1997) evaluated the concurrent validity of the IMM scale for 66 adolescents aged 13–18 in a residential treatment setting. They reported that elevated IMM scales were related to greater impulsivity and lower levels of intelligence. Similar IMM scales correlates have been reported by Milne and Greenway (1999) and by Zinn, McCumber, and Dahlstrom (1999).

Another area of MMPI–A research interest has been the issue of critical items. Archer and Jacobson (1993) examined the endorsement frequency of the Koss-Butcher (1973) and the Lachar-Wrobel (1979) critical items for normative and clinical samples for the MMPI–A and the MMPI-2. They found that adolescents in both the normative and clinical samples endorsed items at a higher frequency than did normal adults. Further, results indicated that adolescents in clinical settings did not generally endorse critical items with a higher frequency than normal adolescents. The authors observed that these findings underscored the difficulties inherent in creating a critical item list for adolescents by selecting items with differences in endorsement frequency between normal and clinical settings. More recently, Forbey and Ben-Porath (1998) developed a set of MMPI–A critical items by comparing the item-level responses of the MMPI–A normative sample with 419 adolescents receiving treatment in a midwestern residential treatment facility. The result of this effort was a critical item set composed of 82 items grouped into 15 content areas, including aggression, conduct problems, and depression-suicidal ideation.

The K-correction procedure used with the original MMPI was not carried over to the MMPI–A. The original MMPI K scale included 30 items that were empirically selected by contrasting the item endorsements of clearly disturbed psychiatric patients who produced normal-range scores on the clinical scales with the item responses of the normative group. The main function of the K scale was to improve the ability of the clinical scales to detect psychopathology by adding varying proportions of K scale raw score values to the scales $Hs, Pd, Pt, Sc,$ and Ma. Although K correction was carried over to the MMPI-2 (Butcher et al., 2001), the procedure was not retained for the MMPI–A. Alperin, Archer, and Coates (1996) derived experimental K-weights for the MMPI–A to determine whether they could improve test accuracy in adolescent samples. Empirically determined K-weights were systematically added to the raw score values from the eight basic scales (excluding *Mf* and *Si*) and used to predict membership in the MMPI–A normative sample versus membership in a clinical sample of 122 adolescents receiving inpatient treatment. The results indicated that the use of the *K*-correction procedure did not lead to any systematic improvement in test accuracy in this classification task. Alperin and her colleagues concluded that their findings failed to provide support for the use of the *K*-correction procedure with the MMPI–A.

In addition to studies of the *K*-correction procedure, a substantial amount of research has been devoted to the effectiveness of the MMPI–A validity scales. Profile validity is a particularly important issue for MMPI–A evaluations of adolescents in a forensic setting. In this setting, response biases involving both underreporting and overreporting frequently occur, depending on the perceived advantages associated with these approaches. In addition, adolescents from lower socioeconomic backgrounds or with various forms of conduct disorder may produce invalid results due to reading deficits and/or carelessness. It is therefore critical for psychologists to be able to use MMPI–A validity scales in order to detect response distortions or biases. Preliminary evaluations of the *VRIN* and *TRIN* validity scales, reported in the test manual (Butcher et al., 1992), indicated that these scales were useful in detecting inconsistent responding *(VRIN)* as well as an acquiescent or nay-saying response style *(TRIN)*. The test manual also noted that the *T*-score difference between *F1* and *F2* could prove useful in identifying changes in an adolescent's test-taking approach between the first and second half of the test. Archer (2005) presented a random response pattern on the MMPI–A, with the resulting profile showing elevations on the scales *L*, *VRIN*, *F1*, and *F2*, an invalid profile easily detected by most interpreters. Baer, Ballenger, Berry, and Wetter (1997) evaluated varying degrees of random responding on the MMPI–A. Their results demonstrated a pattern of increasing scores on *F1*, *F2*, *F*, and *VRIN*, as profile randomness increased. Archer and Elkins (1999) also found that scores on the validity scales *F*, *F1*, and *F2*, were effective in differentiating profiles of a clinical sample of 354 adolescents from randomly generated protocols.

Baer, Ballenger, and Kroll (1998) compared community and clinical adolescent samples instructed to portray themselves as having superior psychological adjustment (i.e., the instructions were designed to produce underreporting of psychopathology). The results included significantly higher scores on the MMPI–A defensiveness scales *L* and *K*, and these scales provided accurate discrimination between underreported and standard profiles. Baer, Kroll, Rinaldo, and Ballenger (1999) further demonstrated that overreporting on the MMPI–A was effectively detected using an *F* scale T-score ≥ 80 as the optimal cutoff value. In addition, the *F* scale was sensitive to both random responding and overreporting of symptoms, whereas *VRIN* scale results were effective only for the identification of random responding. Finally, an Infrequency Psychopathology Scale *(Fp-A)* for the MMPI–A was constructed by McGrath, et al. (2000) that was very similar in purpose to the *Fp* scale developed for the MMPI-2 by Arbisi and Ben-Porath (1995) by selecting items rarely endorsed by normal adults or by VA psychiatric patients. Using a similar approach, McGrath and his colleagues developed the *Fp-A* scale by selecting items that were rarely endorsed by normal adolescents or by two inpatient adolescent clinical samples. The initial results obtained by McGrath et al., however, showed relatively little gain from using the *Fp-A* scale rather than relying on the MMPI–A *F* scale.

Finally, a substantive group of research studies have centered on the factor structure of the MMPI–A. Archer, Belevich, and Elkins (1994) conducted a factor analysis using the MMPI–A normative sample. The results indicated that eight factors accounted for a majority of raw score variance produced by the 69 scales and subscales of the MMPI–A. The factor structure identified by these authors included the following

MMPI-A Structural Summary

Robert P. Archer and Radhika Krishnamurthy

Name: _____ Date: _____

Age: _____ Grade: _____

Gender: _____ School: _____

Test-Taking Attitudes

1. Omissions (raw score total)

_____ ? (Cannot Say scale)

2. Consistency (T-score values)

_____ VRIN

_____ TRIN

_____ F_1 vs. _____ F_2

3. Accuracy (check if condition present)

Overreport

_____ F scale T score ≥ 90

_____ All clinical scales except 5 and 0 ≥ 60

Underreport

_____ High L (T ≥ 65)

_____ High K (T ≥ 65)

_____ All clinical scales except 5 and 0 < 60

Factor Groupings
(enter T-score data)

1. General Maladjustment

_____ Welsh's A

_____ Scale 7

_____ Scale 8

_____ Scale 2

_____ Scale 4

_____ D_1 (Subjective Depression)

_____ D_4 (Mental Dullness)

_____ D_5 (Brooding)

_____ Hy_3 (Lassitude-Malaise)

_____ Sc_1 (Social Alienation)

_____ Sc_2 (Emotional Alienation)

_____ Sc_3 (Lack of Ego Mastery – Cognitive)

_____ Sc_4 (Lack of Ego Mastery – Conative)

_____ Si_3 (Alienation)

_____ Pd_4 (Social Alienation)

_____ Pd_5 (Self-Alienation)

_____ Pa_2 (Poignancy)

_____ A-dep

_____ A-anx

_____ A-lse

_____ A-aln

_____ A-obs

_____ A-trt

_____ /23 Number of scales with T ≥ 60

2. Immaturity

_____ IMM

_____ Scale F

_____ Scale 8

_____ Scale 6

_____ ACK

_____ MAC-R

_____ Pa_1 (Persecutory Ideas)

_____ Sc_2 (Emotional Alienation)

_____ Sc_6 (Bizarre Sensory Experiences)

_____ A-sch

_____ A-biz

_____ A-aln

_____ A-con

_____ A-fam

_____ A-trt

_____ /15 Number of scales with T ≥ 60

FIG. 3.1. MMPI-A Structural Summary form Reprinted by Permission. Copyright © 1994 by Psychological Assessment Resources, Inc.

3. Disinhibition/Excitatory Potential

______ Scale 9
______ Ma_2 (Psychomotor Acceleration)
______ Ma_4 (Ego Inflation)
______ Sc_5 (Lack of Ego Mastery, Defective Inhibition)
______ D_2 (Psychomotor Retardation) (low score)*
______ Welsh's R (low score)*
______ Scale K (low score)*
______ Scale L (low score)*
______ A-ang
______ A-cyn
______ A-con
______ MAC-R

___/12 Number of scales with $T \geq 60$ or ≤ 40 for scales with asterisk

4. Social Discomfort

______ Scale 0
______ Si_1 (Shyness/Self-Consciousness)
______ Hy_1 (Denial of Social Anxiety) (low score)*
______ Pd_3 (Social Imperturbability) (low score)*
______ Ma_3 (Imperturbability) (low scores)*
______ A-sod
______ A-lse
______ Scale 7

___/8 Number of scales with $T \geq 60$ or $T \leq 40$ for scales with asterisk

5. Health Concerns

______ Scale 1
______ Scale 3
______ A-hea
______ Hy_4 (Somatic Complaints)
______ Hy_3 (Lassitude-Malaise)
______ D_3 (Physical Malfunctioning)

___/6 Number of scales with $T \geq 60$

6. Naivete

______ A-cyn (low score)*
______ Pa_3 (Naivete)
______ Hy_2 (Need for Affection)
______ Si_3 (Alienation-Self and Others) (low score)
______ Scale K

___/5 Number of scales with $T \geq 60$ or $T \leq 40$ for scales with asterisk

7. Familial Alienation

______ Pd_1 (Familial Discord)
______ A-fam
______ Scale 4
______ PRO

___/4 Number of scales with $T \geq 60$

8. Psychoticism

______ Pa_1 (Persecutory Ideas)
______ Scale 6
______ A-biz
______ Sc_6 (Bizarre Sensory Experiences)

___/4 Number of scales with $T \geq 60$

Note. The presentation of scales under each factor label is generally organized in a descending order from the best to the least effective marker. Within this overall approach, scales are grouped logically in terms of basic clinical scales, Harris-Lingoes and *Si* subscales, and content scales. The majority of scales included in this summary sheet were correlated ≥ .60 or ≤ –.60 with the relevant factor for the MMPI-A normative sample.

PAR Psychological Assessment Resources, Inc.
P.O. Box 998/Odessa, Florida 33556/Toll-Free 1-800-331-TEST

9 8 7 6 5 4 3 2 1 Reorder #RO-2698 Printed in the U.S.A.
This form is printed in blue ink on white paper. Any other version is unauthorized.

FIG. 3.1. (*continued*)

dimensions: General Maladjustment, Immaturity, Disinhibition-Excitatory Potential, Social Discomfort, Health Concerns, Naiveté, Familial Alienation; and Psychoticism. These factor analysis results were used by Archer and Krishnamurthy (1994a,1994b) to construct the MMPI–A Structural Summary. The Structural Summary is a means of effectively focusing a clinician's attention on the dimensions of greatest importance for understanding an adolescent's performance on the MMPI–A. Archer and Krishnamurthy (1994b) recommended that more than half of the scales and subscales associated with each factor should reach critical values before an interpreter emphasizes a given dimension in describing an adolescent's functioning. Additionally, these authors recommended that when more than one factor structure was suggested, the factor with the highest percentage of scales or subscales producing clinical values should receive greater weight in the interpretation. Archer, Krishnamurthy, and Jacobson (1994) provided factor descriptions for all of the external correlates that have been identified for the Structural Summary factors, and these factor correlates are also found in Archer (2005). Figure 3.1 presents the MMPI–A Structural Summary form developed by Archer and Krishnamurthy (1994a).

Archer and Krishnamurthy (1997) replicated the structural summary in a clinical sample of adolescents, and the same authors provided an extensive array of empirical correlates for each factor dimension (1994). This work was recently extended to juvenile forensic populations by Archer, Bolinskey, Morton, and Farris (2003). Most recently, Krishnamurthy, Bolinskey, and Archer (2005) showed the viability of the eight-factor Structural Summary model when the 69 standard MMPI–A scales and subscales are factored in combination with new MMPI–A scales, including the Content Component scales and the Personality Psychopathology Five (PSY-5) scales developed by McNulty, Harkness, Ben-Porath, and Williams (1997).

CLINICAL USES AND LIMITATIONS

The MMPI–A was developed to evaluate adolescent psychopathology in a variety of settings, particularly outpatient and inpatient psychiatric and alcohol/drug treatment settings, schools, and medical clinics and hospitals. The MMPI–A is typically administered at the beginning of treatment in order to assess an adolescent's ability to actively participate and engage in the therapeutic process and to provide a baseline of psychological functioning. The information gathered from the MMPI–A is routinely integrated with data from other tests, such as reports and/or ratings provided by teachers, parents, and treatment team members, as well as the adolescent's treatment history and any interview findings, to allow a comprehensive overview of the adolescent's psychological functioning.

The MMPI–A serves as an important indicator of therapeutic progress when administered on a follow-up basis to evaluate treatment effectiveness. It is particularly useful in this regard because the test is capable of reflecting changes in psychological functioning over relatively short periods of time. Archer (2005) observed that most adolescents are not resistant to the readministration of the MMPI–A to evaluate treatment progress if they receive feedback on the test and thus have an investment in the testing outcome. Archer and Krishnamurthy (2002) noted that adolescents are capable of receiving and utilizing a great deal of feedback information from the MMPI–A if the examiner avoids technical jargon and articulates the feedback in a manner that provides information to them concerning issues they perceive as important.

Like all psychometric instruments, the MMPI–A also has several limitations. It requires a substantial amount of cognitive maturation and reading ability for successful administration, and these factors are likely to be particularly important in the assessment of adolescents in the juvenile justice system, where problems in reading comprehension are frequently encountered. Further, adolescents completing the MMPI–A must have the capacity and motivation to complete a relatively long and demanding test instrument. Although short forms have been developed for the MMPI–A, these are not recommended for the evaluation of adolescents in forensic settings. Archer, Tirrell, and Elkins (2001), for example, developed an MMPI–A short form based on the on the administration of the first 150 items of the test and it illustrates the limitations of all short-form approaches. It is useful for detecting the presence of psychopathology, but the profiles it produces often differ significantly from those produced by full-length test administrations.

Another area of potential limitation is the tendency of the MMPI–A to produce relatively low basic scale elevations, even for adolescents who display significant psychiatric symptoms. This problem was originally noted by Archer (1987) in reference to the Marks and Briggs (1972) norms for the original MMPI, and it continues to occur with adolescents who complete the MMPI–A (e.g., Archer, 2005; Archer & Krishnamurthy, 2002). Alperin and her colleagues (1996) evaluated the relative efficacy of applying an MMPI–A T-score value of 60 or above (as opposed to the standard value of 65) to define "clinical levels" of symptomatology, Lowering the clinical criterion T-score in this study reduced rather than increased the overall classification accuracy. These results are consistent with guidance provided in the MMPI–A manual (Butcher et al., 1992), specifically the statement that "a clinically significant elevation is defined as an MMPI–A T-score $\geq$ 65" (p. 43). Fontaine, Archer, Elkins, and Johansen (2001) replicated and expanded the work of Alperin et al., by comparing the accuracy of the MMPI–A in identifying normal and clinical adolescents utilizing the $T \geq 60$ and $T \geq 65$ criteria at differing base rates for the occurrence of psychopathology. Once again, the $T \geq 65$ criterion resulted in a higher level of accuracy, minimizing misclassification of both normal and clinical cases. Most recently, Archer, Handel, and Lynch (2001) showed that the MMPI–A item endorsement frequencies for normal and clinical adolescent samples often exhibit no significant differences, in contrast to the MMPI-2, which typically demonstrates a high rate of effectiveness in separating normal from clinical samples. Archer et al. concluded that a markedly high rate of MMPI–A item endorsement in the normative sample (rather than unusually high rates of item endorsement associated with adolescents in clinical samples) was most likely responsible for this phenomenon. Overall, these research studies indicate that there is a high rate of within-normal-limits (W-N-L) MMPI–A profiles among adolescents in treatment settings, and recent findings by Archer, et al. (2003) indicate that the high frequency of W-N-L profiles is also found among adolescents evaluated in juvenile justice or forensic settings.

The MMPI–A, like the MMPI-2, is best viewed as an instrument that provides a description of an individual's psychological functioning at a "moment in time" (Archer and Baker, 2005). MMPI–A profiles have a very limited capacity for making long-term behavioral or diagnostic predictions regarding adult functioning (Gottesman & Hanson, 1990; Lowman, Galinsky, & Gray-Little, 1980). This limitation is not unique to the MMPI–A but is possessed by all psychological instruments because of the behavioral and affective instability characteristic of adolescent development (Archer, 2005). This fluidity in personality structure is a major reason why the *Diagnostic and Statistic Manual of Mental Disorders*, fourth edition, test revision (*DSM–V–TR*, American Psychiatric Association, 2000) strongly encourages clinicians to avoid the application of personality disorder diagnoses to adolescents. Further, the manual explicitly prohibits the use of the Antisocial Personality Disorder diagnosis with individuals under the age of 18.

FORENSIC USES AND LIMITATIONS

Common Uses

Hathaway and McKinley (1943) did not develop the MMPI with the intent of utilizing this instrument in forensic evaluations, and the MMPI–A manual (Butcher et al., 1992) provides little guidance on the application of this instrument in forensic settings. Therefore, the use of the MMPI–A in forensic settings represents an extension of this instrument in which test findings must be "translated" to address questions beyond the original scope of the instrument. There are a variety of referral questions that the MMPI–A can be useful for answering, as the clinical constructs assessed by this instrument are often relevant to forensic issues or to individuals being treated in forensic settings. Examples include competency to stand trial and insanity evaluations, personal injury and disability assessments, and assessment of general mental functioning for purposes of placement and treatment planning. However, caution should always be used in making the transition from clinical conclusions to inferences regarding forensic issues. As the area of forensic psychology has rapidly expanded, the opportunities for the use and misuse of traditional clinical assessment instruments in forensic settings have also dramatically increased.

Grisso (1998) noted that juvenile courts, prosecutors, and defense attorneys may request a clinical evaluation of an adolescent at a number of points in the juvenile justice system. The most frequent requests for an evaluation are to assist the court in dispositional decisions prior to adjudication and/or to assist in identifying appropriate sentencing after adjudication. Psychologists may also be asked to evaluate the emergency medical needs of an adolescent who is being held in detention and exhibiting severely disorganized or depressed (and potentially suicidal) behaviors. Forensic evaluations may also be requested at the pretrial stage to determine whether the adolescent should be retained in a secure facility or could be released back to the community to await trial.

Psychological evaluations may also be requested in preparation for hearings on the waiver of adolescents from juvenile courts to the adult criminal justice system. Competence to stand trial is another type of pretrial issue for which evaluations may be requested by the court. These evaluations typically focus on the juvenile's awareness and understanding of the charges, knowledge of the legal system, and ability to meaningfully assist an attorney with defense preparations. Psychologists may also be asked to perform evaluations of a juvenile's competence to waive Miranda rights "knowingly, intelligently, and voluntarily." Finally, psychologists may be asked to evaluate an adolescent's mental state at the time of the offense, although this latter issue rarely arises. Grisso (1998), for example, noted that many clinicians working in the juvenile justice system have never been asked to evaluate an adolescent's sanity at the time of the offense.

While the most frequent forensic use of the MMPI–A is within the juvenile justice system, another important application is the assessment, in personal injury cases, of adolescents who may have suffered emotional damage. The legal framework for personal injury litigation differs substantially from the criminal justice system, in that the former is largely defined by the accumulation of relevant case law whereas criminal cases are typically tried on state or federal statutes. The basis of personal injury litigation is tort, defined by Greenberg, Otto, and Long (2003) as "a civil wrong that gives rise to a remedy in the form of a claim for compensation that is commenced with the filing of a complaint or petition" (p. 412). The usefulness of the MMPI–A for evaluating adolescents in civil cases rests on its ability to provide an overview of the plaintiff's psychological or emotional functioning in reference to well-established adolescent norms. Additionally, the MMPI–A provides an important opportunity to evaluate an adolescent's response style, such as a tendency to overreport symptomatology, a dimension particularly relevant to examinations in personal injury cases.

Other uses of the MMPI–A in forensic settings include the evaluation of adolescents who have been sexually abused. The literature on the use of the MMPI and MMPI–A with this population was briefly reviewed by Archer and Krishnamurthy (2002). As noted by these authors, the MMPI–A profiles of sexually abused adolescents typically contain multiple basic scale elevations reflective of general emotional distress. In addition, these adolescents are likely to produce elevations on scales reflecting alienation, interpersonal sensitivity, and social withdrawal. Hillary and Schere (1993), for instance, found that sexually abused adolescents typically produced elevations on scales measuring depression (*D*) and anxiety (*Pt*), with elevations on scales *Sc* and *Ma* occurring frequently as well. Scott and Stone (1986) compared the MMPI profiles of adolescents and adults who had been molested by their fathers and/or stepfathers and found that both groups produced elevations on *Sc*, with adolescents also producing *Ma* scale elevations. Forbey and Ben-Porath (2000) examined the MMPI–A profiles of adolescents receiving residential treatment and reported that sexual abuse histories were related to higher scores on basic scales *D, Pd, Si*, and *Pa* as well as content scales *A-dep, A-lse, A-sod, A-fam*, and *A-ang*. Williams et al. (1992) found a similar content scale pattern for adolescents with histories of sexual abuse, with sexually abused boys particularly likely to produce elevations on scales *A-dep, A-ang, A-lse*, and *A-sch*. Williams and her colleagues also found that sexually abused boys most commonly had higher scores on basic clinical scales *Pt* and *Sc* and that sexually abused girls were more likely to produce elevations on scales *Pd* and *Sc*. Archer and Krishnamurthy (2002) concluded that sexually abused adolescents are likely to produce multiple elevations on the MMPI–A scales, and no single profile can be used to identify sexually abused adolescents effectively.

The MMPI–A is also frequently used in child custody evaluations. Most domestic or family relations courts render decisions concerning child custody based on a generally accepted standard involving "the best interests of the child." The MMPI–A can be used to evaluate the emotional and psychological needs of adolescents involved in child custody proceedings and to provide information or offer recommendations to the court regarding optimal custodial placements. Otto and Collins (1995) noted that the MMPI–A provides a well-researched basis for describing the emotional needs of adolescents, although they caution that little is currently known about how to use the MMPI-2 characteristics of parents and the MMPI–A characteristics of adolescents in combination to predict specific outcomes of child placement decisions.

Research on Forensic Uses of the MMPI/MMPI–A

The history of the research on the MMPI and MMPI–A in juvenile offender populations spans 6 decades. As previously noted, Dora Capwell (1945a, 1945b) examined the effectiveness of scale *Pd* in accurately identifying delinquent and nondelinquent girls. Hathaway and Monachesi (1952, 1953, 1961, 1963) launched a landmark study of the ability of the MMPI to predict delinquent and antisocial behavior. They administered the MMPI to 3,971 ninth graders during the 1947–1948 school year and combined these data with the results of a statewide sample collected in 1954 on an addition 3,329 ninth graders in 86 Minnesota communities. Their researchers also collected data from school records, teacher ratings, and follow-up data from public agencies, including police and court reports. Hathaway and Monachesi undertook collection of this massive data set in order to implement a longitudinal study that would potentially identify personality variables related to the later onset of delinquent behaviors. Extensive follow-up research based on the data originally collected by Hathaway and Monachesi has provided mixed support for their proposal that elevations on scales *Pd, Sc,* and *Ma* tend to increase the probability of adolescent delinquency. Some early studies did appear to demonstrate the usefulness of the MMPI for identifying adolescent predisposal to delinquency (e.g., Briggs, Wirt, & Johnson, 1961; Huesmann, Lefkowitz, & Eron, 1978; Wirt & Briggs, 1959). More recent studies, however, have produced mixed results on the usefulness of the excitatory scales in predicting delinquent behavior (e.g., Archer et al., 2003).

The MMPI–A does appear to hold promise as a means of effectively identifying and describing juvenile delinquents, however. For example, Cashel, Rogers, Sewell, and Holliman (1998) examined the MMPI–A scale correlates for 99 male delinquents held in a Texas juvenile correction facility. These adolescents were also evaluated with the Schedule of Affective Disorders and Schizophrenia with School Age Children (Angold, 1989). Cashel and colleagues found an association between *Ma* scale elevations and higher levels of hyperactivity and greater mood and conduct disturbance; addition, elevations on the *Hy* scale were related to cruelty toward others and increased suicidal ideation. Thus, this study offered limited support for the excitatory scale concept developed by Hathaway and Monachesi. Hicks, Rogers, and Cashel (2000) evaluated the usefulness of the screening version of the Psychopathology Checklist (PCL–SV) and the MMPI–A for predicting violent, nonviolent, self-injurious, and total infractions in male adolescent offenders. Among the findings of this study, the MMPI–A proved to be more effective than the PCL–SV in predicting the total number of infractions during incarceration. The combination of scores from the MMPI–A *Pa* and *Ma* basic scales, for example, resulted in the accurate classification of 60% of residents with violent infractions and 66% of residents without violent infractions. Hicks and his colleagues suggested that clinicians routinely evaluate scale *Pa* elevations in assessing the risk of violent infractions among adolescent offenders. Interestingly, *Pd* scale elevations in this study were not correlated with scores from the PCL–SV, the number of infractions, or the presence of conduct disorder symptoms. Thus, Hicks et al. also provided limited support for the predictive utility of *Ma* as one of Hathaway and Monachesi's excitatory scales but no support for the predictive utility of excitatory scales *Pd* and *Sc.*

A number of other researchers have also examined the MMPI–A characteristics of male juvenile offenders. Hume, Kennedy, Patrick, and Partyka (1996) evaluated the relationship between the MMPI–A and the Psychopathy Checklist–Revised (PCL–R) by Hare (1991) in a sample of 101 male juvenile delinquents in a state correctional facility. The authors reported that scores from these two instruments were essentially independent and unrelated. Pena, Megargee, and Brody (1996) compared the MMPI–A profiles of 162 incarcerated delinquent boys with several groups, including 805 nondelinquent male adolescents from the MMPI–A normative sample. The results indicated that the profiles of delinquents often showed elevations on *Pa, Pd,* and *Ma* and that the most frequent two-point codetype classification was the 4-9/9-4. Pena et al. concluded that their findings supported the construct validity of the MMPI–A in forensic settings and also noted it was possible to evaluate 94% of the boys in the sample by using an oral administration of the test instrument. Glaser, Calhoun, and Petrocelli (2002) also evaluated the ability of the MMPI–A to classify 72 male juvenile offenders according to whether they committed crimes against person, crimes against property, or alcohol/drug-related offenses. The instrument correctly classified 79.2% of these adolescents. Adolescents who scored higher on scales *Hs* and *Si,* for example, were less likely to develop alcohol and drug problems and more likely to engage in property crimes. In contrast, adolescents who produced lower scores on the basic scale *Ma* and higher scores on the *A-sch* content scale were more likely to have committed drug-related offenses.

Morton, Farris, and Brenowitz (2002) examined the ability of the MMPI–A to discriminate accurately between 855 male delinquents in a South Carolina correctional facility and 805 males from the MMPI–A normative sample. The single most effective scale in accurately discriminating normal from delinquent adolescents was MMPI–A basic scale *Mf*, with more masculine scores characteristic of the delinquent sample. In addition, elevations on MMPI–A basic scales *Pd* and *Pa* were also found to be more frequent among male delinquents. These latter findings are consistent with the findings of Pena et al. (1996), but the relative importance of scale *Mf* found by Morton et al. has not yet been confirmed by other researchers. The results of these MMPI–A studies indicate that conduct disorder (*Pd* scale), identification with a stereotypically male gender role (*Mf* scale), and interpersonal suspiciousness, distrust, and sensitivity to injury or slight (*Pa* scale) are characteristics that distinguish male juvenile delinquents from their nondelinquent adolescent counterparts.

Archer et al. (2003) followed up the Morton et al. (2002) study to further evaluate the extent to which MMPI–A profiles from 196 male juveniles in detention facilities could be successfully discriminated from the MMPI–A protocols produced by 200 adolescent male psychiatric patients and 151 dually diagnosed adolescent males receiving inpatient treatment for comorbid substance abuse and psychiatric disorders. The findings included significant differences in mean *T*-score elevations between these three groups of adolescents across a variety of MMPI–A scales and subscales. The profiles of delinquent boys were characterized by greater psychological immaturity as seen on the *IMM* scale and by superficial efforts to appear emotionally controlled and well adjusted as seen on the *Hy* scale. Although the MMPI–A profiles of adolescents in detention, psychiatric, and dual diagnosis facilities showed some distinctive features, Archer and his colleagues also noted that these adolescents shared many common MMPI–A profile features across settings.

Katz and Marquette (1996) attempted to identify personality features exhibited on the MMPI–A for a group of 29 males aged 16–23 who were convicted of first- or second-degree murder. This group was contrasted with a cohort of nonviolent juvenile offenders as well as a group of normal high school students. Contrary to the researchers' expectations, the MMPI–A profiles for the murderers in this study demonstrated little evidence of serious psychopathology. Further, the MMPI–A profiles of the murderers did not differ significantly from the profiles of their nonviolent counterparts or from the normal high school student group. These authors concluded that adolescent males who commit violent crimes may do so for reasons that extend beyond traditionally defined psychopathology, including such factors as involvement with violent gangs. Kaser-Boyd (2002), in studying children who commit murder, observed that no single personality style or dynamic appears to be common to juveniles who commit homicide. The histories of these children, however, often include exposure to family violence and abuse.

Strengths of the MMPI–A in Forensic Settings

Several factors contribute to the value of the MMPI–A as a potential component of a comprehensive forensic evaluation. It is the most widely researched and validated objective personality assessment measurement for adolescents (Archer, 2005; Forbey, 2003) and more widely used with adolescents than any other objective test (Archer & Newsom, 2000). The MMPI–A contains a number of validity scales, including measures of consistency (*VRIN* and *TRIN*), defensiveness (*L* and *K*), and overreporting (*F, F1*, and *F2*).

These validity scales provide detailed and reliable information concerning the test-taking attitudes of the adolescent. The MMPI–A clinical scales and subscales have extensive reliability and validity data, and test-retest studies have demonstrated that the MMPI–A is sensitive to changes in psychological functioning over time (Archer & Baker, 2005). The MMPI–A provides important information concerning an adolescent's emotional distress, drug and alcohol abuse problems, perception of family relationships, and overall degree of impulse control. The MMPI–A also appears to have usefulness in predicting violent or aggressive behaviors in detention or correctional settings, a feature particularly important in the juvenile justice system. A valuable area of future research in forensic psychology is the usefulness of the MMPI–A in assessing the potential risk of development of conduct problems, including aggression, among adolescents receiving treatment in psychiatric settings.

Given the widespread use of the MMPI-2 and MMPI–A among psychologists and other mental health professionals, it is not surprising that these instruments are well accepted as the basis of expert opinions in the courtroom. Pope, Butcher, and Seelen (2000), for example, noted that the MMPI-2 and MMPI–A have become widely used for the assessment of personality features in forensic settings because the validity scales of these instruments allow for the evaluation of the credibility of an individual's responses. These authors also underscored the ability of these tests to provide important descriptive data through well-established empirically based correlates. Finally, Pope and his colleagues suggested that the MMPI-2 and MMPI–A are extensively used in forensic settings because the results produced by these instruments are relatively easy to communicate to nonpsychologists in such settings. The MMPI–A scoring procedure, scale structure, and interpretation process can be presented to laypeople in a manner that requires little psychological training on the part of the audience. Pope et al. recommended that experts utilizing MMPI–A or MMPI-2 test results in forensic settings be prepared to present data relevant to the admissibility of these instruments. Decisions concerning admissibility tend to focus on the relevance of test results to the issue before the trier of fact and on evidence that the MMPI–A has adequate reliability to serve as a component of the assessment performed by the forensic psychologist to address a specific standard or legal question. Pope and his colleagues concluded that MMPI-2 results should be admissible under most interpretations of the *Daubert* standard established by the U.S. Supreme Court in 1993 and as subsequently refined by the Court in *Kumho* (1999) and other rulings.

Limitations of the MMPI–A in Forensic Settings

Even though the MMPI–A has an extensive number of advantages when used in forensic settings, there are also a number of limitations. First, the MMPI–A (as well as the original form of the MMPI) was developed as a measure of psychopathology rather than to address forensic issues. Therefore, the examiner must be aware that the forensic use of the MMPI–A represents a substantive extension of the instrument, and the applicability of MMPI–A findings to specific forensic issues will vary widely depending on the nature of the legal issue or standard. In addition, the correlates developed for the MMPI–A scales have predominantly been based on clinical populations rather than on the behaviors, attitudes, and beliefs of adolescents in the juvenile justice system or involved in civil litigation (e.g., a personal injury suit). Therefore, the MMPI–A is more valuable for describing an adolescent's psychological functioning, for example, than for predicting his or her behavior in detention or correctional facilities. Second, as previously noted, it is important to recognize that the MMPI–A is best viewed as an assessment instrument that can only provide a description of an adolescent's current psychological functioning. Although there is some research evidence that certain psychological features tend to be more stable than others in the description of both adolescents and adults, the MMPI–A remains quite limited in its ability to make long-term behavioral or diagnostic predictions. The turbulent and flexible nature of adolescent personality and the difficulty inherent in making long-term predictions based on adolescent characteristics served as an important basis of the U.S. Supreme Court decision in *Roper v. Simmons* (2005), in which the court forbade the execution of juveniles.

A practical limitation of the MMPI–A involves the restrictions imposed by the reading requirement for this test instrument. The MMPI–A test manual (Butcher et al., 1992) reports the reading difficulty level for each item in the MMPI–A test booklet based on indices of reading ease, reading difficulty, and sentence structure. Results showed that most test items are at a fifth- to seventh-grade reading level. Archer and Krishnamurthy (2002), offering a conservative estimate, recommended a seventh-grade reading level for the successful administration of the MMPI–A, a standard which is not always met by adolescents in the criminal justice system. For some adolescents with problems in the area of reading disability, an audiocassette administration of the MMPI–A may render testing possible.

Forensic Utility of the MMPI–A With American Minorities

A controversial issue for almost every psychological assessment instrument concerns the appropriate use of the instrument with ethnic minorities. Fortunately, an extensive amount of research data regarding this issue is available for the MMPI, MMPI-2, and MMPI–A. Research on the effect of ethnic background on MMPI and MMPI–A profiles has produced mixed results (Archer, 2005). Some earlier investigations found that Black adults, for example, produced higher scores than White adults on scales *F*, *Sc*, and *Ma* (e.g., Gynther, 1972). Early research studies with adolescents yielded similar findings. For example, a study by Ball (1960) found that Black ninth graders scored higher than their White counterparts on scale *Hs* for boys and scales *F, Sc,* and *Si* for girls. Archer (1987) found minimal differences between the MMPI profiles of Black and White adolescents in a sample obtained from a middle-class public high school. Dahlstrom, Lachar, and Dahlstrom (1986) found that MMPI differences between ethnic groups were typically small and frequently nonsignificant when the groups were matched on demographic variables such as socioeconomic status and education. Based on an extensive review, Greene (2000) concluded that no significant or consistent patterns of ethnic differences were discernible on the MMPI when other demographic factors were controlled.

More recent MMPI-2 studies involving adult samples have generally failed to find meaningful differences in profile elevation between Blacks and Whites. Timbrook and Graham (1994) compared the responses of 75 Black men and 65 Black women with those of 725 White men and 724 White women from the MMPI-2 normative sample. They found that the mean differences between ethnic groups on the MMPI-2 basic scales were relatively small in magnitude for both genders, and these differences were further reduced when groups were matched for age, socioeconomic status, and income level. Similarly, Archer (2005) noted that there are few differences between Black and White adolescents in the MMPI–A normative sample for the basic scales. Archer and Krishnamurthy (2002) concluded that the current literature indicates that the standard norms for adult and adolescent forms of the MMPI may be used for assessing individuals from ethnic minority groups and that norms specifically developed for various ethnic groups are not required.

Archer and Krishnamurthy offer several cautions, however, when the MMPI–A is used with ethnic minorities. First, because the bulk of MMPI research studies on the effects of ethnicity have been focused on the profiles of Blacks and Whites, relatively less is known about the response patterns of Hispanics, Asian Americans, Native Americans, and other ethnic minorities. One exception is a comparative study by Gomez, Johnson, Davis, and Velasquez (2000) that examined the MMPI–A scale elevations of Black and Mexican-American youthful offenders. Gomez and his colleagues found few significant differences in MMPI–A response patterns related to ethnicity. Among individual MMPI–A scales, for example, they found only one scale (i.e., the Repression or *R* scale) on which Black adolescents scored significantly higher than Mexican-American teenagers. In addition to normative differences between ethnic groups, we also know significantly less about the correlate patterns of some minority groups. Archer and Krishnamurthy (2002) reviewed evidence indicating that the *MAC*–R scale may produce higher rates of false classification with ethnic minorities than with White respondents (e.g., Gottesman & Prescott, 1989). Similarly, Wrobel and Lachar (1995) cautioned that MMPI content scale elevations produced by minorities, including Blacks, may be related to a different set of correlates than those typically found for Whites. Although the research by Wrobel and Lachar focused on the Wiggins content scales developed for the original MMPI, it is possible that these concerns may also be applicable to the MMPI–A content scales.

ADMINISTRATION AND INTERPRETATIVE ISSUES IN FORENSIC APPLICATIONS

Archer and Krishnamurthy (2002) suggested that examiners rule out the presence of detrimental factors such as intoxication, disorientation, or confusional states that might inhibit an adolescent's ability to respond to the MMPI–A reliably and accurately. It is also imperative that a quiet, comfortable test environment be provided (an admittedly difficult task in some correctional settings) and that supervision is provided during the entirety of the testing session. It is permissible to provide breaks in the administration as needed to prevent excessive fatigue or distractibility, which may interfere with test validity. It is also important to review item omissions with the adolescent before leaving the testing setting and to have the examinee fill in missing information if he or she is capable of reading and understanding the items. Several available sources provide extensive information on appropriate administration and scoring procedures (e.g., Butcher et al., 1992; Archer, 2005).

Administrative guidelines and standards do not change as a function of administrating the MMPI–A in a forensic setting, but it is reasonable to conclude that even relatively small variations from standard administrative practice can cause substantive problems in forensic uses. For example, the MMPI–A is essentially designed to evaluate adolescents 14 to 18 years old, but the MMPI manual (Butcher et al., 1992) also observes that the test may be administered to 12- and 13-year-olds who are developmentally and cognitively capable of responding to the MMPI–A item pool. In most forensic applications, it would be reasonable to assume that a psychologist might be required to render some independent evidence that a 12- or 13-year-old respondent had the cognitive capacity and reading ability necessary to respond meaningfully to the MMPI–A. This issue extends to older adolescents (in the 14- to 18-year-old range) with receptive language disorders, reading disorders, or other learning disorders or cognitive deficits that might impair their ability to understand the items. It is also particularly critical that nonstandard or short forms of the MMPI–A be avoided in the forensic setting. In addition, supervision standards in the testing environment take on additional importance in forensic applications, as "chain of evidence" requirements may apply. The MMPI–A should never be left with an adolescent to complete in an unsupervised environment or be sent home with the adolescent to be completed under the supervision of parents. Such concessions would severely compromise the usefulness of test results in a courtroom setting, and issues regarding supervision often result in the exclusion of test results.

Scoring accuracy is also crucial in forensic settings. Hand-scoring procedures exist for all MMPI–A scales, and these require the examiner to ensure that separate score templates are available for each scale and that gender-appropriate templates and profile sheets are utilized. Hand-scoring templates for the MMPI–A may be purchased from Pearson Assessments, with different answer keys required for the MMPI–A softcover and hardcover test booklets. In scoring *VRIN/TRIN*, the examiner must remember to first transfer the relevant item responses to the recording grid. Given the large number of MMPI–A scales and subscales, hand-scoring procedures tend to produce a significant amount of error, even when the MMPI–A is administered and scored with the anticipation that the data will serve as a foundation for expert testimony. For this reason, it is highly desirable to employ computerized scoring methods available through Pearson Assessments for MMPI-2 and MMPI–A profiles that will be used in court. Computerized scoring yields a Basic Scale Profile Report or an Extended Score Report, depending on the amount of information sought by the examiner. The Basic Scale Profile Report provides a single-page profile for the validity and clinical scales, with raw scores and *T*-scores for each scale. The Extended Score Report offers additional content and supplementary scale scoring as well as the raw scores and *T*-scores for the Harris-Lingoes and *Si* subscales. Computerized scoring procedures are particularly appropriate for adolescents evaluated for forensic purposes because the frequency of errors generated by hand-scoring procedures are relatively high. Some forensic psychologists follow a process of entering the item-level responses into the computerized scoring package (i.e., the Microtest system) twice in order to rule out the possibility of data entry error through comparison of the resulting profile scores.

In addition to the administration and scoring issues just noted, there may be some differences in interpretive emphasis associated with using the MMPI–A in forensic settings. Although the MMPI–A validity scale findings are always important in terms of evaluating the reliability and validity of the adolescents' self-reports, they are likely to be particularly crucial in forensic settings. Individuals evaluated in a criminal justice setting or as part of a civil law case (e.g., a child custody or personal injury case) may have a substantial motivation to overreport or underreport symptomatology in order to influence the testing outcome. Adolescents charged with serious crimes, for example, may attempt to convince the court that the crime was committed when they were in a psychotic state; adolescents involved in personal injury litigation may exaggerate psychological dysfunction and emotional distress to influence jury awards; and adolescents involved in a child custody dispute may underreport or overreport symptoms depending on the manner in which they perceive these self-reports to influence the custody process. The MMPI–A defensiveness scales (*L* and *K*) are particularly useful in accurately identifying conscious and unconscious attempts to underreport symptoms, and the frequency scales (*F*, *F1*, and *F2*) are reliable indicators of the tendency to overreport or exaggerate symptoms. Given that adolescents evaluated in forensic settings may be less cooperative than those assessed in clinical settings, the value of validity scale information is correspondingly increased in forensic evaluations.

It should also be noted that computerized test interpretation packages are available for the MMPI–A, including the Interpretive System (third edition) developed by Archer and distributed by Psychological Assessment Resources (PAR), and the Minnesota Report: Adolescent Interpretive System developed by Butcher and Williams and distributed by Pearson Assessments. Both of these computer reports provide interpretive output specifically designed for adolescents evaluated in forensic settings. Automated computer interpretive reports for the MMPI–A are based on combinations of research findings and clinical experiences, resulting in what has been described as an actuarial-clinical approach to test interpretation (Graham, 2000). Specifically, a series of interpretive statements are generated to match particular sets of test scores based on the research literature combined with the authors' clinical hypotheses and experiences. Therefore, the accuracy of computer-based test interpretations depends heavily on the knowledge and skill of the individual generating the interpretive statements.

CLINICAL CASE EXAMPLE

Brian W., a 16-year-old Caucasian male, is the only child of an upper-middle-class Jewish family. Brian's parents are divorced, and he was living with his mother at the time of the evaluation. He was court referred for a preadjudication evaluation following his arrest for possession of a gun on school property. The purpose of the assessment was to provide the court with information pertaining to Brian's psychological functioning and to make recommendations for interventions to meet possible mental health needs prior to and following adjudication. Brian had no prior history of criminal charges, but he did have a history of conduct problems that resulted in his expulsion from a private school and recent transfer to a public school, where he committed the current offense. Following his arrest on school property, Brian was briefly held in a juvenile detention facility and subsequently released to his family to await adjudication. Brian had obtained the gun from his father's home three days prior to his arrest, during a scheduled weekend visitation. He used the unloaded gun to threaten another student, who then alerted school officials to Brian's possession of the weapon.

Brian was originally suspended from a private school, then expelled due to a series of confrontations and fights with his peers and a pattern of bullying and intimidating behaviors. These problem behaviors included aggressive and threatening verbal and physical actions with his classmates. His behavioral problems in school were extensive and well documented in teacher evaluations; they included repeated outbursts of anger and hostility, combined with substantial interpersonal manipulativeness. For example, Brian had frequently manipulated younger and more impressionable children into engaging in inappropriate behaviors yet denied any responsibility for involvement in their actions. His expulsion resulted from involvement in influencing younger children to distribute marijuana to their classmates, drugs ultimately traced back to Brian by school authorities. Brian's academic performance has suffered over the last two years, and he dropped from a grade point average of 3.2 in the ninth grade to getting Cs and Ds during the current academic year.

Although Brian's problems in the academic environment were clearly evident, he was substantially more compliant and less openly hostile and rebellious within his home setting. Brian's parents were quite divergent in their perceptions of the seriousness of his problem behaviors. Brian's mother provided ratings for Brian on the Child Behavior Checklist (Achenbach & Edelbrock, 1983), and the resulting CBCL profile showed marked elevations on Delinquency Behavior, Aggressive Behavior, and Social Problems. In contrast, the CBCL ratings of Brian by his father reflected his perception that Brian was a moderately anxious and depressed child with few significant interpersonal conflicts or problem behaviors. On the Wechsler Intelligence Scale–3, Brian produced a full scale IQ score of 113, a verbal IQ score of 115, and a performance IQ score of 110. Brian's scores on the Stanford Achievement Test, however, were below expected grade-level performance, with a spelling score at the 26th percentile and an arithmetic performance score at the 30th percentile.

Brian was administered the MMPI–A as part of a comprehensive evaluation that included an extensive clinical interview, collateral teacher and parent interviews, and school and arrest record reviews. His MMPI–A basic scale profile can be seen in Fig. 3.2.

The first step in the profile interpretation is to assess the technical validity of this protocol using the validity assessment model proposed by Greene (2000). Brian produced no item omissions on the Cannot Say (?) scale, and his T-scores on the $VRIN$ ($T = 51$) and $TRIN$ ($T = 54$) scales fall well within acceptable ranges provided in the MMPI–A manual (Butcher et al., 1992). Brian's scores on the scales related to defensiveness, L ($T = 42$) and K ($T = 51$), indicate a relatively candid and accurate self-report. Brian's elevations on scales $F1$ ($T = 47$) and $F2$ ($T = 42$) also suggest an accurate self-report without evidence of exaggerated or overreported symptomatology. Thus, Brian's validity scale configuration indicates that his responses are both consistent and accurate, and his profile is subject to valid and meaningful interpretation.

Brian's basic scale profile shows a single clinical range elevation on MMPI–A basic scale Pd ($T = 72$), with all other basic scales producing T-score values ≥ 55. Elevations on the Pd scale are common in adolescents in criminal justice and psychiatric settings (Archer, 2005). Scores in this range are typically produced by juveniles characterized as rebellious, hostile toward authority figures, and defiant. These adolescents often have histories of poor school adjustment and conduct problems in school. The greater the elevation on scale Pd, the more likely the adolescent exhibits a variety of overtly delinquent behaviors. Adolescents who produce Pd scale scores in ranges similar to Brian's typically display problems in delaying gratification and are described as impulsive and easily bored and frustrated (Archer, 2005). The most common diagnosis for individuals with MMPI–A profiles similar to Brian's is conduct disorder. Elevations on scale Pd are common among adolescents who engage in criminal and antisocial behaviors. Their primary defense mechanisms involve acting out, and their acting-out behavior is often not accompanied by feelings of guilt or remorse. These adolescents may create a good first impression and maintain a relatively extroverted interpersonal style, but they are eventually viewed by others as self-centered, egocentric, and selfish (Archer & Krishnamurthy, 2002). In detention or correctional facilities, these adolescents are more likely to commit institutional infractions and become involved in conflicts and altercations with other residents. In addition to his clinical range elevation on Pd, other basic scale test results produced by Brian indicate a marked lack of emotional distress (reflected by his normal-range scores on scales D and Pt). The low scale Mf score (in the masculine direction) seen in Brian's profile is often found among boys who externalize the blame or responsibility for problems and place great value on characteristics such as strength and dominance (Archer, 2005).

Although high scores on scale Mf have been related to a lower likelihood of acting out behaviors (e.g., Hathaway & Monachesi, 1963), low scores similar to Brian's have been associated with a greater propensity to engage in antisocial or delinquent behaviors. For example, research findings by Archer et al. (2003) show that boys in correctional facilities produce lower Mf scores than boys in psychiatric or substance abuse treatment settings. Further, Hathaway and Monachesi (1963) associated low scale Mf scores among boys with a substantially higher rate of delinquency and school dropout.

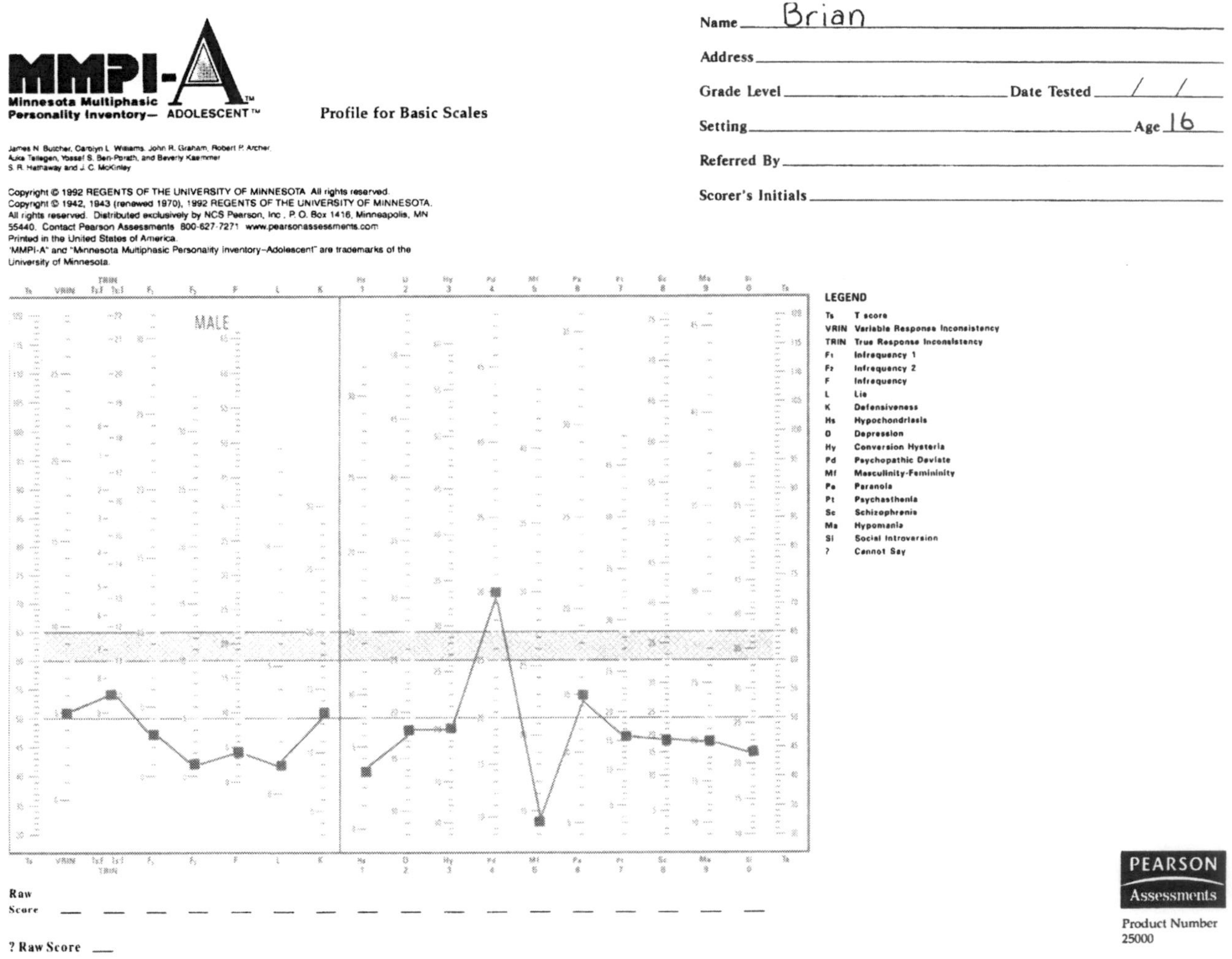
MMPI-A
Minnesota Multiphasic Personality Inventory— ADOLESCENT™
Profile for Basic Scales
James N. Butcher, Carolyn L. Williams, John R. Graham, Robert P. Archer, Auke Tellegen, Yossef S. Ben-Porath, and Beverly Kaemmer
S. R. Hathaway and J. C. McKinley
Copyright © 1992 REGENTS OF THE UNIVERSITY OF MINNESOTA. All rights reserved.
Copyright © 1942, 1943 (renewed 1970), 1992 REGENTS OF THE UNIVERSITY OF MINNESOTA. All rights reserved. Distributed exclusively by NCS Pearson, Inc., P. O. Box 1416, Minneapolis, MN 55440. Contact Pearson Assessments 800-627-7271 www.pearsonassessments.com
Printed in the United States of America.
"MMPI-A" and "Minnesota Multiphasic Personality Inventory–Adolescent" are trademarks of the University of Minnesota.
Name Brian
Address
Grade Level
Date Tested / /
Setting
Age 16
Referred By
Scorer's Initials
MALE
Ts VRIN TRIN F1 F2 F L K Hs 1 D 2 Hy 3 Pd 4 Mf 5 Pa 6 Pt 7 Sc 8 Ma 9 Si 0 Ts
LEGEND
Ts T score
VRIN Variable Response Inconsistency
TRIN True Response Inconsistency
F1 Infrequency 1
F2 Infrequency 2
F Infrequency
L Lie
K Defensiveness
Hs Hypochondriasis
D Depression
Hy Conversion Hysteria
Pd Psychopathic Deviate
Mf Masculinity-Femininity
Pa Paranoia
Pt Psychasthenia
Sc Schizophrenia
Ma Hypomania
Si Social Introversion
? Cannot Say
Raw Score
? Raw Score
PEARSON Assessments
Product Number 25000

FIG. 3.2. MMPI–A Profile for Basic Scales for Brian. MMPI–A Profile Sheet Reprinted by Permission. Copyright © 1992 by the Regents of the University of Minnesota.

Brian's MMPI–A content and supplementary scale profiles are shown in Fig. 3.3.

Brian's content and supplementary scale profile features are relatively consistent with his basic scale profile in showing little evidence of emotional or affective distress, including anxiety (A-ang, $T = 54$) or depression (A-dep, $T = 47$). In contrast, Brian does display a clinical range elevation on the A-ang scale ($T = 79$), characteristic of adolescents with hostile and misanthropic attitudes (Butcher et al., 1992). Adolescents producing similar A-ang scores feel misunderstood and believe that others are jealous of their accomplishments. They are likely to be perceived as irritable, inpatient, angry, and hostile, and their problems often include physical aggressiveness. In addition, Brian also produced a marked elevation on the A-con scale ($T = 84$), typically of adolescents who are impulsive and exhibit a variety of conduct-related problems. These adolescents often hold beliefs and attitudes that conflict with societal norms, and they have particular difficulty dealing with authority figures. Their problem behaviors may include lying, cheating, and disrespectful or oppositional behaviors with others (Williams et al., 1992). Adolescents with similar A-con scores often socialize with delinquent peer groups and may derive satisfaction from intimidating and evoking fear and in others. They also have difficulty in following rules or instructions in clinical, educational, and juvenile justice settings.

Brian also produced moderate clinical-range scores on the content scales A-las ($T = 69$) and A-sch ($T = 65$), the former scale indicating that Brian has few or no educational or life goals, a feature often found among adolescents who have poor academic achievement. These adolescents tend to become frustrated quickly and do not apply themselves in challenging situations. Brian's elevated score on A-sch is typical of adolescents who experience significant behavioral and academic problems in the school setting. These adolescents maintain a negative attitude toward academic achievement and are commonly viewed as lazy or unmotivated by others (Archer, 2005). Finally, Brian's moderate clinical-range elevation on the Alcohol-Drug Problem Proneness (PRO) scale ($T = 67$) is characteristic of adolescents who are at increased risk for drug and alcohol problems. In contrast, Brian's scores on the MAC-R scale and the Alcohol Drug Acknowledgement Scale (ACK) are well within normal limits. This mixed pattern of findings on the three supplementary scales related to drug or alcohol use problems clearly warrants further assessment of Brian's history of drug and alcohol use.

Clinical Case Recommendations

The MMPI–A findings presented in this chapter, in combination with results from other components of this forensic evaluation, suggested that Brian was at low to moderate risk for recidivism. It was recommended that his rehabilitation needs could be best served by placement on probationary status, with the requirement that Brian undergo a comprehensive drug and alcohol abuse evaluation, that he engage in individual psychotherapy, and that he and his parents participate in family therapy sessions. It was further recommended that family therapy focus on increasing communication between Brian and his parents as well as providing assistance to his parents in placing firm limits and controls on Brian's behaviors. Individual psychotherapy was encouraged in part to explore the underlying aspects of Brian's frustration and anger but also to assist Brian in developing more appropriate anger management techniques. Finally, it was suggested that Brian's probationary period be closely supervised and that any significant occurrence of antisocial or conduct disordered behaviors might serve as a basis for reevaluation of Brian's probationary status and placement in a juvenile correctional facility.

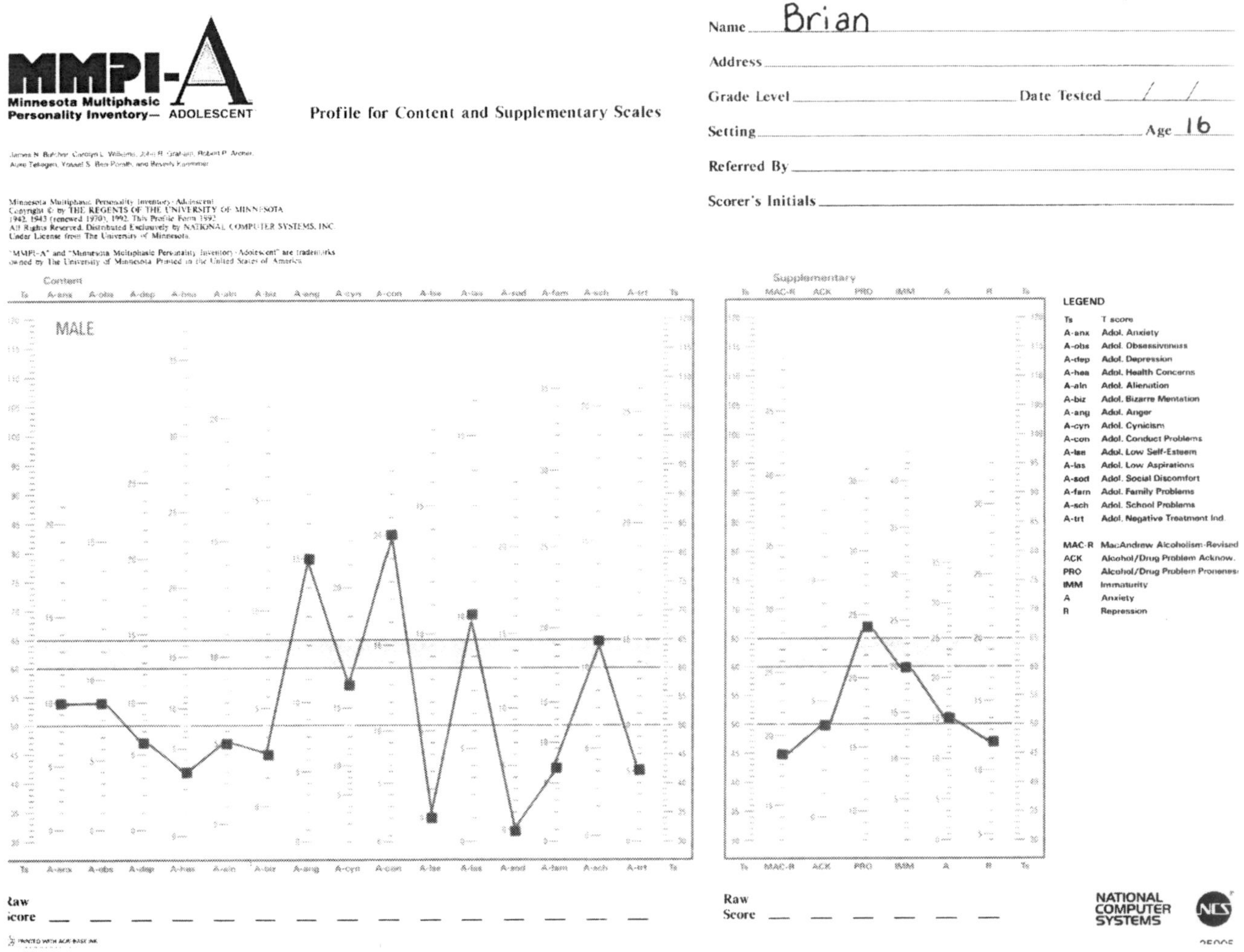

FIG. 3.3. MMPI–A Profile for Content and Supplementary Scales for Brian. MMPI–A Profile Sheet Reprinted by Permission. Copyright © 1992 by the Regents of the University of Minnesota.

REFERENCES

Achenbach, T.M., & Edelbrock, C.S. (1983). *Manual for the Child Behavior Checklist and revised child behavior profile.* Burlington: University of Vermont.

Ackerman, M.J., & Ackerman, M.C. (1997). Custody evaluation practices: A survey of experienced professionals (revised). *Professional Psychology Research and Practice, 28,* 137–145.

Alperin, J.J., Archer, R.P., & Coates, G.D. (1996). Development and effects of an MMPI-A K-correction procedure. *Journal of Personality Assessment, 67,* 155–168.

American Psychiatric Association. (1994). *Diagnostic and statistical manual of mental disorders* (4th ed.). Washington, DC: Author.

Angold, A. (1989). Structured assessments of psychopathology in children and adolescents. In C. Thompson, (Ed.), *The instruments of psychiatric research.* New York: J. Wiley.

Arbisi, P.A., & Ben-Porath, Y.S. (1995). An MMPI-2 infrequent response scale for use with psychopathological populations: The infrequency psychopathology scale F(p). *Psychological Assessment, 7,* 424–431.

Archer, R.P. (1987). *Using the MMPI with adolescents.* Hillsdale, NJ: Lawrence Erlbaum Associates.

Archer, R.P. (1997). *MMPI-A: Assessing Adolescent Psychopathology* (2nd ed.). Mahwah, NJ: Lawrence Erlbaum Associates.

Archer, R.P. (2003). MMPI-A Interpretive System (Version 3) [Computer software]. Tampa, FL: Psychological Assessment Resources.

Archer, R.P. (2005). *MMPI-A: Assessing Adolescent Psychopathology* (3rd ed.). Mahwah, NJ: Lawrence Erlbaum Associates.

Archer, R.P., & Baker, E.M. (2005). Use of the Minnesota Multiphasic Personality Inventory–Adolescent (MMPI-A) in juvenile justice settings. In D. Seagraves & T. Grisso (Eds.), *Handbook of screening and assessment tools for juvenile justice.* New York: Guilford Press.

Archer, R.P., Belevich, J.K.S., & Elkins, D.E. (1994). Item-level and scale-level factor structures of the MMPI-A. *Journal of Personality Assessment, 62,* 332–345.

Archer, R.P., Bolinskey, P.K., Morton, T.L., & Farris, K.L. (2003). MMPI-A characteristics of male adolescents in juvenile justice and clinical treatment settings. *Assessment, 10,* 400–410.

Archer, R.P., & Elkins, D.E. (1999). Identification of random responding on the MMPI-A. *Journal of Personality Assessment, 73,* 407–421.

Archer, R.P., Gordon, R.A., Anderson, G.L., & Giannetti, R.A. (1989). MMPI special scale clinical correlates for adolescent inpatients. *Journal of Personality Assessment, 53,* 654–664.

Archer, R.P., Gordon, R.A., Giannetti, R.A., & Singles, J.M. (1988). MMPI scale clinical correlates for adolescent inpatients. Journal of Personality Assessment, 52, 707–721.

Archer, R.P., Handel, R.W., & Lynch, K.D. (2001). The effectiveness of MMPI-A items in discriminating between normative and clinical samples. *Journal of Personality Assessment, 77,* 420–435.

Archer, R.P., & Jacobson, J.M. (1993). Are critical items "critical" for the MMPI-A? *Journal of Personality Assessment, 61,* 547–556.

Archer, R.P., & Krishnamurthy, R. (1994a). *MMPI-A Structural Summary* [Summary form]. Odessa, FL: Psychological Assessment Resources.

Archer, R.P., & Krishnamurthy, R. (1994b). A structural summary approach for the MMPI-A: Development and empirical correlates. *Journal of Personality Assessment, 63,* 554–573.

Archer, R.P., & Krishnamurthy, R. (1997). MMPI-A scale-level factor structure: Replication in a clinical sample. *Assessment, 4,* 337–349.

Archer, R.P., & Krishnamurthy, R. (2002). *Essentials of MMPI-A assessment.* New York: Wiley.

Archer, R.P., Krishnamurthy, R., & Jacobson, J.M. (1994). *MMPI-A casebook.* Tampa, FL: Psychological Assessment Resources.

Archer, R.P., Maruish, M., Imhof, E.A., & Piotrowski, C. (1991). Psychological test usage with adolescent clients: 1990 survey findings. *Professional Psychology: Research and Practice, 22,* 247–252.

Archer, R.P., & Newsom, C.R. (2000). Psychological test usage with adolescent clients: Survey update. *Assessment, 7,* 227–235.

Archer, R.P., Pancoast, D.L., & Gordon, R.A. (1994). The development of the MMPI-A Immaturity (IMM) scale: Findings for normal and clinical samples. *Journal of Personality Assessment, 62,* 145–156.

Archer, R.P., Tirrell, C.A., & Elkins, D.E. (2001). Evaluation of an MMPI-A short form: Implications for adaptive testing. *Journal of Personality Assessment, 76*, 76–89.

Baer, R.A., Ballenger, J., Berry, D.T.R., & Wetter, M.W. (1997). Detection of random responding on the MMPI-A. *Journal of Personality Assessment, 68*, 139–151.

Baer, R.A., Ballenger, J., & Kroll, L.S. (1998). Detection of underreporting on the MMPI-A in clinical and community samples. *Journal of Personality Assessment, 71*, 98–113.

Baer, R.A., Kroll, L.S., Rinaldo, J., & Ballenger, J. (1999). Detecting and discriminating between random responding and overreporting on the MMPI-A. *Journal of Personality Assessment, 72*, 308–320.

Ball, J.C. (1960). Comparison of MMPI profile differences among Negro-White adolescents. *Journal of clinical Psychology, 16*, 304–307.

Ball, J.C., & Carroll, D. (1960). Analysis of MMPI Cannot Say scores in an adolescent population. *Journal of Clinical Psychology, 16*, 30–31.

Ben-Porath, Y.S., Hostetler K., Butcher, J.N., & Graham, J.R. (1989). New subscales for the MMPI-2 Social Introversion (Si) scale. *Psychological Assessment, 1*, 169–174.

Black, K. (1994). A critical review of the MMPI-A. *Child Assessment News, 4*, 9–12.

Briggs, P.F., Wirt, R.D., & Johnson, R. (1961). An application of prediction tables to the study of delinquency. *Journal of Consulting Psychology, 25*, 46–50.

Butcher, J.N., Graham, J.R., Ben-Porath, Y.S., Tellegen, A., Dahlstrom, W.G., & Kaemmer, B. (2001): *Minnesota Multiphasic Personality Inventory-2 (MMPI-2): Manual for administration, scoring, and interpretation* (rev. ed.).

Butcher, J.N., & Williams, C.L. (2000). *Essentials of MMPI-2 and MMPI-A interpretation* (2nd ed.). Minneapolis: University of Minnesota Press.

Butcher, J.N., Williams, C.L., Graham, J.R., Archer, R.P., Tellegen, A., Ben-Porath, Y.S., & et al. (1992). *Minnesota Multiphasic Personality Inventory–Adolescent (MMPI-A): Manual for administration, scoring, and interpretation. Minneapolis*: University of Minnesota Press.

Capwell, D.F. (1945a). Personality patterns of adolescent girls: I. Girls who show improvement in IQ. *Journal of Applied Psychology, 29*, 212–228.

Capwell, D.F. (1945b). Personality patterns of adolescent girls: II. Delinquents and non-delinquents. *Journal of Applied Psychology, 29*, 284–297.

Cashel, M.L., Rogers, R., Sewell, K.W., & Holliman, N.G. (1998). Preliminary validation of the MMPI-A for a male delinquent sample: An investigation of clinical correlates and discriminant validity. *Journal of Personality Assessment, 71*, 46–69.

Colligan, R. C., & Offord, K. P. (1992). Age, stage, and the MMPI: Changes in response patterns over an 85-year age span. Journal of Clinical Psychology, *48*, 476–493.

Dahlstrom, W.G., Archer, R.P., Hopkins, D.G., Jackson, E., & Dahlstrom, L.E. (1994). *Assessing the readability of the Minnesota Multiphasic Personality Inventory Instruments: The MMPI, MMPI-2, MMPI-A* (MMPI-2/MMPI-A Test Rep. No.2). Minneapolis: University of Minnesota Press.

Dahlstrom, W. G., Lachar, D., & Dahlstrom, L.E. (1986). *MMPI patterns of American minorities*. Minneapolis: University of Minnesota Press.

Fontaine, J.L., Archer, R.P., Elkins, D.E., & Johansen, J. (2001). The effects of MMPI-A T-score elevation on classification accuracy for normal and clinical adolescent samples. *Journal of Personality Assessment, 76*, 264–281.

Forbey, J.D. (2003, June). *A review of the MMPI-A research literature*. Paper presented at the 38th Annual Symposium on Recent Developments in the Use of the MMPI-2 and MMPI-A, Minneapolis, MN.

Forbey, J.D., & Ben-Porath, Y.S. (1998). *A critical item set for the MMPI-A* (MMPI-2/MMPI-A Test Rep. No. 4). Minneapolis: University of Minnesota Press.

Forbey, J.D., & Ben-Porath, Y.S. (2000). A comparison of sexually abused and non-sexually abused adolescents in a clinical treatment facility using the MMP1–A. *Child Abuse and Neglect, 24*, 557–568.

Glaser, B.A., Calhoun, G.B., & Petrocelli, J.V. (2002). Personality characteristics of male juvenile offenders by adjudicated offenses as indicated by the MMPI-A. *Criminal Justice and Behavior, 29*, 183–201.

Gomez, F.C., Johnson, R., Davis, Q., & Velasquez, R.J. (2000). MMPI-A performance of African and Mexican American adolescent first-time offenders. *Psychological Reports, 87*, 309–314.

Gottesman, I.I., & Hanson, D.R. (1990, August). Can the MMPI at age 15 predict schizophrenics-to-be? In R.C. Colligan (Chair), *The MMPI and adolescents: Historical perspective, current research, future developments.* Symposium conducted at the annual convention of the American Psychological Association, Boston.

Gottesman, I.I., & Prescott, C.A. (1989). Abuses of the MacAndrew Alcoholism scale: A critical review. *Clinical Psychology Review, 9,* 223–242.

Greenberg, S.A., Otto, R.K., & Long, A.C. (2003). The utility of psychological testing in assessing emotional damages in personal injury litigation. *Assessment, 10,* 411–419.

Greene, R.L. (2000). *MMPI-2: An interpretive manual* (2nd ed.). Boston: Allyn & Bacon.

Grisso, T. (1998). *Forensic evaluation of juveniles.* Sarasota, FL: Professional Resources Press.

Graham, J.R. (2000). *MMPI-2: Assessing personality and psychopathology* (3rd ed.). New York: Oxford University.

Gynther, M.D. (1972). White norms and Black MMPIs: A prescription for discrimination? *Psychological Bulletin, 78,* 386–402.

Hare, R.D. (1991). *The Hare Pschopathy Checklist–Revised.* Toronto, Ontario, Canada: Multi-Health Systems.

Hathaway, S.R., & McKinley, J.C. (1943). *The Minnesota Multiphasic Personality Inventory* (rev. ed.). Minneapolis: University of Minnesota Press.

Hathaway, S.R., & Monachesi, E.D. (1952). The Minnesota Multiphasic Personality Inventory in the study of juvenile delinquents. *American Sociological Review, 17,* 704–710.

Hathaway, S.R., & Monachesi, E.D. (Eds.). (1953). *Analyzing and predicting juvenile delinquency with the MMPI.* Minneapolis: University of Minnesota Press.

Hathaway, S.R., & Monachesi, E.D. (1961). *An atlas of juvenile MMPI profiles.* Minneapolis: University of Minnesota Press.

Hathaway, S.R., & Monachesi, E.D. (1963). *Adolescent personality and behavior: MMPI patterns of normal, delinquent, dropout, and other outcomes.* Minneapolis: University of Minnesota Press.

Hicks, M.M., Rogers, R., & Cashel, M.L. (2000). Prediction of violent and total infractions among institutionalized male juvenile offenders. *Journal of the American Academy of Psychiatry and Law, 28,* 183–190.

Hillary, B.E., & Schare, M.L. (1993). Sexually and physically abused adolescents: An empirical search for PTSD. *Journal of Clinical Psychology, 49,* 161–165.

Huesmann, L.R., Lefkowitz, M.M., & Eron, L.D. (1978). Sum of MMPI Scales F, 4, and 9 as a measure of aggression. *Journal of Consulting and Clinical Psychology, 46,* 1071–1078.

Hume, M.P., Kennedy, W.A., Patrick, C.J., & Partyka, D.J. (1996). Examination of the MMPI-A for the assessment of psychopathy in incarcerated adolescent male offenders. *International Journal of Offender Therapy and Comparative Criminology, 40,* 224–233.

Imhof, E.A., & Archer, R.P. (1997). Correlates of the MMPI-A immaturity (IMM) scale in an adolescent psychiatric sample. *Assessment, 5,* 169–179.

Kaser-Boyd, N. (2002). Children who kill. In N.G. Ribner (Ed.), *The California School of Professional Psychology handbook of juvenile forensic psychology* (pp. 195–229). San Francisco: Jossey-Bass.

Katz, R.C., & Marquette, J. (1996). Psychosocial characteristics of young violent offenders: A comparative study. *Criminal Behaviour and Mental Health, 6,* 339–348.

Keilin, W.G., & Bloom, L.J. (1986). Child custody evaluation practices: A survey of experienced professionals. *Professional Psychology: Research and Practice, 17,* 338–346.

Koss, M.P., & Butcher, J.N. (1973). A comparison of psychiatric patients' self-report with other sources of clinical information. *Journal of Research in Personality, 7,* 225–236.

Krishnamurthy, R., Archer, R.P., & House, J.J. (1996). The MMPI-A and Rorschach: A failure to establish convergent validity. *Assessment, 3,* 179–191.

Krishnamurthy, R., Bolinskey, P.K., & Archer, R.P. (2005, March). *MMPI-A Structural Summary: Integrating new scales and subscales.* Paper presented at the Annual Conference of the Society for Personality Assessment, Chicago.

Lachar, D., & Wrobel, T.A. (1979). Validating clinicians' hunches: Construction of a new MMPI critical item set. *Journal of Consulting and Clinical Psychology, 47,* 277–284.

Lowman, J., Galinsky, M.D., & Gray-Little, B. (1980). *Predicting achievement: A ten-year follow-up of black and white adolescents.* Chapel Hill: University of North Carolina at Chapel Hill, Institute for Research in Social Science (IRSS Research Reports).

Lubin, B., Larsen, R.M., & Matarazzo, J.D. (1984). Patterns of psychological test usage in the United States: 1935–1982. *American Psychologist, 39,* 451–454.

Lubin, B., Larsen, R.M., Matarazzo, J.D., & Seever, M.F. (1985). Psychological test usage patterns in five professional settings. *American Psychologist, 40,* 857–861.

Lubin, B., Wallis, R.R., & Paine, C. (1971). Patterns of psychological test usage in the United States: 1935–1969. *Professional Psychology, 2,* 70–74.

Marks, P.A., & Briggs, P.F. (1972). Adolescent norm tables for the MMPI. In W.G. Dahlstrom, G.S. Welsh, & L.E. Dahlstrom (Eds.), *An MMPI handbook: Vol. 1. Clinical interpretation* (rev. ed., pp. 388–399). Minneapolis: University of Minnesota Press.

Marks, P.A., Seeman, W., & Haller, D.L. (1974). *The actuarial use of the MMPI with adolescents and adults.* Baltimore: Williams & Wilkins.

McGrath, R.E., Pogge, D.L., Stein, L.A.R., Graham, J.R., Zaccario, M., & Piacentini, T. (2000). Development of the infrequency-psychopathology scale for the MMPI-A: The Fp-A scale. *Journal of Personality Assessment, 74,* 282–295.

McKinley, J.C., & Hathaway, S.R. (1943). The identification and measurement of the psychoneuroses in medical practice. *Journal of the American Medical Association, 122,* 161–167.

McKinley, J.C., Hathaway, S.R., & Meehl, P.E. (1948). The Minnesota Multiphasic Personality Inventory: VI. The K scale. *Journal of Consulting Psychology, 12,* 20–31.

McNulty, J.L., Harkness, A.R., Ben-Porath, Y.S., & Williams, C.L. (1997). Assessing the Personality Psychopathology Five (PSY-5) in adolescents: New MMPI-A scales. *Psychological Assessment, 9,* 250–259.

Millon, T. (1993). *Millon Adolescent Clinical Inventory.* Minneapolis, MN: Pearson Assessments.

Milne, L.C., & Greenway, P. (1999). Do high scores on the adolescent-school problems and immaturity scales of the MMPI-A have implications for cognitive performance as measured by the WISC-III? *Psychology in the Schools, 36,* 199–203.

Monachesi, E.D., & Hathaway, S.R. (1969). The personality of delinquents. In J.N. Butcher (Ed.) *MMPI: Research developments and clinical applications* (pp. 207–219). Menneapolis: University of Minnesota Press.

Morey, L.C. (2000). The challenge of construct validity in the assessment of psychopathology. In R.D. Goffin & E. Helmes (Ed.), *Problems and solutions in human assessment: Honoring Douglas N. Jackson at seventy* (pp. 141–171). New York: Kluwer Academic/Plenum Publishers.

Morton, T.L., Farris, K.L., & Brenowitz, L.H. (2002). MMPI-A scores and high points of male juvenile delinquents: Scales 4, 5, and 6 as markers of juvenile delinquency. *Psychological Assessment, 14,* 311–319.

Otto, R.K., & Collins, R.P. (1995). Use of the MMPI-2/MMPI-A in child custody evaluations. In Y.S. Ben-Porath, J.R. Graham, G.C.N. Hall, R.D. Hirschman, & M.S. Zaragoza (Eds.), *Forensic applications of the MMPI-2* (pp. 222–252). Thousand Oaks, CA: Sage.

Pancoast, D.L., & Archer, R.P. (1988). MMPI adolescent norms: Patterns and trends across four decades. *Journal of Personality Assessment, 52,* 691–706.

Pena, L.M., Megargee, E.I., & Brody, P. (1996). MMPI-A patterns of male juvenile delinquents. *Psychological Assessment, 8,* 388–397.

Piotrowski, C., & Keller, J.W. (1989). Psychological testing in outpatient mental health facilities: A national study. *Professional Psychology: Research and Practice, 20,* 423–425.

Pope, H.S., Butcher, J.N., & Seelen, J. (2000). *The MMPI, MMPI-2, MMPI-A in court: A practice guide for expert witnesses and attorneys* (2nd ed.). Washington, DC: American Psychological Association.

Roper v. Simmons, 03-0633 U.S. (2004).

Scott, R., & Stone, D. (1986). MMPI measures of psychological disturbance in adolescent and adult victims of father-daughter incest. *Journal of Clinical Psychology, 42,* 251–259.

Sherwood, N.E., Ben-Porath, Y.S., & Williams, C.L. (1997). *The MMPI-A content component scales: Development, psychometric characteristics and clinical application.* (MMPI-2/MMPI-A Test Rep. No. 3.) Minneapolis: University of Minnesota Press.

Stein, L.A.R., McClinton, B.K., & Graham, J.R. (1998). Long-term stability of MMPI-A scales. *Journal of Personality Assessment, 70,* 103–108.

Timbrook, R.E., & Graham, J.R. (1994). Ethnic differences on the MMPI-2? *Psychological Assessment, 6,* 212–217.

Weed, N.C., Butcher, J.N., & Williams, C.L. (1994). Development of the MMPI-A alcohol/drug problem scales. *Journal of Studies on Alcohol, 55*, 296–302.

Williams, C.L., & Butcher, J.N. (1989). An MMPI study of adolescents: II. Verification and limitations of code type classifications. *Psychological Assessment, 1*, 260–265.

Williams, C.L., Butcher, J.N., Ben-Porath, Y.S., & Graham, J.R. (1992). *MMPI-A content scales: Assessing psychopathology in adolescents.* Minneapolis: University of Minnesota Press.

Wirt, R.D., & Briggs, P.F. (1959). Personality and environmental factors in the development of delinquency. *Psychological Monographs: General and Applied* (Whole No. 485), 1–47.

Wrobel, N.H., & Lachar, D. (1995). Racial differences in adolescent self-report: A comparative validity study using homogeneous MMPI content measures. *Psychological Assessment, 7*, 140–147.

Zinn, S., McCumber, S., & Dahlstrom, W.G. (1999). Cross-validation and extension of the MMPI-A IM scale. *Assessment, 6*, 1–6.

4

THE PERSONALITY ASSESSMENT INVENTORY

LESLIE C. MOREY

CHRISTOPHER J. HOPWOOD

TEXAS A&M UNIVERSITY

The Personality Assessment Inventory (PAI; Morey, 1991) was designed to provide psychological assessment information in a variety of contexts in which psychopathology, personality, and psychosocial environment are a concern. The breadth of coverage of important psychological constructs allows for a smooth translation to forensic settings (Boccaccini & Brodsky, 1999; Edens, Cruise, & Buffington-Vollum, 2001). This chapter provides a brief overview of the theory and procedures employed in developing the PAI; a review of PAI psychometric and validity data, with particular emphasis on forensic research; a discussion of the use of the PAI in forensic settings; and an illustrative case example. More detailed coverage than is possible in this chapter can be found in several primary sources (Morey, 1991, 1996, 2003), and an independent review of the PAI in forensic settings is also available (Edens et al., 2001). To orient the reader to the structure of the PAI, scale and subscale descriptions are listed in Table 4.1, and validity and predictive indices developed following the construction of the PAI are listed in Table 4.2.

THEORETICAL BASIS AND TEST DEVELOPMENT

The development of the PAI was based on a construct validation framework that emphasized a theoretical/rational as well as a quantitative method of scale development. This framework places a strong emphasis on a theoretically informed approach to the development and selection of items as well as on the assessment of their stability and correlates. As a first step, the theoretical and empirical literature for each of the constructs to be measured was closely examined, since this articulation had to serve as a guide to

TABLE 4.1
PAI Scales and Subscales

Scale		Interpretation of High Scores
		Validity Scales
ICN	Inconsistency	Poor concentration or inattention
INF	Infrequency	Idiosyncratic or random response set
NIM	Negative Impression Management	Negative response set due to pessimistic worldview and/or intentional dissimulation
PIM	Positive Impression Management	Positive response set due to naïveté or intentional dissimulation
		Clinical Scales
SOM	Somatic Complaints	
SOM-C	Conversion	Rare sensorimotor symptoms associated with conversion disorders or certain medical conditions
SOM-S	Somatization	The occurrence of common physical symptoms or vague complaints of ill health or fatigue
SOM-H	Health Concerns	Preoccupation with physical functioning and symptoms
ANX	Anxiety	
ANX-C	Cognitive	Ruminative worry and impaired concentration and attention
ANX-A	Affective	Experience of tension, difficulty relaxing, nervousness, and fatigue
ANX-P	Physiological	Overt signs of anxiety, including sweat, trembling, shortness of breath, and irregular heartbeat
ARD	Anxiety-Related Disorders	
ARD-O	Obsessive-Compulsive	Intrusive thoughts, compulsive behaviors, rigidity, indecision, perfectionism, and affective constriction
ARD-P	Phobias	Common fears, including fear of social situation, heights, and public or enclosed places; low scores suggest fearlessness
ARD-T	Traumatic Stress	Experience of trauma that continues to cause distress
DEP	Depression	
DEP-C	Cognitive	Worthlessness, hopelessness, indecisiveness, and difficulty concentrating; low scores indicate personal confidence
DEP-A	Affective	Feelings of sadness, diminished interest, and anhedonia
DEP-P	Physiological	Level of physical functioning, and activity; sleep and diet patterns
MAN	Mania	
MAN-A	Activity Level	Disorganized overinvolvement in activities, accelerated thought processes and behavior
MAN-G	Grandiosity	Inflated self-esteem and expansiveness; low scores indicate low self-esteem
MAN-I	Irritability	Frustration intolerance, impatience, and resulting strained relationships
PAR	Paranoia	
PAR-H	Hypervigilance	Suspiciousness and tendency to closely monitor environment; low scores suggest interpersonal trust
PAR-P	Persecution	Belief that others have intentionally constructed obstacles to one's achievement
PAR-R	Resentment	Bitterness and cynicism in relationships, tendency to hold grudges, and externalization of blame
SCZ	Schizophrenia	
SCZ-P	Psychotic Experiences	Unusual perceptions and sensations, magical thinking, and unusual ideas

TABLE 4.1

(Continued)

SXZ-S	Social Detachment	Social isolation, discomfort, and awkwardness
SCZ-T	Thought Disorder	Confusion, concentration difficulties, and disorganization
BOR	Borderline Features	
BOR-A	Affective Instability	Emotional responsiveness, rapid mood change, poor modulation
BOR-I	Identity Problems	Uncertainty about major life issues and feelings of emptiness or lack of fulfillment or purpose
BOR-N	Negative Relationships	History of intense, ambivalent relationships and feelings of exploitation or betrayal
BOR-S	Self-Harm	Impulsivity in areas likely to be dangerous
ANT	Antisocial Features	
ANT-A	Antisocial Behaviors	History of antisocial and illegal behavior
ANT-E	Egocentricity	Lack of empathy or remorse, exploitative approach to relationships
ANT-S	Stimulus-Seeking	Cravings for excitement, low boredom tolerance, recklessness
ALC	Alcohol Problems	Use of and problems with alcohol
DRG	Drug Problems	Use of and problems with drugs
		Treatment Consideration Scales
AGG	Aggression	
AGG-A	Aggressive Attitude	Hostility, poor control over anger, and belief in instrumental utility of violence
AGG-V	Verbal Aggression	Assertiveness, abusiveness, and readiness to express anger to others
AGG-P	Physical Aggression	Tendency to be involved in physical aggression
SUI	Suicidal Ideation	Frequency and intensity of thoughts of self-harm or fantasies about suicide
STR	Stress	Perception of an uncertain or difficult environment
NON	Nonsupport	Perception that others are not available or willing to provide support
RXR	Treatment Rejection	Attitudes that represent obstacles or indicate low motivation for treatment
		Interpersonal Scales
DOM	Dominance	Desire for and tendency toward control in relationships; low scores suggest meekness and submissiveness
WRM	Warmth	Interest and comfort with close relationships; low scores suggest hostility, anger, and mistrust

the content of information sampled and to the subsequent assessment of content validity. The development of the test then went through four iterations in a sequential construct validation strategy similar to that described by Loevinger (1957) and Jackson (1970) but including the consideration of a number of item parameters not described by those authors. Of paramount importance at each point of the development process was the assumption that no single quantitative item parameter should be used as the sole criterion for item selection. An overreliance on a single parameter typically leads to a scale with one desirable psychometric property and numerous undesirable ones. Both the conceptual nature and empirical adequacy of the items played an important role in their inclusion in the final version of the PAI.

TABLE 4.2
Supplementary PAI Indices

	Index	Development	Interpretation of High Scores
		Validity Indices	
MI	Malingering Index	Eight configural features observed with relatively high frequency in malingering samples	Negative response set, malingering
RDF	Rogers Discriminant Function	Function found to discriminate patients from naïve and coached malingerers	Malingering
DI	Defensiveness Index	Eight configural features observed with relatively high frequency in positive dissimulation samples	Self-deception and/or other deception in the positive direction
CDF	Cashel Discriminant Function	Function found to discriminate real from fake good inmates and college students	Intentional concealment of specific problems
ALCp	ALC Predicted Score	ALC Predicted by other elements of the profile	ALCp > ALC suggests deception regarding alcohol use
DRGp	DRG Predicted Score	DRG predicted by other elements of the profile	DRGp > DRG suggests deception regarding drug use
BRR	Back Random Responding	Differences > 5T on front and back halves of ALC and SUI scales	Random responding on back half of PAI
ACS*	Addictive Characteristics Scale	Algorithm of BOR-A, BOR-S, and ANT-E used to predict addictive potential	Deception regarding substance use (with low ALC, DRG)
INF-F*	Infrequency-Front	First four INF items	Random responding on first half of PAI
INF-B*	Infrequency-Back	Last four INF items	Random responding on second half of PAI
ICN-C*	Inconsistency-Corrections	Inconsistent responses to two similar items regarding illegal behavior	Inattention
		Predictive Indices	
TPI	Treatment Process Index	Twelve configural features of the PAI associated with treatment amenability	Difficult treatment process, high probability of reversals
VPI	Violence Potential Index	Twenty configural features of the PAI associated with dangerousness to others	Increased likelihood of violence to others
SPI	Suicide Potential Index	Twenty configural features of the PAI associated with suicide	Increased likelihood of suicide

*Developed for use in correctional settings (Edens & Ruiz, 2005).

The goal of the construction of the PAI was to develop scales that provided a balanced sampling of the most important elements of the constructs being measured. This content coverage was designed to include a consideration of both the *breadth* and the *depth* of the construct. The "breadth" of content coverage refers to the diversity of elements subsumed within a construct. For example, in measuring depression, it is important to inquire about physiological and cognitive symptoms as well as features of affect. Depression scales that focus exclusively on one of these elements have limited breadth of coverage and compromised content validity. The PAI sought to insure breadth of content coverage through the use of subscales representing the major elements of the measured constructs, as indicated by the theoretical and empirical literature.

The "depth" of content coverage refers to the need to sample across the full range of construct severity. To ensure adequate depth of coverage, the scales were designed to include items reflecting both its milder and its most severe forms. The use of four-alternative scaling provides each item with the capacity to capture differences in the severity of the manifestation of a feature of a particular disorder and is further justified psychometrically in that it allows a scale to capture more true variance per item, meaning that even scales of modest length can achieve satisfactory reliability. This item type may also be preferred by clinicians who are considering particular items (e.g., risk indicators) or by clients, who often express dissatisfaction with forced-choice alternatives because they feel that the truth is between the two extremes presented.

In addition to differences in depth of severity reflected in response options, the items themselves were constructed to tap different levels of severity. For example, cognitive elements of depression can vary from mild pessimism to severe feelings of hopelessness, helplessness, and despair. Item characteristic curves were used to select items that provide information across the full range of construct severity. The nature of the severity continuum varies across the constructs. For example, severity on the Suicidal Ideation (SUI) scale involves the imminence of the suicidal threat. Thus, items on this scale vary from vague and ill-articulated thoughts about suicide to immediate plans for self-harm.

The construct validation approach to test construction assumes that item content is critical in determining an item's ability to capture the phenomenology of various disorders and traits and hence its relevance for the assessment of the construct. Empirically derived tests may include items on a construct scale that have no apparent relation to the construct in question. However, research (e.g., Holden, 1989; Holden & Fekken, 1990; Peterson, Clark, & Bennett, 1989) has consistently indicated that such items add little or no validity to self-report tests. The available empirical evidence is entirely consistent with the assumption that the content of a self-report item is critical in determining its utility in measurement. This assumption does not preclude the potential utility of items that are truly "subtle" in the sense that a lay audience cannot readily identify the relationship of the item to mental health status. However, the assumption does suggest that the implications of such items for mental health status should be apparent to expert diagnosticians for the item to be useful.

Although discriminant validity has been long recognized as an important facet of construct validity, it traditionally has not played a major role in the construction of psychological tests, and it continues to represents one of the largest challenges in the assessment of psychological constructs. There are a variety of threats to validity where discriminability plays a vital role. One such area involves *test bias*. A test that is intended to measure a psychological construct should not be measuring a demographic variable, such as gender, age, or sex. This means, not that psychological tests should never be correlated with demographic variables, but that the magnitude of any such correlations should not exceed the theoretical overlap of the demographic feature with the construct. For example, nearly every indicator of antisocial behavior suggests that it is more common in men than in women; thus, it would be expected that an assessment of antisocial behavior would yield average scores for men that are higher than those for women. However, the instrument should demonstrate a considerably greater correlation with other indicators of antisocial behavior than it does with gender; otherwise, it may be measuring gender rather than measuring the construct it was designed to assess.

The issue of test bias is one that is particularly salient in light of past abuses of testing and current legislation designed to prevent such abuses. However, test bias is just one of the potential problems regarding discriminant validity. It is particularly common in the field of clinical assessment to find that a measure that supposedly measures one construct (such as anxiety or schizophrenia) is in fact highly related to many constructs. It is this tendency that makes many instruments quite difficult to interpret. How does the clinician evaluate an elevated score on a scale measuring "schizophrenia" if that scale is also a measure of alienation, indecisiveness, family problems, and depression? At each stage of the development of the PAI, items were selected that had maximal associations with indicators of the pertinent construct and minimal associations with the other constructs measured by the test.

NORMATIVE DATA

The PAI was developed and standardized for use in the assessment of individuals in the age range of 18 through adulthood, and it has been translated into several languages. Items were written to be easily understood and applicable across cultures; the initial reading level analyses of the PAI test items indicated that reading ability at the fourth-grade level was necessary to complete the inventory. A comparative study of similar instruments by Schinka and Borum (1993) supported the conclusion that the PAI items are written at a grade equivalent lower than estimates for comparable instruments, an important issue in forensic settings, where reading ability is commonly lower than average.

PAI scale and subscale raw scores are transformed to T-scores ($M = 50$, $SD = 10$) in order to provide interpretation relative to a standardization sample of 1,000 community-dwelling adults. This sample was carefully selected to match 1995 U.S. census projections on the basis of gender, race, and age; the educational level of the standardization sample ($M = 13.3$ years) was representative of a community group with the required fourth-grade reading level. For each scale and subscale, the T-scores were linearly transformed from the means and standard deviations derived from the census-matched standardization sample. Unlike several similar instruments, the PAI does not calculate T-scores differently for men and women; instead, combined norms are used for both genders. Separate norms are only necessary when the scale contains some bias that alters the interpretation of a score based on the respondent's gender. To use separate norms in the absence of such bias would only distort the natural epidemiological differences between genders. As mentioned, women are less likely than men to receive the diagnosis of antisocial personality disorder, and this is reflected in the lower mean scores for women on the Antisocial Features (ANT) scale. A separate normative procedure for men and women would result in similar numbers of each gender scoring in the clinically significant range, a result that does not reflect the established gender ratio for this disorder. The PAI included several procedures to eliminate items that might be biased due to demographic features, and items that displayed any signs of being interpreted differently as a function of these features were eliminated in the course of selecting final items for the test. As it turns out, with relatively few exceptions, differences as a function of demography were negligible in the community sample. The most noteworthy effects involve the tendency for younger adults to score higher on the Borderline Features (BOR) and ANT scales than older adults and the tendency for men to score higher on the ANT and Alcohol Problems (ALC) scales than women.

Because T-scores are derived from a community sample, they provide a useful means for determining if certain problems are clinically significant, because relatively few normal adults will obtain markedly elevated scores. However, other comparisons are often of equal importance in clinical decision making. For example, nearly all patients report depression at their initial evaluation; the question confronting the clinician considering a diagnosis of major depressive disorder concerns the relative severity of symptomatology. Knowing the individual's score on the PAI Depression scale is elevated in comparison with the standardization sample is of value, but a comparison of the elevation relative to a clinical sample may be more critical in forming diagnostic hypotheses.

To facilitate these comparisons, the PAI profile form also indicates the T-scores that correspond to marked elevations when referenced against a representative clinical sample. This profile "skyline" indicates for each scale and subscale the score that represents the raw score 2 standard deviations above the mean for a clinical sample of 1,246 patients selected from a wide variety of professional settings. Scores above this skyline represent a marked elevation of scores relative to those of patients in clinical settings. Thus, interpretation of the PAI profiles can be accomplished in comparison to both normal and clinical samples.

The PAI manual provides normative transformations for a number of different comparisons. Various appendices provide T-score transformations referenced against the clinical sample and a large sample of college students as well as for various demographic subgroups of the community standardization sample. Although the differences between demographic groups were generally quite small, there are occasions where it may be useful to make comparisons with reference to particular groups. Thus, the raw score means and standard deviations needed to convert raw scores to T-scores with reference to normative data provided by particular groups are provided in the manual for this purpose. Personnel selection norms and scoring software are also available through the test publisher. Although it is appropriate to make normative comparisons to a sample most representative of the individual being assessed, for most clinical and research applications the use of T-scores derived from the full normative data set is strongly recommended because of its representativeness and large sample size.

However, comparison to correctional norms may importantly supplement decisions made in correctional settings. Edens and Ruiz (2005) have recently developed correctional software using normative data gathered from multiple correctional settings in order to enhance the forensic utility of the PAI. Their normative sample consisted of inmates in a prerelease treatment facility in New Jersey ($n = 542$), a treatment program for convicted sex offenders in Texas ($n = 98$), state prison inmates in Washington ($n = 515$), and forensic inpatients in New Hampshire ($n = 57$). Overall, the sample averaged 33.6 years of age ($SD = 8.9$) and 10.8 years of education. A large proportion of the sample were male (68.1%), and the racial/ethnic mix mirrored that of corrections settings (45.2% African American, 37.7% Caucasian, 7.8% Hispanic). As would be predicted, the correctional norm group tended to score roughly a standard deviation higher than the community standardization sample on Antisocial Features ($d = 1.15$), Drug Problems ($d = 1.62$), Stress ($d = 0.99$), and Borderline Features ($d = 0.84$), whereas they scored roughly a standard deviation lower on Treatment Rejection ($d = -0.96$).

RELIABILITY

The reliability of the PAI scales and subscales has been examined in terms of internal consistency (Alterman et al., 1995; Boyle & Lennon, 1994; Morey, 1991; Rogers, Flores, Ustad, & Sewell, 1995; Schinka, 1995), test-retest reliability (Boyle & Lennon, 1994; Morey, 1991; Rogers et al., 1995), and configural stability (Morey, 1991). Internal consistency alphas for the full scales are generally found to be in the .80s, whereas the subscales yield alphas in the .70s. The reliability of the PAI in corrections populations appears similar to that in the standardization sample (Edens & Ruiz, 2005). Although these numbers are acceptable, internal consistency estimates are generally not the ideal basis for deriving the standard error of measurement (*SEM*) in clinical measures, because temporal instability is often of greater concern than interitem correlations.

For the standardization studies, the median test-retest reliability value over a 4-week interval for the 11 full clinical scales was .86 (Morey, 1991), leading to *SEM* values for these scales on the order of 3 to 4*T*-score points, with 95% confidence intervals of plus or minus 6 to 8*T*-score points. Absolute *T*-score change values over time were quite small across scales, on the order of 2 to 3*T*-score points for most of the full scales (Morey, 1991). Boyle and Lennon (1994) reported a median test-retest reliability of .73 in their normal sample over 28 days. Rogers et al. (1995) found an average stability of .71 for the Spanish version of the PAI administered over a 2-week interval.

Because multiscale inventories are often interpreted configurally, additional questions should be asked concerning the stability of configurations on the 11 PAI clinical scales. One such analysis involved determining the inverse (or Q-type) correlation between each participant's profile at Time 1 and the profile at Time 2. Correlations were obtained for each of the 155 participants in the full retest sample, and a distribution of the within-subject profile correlations was obtained. With the analysis conducted in this manner, the median correlation of the clinical scale configuration was .83, indicating a substantial degree of stability in profile configurations over time (Morey, 1991).

VALIDITY

In the examination of test validity presented in the manual (Morey, 1991), a number of the best available clinical indicators were administered concurrently to various samples to determine their convergence with corresponding PAI scales. Since that time, a number of studies have investigated the validity of the PAI in a variety of populations and for numerous purposes. A comprehensive presentation of available validity evidence for the various scales is beyond the scope of this chapter; the PAI manual alone contains information about correlations of individual scales with over 50 concurrent indices of psychopathology (Morey, 1991). The following paragraphs provide some of the more noteworthy findings from such studies, in particular those related to forensic assessment. The findings are organized based on the four broad classes of PAI scales: Validity, Clinical, Treatment Consideration, and Interpersonal.

Validity Scales

The assessment of profile validity is a critical component of any method intended for use in an evaluative context; the issue is compounded in most forensic settings where incentives for dishonest responding often exist. The PAI validity scales were developed to provide an assessment of the potential influence of certain response tendencies on PAI test performance, including both random and systematic influences upon test responding. A comparison of profiles derived from normal subjects, clinical subjects, and random response simulations in the standardization sample demonstrated a clear separation of scores of actual respondents from the random simulations, and 99% of these random profiles were identified as such by either the Inconsistency (*ICN*) scale or the Infrequency (*INF*) scale (Morey, 1991). To address the potential problem of partially random response sets, Morey and Hopwood (2004) developed an indicator of back random responding (e.g., a respondent discontinues attending to item content midway through the examination) involving front to back scaled score discrepancies on two PAI scales (*ALC* and *SUI*) with satisfactory positive and negative predictive power across levels and base rates of back random responding. Using another approach, Edens and Ruiz (2005) divided the *INF* scale into a front (*INF-F*) and a back (*INF-B*) in the correctional software to assess partial random responding. They also introduced an Inconsistency scale for use in correctional settings (*ICN-C*); this scale is composed of a single pair of items regarding admitting illegal behavior in the past. Individuals who admit to illegal behavior on one item and deny it on the other are suspected of inattention, as this occurred in only 4% of the correctional standardization sample.

Systematic profile distortion can occur in the positive or negative directions (Caruso, Benedek, Auble, & Bernet, 2003; Holden, Book, Edwards, Wasylkiw, & Starzyk, 2003). It can also occur in both directions on the same profile. For example, an individual may wish to emphasize feelings of anxiety and depression (i.e., negatively dissimulate) and also disguise his or her use of alcohol or drugs (i.e., positively dissimulate). Systematic profile distortion can also occur in at least two ways. Individuals may consciously present themselves in a manner that is inconsistent with their experience or historical fact based on their perception of the consequences of their presentation (i.e., malinger or fake good). Conversely, individuals may present themselves in a way that is consistent with their subjective experience but that most other individuals would see as an exaggeration (if overly negative) or lack of insight (if overly positive). This latter type of profile distortion has been referred to as self-deception and is related to specific forms of psychopathology. For example, cognitive symptoms of depression involve an underestimation of one's own abilities and worth and an overestimation of obstacles to emotional health or achievement. Conversely, narcissistic or manic disorders often involve an expansive approach to life and a limited capacity for a critical appraisal of one's real abilities and prospects. PAI indices of systematic profile distortion were developed to assess self- and other-deception in both the positive and negative directions.

The three indices developed to directly assess positive dissimulation have been subjected to numerous empirical studies. In the initial validation studies described in the test manual, individuals scoring above the threshold on the Positive Impression Management (*PIM*) scale were 13.9 times more likely to be in the positive dissimulation sample than a community sample (Morey, 1991). Subsequent studies have generally supported the ability of these scales to distinguish simulated protocols from actual protocols under a variety of response set conditions. For example, the studies described in the test manual found that the point of rarity on PIM between the distributions of the impression management sample (i.e., "fake good") and the community normative sample was at a raw score of 57*T*. Application of this cut score resulted in a sensitivity in the identification of defensiveness of 82% and a specificity with respect to normal individuals of 70%. Although not reported in the manual, Positive and Negative Predictive Power (PPP, NPP) can be computed from these values given a base-rate value for intentional positive distortion. For example, at a base rate of 50%, PPP = 73% and NPP = 79.5%; at a base rate of 25%, PPP = 57.7% and NPP = 88.6%. These findings have been replicated in several samples (Morey & Lanier, 1998); for example, a study by Cashel, Rogers, Sewell, and Martin-Cannici (1995) also identified 57*T* as the optimal cutting score for their sample. Their study, in which respondents were coached on the believability of results, yielded sensitivity and specificity rates of 48% and 81%, respectively (PPP = 71.6% and NPP = 60.9% when the base rate = 50%; PPP = 55.8% and NPP = 75.7% when the base rate = 25%). Peebles and Moore (1998) also found a cutting score of 57*T* to be optimal for their sample, resulting in a hit rate of 85% in distinguishing forthright from fake-good responders. Finally, a study by Fals-Stewart (1996) found that the 57*T* cut score on PIM had a sensitivity of 88% in identifying "questionable responding" in substance abusers (e.g., forensic patients who denied substance use but had positive urine screens), with a specificity of 80% in honest responding groups (PPP = 81.5% and NPP = 87.0% when the base rate = 50%; PPP = 68.8% and NPP = 93.0% when the base rate = 25%).

The Defensiveness Index (*DEF*; Morey, 1996) is a composite of PAI scale configurations that tend to occur more frequently in profiles of individuals instructed to form a positive impression than in honest respondents from clinical or community populations. Peebles and Moore (1998) reported a hit rate of 83% in distinguishing honest from fake-good respondents with the *DEF*. However, Cashel et al. (1995) reported that coached dissimulators obtained a lower mean score on the *DEF* than naïve dissimulators, though the coached mean was still roughly 1 standard deviation above the norm for community samples. Cashel et al. (1995) developed the Cashel Discriminant Function (*CDF*) to measure positive dissimulation unassociated with self-deception to indicate the possibility that an examinee is "faking good." The *CDF* is a function composed of weighted scale scores that was found to optimally distinguish defensive and honest respondents in their study. Cashel et al. demonstrated *CDF* sensitivies ranging from 79% to 87% in identifying the falsified profiles of college students and jail inmates and a specificity of 88%. Using the conservative value of 79% as the sensitivity estimate, PPP = 86.8% and NPP = 80.7% at the 50% base rate, and PPP = 76.9% and NPP = 88.9% at the 25% base rate. These results, which have been replicated with naïve dissimulators (Morey, 1996; Morey & Lanier, 1998), suggest the ability of the *CDF* to increment *PIM* and *DEF* in the detection of positive dissimulation.

A number of examinations of the utility of the Negative Impression Management (*NIM*) scale in the evaluation of malingering have also been reported in the literature. In the initial validiation studies cited in the test manual, individuals scoring above the critical level of *NIM* were 14.7 times more likely to be a member of the malingering group than of the clinical sample. Rogers, Ornduff, and Sewell (1993) examined the effectiveness of *NIM* in identifying both naïve and sophisticated simulators (advanced graduate students in clinical and counseling psychology) who were given a financial incentive to avoid detection as malingerers while attempting to feign specific disorders. Rogers et al. found that the recommended *NIM* scale cutoff (84*T*) successfully identified 91% of participants attempting to feign schizophrenia, 56% of participants simulating depression, and 39% of participants simulating an anxiety disorder. In contrast, only 3% of control participants were identified as simulators. Rogers et al. concluded that *NIM* is most effective in identifying the feigning of more severe mental disorders. Interestingly, there was no effect of subject sophistication; the scale was equally effective in identifying naïve and sophisticated malingerers. Along similar lines, Bagby, Nicholson, Bacchiochi, Ryder, and Bury (2002) found *NIM* to yield only a moderate effect size ($d = .44$ for coached and .53 for uncoached malingerers vs. bona fide patients) in detecting a group that appeared to be feigning depression, with average *NIM* scores of 74*T* for uncoached and 72*T* for coached malingerers. Gaies (1993) conducted a similar study of malingering that focused on the feigning of clinical depression and reported average scores on *NIM* of 92*T* for sophisticated malingerers and 81*T* for naïve malingerers. Although the Gaies (1993) and Bagby et al. (2002) studies demonstrated that *NIM* was elevated relative to honest responding groups, the results are similar to those of Rogers et al. (1993) in suggesting that individuals attempting to simulate milder forms of mental disorder (in these studies, depression) will obtain more "moderate" elevations on *NIM*.

The utility of *NIM* in detecting simulated posttraumatic stress disorder (PTSD) has also received attention. Liljequiest, Kinder, and Schinka (1998) reported significant NIM elevations in both clinical (alcohol, $M = 62.93$, $SD = 18.25$; PTSD, $M = 67.93$, $SD = 16.94$) and malingering ($M = 92.48$, $SD = 28.40$) groups relative to community norms or their college student samples. Calhoun, Earnst, Tucker, Kirby, and Beckham (2000) compared PAI scores among PTSD diagnosed veterans, college student PTSD simulators, and community controls. A *NIM* score of 80T detected 75% of feigned protocols and demonstrated a hit rate of 59%, whereas a score of 102T detected 44% of simulators and demonstrated a hit rate of 63%. Finally, Scragg, Bor, and Mendham (2000) reported a sensitivity of 54% and a specificity of 100% for distinguishing malingered from true PTSD with the *NIM* scale (PPP = 100.0% and NPP = 68.5% when the base rate = 50%, PPP = 100.0% and NPP = 81.3% when the base rate = 25%).

The Malingering Index (*MAL*; Morey, 1996), a composite of PAI configural indicators, was introduced to measure malingering more directly than *NIM*, which is often affected by response styles consequent to psychopathology in addition to overt attempts at negative dissimulation. *MAL* has been shown to differentiate individuals in a malingering sample from the community and clinical standardization samples (Morey, 1996). Wang et al. (1997) reported a statistically significant positive correlation between the *MAL* and two scales of the Structured Interview of Reported Symptoms (SIRS; Rogers, Bagby, & Dickens, 1992): Improbable or Absurd Symptoms ($r = 0.39$) and Symptom Combinations ($r = 0.42$). Gaies (1993) reported *MAL* (cut score = 3) sensitivity estimates of 56.6% and 34.2% in identifying informed and naïve malingerers, respectively. The specificity with respect to depressed controls in that study was 89% and with respect to community controls was 100%. Calhoun et al. (2000) reported that a *MAL* cut score of 3 detected 44% of simulators in their sample and misclassified several individuals with PTSD as malingerers. Scragg et al. (2000) reported a sensitivity of 45% and a specificity of 94% in distinguishing malingered from true PTSD with *MAL* (PPP = 88.2% and NPP = 63.1% when the base rate = 50%, PPP = 78.6% and NPP = 77.7% when the base rate = 25%). These results suggest both an association with psychopathology, though less so than is the case with *NIM*, and a sensitivity that declines to the extent that less severe forms of psychopathology are feigned. However, Blanchard, McGrath, Pogge, and Khadivi (2003) reported that *MAL* was the most efficient PAI indicator of malingering in their data set, with a hit rate of 94%, a PPP of 96%, and a NPP of 94% at their base rate of 11% malingerers. On a cautionary note, Bagby et al. (2002) found that *MAL* yielded a moderate effect size in distinguishing actual patients from uncoached malingerers, but their coached malingering group achieved *MAL* scores similar to those of their patient sample, suggesting that *MAL* may not be as effective in detecting sophisticated malingerers.

Rogers and colleagues (1996) developed the Rogers Discriminant Function (*RDF*), an index that appears able to indicate malingering but is not associated with psychopathology (i.e., does not systematically correlate with the clinical scales). This research group demonstrated and cross-validated sensitivity and specificity estimates above 80% in distinguishing both coached and naïve malingerers from honest respondents. Morey (1996) replicated these results using naïve college student simulators and found *RDF* to be the most accurate among the PAI negative validity indicators in identifying malingerers. In fact, *RDF* resulted in PPP estimates greater than .80 across malingering base rates of 20%, 50%, and 80%. The Bagby et al. (2002) study found that *RDF* was superior to *NIM* and *DEF* and incremented every Minnesota Multiphasic Personality Inventory–2 (MMPI–2; Butcher, Dahlstrom, Graham, Tellegen, & Kaemmer, 1989) malingering index, although the MMPI–2 indices F and $F(p)$ were able to increment the predictive capability of *RDF*. In a similar study, Blanchard et al. (2003) reported that *NIM, MAL*, and *RDF* all demonstrated hit rates greater than .93 in identifying simulators and that the PAI indicators significantly incremented MMPI–2 indicators of malingering, and vice versa. However, these authors also noted that eight MMPI–2 malingering indicators, considered as a group, yielded a larger r^2 in regression prediction of malingering status than the grouping of the four PAI indicators (including the *CDF*) studied. Scragg et al. (2000) reported a sensitivity of 63% and a specificity of 94% for the *RDF* in their study of malingered PTSD (PPP = 91.3% and NPP = 71.8% when the base rate = 50%; PPP = 83.8% and NPP = 83.9% when the base rate = 25%). However, Wang et al. (1997) failed to find a relationship between *RDF* and the SIRS malingering classification in a small correctional sample, and several authors have suggested that the translation of *RDF* from clinical to forensic settings is problematic (e.g., Edens et al., 2001). Rogers, Sewell, Morey, and Ustad (1996) tested *RDF* in a forensic setting and observed a classification rate shrinkage to 62%. Based on these results, Rogers et al. recommended use of *RDF* to screen for but not directly indicate malingering in forensic settings.

Clinical Scales

The clinical scales of the PAI were assembled to provide information about clinical constructs relevant in a variety of forensic and clinical contexts. A number of instruments have been used to provide information on the convergent and discriminant validity of the PAI clinical scales. Correlations tend to follow hypothesized patterns; for example, strong associations are found between neurotic spectrum scales such as Anxiety (*ANX*), Anxiety Related Disorder (*ARD*), and Depression (*DEP*) and other psychometric measures of neuroticism (Costa & McCrae, 1992; Montag & Levin, 1994; Morey, 1991). The *ARD* scale has also been found to correlate with the probability of experiencing nightmares, with *ARD-T* in particular being associated with night terrors (Greenstein, 1995). The *ARD* scale (particularly *ARD-T*) has also been found to differentiate women psychiatric patients who were victims of childhood abuse from other women patients who did not experience such abuse (Cherepon & Prinzhorn, 1994). Edens and Ruiz (2005) reported that *ARD-T* was effective at detecting inmates released from a forensic inpatient unit with a diagnosis of PTSD (*AUC* = 0.83, *SE* = .05). The *DEP* scale demonstrates its largest correlations with various widely used indicators of depression, such as the Beck Depression Inventory (BDI; Beck & Steer, 1987), the Hamilton Rating Scale for Depression (Hamilton, 1960), and the Wiggins (1966) MMPI Depression content scale (Morey, 1991; Ban, Fjetland, Kutcher, & Morey, 1993). Several indicators have been found useful in discriminating PTSD from ASD among individuals traumatized in motor vehicle accidents (G. E. Holmes, Williams, & Haines, 2001), and the PAI has demonstrated effectiveness in distinguishing true from malingered PTSD in psychiatric (Liljequist et al., 1998) and VA (Calhoun et al., 2000) samples. It has also been suggested that the PAI might provide important diagnostic information for individuals with pain (George & Wagner, 1995; Karlin et al., in press) and eating disorders (Tasca, Wood, Demidenko, & Bissada, 2002). Interestingly, the Somatic Complaints (*SOM*) scale, particularly *SOM-C*, has proven useful in the distinguishing between epileptic and nonepileptic seizures (Wagner, Wymer, Topping, & Pritchard, in press), suggesting that the PAI may be helpful in cases where functional versus organic origins of physical complaints are an issue.

The assessment of psychotic disorders is particularly relevant in forensic settings, where the base rate of psychosis is often higher (e.g., correctional settings) and where individuals' mental status is often a prominent issue. Within the psychotic spectrum, PAI scales such as Paranoia (*PAR*), Mania (*MAN*), and Schizophrenia (*SCZ*) have been correlated with a variety of other indicators of severe psychopathology (Morey, 1991). For example, *PAR* has been found to correlate particularly well with diagnostic assessments of paranoia made via a structured clinical interview (Rogers, Ustad, & Salekin, 1998). Also, the *SCZ* scale has been found to distinguish schizophrenic patients from controls (Boyle & Lennon, 1994). In that study, the schizophrenic sample did not differ significantly from a sample of alcoholics on *SCZ* scores, although certain characteristics of the criterion group (patients on medication maintenance) and the alcoholic group (alcoholics undergoing detoxication) might have in part accounted for their findings (Morey, 1995). *SCZ* has also been shown to significantly increment the Rorschach Comprehensive System Schizophrenia Index (SCZI; Exner, 1993) in differentiating inpatients with schizophrenic spectrum disorders from inpatients with other diagnoses, whereas SCZI was unable to increment *SCZ* (Klonsky, 2004). These data suggest that efforts during the construction of the PAI to enhance discriminant validity on the *SCZ* scale were justified, as the control group were psychiatric inpatients, many of whom met criteria for disorders with symptoms similar to schizophrenia (e.g., organic psychoses, cognitive deficits). Nonetheless, given the limited research and mixed findings (e.g., Edens & Ruiz, 2005) with the *SCZ* scale, some have suggested it be interpreted as a measure of general impairment rather than as a specific marker of schizophrenia (Rogers, Sewell, et al., 1995). Combining the PAI profile with information from other assessment sources may be particularly important for differential diagnosis of psychotic disorders (Edens et al., 2001).

Personality disorders are common in forensic examinees and represent risk factors for a variety of problematic behaviors common in forensic settings, such as violence, substance use, and poor treatment response. Two scales on the PAI directly target personality disorders, the Borderline Features (*BOR*) scale and the Antisocial Features (*ANT*) scale. The choice to include these two constructs on the PAI was based on the fact that the majority of the literature on personality disorders relates to these constructs. Both *BOR* and *ANT* have been found to relate to other measures of these constructs as well as to predict relevant behavioral outcomes (e.g., Salekin, Rogers, Ustad, & Sewell, 1998; Trull, Useda, Conforti, & Doan, 1997). BOR has been found to correlate with the MMPI Borderline scale (Morey, 1991), the Bell Object Relations Inventory (Bell, Billington, & Becker, 1985; Kurtz, Morey, & Tomarken, 1992), and the *NEO–Personality Inventory* (NEO–PI; Costa & McCrae, 1992) Neuroticism scale (Costa & McCrae, 1992). Edens and Ruiz (2005) reported that *BOR* showed an impressive ability to detect forensic inmates discharged with a diagnosis of borderline personality disorder ($AUC = 0.97, SE = .032$). Other studies have supported the validity and utility of this scale in borderline treatment samples (e.g., Evershed et al., 2003; Yeomans, Hull, & Clarkin, 1994) and in predicting general maladjustment in college students (Bagge et al., 2004). It has also been demonstrated that an assessment of *BOR* increments the information provided by a diagnosis of major depressive disorder (Kurtz & Morey, 2001). The *BOR* scale in isolation was able to distinguish borderline patients from unscreened controls with an 80% hit rate, and it successfully identified 91% of these participants as part of a discriminant function (Bell-Pringle, 1997). Classifications based on the *BOR* scale have been validated in a variety of domains related to borderline functioning, including depression, personality traits, coping, Axis I disorders, and interpersonal problems (Trull, 1995). These *BOR* scale classifications were also found to be predictive of 2-year outcome on academic indices in college students, even controlling for academic potential and substance abuse (Trull, Useda, Conforti, & Doan, 1997).

The *ANT* scale demonstrated its largest correlations in initial validation studies (Morey, 1991) with the MMPI antisocial personality disorder diagnosis (Morey, Waugh, &

Blashfield, 1985) and the Self-Report Psychopathy test designed by Hare (1985) to assess his model of psychopathy. Subsequent studies have also supported the validity of *ANT*. Salekin, Rogers, and Sewell (1997) examined the relationship between *ANT* and psychopathic traits in a sample of female offenders and found that elevations on *ANT* among this population were primarily the result of endorsements on Antisocial Behaviors (*ANT-A*). Also, support was found for the convergent validity of *ANT* with other measures of psychopathy, including the Psychopathy Checklist–Revised (PCL–R; Hare, Harpur, Hakstion, Forth, Hart, & Newman, 1990) total score and the Personality Disorder Examination (Loranger, 1988) Antisocial scale. Edens, Hart, Johnson, Johnson, and Olver (2000) examined the relationship of the *ANT* scale to the screening version of the *Psychopathy Checklist* (PCL:SV; Hart, Cox, & Hare, 1995) and the PCL–R. Moderately strong correlations were found between *ANT* and the PCL:SV and PCL–R total scores (ANT-A showed the highest correlations with these measures). Salekin et al. (1998) demonstrated the ability of *ANT* and the Aggression (*AGG*) scale of the PAI to predict recidivism among female inmates over a 14-month follow-up interval. *ANT* has also demonstrated validity in predicting violence in a sample of incarcerated mentally ill individuals (Wang & Diamond, 1999) and in predicting treatment course for a sample of borderline females (Clarkin, Hull, Yeomans, Kakuma, & Caitor, 1994). *ANT* was shown to both increment and outperform the PCL-R in predicting disciplinary infractions among incarcerated sex offenders over a 2-year follow-up period, demonstrating an overall hit rate of 0.70 with a cut score of 70*T* (Buffington-Vollum, Edens, Johnson, & Johnson, 2002). Finally, the PAI, (in particular, *BOR, ANT*, and *AGG*) has demonstrated the capacity to differentiate various types of antisocial individuals, such as generally violent men versus men who abuse family members but are not violent outside the home (DelSol, Margolin, & John, 2003) and individuals convicted of violent versus nonviolent crimes (Edwards, Scott, Yarvis, Paizis, & Panizzon, 2003).

The PAI contains two scales, Alcohol Problems (*ALC*) and Drug Problems (*DRG*), that inquire directly about behaviors and consequences related to alcohol and drug use, abuse, and dependence. These scales demonstrate a similar pattern of correlates: strong correlations with corresponding measures of substance abuse and moderate associations with indicators of behavior problems and antisocial personality (Alterman, et al., 1995; Parker, Daleiden, & Simpson, 1999). The *ALC* scale has been found to differentiate patients in an alcohol rehabilitation clinic from patients with schizophrenia (Boyle & Lennon, 1994) as well as normal controls (Ruiz, Dickinson, & Pincus, 2002). The *DRG* scale has been found to successfully discriminate drug abusers and methadone maintenance patients from general clinical and community samples (Alterman et al., 1995; Kellogg et al., 2002). *DRG* has also demonstrated strong correlations with the Addiction Severity Index (*ASI*; McLellan et al., 1992) and predicted both involvement (as measured by urine samples) with and negative consequences of substance use in a clinical sample (Kellogg et al., 2002). Another interesting finding from the Kellogg et al. study was that individuals who had been in methadone maintenance treatment for more than 1 year produced lower *DRG* scores than individuals who had been treated for less than 1 year. The authors attributed this effect to the biological and psychosocial stabilization that occurs as individuals maintain successful methadone treatment. Because the items for *ALC* and *DRG* inquire directly about substance use, the scales are susceptible to denial. Empirically derived procedures to assess the likelihood that a profile underrepresents the extent of alcohol or drug problems (Edens & Ruiz, 2005; Fals-Stewart, 1996; Fals-Stewart & Lucente, 1997; Morey, 1996) are described later.

Treatment Consideration Scales

The treatment consideration scales of the PAI were assembled to provide indicators of potential complications in treatment that would not necessarily be apparent from diagnostic data, although they also have a variety of applications to forensic settings, where issues such as aggression, suicide, and stress are important and commonly encountered. The treatment consideration scales were developed to specifically assess the potential for harm to self or others, environmental circumstances, and motivation for psychological treatment.

Correlations between the PAI treatment consideration scales and an array of validation measures provide support for the construct validity of these scales (Costa & McCrae, 1992; Morey, 1991). Substantial correlations are described between the *AGG* scale and the NEO-PI Hostility scale (.83), the Spielberger State-Trait Anxiety Inventory (STAXI; Spielberger, 1988) Trait Anger scale (.75), and the STAXI Anger Control scale (−.57) in the test manual. *AGG* has also been extensively researched in forensic settings. Wang et al. (1997) found significant positive relations between *AGG* and all three of its subscales to the Overt Aggression Scale (OES; Yudofsky, Silver, Jackson, Endicott, & Williams, 1986) in a sample of inmates receiving or requesting psychiatric services. Wang and Diamond identified the Physical Aggression (*AGG-P*) and Verbal Aggression (*AGG-V*) scales as related to institutional misbehavior among mentally ill offenders. Salekin et al. (1998) found that *AGG* predicted recidivism among female offenders over a 14-month follow-up. Walters, Duncan, and Geyer (2003) reported that *AGG* significantly incremented the PCL–R and demographic variables in predicting disciplinary adjustment in prison inmates. *AGG* can also be used in conjunction with *ANT, BOR*, and other scales in risk assessments (e.g., DelSol et al., 2003).

The Suicidal Ideation (*SUI*) scale was positively correlated with the Beck Hopelessness Inventory (Beck & Steer, 1988; .64), the BDI, and the Suicidal Ideation scale (.56) and Total Score (.40) of the Suicide Probability Scale (SPS; Cull & Gill, 1982). It was also found to be negatively correlated with the Perceived Social Support (PSS; Procidano & Heller, 1983) scales in the standardization studies. Wang et al. (1997) found that *SUI* had the largest correlation among PAI scales to the number of suicide risk assessments in a large sample of incarcerated men and that the scale could reliably differentiate individuals who had or had not made suicidal gestures. Rogers and Ustad et al. (1998) found that *SUI* demonstrated moderate to large correlations with other self-report measures of suicidal ideation in a sample of correctional emergency referrals.

As expected, the Nonsupport (*NON*) scale was found to be highly (and inversely) correlated with the social support measures (−.67 with PSS-Family and −.63 with PSS-Friends in the standardization studies). It was also moderately associated with numerous measures of distress and tension. The Stress (*STR*) scale displayed its largest correlations with the Schedule of Recent Events (SRE; .50), a unit-scoring adaptation of the widely used Holmes and Rahe (1967) checklist of recent stressors, and it was also associated with various indices of depression and poor morale. Finally, the Treatment Rejection (*RXR*) scale was found to be negatively associated with the Wiggins Poor Morale scale (−.78) and the NEO–PI Vulnerability scale (−.54), consistent with the idea that distress motivates treatment utilization and effort. *RXR* has been shown to be positively associated with indices of social support, implying that people are less likely to be motivated to pursue treatment if they have an intact and available support system as an alternative. This scale has predicted treatment noncompliance in a sample of sex-offending inmates (Caperton, Edens, & Johnson, 2004).

Interpersonal Scales

The interpersonal scales of the PAI were designed to provide an assessment of the interpersonal style of subjects along two dimensions: (a) a warmly affiliative versus a cold rejecting axis and (b) a dominating, controlling versus a meekly submissive style. These axes provide a useful way of conceptualizing variation in normal personality as well as many different mental disorders, and people at the extremes of these dimensions may present with a variety of disorders. The PAI manual describes a number of studies indicating that diagnostic groups differ on these dimensions; for example, spouse abusers usually score relatively high on the Dominance (*DOM*) scale, whereas schizophrenics tend to score low on the Warmth (*WRM*) scale (Morey, 1991). Correlations with related measures also provide support for the construct validity of these scales. For example, the correlations with the Interpersonal Adjective Scales–Revised (IAS–R; Wiggins, 1979) vector scores are consistent with expectations: *DOM* is associated with the IAS–R dominance vector (.61) and *WRM* is associated with the IAS–R love vector (.65). The NEO–PI Extroversion scale roughly bisects the high *DOM*–high *WRM* quadrant, as it is moderately positively correlated with both scales; this finding is consistent with previous research (Trapnell & Wiggins, 1990). *WRM* was also correlated with the NEO–PI Gregariousness scale (.46), and *DOM* was associated with the NEO–PI Assertiveness facet (.71).

FORENSIC ASSESSMENT WITH THE PAI

Forensic assessment may involve questions of competency, criminal responsibility, diagnosis, treatment planning, or risk prediction in correctional, child custody, emotional injury, disability, or other psycholegal contexts as well as questions regarding the valid use of the instrument in forensic decision-making. A multiscale instrument used in forensic settings must be able to answer questions regarding response distortion, clinical diagnosis, substance abuse, risk of violence, suicide, and treatment planning. The PAI appears to be especially useful in a forensic context because of its ability to measure constructs related to that population (e.g., *BOR, ANT, DRG*, and *ALC*) as well as its ability to detect invalid profiles (e.g., Douglas, Hart, & Kropp, 2001; Edens et al., 2001; Wang et al., 1997). The following is a brief review of the PAI with respect the areas most relevant to forensic issues.

Response Distortion

The accuracy of information provided in forensic assessments is a persistent concern; in addition to the possibility of inattention or poor concentration leading to random responding, individuals often have a motivation in such settings to appear more or less pathological than they actually are (Caruso et al., 2003). For example, inmates in correctional settings may feign psychopathology in order to procure services (e.g., psychopharmacological agents), whereas individuals on probation may effortfully disguise substance use in order to avoid more stringent probationary requirements. The PAI offers a number of validity indices designed to assess the factors that could lead to distorted profiles.

As discussed earlier, *INF* and *ICN* are useful as indicators of random responding. A moderate elevation on *INF* may additionally suggest an idiosyncratic, as opposed to a random, approach to the test, as might be expected from an individual with a cognitive deficit or psychotic disorder. Such an elevation should be followed up by asking the individual to explain his or her responses to particular *INF* items if a nonrandom and nonnormative response set is suspected. A moderate *ICN* elevation may suggest inattention, as might occur if the respondent is agitated, is intoxicated, or has attentional problems. Finally, if it is suspected that the respondent began attending appropriately but finished the test randomly, the first half of the test can be used to estimate the full scale scores for the entire profile. Back random responding can be detected by comparing discrepancies on the first and last half of the *SUI* and *ALC* scales; differences greater than 5*T* on both scales suggest that the two halves of the test were not approached in the same way.

The pattern of correlations between the validity indices for both positive and negative dissimulation and clinical phenomena suggests that, whereas *NIM* and *PIM* are heavily influenced by self-deception, *MAL* and *DEF* are less so; further, it suggests that neither *RDF* and *CDF* is associated with psychopathology, *RDF* is not associated with *NIM*, and *CDF* is not associated with *PIM*. Consequently, the combination of three scales representative of positive and negative distortion provides the evaluator with a method to tease out the relative influences of psychopathology and intentional distortion in making decisions about invalidity (Morey, 2003), as discussed later.

Although moderate elevations may be due to either conscious or unconscious response bias, more extreme *NIM* elevations make malingering the more likely hypothesis. *RDF* does not correlate with *NIM* or with psychopathology, and it displays moderate correlations with *MAL*. This suggests that an *RDF* elevation represents intentional malingering and is free from the negative response set common among individuals with clinical disorders. This pattern of correlations also suggests that *MAL* is somewhere between *NIM* and *RDF*, in that it is less prone to ego-syntonic negative coloration than *NIM* but is not as clean a measure of malingering as *RDF*. As a result, a configuration in which *NIM* is moderately elevated, *MAL* is mildly elevated, and *RDF* is in the moderate range suggests an individual who is not intentionally misrepresenting his or her experience. Nevertheless, the profile ought to be viewed with the respondent's generally negative view of him- or herself and his or her situation in mind. Conversely, an elevation on *RDF*, which may also typically involve elevations on *NIM* and is likely to involve an elevation on *MAL*, suggests conscious malingering.

There are also three main indices of positive distortion. The *PIM* scale is affected by both self- and other-deception. Some individuals may obtain moderate elevations on *PIM* because they have a Pollyannish view of life and their situation and may also underreport clinical phenomena for the same reason. Individuals who are naïve about psychopathology and are trying to present themselves in a favorable light may also obtain elevations on PIM. DEF is somewhat less prone to the influence of self-deception, as it is moderately correlated with *PIM* and has been shown to increment *PIM* in distinguishing individuals trying to fake good. *CDF* is uncorrelated with *PIM* and moderately correlated with *DEF* and thus provides an index of intentional deception free from the effects of repression or naïveté. Thus, a similar strategy as was used with respect to negative dissimulation can be employed here, with elevations on *PIM* in the absence of *CDF* representing naïveté and elevations on *CDF* more likely representing conscious distortion.

Clinical Diagnosis

Clinical diagnosis may be relevant in a variety of forensic contexts, including the assessment of risk factors, treatment selection, and determining an individual's mental status where competency is an issue. No single method should be used in isolation to make psychiatric diagnoses in any setting. However, the PAI provides several scales that are useful in suggesting or confirming diagnoses in conjunction with other methods. In addition, several configural algorithms have been suggested as indicative of particular diagnoses (Morey, 1996).

Disorders associated with high degrees of negative affect—disorders that have high base rates in clinical and forensic settings relative to the community—are assessed by four PAI full scales (each with three subscales): *SOM, ARD, ANX,* and *DEP.* The Somatic Complaints (*SOM*) scale is designed to address the phenomenology of individuals reporting pain or somatic deficits. It includes the Conversion Disorders (*SOM-C*), Somatic Complaints (*SOM-S*), and Health Concerns (*SOM-H*) subscales. The use of *SOM* in diagnostic formulations is most helpful when combined with medical information, reported symptoms, and an understanding of the assessment context. *SOM* subscales can be used in combination with the validity indices and external data to differentiate individuals who are malingering somatic problems, converting psychological problems to somatic symptoms as a characteristic strategy to minimize anxiety, or reporting genuine symptoms and severity (e.g., Wagner et al., in press). Distinguishing these classes of individuals, all of whom are likely to obtain elevations on *SOM,* is a common and important forensic issue, particularly in contexts where there is motivation to exaggerate symptoms, such as a disability evaluation. The administration of a self-report instrument such as the PAI is the industry standard in these cases (Bianchini, Etherton, & Greve, 2004; Slick, Sherman, & Iverson, 1999).

The Anxiety Related Disorders (*ARD*) scale assesses three anxiety phenomena: fears and phobias (*ARD-T*), compulsions and overall need for order (*ARD-O*), and trauma history and posttraumatic symptoms (*ARD-T*). *ARD* is one of the least internally consistent PAI scales (Morey, 1991) because the disorders represented by the *ARD* subscales represent somewhat distinct clinical phenomena, although all have in common a high degree of negative affect. Thus, it is common for the subscales to operate independently and reflect specific anxiety reactions rather than generalized anxiety. In concert with other scales, these subscales can also indicate personological factors important in clinical and forensic prediction, such as likely reaction to stress, interpersonal style, and organization of experience. For example, individuals with *ARD-O* elevations tend to be affectively constricted and interpersonally rigid, whereas individuals with *ARD-P* elevations tend to be cautious and fearful.

An *ANX* elevation indicates general tension or agitation and is useful as an indication of the individual's capacity to cope with stressful environments (e.g., incarceration). The *ANX* subscales can be used to predict whether anxiety symptoms will be expressed as subjective feelings of distress and nervousness (*ANX-A*), rumination and obsessive or chaotic thinking (*ANX-C*), or physical symptoms (*ANX-P*).

The Depression (*DEP*) scale measures depressive symptoms, and a diagnosis of major depressive disorder is most likely if all three subscales are elevated. The *DEP* subscales assess cognitive (*DEP-C*), affective (*DEP-A*), and physiological (*DEP-P*) aspects of depression. DEP-C can be thought of as a measure of self-efficacy, and higher scores suggest less confidence in one's ability to master one's environment. Elevations are also common among individuals who are ruminating about their situation or have cognitive deficits, such as problems with attention or concentration. *DEP-A* is perhaps the most direct measure of overall life satisfaction on the PAI and is thus often elevated in clinical and correctional settings. *DEP-P* elevations are also likely to occur where exercise, sleep, and dietary schedules are abnormal or restricted, such as in correctional settings.

The PAI includes three full scales related to the psychotic spectrum of disorders. *MAN* was developed to measure symptoms of a manic disorder, although its subscales also have utility independent of that diagnosis. An elevation on *MAN-A* suggests someone who is overactive, and the higher the score, the less ability the individual is likely to demonstrate in managing his or her activity level effectively. Individuals with *MAN-A* elevations tend to do poorly in restricted environments and are at high risk for poorly planned behavior. High scores on *MAN-G* suggest the kind of grandiosity associated with bipolar and narcissistic disorders and also commonly observed in individuals with an incentive to represent themselves in a positive manner, such as those undergoing personnel selection or child custody evaluations. *MAN-G* can also be conceptualized as a measure of self-esteem, so both high and low scores on the scale are meaningful. *MAN-I* is a measure of irritability and is likely to be predictive of poor response to incarceration, probation, employment, and treatment.

PAR and its subscales are useful in assessing the level of trust with which an individual is likely to approach most situations. The Resentment (*PAR-R*) and Hypervigilance (*PAR-H*) subscales address personological issues of hostility and bitterness and predisposition to distrust others, respectively. Low scores on *PAR-H* are interpretable as indicating high levels of interpersonal trust, an important factor in most assessment contexts. (Conversely high scores indicate lack of trust.) High scores on Persecution (*PAR-P*) indicate the behaviors and experiences of individuals diagnosed with delusional or other paranoid disorders, particularly if *SCZ-P* is also elevated.

An elevation on the Schizophrenia (*SCZ*) scale may suggest a psychotic disorder or high levels of psychological impairment associated with other clinical disorders. The *SCZ* subscales Pscyhotic Experiences (*SCZ-P*) and Social Detachment (*SCZ-S*) were designed to represent positive and negative symptoms of schizophrenia, respectively. *SCZ-S* is also useful as an indicator of introversion, which may range from quiet and self-interested to schizoid or socially phobic. The Thought Disorder (*SCZ-T*) subscale measures organization of thought processes and may suggest thought disorder related to nonpsychotic disorders, such as severe depression or dementia.

Although most personality disorders have characteristic profile configurations (Morey, 2003), two full scales, Borderline Features (*BOR*) and Antisocial Features (*ANT*), directly assess the most commonly researched personality disorders: Individuals with moderate elevations on all four *BOR* subscales are very likely to meet diagnostic criteria for borderline personality disorder and probably several other personality disorders. *BOR* can be thought of as an index of overall psychological maturity, with low scorers being characteristically immature. The Identity Problems (*BOR-I*) and Negative Relationships (*BOR-N*) subscales reflect the common interpersonal pattern of need for interpersonal affection combined with the expectation and experience of disappointment and rejection characteristic of borderline personality disorder. Elevations on the Affective Instability (*BOR-A*) and Self-Harm (*BOR-S*) subscales suggest emotional lability and impulsivity, respectively, traits likely to be common and problematic in forensic correctional settings. Antisocial personality is among the most common diagnoses in correctional settings, and the *ANT* scale measures three key aspects of the disorder. *ANT-A* is a measure of historical and current antisocial behavior; it correlates most highly with the notoriously behavioral diagnosis of antisocial personality disorder. *ANT-E* reflects the character trait egocentricity, which is also common in individuals diagnosed as antisocial. High scorers are likely to be callous and unremorseful about past or future crimes. Elevations on the Stimulus-Seeking (*ANT-S*) subscale suggest an increased risk of substance use or other potentially self- or other-harming behaviors.

Substance Use

The Alcohol Problems (*ALC*) and Drug Problems (*DRG*) scales directly assess the degree to which alcohol or substance use is involved in the clinical picture. Each scale includes items addressing historical and current substance involvement and adverse consequences of substance use. Moderate elevations (e.g., 70*T*) suggest abuse, whereas marked elevations (e.g., 85*T*) suggest dependence. It is also possible to get a moderate elevation if the individual reports past substance use problems but does not admit to current use. Individuals entering substance abuse treatment often demonstrate elevations on *NIM* and other indicators of negative dissimulation (Alterman et al., 1995; Boyle & Lennon, 1994), a phenomenon that may be related to state affects associated with intoxication or the detoxification process.

As items on *ALC* and *DRG* are face valid, individuals who wish to avoid disclosing the full extent of their substance use can obtain low scores somewhat easily. Therefore, several empirically derived procedures to assess the likelihood that a profile underrepresents the extent of alcohol or drug problems (Fals-Stewart, 1996; Morey, 1996) have been described. As discussed above, Fals-Stewart and his research group have demonstrated some success using *PIM* and a combination of *PIM, ALC*, and *DRG* in identifying questionable substance use respondents. Additionally, Morey (1996, 2003) described a linear regression strategy that successfully distinguished the groups described in Fals-Stewart's study with greater accuracy than the composite of *PIM, ALC*, and *DRG*. In this strategy, a predicted score is derived for both *ALC* and *DRG* based on the scores of other scales in the regression model. The difference between the predicted and observed scores is then used to indicate the probability of underreporting; this is thought to be a linear relation. Edens and Ruiz (2005) developed the Addictive Characteristics Scale (*ACS*) to assess personality characteristics indicative of addictive behavior. Their scale consists of the summed raw scores on *BOR-A*, *BOR-S*, and *ANT-E*. As these authors note, this algorithm is very similar to that described by Morey (1996), and these indicators have yet to be compared empirically.

Risk of Violence

The Aggression (*AGG*) scale of the PAI was constructed to estimate aggressive potential, a common assessment issue in forensic settings. Moderate scores on *AGG* indicate chronic anger, whereas marked elevations suggest substantial risk for the expression of anger. As discussed earlier, *AGG* has been found useful in the prediction of violence, institutional misbehavior, and recidivism in forensic settings. Because of the scale's soft floors, low scores can be interpreted as meekness or aggression avoidance. *AGG* subscales correspond to the three major elements of aggression identified in factor analytic work on the construct (e.g., Riley & Treiber, 1989): Aggressive Attitude (*AGG-A*), Verbal Aggression (*AGG-V*), and Physical Aggression (*AGG-P*). The relative elevation of subscales suggests the typical mode through which anger is expressed. For example, a moderate elevation on *AGG-A* but not the other subscales would suggest an individual who experiences but does not express anger, whereas more explosive individuals might be likely to demonstrate elevations on *AGG-P*.

Elevations on several other scales (e.g., *ANT, BOR*, and *MAN*) also elevate the risk of behavioral acting out and recidivism. Research has found *ANT* and *ANT-E* in particular to exhibit accuracy in the classification of recidivists (Salekin et al., 1998). In addition, Morey (1996) developed the Violence Potential Index (*VPI*) to increment the utility of the PAI in assessing risk. The *VPI* samples 20 indicators of violence potential based on PAI scale elevations or configurations, such as impulsivity and sensation seeking. The *VPI* has demonstrated an anticipated pattern of correlations (Edens et al., 2001; Morey, 1996; Wang et al., 1997). Scores of 9 (1 standard deviation above the mean of the clinical standardization sample) and 17 (2 *SD*s) were suggested by Morey (2003) as indicative of moderate and marked risk for violence, respectively.

Suicide

Suicide risk is another common concern in forensic settings. The Suicidal Ideation (*SUI*) scale was designed to indicate suicide potential, and, as discussed, encouraging validity data exist for *SUI* from several forensic samples. Several issues should be kept in mind when predicting suicide based on an observed score on *SUI*. First, the base rate of suicide is generally quite low and is variable across populations. The base rate in the sample from which the data are being collected must be kept carefully in mind, and inflexible cut scores are not recommended. However, scores above 85*T* typically suggest a need for close monitoring or other precautions. Second, *SUI* is a measure of ideation, not probability, and it has an extremely high ceiling. Individuals can achieve scores well above 70*T* without being at imminent risk for suicide. In fact, most clinical patients score between 60 and 69*T*. Third, the adverse consequences of a false negative are typically worse than those of a false positive. Therefore, despite the facts just mentioned, it is a good idea to follow up even moderate elevations on *SUI*. For example, it may be useful to know if current ideation is associated with past attempts by an individual who appears to have learned more adaptive coping strategies or is an emerging tendency to see suicide as a solution to the individual's problems. Finally, *SUI* is a measure of suicidal ideation, not a measure of the probability of the occurrence of suicide. Although most individuals who commit suicide tend to ideate around the issue as well, the two factors are somewhat independent. Many individuals in clinical samples ideate without acting on their suicidal thoughts, whereas some suicides are committed by individuals who appear to spend little time planning or ruminating about the act. The Suicide Potential Index (*SPI*) is composed of 20 configural indices of suicide potential independent of *SUI* (e.g., substance use, impulsivity), and it was developed to increment *SUI* in the prediction of suicidal behavior. The Wang and Rogers et al. (1997) and Rogers et al. (1998) studies cited earlier found significant positive correlations between suicidal behavior and other measures of suicidality. Morey (1996) recommends a score of 13 on the *SPI*, which is 1 *SD* above the mean of the clinical standardization sample and 2 *SDs* above the mean of the community sample, as indicative of increased risk for suicide. However, the *SPI* may also be treated as a dimension higher scores on which are associated with higher suicide risk. *NIM* appears to moderate the relation between *SUI* and *SPI*, suggesting that an elevated *SPI* score with a *NIM* score in the normal range is worthy of particular attention (Morey, 2003).

Treatment Planning

The PAI includes two indices directly relevant to treatment planning. The Treatment Rejection Scale (*RXR*) is a measure of attitudes that could negatively affect motivation for treatment. Individuals achieving high scores on *RXR* may be unmotivated to change, may be unable to recognize problems or their responsibility in the generation or maintenance of problems, or may lack psychological mindedness or interest in self-improvement. It is quite rare for treatment-seeking individuals to achieve scores in the moderate range, as 50*T* on the PAI profile represents the average treatment resistance of community individuals, which is predictably quite high. Conversely, scores below 20*T* may represent desperation or negative dissimulation, neither of which are typically associated with smooth and productive treatment.

Motivation for treatment is not the lone indicator of good treatment response. The Treatment Process Index (*TPI*) is a configural index developed to predict treatment amenability (Morey, 1996). Indices such as hostility, low insight, and limited social supports are harbingers of a difficult treatment process independent of motivation for change. High scores on *RXR* generally indicate resistance to beginning therapy. Individuals without *RXR* elevations but with TPI elevations may be motivated, at least initially, but the treatment is likely to be characterized by either early discontinuation or long length as well as reversals and high levels of therapist frustration.

LIMITATIONS OF THE PAI IN FORENSIC SETTINGS

The validity data presented earlier suggest that the PAI is amenable to use in a wide variety of forensic assessment contexts. Any self-report instrument has unique advantages over other methods of forensic assessment, including efficiency, standardization, large normative samples, and the capacity to capture the phenomenology of the respondent from his or her point of view. The low reading requirements, breadth of coverage, relative brevity, and ease of interpretation due to recognizable scale names related to commonly used constructs represent advantages over other self-report methods of forensic assessment. The PAI also appears to stand up well against contemporary legal criteria (Morey, Warner, & Hopwood, in preparation) and has several advantages over other multiscale instruments. Administrative advantages include short length, low required reading level, and scale names that represent the constructs being measured (Rogers, 2003). One psychometric advantage is that, because the scales are composed of nonoverlapping items, artifactual scale intercorrelations are reduced and discriminant validy is thereby enhanced. Also, item response theory was used in item selection to ensure the appropriate depth of coverage across the full range of severity for each clinical construct.

Despite these reasons to recommend the PAI in forensic settings, several limitations of the PAI in these settings should be noted. These have to do with both its structure and the current lack of research on some of its specific uses. One structural limitation of any self-report instrument is that it requires the examinee to be literate. If the examinee is illiterate, the items could be administered in interview format, although no research has been conducted thus far on the effects of this deviation from standardized administration on the validity of the test. Another feature of any self-report instrument is that response sets must be kept carefully in mind, and forensic decisions based on PAI data should always be incremented with data from other sources. The PAI is equipped with validity and clinical scales to assess the effects of disordered or compromised thinking on test validity, but individuals with severe cognitive deficits or disordered thinking are likely to produce a profile with significant distortion due to idiosyncratic or random responding. Additionally, the PAI does not measure every potentially relevant construct of clinical interest. For example, eating disorders are not directly assessed by the PAI, although these and other clinical disorders tend to produce characteristic profiles (Tasca et al., 2002). Finally, more research on the PAI in forensic contexts would be helpful. For example, research on the validity of *DRG* and *SCZ* has been mixed (e.g., Edens et al., 2001), and more work is necessary before firm conclusions (e.g., norm-specific cut scores) can be drawn about these scales.

CASE EXAMPLE

Lionel was a single, 26-year-old African-American man with 12 years of education employed as a fry cook at the time of the evaluation. He was serving a 3-year probation for writing checks with insufficient funds, which his probation officer suspected was related to his maintenance of a cocaine (crack) habit. Lionel denied any current or past problems with substance abuse, said that he had only experimented with drugs as a teenager, and had generally complied with probation conditions. However, he was videotaped leaving the residence of a known crack dealer and tested positive for cocaine shortly thereafter. He was informed by his probation officer that he must either comply with a full substance abuse evaluation and a week of daily urine screens or be in violation of probation. He complied but asserted that the positive drug test results were wrong and that his probation officer was out to get him.

Upon presenting for the evaluation, Lionel completed the PAI and a clinical interview. During the interview, he reiterated that he felt he had no mental health or substance abuse problems requiring treatment. He did describe a long history of legal problems of an aggressive nature. He noted that his attitude had always been that "the only way to survive is to cover your back and look over your shoulder." He had been fired from several jobs during the previous 5 years for poor performance. He declined to discuss his family history, but records indicated that he was the only child of separated parents from a low-income urban area and that his parents endured many legal problems of their own.

During the week-long series of daily drug screens that followed completion of the PAI, two of the tests were positive for cocaine. At this point, Lionel was referred for outpatient substance abuse treatment. After 2 weeks of treatment and two more positive screens following the evaluation, he finally admitted to the daily use of cocaine for nearly 9 years. He also described, somewhat boastfully, how he had avoided detection. During the first 6 weeks of treatment, nearly all of the urine samples were positive for cocaine. Clinical staff described him as defiant and hostile during this time, and he was sent to a therapeutic community. However, he was removed after 2 months due to frequent aggressive behavior and lack of clinical improvement. He was then placed in a 28-day inpatient program, from which he graduated successfully. He returned to the original outpatient facility and graduated, then completed his probation with no further incident. He went on to take a job in landscaping and enroll in a community college part-time.

Lionel's PAI full scale and subscale profiles are presented in Figures 4.1 and 4.2, respectively, and his supplemental indices are shown in Table 4.3. The following sections discuss various elements of the test results as they pertain to this case.

Validity of Test Results

Positive impression management is a high base rate phenomenon in many forensic evaluation settings but is particularly prevalent under conditions such as those in this case. Lionel's PIM and Defensiveness Index scores fall within normal limits, likely indicating his ability and willingness to admit to certain problems unrelated to substance use. However, the Cashel Discriminant Function was extremely high, which is typical of the protocols of individuals who intentionally positively dissimulate. In addition, Lionel's ALC and DRG predicted scores were far higher than the obtained scores, indicating a personality highly prone to substance use but not forthcoming regarding substance use. Interestingly, his Rogers Discriminant Function was also somewhat elevated, suggesting some negative impression management, perhaps related to his expression of anxiety, trauma, or self-harm. In any case, his validity profile suggests efforts at distorting his self-presentation, and certain clinical scale elevations (e.g., the ANT-E elevation and the high DOM–low WRM configuration) suggest an individual who may value his ability to mislead or deceive people. The remainder of the profile should be interpreted with these results in mind.

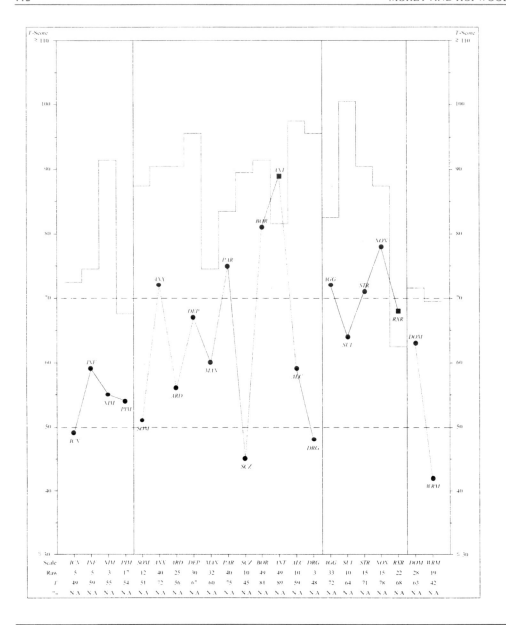

Plotted *T*-scores are based on a census-matched standardization sample of 1,000 normal adults.
■ indicates that the score is more than two standard deviations above the mean for a sample of 1,246 clinical patients.
◆ indicates that the scale has more than 20% missing items.

FIG. 4.1.   PAI full scale profile for Lionel.

Clinical Features

Lionel's clinical scale configuration depicts him as impulsive (*ANT-S*), labile (*BOR-A*),
hostile (*PAR-R*), hypervigilant (*PAR-H*), egocentric (*ANT-E*), and aggressive (*AGG*). These
traits may have helped him survive in a difficult early environment, as he suggested during
the interview, but they have led to interpersonal impoverishment, abuse, and mistrust

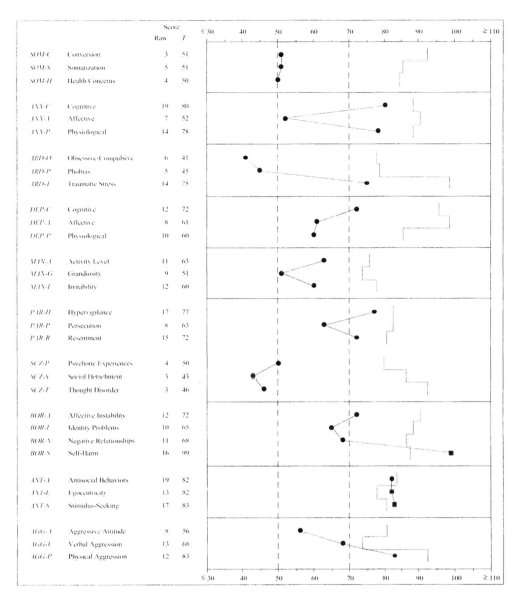

		Score		≤ 30	40	50	60	70	80	90	100	≥ 110
		Raw	T									
SOM-C	Conversion	3	51									
SOM-S	Somatization	5	51									
SOM-H	Health Concerns	4	50									
ANX-C	Cognitive	19	80									
ANX-A	Affective	7	52									
ANX-P	Physiological	14	78									
ARD-O	Obsessive-Compulsive	6	41									
ARD-P	Phobias	5	45									
ARD-T	Traumatic Stress	14	75									
DEP-C	Cognitive	12	72									
DEP-A	Affective	8	61									
DEP-P	Physiological	10	60									
MAN-A	Activity Level	11	63									
MAN-G	Grandiosity	9	51									
MAN-I	Irritability	12	60									
PAR-H	Hypervigilance	17	77									
PAR-P	Persecution	8	63									
PAR-R	Resentment	15	72									
SCZ-P	Psychotic Experiences	4	50									
SCZ-S	Social Detachment	3	43									
SCZ-T	Thought Disorder	3	46									
BOR-A	Affective Instability	12	72									
BOR-I	Identity Problems	10	65									
BOR-N	Negative Relationships	11	68									
BOR-S	Self-Harm	16	99									
ANT-A	Antisocial Behaviors	19	82									
ANT-E	Egocentricity	13	82									
ANT-S	Stimulus-Seeking	17	83									
AGG-A	Aggressive Attitude	8	56									
AGG-A	Verbal Aggression	13	68									
AGG-P	Physical Aggression	12	83									

Plotted T-scores are based on a census-matched standardization sample of 1,000 normal adults.
■ indicates that the score is more than two standard deviations above the mean for a sample of 1,246 clinical patients.
◆ indicates that the scale has more than 20% missing items.

FIG. 4.2. PAI subscale profile for Lionel.

(*NON, BOR, PAR, AGG*) and intrapersonal turmoil and dissatisfaction (*ANX-C, ANX-P, BOR-S*). Substance use is common among individuals with similar profiles (predicted *ALC* and *DRG* scores), and if present, it complicates the clinical picture and treatment process.

Lionel's clinical scale profile suggests antisocial personality disorder; he is likely to be unreliable and irresponsible and, as his intake data suggest, has had difficulties in the past with occupational or educational responsibilities. Also consistent with his intake, the data suggest a history of antisocial behavior that may have manifested as a conduct disorder

TABLE 4.3
PAI Supplemental Indices for Case Example: Lionel

Index	Value	T
Defensiveness Index	3	51
Cashel Discriminant Function	192.69	87
Malingering Index	0	44
Rogers Discriminant Function	1.91	77
Suicide Potential Index	12	78
Violence Potential Index	11	93
Treatment Process Index	12	107
ALC Estimated Score	(25*T* higher than *ALC*)	84
DRG Estimated Score	(41*T* higher than *DRG*)	89

during adolescence (*ANT-A*). His practice of manipulating his probation officer in order to maintain his drug use while passing urine tests is typical of such individuals. He is likely to be egocentric and show little regard for others or normative societal expectations (*ANT-E*). He is likely to be willing to do nearly anything to meet his own needs and to experience little lasting remorse about his effect on others. His behavior is also likely to be reckless; he can be expected to entertain risks that are potentially dangerous to himself and to those around him (*ANT-S*).

In addition to antisocial traits, he obtained significant clinical elevations across the BOR subscales. His emotional lability and mood swings (*BOR-A*) are likely to interfere significantly with his interpersonal life (*BOR-N, NON*) and to unpredictably manifest as anger (*AGG-P*). Associated with unstable affect is marked impulsivity (*BOR-S*); this may indicate his substance use or other masochistic behaviors involving spending, sex, or self-harm, particularly during times of affective turmoil. The combination of *BOR, ANT, ARD-T*, and *AGG* elevations, as well as his reluctance to discuss his family history, increases the probability that he experienced violence or abuse during his childhood.

Not surprisingly, given what is known about his development and the picture emerging from the clinical scales, he is likely to be a hypervigilant individual who often questions and mistrusts the motives of those around him (*PAR-H*). Lionel's interview and PAI data indicate that he believes others will reliably misuse him if given the opportunity, and he has decided to get to them first. He is probably extremely sensitive to perceived slights (*PAR-R*) and is likely to be cold, suspicious, and hostile in daily interactions, to expect the worst from others, and to have few (*NON*), heavily strained, relationships (*BOR-N*).

Lionel indicated some experience of overt physical signs of tension and stress, such as sweaty palms, trembling hands, irregular heartbeat, and shortness of breath (*ANX-P*), as well as some cognitive anxiety and depression (*ANX-C, DEP-C*). This pattern suggests that Lionel may occasionally experience panic symptoms. However, he does not report a strong subjective experience of tension or major difficulties relaxing (*ANX-A*). This may represent the experience of a man who continues to rationalize a way of life that he is increasingly dissatisfied with and may help explain what appears to be a relatively dramatic turnaround in the following months.

Finally, the low score on *DRG*, coupled with the high estimated score on *DRG*, suggests that underreporting of substance misuse is likely. The estimated *DRG* score of 89*T* would place him in a range typical of individuals receiving a substance dependence diagnosis.

Self-Concept

Given the contrast between his attitude at intake and what is presumed to have been a subsequent turn toward a healthier lifestyle, his self-concept appears to have been shifting at the time of the evaluation. His posture was tough, cold, and guarded, and he gave the impression that he was uninterested in change (*RXR*), but underneath this veneer he was anxious and dissatisfied with his life (*DEP, ANX-P, ANX-C, STR*). Although he maintained his independence and attributed most of his problems to others (*PAR-R*), his inability to tolerate negative interpersonal transactions (*BOR-N*) likely had a strong influence on his self-concept, often causing him to lash out impulsively at others or himself (*AGG-P, BOR-S*) in response to interpersonal disappointment or frustration. This pattern may have contributed to Lionel's involvement with an impoverished social network with little prospects for improvement (*NON*), typical of a crack cocaine–using population, and Lionel probably considered solitary substance use a more satisfying alternative.

Interpersonal and Social Environment

Lionel's PAI profile suggests that he views relationships as a means to an end rather than as a source of satisfaction and that he anticipates others will do the same (*ANT-E, DOM*). He is not likely to be perceived by others as a warm and friendly person (*WRM*), although he is not necessarily lacking in social skills and he appears to have the capacity to be reasonably effective in social interactions. Those who know him well are likely to see him as shrewd, competitive, and independent. As discussed previously, Lionel was experiencing considerable turmoil at the time of the evaluation, largely as a result of environmental stressors, including legal, occupational, and financial problems (*STR*). A primary source of stress probably involves relationship issues because he believes that his social relationships offer him little support; family relationships may be somewhat distant or ridden with conflict, and friends may not be available when needed (*NON*).

Treatment Considerations

Lionel's angry (*AGG-V*), resentful (*PAR-R*), and combative (*AGG-P*) style proved to be difficult for treatment staff. His responses suggest that he believes that he is generally in control of angry feelings and impulses and expresses an angry outburst relatively infrequently. However, when he loses control of his anger, he is likely to respond with more extreme displays of anger, including damage to property and threats to assault others (*ANT-A, AGG-P*). Some of these displays may be sudden and unexpected, as he may not display his anger readily when it is experienced. It is likely that those around him are intimidated by his temper and the potential for physical violence. It should also be noted that his risk for aggressive behavior is further exacerbated by the presence of a number of features—such as agitation (*ANX-C*), a limited capacity for empathy (*ANT-E*), impulsivity (*BOR-S, ANT-S*), and affective lability (*BOR-A*)—that have been found to be associated with increased potential for violence.

Based on the PAI, Lionel would appear to be a very poor candidate for psychotherapy (*TPI, RXR*) at the time of the evaluation. Lionel's stated interest in and motivation for treatment is well below the average for adults who are not being seen in a therapeutic setting, and his treatment motivation is substantially lower than is typical of individuals being seen in such a setting (*RXR*). His responses suggest that he was willing to take little responsibility for the many difficulties in his life and that he has no desire to make personal changes, despite the fact that several areas of his life did not seem to be going well. He seemed to put the responsibility for changing his life on treatment staff but was openly hostile to them, indicating an area of conflict that may have been useful in engaging Lionel in treatment. However, suggesting such conflict directly with Lionel would likely be ineffective, given his affective lability and interpersonal mistrust. One would not predict based on the PAI results that Lionel would seek therapy on his own initiative, and resistance would be considerable in any nonvoluntary treatment. In addition, the elevated *TPI* indicates that the combination of problems that he reported portend that treatment would be an uphill struggle and that the treatment process would likely be arduous, with numerous reversals. These reversals were evident in his progression through three progressively more restrictive treatment programs; the *TPI* also suggests that his dramatic improvement during inpatient treatment should be regarded with some suspicion. Either he responded well to a heavily structured and restrictive environment or he continued his pattern of manipulating the authorities in order to maintain his self-defeating habits. Follow-up data would be useful in tracking the effects of treatment and his apparent turnaround as well as providing confirmatory evidence that he was not, in fact, still "fooling" the system by faking good.

Special Considerations

This case illustrates a number of features common in forensic settings, including impression management, substance misuse, poor treatment compliance, and impulse control problems. Lionel's apparent turnaround after progressively more intensive treatment efforts may suggest that removing an individual with an unstable and poorly articulated sense of self from a malignant environment (the culture of crack users) may have been a necessary first step in treatment. Typically, individuals with deep-seated character pathology such as is depicted in his PAI profile have very poor prognoses in psychotherapy, and when psychosocial treatment is successful, it is long and difficult. His intake profile indicates little interest in change and a tendency to attribute responsibility for his problems to others. However, subsequent information suggests an individual who, once off the substances and away from the environment that got him into trouble, was able to take some responsibility for change and to succeed. The relationship between his personality and his drug use would be clarified by follow-up PAI data, which would also be very helpful in confirming this change. If his tendency to be suspicious, hostile, and cold was mostly a function of his environment and his need to hide from the police, if his affective lability and stress were the physiological and financial results of substance abuse, and if his feelings of nonsupport were the result of a support network that had given up on him or was genuinely untrustworthy, these problems might remit given a clean lifestyle. However, in the presence of the prominent antisocial traits indicated by the PAI, it is reasonable to be skeptical about a full recovery and to anticipate and plan for eventual relapse.

REFERENCES

Alterman, A.I., Zaballero, A.R., Lin, M.M., Siddiqui, N., Brown, L.S, Rutherford, M.J., & McDermatt, P.A. (1995). Personality Assessment Inventory (PAI) scores of lower-socioeconomic African American and Latino methadone maintenance patients. *Assessment, 2*, 91–100.

Bagby, M.R., Nicholson, R.A., Bacchiochi, J.R., Ryder, A.G., & Bury, A.S. (2002). The predictive capacity of the MMPI-2 and PAI validity scales and indexes to detect coached and uncoached feigning. *Journal of Personality Assessment, 78*, 69–86.

Bagge, C., Nickell, A., Stepp, S., Durrett, C., Jackson, K., & Trull, T.J. (2004). Borderline personality disorder features predict negative outcomes 2 years later. *Journal of Abnormal Psychology, 113*, 279–288.

Ban, T.A., Fjetland, O.K., Kutcher, M., & Morey, L.C. (1993). CODE-DD: Development of a diagnostic scale for depressive disorders. In I. Hindmarch & P. Stonier (Eds.), *Human psychopharmacology: 4.* Measures and methods (pp. 73–85). Chichester, UK: John Wiley and Sons.

Beck, A.T., & Steer, R.A. (1987). *Beck Depression Inventory manual.* San Antonio: The Psychological Corporation.

Beck, A.T., & Steer, R.A. (1988). *Beck Hopelessness Scale manual.* San Antonio: The Psychological Corporation.

Bell, M.J., Billington, R., & Becker, B. (1985). A scale for the assessment of object relations: Reliability, validity, and factorial invariance. *Journal of Clinical Psychology, 42*, 733–741.

Bell-Pringle, V.J., Pate, J.L., & Brown, R.C. (1997). Assessment of borderline personality disorder using the MMPI-2 and the Personality Assessment Inventory. *Assessment, 4*, 131–139.

Bianchini, K.J., Etherton, J.L., & Greve, K.W. (2004). Diagnosing cognitive malingering in patients with work-related pain: Four cases. *Journal of Forensic Neuropsychology, 4*(1), 65–85.

Blanchard, D.D., McGrath, R.E., Pogge, D.L., & Khadivi, A. (2003). A comparison of the PAI and MMPI-2 as predictors of faking bad in college students. *Journal of Personality Assessment, 80*, 197–205.

Boccaccini, M.T., & Brodsky, S.L. (1999). Diagnostic test usage by forensic psychologists in emotional injury cases. *Professional Psychology: Research and Practice, 30*, 253–259.

Boyle, G.J., & Lennon, T. (1994). Examination of the reliability and validity of the Personality Assessment Inventory. *Journal of Psychopathology and Behavioral. Assessment, 16*, 173–187.

Buffington-Vollum, J., Edens, J.F., Johnson, D.W., & Johnson, J.K. (2002). Psychopathy as a predictor of institutional misbehavior among sex offenders: A prospective replication. *Criminal Justice and Behavior, 29*, 497–511.

Butcher, J.N., Dahlstrom, W.G., Graham, J.R., Tellegen, A., & Kaemmer, B. (1989). *Minnesota Multiphasic Personality Inventory-2* (MMPI-2): Manual for administration and scoring. Minneapolis: University of Minnesota Press.

Calhoun, P.S., Earnst, K.S., Tucker, D.D., Kirby, A.C., & Beckham, J.C. (2000). Feigning combat-related posttraumatic stress disorder on the Personality Assessment Inventory. *Journal of Personality Assessment, 75*, 338–350.

Caperton, J.D., Edens, J.F., & Johnson, J.K. (2004). Predicting sex offender institutional adjustment and treatment compliance using the Personality Assessment Inventory. *Psychological Assessment, 16*, 187–191.

Caruso, K.A., Benedek, D.M., Auble, P.M., & Bernet, W. (2003). Concealment of psychopathology in forensic evaluations: A pilot study of intentional and uninsightful dissimulators. *Journal of the American Academy of Psychiatry and Law, 31*, 444–450.

Cashel, M.L., Rogers, R., Sewell, K., & Martin-Cannici, C. (1995). The Personality Assessment Inventory (PAI) and the detection of defensiveness. *Assessment, 2*, 333–342.

Cherepon, J.A., & Prinzhorn, B. (1994). Personality Assessment Inventory (PAI) profiles of adult female abuse survivors. *Assessment, 1*, 393–399.

Clarkin, J.F., Hull, J.W., Yeomans, F., Kakuma, T., & Caitor, J. (1994). Antisocial traits as modifiers of treatment response in borderline inpatients. *Journal of Psychotherapy Practice and Research, 3*, 307–312.

Costa, P.T., & McCrae, R.R. (1992). Normal personality in clinical practice: The NEO Personality Inventory. *Psychological Assessment, 4*, 5–13.

Cull, J.G., & Gill, W.S. (1982). *Suicide Probability Scale manual.* Los Angeles, CA: Western Psychological Services.

DelSol, C., Margolin, G., & John, R.S. (2003). A typology of maritally violent men and correlates of violence in a community sample. *Journal of Marriage and Family, 65*, 635–651.

Douglas, K.S., Hart, S.D., & Kropp, P.R. (2001). Validity of the Personality Assessment Inventory for forensic assessments. *International Journal of Offender Therapy and Comparative Criminology, 45*(2), 183–197.

Edens, J.F., Cruise, K.R., & Buffington-Vollum, J.K. (2001). Forensic and correctional applications of the Personality Assessment Inventory. *Behavioral Sciences and the Law, 19*, 519–543.

Edens, J.F., Hart, S.D., Johnson, D.W., Johnson, J.K., & Olver, M.E. (2000). Use of the Personality Assessment Inventory to assess psychopathy in offender populations. *Psychological Assessment, 12*, 132–139.

Edens, J.F., & Ruiz, M.A. (2005). *PAI Interpretive Report for Correctional Settings (PAI-CS)*. Odessa, FL: Psychological Assessment Resources.

Edwards, D.W., Scott, C.L., Yarvis, R.M., Paizis, C.L., & Panizzon, M.S. (2003). Impulsiveness, impulse aggression, personality disorder, and spousal violence. *Violence and Victims, 18*, 3–14.

Evershed, S., Tennant, A., Boomer, D., Rees, A., Barkham, M., & Watson, A. (2003). Practice-based outcomes of dialectical behaviour therapy (DBT) targeting anger and violence, with male forensic patients: A pragmatic and non-contemporaneous comparison. *Criminal Behaviour and Mental Health, 13*, 198–213.

Exner, J.E. (1993). *The Rorschach: A comprehensive system*. Asheville, NC: Rorschach Workshops.

Fals-Stewart, W. (1996). The ability of individuals with psychoactive substance use disorders to escape detection by the Personality Assessment Inventory. *Psychological Assessment, 8*, 60–68.

Fals-Stewart, W., & Lucente, S. (1997). Identifying positive dissimulation substance-abusing individuals on the Personality Assessment Inventory: A cross-validation study. *Journal of Personality Assessment, 68*, 455–469.

Gaies, L.A. (1993). Malingering of depression on the Personality Assessment Inventory. (Doctoral dissertation, University of South Florida, 1993). *Dissertation Abstracts International, 55*, 6711.

George, J.M., & Wagner, E. (1995). Correlations between the Hand Test Pathology score and Personality Assessment Inventory scales for pain clinic patients. *Perceptual and Motor Skills, 80*, 1377–1378.

Greenstein, D.S. (1995). Relationship between frequent nightmares, psychopathology, and boundaries among incarcerated male inmates. (Doctoral dissertation, Adler School of Professional Psychology, 1995). *Dissertation Abstracts International, 55*, 4119.

Hamilton, M. (1960). A rating scale for depression. *Journal of Neurology, Neurosurgery, and Psychiatry, 23*, 56–62.

Hare, R.D. (1985). Comparison of procedures for the assessment of psychopathy. *Journal of Consulting and Clinical Psychology, 53*, 7–16.

Hare, R.D., Harpur, T.J., Hakstian, A.R., Forth, A.E., Hart, S.D., & Newman, J.P. (1990). The Revrsed Psychopathy Checklist: Reliability and Factor structure. *Psychological Assessment: A Journal of Consulting and Clinical Psychology, 2*(3), 338–341.

Hart, S.D., Cox, D.N., & Hare, R.D. (1995). *Psychopathy Checklist: Screening version*. Toronto, Ontario, Canada: Multi-Health Systems.

Holden, R.R. (1989). Disguise and the structured self-report assessment of psychopathology: II. A clinical replication. *Journal of Clinical Psychology, 45*, 583–586.

Holden, R.R., Book, A.S., Edwards, M.J., Wasylkiw, L., & Starzyk, K.B. (2003). Experimental faking in self-reported psychopathology: Unidimensional or mulitidimensional? *Personality and Individual Differences, 35*, 1107–1117.

Holden, R.R., & Fekken, G.C. (1990). Structured psychopathological test item characteristics and validity. *Psychological Assessment, 2*, 35–40.

Holmes, G.E., Williams, C.L., & Haines, J. (2001). Motor vehicle accident trauma exposure: Personality profiles associated with posttraumatic diagnoses. *Anxiety, Stress and Coping, 14*, 301–313.

Holmes, T.H., & Rahe, R.H. (1967). The social readjustment rating scale. *Journal of Psychosomatic Research, 11*, 213–218.

Jackson, D.N. (1970). A sequential system for personality scale development. In C.D. Spielberger (Ed.), *Current topics in clinical and community psychology*, Vol. 2 (pp. 62–97). New York: Academic Press.

Karlin, B.E., Creech, S.K., Grimes, J.S., Clark, T.S., Meagher, M.W., & Morey, L.C. (in press). The use of the Personality Assessment Inventory with individuals with chronic pain. *Journal of Clinical Psychology*.

Kellogg, S.H., Ho, A., Bell, K., Schluger, R.P., McHugh, P.F., McClary, K.A., & Kreek, M.J. (2002). The Personality Assessment Inventory Drug Problems Scale: A validity analysis. *Journal of Personality Assessment, 79*, 73–84.

Klonsky, E.D. (2004). Performance of Personality Assessment Inventory and Rorschach indices of schizophrenia in a public psychiatric hospital. *Psychological Services, 1*(2), 107–110.

Kurtz, J.E., & Morey, L.C. (2001). Use of structured self-report assessment to diagnose borderline personality disorder during major depressive episodes. *Assessment, 8*, 291–300.

Kurtz, J.E., Morey, L.C., & Tomarken, A. (1992, March). *The concurrent validity study of three self-report measures of borderline personality.* Paper presented at the meetings of the Society for Personality Assessment, Washington, DC.

Lally, S.J. (2003). What tests are acceptable for use in forensic evaluations? A survey of experts. *Professional Psychology: Research and Practice, 34*, 491–498.

Liljequist, L., Kinder, B.N., & Schinka, J.A. (1998) An investigation of malingering posttraumatic stress disorder on the Personality Assessment Inventory. *Journal of Personality Assessment, 71*, 322–336.

Loevinger, J. (1957). Objective tests as instruments of psychological theory. *Psychological Reports, 3*, 635–694.

Loranger, A.W. (1988). *Personality disorders examination manual.* Yonkers, NY: DV Communications.

McLellan, A.T., Kushner, H., Metzger, D., Peters, R., Smith, I., Grissam, G., et al. (1992). The fifth edition of the Addiction Severity Index. *Journal of Substance Abuse Treatment, 9*, 199–213.

Montag, I., & Levin, J. (1994). The Five Factor Model and psychopathology in nonclinical samples. *Personality and Individual Differences, 17*, 1–7.

Morey, L.C. (1991). *The Personality Assessment Inventory professional manual.* Odessa, FL: Psychological Assessment Resources.

Morey, L.C. (1995). Critical issues in construct validation: Comment on Boyle and Lennon (1994). *Journal of Psychopathology and Behavioral Assessment, 17*, 393–401.

Morey, L.C. (1996). *An interpretive guide to the Personality Assessment Inventory.* Odessa, FL: Psychological Assessment Resources.

Morey, L.C. (2003). *Essentials of PAI assessment.* Hoboken, NJ: Wiley.

Morey, L.C., & Hopwood, C.J. (2004). Efficiency of a strategy for detecting back random responding on the Personality Assessment Inventory. *Psychological Assessment, 16*, 197–200.

Morey, L.C., & Lanier, V.W. (1998). Operating characteristics of six response distortion indicators for the Personality Assessment Inventory. *Assessment, 5*, 203–214.

Morey, L.C., Waugh, M.H., & Blashfield, R.K. (1985). MMPI scales for DSM-III personality disorders: Their derivation and correlates. *Journal of Personality Assessment, 49*, 245–251.

Parker, J.D., Daleiden, E.L., & Simpson, C.A. (1999). Personality Assessment Inventory substance-use scales: Convergent and discriminant relations with the Addiction Severity Index in a residential chemical dependence treatment setting. *Psychological Assessment, 11*, 507–513.

Peebles, J., & Moore, R.J. (1998). Detecting socially desirable responding with the Personality Assessment Inventory: The Positive Impression Management scale and the Defensiveness index. *Journal of Clinical Psychology, 54*, 621–628.

Peterson, G.W., Clark, D.A., & Bennett, B. (1989). The utility of MMPI subtle, obvious scales for detecting fake good and fake bad response sets. *Journal of Clinical Psychology, 45*, 575–583.

Procidano, M.E., & Heller, K. (1983). Measures of perceived social support from friends and from family: Three validation studies. *American Journal of Community Psychology, 11*, 1–24.

Riley, W.T., & Treiber, F.A. (1989). The validity of multidimensional self-report anger and hostility measures. *Journal of Clinical Psychology, 45*, 397–404.

Rogers, R. (2003). Forensic uses and abuses of psychological tests: Multi-scale inventories. *Journal of Psychiatric Practice, 9*, 316–320.

Rogers, R., Bagby, R.M., & Dickens, S.E. (1992). *Structured Interview of Reported Symptoms: Professional manual.* Odessa, FL: Psychological Assessment Resources.

Rogers, R., Flores, J., Ustad, K., & Sewell, K.W. (1995). Initial validation of the Personality Assessment Inventory: Spanish version with clients from Mexican American communities. *Journal of Personality Assessment, 64*, 340–348.

Rogers, R., Ornduff, S.R., & Sewell, K. (1993). Feigning specific disorders: A study of the Personality Assessment Inventory (PAI). *Journal of Personality Assessment, 60*(3), 554–561.

Rogers, R., Sewell, K.W., Morey, L.C., & Ustad, K.L. (1996). Detection of feigned mental disorders on the Personality Assessment Inventory: A discriminant analysis. *Journal of Personality Assessment, 67*, 629–640.

Rogers, R., Sewell, K.W., Ustad, K., Reinhardt, V., Edwards, W. (1995). The Referral Decision Scale with mentally disorder inmates: A preliminary study of convergent and discriminant validity. *Law and Human Behavior, 19*, 481–492.

Rogers, R., Ustad, K.L., & Salekin, R.T. (1998). Convergent validity of the Personality Assessment Inventory: A study of emergency referrals in a correctional setting. *Assessment, 5*, 3–12.

Ruiz, M.A., Dickinson, K.A., & Pincus, A.L. (2002). Concurrent validity of the Personality Assessment Inventory Alcohol Problems (ALC) scale in a college student sample. *Assessment, 9*, 261–270.

Salekin, R.T., Rogers, R., & Sewell, K.W. (1997). Construct validity of psychopathy in a female offender sample: A multitrait-multimethod evaluation. *Journal of Abnormal Psychology, 106*, 576–585.

Salekin, R.T., Rogers, R., Ustad, K.L., & Sewell, K.W. (1998). Psychopathy and recidivism among female inmates. *Law and Human Behavior, 22*, 109–128.

Schinka, J.A. (1995). PAI profiles in alcohol-dependent patients. *Journal of Personality Assessment, 65*, 35–51.

Schinka, J.A., & Borum, R. (1993). Readability of adult psychopathology inventories. *Psychological Assessment, 5*, 384–386.

Scragg, P., Bor, R., & Mendham, M.C. (2000). Feigning post-traumatic stress disorder on the PAI. *Clinical Psychology and Psychotherapy, 7*, 155–160.

Slick, D.J., Sherman, E.M.S., & Iverson, G.L. (1999). Diagnosing criteria for malingering neurocognitive dysfunction: Proposed standards for clinical practice and research. *The Clinical Neuropsychologist, 13*, 545–561.

Spielberger, C.D. (1988). State-Trait Anger Expression Inventory. Odessa, FL: Psychological Assessment Resources.

Tasca, G.A., Wood, J., Demidenko, N., & Bissada, H. (2002). Using the PAI with an eating disordered population: Scale characteristics, factor structure and differences among diagnostic groups. *Journal of Personality Assessment, 79*, 337–356.

Trapnell, P.D., & Wiggins, J.S. (1990). Extension of the Interpersonal Adjective Scale to include the big five dimensions of personality. *Journal of Personality and Social Psychology, 59*, 781–790.

Trull, T.J. (1995). Borderline personality disorder features in nonclinical young adults: I. Identification and validation. *Psychological Assessment, 7*, 33–41.

Trull, T.J., Useda, J.D., Conforti, K., & Doan, B.T. (1997). Borderline personality features in nonclinical young adults: Two year outcome. *Journal of Abnormal Psychology, 106*, 307–314.

Wagner, M.T., Wymer, J.H., Topping, K.B., & Pritchard, P.B. (in press). Use of the Personality Assessment Inventory as an efficacious and cost effective diagnostic tool for nonepileptic seizures. *Epilepsy and Behavior*.

Walters, G.D., Duncan, S.A., & Geyer, M.D. (2003). Predicting disciplinary adjustment in inmates undergoing forensic evaluation: A direct comparison of the PCL-R and the PAI. *Journal of Forensic Psychiatry and Psychiatry, 14*, 382–393.

Wang, E.W., & Diamond, P.M. (1999). Empirically identifying factors related to violence risk in corrections. *Behavioral Sciences and the Law, 17*, 377–389.

Wang, E.W., Rogers, R., Giles, C.L., Diamond, P.M., Herrington-Wang, L.E., & Taylor, E.R. (1997). A pilot study of the Personality Assessment Inventory (PAI) in corrections: Assessment of malingering, suicide risk, and aggression in male inmates. *Behavioral Sciences and the Law, 15*, 469–482.

Wiggins, J.S. (1966). Substantive dimensions of self-report in the MMPI item pool. *Psychological Monographs, 80* (22, Whole No. 630).

Wiggins, J.S. (1979). A psychological taxonomy of trait-descriptive terms: The interpersonal domain. *Journal of Personality and Social Psychology, 37*, 395–412.

Yeomans, F.E., Hull, J.W., & Clarkin, J.C. (1994). Risk factors for self-damaging acts in a borderline population. *Journal of Personality Disorders, 8*(1), 10–16.

Yudofsky, S.C., Silver, J.M., Jackson, W., Endicott, J., & Williams, D. (1986). The Overt Aggression Scale for the objective rating of verbal and physical aggression. *American Journal of Psychiatry, 143*, 35–39.

5

THE MILLON CLINICAL MULTIAXIAL INVENTORY—III

ROBERT J. CRAIG

JESS BROWN VA MEDICAL CENTER

DESCRIPTION AND PURPOSE OF THE INSTRUMENT

The Millon Clinical Multiaxial Inventory (Millon, 1983) as revised (MCMI II and MCMI–III; Millon, 1987, 1994, 1997) is a clinical test of personality designed to measure personality disorders and major psychiatric syndromes. The personality disorders assessed by the instrument are not isomorphic with official nomenclature (e.g., that in the *Diagnostic and Statistical Manual of Mental Disorders*, American Psychiatric Association [APA], 1983, 1987, 1994); rather they emanate from Millon's (1990) theory of the derivation of personality disorders. However, recent changes in the instrument bring it closer to the *DSM–IV* classification of personality disorders, although still not identical to it.

In its original version, the MCMI–I consisted of 11 personality scales (Schizoid-Asocial, Avoidant, Dependent-Submissive, Histrionic-Gregarious, Narcissistic, Antisocial-Aggressive, Compulsive-Conforming, Passive-Aggressive-Negativistic, Schizotypal-Schizoid, Borderline-Cycloid, and Paranoid) and 9 clinical syndrome scales (Anxiety, Somatoform, Hypomanic, Dysthymia, Alcohol Abuse, Drug Abuse, Psychotic Thinking, Psychotic Depression, and Psychotic Delusions). When the *DSM–III* was revised (*DSM–III–R*, APA, 1987), the MCMI–I was also revised, in part to account for additional personality disorders that were then added to the official diagnostic classification system. Thus the MCMI–II separated the Antisocial-Aggressive scale into two separate scales, Antisocial and Aggressive-Sadistic, and also added a Self-Defeating (Masochistic) Personality Disorder scale, bringing the number of personality disorder scales to 13, with no change in the number of clinical syndrome scales. When the *DSM–IV* (APA,

1994) was published, the aggressive and self-defeating personality disorders were eliminated from consideration in official classification, but a depressive personality disorder was added. The MCMI–II was then revised (Millon, 1994), in part to bring it closer to *DSM–IV*.

Millon believes that the self-defeating and aggressive personality styles/disorders "exist in nature," and hence they were retained as scales in the revision. However, a Depressive Personality Disorder scale was added as well as a scale measuring Post-Traumatic Stress Disorder. Hence the MCMI–III consists of 175 items assigned to 11 scales measuring "clinical personality patterns" (Schizoid, Avoidant, Depressive, Dependent, Histrionic, Narcissistic, Antisocial, Aggressive, Compulsive, Negativistic [Passive-Aggressive (Negativistic)], Self-Defeating [Masochistic], 3 scales measuring "severe personality pathology" (Schizotypal, Borderline, Paranoid), 8 "clinical syndrome" scales (Anxiety, Somatoform, Bipolar: Manic, Dysthymia, Alcohol Dependence, Drug Dependence, and Post-Traumatic Stress Disorder), and 3 "severe clinical syndrome" scales (Thought Disorder, Major Depression, Delusional Disorder).

The test also features four validity scales, termed "modifier indices." A Validity Index consists of improbable items, which, if endorsed "true," bring the test answers into question. An example of such an improbable item would be "I play quarterback for the Chicago Bears" (this is not an actual item on the test but is presented here as an illustration). The Disclosure scale assesses the degree to which a respondent is providing too little information and thus is essentially secretive and withholding or frank and self-revealing. The Desirability Index assesses whether the respondent endorsed items in an overly positive manner, and the Debasement Index assesses whether the respondent endorsed items to present an unfavorable picture of present functioning. Disclosure, Desirability, and Debasement are referred to as "modifier indices" rather than validity scales because high or low scores on these scales result in adjustment in scores on the other MCMI–III scales.

Administration time is approximately 30 minutes. The instrument was designed for use with adults who are seeking mental health services and have at least a eighth-grade education, and it is available in English and in Spanish in paper-and-pencil or computer-administered formats. Audiocassette recordings are also available for clients with special needs. It may be hand-scored, using templates available from the test's distributor, or computer-scored. Two computer narrative interpretive reports are available. One is published by Pearson Assessments (Millon, Millon, & Davis, 2003), and the other is marketed through Psychological Assessment Resources (Craig, 2006). Pearson Assessments also distributes an interpretive report specific to correctional settings that presents information on reaction to authority, risk of violence, risk of escape, impulsivity, sexual victimization, malingering potential, response to crowding or isolation, suicidal potential, and amenability to treatment and rehabilitation. However, graduate training in psychodiagnostic assessment is required for test interpretation, and users of these interpretive reports should adhere to test ethics of the American Psychological Association pertaining to computer interpretive reports.

HISTORY OF THE TEST'S DEVELOPMENT

The *DSM–III* (APA, 1983) introduced the multiaxial format that required diagnostic information on five axes. Axis II required an evaluation to determine whether the patient had a personality disorder. Personality assessment achieved a new focus, since it became apparent that (a) an understanding of the patients's personality was required to understand the patient's clinical condition, (b) personality disorders affect the course and treatment of Axis I conditions, and (c) personality disorders could be the focus of treatment in their own right. Furthermore, the transition of the locus of care from inpatient to outpatient settings made the treatment of personality disorders more feasible. These developments stimulated new interest and research into personality and personality disorders in both psychiatry and psychology.

Psychiatry placed emphasis on its historical strength and developed a spate of structured and semistructured clinical interviews to assess for Axis II disorders. These structured interviews were subsequently revised with the publication of the *DSM–IV*. Concurrently psychology relied on one of its historical strengths—knowledge of test construction—and developed a spate of tests for personality disorders primarily using self-report methodology. The MCMI, as revised, is by far the most frequently used and researched instrument of its kind.

Millon argued that the structure of a clinical science consists of a *theory* that explained why natures takes the observed form, a *taxonomy* that classifies these observations into a coherent whole, *instrumentation* that measures these observations, and *intervention* to remediate outliers. Thus his theory of personality development and personality disorders preceded the development of instrumentation to measure them.

Millon's originally relied on biopsychosocial levels of explanation with which to begin theory construction but since has developed a bioevolutionary theory of the science he calls "personology." Millon relied, in part, on knowledge of evolutionary biology to build a comprehensive evolutionary ecological model that has, at its core, three polarity structures that are considered universal motivating aims in both the animal and plant world. These, in turn, are connected to principles found in studies of chemistry, biology, particle physics, and other natural sciences.

Millon argued that the first task of an orgasm is to *survive*. Once survival is assured, the next task is to *adapt* to the environment in which existence has been assured, and the final task is to *replicate* to ensure the preservation of the species. These three survival aims or polarities have corollaries at the psychological level, namely, *pain-pleasure* (a survival aim), *active-passive* (adaptational strategies), and *self-other* (replication polarity). (Millon has subsequently added a fourth polarity called "abstraction" but has not yet developed this into changes in instrumentation.)

Adaptation may be thought of as how we seek reinforcement (active or passive), and where we seek reinforcement is deemed a replication polarity. Millon theorizes that there are five such ways: (a) independent (self), (b) dependent (others), (c) ambivalent (self-other conflict), (d) discordant (a reversal of pain-pleasure gratification), and (e) detached (no pleasure). From this theoretical 2×5 model are derived the basic personality styles. Table 5.1 depicts Millon's theory-derived models of personality and personality disorders. He believes that personality disorders emanate from environmental stress and/or compromised biology but are basic extensions of the underlying personality style. Thus, by knowing the basic style we can predict the personality disorder that may ensue in times of psychological turmoil. It should be noted that Millon's theory *predicted* the presence of an avoidant personality disorder, which was subsequently added to the official classification in the *DSM–III*.

Once he developed (and continues to develop) his theory and taxonomy, he pursued the development of instrumentation to assess the syndromes predicted by the theory and observed in nature. One result was the MCMI–I, which was constructed as a measure of personality styles and personality disorders as well as major clinical syndromes.

TABLE 5.1
Millon's Bioevolutionary Characterization of Personality Styles and Personality Disorders

| | Sources of Reinforcement | | | | |
Adaptation	Independent	Dependent	Ambivalent	Discordant	Detached
Active					
Normal	Unruly	Sociable	Sensitive	Forceful	Inhibited
Disordered	Antisocial	Histrionic	Passive - aggressive	Aggressive	Avoidant
Passive					
Normal	Confidant	Cooperative	Respectful	Defeatist	Introversive
Disordered	Narcissistic	Dependent	Compulsive	Self-defeating	Schizoid

PSYCHOMETRIC CHARACTERISTICS

In constructing the MCMI–I (and the subsequent revisions), Millon used a three-stage validation process consisting of theoretical-substantive, internal-structural, and external-criterion validation. In the first stage, test items are developed and then assessed according to the degree to which they fit the theory. In stage two, the items are assessed to see how well they interrelate, and the psychometric properties of the test are determined. In stage 3, the convergent and discriminative validity of the test is assessed by correlating the test with similar (or dissimilar) instruments.

For the MCMI–I, face-valid items were written, items were eliminated after clinician sorting and patient judging, and a split 1,100-item pool was divided into two equivalent forms. This represented the processes involved in stage 1 validation (theoretical-substantive). For internal-structural validation, these two forms were given to clinical samples, and items were retained that had the highest item–total score correlations. Endorsement frequencies were determined and item-scale correlations were run; items with endorsement frequencies less than .15 or greater than .85 were then eliminated. The remaining 440 items were screened to ensure there were an adequate number of items for each scale, and the total number of items was reduced to 289. An external-criterion validation was then conducted in which 167 clinicians gave the test to their patients and completed a diagnostic form. Based on the results, the total number of items was reduced to 150, three scales were eliminated, and three scales were added. Then the entire process was repeated, resulting in a 175-item test.

The standardization sample eventually consisted of 1,591 clinical patients (58% males, 42% females) ranging in age from 18 to 66 and another 256 patients (57% males, 43% females) selected for cross-validation. MCMI–I test protocols were obtained from 223 clinicians at 108 hospitals and outpatient clinics and 39 private practitioners from 27 states and Great Britain The nonclinical population consisted of 297 people from a variety of community settings (48% males, 52% females) and ranging in age from 18 to 66.

Millon revised the MCMI–I because of new personality disorders were included in his theory, the *DSM* had been modified, and a comprehensive set of diagnostic criteria for personality disorders had been defined. Validation studies assisted in determining which items should be retained and which items should be eliminated. The MCMI–II standardization and validation process used the same procedures described for the MCMI–I. A provisional form of the MCMI–II was developed; it contained 368 items, including added items for a Sadistic and a Self-Defeating scale. A total of 45 items were subsequently changed in validation, and an item-weighting system was introduced, with prototype items that were isomorphic with theory receiving the highest weight in scoring. The Disclosure, Desirability, and Debasement scales were added. The MCMI–I Antisocial Personality Disorder scale was divided into an Antisocial scale and an Aggressive Personality Disorder scale. The MCMI–II normative sample consisted of 1,292 clinical patients, 50% male and 50% females and 88% White, 7% Black, 4 % Hispanic, and 1% other races. The age range was similar to that of the MCMI–I.

The MCMI–III standardization sample consisted of 600 clinical patients and another 398 for cross-validation. The sample was 86% White, 9% Black, 3% Hispanic, and 2% other races, and the sample participants ranged in age from 18 to 88. Correctional inmates represented 8.5% of the standardization sample. Two new scales were added (Depressive Personality Disorder and Post-Traumatic Stress Disorder), up to 50% of the MCMI–II items were changed, and scales were reduced in length. Items dealing with child abuse and eating disorders were added but not scored on any scale, and the prototype item-weighting system was changed from a 3-point to a 2-point scale. Again, Millon emphasized and employed the three-stage validation process previously described.

Millon persuasively argued that personality disorders and clinical syndromes are not normally distributed in the general population. Therefore, transforming raw scores to a normalized distribution, using T-scores or standard scores is not statistically appropriate. Millon then developed a *base rate (BR) score* that addresses the issue of prevalence rates of the disorder being measured. Millon arbitrarily set a BR of 60 as representing the mean raw score of the clinical standardization sample on each scale and a BR of 30 as the mean raw score of the nonclinical standardization sample. He then found that point in the distribution of scores where the patient had all of the traits and behaviors of the disorder or syndrome at the diagnostic level and assigned a BR score of 85 to that score. He interpolated BR scores between 75 and 84 for patients who had some of the features of the disorder or syndrome but not at the diagnostic level. A unique aspect of the instrument's BR score is that *BR greater than 84 is that point in the distribution where the percentage of scores is equal to the rate of occurrence of that disorder within the population.* Ordinal values for other points in the distribution were assigned BR scores, and then conversion tables were added to the test manual.

However, additional scoring adjustments are needed based on whether the respondent has endorsed an excessive number of items, resulting in the appearance of a favorable (Desirability scale) or an unfavorable (Debasement scale) impression. The Denial versus Complaint Adjustment alters scores upward for respondents who deny or accentuate problems. Their scores are adjusted upward if they obtained high scores on the Personality Disorder scales of Histrionic, Narcissistic, and Compulsive, and their scores are lowered if they obtained high scores on Avoidant and Self-Defeating. These adjustments are made to the Schizoid, Borderline, Paranoia, Anxiety, Dysthymia, and Somatoform scales. Scores on the Disclosure scale either increase or decrease scores on many of the MCMI–III scales, with the specific amount depending on the magnitude of the Disclosure score. Finally, adjustments are made for those experiencing more acute psychological turmoil as manifested by high scores on Anxiety and Dysthymia and are also made based on the setting in which the patient took the test (e.g., outpatient, inpatient, length of time as an inpatient). The test manual provides exact details on which scales are increased or decreased as a result of these multiple adjustments. As one can see, scoring the MCMI–III is a time-consuming and cumbersome process, and computer scoring of the test is definitely recommended.

TABLE 5.2
Stability Reliability of Scale 6A

Author(s)	MCMI	Population	Sample Size	Interval	r'
Millon (1983)	I	Psych. pts.	59	5–9 days	.90
			86	4–6 weeks	.83
McMahon, Flynn, &	I	Alcoholics	96	4–6 weeks	.63
Davidson (1985)		Drug Addicts	33	4–6 weeks	.72
		Drug Abusers	33	3–5 weeks	.79
Piersma (1986)	I	Psych. inpts.	151	4–6 weeks	.55
Wheeler & Schwartz (1989)	I	College stds.	225	3 years	.60
Hyer et al. (1989)	I	PTSD vets	50	35 days	.79
Murphy et al. (1991)	I	Psych. inpts.	150	ca. 6 months	.64
Libb et al. (1990)	I	Depressed pts.	28	3 months	.62
Overholser (1990)	I	Psych. pts.	28	ca. 1 year	.85
		Major depress.	15	6 weeks	.79
Millon (1987)	II	Nonclinical	91	3–5 weeks	.88
Millon (1987)	II	Psych. outpts.	37	3–5 weeks	.73
		Psych. inpts.	47	3–5 weeks	.64
Piersma (1989)	II	Psych. inpts.	98	21 days	.84
McMahon &	II	Cocaine Addicts	109	ca.3 months	.79
Richards (1996)			102	c4 months	.63
			38	ca. 30 days	.74
Lenzenweger (1999)	II	College stds.	250	1 year	.74
				1 year	.70
				2 years	.70
Millon (1994)	III	Misc. psych.	87	5–14 days	.93
Piersma & Boes (1997)	III	Psych. inpts.	97	7–10 days	.76
Craig & Olson (1998)	III	Drug inpts	35	ca. 6 months	.62

Reliability

Information on the reliability and validity of the MCMI–I and MCMI–II has been extensively presented in the literature; similar information on the MCMI–III is not as substantial. Also, with 24 scales on the MCMI–III, the reliability of each scale would have to be determined by means of a multitrait-multimethod nomothetic network of studies among different populations. Details are presented here on the reliability of just one personality disorder scale—the Antisocial PD (scale 6A)—for illustrative purposes.[1] This scale was chosen because the disorder is well described and had the highest reliability correlation in *DSM–IV* field trials among all personality disorders.

Table 5.2 presents the research data on the test-retest correlations from all studies on scale 6A from all three versions of the test. There have been 15 studies on the stability and reliability of scale 6A, covering 20 clinical samples and 3 nonclinical samples. For the MCMI–I, there are 11 data sets for clinical populations and 1 for a nonclinical sample. For the MCMI–II, there are 10 data sets from five studies. For the MCMI–III, there are

---

[1]Readers interested in obtaining information about the reliability, validity, and diagnostic power of any MCMI scales are invited to send a request to RJCraig41@comcast.net.

3 data sets. Stability estimates for a variety of clinical groups (inpatient and outpatient psychiatric patients, PTSD patients, and drug and alcohol abusers) ranged from .55 to .90 for clinical samples across a variety of test-retest intervals for scale 6A of MCMI–I, with a median of .79; for the MCMI–II scale, stability estimates for clinical groups ranged from .63 to .84, with a median of .73, for up to 4 months. For the MCMI–III scale, the median correlation was .76, based on three samples.

Internal consistency studies have also been published, although far fewer than test-retest reliability studies. Langevin, Paitich, Freeman, Mann, and Handy (1979) reported an internal consistency estimate of .61 for MCMI–I scale 6A, with a sample of 419 sex offenders. Millon (1987) reported an internal consistency estimate for MCMI–II scale *T* of .88. Sinha and Watson (2001) reported a median internal consistency estimate for MCMI–II of .79 with university students. Millon reported an internal consistency for MCMI–III scale 6A of .77, and an internal consistency for MCMI–III of .73 was also reported (Dyce, O'Connor, Parkins, & Janzen, 1997).

The data indicate that scale 6A of each version of the MCMI remains generally stable, suggesting that it is measuring rather enduring personality traits. The internal consistency of the scale appears good.

Validity

As with reliability, it would be difficult to describe the validity of the MCMI given the limited space. Again, within a multitrait-multimethod nomothetic network, we would have to present data on the convergent and discriminative validity on each scale of the MCMI (III) for a variety of populations. Again, for illustrative purposes I present convergent validity data for scale 6A as well as for scale *CC* (Major Depression). Again, the latter scale was selected for presentation because depression is largely an observable behavior.

Table 5.3 presents convergent validity data on MCMI scale 6A (all test versions). Researchers have most often correlated the MCMI Antisocial PD scale with the MMPI Antisocial scale (a personality disorder scale). Correlations ranged from −.08 to .30, with a median r' of .15, for the MCMI–I; correlations ranged from .46 to .61, with a median of .57, for MCMI–II scale 6A and the MMPI and MMPI–2 Antisocial scale (three studies); correlations for MCMI–III scale 6A and the MMPI–2 Antisocial scale ranged from .57 to .70, with a median of .65, (five studies). The data in Table 5.3 show that the median correlation of MCMI scale 6A (all versions) with similar constructs from structured clinical interviews was .37 and that the median correlation with self-report inventories was .45. This suggests that method variance affects the convergent validity of these instruments, and a pattern of attaining higher correlations within methods (i.e., self-report inventories) than across methods (i.e., correlating a self-report measure with a structured clinical interview of that same construct) has been reported for many instruments that screen for personality disorders (Craig, 2003a).

The Psychopathy Checklist (PCL) has become the standard measure for the diagnosis of antisocial personality disorder within a correctional setting. It shows the highest correlation with other measures of criminality (Salekin, Rogers, & Sewell, 1996). Only one study has correlated the PCL with MCMI scale 6A. Hart, Forth, and Hare (1991) reported a correlation of .45 between these two instruments. This brings us to an interesting point. The item content of scale 6A was theory driven and consists of two "types" of items. One group of items are consistent with the *DSM–IV* characterization of the antisocial disorder, which emphasizes conduct disordered behavior and criminality. However, the second group of items pertains to Millon's *theory* as to what constitutes the essential

TABLE 5.3

Convergent Validity of the MCM–III Antisocial *PD* Scale with Similar Measures

Author(s)	Instrument	MCMI	r'
Marsh et al. (1988)	MMPI PD	I	−.08
Morey & Levine (1988)	MMPI PD	I	.30
Dubro & Wetzler (1989)	MMPI PD	I	.14
McCann (1989)	MMPI PD	I	.15
Zarella et al. (1990)	MMPI PD	I	.14
		I	.13
Schuler et al. (1994)	MMPI PD	I	.25
Wise (1994a)	MMPI PD	I	.09
Widiger & Sanderson (1987)	PIQ	I	.81
Hogg et al. (1990)	SIDP	I	.23
Klein et al. (1993)	Wisc PDI	I	.11
Morey (1985)	ICL Agg/Sad	I	.45
Chick et al. (1993)	*DSM–III–R* Cklt	I	.04
Wise (1994b)	MBHI Forceful	I	.54
McCann (1991)	MMPI PD	II	.57
Wise (1996)	MMPI–2 PD	II	.46
Wise (2001)	MMPI–2 PD	II	.61
Turley et al. (1992)	SIDP	II	.47
Hart et al. (1991)	PCL	II	.45
Coolidge & Merwin (1992)	Coolidge	II	.53
Soldz et al. (1993)	PDE	II	.37
Hart et al. (1993)	PDE sym. count	II	.41
Kennedy et al. (1995)	SCID–II	II	.17
Messina et al. (2001)	SCID–II	II	.27
Wierzbicki & Gorman (1995)	PDQ–R	II	.37
Bayon et al. (1996)	TCI Novelty Seeking	II	.4
Marlowe et al. (1997)	SCID–II	II	.49
Silberman et al. (1997)	Coolidge	II	.70
Rossi et al. (2003)	MMPI PD	III	.66
Hicklin & Widiger (2000)	MMPI PD	III	.57
Lindsay et al. (2000)	MMPI–2 PD	III	.57
Hicklin & Widiger (2000)	MMPI–2 PD	III	.70
Rossi, Hauben, et al. (2003)	MMPI–2 PD	III	.65
Rossi, Van den Brande, et al. (2003)	MMPI–2 PD	III	.65
Lindsay et al. (2000)	PDQ–4	III	.67

Coolidge = Coolidge Axis II Inventory; *DSM–III–R* Cklt = *DM–III–R* Checklist; ICL Agg/Sad = Interpersonal Checklist for Aggressive/Sadistic Personality Disorder; MBHI = Millon Behavioral Health Inventory Forceful scale; MMPI PD = Personality disorder scales from the Minnesota Multiphasic Personality Inventory; PCL = Psychopathy Check List; PDE = Personality Disorder Examination; PDE Sym. Count = Personality Disorder Examination symptom count; PDQ–4 = Personality Diagnostic Questionnaire, fourth edition. PIQ = Personality Inventory Questionnaire; SCID–II = Structured Clinical Inventory for *DSM–IV* Personality Disorders; SIDP = Structured Inventory for *DSM* Personality Disorders; TCI Novelty Seeking = Temperament and Character Inventory Novelty Seeking scale; Wisc. PDI = Wisconsin Personality Disorder Inventory.

TABLE 5.4
Correspondence of MCMI Major Depression Scale with Similar Measures

Author(s)	Instrument	MCMI	r'
Millon (1983)	MMPI D	I	.67
Smith et al. (1988)	MMPI D	I	.57
Millon (1983)	Wiggins Depress	I	.83
Millon (1983)	SCL–90 Depress	I	.75
McMahon & Davidson (1985)	POMS Depress	I	.54
	POMS Confusion	I	.56
Goldberg et al. (1987)	Beck Depress Inv	I	.62
	Hamilton DRI	I	.45
Choca et al. (1988)	Hamilton DRI	I	.56
Holliman & Guthrie (1989)	CPI Well Being	I	−.58
McCann (1990)	MMPI D	II	.58
Blais et al. (1994)	MMPI–2 D	II	.46
Craig & Olson (1992)	16 PF Emotionally Stable	II	−.34
Bayon et al. (1996)	TCI Harm Avoid	II	.65
Millon (1994)	MMPI–2 D	III	.71
Millon (1994)	SCL\CL–90R Depres	III	.74
Millon (1994)	Beck Depress Inv	III	.74

Beck Depress Inv = Beck Depression Inventory; CPI Well Being = California Personality Inventory Well Being; Hamilton DRI = Hamilton Depression Inventory; MMPI D = Minnesota Multiphasic Personality Inventory Depression (scale 2); POMS Depress = Profile of Mood States Depression; SCL–90 Depress = Symptom Check List–90 Depression; 16 PF Emotionally Stable = Sixteen Personality Factors Questionnaire Emotionally Stable; TCI Harm Avoid = Temperament and Character Inventory Harm Avoidance; Wiggins Depress = MMPI Wiggins Content scale Depression.

behavior of the antisocial style. Millon believed that the antisocial personality type is motivated primarily by a desire to avoid being controlled by others and so acts in ways to dominate others before others control him or her. Given this motivational attribution, the MCMI, as revised, contains several items that tap this fiercely independent stance. This sense of independence is not contained in other measures of this style/disorder, and as a consequence the correlations between these instruments and scale 6A are lower than they otherwise would be.

Table 5.4 presents convergent validity data for the Major Depression scale (CC). The median correlation between MCMI–I scale CC was .57 based on eight studies with 10 data points; the median correlation between MCMI–II scale CC and similar measures ($N = 4$) was .52; the median correlation between MCMI–III scale CC and other measures, was .74, but the three studies in question were based on information from the test manual and have not been independently validated. Prior versions of the MCMI depression scale were criticized because they did not contain items pertaining to the vegetative signs of depression, and these symptoms are the hallmarks of the disorder. The MCMI–III now includes these types of items in scale CC, and the correlations with similar instruments are now quite robust.

Unlike many other omnibus personality instruments, the MCMI (all versions) has determined precise cutting points to establish a diagnosis. This allows researchers to evaluate the accuracy of the MCMI diagnostic decisions using diagnostic power statistics (Gibertini, Brandenberg, & Retzlaff, 1986). This is particularly important in forensic application because the *Daubert* (1993) standard for federal rules of evidence stipulate that the trier

TABLE 5.5
Diagnostic Power of the Borderline *PD* Scale

	Classification	MCMI	Prev	Sens	Spec	PPP	NPP	D×P
(1)	BR > 74	I	.20	.77	.92	.71	.94	.89
	BR > 84		.13	.60	.95	.64	.94	.90
(2*)	BR > 75[a]	I	.15	.64	.64	.25	.91	X
	BR > 85[a]		.33	.86	.30	.88	X	X
(3)		I	.14	.77	.93	.64	.96	X
(4)	BR > 84	I	.08	.42	.80	.17	.96	X
	Clin Dx		.33	.60	.43	.35	.68	X
(5)	BR > 74	I	.05	.40	.78	.09	.96	.76
	BR > 84		.05	.20	.91	.10	.96	.87
(6)	Two highest scales	II	.15	.72	.93	.66	.95	.90
	Highest in code		.11	.67	.95	.60	.96	.92
(7)	*DSM–III* Dx BR > 74	II	.65	.74	.61	.78	.71	X
	DSM–III Dx BR > 84	II		.58	.83	.68	.76	.74
(8)	SCID Dx	II	.17	.50	.91	.56	.89	.83
(9)	SCID–II	II	XX	.70	.70	.49	.84	.70
(10)	BR > 74	III	.27	.46	.77	.30	X	.68
	BR > 84	III	.10	.20	.90	.11	X	.83
(11)	BR > 74	II	XX	.57	.66	.30	.85	.64
	BR > 84	II	XX	.48	.82	.41	.86	.75
(12)	Clin Dx	III	XX	.71	X	.60	X	X

Clin Dx = clinical diagnosis; D×P = overall diagnostic power; NPP = negative predictive power; PPP = positive predictive power; Prev = prevalence; Sens = sensitivity; Spec = specificity.
(1) Gibertini, Brandenberg, and Retzlaff, (1986); (2) Torgersen and Alnaes, (1990); (3) Miller et al. (1992); (4) Patrick (1993); (5) Chick et al. (1993; *N* = 107 miscellaneous psychiatric patients); (6) Millon (1987); (7) McCann et al. (1992); (8) Guthrie & Mobley (1994; *N* = 55 outpatients); (9) Hills (1995; *N* = 125); (10) Millon (1994; *N* = 398); (11) Marlowe et al. (1997; *N* = 144); (12) Millon (1997; *N* = 321).
[a] Norwegian sample.

of fact (i.e., the judge or jury) must make a preliminary assessment as to whether an expert witness's methodology is scientifically valid. The assessment would consider the error rate, and whether the methodology was capable of being tested, had been subjected to peer review, and had achieved general acceptance in the field. The standard error-of-measurement statistic would provide this information, but there are no such data in any of the MCMI test manuals. Instead, researchers have reported on the test's diagnostic accuracy using diagnostic power statistics. Among these data, the test's positive predictive power (PPP) may be salient in expert testimony because that statistic indicates the test's ability to successfully detect a condition/disorder (i.e., the test indicates the condition/disorder is present and it actually is present). Of course, in some circumstances it would also be desirable to know the test's negative predictive power (NPP), that is, its ability to successfully rule out a condition/disorder. Keep in mind that the MCMI–III has 24 scales and that the PPP and NPP would have to be determined for each one. The data are too voluminous to present here. Instead, I present diagnostic power data for the Borderline Personality Disorder scale in Table 5.5.

The diagnostic power of a test is dependent, in part, on the prevalence rate of the disorder within the researched sample as well as the criteria used to determine the presence or absence of the disorder. Although Millon has indicated that a BR score greater than 84 reflects the disorder at the diagnostic level, most researchers have also reported diagnostic power statistics at the BR greater than 74 level as well. The data indicate that the Borderline PD scale PPP ranges from .09 to .88, with a median value of .56, for all test versions across all criteria. The NPP ranges from .68 to .96, with a median of .94. This suggests that the Borderline PD scale is excellent at ruling out a disorder and is able to detect the disorder slightly better than half the time, on average. This is not an unusual finding, for assessment measures have historically been better at ruling out a disorder than ruling it in. Of course, the forensic psychologist will need to know the diagnostic power statistics for any scale used as part of expert testimony. Most of the MCMI scales have a diagnostic power beyond chance when used to help establish an individual diagnosis (McCann, 2002).

Some dismiss the idea that diagnoses are relevant to forensic assessments. However, a diagnosis and the *consequences* of that diagnosis are relevant to many forensic issues that come before the court. A recent case illustrates this.

The examinee was a 42-year-old married housewife with a history of schizophrenia. She had been under psychiatric care for many years and had periods of remission; in fact, most recently she had been symptom-free. She had three children, and her husband was a successful businessman. Recent business required him to travel to Europe during the summer for 3 months. He periodically kept in touch with his wife, who told him things were going well. Because of his wife's past history, her husband had been managing their financial affairs, and he continued to do so while in Europe. However, upon his return home he found the house in disarray, the children emaciated and sickly, and his wife depressed, lethargic, and anergic, with suicidal ideation. He then called the police, and the child protective agency became involved. The children were temporarily removed from the home and placed out of state with near relatives after receiving medical treatment.

The wife was charged with neglect and jailed. The court eventually ordered a psychological evaluation, and after reviewing the results of this examination, her attorney hired an independent psychologist as an expert witness. Both examiners agreed that the examinee was not experiencing any symptoms associated with schizophrenia, and hence this condition was ruled out as a reason for the neglect. Both examiners diagnosed major depression, single episode without psychotic features. However, although one expert testified that her depression was not severe enough to have caused the neglect and hence she should be held culpable, the other expert testified that her symptoms of depression were directly related to her inability to properly care for her children.

Hence diagnosis is relevant in many assessments, and the diagnostic power of an assessment measure also becomes relevant in that assessment.

CLINICAL USES AND LIMITATIONS

All versions of the MCMI have been used primarily with clinical patients in both inpatient and outpatient venues. There is an especially large literature on using the MCMI with drug addicts (Craig & Weinberg, 1992a), alcoholics (Craig & Weinberg, 1992b), patients with posttraumatic stress disorder (Hyer, Brandsma, & Boyd, 1997; Hyer, Melton, & Gratton, 1993), and spouse abusers (Craig, 2003b), and I will briefly summarize the major findings with these populations to date.

Drug Addiction

MCMI-based studies have reported that the modal profile of drug addicts (users of heroin and/or cocaine) reflects antisocial and narcissistic traits along with elevations on the Paranoia (*P*), Drug Abuse (*T*), and Alcohol Abuse (*B*) syndrome scales. The elevations on scale *P* do not reflect clinical paranoia but a wary alertness associated with the drug addict lifestyle. Although the MCMI has shown higher prevalence rates than other measures, almost all studies have reported that drug addicts have higher rates of antisocial personality disorders than other disorders (Craig, 2003c). Female addicts score higher than male addicts on the Self-Defeating PD scale (Haller, Miles, & Dawson, 2002). However, investigators have found up to six types of personality profiles upon typological analysis, including a within-normal-limit profile (Calsyn, Fleming, Wells, & Saxon, 1996; Craig, Bivens, & Olson, 1997). Drug addicts have been able to avoid detection of their substance abuse on the MCMI (Craig, Kuncel, & Olson, 1994; Fals-Stewart, 1995), and few studies have found detection rates for scale T greater than 50% (Calsyn, Saxon, & Daisy, 1990).

Alcoholism

A literature review suggested that the personality disorder of passive-aggressive (negativistic) antisocial, with elevations on Anxiety, Depression, Alcohol Abuse, and Drug Abuse, predominated in the MCMI profiles of male alcoholics (Craig & Weinberg, 1992b). Subsequent research also found this character type in cluster analysis, along with elevations on Avoidant, and within-normal-limit profiles reflecting narcissistic traits (Donat, 1994; Matano, Locke, & Schwartz, 1994; McMahon, Malow, & Peneod, 1998). Female aloholics were typed with passive-aggressive (negativistic) personality disorder and within-normal-limit profile types with Compulsive and Histrionic/Narcissistic at subclinical elevations. Having an elevation on the Compulsive PD scale has been associated with higher social functioning, episodic rather than continuous drinking, and positive treatment outcomes.

For an in-depth presentation and discussion of issues pertaining to assessing substance abusers with the MCMI, see Craig (2005c) and Flynn, McCann, and Fairbank (1995).

PTSD

The MCMI has been extensively used with Vietnam combat veterans (Craig & Olson, 1997; Hyer Brandsma et al., 1997). The personality styles of schizoid/avoidant, passive-aggressive (negativistic) avoidant, and compulsive/dependent are most prominent in the MCMI protocols of Vietnam veterans with PTSD. These findings led Hyer to conclude that the MCMI 8A2 (Passive-Aggressive/Avoidant) profile has appeared with such consistency in this population that it can be construed as a "traumatogenic" profile. However, this codetype has also appeared in populations without trauma (Craig, 1995). The personality styles of avoidant, passive-aggressive (negativistic), and borderline demonstrate conceptual closeness to the PTSD construct, and how people cope with traumatic memories is intrinsically related to their personality styles (Hyer, Brandsma, et al., 1997). Recent research has begun to use the MCMI for investigating civilian trauma as well (Alexander et al., 1998; Allen, Coyne, & Huntoon, 1998; Lecic-Tosevski, Gavrilovic, Knezevic, & Priebe, 2003).

Preliminary results on the MCMI–III PTSD scale (*R*) suggest good concurrent validity in distinguishing combat veterans with and without PTSD (Hyer, Boyd, Stanger, Davis, & Walters, 1997). Also, scale *R* was able to successfully discriminate between PTSD and a non-PTSD patients, it was the best predictor of PTSD in a multiple regression equation, and its sensitivity and specificity were higher than those provided in the MCMI–III test manual (Craig & Olson, 1997).

Domestic Violence

Personality disorders are quite prevalent among male domestic abusers, with antisocial, aggressive, and passive-aggressive (negativistic) disorders demonstrating higher prevalence rates in this population than other personality disorders. However, some male spouse abusers produce a within-normal-limit MCMI profile, and their domestic violence may not be a product of a personality disorder. MCMI test results suggest a relative absence of Axis I syndromes, except for substance abuse. Elevations on the Antisocial, Aggressive, and Passive-Aggressive (Negativistic) scales may constitute a psychological marker for risk of domestic violence and abuse and even be able to predict it, although no study has tested this latter hypothesis (Craig, 2003b). Female batterers were more likely than their male counterparts to score in the clinical range on the Borderline, Somatoform, Major Depression, Bipolar Disorder, and Delusional Disorder syndrome scales (Henning, Jones, & Holdford, 2003).

FORENSIC USES AND LIMITATIONS

In *People v. Stoll* (1989), the court upheld the admissibility of the MCMI in court testimony. McCann and Dyer (1996) found 22 cases through 1994 that have allowed MCMI-based testimony pertaining to a variety of issues, including child custody, personal injury, classification of sex offenders, domestic violence, determination of disability, employment discrimination, assessment of malingering and deception, and termination of parental rights.

The MCMI has an increasing literature covering forensic populations. Within the past 10 years, it has been used with correctional inmates (Blackburn, 1998; Kelln, Dozois, & McKenzie, 1998; Retzlaff, Stoner, & Kleinasser, 2002; Schwartz, Seemann, Buboltz, & Flye, 2004; White, Ackerman, & Caraveo, 2001; Wise, 2001) and sexual offenders (Ahlmeyer, Kleinsasser, Stoner, & Retzlaff, 2003; Carpenter, Peed, & Eastman, 1995; Cohen et al., 2002; Holt, Meloy, & Strack, 1999; Lehne, 2002).

Nevertheless, use of the MCMI in forensic work remains controversial (Lally, 2003; Rogers, 2003). Some have argued that the MCMI was standardized on a clinical population and did not include normals and hence does not allow for discrimination between patients and normals (Butcher & Miller, 1999; Hess, 1998). This issue may be especially salient in child custody evaluations, where parents often are free of personality disorders, compared with other types of forensic assessments (Otto & Butcher, 1995). In a recent survey, 201 psychologists from 39 states were questioned on multiple aspects of child custody evaluations. The MCMI was used by 34% of the sample (Ackerman & Ackerman, 1997). Surprisingly, 10 years before the MCMI was not used at all (Keilin & Bloom, 1986). The MCMI is the second most frequently used personality test in civil (Boccaccini & Brodsky, 1999), criminal (Borum & Grisso, 1995), and in child custody evaluations (Quinnell & Bow, 2001). Use of the MCMI in forensic work is beginning to receive more favorable comments by forensic psychologists (Camara, Nathan, & Ouente, 2000; Lampel, 1999; Schutte, 2001). However, attorneys will pick up the criticisms of the use of the MCMI and attempt to have MCMI-based testimony dismissed on the grounds that it does not meet the *Daubert* standards. In fact, the arguments proffered by Rogers, Salekin, and Sewell (1999) were cited in an Alabama plaintive brief that objected to MCMI-based testimony concerning the psychologist's evaluation of the plaintive in an employment-related case. However, the trial judge rejected the motion, which sought to exclude anything related to the MCMI–II on the grounds that the test did not meet the *Daubert* standards (*Jeffrey V. Dillard's Department Store and Dillard's Bel Air Mall*, 2000).

In fact, 8% of the standardization sample for the MCMI–III were from a correctional setting. Also, it could be argued that, in the case of forensic examinees, the test does meet the criteria for usage because these examinees are in a setting in which they are being evaluated by a mental health expert and hence could meet the definition of a "clinical" patient. Furthermore, the literature base of the MCMI (III) continues to expand, and published normative data on the use of the MCMI–III in custody evaluations now exist (McCann et al., 2001).

One of the more serious assaults on the MCMI questioned whether the MCMI scales meet the *Daubert* standard as to admissibility based on scientific merit (Rogers, 2003; Rogers, Salekin, & Sewell, 1999, 2000). One argument was that only the Avoidant, Schizo-typal, and Borderline scales (of the MCMI–II) have been the subject of sufficient conver-gent and discriminant validity studies to meet the admissibility criteria, whereas the other scales have not been. A second argument was that there are insufficient research data on which to base expert evaluations in many common forensic applications, such as insanity evaluations.

Dyer and McCann (2000) rebutted these arguments and concluded that "while the MCMI–II meets . . . [the] .80 criterion for all personality disorder scales and the MCMI–III meets it for most scales, other instruments do not fare as well. . . . The MMPI–2 has several scales that have a reliability of less than .50" (p. 493).

In contrast, one rule of evidence is that the method be in frequent use in psychological practice—a criterion that is clearly met based on test usage surveys (Butcher & Rouse, 1996). Furthermore, no rules of evidence mandate that a test or method be without contro-versy before material based on that technique is admissible (Craig, 2005). Still, the prudent forensic psychologist would be well served to be aware of the arguments surrounding this debate.

One problem area for a forensic psychologist using the MCMI–III as part of expert testimony pertains to the (mis)interpretation of BR scores in cross-examination. Suppose you render an opinion that the examinee is suffering with schizophrenia and that this conclusion was based, in part, on the examinee's BR score on the Thought Disorder scale. During cross-examination, the attorney asks you if the MCMI–III test manual is an authoritative source on the test, and you assert that it is. The attorney points out that the PPP of scale *SS* (Thought Disorder) is .52 and asks if this means that the scale is able to detect the disorder 52% of the time, and you agree that this is what it means. Then the attorney suggests that this must mean that the test fails to diagnose the disorder 48% of the time, and again you agree. Finally, the attorney asks you, "Isn't it fair to conclude that this test is no better than flipping a coin in making this diagnosis because in a coin flip we would be right 50% of the time?" What is your response?

The attorney is attempting to mislead the jury, or perhaps she does not really under-stand diagnostic power statistics as applied to the MCMI–III. Since the prevalence rate of patients with a thought disorder in the MCMI–III standardization sample was 10%, a coin flip would be incorrect 90% of the time and correct only 10% of the time, whereas the MCMI–III would achieve an immense improvement over the base rate (five times better).

Another criticism of the MCMI is that it overpathologizes. This contention was ini-tially proposed by Dana and Cantrell (1988) and was voiced by Widiger (2001) in the test's most recent review. In settings where substantial clinical symptomotology would not be expected, such as in college counseling or divorce mediation, it is argued that the MCMI–III overestimates the extent of personality disorders. If this were true, then the MCMI operating statistics would demonstrate weak specificity statistics across most scales. However, the opposite is true. Specificity statistics across MCMI scales has been excellent. This suggests that the test does not incorrectly label a person as having a particular disorder (Dyer, 2005).

There is a potential for response bias to distort test results. This is not unique to the MCMI but the scoring adjustments make it almost impossible to invalidate the test by symptoms exaggeration (Morgan, Schoenberg, Dorr, & Burke, 2002).

RACE AND GENDER ISSUES

Two studies have explicitly researched the question of racial bias in the MCMI–I (Choca, Shanley, Peterson, & VanDenburg, 1990; Hamberger & Hastings, 1989), one has investigated racial bias in the MCMI–II (Munley, Vacha-Haase, Busby, & Paul, 1998), and six other studies have reported on differences between Blacks and Whites and between men and women on MCMI scales, although these difference were not the main focus of the studies (Davis, Greenblatt, & Pochyly, 1990; Dillon, 1988; Donat, Walters, & Hume, 1992; Gabrys, 1988; Matano et al., 1994; Piersma, 1986). The data indicated that Blacks scored higher than Whites on the Narcissistic, Paranoid, Drug, and Delusional Disorder scales; Whites scored higher than Blacks on the Dysthymia scale. Males scored higher on Antisocial, and females scored higher on Somatoform and Major Depression. Bornstein (1995) reported that women of all ages consistently score higher than men on dependency on all self-report and projective test measures of dependency. These data were all based on MCMI–I and MCMI–II research. The real (unanswered) question is whether these differences represent true differences between men and women and between Blacks and Whites or whether they are suggestive of racial and/or gender bias. One study concluded that some of the items of the MCMI–III had the *potential* for gender bias, primarily those on the Narcissistic scale (Lindsay & Widiger, 1995). Also, although the BR scores on the aforementioned scales reached statistical significance, they would not have changed the diagnostic decision based on those scores!

OVERVIEW OF STRENGTHS AND WEAKNESSES

The strengths of the MCMI include these: (a) test development was anchored to theory, (b) the scales are reliable and internally consistent, (c) there are precise cutting rules for the classification of personality disorders, (d) and there is more research on all versions of the MCMI than on all other self-report personality disorder assessment instruments combined.

Two interesting developments pertain to the effort to refine personality disorder assessment and make it more precise. The refinement began as theory-driven characterizations but will eventuate in new scales for the measurement of personality disorder subtypes. Millon theorized that there are subtypes of personality disorders and that each has the essential characteristics that define the parent disorder but contributes a unique aspect of the disorder (Millon & Davis, 1997). Roger Davis has presented ways that the MCMI–III can be used to assess these theorized subtypes (Davis & Patterson, 2005).

Furthermore, Seth Grossman has developed a set of facet subscales for the MCMI–III (Grossman & del Rio, 2005), and these will soon be made available for scoring through the test's publisher. Theoretically, two individuals may have identical BR scores on a given scale by differentially endorsing different sets of items within the scale. Facet subscales allow the assessor to determine the salient dimensions endorsed by the respondent, thereby refining the psychological assessment of that disorder. These facet scales are somewhat analogous to the Harris and Lingoes subscales of the MMPI–2. However, the Harris and Lingoes scales were rationally derived, whereas the Grossman facet subscales were developed using sound scale construction techniques.

Continuing problems with this test include these: (a) Research with the MCMI–III has been insufficient (though this will certainly change with time). (b) There is a question as to how much research on the MCMI–I and –II can be applied to the MCMI–III. Some research suggests that applying previous research to the new version may be a questionable practice. For example, the PTSD profile codes in MCMI–I and –II differ from those in MCMI–III, and possibly the modal profiles of drug addicts differ as well. (c) Forensic psychologists may need to evaluate the extent of possible trauma, but the literature on use of the MCMI with a civilian population is limited. (d) Finally, the issue of whether the MCMI overpathologizes personality disorders continues to haunt this test, and additional research is needed on the MCMI–III to address this lingering question.

CASE EXAMPLE

The examinee was a 39-year-old, married White male who was originally seen by me for an initial evaluation by an HMO after he requested help for an alcohol problem.

His presenting complaints in the diagnostic interview were "emotional stress and alcohol." He reported a drinking history since age 16 and problematic drinking for about the last 2 years. He drank only on weekends and only a half pint of vodka. He said that alcohol "acts like medicine" and calms him down. He reported an ability to go to a party and have only two or three drinks, but the next day he would feel a need to drink upon awakening, and he said that he "binged" on Saturday and Sunday, again claiming that he did not drink more than a half pint during each "binge." He denied tolerance and said that he thought he could no longer drink as much as previously. He denied a history of blackouts, DTs, memory problems, hepatitis, or diminished sexual activity or drive. He did report mild "shakes," that dissipated with drinking. When asked if he was physically dependent on alcohol, he replied, "Probably." He reported early morning awakenings and "tossing and turning" in his sleep. He denied any depression, said that his appetite was good, and denied the use of other drugs.

He was treated once, in a 28-day inpatient alcohol treatment ward in a private hospital 1 and a half years ago. He attended AA for about 3 months but discontinued it because he thought that he did not need it. He was initially sent there by a psychologist who had seen the examinee for four sessions. He also reported no other treatment history and said that a physical exam had found no problems. He had recently gone to his physician, who prescribed a tranquilizer, but the examinee did not fill the prescription, fearing he would become physically dependent on the drug.

He was the director of engineering at a moderately sized manufacturing facility. He did not believe that his peers or his boss knew about his drinking problem. He said that his performance evaluations were high, but his peers saw him sweating at work, and he had had some recent absenteeism, particularly during the early part of the week, which they were beginning to notice. He denied using vodka to avoid detection at work and seemed genuinely naïve about this.

TABLE 5.6
MCMI–III Scores

Disclosure	15	Schizotypal	19
Desirability	78	Borderline	13
Debasement	12	Paranoid	31
Schzoid	38	Anxiety	27
Avoidant	11	Somatiform	40
Depressive	30	Bipolar	52
Dependent	64	Dysthymic	27
Histrionic	62	Alcohol	60
Narcissistic	49	Drug	35
Antisocial	32	PTSD	27
Aggressive	52	Thought Disorder	2
Compulsive	80	Major Depression	2
Passive-Aggressive	5	Delusional	37
Self-Defeating	5		

He had been married for four years. It was the first marriage for both him and his wife. He said that his wife thought he drank too much, and he had been hiding his drinking because he did not want to get into any fights with her. He reported no martial problems. He had no legal history and denied any DUI arrests, charges, or even driving after he had been drinking at all.

His family history indicated that his mother abstained and his father "drank too much" but was never treated for alcoholism and had no family problems due to drink. His sister did not drink.

When pressed about his "emotional stress," which he said precipitated his drinking, he was unable to elaborate or specify. He complained about his long drive at night and some job pressures, which he later said were "not too great," and he said that he drank more during "good and happy times" (i.e., birthdays, holidays).

During the interview, the examinee sweated frequently, using tissue to wipe his face. No other symptoms were noticeable. He said that he had last drank 2 days ago, half a pint of vodka.

I diagnosed him as alcohol dependent and sent in my report with treatment recommendations. Several months later, he contacted me because his company had fired him for tardiness and absenteeism. He had retained an attorney and filed a civil suit, under Title 56, chapter II of the Department of Human Rights section on Handicap Discrimination in Employment Act, arguing that he was handicapped due to alcoholism and that, contrary to law, he was not given the chance to seek treatment prior to his termination. He retained me as an expert witness to testify that he did have alcoholism. I gave him another clinical interview and psychological testing. Table 5.6 presents his MCMI–III scores. The results suggest that he had a compulsive personality style. These traits would serve him well in his capacity as an engineer and manager. A compulsive style has also been shown to have positive prognostic value in the treatment for alcoholism (McMahon, Davidson, & Flynn, 1986). The problem was that the Alcohol Scale (*B*) was in the normal range (BR = 60). (His *MAC–R, APS,* and *AAS* on the MMPI–2 were also in the normal range.)

The examinee, in a clinical interview, was diagnosed as alcohol dependent based on the following: sleep disturbance with early morning awakenings, sweating (early withdrawal), absenteeism, surreptitious drinking, and complaints by his wife about his drinking. Based on the disease model of alcoholism, he was in the early phase of alcoholism on a Jellinek chart and would probably be classified as a gamma alcoholic, although he showed some signs of the delta type. Why wasn't his substance abuse scale elevated?

I had to do an item analysis, going over his responses to each item on the scale (and on the other substance abuse scales as well) to be able ask him why he answered the questions in the manner he did. His explanations were quite revealing. For example, he doesn't have trouble controlling his drinking because he doesn't drink anymore. He doesn't experience physical problems from drinking because he doesn't drink anymore. He doesn't have trouble stopping himself from using alcohol because he doesn't drink anymore and goes to AA. He said his habit of abusing drugs didn't cause him to miss work in the past because he never used drugs and only missed work because of his use of alcohol.

In subsequent testimony, I presented the court with a copy of the Jellinek chart depicting the progressive nature of alcoholism, indicated the examinee's symptoms, and showed the judge where on the chart the examinee was functioning. I presented the results of my findings from psychological testing, cited the (negative) results from the substance abuse scales, and then detailed the examinee's individual answers to these items upon a detailed inquiry. The testimony was apparently so thorough that the defendant's attorney had few questions upon cross-examination.[2]

Some guidelines for use of the MCMI in forensic work have been published (Craig, 1999; McCann, 2002). These guidelines include the following recommendations:

- Make sure that the MCMI is an appropriate instrument for the situation in which it is being used.

- Be prepared to cite evidence on the reliability and validity of the MCMI validity scales.

- Maintain knowledge on the reliability, validity, and other technical aspects, especially in the area of diagnostic power, of the scales on which you are basing expert testimony.

- Ensure that there are a sufficient number of criterion-related MCMI–III validity studies that address the issue before the court.

- Test the examinee individually and do not violate chain-of-custody procedures.

- Be prepared to explain the BR score and use computer scoring to avoid scoring errors.

- Maintain currency on recent test developments and interpretations as they apply to certain MCMI–III scales (Craig, 2005; Halon, 2001; Lampel, 1999).

- Be prepared to defend applicability to the MCMI–III of any research done with the MCM–I and –II.

- Be prepared to explain in lay terms the meaning of diagnostic efficiency statistics and how they differ from decisions based on chance alone.

- Do not use a computerized interpretive report in forensic cases but use a computer-scoring report. This is to avoid a situation in which your conclusions differ from those contained in the computer report, placing you in disagreement with the "expert" who wrote the computer interpretation and hence putting you on the defensive.

- Finally, be prepared to accept and report the limitations of the test and use the test in a manner that can be supported by empirical evidence (McCann, 2002).

---

[2]This case raises the question of potential dual relations. I was not treating this person and merely did a clinical evaluation for an insurance company. Subsequently he retained me independently as part of his civil suit. Hence there was no dual relationship.

REFERENCES

Ackerman, M.J., & Ackerman, M.C. (1997). Custody evaluations practices: A survey of experiences professionals revisited. *Profession Psychology: Research and Practice, 28*, 137–145.

Ahlmeyer, S., Kleinsasser, D., Stoner, J., & Retzlaff, P. (2003). Psychopathology of incarcerated sex offenders. *Journal of Personality Disorders, 17*, 306–318.

Alexander, P.C., Anderson, C.L., Brand, B., Schaffer, C.M., Grelling, B.Z., & Kretz, L. (1998). Adult attachment and long-term effects in survivors of incest. *Child Abuse and Neglect, 22*, 45–61.

Allen, J.G., Coyne, L., & Huntoon, J. (1998). Complex posttraumatic stress disorder in women from a psychometric perspective. *Journal of Personality Assessment, 70*, 277–298.

American Psychiatric Association. (1983). *Diagnostic and statistical manual of mental disorders* (3rd ed.). Washington, DC: Author.

American Psychiatric Association. (1987). *Diagnostic and statistical manual of mental disorders* (3rd ed., revised). Washington, DC: Author.

American Psychiatric Association. (1994). *Diagnostic and statistical manual of mental disorders* (4th ed.). Washington, DC: Author.

Bayon, C., Hill, K., Svrakic, D.M., Przybeck, T.R., & Cloninger, C.R. (1996). Dimensional assessment of personality in an outpatient sample: Relations of the systems of Millon and Cloninger. *Journal of Psychiatric Research, 30*, 341–352.

Blackburn, R. (1998). Relationship of personality disorders to observer ratings of interpersonal style in forensic psychiatric patients. *Journal of Personality Disorders, 12*, 77–85.

Blais, M.A., Benedict, K., & Norman, D. (1994). Associations among MCMI-II clinical syndrome scales and the MMPI-2 clinical scales. *Assessment, 1*, 401–413.

Boccaccini, M.T., & Brodsky, S. L. (1999). Diagnostic test usage by forensic psychologists in emotional injury cases. *Professional Psychology: Research and Practice, 30*, 253–259.

Bornstein, R.F. (1995). Sex differences in objective and projective dependency tests: A meta-analytic review. *Assessment, 2*, 319–331.

Borum, R., & Grisso, T. (1995). Psychological test use in criminal forensic evaluations. *Professional Psychology: Research and Practice, 26*, 465–473.

Brodie, L.A. (2003). *Child custody: Issues and techniques* (Part 1). PsychCredits.com.

Butcher, J.N., & Miller, K. B. (1999). Personality assessment in personal injury litigation. In A. K. Hess & I. B. Weiner (Eds.), *The handbook of forensic psychology* (2nd ed., pp. 104–126). New York: Wiley.

Butcher, J.N., & Rouse, S. (1996). Clinical personality assessment. *Annual Review of Psychology, 47*, 87–111.

Calsyn, D.A., Fleming, C., Wells, E. A., & Saxon, A. J. (1996). Personality disorder subtypes among opiate addicts in methadone maintenance. *Psychology of Addictive Behaviors, 10*, 3–8.

Calsyn, D.A., Saxon, A. J., & Daisy, F. (1990). Validity of the MCMI drug abuse scale with drug abusing and psychiatric samples. *Journal of Clinical Psychology, 46*, 244–246.

Camara, W., Nathan, J., & Ouente, A. (2000). Psychological test usage: Implications in professional use. *Professional Psychology: Research and Practice, 31*, 141–154.

Carpenter, D.R., Peed, S. F., & Eastman, B. (1995). Personality characteristics of adolescent sexual of fenders: A pilot study. *Sexual Abuse, 7*, 195–202.

Chick, D., Sheaffer, C.I., & Goggin, W.C. (1993). The relationship between MCMI personality scales and clinician-generated *DSM–III–R* personality disorder diagnoses. *Journal of Personality Assessment, 61*, 264–276.

Choca, J.P., Bresolin, L., Okonek, A., & Ostrow, D. (1988). Validity of the MCMI in the assessment of affective disorders. *Journal of Personality Assessment, 52*, 96–105.

Choca, J.P., Shanley, L.A., Peterson, C.A., & VanDenburg, E. (1990). Racial bias and the MCMI. *Journal of Personality Assessment, 54*, 479–490.

Cohen, L.J., Gans, S.W., McGeoch, P. G., Poznansky, O., Itskovich, Y., Murphy, S., et al. (2002). Impulsive personality traits in male pedophiles versus healthy controls: Is pedophilia an impulsive-aggressive disorder? *Comprehensive Psychiatry, 43*, 127–134.

Coolidge, F.L., & Merwin, M.M. (1992). Reliability and validity of the Coolidge Axis II Inventory: A new inventory for the assessment of personality disorders. *Journal of Personality Assessment, 59*, 233–238.

Craig, R.J. (2006). *MCMI-II/III computer narrative report.* Odessa, FL: Psychological Assessment Resources.

Craig, R.J. (1995). Clinical diagnoses and MCMI codetypes. *Journal of Clinical Psychology, 51,* 352–360.

Craig, R.J. (1999). Testimony based on the Millon Clinical Multiaxial Inventory: Review, commentary, and guidelines. *Journal of Personality Assessment, 73,* 290–316.

Craig, R.J. (2003a). Assessing personality and psychopathology with interviews. In I.B. Weiner (Series Ed.) & J.R. Graham & J.A. Neglieri (Vol. Eds.), *Handbook of psychology: Vol. 10. Assessment Psychology* (pp. 487–508). New York: Wiley.

Craig, R.J. (2003b). Use of the Millon Clinical Multiaxial Inventory in the psychological assessment of domestic violence: A review. *Aggression and Violent Behavior, 8,* 235–243.

Craig, R.J. (2003c). Prevalence of personality disorders among cocaine and heroin addicts. *Directions in Addiction Treatment and Prevention, 7,* 33–42.

Craig, R.J. (2005a). Alternative interpretations for the Histrionic, Narcissistic, and Compulsive personality disorder scales of the Millon Clinical Multiaxial Inventory. In R.J. Craig (Ed.), *New Directions in interpreting the Millon Clinical Multiaxial Inventory.* (pp. 71–93). New York: Wiley.

Craig, R.J. (2005b). *Personality-guided forensic psychology.* Washington, DC: American Psychological Association.

Craig, R.J. (2005c). *Assessing substance abusers with the Millon Clinical Multiaxial Inventory.* Springfield, IL: Charles C Thomas.

Craig, R.J. (2003). Use of the Millon Clinical Multiaxial Inventory in the psychological assessment of domestic violence: A review. *Aggression and Violent Behavior, 8,* 235–243.

Craig, R.J., Bivens, A., & Olson, R. (1997). MCMI-III-derived typological analysis of cocaine and heroin addicts. *Journal of Personality Assessment, 69,* 583–595.

Craig, R.J., Kuncel, R., & Olson, R. (1994). Ability of drug abusers to avoid detection of substance abuse on the MCMI-II. *Journal of Social Behavior and Personality, 9,* 95–106.

Craig, R.J., & Olson, R. E. (1992). Relationship between MCMI-II scales and normal personality traits. *Psychological Reports, 71,* 699–705.

Craig, R.J., & Olson, R. (1997). Assessing PTSD with the Millon Clinical Multiaxial Inventory–III. *Journal of Clinical Psychology, 53,* 943–952.

Craig, R.J., & Olson, R. (1998). Stability of the MCMI-III in a substance-abusing inpatient sample. *Psychological Reports, 83,* 1273–1274.

Craig, R.J., & Weinberg, D. (1992a) Assessing drug abusers with the Millon Clinical Multiaxial Inventory: A review. *Journal of Substance Abuse Treatment, 9,* 249–255.

Craig, R.J., & Weinberg, D. (1992b) Assessing alcoholics with the Millon Clinical Multiaxial Inventory: A review. *Psychology of Addictive Behaviors, 6,* 200–208.

Dana, R., & Cantrell, J. (1988). An update on the Millon Clinical Multiaxial Inventory (MCMI). *Journal of Clinical Psychology, 44,* 760–763.

Davis, R. (2005). Diagnosis of personality disorder subtypes. In R.J. Craig (Ed)., *New interpretations of the Millon Clinical Multiaxial Inventory–III* (pp. 32–70). New York: Wiley.

Davis, R.A. & Patterson, M.P. (2005). Diagnosing personality disorder subtypes with the MCMI-III. In R.J. Craig (Ed.). *New directions in interpreting the Millon Clinical Personality Inventory.* New York: John Wiley & Sons. pp. 32–70.

Davis, W.E., Greenblatt, R.L., & Pochyly, J.M. (1990). Test of MCMI Black norms for five scales. *Journal of Clinical Psychology, 46,* 175–178.

Daubert v. Merrell Dow Pharmaceuticals, Inc., 113 S. Ct. 2786 (1993).

Dillon, S.K. (1988). Narcissism and embellishments of signature. *Psychological Reports, 62,* 152–154.

Donat, D.C. (1994). Empirical groupings of perceptions of alcohol use among alcohol dependent persons: A cluster analysis of the alcohol use inventory (AUI) scales. *Assessment, 1,* 103–110.

Donat, D.C., Walters, J., & Hume, A. (1992). MCMI differences between alcoholics and cocaine abusers: Effects of age, sex, and race. *Journal of Personality Assessment, 58,* 96–104.

Dubro, A. F., & Wetzler, S. (1989). An external validity study of the MMPI personality disorder scales. *Journal of Clinical Psychology, 45,* 570–575.

last-page-books-Columbus
3860 La Reunion Pkwy.
Dallas, TX 75212
outletohio@hpb.com

Items:

Qty	Title	Locator
1	Forensic Uses of Clinical Asse...	L01-2-74-012-001-3062

Marketplace: AmazonMarketplaceUS
Order Number: 6944296
Ship Method: Standard
Customer Name: Loren M
Order Date: 9/2/2017 9:22:04 AM
Marketplace Order #: 111-5449925-1297035
Email: 31pc635lj52p53k@marketplace.amazon.com

If you have any questions or concerns regarding this order, please contact us at outletohio@hpb.com

Dyce, J.A., O'Connor, B.P., Parkins, S. Y., & Janzen, H.L. (1997). Correlational structure of the MCMI-III personality disorder scales and comparisons with other data sets. *Journal of Abnormal Psychology, 69,* 568–582.

Dyer, F.J. (2005). Forensic application of the MCMI-III in light of recent controversies. In R.J. Craig (Ed.), *New directions in interpreting the Millon Clinical Multiaxial Inventory* (pp. 201–226). New York: Wiley.

Dyer, F.J., & McCann, J.T. (2000). The Millon clinical inventories, research critical of their application, and *Daubert* criteria. *Law and Human Behavior, 24,* 487–497.

Fals-Stewart, W. (1995). The effect of defensive responding by substance-abusing patients on the Millon Clinical Multiaxial Inventory. *Journal of Personality Assessment, 64,* 540–551.

Flynn, P.M., McCann, J.T., & Fairbank, J.A. (1995). Issues in the assessment of personality disorder and substance abuse using the Millon Clinical Multiaxial Inventory (MCMI-II). *Journal of Clinical Psychology, 51,* 415–421.

Gabrys, J.B., Kent, A., Utendale, D.S., Phillips, N., Peters K., Robertson, G., et al. (1988). Two inventories for the measurement of psychopathology: Dimensions and common factorial space on Millon's clinical and Eysenck's general personality scales. *Psychological Reports, 62,* 591–601.

Gibertini, M., Brandenberg, N., & Retzlaff, P. (1986). The operating characteristics of the Millon Clinical Multiaxial Inventory. *Journal of Personality Assessment, 50,* 554–567.

Goldberg, J.O., Shaw, B., & Segal, Z.V. (1987). Concurrent validity of the MCMI depression scales. *Journal of Consulting and Clinical Psychology, 55,* 785–787.

Grossman, S., & del Rio, C. (2005). The MCMI-III facet subscales. In R.J. Craig (Ed.), *New interpretations for the Millon Clinical Multiaxial Inventory–III* (pp. 3–31). New York: Wiley.

Guthrie, P.C., & Mobley, B.D. (1994). A comparison of the differential diagnostic efficiency of three personality disorder inventories. *Journal of Clinical Psychology, 50,* 656–665.

Haller, D.L., Miles, D.R., & Dawson, K.S. (2002). Psychopathology influences treatment retention among drug-dependent women. *Journal of Substance Abuse Treatment, 23,* 431–436.

Halon, R.L. (2001). The Millon Clinical Multiaxial Inventory–III: The normal quartet in child custody cases. *American Journal of Forensic Psychology, 19,* 57–75.

Hamberger, L.K., & Hastings, J.E. (1989). Counseling male spouse abusers: Characteristics of treatment completers and dropouts. *Violence and Victims, 4,* 275–286.

Hart, S.D., Dutton, D.G., & Newlove, T. (1993). The prevalence of personality disorder among wife assaulters. *Journal of Personality Disorders, 7,* 329–341.

Hart, S.D., Forth, A.E., & Hare, R.D. (1991). The MCMI-II and psychopathy. *Journal of Personality Disorders, 5,* 318–327.

Henning, K., Jones, A., & Holdford, R. (2003). Treatment needs of women arrested for domestic violence: A comparison with male offenders. *Journal of Interpersonal Violence, 18,* 839–856.

Hess, A.K. (1998). Review of the Millon Clinical Multiaxial Inventory–III. In J. Mitchell (Ed.), *Mental measurements yearbook.* Lincoln: University of Nebraska Press. 984–986.

Hicklin, J., & Widiger, T.A. (2000). Convergent validity of alternative MMPI–2 personality disorder scale. *Journal of Personality Assessment, 75,* 502–518.

Hills, H.A. (1995). Diagnosing personality disorders: An examination of the MMPI–2 and MCMI-II. *Journal of Personality Assessment, 65,* 21–34.

Hogg, B., Jackson, H.J., Rudd, R.P., & Edwards, J. (1990). Diagnosing personality disorders in recent-onset schizophrenia. *Journal of Nervous and Mental Disease, 179,* 194–199.

Holliman, N., & Guthrie, P. (1989). A comparison of the MCMI and the CPI in assessment of a nonclinical population. *Journal of Clinical Psychology, 45,* 373–382.

Holt, S.E., Meloy, J. R., & Strack, S. (1999). Sadism and psychopathy in violent and sexually violent offenders. *Journal of the American Academy of Psychiatry and Law, 27,* 23–32.

Hyer, L., Boyd, S., Stanger, E., Davis, H., & Walters, P. (1997). Validation of the MCMI-III PTSD scale among combat veterans. *Psychological Reports, 80,* 720–722.

Hyer, L., Brandsma, J., & Boyd, S. (1997). The MCMIs and posttraumatic stress disorder. In T. Millon (Ed.), *The Millon inventories: Clinical and personality assessment* (pp. 191–216.) New York: Guilford Press.

Hyer, L., Melton, M., & Gratton, C. (1993). Posttraumatic stress disorders and MCMI-based assessment. In R. J. Craig (Ed.), *The Millon Clinical Multiaxial Inventory: A clinical and research information synthesis.* (pp. 159–172) Hillsdale, NJ: Erlbaum.

Hyer, L., Woods, M.G., Bruno, R., & Boudewyns, P. (1989). Treatment outcomes of Vietnam veterans with PTSD and consistency of the MCMI. *Journal of Clinical Psychology, 45,* 547–552.

Jeffrey v. Dillard's Department Stores and Dillard's Bel Air Mall, United States District Court for the Southern District of Alabama, Southern Division, 2000.

Keilin, W.J., & Bloom,. L.J. (1986). Child custody evaluation practices: A survey of experienced professionals. *Professional Psychology: Research and Practice, 17,* 338–346.

Kelln, B.R., Dozois, D.J., & McKenzie, I.E. (1998). An MCMI-III discriminant function analysis of incarcerated felons: Prediction of subsequent institutional misconduct. *Criminal Justice and Behavior, 25,* 177–189.

Kennedy, S.H., Katz, R., Rockert, W., Mendlowitz, S., Ralevski, E., & Clewes, C.J. (1995). Assessment of personality disorders in anorexia nervosa and bulimia nervosa: A comparison of self-report and structured interview methods. *Journal of Nervous and Mental Disease, 183,* 358–364.

Klein, M.H., Benjamin, L.S., Rosenfeld, R., Treece, C., Husted, J., & Greist, J. H. (1993). The Wisconsin Personality Disorders Inventory: Development, reliability, and validity. *Journal of Personality Disorders, 7,* 285–303.

Lally, S.J. (2003). What tests are acceptable for use in forensic evaluations? A survey of experts. *Professional Psychology: Research and Practice, 26,* 54–60.

Lampel, A.K. (1999). Use of the Millon Clinical Multiaxial Inventory–III in evaluating child custody litigants. *American Journal of Forensic Psychology, 17,* 19–31.

Langevin, R., Paitich, D., Freeman, R., Mann, K., & Handy, L. (1979). Personality and sexual anomalies: An examination of the Millon Clinical Multiaxial Inventory. *Annals of Sex Research, 1,* 13–32.

Lecic-Tosevski, D., Gavrilovic, J., Knezevic, G., & Priebe, S. (2003). Personality factors and posttraumatic stress: Associations in civilians one year after air attacks. *Journal of Personality Disorders, 17,* 537–549.

Lehne, G.K. (2002). The NEO Personality Inventory and the Millon Clinical Multiaxial Inventory in the forensic evaluation of sex offenders. In P. T. Costa & T. A. Widiger (Eds.), *Personality disorders and the five-factor model of personality* (2nd ed., pp. 269–282). Washington, DC: American Psychological Association.

Lenzenweger, M.F. (1999). Stability and change in personality disorder features. *Archives of General Psychiatry, 56,* 1009–1018.

Libb, J.W., Stankovic, S., Sokol, A., Houck, C., & Switzer, P. (1990). Stability of the MCMI among depressed psychiatric outpatients. *Journal of Personality Assessment, 55,* 209–218.

Lindsay, K.A., Sankis, L.M., & Widiger, T.A. (2000). Gender bias in self-report personality disorder inventories. *Journal of Personality Disorders, 14,* 218–232.

Lindsay, K.A., & Widiger, T.A. (1995). Sex and gender bias in self-report personality disorder inventories: Item analysis of the MCMI-II, MMPI, and PDQ-R. *Journal of Personality Assessment, 65,* 1–20.

Marlowe, D.B., Husband, S.D., Bonieskie, L.M., Kirby, K.C., & Platt, J.J. (1997). Structured interview versus self-report test advantages for the assessment of personality pathology in cocaine dependence. *Journal of Personality Disorders, 11,* 177–190.

Marsh, D.T., Stile, S.A., Stoughton, N.L., & Trout-Landen, B.L. (1988). Psychopathology among opiate addiction: Comparative data from the MMPI and MCMI. *American Journal of Drug and Alcohol Abuse, 14,* 17–27.

Matano, R.A., Locke, K.D., & Schwartz, K. (1994). MCMI personality subtypes for male and female alcoholics. *Journal of Personality Assessment, 63,* 250–264.

McCann, J.T. (1989). MMPI personality disorder scales and the MCMI: Concurrent validity. *Journal of Clinical Psychology, 45,* 365–369.

McCann, J.T. (1990). A multitrait-multimethod analysis of the MCMI-II clinical syndrome scales. *Journal of Personality Assessment, 55,* 465–476.

McCann, J.T. (1991). Convergent and discriminant validity of the MCMI-II and MMPI personality disorder scales. *Psychological Assessment, 3,* 9–18.

McCann, J.T. (2002). Guidelines for forensic application of the MCMI-III. *Journal of Forensic Psychology Practice, 2,* 55–69.

McCann, J., & Dyer, F.J. (1996). *Forensic assessment with the Millon inventories.* New York: Guilford Press.

McCann, J.T., Flens, J.R., Campagna, V., Collman, P., Lazarro, T., & Connor, E. (2001). The MCMI-III in child custody evaluations: A normative study. *Journal of Forensic Psychology Practice, 1*, 27–44.

McCann, J.T., Flynn, P.M., & Gersh, D.M. (1992). MCMI-II diagnosis of borderline personality disorders: Base rates versus prototypic items. *Journal of Personality Assessment, 58*, 105–114.

McMahon, R.C., & Davidson, R. S. (1985). An examination of the relationship between personality patterns and symptom/mood patterns. *Journal of Personality Assessment, 49*, 552–556.

McMahon, R.C., Davidson, R.S., & Flynn, P. M. (1986). Psychological correlates and treatment outcomes for high and low social functioning alcoholics. *International Journal of the Addictions, 21*, 819–835.

McMahon, R.C., Flynn, P.M., & Davidson, R.S. (1985). Stability of the personality and symptom scales of the Millon Clinical Multiaxial Inventory. *Journal of Personality Assessment, 49*, 231–234.

McMahon, R.C., Malow, R.M., & Peneod, F.J. (1998). Substance abuse problems, psychiatric severity, and HIV risk in Millon Clinical Multiaxial Inventory–II personality subgroups. *Psychology of Addictive Behaviors, 12*, 3–13.

McMahon, R.C., & Richards, S.K. (1996). Profile patterns, consistency, and change in the Millon Clinical Multiaxial Inventory–II in cocaine abusers. *Journal of Clinical Psychology, 52*, 75–79.

Messina, N., Wish, E., Hoffman, J., & Nemes, S. (2001). Diagnosing antisocial personality disorder among substance abusers: The SCID versus the MCMI-II. *American Journal of Drug and Alcohol Abuse, 27*, 699–717.

Miller, H.R., Streiner, D.L., & Parkinson, A. (1992). Maximum likelihood estimates of the ability of the MMPI and MCMI personality disorder scales and the SIDP to identify personality disorders. *Journal of Personality Assessment, 59*, 1–13.

Millon, T. (1983). *Millon Clinical Multiaxial Inventory manual.* New York: Holt, Rinehart & Winston.

Millon, T. (1987). *Millon Clinical Multiaxial Inventory–II: Manual for the MCMI-II.* Minneapolis, MN: Pearson Assessments.

Millon, T. (1990). *Toward a new personology.* New York: Wiley.

Millon, T. (1994). *Millon Clinical Multiaxial Inventory–III: Manual.* Minneapolis, MN: Pearson Assessments.

Millon, T. (1997). *Millon Clinical Multiaxial Inventory–III: Manual* (2nd ed.). Minneapolis, MN: Pearson Assessments.

Millon, T., & Davis, R. (1997). *Disorders of personality.* New York: Guilford Press.

Millon, T., Millon, C., & Davis, R. (2003). *MCMI-III corrections report.* Minneapolis, MN: Pearson Assessments.

Morgan, C.D., Schoenberg, M.R., Dorr, D., & Burke, M.J. (2002). Overreport on the MCMI-III: Concurrent validation with the MMPI-2 using a psychiatric inpatient sample. *Journal of Personality Assessment, 78*, 288–300.

Morey, L.C. (1985). An empirical approach of interpersonal and DSM–III approaches to classification of personality disorders. *Psychiatry, 48*, 358–364.

Morey, L.C., & Levine, D.J. (1988). A multitrait-multimethod examination of Minnesota Multiphasic Personality Inventory (MMPI) and Millon Clinical Multiaxial Inventory (MCMI). *Journal of Psychopathology and Behavioral Assessment, 10*, 333–344.

Munley, P.H., Vacha-Haase, T., Busby, R.M., & Paul, B.D. (1998). The MCMI-II and race. *Journal of Personality Assessment, 70*, 183–189.

Murphy, T.J., Greenblatt, R.L., Modzierz, G.J., & Trimakas, K.A. (1991). Stability of the Millon Clinical Multiaxial Inventory among psychiatric inpatients. *Journal of Psychopathology and Behavioral Assessment, 12*, 143–150.

Otto, R.K., & Butcher, J.N. (1995). Computer-assisted psychological assessment in child custody evaluations. *Family Law Quarterly, 29*, 79–96.

Overholser, J.C. (1990). Retest reliability of the Millon Clinical Multiaxial Inventory. *Journal of Personality Assessment, 55*, 202–208.

Patrick, J. (1993). Validation of the MCMI-1 borderline personality disorder scale with a well-defined criterion sample. *Journal of Clinical Psychology, 49*, 29–32.

Piersma, H.L. (1986). The Millon Clinical Multiaxial Inventory (MCMI) as a treatment outcome measure for psychiatric inpatients. *Journal of Clinical Psychology, 42,* 493–499.

Piersma, H.L. (1989). The stability of the MCMI-II for psychiatric inpatients. *Journal of Clinical Psychology. 45,* 781–785.

Piersma, H.L., & Boes, J.L. (1997). The relationship between length of stay to MCMI-II and MCMI-III change scores. *Journal of Clinical Psychology, 53,* 535–542.

Quinnell, F.A., & Bow, J.N. (2001). Psychological tests used in child custody evaluations. *Behavioral Science and the Law, 19,* 491–501.

Retzlaff, P., Stoner, J., & Kleinasser, D. (2002). The use of the MCMI-III in the screening and triage of offenders. *International Journal of Offender Therapy and Comparative Criminology, 46,* 319–332.

Rogers, R. (2003). Forensic use and abuse of psychological tests: Multiscale inventories. *Journal of Psychiatric Practice, 9,* 316–320.

Rogers, R., Salekin, R.T., & Sewell, K.W. (1999). Validation of the Millon Clinical Multiaxial Inventory for Axis II disorders: Does it meet the *Daubert* standard? *Law and Human Behavior, 23,* 425–443.

Rogers, R., Salekin, R.T., & Sewell, K.W. (2000). The MCMI-III and the *Daubert* standard: Separating rhetoric from reality. *Law and Human Behavior, 24,* 501–506.

Rossi, G., Hauben, C., Van den Brande, I., & Sloore, H. (2003). Empirical evaluation of the MCMI-III personality disorder scales. *Psychological Reports, 92,* 627–642.

Rossi, G., Van den Brande, I., Tobac, A., Sloore, H., & Hauben, C. (2003). Convergent validity of the MCMI-III personality disorder scales and the MMPI-2 scales. *Journal of Personality Disorders, 17,* 330–340.

Salekin, R.T., Rogers, R., & Sewell, K. W. (1996). Review and meta-analysis of the Psychopathy Checklist and Psychopathy Checklist–Revised. *Clinical Psychology: Science and Practice, 3,* 203–215.

Schwartz, J.P., Seemann, E., Buboltz, W.C., & Flye, A. (2004). Personality styles: Predictors of masculine gender role conflict in male prison inmates. *Psychology of Men and Masculinity, 5,* 59–64.

Schuler, C.E., Snibbe, J.R., & Buckwalter, J.G., (1994). Validity of the MMPI personality disorder scales (MMPI-Pd). *Journal of Clinical Psychology, 50,* 220–227.

Schutte, J.W. (2001). Using the MCMI-III in forensic evaluations. *American Journal of Forensic Psychology, 19,* 5–20.

Silberman, C.S., Roth, L., Segal, D.L., & Burns, W. J. (1997). Relationship between the Millon Clinical Multiaxial Inventory–II and Coolidge Axis II Inventory in chronically mentally ill older adults: A pilot study. *Journal of Clinical Psychology, 53,* 559–566.

Sinha, B.K., & Watson, D.C. (2001). Personality disorder in university students: A multitrait-multimethod matrix study. *Journal of Personality Disorders, 15,* 235–244.

Smith, D., Carroll, J.L., & Fuller, G. (1988). The relationship between the Millon Clinical Multiaxial Inventory and the MMPI in a private outpatient mental health clinic population. *Journal of Clinical Psychology, 44,* 165–174.

Soldz, S., Budman, S., Demby, A., & Merry, J. (1993). Diagnostic agreement between the Personality Disorder Examination and the MCMI-II. *Journal of Personality Assessment, 60,* 486–499.

Torgersen, S., & Alnaes, R. (1990). The relationship between the MCMI personality scales and DSM–III, Axis II. *Journal of Personality Assessment, 55,* 698–707.

Turley, B., Bates, G.W., Edwards, J., & Jackson, H. J. (1992). MCMI-II personality disorders in recent-onset bipolar disorders. *Journal of Clinical Psychology, 48,* 320–329.

Watkins, C., Campbell, V., Nieberding, R., & Hallmark, R. (1995). Contemporary practice of psychological assessment by clinical psychologists. *Professional Psychology: Research and Practice, 26,* 54–60.

Wheeler, D.S., & Schwartz, J.C. (1989). Millon Clinical Inventory (MCMI) scores with a collegiate sample: Long term stability and self-other agreement. *Journal of Psychopathology and Behavioral Assessment, 11,* 339–352.

White, R.J., Ackerman, R.J., & Caraveo, L.E. (2001). Self-identified alcohol abusers in a low-security federal prison: Characteristics and treatment implications. *International Journal of Offender Therapy and Comparative Criminology, 45,* 214–227.

Widiger, T. (2001). Review of the Millon Clinical Multiaxial Inventory. In J. V. Mitchell, Jr. (Ed.), *The ninth mental measurements yearbook* (Vol. 1, pp. 986–988). Lincoln: University of Nebraska Press.

Widiger, T., & Sanderson, C. (1987). The convergent and discriminant validity of the MCMI as a measure of the *DSM III* personality disorders. *Journal of Personality Assessment, 51,* 228–242.

Wierzbicki, M., & Gorman, J. L. (1995). Correspondence between students' scores on the Millon Clinical Multiaxial Inventory–II and Personality Diagnostic Questionnaire–Revised. *Psychological Reports, 77,* 1079–1082.

Wise, E. A. (1994a). Managed care and the psychometric validity of the MMPI and MCMI personality disorder scales. *Psychotherapy in Private Practice, 13,* 81–97.

Wise, E. A. (1994b). Personality style codetype concordance between the MCMI and MBHI. *Journal of Clinical Psychology, 50,* 367–380.

Wise, E. A. (1996). Comparative validity of MMPI-2 and MCMI-II personality disorder classifications. *Journal of Personality Assessment, 66,* 569–582.

Wise, E. A. (2001). The comparative validity of MCMI-II and MMPI-2 personality disorder scales with forensic examinees. *Journal of Personality Disorders, 15,* 275–279.

Zarella, K. L., Schuerger, J. M., & Ritz, G. H. (1990). Estimation of MCMI DSM–III Axis II constructs from MMPI scales and subscales. *Journal of Personality Assessment, 55,* 195–201.

6

THE PSYCHOPATHY CHECKLIST–REVISED AND THE PSYCHOPATHY CHECKLIST: YOUTH VERSION

ANGELA S. BOOK

BROCK UNIVERSITY

HEATHER J. CLARK
ADELLE E. FORTH

CARLETON UNIVERSITY

ROBERT D. HARE

UNIVERSITY OF BRITISH COLUMBIA

In 1941, Hervey Cleckley described a subgroup of patients who appeared to be normal (i.e., not insane) and yet lacked remorse and empathy and were very impulsive, deceptive, and manipulative. He suggested that these individuals suffered from "emotional poverty," and he described in detail a number of symptoms, subsequently operationalized for research purposes by Hare (1980) in the Hare Psychopathy Checklist (PCL). A large number of studies using the PCL and its successor (the Hare Psychopathy Checklist–Revised [PCL–R]; Hare, 1991, 2003) have established the importance of these instruments in research and in clinical and forensic practice (Cooke, Forth, & Hare, 1998; Fulero, 1995; Gacono, 2000; Patrick, 2005).

The PCL–R describes psychopathy as a constellation of interpersonal, affective, and behavioral characteristics. As discussed later, there is converging evidence for a strong association between psychopathy and serious repetitive crime, violent behavior and recidivism, instrumental and "cold-blooded" violence, and poor treatment prognosis.

The construct of psychopathy, as applied to children and adolescents, has received increasing attention (Forth & Burke, 1998; Forth & Mailloux, 2000; Frick, 2000; Frick, O'Brien, Wootton, & McBurnett, 1994; Kosson, Cyterski, Steurerwald, Neumann, & Walker-Matthews, 2002; Lynam, 1996). Psychopathy does not emerge suddenly in adulthood. Many researchers and clinicians believe that psychopathic traits and behaviors are first manifested early in life. Consequently, there have been attempts to develop measures to identify psychopathic traits early in development. There is increasing evidence that potential precursors of these traits can be identified as early as 5 or 6 years of age (Dadds, Fraser, Frost, & Hawes, 2005; Frick & Hare, 2001; Lynam, 1998; Lynam & Gudonis, 2005) and that psychopathic features can be measured in adolescence. Forth, Kosson, and Hare (2003) modeled the Psychopathy Checklist: Youth Version (PCL:YV) on the PCL–R items, modifying those that were applicable only to adult offenders (e.g., many short-term marital relationships). As with adults, psychopathic features in youth are associated with negative outcomes, such as disruptive behavior disorders (Salekin, Neumann, Leistico, DiCicco, & Duros, 2004), number of offences (Kosson et al., 2002; Murrie, Cornell, Kaplan, McConville, & Levy-Elkon, 2004), institutional violence (Murrie et al., 2004), and general and violent recidivism (Corrado, Vincent, Hart, & Cohen, 2004; Gretton, McBride, Hare, O'Shaughnessy, & Kumka, 2001).

The purpose of this chapter is to discuss the development, psychometric properties, strengths, and limitations of the PCL–R (Hare, 1991, 2003) and the PCL:YV (Forth et al., 2003) in forensic settings. The measures are discussed separately, beginning with the PCL–R.

HARE PSYCHOPATHY CHECKLIST–REVISED

Description

The PCL–R (Hare, 1991, 2003) is a 20-item construct rating scale widely used in research, clinical, and forensic settings for the assessment of psychopathy in adults. The scale items measure personality traits and behaviors related to traditional conceptions of psychopathy, such as impulsivity, lack of empathy, lack of remorse, and grandiosity (see Berrios, 1996; Cleckley, 1976; Coid, 1993; Cooke et al., 1998; Millon, Simonsen, Birket-Smith, & Davies, 1998; Pichot, 1978). Each item is rated on a 3-point scale (0, 1, or 2) according to the extent to which an individual exhibits the trait or behavior being rated. The total score varies from 0 to 40, reflecting the degree to which the individual matches the prototypical psychopath. This score can also be used to classify individuals as psychopathic. Typically, a cut score of 30 is used, although other cut scores have been used periodically in research contexts (Hare, 2003; Hare & Neumann, 2005a). In the 1991 manual, this score appeared to have the best diagnostic efficiency with respect to clinical assessments of psychopathy in use prior to the inception of the precursor of the PCL–R, the PCL (Hare, 1980). A score of 30 was approximately 1 standard deviation above the mean for pooled samples of offenders.

The standard procedure for administration of the PCL–R involves a semistructured interview and a review of available file and collateral information (Hare, 2003). The interview typically covers education, employment and family background, relationships, substance use, and antisocial behaviors from adolescence on. It usually takes between 90 and 120 minutes and may be spread over several sessions, allowing for a more representative sample of the individual's interactional style.

The interview itself has several purposes. First, certain historical information about the individual is required for scoring PCL–R items. Second, the interview often provides clues as to the individual's interpersonal style. It also gives the assessor a chance to evaluate consistency (and deception) within the interview and between the interview and collateral information. Finally, the use of an interview allows probes and challenges when further information is required or inconsistencies are encountered. The latter purpose is facilitated if the file review is conducted prior to the interview, giving the interviewer a basis for challenging or probing.

The second part of the assessment involves reviewing any collateral and/or file information that is available; this is a mandatory aspect of the assessment. The use of collateral information allows the rater to evaluate the truth or reliability of the information given in the interview, determine the representativeness of the interactional style during the interview, and gain access to primary data for scoring several of the PCL–R items. A collateral review typically takes about 60 minutes but can be longer if the file information is extensive and detailed.

Available collateral information will depend on the setting in which the assessment is conducted. In correctional settings, files typically contain a variety of official records that may be helpful in scoring the items of the PCL–R and usually are adequate for collateral review (Hare, 2003). In forensic psychiatric and pretrial settings, raters may have access to official reports but may also be able to examine reports of interviews with family members, friends and employers, as well as the results of medical and psychological assessments. When dealing with nonoffenders it may be difficult to obtain sufficient collateral information, although there may be methods available for accessing some useful information, such as telephone interviews, work records, peer ratings, and so forth. Regardless of the context in which the assessment is conducted, information should come from as many different sources as possible. Scores for items should not be calculated unless there is adequate collateral information.

History of the Instrument's Development

The PCL

The development of the PCL was initiated in part because of concerns about extant assessment procedures, including clinical diagnosis and the use of self-report instruments, as these did not demonstrate adequate reliability or validity (Hare, 1980, 2003; Hare & Neumann, 2005a). The first step in its development involved psychometric analyses of the features of psychopathy described by Cleckley (1976), along with a compilation of traits and behaviors Hare and his colleagues found useful in the assessment of psychopathy in a prison setting. This process resulted in a pool of more than 100 items. Those that were overly redundant or would be next to impossible to rate reliably were eliminated from the pool. Preliminary scoring criteria were developed for the remaining items. Items were scored by two investigators, who used both interview and file information. Each item was scored on a 3-point ordinal scale, as noted earlier. Analyses were conducted to ascertain which items were most psychometrically sound and were able to discriminate between inmates with low and high (7-point) global ratings of psychopathy. After this procedure, only 22 items remained. Hare and Frazelle (1980) disseminated a mimeographed manual for other investigators to use. Amongst the items, some were intended to measure complex behaviors and traits, and scoring these items required the use of clinical judgment. In spite of this, the items had acceptable interrater reliabilities (Hare, 1980). The total scores, which could range from 0 to 44, also displayed high interrater reliability ($r = .93$) and internal consistency (Cronbach's alpha = .88). Total scores were highly correlated with global ratings of psychopathy ($r = .83$). Numerous studies have indicated that the PCL was both reliable and valid (see Hare, 2003, for a review).

Revision: The PCL–R

Comments and concerns from fellow researchers indicated that it was important to make a number of improvements to the PCL (Hare, 2003). Two items were deleted because of scoring difficulties, and one item was altered to be more general: Item 6 ("irresponsible behavior as a parent") was deemed to be too specific and was changed to "irresponsibility" in general. Further, item content and scoring procedures were described in greater detail. Finally, the procedure for dealing with inadequate information was revised. Originally, a score of 1 could be assigned where there was not enough evidence or information to score an item with confidence. For the PCL–R, the item simply would be omitted and the total score would be prorated. A draft version of the PCL–R was created based on these revisions (Hare, 1985) and was circulated throughout the research community. Subsequently, the draft was fine-tuned and the scoring criteria clarified in order to make the manual (and the instrument) easier for other investigators to use. These changes did not affect the actual scores assigned to an item. A formal manual was published as *The Hare PCL–R* (Hare, 1991).

The PCL–R Second Edition (2003)

Although no changes were needed in the wording or scoring of the PCL–R items, a revision to the manual was deemed necessary for several reasons. First, the authors sought to minimize the misuse of the PCL–R, especially where it is used to guide adjudication and treatment decisions. One of the most important requirements for proper use of the PCL–R is familiarity with the current literature. However, it was apparent that many of those who produced psychological reports for the criminal justice system or who testified in court relied primarily on material published in the 1991 manual. The inclusion of more recent research in the 2003 manual was intended to provide users with more information about the PCL–R assessment of psychopathy. Nontheless, it is still extremely important for users to keep abreast of the current literature, especially with regard to its implications for minority and legal issues.

The second reason for the revision was that a large amount of data had been generated since the original manual was written. The explosion in research provided extensive data for establishing comparison tables and for addressing issues concerning the factor structure, reliability, validity, and generalizability of the PCL–R. Psychometric analyses were conducted on 10,896 North American and European offenders and forensic patients, and these are fully detailed in the manual (Hare, 2003).

Factor Structure, Reliability, and Generalizability

Factor Structure

Exploratory factor analyses of the data sets used in the 1991 manual yielded two correlated factors. Factor 1 reflected interpersonal and affective features (items 1, 2, 4, 5, 6, 7, 8, and 16), whereas Factor 2 reflected social deviance features (items 3, 9, 10, 12, 13, 14, 15, 18, and 19). Items 11, 17, and 20 did not load on either of the factors (see Table 6.1).

TABLE 6.1
Factors, Facets, and Items in the PCL–R

Factor 1: Interpersonal/Affective

Interpersonal	*Affective*
1. Glibness/superficial charm	6. Lack of remorse
2. Grandiose self-worth	7. Shallow affect
4. Pathological lying	8. Lack of empathy
5. Conning/manipulative	16. Will not accept responsibility

Factor 2: Lifestyle/Antisocial

Lifestyle	*Antisocial*
3. Need for stimulation	10. Poor behavioral controls
9. Parasitic lifestyle	12. Early behavioral problems
13. Lack of goals	18. Juvenile delinquency
14. Impulsivity	19. Revocation conditional release
15. Irresponsibility	20. Criminal versatility

Note: From Hare, 2003. Item 11, Promiscuous sexual behavior, and Item 17, Many short-term marital relationships, contribute to the total PCL–R score but do not load on any factors. The Interpersonal and Affective factors underpin a broad factor (Interpersonal/Affective) identical with the original Factor 1 described in the 1991 manual. The Lifestyle and Antisocial factors underpin a broad factor (Lifestyle/Antisocial) identical with the original Factor 2 described in the 1991 manual except for the addition of item 20.

This two-Factor structure has been replicated several times, and it formed the early basis for exploring the differential correlates of the components of psychopathy.

More recently, Cooke and Michie (2001) argued that the two-factor model was untenable when evaluated with current statistical methods. They performed a confirmatory factor analysis on a selected set of 13 PCL–R items and reported that the set was underpinned by three correlated factors reflecting interpersonal, affective, and lifestyle features of psychopathy (Factors 1, 2, and 3, respectively, in Table 6.1). The first two factors were a split of the original Factor 1, and the third factor consisted of five of the original Factor 2 items. Cooke and Michie (2001) argued that the seven excluded items were not essential to the psychopathy construct because they measured antisociality. However, the procedures used to select the items and to conduct the analyses have been criticized on statistical and conceptual grounds (see Hare, 2003; Hare & Neumann, 2005; Hill, Neumann, & Rogers, 2004; Vitacco, Neumann, & Jackson, 2005). Among other things, the decision to exclude items related to antisociality was based on subjective and inconsistent procedures, a failure to appreciate the role of antisociality in traditional conceptions of psychopathy, and the use of analytical methods that treated the items as interval rather than as ordinal scales.

Recent exploratory and confirmatory factor analyses clearly indicate that a four-factor model of psychopathy is statistically and conceptually more defensible than a three-factor model, not only for the PCL–R but for its derivatives, the PCL:SV and the PCL:YV (Forth et al., 2003; Hare, 2003; Hare & Neumann, 2005a, 2005b; Vitacco et al., 2005; Vitacco, Rogers, Neumann, Harrison, & Vincent, 2005). These four first-order factors are listed in Table 6.1. The Interpersonal, Affective, and Lifestyle factors are identical with the Cooke and Michie (2001) factors. The Antisocial factor consists of five of the items excluded by Cooke and Michie. In the second edition of the PCL–R manual, these four factors are described as facets. The pattern of correlations among the facets implies the presence

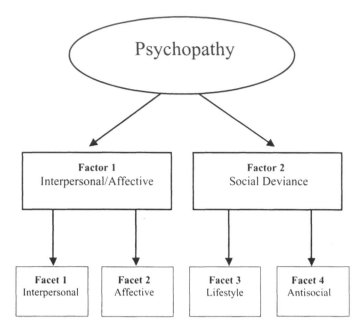

FIG. 6.1.   Scale structure of the PCL–R.

of two second-order factors, with the Interpersonal and Affective facets underpinning a broad Interpersonal/Affective factor (the original Factor 1 described in the 1991 manual) and the Lifestyle and Antisocial facets underpinning a broad Lifestyle/Antisocial factor (the original Factor 2, with the addition of Criminal Versatility). As in the original factor structure, "Promiscuous sexual behavior" and "Many short-term marital relationships" contribute to the total PCL–R score but do not load on any factor or facet. As in the second edition of the manual, the terms "Factor 1" and "Factor 2" in this chapter refer to the broad PCL–R factors; the facets are referred to by name (i.e., Interpersonal, Affective, Lifestyle, and Antisocial). The scale structure of the PCL–R is depicted in Fig. 6.1.

Debates about the factor structure of the PCL–R should not obscure the fact that the most reliable and important information for the clinician is the total score, to which all items contribute (Bolt, Hare, Vitale, & Newman, 2004). Inspection of Factors 1 and 2 and the four facets may help the clinician with the interpretation of an individual's PCL–R protocol. The publisher of the PCL–R second edition, Multi-Health Systems, provides QuikScore Forms that facilitate calculation of total, factor, and facet scores.

Reliability

Hundreds of studies confirm the reliability (internal consistency and interrater reliability) of the PCL–R in research and applied settings (for a full review, see Hare, 2003). Reliabilities for individual items are moderate and acceptable, with intraclass correlation coefficients (ICCs) for male offenders varying from .41 for single ratings to .57 for averaged ratings. Similar values have been obtained with female offenders. Interrater reliabilities for total scores based on standard and file reviews are high. The ICC is above .85 for a single rating and above .90 for the average of two ratings. The reliabilities of the PCL–R factors are adequate for research and clinical purposes. Finally, the standard error of measurement (*SEM*) of the PCL–R for the total score is approximately 3 for a single rating and 2 for the average of two ratings. The *SEM* is the standard deviation of observed scores if the true score is held constant. This means that if 100 trained raters assessed the same subject at the same time, about 68% of the scores would fall within ±1 SEM unit of the subject's obtained total score, and about 95% would fall within ±2 *SEM* units. The *SEM* can be used as an estimate of "the reasonable limits of the true score for (an individual) with any given obtained score" (Anastasi, 1982).

Generalizability

Although several of the samples described in the second edition of the manual are representative of the forensic populations from which they were obtained, many were "samples of convenience" provided by researchers and institutions. However, the distributions of PCL–R scores in the samples that *were* representative were similar to those obtained from convenience samples. Moreover, the means, standard deviations, and other psychometric properties of samples described in the published literature generally are consistent across samples and similar to those in the manual. Nonetheless, because the samples were not randomly selected from forensic populations, the percentile and T-score tables provided in the manual are meant only to be frameworks or guidelines ("comparison tables") for evaluating the scores of inmates or patients similar to those for whom the tables were constructed.

Although PCL–R scores are based on samples that appear to be representative, possible moderating variables need to be mentioned and discussed. A number of variables could influence the scoring and interpretation of PCL–R scores, including type of sample, age, gender, method of assessment (standard vs. file review alone), culture, and ethnic background.

Type of Sample. Samples of sex offenders, substance-dependant offenders, and noncriminals are described in the manual. Compared with offenders in general, child molesters score lower, and rapists and rapists/molesters higher, on the PCL–R. The differences between sex offenders and general offenders were not large enough to warrant the construction of separate percentile and T-score tables.

There is a considerable amount of research on the association between the PCL–R and substance use in prison inmates and forensic psychiatric inpatients and outpatients (Darke, Kaye, Finlay-Jones, & Hall, 1998; Hare, 2003; McDermott et al., 2000; Windle & Dumenci, 1999). However, substance use in these populations is so extensive that there was little to be gained by providing in the manual separate descriptive statistics or percentile and T-score tables for those who do and do not use and abuse alcohol and drugs. In general, substance use is strongly associated with PCL–R scores, though more so with Factor 2 than with Factor 1 (Hemphill, Hart, & Hare, 1994).

There has been very little systematic research examining PCL–R scores in noncriminals (Babiak, 2000; Hare, 2003), mostly because of problems in obtaining adequate collateral information to score the items with confidence. Weiler and Widom (1996) obtained a mean PCL–R score of 6.8 ($SD = 5.9$) for a sample of 489 adults who had been the control group for a study of abused children. This study, along with several other small-sample studies (Hare, 2003), suggests that most individuals in the general population would obtain a score of less than 4 or 5.

The PCL: SV has been employed in a variety of samples, including samples of college students (e.g., Forth, Brown, Hart, & Hare, 1996; Hart, Cox, & Hare, 1995), community samples (e.g., Coid et al., 2005; Monahan & Steadman, 1994), and samples of civil psychiatric patients (e.g., Steadman et al., 2000). PCL: SV scores in these samples are very low. For example, in the MacArthur Risk Study community samples (Monahan & Steadman, 1994), the mean PCL: SV score was 3.6 ($SD = 3.8$) for 197 males and 2.2 ($SD = 3.2$) for 318 females. Similar scores were obtained in a large representative sample of the UK population (Coid et al., 2005). The 12-item PCL: SV is conceptually and empirically equivalent to the 20-item PCL–R (Cooke, Michie, Hart, & Hare, 1999), making it possible to convert scores from one to the other. For example, a PCL: SV community sample score of 3 would be approximately equivalent to a PCL–R score of 5.

Age.   Cross-sectional analyses indicate that PCL–R scores obtained with the standard procedure are only weakly associated with the age of assessment among male offenders and male forensic psychiatric patients. Factor 1 scores in particular appear to be very stable, while Factor 2 scores decline slightly with age of assessment. For female offenders, there is a slight decrease in PCL–R total, Factor 1, and Factor 2 scores with age of assessment. Because the association between age and PCL–R scores is weak, comparison tables based on age of assessment were not composed.

Gender.   The PCL–R is a useful tool for assessing psychopathy in female offenders (Hare, 2003), and the descriptive properties and correlates are similar to those found with male offenders (e.g., Loucks & Zamble, 2000; McDermott et al., 2000; Richards, Casey, & Lucente, 2003; Richards, Casey, Lucente, & Kafami, 2003; Vitale & Newman, 2001; Vitale, Smith, Brinkley, & Newman, 2002; Warren et al., 2003; Windle & Dumenci, 1999). Mean PCL–R scores are several points lower in female than in male offenders (19.0 vs. 22.1). Separate percentile and T-score tables therefore are given for female and male offenders.

Item response theory (IRT) provides a mathematical expression of the relationship between a score on an individual item or group of items (e.g., total score) and the underlying construct or latent trait of psychopathy. IRT analyses described in the second edition and by Bolt and colleagues (2004) indicate that PCL–R total scores are related to the construct of psychopathy in much the same way in female as in male offenders, particularly at middle and upper ranges of PCL–R scores. For example, a score of 28 reflects approximately the same level of psychopathy in female offenders as does a score of 30 in male offenders.

Method of Assessment.   The standard (and recommended) assessment procedure for the PCL–R involves a semistructured interview and a review of collateral information (Hare, 2003). Assessments that do not include an interview typically yield lower scores than do standard assessments. The second edition of the manual lists the mean score for male offenders assessed with the standard procedure as 22.1 ($SD = 7.9$) and for those assessed from file reviews as 16.5 ($SD = 8.3$). Part of this difference may be due to sampling issues. Although IRT analyses indicate that a given PCL–R score obtained with either method reflects much the same level of psychopathy (Bolt et al., 2004), the interview is important for scoring many of the interpersonal and affective items, and the standard procedure should be used when possible.

Culture.   In recent years, the PCL–R has been used extensively in several countries outside of North America. PCL–R total scores for male offenders and forensic psychiatric patients are somewhat lower in the United Kingdom and in several European countries than in North America. The second edition provides separate percentile and T-score tables for the United Kingdom (samples from other countries were not large enough to construct such tables). IRT analyses indicate that some of the items may not function the same in North America as in Britain (Hare, 2003) and in several European countries (Sweden, Denmark, Germany, Belgium, Norway, and Spain; Cooke, Michie, Hart, & Clark, 2005). That is, there are cultural differences in the extent to which some items are discriminating of psychopathy. However, IRT analyses indicate that in the middle to upper ranges a given total score appears to have much the same meaning in Britain (Hare, 2003) and in the European countries as in North America (Cooke et al., 2005). That is, there is considerable metric equivalence of PCL–R scores (most notably for the Interpersonal and Affective facets) across countries and cultures. However, considerably more cross-cultural research is needed. This work will be facilitated by the current availability of the PCL–R manual in several languages, including Dutch, Spanish, Portugese, Swedish , Norwegian, French, German, and Japanese.

Ethnic Background. Early data on the PCL–R were obtained predominantly from Caucasian samples. However, over the past few years, efforts have been made to assess the applicability of the PCL–R across ethnic groups. Although Lynn (2002) has asserted that certain races or ethnic groups are more psychopathic than others, the scientific evidence, reviewed by Zuckerman (2003), suggests otherwise. In the second edition of the PCL–R manual, the PCL–R was assessed in a large number of African-American offenders and in smaller samples of Native-American and Hispanic-American offenders. The PCL–R scores did not appear to be influenced by ethnicity. Similar results were obtained in a meta-analysis by Skeem, Edens, Camp, and Colwell (2004). Further IRT analyses suggest that the PCL–R has metric equivalence for Caucasian and African-American male offenders (Cooke, Kosson, & Michie, 2001).

Nonetheless, there are still several issues that need to be addressed. For example, there are ethnic and cultural factors that may influence the expression of the disorder, particularly as reflected in Factor 2 items. In addition, research indicates that some of the "deficits" observed in laboratory research with Caucasian offenders are not observed in African Americans (Doninger & Kosson, 2001; Lorenz & Newman, 2002; Newman & Schmitt, 1998). It is uncertain whether these differences are due to ethnic factors related to psychopathy or to the tasks involved in the research. More research is required to understand the nature and implications of the psychopathy construct in different ethnic groups. At present, we have little information about potential rater bias when the rater and the individual being rated are from different ethnic backgrounds.

Conclusion. The available evidence indicates that the PCL–R and the construct it measures are generalizable across a variety of populations and contexts. Enough data are available for the use of separate percentile and T-score comparison tables for North American male offenders, male forensic psychiatric patients, female offenders, and British male offenders. The effects of other variables were either based on a small number of samples or yielded minimal differences. Therefore, separate tables were not deemed necessary or possible at this point.

Validity

Because of the strong association between the PCL–R and its predecessor, the PCL, evidence in support of the validity of the latter is applicable to the former. Evidence for the validity of the PCL–R is extensive (see Hare, 2003) and comes from research examining its relationship to a variety of other instruments and scales; its association with behavioral data, such as data on recidivism and violence; and its role in basic laboratory research (the latter is not discussed here; see Hare, 2003).

Correlations With Other Measures

As expected, the PCL and PCL–R scores are strongly correlated with other conceptually relevant clinical assessment tools, including global ratings of psychopathy (used to assess psychopathy prior to 1980), *DSM–III, DSM–III–R*, and *DSM–IV* diagnoses of Antisocial Personality Disorder (APD; American Psychiatric Association, 1994), prototypicality ratings of APD, and APD symptom counts (Hart & Hare, 1989; Hildebrand & de Ruiter, 2004). The PCL–R is also moderately correlated with various self-report measures of psychopathy, including the Psychopathic Personality Inventory (PPI; Lilienfeld & Andrews, 1996), the Interpersonal Measure of Psychopathy (IMP; Kosson, Steuerwald, Forth, & Kirkhart, 1997), Levenson's Self-Report Psychopathy Scale (SRPS; Levenson, Kiehl, & Fitzpatrick, 1995), and the Self-Report Psychopathy scale (SRP; Hare, 1985), including its most recent version, the SRP–III (Paulhus, Hemphill, & Hare, in press; Williams, Paulhus, & Hare, in press). Similarly, PCL–R scores are correlated with relevant scales in omnibus personality inventories, including the Multidimensional Personality Questionnaire (MPQ; Tellegen, in press) and the Five-Factor Model of Personality (Costa & McCrae, 1992; Costa & Widiger, 2002; Hicklin & Widiger, 2005; Lynam, 2002). Finally, psychopathy, as measured by the PCL–R, is correlated in a theoretically relevant manner with a wide variety of personality scales and with subscales on omnibus measures of psychopathology, including the Minnesota Multiphasic Personality Inventory (MMPI; Dahlstrom & Welsh, 1960), the Millon Clinical Multiaxial Inventory (MCMI; Millon, 1987) and its revisions (Millon, 1987; Millon, Davis, & Millon, 1997), and the Personality Assessment Inventory (PAI; Morey, 1991).

Relation to Criminal Behavior

The PCL–R distinguishes a distinct subgroup within offender populations, a group that is persistently violent across the lifespan (Porter, Birt, & Boer, 2001), engages in a large number of criminal acts (Blackburn & Coid, 1998; Brown & Forth, 1997; Douglas & Webster, 1999; Porter et al., 2000), is predatory in its aggression (Cornell et al., 1996; Williamson, Hare, & Wong, 1987; Woodworth & Porter, 2002), presents management problems within the institution (Hare, Clark, Grann, & Thornton, 2000; Kroner & Mills, 2001; Shine & Hobson, 2000; Walters, 2003), and is more likely to engage in violence after release from an institution than are other offenders (Glover, Nicholson, Hemmati, Bernfeld, & Quinsey, 2002; Hemphill, Hare, & Wong, 1998; Kroner & Mills, 2001; Serin, 1996; Serin & Amos, 1995; see meta-analyses by Dolan & Doyle, 2000; Gendreau, Goggin, & Smith, 2002; Hemphill & Hare, 2004; Hemphill et al., 1998; Salekin, Rogers, & Sewell, 1996). In addition, psychopaths with deviant sexual interests pose a high risk for sexual crimes (Hildebrand, de Ruiter, & de Vogel, 2004; Rice & Harris, 1997; Serin, Mailloux, & Malcolm, 2001). Although PCL–R scores are somewhat lower in forensic psychiatric patients than in offender populations, the predictive power of the instrument is about the same in patients as in offenders (Gray et al., 2003; Hart & Hare, 1989; Rice, Harris, & Cormier, 1992; Tengström, Grann, Långström, & Kullgren, 2000). The presence of psychopathic traits in forensic psychiatric patients greatly increases the risk of violent recidivism.

Response to Treatment

There is little convincing scientific evidence that psychopathic individuals respond favorably to traditional treatments and interventions (see Dolan & Coid, 1993; Hare, 1998a; Losel, 1998; Wong & Hare, 2005). This does not mean that their attitudes and behaviors are immutable, only that there have been no methodologically sound treatment or "resocialization" programs that have been shown to work with psychopaths. But there are legitimate concerns that the "nothing works" philosophy is not grounded in solid research (D'Silva, Duggan, & McCarthy, 2004; Hemphill & Hart, 2004; Wong & Hare, 2005).

Unlike most other offenders, psychopaths suffer little personal distress, see little wrong with their attitudes and behavior, and seek treatment only when it is in their best interest to do so, such as when seeking probation or parole. It is therefore not surprising that they derive little benefit from traditional prison programs, particularly those aimed at the development of empathy, conscience, and interpersonal skills. Programs that do not take into account the nature of psychopathic offenders are unlikely to be effective. Indeed, several studies indicate that such programs may help them to develop their manipulative skills and, apparently, to "make them worse," at least in terms of postrelease behavior (Hare et al., 2000; Hobson, Shine, & Roberts, 2000; Rice et al., 1992). There is some evidence that psychopathic sex offenders are able to manipulate skilled therapists into wrongly concluding that they have made good progress (Looman, Abracen, Serin, & Marquis, 2005).

An extensive set of guidelines for development of a program specifically designed for psychopaths is now available (Wong & Hare, 2005). In brief, we propose that relapse-prevention techniques should be integrated with elements of the best available cognitive-behavioral correctional programs. The program is less concerned with developing empathy and conscience or effecting changes in personality than with convincing participants that they alone are responsible for their behavior and that it is in their own interest to adopt more prosocial ways of using their strengths and abilities to satisfy their needs and wants.

Forensic Uses

Because of its demonstrated reliability and validity, the PCL–R is widely used in research and applied settings, including the mental health and criminal justice systems. Scoring is standardized, allowing for easy replication of the assessment protocol and communication of results. The comparison tables for the PCL–R are based on large samples (Hare, 2003), and scores on the instrument appear to have much the same explanatory and predictive value in a wide range of groups and contexts.

The number and variety of situations in which the PCL–R is applied are increasing. It has been employed in child custody hearings, risk assessments, parole evaluations, decisions about treatment suitability, civil commitment proceedings and death penalty hearings (in the United States), dangerous and long-term offender hearings (in Canada), and severe dangerous personality disorder evaluations (in the United Kingdom).

The actual frequency with which the PCL–R is used in civil commitment hearings, capital sentencing cases, and severe dangerous personality disorder evaluations is not known, but clearly it is increasing. A recent study found that psychopathy was mentioned in 63% of a random sample of dangerous offender and long-term offender cases in Canada (Clark & Forth, 2004). Examples of the PCL–R being used in some controversial contexts are reviewed below.

Child Custody Hearings

The PCL–R has been used in child custody hearings, including custody battles where the parents may lose custody to the state and custody hearings that result from divorce. The most frequent use of the PCL–R appears to be in helping to decide whether a parent poses a risk to the child. For example, in a recent case an application was made to terminate contact between father and daughter. The man's high PCL–R score was treated as a risk variable and contributed to the judge's decision to bar the man from seeing his daughter because of the risk he posed for sexually offending against his daughter and her friends.

In child custody hearings the PCL–R may address the personality of an individual, and although it may seem reasonable that a high PCL–R score would increase the risk of child neglect or abuse, there are as yet no empirical studies for the expert to draw upon.

Capital Sentencing Hearings

There is considerable debate regarding the use of the PCL–R in capital punishment hearings, in large part because it represents such a powerful aggravating factor (Cunningham & Reidy, 2001; Edens, Desforges, Fernandez, & Palac, 2004). One of the important issues in capital cases is whether the offender presents a serious continuing threat to society (Ogloff & Chopra, 2004). Although the specific criteria vary across jurisdictions, in general an offender in a capital case who does not receive the death penalty may be sentenced to either life or a very long term, usually without parole. Therefore, some argue that in order to be useful in capital punishment trials, violence risk predictions should provide information regarding institutional adjustment or violence risk after a lengthy period of incarceration (Edens, Buffington-Vollum, Keilen, Roskamp, & Anthony, 2005). To date, no research has been conducted to assess the predictive validity of the PCL–R with samples of death row inmates. However, in light of the very low base rate of institutional violence within this group of offenders, it is unlikely any risk assessment scale would be able to accurately predict this outcome.

A moderate association between PCL–R score and measures of institutional adjustment exists (Hare et al., 2000; Heilbrun et al., 1998; Hicks, Rogers, & Cashel, 2000; Hobson et al., 2000; Kroner & Mills, 2001; see meta-analysis by Walters, 2003). However, relatively little research has assessed the predictive validity of the PCL–R in U.S. male prison inmates (Buffington-Vollum, Edens, Johnson, & Johnson, 2002; Walters, 2003). In addition, institutional misconduct includes a range of behaviors from verbal infractions to assault with a weapon. Not all of these behaviors are likely to apply to the question of whether an offender presents a continuing threat.

Nevertheless, experts are still called upon to address the issue of whether an offender presents a continuing danger to society. If the context in which this issue arises is an institutional setting, the expert should evaluate a range of variables that may be of help to the courts. Recent research suggests the PCL–R and actuarial factors such as age, education, and type of sentence may be useful when predicting institutional violence (Cunningham, Sorensen, & Reidy, 2005; Walters, 2003). Experts who use the PCL–R in their assessment of future dangerousness should be explicit about the limitations of the research upon which their evaluations are based.

Besides its predictive role in capital sentencing hearings, the PCL–R may be helpful in the evaluation of the capacity for empathy, guilt, and remorse, each of which might be considered as mitigating or aggravating factors in sentencing. In such a case, the clinician should be explicit about the reliability and measurement error involved in assessing these features.

Preventative Detention

In addition to capital sentencing cases, the PCL–R is frequently used in preventative detention hearings. Many states have legislation that allows for the civil commitment of sexually violent predators. For example, in Washington State a sexually violent predator is an offender convicted of a sexual offence who is judged likely to engage in future predatory sexual violence (Washington Laws, 1990, 71.09.030). These offenders are committed for an indeterminate time until they no longer pose a threat to society (Washington Laws,

1990, 71.09.100). The specifics of these laws, including the need for a prior conviction and the length of commitment, vary across jurisdictions.

In the United Kingdom there is an initiative to identify and treat people with dangerous and severe personality disorder. The initiative is a joint effort by the Home Office, Prison Service, and Department of Health. It is aimed at people who are regarded as a risk at the time of release from either a hospital or prison or those in the community who exhibit dangerous behavior (Home Office & Department of Health, 1999). The PCL–R plays a major role in the determination, management, and treatment of dangerous and severe personality disorder (Home Office & Department of Health, 2005). For this reason, special efforts are taken to ensure that the administrators of the instrument are well trained.

In Canada preventative detention laws are found in the long-term offender and dangerous offender provisions of the criminal code. These offenders are dealt with through the criminal justice system. Long-term offender provisions require a significant probability of future violence and involve a community supervision order (Criminal Code of Canada, 1985, C-46, s.753.1). Alternately, a dangerous offender declaration requires the additional criterion of lack of prospects for community control and involves an indeterminate sentence (Criminal Code of Canada, 1985, C-46, s.753).

The PCL–R can provide useful information within each of these legislative frameworks. It can indicate future risk and potential treatment concerns, and provide information about interpersonal and affective characteristics, thus aiding in the development of a more complete picture of the person. The total score is the most important and most reliable information provided by a PCL–R assessment. However, it is possible to supplement this score with information about the clusters of items (factors and facets) that contribute to the total score. In some cases, reference to Factor 1 and Factor 2 may suffice, whereas in others the user may wish to conduct a finer descriptive analysis of the individual by inspecting the scores on the Interpersonal, Affective, Lifestyle, and Antisocial facets (see Fig. 6.1).

Potential for Misuse

Although the research evidence for the reliability and validity of the PCL–R is extensive, this does not ensure that an individual assessment will be reliable or valid. In a research context, misuse of the PCL–R will have few negative consequences for the individual. However, when PCL–R scores are used in clinical and criminal justice contexts, the implications of misuse are potentially very serious, especially if the scores are used to guide treatment or adjudication decisions (Hare, 1998b, 2003). In addition, it is important when conducting an assessment to use all information available to provide a complete picture of the person. In each case, it behooves the evaluator to ensure that the PCL–R is used properly and in accordance with the highest ethical and professional standards. Needless to say, the items must be scored in accordance with the criteria listed in the manual or not scored at all. Unfortunately, there have been cases in which a clinician has scored the PCL–R entirely from the item titles, without reference or access to the manual (Hare, 1998b). Presumably the item titles were obtained from a journal article. Clinicians who use the PCL–R must be prepared to outline the information used to score the items and to explain and justify the manner in which they scored the items.

Risk

The PCL–R can provide information able to aid decision makers in a wide range of cases, but it is possible that professionals may misuse or misinterpret the instrument. Edens

(2001) provides two examples where this occurred in capital sentencing hearing in the United States. One expert interpreted a low PCL–R score as indicating that a man was not guilty of molesting his daughter. This is clear misuse an instrument that provides evidence about risk of future behavior, not indications of guilt or innocence. In the second case, an expert testified that the offender was at high risk for violence in the institution because of his high PCL–R score. Although PCL–R scores may provide information regarding an offender's risk for institutional violence, it is important to consider the predictive limitations of the PCL–R in this context and to take into account other risk and protective factors. The evidence is not sufficient to warrant strong statements regarding risk in an institutional setting based solely on a PCL–R score.

Cut Scores

An important issue is the use of cut scores to diagnose psychopathy. The PCL–R provides a dimensional score that represents the extent to which a given individual is judged to match the "prototypical psychopath." The higher the score, the closer the match. These dimensional ratings are more useful than categorical diagnoses in several respects. For example, they have superior psychometric properties, and they do not require that assumptions be made about whether the underlying construct is continuous or categorical. Moreover, there is recent evidence that the construct underlying the PCL–R is dimensional in nature (Guay, Ruscio, Hare, & Knight, 2004). Nevertheless, categorical diagnoses of psychopathy may be useful or required for some research and clinical applications. The difficulty is to determine the most appropriate cut score to use for these purposes. For research purposes, a cut score of 30 has proven useful, for it provides researchers with a common working definition of psychopathy. Problems arise when clinicians and investigators treat a cut score of 30 as if it were a sharp dividing line between offenders and patients who are psychopaths (members of a taxon) and those who are not. The problems are compounded when the judicial system makes the same assumption. Hare (1998b) described a case in which a judge in a dangerous offender hearing questioned the prosecution psychiatrist's PCL–R assessment, "scored" it himself, managed to get the score down to 29, and concluded that if 30 means that the defendant is a psychopath, 29 must mean that he is not a psychopath. Hare provided several other examples of misuse of the PCL–R in forensic practice.

Labels

Those who wish to avoid diagnostic labels or categories may convert PCL–R and factor scores to percentiles or T-scores using the appropriate tables provided in the second edition of the manual. An alternative strategy for reporting PCL–R scores would be to group them into several levels or descriptive categories and then determine the risk associated with a particular level or category. One such scheme is depicted in the manual. In any case, the practical implications of a PCL–R score will depend on the population involved (e.g., offenders, forensic psychiatric, patients, men vs. women, etc.), the context in which the score is used (e.g., treatment options, conditional release, risk assessment, research, etc.), and its integration with other relevant information and variables.

Qualifications

Because of the potentially serious consequences associated with an assessment of psychopathy, the PCL–R has been subjected to psychometric and legal scrutiny that is more intense than is the case with most other psychological instruments (Hare, 2003). To ensure that the PCL–R is used as intended, individual raters must meet certain criteria prior to conducting assessments. The qualifications for use of the PCL–R in clinical and forensic work are stricter than they are for research purposes because of the potentially serious consequences in the former (Edens et al., 2004; Hare, 1998b, 2003). A list of criteria is given by Hare (2003). First, clinicians who use the PCL–R (or who supervise its use) must possess an advanced degree and must have completed graduate courses in psychopathology, statistics, and psychometric theory. This enables them to interpret the statistics and research given in the manual and in the literature. Further, users of the PCL–R need to be familiar with the current clinical and empirical literature on psychopathy. This will help in the interpretation and practical implications of psychopathy scores. It is important for the user to have the appropriate professional credentials (e.g., registration, licensing), and to have experience with the populations in which PCL–R assessments will be conducted. That is, users must understand the principles and limitations of such assessments and must ensure that they are conducting assessments in accordance with professional and legal standards for psychological testing.

Individuals wishing to use the PCL–R (in any context) must have adequate training and experience. Scoring the PCL–R involves clinical judgment, and specific training and experience are warranted (Campbell, 2000). Clinicians who do court reports or who testify in court should be aware that prosecutors and defense attorneys are becoming increasingly knowledgeable about the PCL–R and that their knowledge will be reflected in detailed examination of the clinicians' credentials, assessments, and testimony.

Confusion With APD

Problems can arise when experts use their clinical judgment to diagnose psychopathy or confuse psychopathy with antisocial personality disorder (APD). Little is known about the validity and reliability of unstructured clinical diagnoses, but the association between the PCL–R and APD is well-known. Briefly, the PCL–R has an asymmetric relationship with APD; the majority of offenders with high PCL–R scores meet the diagnostic criteria for APD, whereas the reverse is not true (Hare, 1996, 2003; Hart & Hare, 1989). The PCL–R is able to target a subgroup within the forensic population for which there is a great deal of empirical evidence concerning implications for risk and for treatment suitability. If an offender with APD does not also have a high PCL–R score, it would be inappropriate to use the extensive literature on PCL–R psychopathy to draw inferences about the offender's risk or treatment suitability. An example of the problem is court testimony by a prosecution expert that "persons with antisocial personality disorder are psychopaths; they are some of the most dangerous people alive" (citations for the cases described in this section can be obtained from Heather Clark).

Familiarity With the Literature

Experts clearly should keep up to date on the empirical literature regarding psychopathy, and they should not misinterpret or go beyond the literature in their testimony. For example, in a recent case an expert testified that "there is a growing body of evidence to suggest that individuals with high PCL–R scores not only do not benefit from treatment but may in fact recidivate more frequently, and more quickly when they have been treated (for a variety of reasons). Accordingly, in keeping with the current empirical evidence on the subject, it is my recommendation that (the offender) receive no psychological treatment of any kind." Or as put by another expert, "Psychopathy is a very significant consideration in dangerous offender proceedings. That is so because it appears to be common ground that truly psychopathic offenders cannot be cured and that treatment of a psychopath is virtually impossible because a true psychopath will often use treatment to mask a cure while in fact improving his or her re-offence capabilities." As Wong and Hare (2005) have argued, the treatability issue with respect to psychopathy is somewhat more complex and uncertain than these recommendations indicate.

Research Context

The criteria for using the PCL–R in a research setting are less stringent than they are for clinical purposes. In research settings, individual PCL–R scores typically are kept confidential and not made available to correctional or institutional staff, parole boards, and so forth. Still, researchers must follow reasonable guidelines in using the PCL–R. Like clinicians, they should possess an advanced degree in the social, medical, or behavioral sciences; have completed graduate-level courses in psychopathology, statistics; and psychometric theory, and accept responsibility for the supervision of raters with lesser qualifications (e.g., research assistants with an undergraduate degree in the social or behavioral sciences, counseling psychology, or social work, plus some experience in interviewing).

PSYCHOPATHY CHECKLIST: YOUTH VERSION

Description

The PCL:YV was derived from the PCL–R as a measure of psychopathic traits in adolescents aged 12–18 years. Both instruments emphasize the need for information from several sources and domains in order to adequately assess 20 characteristics (Table 6.2). The PCL:YV uses the same rating format as the PCL–R, and there is a considerable overlap between the two instruments with respect to user qualifications. In addition, users of the PCL:YV must be familiar with theory and research on adolescent development. In contrast to the PCL–R, there is no PCL:YV cut score for a diagnosis of psychopathy. The

TABLE 6.2
Factors and Items in the PCL:YV

Factor 1: Interpersonal	Factor 2: Affective
1. Impression management	6. Lack of remorse
2. Grandiose sense of self-worth	7. Shallow affect
4. Pathological lying	8. Callous/lack of empathy
5. Manipulation for personal gain	16. Will not accept responsibility
Factor 3: Behavioral	Factor 4: Antisocial
3. Need for stimulation	10. Poor anger control
9. Parasitic orientation	12. Early behavioral problems
13. Lack of goals	18. Serious criminal behavior
14. Impulsivity	19. Serious violations of release
15. Irresponsibility	20. Criminal versatility

Note: Item 11, Impersonal sexual behavior, and Item 17, Unstable interpersonal relationships, contribute to the total PCL:YV score but do not load on any factors.

manual provides T-scores and percentiles for total and factor scores for institutionalized male offenders, male probationers, and small samples of female offenders and community males. All individuals in the samples were between the ages of 12 to 18 years. The rater should choose the most appropriate comparison sample and then obtain the T-score or percentile rank for the individual being assessed.

PCL:YV items are scored from both a semistructured interview with the youth and a review of available file and collateral information. The PCL:YV interview requires more coverage of school, peer, and family relationships than does the PCL–R interview. The other major source of information used in the PCL:YV is a review of charts and collateral information. Depending on the amount of file information available, an interview with a caregiver or guardian may be needed. Some researchers (Campbell, Porter, & Santor, 2004; Gretton, Hare, & Catchpole, 2004; Gretton et al., 2001; Marczyk, Heilbrun, Lander, & DeMatteo, 2003; O'Neill, Lidz, & Heilbrun, 2003a, 2003b) have used extensive file information to generate PCL:YV scores (i.e., no interview was conducted). Although not optimal, file-only PCL:YV scores are acceptable when it is impossible to conduct an interview or when an archival study is being conducted.

History of the Instrument's Development

A key decision made by the authors was to use the item content of the PCL–R to guide development of the PCL:YV. Thus, the PCL:YV is a downward extension of the PCL–R that assesses similar content domains. The first study to examine these domains in adolescents was by Forth, Hart, and Hare (1990), who modified several PCL–R items. Because adolescents have a limited work history and few marital relationships, PCL–R items 9 ("Parasitic lifestyle") and 17 ("Many short-term marital relationships") were deleted. Furthermore, because adolescent offenders have had less opportunity than adult offenders to come into contact with the judicial system, it was necessary to modify two other items: item 18 ("Juvenile delinquency") and item 20 ("Criminal versatility"). This original version of the scale has been referred to as the modified PCL–R or the 18-item PCL–R. Several studies used this version to study psychopathic traits in adolescents (e.g., Brandt, Kennedy, Patrick, & Curtin, 1997; Harvey, Stokes, Lord, & Pogge, 1996; Myers, Burket, & Harris, 1995; Rogers, Johansen, Chang, & Salekin, 1997).

Subsequently, additional modifications were made. First, raters were required to compare the behavior of the adolescent being assessed to the general behavior of same-age peers. This was done to ensure the trait or behavior being rated is more extreme than what is normative for that age group. Second, items were modified to include descriptions of life domains more relevant to adolescents, such as peers, family, and school. Third, items 9 and 17 were modified to permit assessments of the intent of these items in youths (item 9 became "Parisitic orientation," and item 17 became "Unstable interpersonal relationships"). Fourth, when scoring individual items, the focus was placed on relatively enduring features of the individual, displayed across settings and situations since late childhood. This modified version of the PCL–R was named the "Psychopathy Checklist: Youth Version" (PCL:YV).

The PCL:YV was published in 2003 in order to provide researchers and clinical users with a common metric to assess psychopathy in adolescents and to encourage systematic research. Future research and input from practitioners will play an integral role clarifying and refining the construct, identifying casual mechanisms, delineating the psychobiological correlates, and designing effective intervention programs.

Factor Structure, Reliability, and Generalizability

Factor Structure

Both exploratory and confirmatory factor analyses have been conducted to examine the factor structure of the PCL:YV. Confirmatory factor analyses across all the samples suggested that a model with four correlated first-order factors provided a very good explanation for the pattern of covariation among PCL:YV item scores (Forth et al., 2003). Four items loaded on an Interpersonal dimension (e.g., "Impression management", "Pathological lying") and four items on an Affective dimension (e.g., "Lack of remorse", "Callous/lack of empathy"). Five items loaded on a Behavioral dimension (e.g., "Impulsivity", "Lack goals") and five items on an Antisocial dimension (e.g., "Poor anger control", "Serious criminal behavior"). Unlike with the PCL–R, the pattern of correlations among the factors does not imply second-order factors. The internal consistency of the four factors ranged from .74 to .81. The differential correlates of these factor scores currently are being investigated.

Reliability

The interrater reliability of PCL:YV total scores is high (single rater ICC of .90 to .96; Forth et al., 2003). This high level of interrater agreement may be due to the level of training provided to the raters in the research studies that formed the basis of the manual. Moreover, adolescents who volunteer to participate in research seem less motivated to engage in impression management than those being assessed as part of a forensic evaluation. Whether this high level of interrater reliability will be maintained when the PCL:YV is used for clinical and forensic purposes remains to be seen.

For the data set described in the manual, the internal consistency of PCL:YV total scores is high, with alpha coefficients ranging from .85 to .94. Across settings, the mean interitem correlations were all above .20. These values are consistent with the view that the PCL:YV is a homogeneous scale. There has been only one published study that has assessed the test-retest reliability of the PCL:YV in a sample of incarcerated youths. Skeem and Cauffman (2003) reported a respectable ICC of .66 for the PCL:YV total score over a 1-month follow-up.

Generalizability

Data from 2,438 youths in three countries (Canada, the United States, and the United Kingdom) across 19 different samples are described in the manual. Research has been conducted with institutionalized young offenders, young offenders on probation, psychiatric inpatient youths, and youths in the community.

PCL:YV total scores vary across samples, with institutionalized offenders obtaining a relatively high score, followed closely by youths on probation. Youths in the community have a very low PCL:YV score. Incarcerated adolescents tend to score slightly higher on the PCL:YV than incarcerated adult offenders score on the PCL–R.

To date, there are few longitudinal data on the stability of the PCL:YV items from adolescence into adulthood. Within institutionalized and probation samples, there is a small negative correlation between PCL:YV total score and age at assessment. Younger adolescents score slightly higher on the PCL:YV than do their older counterparts.

There have been few studies assessing psychopathic traits in female adolescents. In the manual data set, both incarcerated and probation female adolescents were rated as slightly less psychopathic than males (about 1 point). Other researchers have reported no gender differences in the prevalence of youths scoring high on the PCL:YV (Campbell et al., 2004; Salekin et al., 2004).

Many of the data on ethnicity compare Caucasians with non-Caucasians. The strength of the correlation between PCL:YV total scores and ethnicity in the manual data set ranges from .03 in probation samples to .17 in institutionalized samples, with non-Caucasians scoring from 1 to 3 points higher than Caucasians. Other studies comparing PCL:YV scores across ethnic groups have reported no significant differences across groups (Gretton et al., 2004; O'Neill et al., 2003a). IRT analyses of the PCL:YV are needed to determine if the instrument is metrically equivalent across different ethnic and cultural groups.

Conclusion

PCL:YV total scores do not appear to be unduly influenced by the youths' age, gender, or ethnicity. However, much of the research has been conducted on older male adolescents who have been in contact with the juvenile justice system. Additional data are needed on female adolescents, younger adolescents, nonadjudicated community youths, and ethnically and culturally diverse groups.

Validity

Face validity is a basic component of any theoretical construct, including psychopathy. Several studies have investigated how clinicians (Salekin, Rogers, & Machin, 2001) and juvenile justice personnel (Cruise, Colwell, Lyons, & Baker, 2003) conceptualize psychopathy in male and female adolescents. Both of these studies asked respondents to rate prototypical features of a male and female adolescent described as psychopathic. Both clinicians and juvenile justice personnel considered a wide range of features as indicators of adolescent psychopathy, including those that are interpersonal (e.g., "Lies easily and skillfully"), affective (e.g., "Emotions seem shallow"), behavioral (e.g., "Dangerous or risky activities"), and antisocial in nature (e.g., "Juvenile delinquency"). The PCL:YV captures the majority of the features identified in these studies as highly prototypical of adolescent psychopathy.

Relations to Other Measures

Several self-report questionnaires have been developed to assess psychopathic traits in adolescents, and these can be used to assess the convergent validity of the PCL:YV. The instrument is moderately correlated with a self-report version of the Antisocial Process Screening Device (see Caputo, Frick, & Brodsky, 1999), with $r = .30$ in the Murrie and Cornell (2002) study and $r = .40$ in the Lee, Vincent, Hart, and Corrado (2003) study. The PCL:YV is also moderately correlated with the Psychopathy Content Scale (from the Millon Adolescent Clinical Inventory; Millon, 1993), with $r = .49$ (Murrie & Cornell, 2002). Skeem and Cauffman (2003) reported a weaker association ($r = .24$) between the PCL:YV and the Youth Psychopathy Scale (Andershed, Gustafson, Kerr, & Stattin, 2002).

The PCL:YV is associated with substance use, conduct disorder, oppositional defiant disorder, and attention-deficit/hyperactivity disorder in adolescents (Campbell et al., 2004; Forth & Burke, 1998; Gretton et al., 2001; Kosson et al., 2002; Mailloux, Forth, & Kroner, 1997). Measuring a broader range of psychopathologies, Salekin et al. (2004) examined the association between the PCL:YV and the clinical and psychosocial scales from the Adolescent Psychopathology Scale (APS). The PCL:YV was significantly correlated with symptoms of conduct disorder ($r = .52$), oppositional defiant disorder ($r = .35$), and adjustment disorder ($r = .31$, and with the following APS psychosocial content scales: Psychosocial Substance Use Difficulties ($r = .35$), Anger ($r = .29$), Aggression ($r = 41$), and Interpersonal Problems ($r = .40$). This study also found that the PCL:YV was able to make an unique contribution to the postdiction of nonviolent and violent offenses over and above symptoms of conduct disorder, oppositional defiant disorder, and attention-deficit/hyperactivity disorder.

Research with the PCL–R has found no or small correlations with anxiety and depression (Hare, 2003). In contrast, PCL:YV scores are correlated with some internalizing disorders. For example, Kosson et al. (2002) reported that the PCL:YV was positively correlated with anxiety ($r = .25$). Salekin et al. (2004) also found that the PCL:YV was positively correlated with internalizing psychosocial problems ($r = .20$). In contrast, Campbell et al. (2004) reported that PCL:YV total scores were unrelated to internalizing symptoms ($r = -.03$).

Relation to Criminal and School Behavior

The PCL:YV has been related to a range of relevant correlates and outcome measures. High PCL:YV scores are associated with academic problems (Campbell et al., 2004; Ridenour, Marchant, & Dean, 2001), early onset of antisocial problems (Corrado et al., 2004; Forth & Burke, 1998), increased frequency and versatility of nonviolent and violent offenses (Gretton et al., 2004; Kosson et al., 2002; Murrie et al., 2004), and increased institutional nonviolent and violent infractions (Murrie et al., 2004; Spain, Douglas, Poythress, & Epstein, 2004; Stafford & Cornell, 2003).

Several studies have been conducted to examine the predictive validity of the PCL:YV. PCL:YV scores were predictive of nonviolent and violent recidivism in juvenile sex offenders (Gretton et al., 2001) and nonviolent and violent recidivism in adjudicated youths (Catchpole & Gretton, 2003; Corrado et al., 2004; Gretton et al., 2004; Vincent, Vitacco, Grisso, & Corrado, 2003).

Response to Treatment

No controlled evaluations of intervention programs for youths scoring high on the PCL:YV have been completed to date. However, O'Neill et al. (2003b) found that PCL:YV scores correlated negatively with days in the program, quality of participation, number of consecutive clean urine screens, and researchers' ratings (from discharge summaries) of clinical improvement in offenders referred to a substance abuse program. Offenders were followed up for 1 year after release from the treatment facility. PCL:YV scores were significantly correlated with the number of times they were arrested. In contrast to the above study, Spain et al. (2004) reported that PCL:YV total scores were not strongly related to treatment progress. In a small study of 30 youths, Caldwell and van Rybroek (2001) reported positive treatment outcome for very psychopathic youths. Forth et al. (2003) summarized studies measuring the association between PCL:YV scores and treatment needs. Treatment targets for psychopathic youths include family problems, education difficulties, substance abuse, delinquent peers, and antisocial attitudes. These findings point to the need for a multimodal (school, family, peers, community) intervention program that is started at an early age, is long-lasting, and targets both the characteristics of the youth and parental behavior. There is some encouraging evidence that adolescent offenders with high PCL:YV scores who complete a treatment program (cognitive-behavioral, relapse prevention) have posttreatment recidivism rates that are lower than those who do not complete the program (Forth & Book, in press; Forth et al., 2003; Gretton et al., 2001, 2005;

Gretton, McBride, Hare, & O'Shaughnessy, 2000). Young offenders are more "malleable" than adult offenders, and early interventions are more likely to be effective than those directed at adults.

Forensic Uses

The PCL:YV has been used in research and juvenile justice settings (Forth et al., 2003) and is well regarded because of its demonstrated reliability and validity in these contexts. It is a standardized method of examining the traits and behaviors considered integral to psychopathy in adolescents. Importantly, the reliability and validity of the PCL:YV extends across age, gender, and several ethnic groups.

The utility of the PCL:YV in various contexts (both research and applied) rests on three separate but related assumptions: (a) It is a good measure of psychopathic traits, (b) it demonstrates reasonable predictive utility, and (c) scores may provide useful information for early intervention.

A good measure of any trait should be reliable and valid and have a standardized scoring method that uses multiple sources of information. These criteria are met by the PCL:YV. The reliability and validity of the PCL:YV have been well established (Forth et al., 2003) and are detailed in the previous sections. The PCL:YV is also a standardized assessment tool, providing comparison tables for several different populations (Forth et al., 2003). It is important to note that the standardized scoring procedures require training and experience to ensure that the instrument is used appropriately. Finally, the PCL:YV is not scored on the basis of information from any one domain. Raters must obtain information from several different domains and from a variety of sources (e.g., institutional files, school records, family reports).

In addition to the preceding requirements, an instrument should also have predictive value if is to be a useful measure of a construct. The predictive validity of the PCL:YV has been demonstrated in several studies. According to Forth and Book (in press), the research literature consistently finds that the PCL:YV, like its adult counterpart, is related to a range of theoretically relevant clinical and forensic correlates and outcome variables.

One of the most important goals in using a measure of psychopathy with youths is to attempt to identify those who might benefit from early intervention and treatment programs. Psychopathic adults do not appear to benefit greatly from traditional treatment programs (Wong & Hare, 2005). However, as noted earlier, it is possible that even adolescents with high PCL:YV scores may be responsive to intervention and treatment.

Overall, the PCL:YV has sound psychometric properties and good predictive utility and may be useful in the development and evaluation of early intervention programs.

Concerns About Misuse

Various authors have considered the potential use (or misuse) of the PCL:YV in mental health and criminal justice settings (Edens, Skeem, Cruise, & Cauffman, 2001; Hare, 1998b; Hart, Watt, & Vincent, 2002; Lyon & Ogloff, 2000; Seagrave & Grisso, 2002; Steinberg, 2002; Zinger & Forth, 1998). Their concerns have included the following: (a) the issue of labeling an adolescent as a psychopath; (b) the implications of the PCL:YV for classification, sentencing, and treatment; (c) the possibility that characteristics of psychopathy are common features of normally developing youths; and (d) the stability of psychopathic traits from late childhood to early adulthood.

Labeling

A major issue is the possibility that PCL:YV scores will be used to diagnose adolescents as "psychopathic." It is common for *researchers* to use cut scores on the PCL–R to diagnose psychopathy in adults, and similar cut scoress have been employed effectively with adolescent offenders for research purposes (e.g., Gretton et al., 2001). However, it would be inappropriate to use the PCL:YV to render a clinical or forensic diagnosis of psychopathy for an adolescent (Forth et al., 2003). Such a diagnosis would require that adolescent psychopathy can be viewed as a taxon or discrete category and that we know what cut score to use for inclusion in the category. However, recent research with adults indicates that a continuum, not a taxon, may underlie PCL–R scores (Guay et al., 2004). It is likely that the same results will be obtained with the PCL:YV. Even if the term "psychopathic" simply is used to describe those with a very high score on the PCL:YV, the effects of measurement error, various rater factors (e.g., inexperience, inadequate training, bias), and the negative impact on the individual would have to be taken into account.

Diagnostic issues are of less concern in research contexts because the consequences for participants are minimal. In forensic contexts, however, the consequences of labeling are potentially very serious for the adolescent. The authors of the PCL:YV note that "psychopathy" is a psychological term, not a legal one, and that it has negative connotations for the general population as well as for mental health and criminal justice professionals (Forth et al., 2003). As stated by Lyon and Ogloff (2000), "Psychopathy is a powerful pejorative diagnostic label that can exert a profound influence over the legal decisions rendered in courts" (p. 139). Scores on the PCL:YV might be used to assist in making decisions in various legal and mental health arenas, including by providing justification for harsher sanctions (e.g., pretrial secure detention, longer sentences, an increased level of supervision after release). Further, with the recent trend toward limited treatment resources, it is possible that clinicians may feel obliged to exclude from treatment young offenders with high scores on the PCL:YV in the belief that psychopaths do not benefit from treatment. This would be contrary to the purpose of the PCL:YV, which is to identify psychopathic traits early enough to provide an opportunity to develop and offer effective intervention, treatment, and management. As noted, psychopathic and related features may be more amenable to treatment in adolescents than in adults, and the PCL:YV may be useful in helping to identify targets for intervention. Several recent studies (cited earlier) suggest that there may be reason for some optimism in this regard.

Age Normative Behavior

Another concern about the measurement of psychopathy in adolescence is that "scores on measures of psychopathy arguably may be inflated by general characteristics of adolescence" (Edens et al., 2001, p. 59). These authors contend that developmental issues may influence the measurement of interpersonal, affective, and social deviance features of psychopathy. Due to changes in perspective-taking ability and cognitive functions, the development of an autonomous identity, and susceptibilty to peer influences, an individual may appear to be grandiose, lacking in remorse or empathy, manipulative, sensation seeking, impulsive, and lacking in goals. Clearly, adolescence itself poses a challenge to any instrument intended to measure psychopathy during this period. Measures of psychopathy that fail to take into account normative adolescent patterns of behavior may well obtain scores that are spuriously high and overestimate the level of psychopathic traits in adolescent samples. Nevertheless, research suggests that it is possible to differentiate normal adolescent behavior from psychopathy. Although some adolescents may exhibit some features of psychopathy in certain contexts or for a limited time, a high score on the PCL:YV requires evidence that the traits and behaviors are extreme and that they are manifested across social contexts and over substantial time periods. High ratings of psychopathic traits are rare in community youths (80% of community males score less than 5 on the PCL:YV; Forth et al., 2003).

Stability

A final concern is the stability of psychopathic traits in adolescents. Adolescence is a period of substantial change in biological, psychological, and social systems (Arnett, 1999). Given the dynamic nature of adolescent development, the question is how much change occurs in personality traits during adolescence. Research measuring the stability of personality traits from childhood to adulthood has indicated that a moderate level of consistency exists and that most change occurs prior to adolescence and not during adolescence itself (Caspi, Roberts, & Shinner, 2005). Caspi et al. (2005) concluded that during adolescence "personality differences remain remarkably consistent during this period" (p. 467). Currently, there are no longitudinal studies assessing psychopathic traits from adolescence to adulthood, making it difficult to draw strong conclusions about the stability of personality traits and behaviors that are measured. However, psychopathic traits appear to be stable from childhood into early adolescence. Frick, Kimonis, Dandreaux, and Farell (2003) assessed the stability of psychopathic traits over a 4-year period using the APSD, a downward extension of the PCL–R (Frick & Hare, 2001). For parent ratings of psychopathic traits, there was a substantial degree of stability across this time period, with an ICC of .80. Most APSD scores remained stable; however, when change did occur, it was rare for those with few psychopathic (callous/unemotional) traits in childhood to develop these traits in adolescence. Lynam (2003) used another downward extension of the PCL–R, the Childhood Psychopathy Scale (CPS; Lynam, 1997), to investigate the stability of psychopathic traits in large samples from the Pittsburgh Youth Study. He reported that mean CPS scores were unrelated to age of assessment, from 7 to 17, and concluded that there was little developmental change in psychopathy and that the traits measured by the CPS were as stable as the major dimensions of personality. He also reported that there was a significant correlation between the CPS administered at age 13 and a derivative of the PCL–R, the 12-item Psychopathy Checklist: Screening Version (PCL:SV; Hart et al., 1995), administered between the ages of 23 and 25.

The stability of personality traits is likely related to the strong genetic influence on personality (Bouchard & Loehlin, 2001). Researchers comparing monozygotic and same-sex dizygotic twins have also found evidence of a substantial genetic influence for psychopathic traits (Blonigen, Carlson, Krueger, & Patrick, 2003; Larsson, Andershed, & Lichtenstein, in press; Taylor, Loney, Bobadilla, Iacono, & McGue, 2003; Viding, Blair, Moffitt, & Plomin, 2005). Although not directly related to the issue of stability of traits in individuals, there is accumulating evidence that some of the biological correlates of adult psychopathy are also found in adolescents with psychopathic traits. For example, Fung et al. (2005) reported that adolescent males with high scores on the CPS showed the same pattern of anticipatory electrodermal hyporesponsivity as found in adult psychopaths. The authors suggested that "this autonomic impairment is present by adolescence and may predispose individuals to adult psychopathy" (p. 187).

Recommendations

Forth et al. (2003) made several recommendations to reduce assessment errors and misuse of information. These recommendations fall into two categories: (a) professional qualifications and (b) professional practices and safeguards. Individuals who use the PCL:YV for forensic purposes must be qualified to do so. In determining the meaning and implications of a given PCL:YV score for a particular individual, the user should take into account the literature on developmental stages, norms, and age-appropriate behaviors (Forth & Book, in press). As stated by Arnett (1999), adolescence can be a period of great stress, and some of the activities in which adolescents engage, while not necessarily prosocial, are part of normal adolescent development.

Clinicians must be able to justify the application, relevance, and implications of their assessments. They must also follow the standard instructions and guidelines in the manual. This includes basing their ratings on reliable multisource information from a variety of domains and on behavior over a substantial period of time (e.g., a year or more).

Because of the increasing importance of the PCL:YV in the juvenile justice system, the manual recommends that it should be used and interpreted in combination with information from a number of sources and should never be the sole criterion for decision making around treatment and/or adjudication (Forth et al., 2003). As well, because the consequences of misuse are especially serious, Forth and colleagues (2003) state that it is inappropriate to label a youth as a psychopath and that it is unethical to use scores to justify exclusion from available treatment programs. Finally, it is not appropriate to rely on PCL:YV scores alone to impose harsher sentences or to use the scores in determining whether a young offender should be tried as an adult.

CLINICAL CASE EXAMPLE

Mark is a 15-year-old White male adolescent offender who was recently convicted of reckless driving, automobile theft, and drug trafficking (all part of the same incident). He had been selling marijuana on a street corner that was well known for being a place to "score drugs." The police began a raid on that particular street, and Mark took off before he could be caught. He saw a woman getting out of her car beside a parking meter. He pushed her aside, jumped into her car, and drove off. During ensuing police chase, Mark ran a red light and hit another car, seriously injuring the 62-year-old driver. Mark received minor injuries and was apprehended about two blocks from the scene of the incident.

An assessment of psychopathic traits was requested to aid in making recommendations regarding risk for future criminal behavior and appropriate level of intervention. A forensic psychologist completed the PCL:YV in a detention facility on the basis of file information; an interview with Mark's mother, stepfather, and probation officer; and a 2-hour interview, with Mark. During the interview, Mark was exceptionally talkative. He tried to control the interview by interrupting and questioning the qualifications of the rater. He reported that his father left his mother before he turned 1 and that he had been raised by his mother and stepfather, whom she had married when he was 5. He stated that his stepfather never liked him and that he was often punished physically, even in public. At around the same time, Mark began stealing toys and candy from the grocery store and from other children at school.

According to file information, Mark began acting out at an early age. He was first suspended from school at the age of 8 for stealing from other students' lockers. His first contact with the local police was at age 9, also for theft. At age 12, he was convicted of his first crime, breaking and entering. He had entered a neighbor's house and had stolen a wallet from the kitchen table. He took the cash from the wallet and threw the wallet in a nearby creek. Mark was expelled from school at age 13 for bringing a large kitchen knife to school. According to his mother's report, he was hanging around with children who were a bad influence on him. In fact, according to school reports and Mark himself, Mark was the bad influence.

Academically, Mark has done quite poorly. He rarely completed homework assignments, was consistently absent, and was suspended numerous times, beginning in elementary school. Although his academic performance was poor, he was always sent on to the next grade. He completed grade 9 and then dropped out of school. He has had a minimal employment history in the community. When he was 14, he had a paper route, although he was consistently reprimanded, and eventually fired, for throwing the newspapers in the trash rather than delivering them.

Mark has an extensive history of substance use, ranging from alcohol and marijuana to heroin, LSD, and ecstasy. He stated that he enjoys using drugs and that when he does not use them, the boredom is unbearable. During the current assessment, he stated that he had started using drugs and alcohol at the age of 13. He also stated that drugs or alcohol preceded most of his criminal activities. He said, however, that he is very proud of not being addicted to anything.

Mark reported having first experienced sexual intercourse when he was 12 years old and stated that he could not count the number of times he had had intercourse since. He has not had any serious girlfriends or even dating partners. He stated that having a girlfriend would be too much of a hassle.

His previous convictions included breaking and entering (two counts), car theft (three counts), and assault causing bodily harm. The assault incident occurred when he was 14, and he received a 6-month sentence. While at a party, he got into a verbal argument with a 16-year-old boy. Mark left the party and returned with a baseball bat and waited outside for the victim. He hit the victim three times with the bat before being restrained by other youths.

Mark has had problems within the institution. He is consistently rude and sarcastic with the staff and has, on occasion, been physically aggressive toward younger offenders. During his previous incarceration for the assault causing bodily harm, he refused to participate in treatment, stating that therapy is for crazy people.

Mark has been on probation for the break and enters and the car thefts. He violated probation once. He missed meetings with his probation officer, and his probation was revoked. He pled guilty at his trial (to all charges). However, when asked about the consequences of his crime, he stated that no one was hurt and that insurance would cover the losses. This statement completely ignored the physical harm to the man whose car he hit. When asked about this, he said, "That part was an accident. As if I should have been charged with that."

Mark exhibits many psychopathic traits. Among institutionalized male adolescent offenders, he would score at the 64th percentile, meaning that 64% of other male offenders would receive a score similar to or lower than his score. Among male adolescent probationers, he would score at the 86th percentile, indicating he has many more psychopathic features than most offenders in such a setting. The PCL:YV is divided into four factors. The Interpersonal factor focuses on such features as grandiosity and manipulativeness. The Affective factor measures such features as callousness and remorseless use of others. The Behavioral factor reflects features such as impulsivity, irresponsibility, and lack of goals. The Antisocial factor reflects poor anger control and the early onset and high frequency of antisocial behaviors. Compared with other adolescent male offenders, he had elevated scores on the Affective, Behavioral, and Antisocial factors. He had some of the Interpersonal (42nd percentile) and Affective (68th percentile) psychopathic features. His score on the Behavioral factor was very high (at the 82nd percentile), and his score on the Antisocial factor was at the 66th percentile. Overall, Mark's score on the PCL:YV is within the range of scores associated with institutional adjustment problems, treatment noncompliance, and an increased risk of future criminal behavior. The evaluator stated that Mark was at high risk for violence and recommended interventions to improve parental management and a high-intensity cognitive-behavioral program focused on the following treatment targets: self-management of negative affect and impulse control, substance use problems, negative attitudes, and antisocial peers.

REFERENCES

American Psychiatric Association. (1994). *Diagnostic and statistical manual of mental disorders* (4th ed.). Washington, DC: Author.

Anastasi, A. (1982). *Psychological testing* (5th ed.). London: Collier Macmillan.

Andershed, H.A., Gustafson, S.B., Kerr, M., & Stattin, H. (2002). The usefulness of self-reported psychopathy-like traits in the study of antisocial behaviour among non-referred adolescents. *European Journal of Personality, 16*, 383–402.

Arnett, J.J. (1999). Adolescent storm and stress, reconsidered. *American Psychologist, 54*, 317–326.

Babiak, P. (1995). When psychopaths go to work: A case study of an industrial psychopath. *Applied Psychology, 44*, 171–178.

Babiak, P. (2000). Psychopathic manipulation at work. In C.B. Gacono (Ed.), *The clinical and forensic assessment of psychopathy: A practitioner's guide* (pp. 287–312). Mahwah, NJ: Lawrence Erlbaum Associates.

Berrios, G.E. (1996). *The history of mental symptoms: Descriptive psychopathology since the nineteenth century*. Cambridge: Cambridge University Press.

Blackburn, R., & Coid, J.W. (1998). Psychopathy and the dimensions of personality disorders in violent offenders. *Personality and Individual Differences, 25*, 129–145.

Blonigen, D.M., Carlson, S.R., Krueger, R.F., & Patrick, C.J. (2003). A twin study of self-reported psychopathic personality traits. *Personality and Individual Differences, 35*, 179–197.

Bolt, D., Hare, R.D., Vitale, J., & Newman, J.P. (2004). A multigroup item response theory analyses of the Hare Psychopathy Checklist-Revised. *Psychological Assessment, 16*, 155–168.

Bouchard, T.J., & Loehlin, J.C. (2001). Genes, evolution, and personality. *Behavioral Genetics, 31*, 243–247.

Brandt, J.R., Kennedy, W.A., Patrick, C.J., & Curtin, J.J. (1997). Assessment of psychopathy in a population of incarcerated adolescent offenders. *Psychological Assessment, 9*, 429–435.

Brown, S.L., & Forth, A.E. (1997). Psychopathy and sexual assault: Static risk factors, emotional precursors, and rapist subtypes. *Journal of Consulting and Clinical Psychology, 65*, 848–857.

Buffington-Vollum, J.K., Edens, J.F., Johnson, D.W., & Johnson, J.K. (2002). Psychopathy as a predictor of institutional misbehaviour in sex offenders: A prospective replication. *Criminal Justice and Behavior, 29*, 497–511.

Caldwell, M.F., & Van Rybroek, G.J. (2001). Efficacy of a decompression treatment model in the clinical management of violent juvenile offenders. *International Journal of Offender Therapy and Comparative Criminology, 45*, 469–477.

Campbell, M.A., Porter, S., & Santor, D. (2004). Psychopathic traits in adolescent offenders: An evaluation of criminal history, clinical, and psychosocial correlates. *Behavioral Sciences and the Law, 22*, 23–47.

Campbell, T.W. (2000). Sexual predator evaluations and phrenology: Considering issues of evidentiary reliability. *Behavioral Sciences and the Law, 18*, 111–130.

Caspi, A., Roberts, B.W., & Shiner, R.L. (2005). Personality development: Stability and change. *Annual Review of Psychology, 56*, 453–484.

Caputo, A.A., Frick, P.J., & Brodsky, S.L. (1999). Family violence and juvenile sex offending: Potential mediating roles of psychopathic traits and negative attitudes toward women. *Criminal Justice and Behavior, 26*, 338–356.

Catchpole, R.E.H., & Gretton, H.M. (2003). The predictive validity of risk assessment with violent young offenders: A 1-year examination of criminal outcome. *Criminal Justice and Behavior, 30,* 688–708.

Clark, H.J., & Forth, A.E. (2004). *Psychopathy in the court.* Unpublished manuscript, Department of Psychology, Carleton University.

Cleckley, H. (1941). *The mask of sanity.* St. Louis, MO: Mosby.

Cleckley, H. (1976). *The mask of sanity* (5th ed.). St. Louis, MO: Mosby.

Coid, J. (1993). Current concepts and classifications of psychopathic disorder. In P. Tyrer & G. Stein (Eds.), *Personality disorder reviewed* (pp. 113–164). London: Royal College of Psychiatrists; Gaskell Press.

Coid, J., Ullrich, S., Yang, M., Roberts, A., Singleton, N., & Hare, R.D. (2005). *Psychopathy in the household population of Great Britain.* Manuscript in preparation.

Cooke, D.J., Forth, A.E., & Hare, R.D. (Eds.). (1998). *Psychopathy: Theory, research, and implications for society.* Dordrecht, The Netherlands: Kluwer Academic Publishing.

Cooke, D.J., Kosson, D.S., & Michie, C. (2001). Psychopathy and ethnicity: Structural, item and test generalizability of the Psychopathy Checklist Revised (PCL–R) in Caucasian and African-American participants. *Psychological Assessment, 13,* 531–542.

Cooke, D.J., & Michie, C. (1999). Psychopathy across cultures: North America and Scotland compared. *Journal of Abnormal Psychology, 108,* 58–68.

Cooke, D.J., & Michie, C. (2001). Refining the construct of psychopathy: Towards a hierarchical model. *Psychological Assessment, 13,* 171–188.

Cooke, D.J., Michie, C. Hart, S.D., & Clarke, D. (2005). Searching for the pan-cultural core of psychopathic personality disorder. *Personality and Individual Differences, 39,* 283–295.

Cooke, D.J., Michie, C., Hart, S.D., & Hare, R.D. (1999). The functioning of the clinical version of the Psychopathy Checklist: An item response theory analysis. *Psychological Assessment, 11,* 3–13.

Cornell, D.G., Warren, J., Hawk, G., Stafford, E., Oram, G., & Pine, D. (1996). Psychopathy in instrumental and reactive violent offenders. *Journal of Consulting and Clinical Psychology, 64,* 3–19.

Corrado, R.R., Vincent, G.M., Hart, S.D., & Cohen, I.M. (2004). Predictive validity of the Psychopathy Checklist: Youth Version for general and violent recidivism. *Behavioral Sciences and the Law, 22,* 5–22.

Costa, P.T., & McCrae, R.R. (1992). The five-factor model of personality and its relevance to personality disorders. *Journal of Personality Disorders, 6,* 343–359.

Costa, P.T., & Widiger, T.A. (2002). *Personality disorder and the five-factor model of personality* (2nd ed.). Washington, DC: American Psychological Association.

Cruise, K.R., Colwell, L.H., Lyons, P.M., & Baker, M.D. (2003). Prototypical analysis of adolescent psychopathy: Investigating the juvenile justice perspective. *Behavioral Sciences and the Law, 21,* 829–846.

Cunningham, M.D., & Reidy, T.J. (2001). A matter of life or death: Special considerations and heightened practice standards in capital sentencing evaluations. *Behavioral Sciences and the Law, 19,* 473–490.

Cunningham, M.D., Sorensen, J.R., & Reidy, T.J. (2005). An actuarial model for assessment of prison violence risk among maximum security inmates. *Assessment, 12,* 40–49.

Dadds, M.R., Fraser, J., Frost, F., & Hawes, D.J. (2005). Disentangling the underlying dimensions of psychopathy and conduct problems in childhood: A community study. *Journal of Consluting and Clinical Psychology, 73,* 400–410.

Dahlstrom, W.G., & Welsh, G.S. (1960). *An MMPI handbook: A guide to use in clinical practice and research.* Minneapolis: University of Minnesota Press.

Darke, S., Kaye, S., Finlay-Jones, R., & Hall, W. (1998). Factor structure of psychopathy among methadone maintenance patients. *Journal of Personality Disorders, 12,* 162–171.

Dolan, M., & Coid, J. (1993). *Psychopathic and antisocial personality disorders: Treatment and research issues.* London: Gaskell Press.

Dolan, M., & Doyle, M. (2000). Violence risk prediction: Clinical and actuarial measures and the role of the Psychopathy Checklist. *British Journal of Psychiatry, 177,* 303–311.

Doninger, N.A., & Kosson, D.S. (2001). Interpersonal construct systems among psychopaths. *Personality and Individual Differences, 30,* 1263–1281.

Douglas, K.S., Strand, S., Belfrage, H., Fransson, G., & Levander, S. (2005). Reliability and validity evaluation of the Psychopathy Checklist: Screening Version (PCL:SV) in Swedish correctional and forensic psychiatric samples. *Assessment, 12,* 145–161.

Douglas, K.S., & Webster, C.D. (1999). The HCR-20 violence risk assessment scheme: Concurrent validity in a sample of incarcerated offenders. *Criminal Justice and Behavior, 26,* 3–19.

D'Silva, K., Duggan, C., & McCarthy, L. (2004). Does treatment really make psychopaths worse? A review of the evidence. *Journal of Personality Disorders, 18,* 163–177.

Edens, J.F. (2001). Misuses of the Hare Psychopathy Checklist–Revised in court: Two case examples. *Journal of Interpersonal Violence, 16,* 1082–1094.

Edens, J.F., Buffington-Vollum, J.K., Keilen, A., Roskamp, P., & Anthony, C. (2005). Prediction of future dangerousness in capital murder trials: Is it time to "disinvent the wheel"? *Law and Human Behavior, 29,* 55–86.

Edens, J.F., Desforges, D.M., Fernandez, K., & Palac, C.A. (2004). Effects of psychopathy and violence risk testimony on mock juror perceptions of dangerousness in a capital murder trial. *Psychology, Crime and Law, 10,* 393–412.

Edens, J.F., Skeem, J.L., Cruise, K.R., & Cauffman, E. (2001). Assessment of "juvenile psychopathy" and its association with violence: A critical review. *Behavioral Sciences and the Law, 19,* 53–80.

Forth, A.E., & Book, A.S. (in press). Psychopathy in youth: A viable construct? In H. Hervé & J. Yuille, J. *Psychopathy in the 21st century.* Mahwah, NJ: Lawrence Erlbaum Associates.

Forth, A.E., Brown, S.L., Hart, S.D., & Hare, R.D. (1996). The assessment of psychopathy in male and female noncriminals: Reliability and validity. *Personality and Individual Differences, 20,* 531–543.

Forth, A.E., & Burke, H. (1998). Psychopathy in adolescence: Assessment, violence, and developmental precursors. In D.J. Cooke, A.E. Forth, & R.D. Hare (Eds.), *Psychopathy: Theory, research, and implications for society* (pp. 205–229). Dordrecht, The Netherlands: Kluwer Academic Publishers.

Forth, A.E., Hart, S.D., & Hare, R.D. (1990). Assessment of psychopathy in male young offenders. *Psychological Assessment, 2,* 342–344.

Forth, A.E., Kosson, D., & Hare, R.D. (2003). *The Hare PCL: Youth Version.* Toronto, Ontario, Canada: Multi-Health Systems.

Forth, A.E., & Mailloux, D.L. (2000). Psychopathy in youth: What do we know? In C.B. Gacono (Ed.), *The clinical and forensic assessment of psychopathy: A practitioner's guide* (pp. 25–54). Mahwah, NJ: Lawrence Erlbaum Associates.

Frick, P.J. (2000). The problems of internal validation without a theoretical context: The different conceptual underpinnings of psychopathy and the disruptive behavior disorder criteria. *Psychological Assessment, 12,* 451–465.

Frick, P.J., & Hare, R.D. (2001). *The Antisocial Process Screening Device.* Toronto, Ontario, Canada: Multi-Health Systems.

Frick, P.J., Kimonis, E.R., Dandreaux, D.M., & Farell, J.M. (2003). The 4 year stability of psychopathic traits in non-referred youth. *Behavioral Sciences and the Law, 21,* 713–736.

Frick, P.J., O'Brien, B.S., Wootton, J.M., & McBurnett, K. (1994). Psychopathy and conduct problems in children. *Journal of Abnormal Psychology, 103,* 700–707.

Fulero, S.M. (1995). Review of the Hare Psychopathy Checklist-Revised. In J.C. Conoley & J.C. Impara (Eds.), *Twelfth mental measurements yearbook* (pp. 453–454). Lincoln, NE: Buros Institute.

Fung, M.T., Raine, A., Loeber, R., Lynam, D.R., Steinhauer, S.S., Venables, P.H., et al. (2005). Reduced electrodermal activity in psychopathy-prone adolescents. *Journal of Abnormal Psychology, 114,* 187–196.

Gacono, C. (Ed.). (2000). *The clinical and forensic assessment of psychopathy: A practitioner's guide.* Mahwah, NJ: Lawrence Erlbaum Associates.

Gendreau, P., Goggin, C., & Smith, P. (2002). Is the PCL–R really the "unparalled" measure of offender risk? A lesion in knowledge cumulation. *Criminal Justice and Behavior, 29,* 397–426.

Glover, A.J., Nicholson, D.E., Hemmati, T., Bernfeld, G.A., & Quinsey, V.L. (2002). A comparison of predictors of general and violent recidivism among high-risk federal offenders. *Criminal Justice and Behavior, 29,* 235–249.

Grann, M., & Tengström, A. (2003). *Hare PCL–R* (2nd ed.). Stockholm: Psychologiförlaget.

Gray, N.S., Hill, C., McGleish, A., Timmons, D., MacCulloch, M.J., & Snowden, R.J. (2003). Prediction of violence and self-harm in mentally disordered offenders: A prospective study of the efficacy of HCR-20, PCL–R, and psychiatric symptomatology. *Journal of Consulting and Clinical Psychology, 71,* 443–451.

Gretton, H.M., Catchpole, R.E.H., McBride, M., Hare, R.D., O'Shaughnessy, R., & Regan, K.V. (2005). The relationship between psychopathy, treatment completion, and criminal outcome over ten years: A study of adolescent sex offenders. In M. Caldwell (Ed.), *Children and young people who sexually abuse: New theory, research, and practice developments* (pp. 19–31). London: Russull House Publishing.

Gretton, H.M., Hare, R.D., & Catchpole, R.E.H. (2004). Psychopathy and offending from adolescence to adulthood: A 10-year follow-up. *Journal of Consulting and Clinical Psychology, 72*, 636–645.

Gretton, H.M., McBride, M., Hare, R.D., & O'Shaughnessy, R. (2000, November). *The developmental course of offending in adolescent offenders; A ten-year follow-up study.* Paper presented at the Association for the Treatment of Sexual Abusers, San Diego, CA.

Gretton, H.M., McBride, M., Hare, R.D., O'Shaughnessy, R., & Kumka, G. (2001). Psychopathy and recidivism in adolescent sex offenders. *Criminal Justice and Behavior, 28*, 427–449.

Guay, J.P., Ruscio, J., Hare, R.D., & Knight, R.A. (2004, October). *The latent structure of psychopathy: When more is simply more.* Paper presented at the Society for Research in Psychopathology, St. Louis MO.

Hare, R.D. (1980). A research scale for the assessment of psychopathy in criminal populations. *Personality and Individual Differences, 1*, 111–119.

Hare, R.D. (1985). Comparison of the procedures for the assessment of psychopathy. *Journal of Consulting and Clinical Psychology, 53*, 7–16.

Hare, R.D. (1991). *The Hare Psychopathy Checklist–Revised.* Toronto, Ontario, Canada: Multi-Health Systems.

Hare, R.D. (1996). Psychopathy and antisocial personality disorder: A case of diagnostic confusion. *Psychiatric Times, 13*, 39–40

Hare, R.D. (1998a). Psychopaths and their nature: Implications for the mental health and criminal justice systems. In T. Millon, E. Simonson, M. Burket-Smith, & R. Davis (Eds.), *Psychopathy: Antisocial, criminal, and violent behavior* (pp. 188–212). New York: Guilford Press.

Hare, R.D. (1998b). The Hare PCL–R: Some issues concerning its use and misuse. *Legal and Criminological Psychology, 3*, 101–123.

Hare, R.D. (2003). *The Hare Psychopathy Checklist–Revised* (2nd ed.). Toronto, Ontario, Canada: Multi-Health Systems.

Hare, R.D., Clark, D., Grann, M., & Thornton, D. (2000). Psychopathy and the predictive validity of the PCL–R: An international perspective. *Behavioral Sciences and the Law, 18*, 623–645.

Hare, R.D., & Frazelle, J. (1980). *Some preliminary notes on the use of a research scale for the assessment of psychopathy in criminal populations.* Unpublished manuscript, University of British Columbia.

Hare, R.D., & Neumann, C.S. (2005a). The PCL–R assessment of psychopathy: Development, structural properties, and new directions. In C. Patrick (Ed.), *Handbook of psychopathy* (pp. 58–88). New York: Guilford Press.

Hare, R.D., & Neumann, C.S. (2005b). The structure of psychopathy. *Current Psychiatry Reports, 7*, 57–64.

Hart, S.D., Cox, D.N., & Hare, R.D. (1995). *Manual for the Psychopathy Checklist: Screening Version (PCL:SV).* Toronto, Ontario, Canada: Multi-Health Systems.

Hart, S.D., & Hare, R.D. (1989). Discriminant validity of the Psychopathy Checklist. *Psychological Assessment, 1*, 211–218.

Hart, S.D., Watt, K.A., & Vincent, G.M. (2002). Commentary on Seagrave and Grisso: Impressions of the state of the art. *Law and Human Behavior, 26*, 241–245.

Harvey, P.D., Stokes, J.L., Lord, J., & Pogge, D.L. (1996). Neurocognitive and personality assessment of adolescent substance abusers: A multidimensional approach. *Assessment, 3*, 241–253.

Heilbrun, K., Hart, S.D., Hare, R.D., Gustafson, D., Nunez, C., & White, A. (1998). Inpatient and post-discharge aggression in mentally disordered offenders: The role of psychopathy. *Journal of Interpersonal Violence, 13*, 514–527.

Hemphill, J.F., & Hare, R.D. (2004). Some misconceptions about the Hare PCL–R and risk assessment: A reply to Gendreau, Goggin, and Smith. *Criminal Justice and Behavior, 31*, 203–243.

Hemphill, J.F., Hare, R.D., & Wong, S. (1998). Psychopathy and recidivism: A review. *Legal and Criminological Psychology, 3*, 139–170.

Hemphill, J.F., & Hart, S.D. (2004). Motivating the unmotivated: Psychopathy, treatment, and change. In M. McMurran (Ed.), *Motivating offenders to change: A guide to enhancing engagement in therapy* (pp. 193–219). Chichester, England: Wiley.

Hemphill, J.F., Hart, S.D., & Hare, R.D. (1994). Psychopathy and substance use. *Journal of Personality Disorders, 8*, 169–180.

Hicklin, J., & Widiger, T.A. (2005). Similarities and differences among antisocial and psychopathic self-report inventories from the perspective of general personality functioning. *European Journal of Personality, 19*, 325–342.

Hicks, M.M., Rogers, R., & Cashel, M. (2000). Predictions of violent and total infractions among institutionalized male juvenile offenders. *Journal of the American Academy of Psychiatry and the Law, 28*, 183–190.

Hildebrand, M., & de Ruiter, C. (2004). PCL-R psychopathy and its relation to *DSM–IV* Axis I and Axis II disorders in a sample of male forensic psychiatric patients in the Netherlands. *International Journal of Law and Psychiatry, 27*, 233–248.

Hildebrand, M., de Ruiter, C., & de Vogel, V. (2004). Psychopathy and sexual deviance in treated rapists: Association with sexual and non-sexual recidivism. *Sexual Abuse, 16*, 1–24.

Hill, C., & Neumann, C.S., & Rogers, R. (2004). Confirmatory factor analysis of the Psychopathy Checklist: Screening Version (PCL:SV) in offenders with Axis I disorders. *Psychological Assessment, 16*, 90–95.

Hill, C.D., Rogers, R., & Bickford, M.E. (1996). Predicting aggressive and socially disruptive behavior in a maximum security forensic psychiatric hospital. *Journal of Forensic Sciences, 41*, 56–59.

Hobson, J., Shine, J., & Roberts, R. (2000). How do psychopaths behave in a prison therapeutic environment? *Psychology, Crime and Law, 6*, 139–154.

Home Office and Department of Health. (1999). *Managing dangerous people with severe personality disorder*. London: Authors. Available at: http://www.homeoffice.gov.uk/docs/persdis.html

Home Office and Department of Health. (2005). *DPSD: Dangerous people with severe personality disorder*. Available at: http://www.dspdprogramme.gov.uk/pages/what we're doing/what we do7.php

Kosson, D.S., Cyterski, T.D., Steuerwald, B.L., Neumann, C.S., & Walker-Matthews, S. (2002). The reliability and validity of the Psychopathy Checklist: Youth Version in nonincarcerated adolescent males. *Psychological Assessment, 14*, 97–109.

Kosson, D.S., Steuerwald, B.L., Forth, A.E., & Kirkhart, K.J. (1997). A new method for assessing the interpersonal behavior of psychopaths: Preliminary validation studies. *Psychological Assessment, 9*, 89–101.

Kroner, D.G., & Mills, J.F. (2001). The accuracy of five risk appraisal instruments in predicting institutional misconduct and new convictions. *Criminal Justice and Behavior, 28*, 471–489.

Larsson, H., Andershed, H., & Lichtenstein, P. (in press). A genetic factor explains most of the variation in the psychopathic personality. *Journal of Abnormal Psychology*.

Lee, Z., Vincent, G.M., Hart, S.D., & Corrado, R.R. (2003). The validity of the Antisocial Process Screening Device as a self-report measure of psychopathy in adolescent offenders. *Behavioral Sciences and the Law, 21*, 771–786.

Levenson, M.R., Kiehl, K.A., & Fitzpatrick, C.M. (1995). Assessing psychopathic attributes in a noninstitutionalized population. *Journal of Personality and Social Psychology, 68*, 151–158.

Lilienfeld, S.O., & Andrews, B.P. (1996). Development and preliminary validation of a self-report measure of psychopathic personality traits in noncriminal populations. *Journal of Personality Assessment, 66*, 488–524.

Looman, J., Abracen, J., Serin, R., & Marquis, P. (2005). Psychopathy, treatment change and recidivism in high risk high need sexual offenders. *Journal of Interpersonal Violence, 20*, 549–568.

Lorenz, A.R., & Newman, J.P. (2002). Do emotion and information processing deficiencies found in Caucasian psychopaths generalize to African-American psychopaths? *Personality and Individual Differences, 32*, 1077–1086.

Lösel, F. (1998). Treatment and management of psychopaths. In D.J. Cooke, R.D. Hare, & A.E. Forth (Eds.), *Psychopathy: Theory, research, and implications for society* (pp. 303–354). Dordrecht, The Nether lands: Kluwer Academic Publishing.

Loucks, A.D., & Zamble, E. (2000). Predictors of criminal behavior and prison misconduct in serious female offenders. *Empirical and Applied Criminal Justice Review, 1*, 1–47.

Lynam, D.R. (1996). Early identification of chronic offenders: Who is the fledging psychopath? *Psychological Bulletin, 120*, 209–234.

Lynam, D.R. (1997). Pursuing the psychopath: Capturing the fledging psychopath in a romological net. *Journal of Abnormal Psychology, 106*, 425–438.

Lynam, D.R. (1998). Early identification of the fledgling psychopath: Locating the psychopathic child in the current nomenclature. *Journal of Abnormal Psychology, 107,* 566–575.

Lynam, D.R. (2002). Psychopathy from the perspective of the five-factor model of personality. In P. T. Costa & T.A. Widiger (Eds.), *Personality disorder and the five-factor model of personality* (2nd ed., pp. 325–348). Washington, DC: American Psychological Association.

Lynam, D.R. (2003, July). *Development and psychopathy.* Paper presented at the Conference on Developmental and Neuroscience Perspectives on Psychopathy, University of Wisconsin, Madison.

Lynam, D.R., & Gudonis, L. (2005). The development of psychopathy. *Annual Review of Clinical Psychology, 1,* 381–407.

Lynn, R. (2002). Racial and ethnic differences in psychopathic personality. *Personality and Individual Differences, 32,* 273–316.

Lyon, D.R., & Ogloff, J.R.P. (2000). Legal and ethical issues in psychopathy assessment. In C.B. Gacono (Ed.), *The clinical and forensic assessment of psychopathy: A practitioner's guide* (pp. 139–173). Mahwah, NJ: Lawrence Erlbaum Associates.

Mailloux, D.L., Forth, A.E., & Kroner, D.G. (1997). Psychopathy and substance use in adolescent male offenders. *Psychological Reports, 81,* 529–530.

Marczyk, G.R., Heilbrun, K., Lander, T., & DeMatteo, D. (2003). Predicting juvenile recidivism with the PCL:YV, MAYSI, and YLS/CMI. *International Journal of Forensic Mental Health, 2,* 7–18.

McDermott, P.A., Alterman, A.I., Cacciola, J.S., Rutherford, M.J., Newman, J.P., & Mulholland, E.M. (2000). Generality of Psychopathy Checklist–Revised factors over prisoners and substance-dependent patients. *Journal of Consulting and Clinical Psychology, 68,* 181–186.

Millon, T. (1987). *Millon Clinical Multiaxial Inventory–II manual.* Minneapolis, MN: National Computer Systems.

Millon, T. (1993). *The Millon Adolescent Clinical Inventory (MACI).* Minneapolis, MN: NCS Assessments.

Millon, T., Davis, R., & Millon, C. (1997). *MCMI-III Manual (2nd ed.).* Minneapolis, MN: National Computer Systems.

Millon, T., Simonson, E., Birket-Smith, M., & Davis, R. D. (Eds.). (1998). *Psychopathy: Antisocial, criminal, and violent behavior.* New York: Guilford Press.

Monahan, J., & Steadman, H.J. (1994). *Violence and mental disorder: Developments in risk assessment.* Chicago: University of Chicago Press.

Morey, L.C. (1991). *Personality Assessment Inventory: Professional manual.* Lutz, FL: Psychological Assessment Resources.

Murrie, D.C., & Cornell, D.G. (2002). Psychopathy screening of incarcerated juveniles: A comparison of measures. *Psychological Assessment, 14,* 390–396.

Murrie, D.C., Cornell, D.G., Kaplan, S., McConville, D., & Levy-Elkon, A. (2004). Psychopathy scores and violence among juvenile offenders: A multi-measure study. *Behavioral Sciences and the Law, 22,* 49–67.

Myers, W.C., Burket, R.C., & Harris, H.E. (1995). Adolescent psychopathy in relation to delinquent behaviors, conduct disorder, and personality disorders. *Journal of Forensic Sciences, 40,* 436–440.

Newman, J.P., & Schmitt, W.A. (1998). Passive avoidance in psychopathic offenders: A replication and extension, *Journal of Abnormal Psychology, 107,* 527–532.

Ogloff, J.P.R., & Chopta, S.R. (2004). Stuck in the dark ages: Supreme Court decision-making and legal developments. *Psychology, Public Policy, and Law, 10,* 379–416.

O'Neill, M.L., Lidz, V., & Heilbrun, K. (2003a). Adolescents with psychopathic characteristics in a substance abusing cohort: Treatment process and outcomes. *Law and Human Behavior, 27,* 299–314.

O'Neill, M.L., Lidz, V., & Heilbrun, K. (2003b). Predictors and correlates of psychopathic characteristics in substance abusing adolescents. *International Journal of Forensic Mental Health, 2,* 35–45.

Patrick, C.J. (Ed.). (2005). *Handbook of psychopathy.* New York: Guilford Press.

Paulhus, D.L., Hemphill, J.F., & Hare, R.D. (in press). *Manual for the Self-Report Psychopathy Scale (SRP-III).* Toronto, Ontario, Canada: Multi-Health Systems.

Pichot, P. (1978). Psychopathic behaviour: A historical overview. In R.D. Hare, & D. Schalling (Eds.), *Psychopathic behaviour: Approaches to research* (pp. 55–70). Chichester, England: Wiley.

Porter, S., Birt, A.R., & Boer D.P. (2001). Investigation of the criminal and conditional release profiles of Canadian federal offenders as a function of psychopathy and age. *Law and Human Behavior, 25,* 647–661.

Porter, S., Fairweather, D., Drugge, J., Hervé, H., Birt, A., & Boer, D.P. (2000). Profiles of psychopathy in incarcerated sexual offenders. *Criminal Justice and Behavior, 27*, 216–233.

Rice, M.E., & Harris, G.T. (1997). Cross-validation and extension of the Violence Risk Appraisal Guide for child molesters and rapists. *Law and Human Behavior, 21*, 231–241.

Rice, M.E., Harris, G.T., & Cormier, C.A. (1992). An evaluation of a maximum security therapeutic community for psychopaths and other mentally disordered offenders. *Law and Human Behavior, 16*, 399–412.

Richards, H.J., Casey, J.O., & Lucente, S.W. (2003). Psychopathy and treatment response in incarcerated female substance abusers. *Criminal Justice and Behavior, 30*, 251–267.

Richards, H.J., Casey, J.O., Lucente, S.W., & Kafami, D. (2003). Differential association of Hare Psychopathy Checklist scores to HIV behaviors in incarcerated female substance abusers. *Individual Differences Research, 2*, 95–107.

Ridenour, T.A., Marchant, G.J., & Dean, R.S. (2001). Is the Psychopathy Checklist-Revised clinically useful for adolescents? *Journal of Psychoeducational Assessment, 19*, 227–238.

Rogers, R., Johansen, J., Chang, J.J., & Salekin, R.T. (1997). Predictors of adolescent psychopathy: Oppositional and conduct-disordered symptoms. *Journal of the American Academy of Psychiatry and the Law, 25*, 261–271.

Salekin, R.T., Neumann, C.S., Leistico, A.R., DiCicco, T.M., & Duros, R.L. (2004). Construct validity of psychopathy in a young offender sample: Taking a closer look at psychopathy's potential importance over disruptive behavior disorders. *Journal of Abnormal Psychology, 113*, 416–427.

Salekin, R.T., Rogers, R., & Machin, D. (2001). Psychopathy in youth: Pursuing diagnostic clarity. *Journal of Youth and Adolescence, 30*, 173–194.

Salekin, R., Rogers, R., & Sewell, K.W. (1996). A review and meta-analysis of the Psychopathy Checklist–Revised: Predictive validity of dangerousness. *Clinical Psychology: Science and Practice, 3*, 203–215.

Seagrave, D., & Grisso, T. (2002). Adolescent development and the measurement of juvenile psychopathy. *Law and Human Behavior, 26*, 219–239.

Serin, R.C. (1996). Violent recidivism in criminal psychopaths. *Law and Human Behavior, 20*, 207–217.

Serin, R.C., & Amos, N.L. (1995). The role of psychopathy in the assessment of dangerousness. *International Journal of Law and Psychiatry, 18*, 231–238.

Serin, R.C., Mailloux, D.L., & Malcolm, P.B. (2001). Psychopathy, deviant sexual arousal, and recidivism among sexual offenders. *Journal of Interpersonal Violence, 16*, 234–246.

Seto, M.C., & Barbaree, H.E. (1999). Psychopathy, treatment behavior, and sex offender recidivism. *Journal of Interpersonal Violence, 14*, 1235–1248.

Shine, J.H., & Hobson, J.A. (2000). Institutional behaviour and time in treatment among psychopaths admitted to a prison-based therapeutic community. *Medicine, Science, and the Law, 20*, 327–335.

Skeem, J.L., & Cauffman, E. (2003). Views of the downward extension: Comparing the Youth Version of the Psychopathy Checklist with the Youth Psychopathic Traits Inventory. *Behavioral Sciences and the Law, 21*, 737–770.

Skeem, J.L., Edens, J.F., Camp, J., & Colwell, L.H. (2004). Are there ethnic differences in levels of psychopathy? A meta-analysis. *Law and Human Behavior, 28*, 505, 527.

Spain, S.E., Douglas, K.S., Poythress, N.G., & Epstein, M. (2004). The relationship between psychopathic features, violence, and treatment outcome: The comparison of three youth measures of psychopathic features. *Behavioral Sciences and the Law, 22*, 85–102.

Stafford, J.E., & Cornell, D. (2003). Psychopathy scores predict adolescent inpatient aggression. *Assessment, 10*, 102–112.

Steadman, H.J., Silver, E., Monahan, J., Appelbaum, P.S., Robbins, P.C., Mulvey, E.P., et al., (2000). A classification tree approach to the development of actuarial violence risk assessment tools. *Law and Human Behavior, 24*, 83–100.

Steinberg, L. (2002). The juvenile psychopath: Fads, fictions, and facts. In *National Institute of Justice Perspectives on Crime and Justice: 2001 Lecture Series*, (Vol. 5, pp. 35–64).

Taylor, J., Loney, B.R., Bobadilla, L., Iacono, W.G., & McGue, M. (2003). Genetic and environmental influences on psychopathy trait dimensions in a community sample of male twins. *Journal of Abnormal Child Psychology, 31*, 633–645.

Tellegen, A. (in press). *Manual for the Multidimensional Personality Questionnaire.* Minneapolis: University of Minnesota Press

Tengström, A., Grann, M., Långström, N., & Kullgren, G. (2000). Psychopathy (PCL–R) as a predictor of violent recidivism among criminal offenders with schizophrenia. *Law and Human Behavior, 24,* 45–58.

Vertommen, H., Verheul, R., de Ruiter, C., & Hildebrand, M. (2002). *Hare's Psychopathie Checklist–Revised.* Lisse, The Netherlands: Swets.

Viding, E., Blair, R.J.R., Moffitt, T.E., & Plomin, R. (2005). Evidence for substantial genetic risk for psychopathy in 7-year-olds. *Journal of Child Psychology and Psychiatry, 46,* 592–597.

Vincent, G.M., Vitacco, M.J., Grisso, T., & Corrado, R.R. (2003). Subtypes of adolescent offenders: Affective traits and antisocial behavior patterns. *Behavioral Sciences and the Law, 21,* 695–712.

Vitacco, M.J., Neumann, C.S., & Jackson, R.L. (2005). Testing a four-factor model of psychopathy and its association with ethnicity, gender, intelligence, and violence. *Journal of Consulting and Clinical Psychology, 73,* 466–476.

Vitacco, M.J., Rogers, R., Neumann, C.S., Harrison, K., & Vincent, G. (2005). A comparison of factor models on the PCL–R with mentally disordered offenders: The development of a four-factor model. *Criminal Justice and Behavior, 32,* 526–545.

Vitale, J.E., & Newman, J.P. (2001). Using the Psychopathy Checklist–Revised with female samples: Reliability, validity, and implications for clinical utility. *Clinical Psychology: Science and Practice, 8,* 117–132.

Vitale, J.E., Smith, S.S., Brinkley, C.A., & Newman, J.P. (2002). The reliability and validity of the Psychopathy Checklist–Revised in a sample of female offenders. *Criminal Justice and Behavior, 29,* 202–231.

Walters, G.D. (2003). Predicting institutional adjustment and recidivism with the Psychopathy Checklist factor scores: A meta-analysis. *Law and Human Behavior, 27,* 541–558.

Warren, J.I., Burnette, M., South, S.C., Chauhan, P., Bale, R., Friend, R., et al. (2003). Psychopathy in women: Structural modeling and co-morbidity. *International Journal of Law and Psychiatry, 26,* 223–242.

Weiler, B.L., & Widom, C.S. (1996). Psychopathy and violent behaviour in abused and neglected young adults. *Criminal Behaviour and Mental Health, 6,* 253–271.

Williams, K.M., Paulhus, D.L., & Hare, R.D. (in press). Capturing the four-facet structure of psychopathy in nonforensic samples: The SRP-III. *Journal of Personality Assessment.*

Williamson, S.E., Hare, R.D., & Wong, S. (1987). Violence: Criminal psychopaths and their victims. *Canadian Journal of Behavioral Science, 19,* 454–462.

Windle, M., & Dumenci, L. (1999). The factorial structure and construct validity of the Psychopathy Checklist–Revised (PCL–R) among alcoholic inpatients. *Structural Equation Modeling, 6,* 372–393.

Wong, S., & Hare, R. D. (2005). *Guidelines for a psychopathy treatment program.* Toronto, Ontario, Canada: Multi-Health Systems.

Woodworth, M., & Porter, S. (2002). In cold blood: Characteristics of criminal homicides as a function of psychopathy. *Journal of Abnormal Psychology, 111,* 436–445.

Zinger, I., & Forth, A. (1998). Psychopathy and Canadian criminal proceedings: The potential for human rights abuses. *Canadian Journal of Criminology, 40,* 237–276.

Zuckerman, M. (2003). Are there racial and ethnic differences in psychopathic personality? A critique of Lynn's (2002) *Racial and ethnic differences in psychopathic personality. Personality and Individual Differences, 35,* 1463–1469.

7

THE RORSCHACH INKBLOT METHOD

IRVING B. WEINER

UNIVERSITY OF SOUTH FLORIDA

The Rorschach Inkblot Method (RIM) is a relatively unstructured, performance-based personality assessment instrument. When properly administered and interpreted, the RIM provides dependable information about how people attend to and perceive their surroundings, how they form concepts and ideas, how they experience and express affect, how they manage stress, and how they view themselves and other people. Rorschach findings can thereby facilitate decision making whenever conclusions and recommendations concerning people are based at least in part on these personality characteristics. The contexts in which personality-based decisions are made include differential diagnosis, treatment planning, and outcome evaluation in clinical work and criminal, personal injury, and child custody determinations in forensic settings. The present chapter elaborates these clinical and forensic applications of Rorschach assessment, preceded by an introductory review of Rorschach procedures, the development of the instrument, and research findings bearing on its psychometric properties.

RORSCHACH PROCEDURES

The Rorschach stimuli comprise 10 standard inkblots, 7 in shades of gray and black, 2 in shades of red as well as gray and black, and 3 in shades of various chromatic and achromatic colors. Respondents are shown these inkblots one at a time and asked, "What might this be?" After presenting the 10 cards in this way, examiners conduct an inquiry in which they show respondents the cards a second time and ask them to indicate for each of their percepts where in the inkblot they saw it and what made it look as it did (see Exner, 2003a, chap. 4, for additional guidelines on standardized procedures used in Rorschach administration).

The time required to conduct a Rorschach examination varies with the number of responses a person gives, the length and complexity of these responses, and the facility with which examiners manage the inquiry. A reasonable estimate based on clinical experience and a smattering of data (Ball, Archer, & Imhof, 1994) is that 40 minutes is the average time needed to take an adequate Rorschach record, with substantial variation both above and below this average.

As elaborated by Weiner (2003a, chaps. 5–7), a Rorschach examination yields three kinds of data, usually referred to as *structural, thematic*, and *behavioral*. The structural data in a Rorschach protocol consist of codes for several aspects of how respondents perceive the inkblots. These codes categorize various objective features of a response, including its location (e.g., whether it is seen in the whole blot or in some blot detail), its determinants (e.g., whether it looks as it does because of its shape or because of its color), its content (e.g., whether it is seen as a human figure or an animal), and whether it is a Popular (defined empirically as a response given by one third or more of nonpsychotic persons).

In the Rorschach Comprehensive System (CS) developed by Exner (2003a), response codes are tabulated and combined to yield over 100 summary scores and indices. These summary scores and indices are interpreted on the basis of two assumptions: first, that the manner in which people perceive the inkblots is representative of how they generally perceive objects and events in their lives, and, second, that how people perceive objects and events in their lives—that is, how they look at their world—reflects the kind of people they are, particularly with respect to their tendencies to think, feel, and act in certain ways.

Rorschach thematic data consist of the imagery with which most respondents embellish their reports of what the inkblots might be. Whereas the structural data derive from a perceptual process attuned to the stimulus properties of the inkblots (form, color, and shading), the thematic data emerge from an associative process in which characteristics not intrinsic to the blot stimuli are nevertheless attributed to them. For example, human figures may be seen as moving even though the blots are in fact static, and they may be described as being happy or sad even though the blots contain no objective indications to this effect. The interpretation of such attributions is based on the assumption that because they are not based directly on what is in the blots, they must come from inside the person. Thematic imagery produced by associations to the blot stimuli is consequently likely to provide clues to a respondent's underlying needs, attitudes, conflicts, and concerns.

Behavioral data in Rorschach examinations consist of the manner in which respondents deal with the test situation, handle the test materials, relate to the examiner, and use language in expressing themselves. Interpretation of these behavioral data is based on the expectation that the way in which respondents approach the Rorschach task and structure their relationship with the examiner constitutes a representative sample of their problem-solving and interpersonal style. As a relatively unstructured verbal interaction between the two parties, the Rorschach situation creates ample opportunity for such characteristic styles to become apparent.

Integrated interpretation of the structural, thematic, and behavioral data generated by a Rorschach examination leads to detailed descriptions of respondents' assets and limitations with respect to how they make decisions, solve problems, cope with the demands in their lives, and prefer to conduct themselves. These Rorschach-based descriptions of adaptive capacities, enriched by thematic clues to a respondent's underlying concerns, facilitate numerous applications of the instrument. As elaborated in the course of this chapter, these applications include clinical decision-making, particularly with regard to differential diagnosis and treatment planning, and forensic determinations related to psycholegal issues in criminal, personal injury, and child custody cases.

DEVELOPMENT OF THE RORSCHACH INKBLOT METHOD

The Rorschach Inkblot Method was created over 85 years ago by Hermann Rorschach, a Swiss psychiatrist. In his youth, Rorschach had been adept at a popular parlor game of his day in which players competed to see who could generate the most interesting descriptions of inkblots made by dropping some ink in the middle of a piece of paper and folding it in half. Working in a large mental hospital after completion of his medical studies and psychiatric training, Rorschach became intrigued with the possibility that patients with different types of mental disorder might perceive inkblots differently from each other and from normally functioning people. He pursued this notion by developing a standard set of inkblots and showing them to a sample of 288 patients and 117 nonpatient volunteers, asking the simple question, "What might this be?"

Rorschach formulated some basic codes for the previously mentioned location, determinant, and content features of the inkblot responses he obtained, and then he compared his subgroups with respect to their percentage frequencies for these codes (e.g., the proportion of responses given to the entire blot as opposed to blot details). From his findings he inferred numerous relationships between certain code frequencies and percentages, on the one hand, and particular mental disorders and personality characteristics, on the other hand. Despite Rorschach's creativity in conceiving the notion of using inkblot percepts to identify personality characteristics, however, he was basically an empiricist rather than a theorist. His methods of coding and interpretation were guided by the data he collected and not by any particular conceptual framework. In his final paper, which became available after his death, he noted, "There has, however, been little progress in the development of the theory of the experiment" (Rorschach, 1921/1942, p. 186).

Rorschach published the findings from his research in *Psychodiagnostics*, the 1921 monograph just cited. The materials and methods he described in this monograph have remained basic to commonly practiced Rorschach procedures since that time. The 10 inkblots published with the original monograph are the standard Rorschach plates in use today, and Rorschach's delineation of test-inferred personality characteristics is a sophisticated treatise that can still be read with pleasure and profit. The 1921 monograph was only a preliminary work, however, and Rorschach died just 1 year after it was published, at the age of 37, leaving development of the instrument largely unfinished.

Over the 50 years following Rorschach's death, many different systems of administering, coding, and interpreting the RIM devolved from his monograph. Some of these systems, best exemplified in the United States by the work of Samuel Beck (Beck, Beck, Levitt, & Molish, 1961), continued, as Rorschach had done, to emphasize a structural approach to the method and an empirical basis for proposing coding refinements and interpretive strategies. Other systems, exemplified by the contributions of Bruno Klopfer (Klopfer, Ainsworth, Klopfer, & Holt, 1954) and Roy Schafer (1954), advocated embellishing Rorschach's approach with expanded attention to thematic imagery and recourse to theoretical formulations, primarily psychoanalytic in nature, for guidance in developing new coding and interpretive guidelines. Rorschach's life and the early development of the RIM are described in further detail by Ellenberger (1954), Exner (2003a, chap. 1), Schwarz (1996), Weiner (2003a, chap. 1), and Wolf (2000).

By the 1970s there were five major Rorschach systems being used in the United States, and several other systems enjoyed popularity abroad. In addition, most Rorschach clinicians were employing some individually preferred blend of these systems (e.g., a Beck coding for locations and a Klopfer coding for determinants). Although personalized embellishments of Rorschach procedures were serving clinical purposes in the individual case, this diversity of method made it difficult for Rorschach scholars to communicate effectively with each other and cumulate systematic data concerning the psychometric properties of the instrument. Exner addressed this problem by combining the clearest and most dependable aspects of the five U.S. systems into a standardized set of procedures for administration and coding that became the previously mentioned Comprehensive System (CS). First published in 1974, the CS has subsequently been modified over the years to take account of both new empirical data and contemporary conceptual formulations (see Exner, 1974, 2003a).

Although focused primarily on the structural features of Rorschach responses, the CS approach includes interpretive strategies that call attention to thematic and behavioral data as well. Psychoanalytic perspectives on the interpretation of Rorschach imagery and behavior have also continued to flourish over the years, as illustrated by the work of Lerner (1991, 1998). Rorschach scholars and practitioners generally concur that the RIM realizes its full potential as a personality assessment instrument only when the interpretive process is guided by a judicious blend of structural and psychodynamic perspectives (Smith, 1994; Weiner, 2003a).

The CS procedures for administering and coding the RIM have become by far the most frequently used approach to Rorschach assessment in the United States and the preferred approach in many other countries as well. Widespread adoption of these standardized procedures has fostered substantial advances in knowledge about the RIM, including collection of large normative reference samples and systematic investigation of the psychometric properties of the instrument.

PSYCHOMETRIC PROPERTIES

The psychometric adequacy of Rorschach assessment has been a topic of debate throughout most of the instrument's history. The advent of Exner's Comprehensive System led to a lull in this storm during the 1980s, mainly by putting to rest concerns that the instrument lacked standardized procedures for administration and coding. Beginning in the mid-1990s, however, a new wave of psychometric challenges directed specifically at the CS has washed over Rorschach assessment. In a series of influential articles, a group of critics has contended that (a) the CS normative data are outdated, overpathologizing (i.e., likely to identify psychological disturbance where none is present), and insufficient to warrant using the RIM with culturally diverse populations; (b) adequate intercoder and retest reliability has not yet been broadly established for CS variables; and (c) for a broad range of purposes, Rorschach assessment lacks criterion and incremental validity (see Garb, Wood, Nezworski, Grove, & Stejskal, 2001; Hunsley & Bailey, 1999; Lilienfeld, Wood, & Garb, 2000; Wood & Lilienfeld, 1999; Wood, Nezworski, Garb, & Lilienfeld, 2001; Wood, Nezworski, & Stejskal, 1996).

Some of these contemporary criticisms of Rorschach assessment have gone beyond scientific discourse and taken a regrettably adversarial stance; examples include a call for a moratorium on use of the RIM (Garb, 1999), reference to Rorschach assessment as an example of "junk science" or "pseudoscience" (Lohr, Fowler, & Lilienfeld, 2002), and the assertion that Rorschach testimony is not sufficiently "relevant and reliable" to be admitted into evidence in the courtroom (Grove & Barden, 1999). Nevertheless, many of the technical points raised in contemporary criticisms of the RIM were well taken and have had the salutary effect of stimulating expanded lines of research, including the collection of a new CS normative sample, and eliciting numerous reanalyses and fresh conceptualizations of the available data.

Abundant research findings now document that, contrary to the technical concerns and extreme negative views expressed by some critics, Rorschach assessment with the CS is a psychometrically sound procedure with a broad and useful normative reference base, good to excellent intercoder agreement, substantial retest reliability, adequate validity when used properly for its intended purposes, and sufficient respectability to provide an acceptable basis for courtroom testimony. The following discussion reviews the key data supporting these assertions.

Normative Reference Base

The development of the Rorschach CS included the compilation of descriptive statistics for each of its codes and summary scores for a sample of 600 nonpatient adults aged 19 to 69 ($M = 31.7$). As described by Exner (2003a, chap. 12), this sample was randomly selected from a larger group of volunteer participants who were informed of the importance of what they were doing—namely, helping to standardize a widely used personality test—and who were examined by well-trained professional psychologists and research technicians. The sample was stratified to include an equal number of males and females and 120 persons from each of five geographic areas that make up the continental United States (Northeast, South, Midwest, Southwest, and West). This nonpatient sample was also generally representative of the patterns of marital status, socioeconomic status, and urban-suburban-rural residence in the United States, and 18% of the respondents were African American, Hispanic, or Asian American.

Two thirds of the 600 persons in the CS nonpatient reference sample were recruited through their place of employment and were given time off from work to participate in the data collection. Another one fourth were recruited through social or interest organizations (e.g., PTA groups, bowling leagues), and the remaining 8% through social service agencies. These 600 persons averaged 13.4 years of education, with 68% having attended college, and none of them had any significant history of mental health problems. Consequently, this nonpatient sample is representative of people who are relatively well educated and appear to be functioning reasonably well socially and vocationally. Reference data were also obtained from 1,390 nonpatient young people aged 5 to 16 and from three groups of adult psychiatric patients: 328 first admission inpatients with schizophrenia, 279 patients hospitalized for depression, and 535 outpatients presenting a diversity of symptoms (Exner, 2001, chap. 11). Taken together, then, the CS reference data identify the frequency with which each of the Rorschach structural variables is likely to occur in nonpatient adults and young people and in persons with various kinds of psychological disorder.

Because these CS reference data were collected mainly from 1973 to 1986, it is reasonable to question whether they remain applicable a generation later. To answer this question, Exner, as previously mentioned, has undertaken a new normative data collection project to update the nonpatient reference information. As in the earlier work, respondents are being solicited to provide a demographically representative U.S. sample, and they are being tested by experienced professional examiners operating with a uniform and carefully formulated set of instructions. Exner (2002, 2003b) published the findings for the first 175 persons tested in this project, and he reported updated results when this new normative sample grew to 350 respondents. With only minor exceptions, the new reference data closely resemble the older data and do not appear to call for any major alterations in interpretive criteria.

As for whether Rorschach assessment is likely to overpathologize, the old ($N = 600$) and new ($N = 350$) nonpatient reference groups showed the following frequencies of elevations on the central CS indices of psychopathology: for the Perceptual Thinking Index (*PTI*), 0% and 0.2%, respectively; for the Depression Index (*DEPI*), 5% and 11%; for the Coping Deficit Index (*CDI*), 4% and 7%; and for the Hypervigilance Index (*HVI*), 3% in both groups. Such infrequent elevations on the Rorschach psychopathology scales in these large, representative, and carefully evaluated samples of nonpatients indicate a very low probability that the RIM will suggest psychological disorder when none is present.

With respect to issues of cross-cultural diversity, moreover, recent studies with U.S. minority groups have found no substantial CS differences among them that would contraindicate cross-ethnic use of the RIM or require modifications in normative expectations. Presley, Smith, Hilsenroth, and Exner (2001) found a clinically significant difference on only 1 of 23 core Rorschach variables between 44 African Americans and 44 demographically matched European Americans in the CS nonpatient reference sample. In a multicultural patient sample of 432 consecutive persons evaluated in a hospital-based psychological testing program, Meyer (2002) found no association between ethnicity and 188 Rorschach summary scores among demographically matched European-American, African-American, Hispanic-American, Asian-American, and Native-American respondents. Meyer concluded from his findings that "the available data clearly support the cross-ethnic use of the Comprehensive System" (p. 127).

Intercoder Agreement

Intercoder agreement for CS Rorschach variables, whether measured by percentage of agreement or by kappa and intraclass correlation coefficients (ICCs) that take account of chance agreement, has proved good to excellent in numerous studies. In one recent instance of such findings, Meyer and colleagues (2002) examined four different samples and 219 protocols containing 4,761 responses and found a median ICC of .93 for intercoder agreement across 138 regularly occurring Rorschach variables, with 134 of these variables falling in the excellent range for chance-corrected agreement. In a similar study, Viglione and Taylor (2003) examined coder concurrence for 84 protocols with 1,732 responses and found a median ICC of .92 for 68 variables considered to be of central interpretive significance in the CS. Earlier meta-analytic reviews and studies with patient and nonpatient samples identified mean kappa coefficients ranging from .79 to .88 across various CS coding categories, which for kappa coefficients is generally regarded as being in the good to excellent range (Acklin, McDowell, Verschell, & Chan, 2000; Meyer, 1997a, 1997b; Viglione & Taylor, 2003).

Research findings have also indicated that Rorschach practitioners in the field can achieve reasonably good agreement in their coding. In one of the samples in the Meyer et al. (2002) study and in a study reported by McGrath et al. (2005), patient protocols that had initially been coded in clinical practice, without any anticipation of their being used in a research project, were later coded independently for research purposes. In both cases, the obtained correlation coefficients for intercoder agreement were more than adequate to demonstrate the potential field reliability of Rorschach coding. Research by McGrath (2003) has indicated further that practicing clinicians can readily reduce their coding errors by attending to the coding criteria and guidelines provided in textbooks and workbooks (e.g., Exner, 2001, 2003a; Viglione, 2002).

Retest Reliability

Retest studies with both children and adults over intervals ranging from 7 days to 3 years have demonstrated substantial reliability for Rorschach summary scores and indices that are conceptualized as relating to trait characteristics, which include almost all of the CS variables (see Exner, 2003a, chap. 11; Gronnerod, 2003; Viglione & Hilsenroth, 2001). In adults, the short- and long-term stability of most CS variables exceed .75, and 19 core variables with major interpretive significance have shown 1-year or 3-year retest correlations of .85 or higher. The only Rorschach summary scores that show low retest correlations, even over brief intervals, are a few variables and combinations of these variables that are conceptualized as measuring situationally influenced state characteristics.

Children show stability coefficients similar to those of adults when retested over brief intervals. When retested over 2-year intervals between the ages of 8 and 16, young people fluctuate considerably in their Rorschach scores early on but then show steadily increasing long-term consistency as they grow older (Exner, Thomas, & Mason, 1985). The increasing long-term stability of Rorschach variables from age 8 to age 16 is consistent with the expected gradual consolidation of personality characteristics that occurs during the developmental years.

Validity

In a carefully designed large-scale examination of Rorschach validity, Hiller, Rosenthal, Bornstein, Berry, and Brunell-Neuleib (1999) conducted a meta-analysis of a random sample of Rorschach and MMPI (Minnesota Multiphasic Personality Inventory) research studies published from 1977 to 1997 in which there was at least one external (nontest) variable and in which some reasonable basis had been posited for expecting associations between variables. In their analysis of these studies, which included 2,276 RIM and 5,007 MMPI protocols, they found the validity of the two measures, as indicated by their average effect sizes, to be virtually identical. The unweighted mean validity coefficients were .29 for RIM variables and .30 for MMPI variables, and there is no significant difference between these two validity estimates. Hiller et al. concluded that these obtained effect sizes are sufficiently large to warrant confidence in using both the RIM and the MMPI for their intended purposes and furthermore that the validity of both instruments "is about as good as can be expected for personality tests" (p. 291).

Hiller et al. also found some noteworthy differences between RIM and MMPI variables in the strength of their relationship with different types of dependent variables. On the average, Rorschach variables proved somewhat superior (mean validity coefficient = .37) to MMPI variables (mean validity coefficient = .20) in predicting behavioral outcomes, such as whether patients remain in or drop out of therapy. MMPI variables, on the other hand, showed higher effect sizes than Rorschach variables in correlating with psychiatric diagnosis and self-reports (.37 vs. .18). These differences probably reflect the particular sensitivity of the RIM to persistent behavioral dispositions, consistent with the primarily trait implications of most of its variables, and the self-report nature of the MMPI, which resembles both the methodology of other self-report measures and the typical method of gaining information on which to base psychiatric diagnoses (i.e., simply to ask patients about their symptoms).

Extending well beyond the boundaries of this meta-analysis, an extensive research base has documented the validity of Rorschach assessment when the instrument is used for its intended purposes. As described in reviews by Hilsenroth and Stricker (2004), Mattlar (2004), Meyer (2004), Stricker and Gold (1999), Viglione (1999), Viglione and Hilsenroth (2001), and Weiner (2001, 2004a), this validating research has additionally demonstrated the incremental validity of Rorschach findings in contributing diagnostic and predictive information above and beyond what can be learned from other sources of information, including self-report inventories and clinical interviews (see Blais, Hilsenroth, Castlebury,

Fowler, & Baity, 2001; Janson & Stattin, 2003; Meyer & Handler, 2000; W. Perry, 2001). By establishing the utility and scientific respectability of Rorschach assessment, these validating data also refute contentions that Rorschach-based testimony is unlikely to be admitted in the courtroom. To the contrary, detailed refutation of such contentions by Hilsenroth and Stricker (2004), McCann (1998), and Ritzler, Erard, and Pettigrew (2002) include survey data indicating that the reliability and relevance of Rorschach findings are in fact seldom challenged in the courtroom and hardly ever challenged successfully.

Finally with respect to the current status of Rorschach controversy, there is good reason to believe that the RIM has been subjected to harsher criticism than it deserves and to more criticism than other assessment instruments with similar psychometric profiles. According to the most recent edition of the *Mental Measurements Yearbook*, "The Rorschach, employed with the Comprehensive System, is a better personality test than its opponents are willing to acknowledge" (A.K. Hess, Zachar, & Kramer, 2001, p. 1037). In a similar vein, Meyer and Archer (2001) drew the following conclusion after examining the available data concerning the comparative validity of the RIM, the MMPI, and the Wechsler Adult Intelligence Scale (WAIS): "There is no reason for the Rorschach to be singled out for particular criticism or specific praise. It produces reasonable validity, roughly on par with other commonly used tests" (pp. 491–492).

Nevertheless, and without discounting the adequately demonstrated validity of Rorschach assessment in general, considerable work remains to be done in this area. Individual Rorschach variables vary widely in the known certainty of their correlates. In the case of the implications of a high $X\text{-}\%$ for impaired reality testing and of an elevated *WSum6* for thought disorder, for example, and the consequent utility of the Perceptual Thinking Index (*PTI*) in identifying schizophrenia spectrum disorders, a substantial array of confirmatory empirical findings buttress these applications (see Hilsenroth & Stricker, 2004; Viglione & Hilsenroth, 2001). On the other hand, many commonly assumed associations between specific Rorschach variables and certain personality characteristics are based on reasonable conceptual formulations but have yet to be examined in appropriately designed research studies. Research to close current gaps in knowledge concerning the empirical correlates of these Rorschach variables is an important agenda item for the future.

CLINICAL USES AND LIMITATIONS

Rorschach assessment contributes to clinical practice by helping to identify the presence and nature of psychological disorder and by elucidating a troubled person's need for, amenability to, and extent of progress in treatments of various kinds. With respect to differential diagnosis, many of the personality characteristics identified by Rorschach variables are associated with particular patterns of psychopathology. For example, schizophrenia is usually defined to involve disordered thinking and poor reality testing, which means that the previously mentioned Rorschach indicators of these cognitive impairments (i.e., elevated *WSum6* and high $X\text{-}\%$) increase the likelihood of a schizophrenia spectrum disorder. Depressive disorder is suggested by Rorschach indices of dysphoria (elevated C', Color-Shading Blends [*Col-Shd Blds*] > 0) and negative self-attitudes (numerous Morbid [*MOR*] responses, $V > 0$, low Egocentricity Ratio [$3r + 2/R$]); obsessive-compulsive personality disorder is suggested by indices of pedantry and perfectionism (positive Obsessive Index [*OBS*]); and so on (see Weiner, 2003a).

One limitation of the RIM in identifying maladaptive personality characteristics, however, is that Rorschach variables differ with respect to whether their interpretive significance is *bidirectional* or *unidirectional*. Bidirectional variables are interpretable when their values fall substantially above or substantially below normative expectation. Unidirectional variables are noteworthy only when they are either unusually high or unusually low but not both. Form level qualifies as a bidirectional variable, in that a low X-% typically indicates good reality testing, in contrast to the impaired reality testing identified by a high X-%. The *OBS*, by contrast, functions as a unidirectional variable, in that it usually identifies obsessive-compulsive characteristics when it is positive, but when negative says nothing at all about whether a respondent has such characteristics.

A unidirectional variable with particularly important implications in clinical decision-making is the Suicide Constellation (*S-Con*). An *S-Con* elevation indicates risk for suicidal behavior (see Fowler, Piers, Hilsenroth, Holdwick, & Padawer, 2001), but a low *S-Con* does not contraindicate suicidal potential and should never be interpreted as doing so. The Depression Index (*DEPI*) is similarly unidirectional for the most part, capturing probable features of mood disorder when it is high but not negating the possibility of mood disturbance when it is low. Whether in identifying adjustment difficulties or personality strengths, then, bidirectional variables provide information both by their presence and by their absence. Unidirectional variables, on the other hand, help mainly to indicate when conditions and characteristics are present but provide little basis for inferring the absence of these conditions and characteristics. Proper application of Rorschach variables in research and practice requires taking adequate account of whether their interpretive significance is bidirectional or unidirectional, in the expectation that unilateral variables may frequently yield false negative findings (see Weiner, 2000).

Moreover, as an instrument more attuned to personality traits than personality states, the RIM is of limited use in identifying the particular symptoms a disturbed person may be having. A respondent with Rorschach indications of an obsessive-compulsive personality style may be a compulsive handwasher, an obsessive prognosticator, or neither; a person with Rorschach indices of dysphoric mood may be having crying spells, disturbed sleep, weight loss, or some other manifestations of depression; someone with Rorschach signs of subjectively felt distress could be experiencing a phobic reaction, a generalized anxiety disorder, a posttraumatic stress disorder, or none of these conditions. The particular symptoms of psychological disorder that are in evidence—which is a central consideration in arriving at a *DSM* diagnosis—are better determined by observing people's behavior and asking about them directly about their symptoms than by attempting to infer their symptoms from their Rorschach responses.

Similarly with respect to determining whether respondents have conducted themselves in certain ways (e.g., abused alcohol or drugs) or had certain life experiences (e.g., been sexually abused), Rorschach data rarely provide powerful indications one way or the other. The RIM can generate dependable postdictions only when there is a substantial known correlation between specific personality characteristics and the likelihood of certain behaviors or experiences having occurred (see Weiner, 2003b). The predictive validity of Rorschach findings likewise depends on how strongly personality factors influence the occurrence of whatever future actions or events are being predicted. As an instance in this latter regard, personality characteristics are known to influence whether and how people usually respond to various kinds of treatment, and Rorschach findings are accordingly pertinent to many of the decisions that therapists make during an intervention process.

For example, the degree of disturbance or coping incapacity reflected in Rorschach responses can assist in determining whether a troubled person requires inpatient care or is functioning sufficiently well to be treated as an outpatient. The personality style and severity of distress or disorganization revealed by the RIM can help to indicate whether a patient's treatment needs will be served best by a supportive approach oriented to relieving distress, a cognitive-behavioral approach designed to modify symptoms or solve problems, or an exploratory approach intended to enhance self-understanding. Whatever treatment approach is implemented, moreover, the maladaptive personality traits and the underlying concerns identified by Rorschach data can help therapists determine, in consultation with their patients, what the goals of the treatment should be and with what priority these treatment targets should be addressed (see Weiner, 2004b).

Predictive utility in treatment planning also derives from the fact that certain personality characteristics measured by Rorschach variables are typically associated with being able to participate in and benefit from psychotherapy. These personality characteristics include being open to experience (*Lambda* not elevated), cognitively flexible (balanced active:passive ratio [$a : p$]), emotionally responsive (adequate *WSumC* and Affective Ratio [*Afr*]), interpersonally receptive ($T > 0$, ample human content [*SumH*]), and personally introspective ($FD > 0$), each of which facilitates engagement and progress in psychological treatment. By contrast, having an avoidant or guarded approach to experience, being set in one's ways, having difficulty recognizing and expressing one's feelings, being interpersonally aversive or withdrawn, and lacking psychological mindedness are often obstacles to progress in psychotherapy (see Beutler, Harwood, & Holaway, 2002; Clarkin & Levy, 2004).

In a research project relevant to the utility of the RIM in guiding therapist activity once treatment is underway, Blatt and Ford (1994) used Rorschach variables to assist in categorizing patients as having problems primarily with forming satisfying interpersonal relationships (*anaclitic* problems) or primarily with maintaining their own sense of identity, autonomy, and self-worth (*introjective* problems). In the course of their psychotherapy, the anaclitic patients studied by Blatt and Ford were more responsive than the introjective patients to their therapist's focusing on relational aspects of the treatment. The introjective patients, by contrast, were more influenced than the anaclitic patients by their therapist's interpretive activity.

By helping to identify treatment goals and targets, Rorschach assessment can also play a role in monitoring treatment progress and evaluating treatment outcome. Suppose that an RIM is administered prior to beginning therapy and that certain treatment targets are identified in Rorschach terms, such as reducing subjectively felt distress, as in changing $D < 0$ to $D = 0$; increasing receptivity to emotional arousal, as in bringing up a low *Afr*; or promoting more careful problem solving, as in elevating a $Zd < -3.0$ to a $Zd \geq -3.0$. Subsequent retesting can then provide quantitative indications of how much progress has been made toward achieving these goals and how much work remains to be done on them. Rorschach evidence concerning the extent to which the goals of the treatment have been achieved can also guide therapists in deciding if and when termination is indicated. At the point of termination or in a follow-up evaluation later on, comparison of Rorschach findings with findings obtained in a pretreatment evaluation can serve usefully as an objective measure of the effects of the treatment.

Studies by Weiner and Exner (1991) and Exner and Andronikof-Sanglade (1992) demonstrated the utility of Rorschach assessment in evaluating treatment progress and outcome. In these studies, patients in long-term, short-term, and brief psychotherapy were examined at several points before, during, and after their treatment. The results of both studies showed significant positive changes over the course of therapy in numerous Rorschach variables considered to have implications for a person's level of adjustment. Of further significance, the amount of improvement in these patients was directly related to the length of their treatment, which corresponds to evidence from psychotherapy research that longer therapies are likely to produce more change than briefer therapies (Lambert & Ogles, 2004). Accordingly, these Rorschach studies attest both the effectiveness of psychotherapy in promoting positive personality change and the validity of the RIM in measuring such change.

Recent studies that demonstrate the utility of Rorschach variables in predicting treatment outcome and monitoring treatment change are reported by Fowler et al. (2004) and Stokes et al. (2003). Also of note is a meta-analysis by Gronnerod (2004) of 38 samples in which repeat Rorschach testing was used to monitor change during psychological treatment. Gronnerod found substantial effect sizes for numerous Rorschach variables as indicators of change, and in parallel with the earlier studies, the degree of change in his samples was positively associated with the length and intensity of the treatment received.

FORENSIC USES AND LIMITATIONS

Like clinical applications, forensic uses of the RIM derive from the relevance of personality characteristics to making various kinds of decisions. In clinical work, personality-based decisions concern differential diagnosis and treatment planning and outcome evaluation, as just discussed. In forensic work, personality characteristics are often relevant to resolving issues that arise in criminal, personal injury, and child custody cases (see Craig, 2005). Rorschach assessors can assist the court in addressing these psycholegal issues by attending to Rorschach variables that measure personality characteristics pertinent to them. In so doing, forensic consultants can benefit from special advantages, including the applicability of Rorschach findings across diverse populations, the resistance of the RIM to impression management, and the objectivity of a structural emphasis in formulating Rorschach interpretations.

Criminal Cases

Psychologists consulting in criminal cases are most commonly asked to assess whether defendants are competent to proceed to trial and, if so, whether they should be held responsible for the alleged offense. Being competent to proceed is defined in legal terms as having a factual and rational understanding of the criminal acts with which one is charged and being able to participate effectively in one's defense. These basic elements of competence consist more specifically of defendants' appreciating of the possible penalties as well as the charges they are facing, comprehending the nature of the adversarial process and the roles of the key people in it, being able to disclose pertinent facts in their case to their attorney, and being capable of conducting themselves appropriately in the courtroom and testifying relevantly in their own behalf (see Roesch, Zapf, Golding, & Skeem, 1999; Stafford, 2003).

With respect to personality characteristics, these components of competence depend heavily on whether defendants can think logically and coherently and perceive people and events realistically. If they lack these capabilities, disordered thinking and impaired reality testing, together with the poor judgment and peculiar behavior they typically engender, may compromise their legal competence. Hence the previously mentioned Rorschach indices of disordered thinking and impaired reality testing (elevated *WSum6* and high *X-%*) warrant some expectation that a defendant will have difficulty demonstrating competency to proceed.

As an indirect measure of personality characteristics, however, the RIM is limited in how much it can reveal about what a respondent actually knows or can do. Consequently,

Rorschach findings of cognitive slippage do not preclude a person's being legally competent. Whether defendants have an adequate grasp of courtroom procedures, for example, is better determined by asking them directly about courtroom procedures than by looking at their X-% or $WSum6$. When defendants cannot give an adequate account of the adversarial process, on the other hand, or fall short in other ways of being able to demonstrate legal competence, Rorschach evidence of disordered thinking or poor reality testing can help examiners inform the court of likely sources of the incompetence. Additionally, for defendants who are adjudicated incompetent and mandated for competency restoration, Rorschach findings can assist in identifying critical treatment targets for the training program. A high X-%, for example, can indicate the importance of improved reality testing in bringing an incompetent defendant into competence.

Criminal responsibility in forensic cases hinges on whether defendants were legally sane when they committed the alleged offense. Insanity at the time of an offense is customarily defined by the presence of either a *cognitive* or a *volitional* incapacity. Cognitive incapacity in this context consists of being unable to recognize the criminality of one's illegal actions or to appreciate the wrongfulness of this conduct (i.e., telling right from wrong). Volitional incapacity consists being unable at the time of the offense to alter or refrain from the alleged criminal conduct (i.e., insufficient self-control). Jurisdictions vary with respect to whether insanity is defined solely by cognitive incapacity or can also be established by volitional incapacity (see Golding, Skeem, Roesch, & Zapf, 1999; Goldstein, Morse, & Shapiro, 2003).

The previously mentioned Rorschach indices of disordered thinking and poor reality testing serve to translate the cognitive prong of legal insanity into the language of personality functioning. As for the volitional prong, susceptibility to losing self-control is suggested by Rorschach indications of acute or chronic stress overload ($D < 0$, $AdjD < 0$), which are commonly associated with limited frustration tolerance, intemperate outbursts of affect, and episodes of impulsive behavior. However, because legal sanity is defined by a person's state of mind at the time of an alleged offense and not at the time of a later examination, Rorschach evidence of either cognitive or volitional incapacity cannot by itself sustain an insanity defense. The critical evidence in determining criminal responsibility comes from defendants' recollections of their mental state preceding, during, and following an alleged offense and from observers' reports of how defendants were behaving at that time. Should evidence from these sources suggest cognitive or volitional incapacity at the time of an offense, then Rorschach indications of incapacity, together with mental health records showing a history of psychological disorder, provide supplementary information that strengthens an insanity plea and clarifies the origins of the disturbed behavior.

In identifying these functioning incapacities, examiners must take into account how the relevant Rorschach scores interact with other structural data. None of the variables in a Structural Summary can be interpreted accurately without attention to other variables that may enhance or attenuate its interpretive significance. In the case of perceptual accuracy, for example, the implications of a high X-% for impaired reality testing vary with the levels of XA%, WDA%, Xu%, and Populars (P) in a record and also with any repetitive association of $FQ-$ responses with particular content categories or embellishments.

Likewise with regard to the implications of an elevated $WSum6$ for disordered thinking; adequate Rorschach assessment of severity of thought disorder calls for considerations that go beyond the magnitude of this particular score. These considerations include the distribution of critical special scores among mild (DV, INC) and serious (DR, FAB, $CONTAM$) indicators of cognitive slippage, the frequency of bizarre (Level 2) as opposed to relatively unremarkable (Level 1) special scores, and the percentage of total R containing a critical special score. As for the D and $AdjD$ scores in a record, their interpretive significance for self-control is a complex function of the R and *Lambda* in the record, the levels of the EA and es, and the extent to which the EB is balanced. Attention to these and other interactive influences, as elaborated in the texts by Exner (2003a, chap. 18) and Weiner (2003a, chap. 5), is essential to adequate interpretation of Rorschach data.

Despite the limitation of the RIM with respect to postdicting mental state at the time of an alleged offense—which is a limitation shared with other personality assessment instruments—test indices of chronicity and stability can sometimes guide estimation of previous functioning capacity from presently obtained data. Evidence of chronicity and stability tend to increase the likelihood that an effectively functioning person has been well adjusted in the past and, correspondingly, that a psychologically disturbed person has probably had previous episodes of disorder. The key Rorschach finding in this regard is $D \geq 0$, which in an unguarded record is usually associated with consistency over time (even when the consistency involves being emotionally unstable), with little sense of needing to change or become a different kind of person, and with ego-syntonic as opposed to ego-alien symptom formation.

The chronicity and stability associated with $D \geq 0$ still does not warrant inferring legal insanity at the time of an offense from presently obtained test findings. On the other hand, should a defendant who appears to be functioning fairly well when examined be claiming temporary insanity at the earlier time of an alleged offense, Rorschach findings may lend themselves to a diathesis-stress perspective on this possibility. Specifically, the less stressful a defendant's circumstances appear to have been at the time of an alleged offense and the more stable and effective the person's coping resources as presently reflected in the test data, the less susceptible this person would have been at the previous time to a psychological breakdown, with loss of cognitive or volitional capacities.

Personal Injury Cases

Personality assessment becomes relevant in personal injury cases when plaintiffs complain of having become emotionally distressed or incapacitated as a consequence of irresponsible behavior by some person or entity (see Greenberg, 2003; Greenberg & Brodsky, 2001). The types of emotional distress or incapacitation most frequently alleged in such circumstances involve posttraumatic stress disorder and other anxiety reactions, affective and cognitive features of depressive disorder, and psychotic breakdowns involving loss of touch with reality and inability to meet the demands of everyday living. Each of these conditions is likely to be reflected in patterns of Rorschach responses that help to identify their presence and severity.

Persons with an anxiety or stress disorder are likely to produce either a *flooded* Rorschach protocol, which is distinguished by pervasive indications of anxiety, or a *constricted* Rorschach protocol, which is notable for guardedness and evasion. When produced by persons who have experienced potentially traumatic events, flooded protocols are usually associated with manifestations of stress disorder in hyperarousal and reexperiencing phenomena. With respect to hyperarousal, the utility of the D scores in assessing whether people are experiencing more demands than they can manage without becoming unduly upset by them—and are thereby experiencing a stress overload—has already been noted. In more specific terms, a combination of $D < -1$ with $AdjD \geq 0$ is likely to indicate a substantial acute or situational stress overload, and $D < -1$ combined with $AdjD < -1$ usually identifies a substantial and persistent stress overload.

Susceptibility to reexperiencing distressing events is suggested on the Rorschach by a high frequency of $FM + m$ responses, which generally serves as an index of intrusive ideation. Troubling preoccupations, particularly about incurring bodily harm, are also likely to be revealed by the Trauma Content Index (TCI; Armstrong, 1991, 2002). The TCI consists of the number of Aggression, Anatomy, Blood, Morbid, and Sex contents in a record divided by R, and $TCI \geq .30$ is commonly associated with having had a traumatic experience (see Kamphuis, Kugeares, & Finn, 2000).

A constricted Rorschach protocol given by persons who are suspected of having been traumatized suggests a stress disorder characterized by defensive avoidance. Instead of becoming excitable, easily upset, and troubled by flashbacks, nightmares, and other types of reexperiencing, traumatized persons who are defensively avoidant do whatever they can to escape from thoughts, feelings, and situations that might precipitate or exacerbate an episode of distress. In the process of this escape, stress avoidant people typically become withdrawn and emotionally numb. The constricted Rorschach protocols that such persons consequently produce usually bear such hallmarks of guardedness as low R, high $Lambda$, low $WSumC$, low Affective Ratio (Afr), and bland or vague content. Research concerning these Rorschach correlates of anxiety and stress disorder is reviewed by Armstrong and Kaser-Boyd (2004), Holaday (2000), Luxenberg and Levin (2004), Sloan, Arsenault, and Hilsenroth (2002), and Sloan, Arsenault, Hilsenroth, Handler, and Harvill (1996).

Neither flooded nor constricted Rorschach protocols are specific to anxiety and stress disorder, however, nor do they provide conclusive evidence of the presence of such a disorder. Given historical and other clinical or test data suggesting an anxiety or stress disorder, they merely increase the likelihood of its presence. Moreover, as in the case of evaluating sanity, the results of a present personal injury examination are useful only when they are interpreted in the context of past events. Personal injury cases require examiners to determine whether a plaintiff's current distress or disability constitutes a decline in functioning capacity from some previously higher level of functioning prior to the defendant's alleged breech of duty or whether instead the distress or disability predated it.

Two other considerations limit the application of these and other Rorschach data in evaluating possible traumatic stress in the individual case. First, like the S-CON and $DEPI$ mentioned earlier, Rorschach stress indices seldom yield false positives but may produce numerous false negatives. Hence, fearfulness, avoidance, and hyperarousal can be inferred with some confidence when the Rorschach index levels discussed in the preceding paragraphs occur, but the absence of these levels does not rule out the possibility of such phenomena. Of particular note in this regard, the type of defensive avoidance that leads to constriction in persons with stress disorder tends to constrain the emergence of the kinds of test responses that identify fearfulness and hyperarousal. Hence, defensive avoidance is likely to result in a bland and guarded Rorschach protocol that reveals little if any distress, despite indications from other sources that the respondent has in fact developed a traumatic stress reaction.

Second, like flooded and constricted records in general, neither fearfulness, constriction, hyperarousal, nor any of the Rorschach index levels associated with them is specific to the experience of traumatic stress. Fearfulness is common among phobic and obsessive worriers, for example, constriction among depressed individuals, and hyperarousal among people with a variety of anxiety disorders, to name just a few alternative explanations for a respondent's showing Rorschach patterns that are sometimes associated with stress disorder.

It is because most Rorschach variables neither rule out nor are specific to any one condition or previous life event that the RIM should not be used as the sole basis for deriving psycholegal inferences. The RIM shares this limitation with other personality assessment instruments, all of which, whether performance based or self-report in nature, work best when they are administered as part of a multifaceted test battery and interpreted in light of the respondent's personal history and sociocultural context. The scientific foundations and clinical utility of such integrative personality assessment are elaborated by Beutler and Groth-Marnat (2003), Meyer (1997a), and Weiner (2003b, 2005).

Similar considerations apply in the assessment of depressive and psychotic features in plaintiffs seeking personal injury damages. Rorschach indices of dysphoric affect and negative cognitions are usually helpful in identifying these features of depression, but the absence of elevations on these indices rarely warrants ruling out depressive disorder. When indications of depression do pervade a Rorschach protocol, forensic examiners must then draw on other sources of information to determine a causative timeline: Did the plaintiff's apparent depressive state emerge subsequent to the defendant's allegedly damaging actions or was the plaintiff already depressed? And if the depression followed the defendant's actions in time, did the plaintiff become depressed in response to events for which the defendant was not responsible?

When psychotic impairments of functioning are at issue, Rorschach findings can be helpful in ruling out as well as identifying this possibility. As previously mentioned, the critical variables in measuring such serious disturbance, $X-\%$ and $WSum6$, are bidirectional in nature and hence unlikely to generate false-negative findings. To the contrary, low scores on these two variables ordinarily provide evidence of adequate reality testing and logical reasoning and would accordingly challenge a plaintiff's claim of being psychotically impaired. When Rorschach findings do identify psychotic impairment, however, the timing of events once more becomes a crucial consideration. Present indications of psychosis would support a personal injury claim only if other reliable data (e.g., previous testing, mental health history) gave good reason to believe that the plaintiff was not psychotic prior to the alleged harmful conduct by the defendant or, if previously disturbed, had shown a demonstrable decline in functioning capacity subsequent to the conduct.

Child Custody Cases

Judges deciding how a child's time and supervision should be divided between separated or divorced parents often seek psychological opinions concerning the personality characteristics of the parties involved. Courts also commonly rely on test indications of the personality strengths and weaknesses of the parents to help determine whether their parental rights should be continued or terminated altogether. No single set of personal qualities defines suitability to parent or makes one person better qualified than another to fill a parent's role. Nevertheless, there are some personality characteristics that are likely to have a bearing on how well parents can meet their children's needs. These characteristics include their general level of adjustment, the adequacy of their coping skills, and the extent of their interpersonal accessibility, each of which can be measured by Rorschach variables.

With respect to level of adjustment, serious psychological disturbance or incapacitation is likely to detract from the clear thinking, emotional stability, and impulse control usually required for effective parental functioning. Rorschach findings that help to identify such serious disturbance or incapacitation include substantial elevations on variables previously mentioned in this chapter as measures of disordered thinking (*WSum6*), impaired reality testing (*X-%*), negative mood states and cognitions (*C'*, *Col-Shd Blds*, *MOR*, *3r + 2/R*, *V*), and excessive anxiety (*D-minus* and *AdjD-minus*).

In terms of coping skills, mental health professionals generally concur that sound judgment, careful decision making, flexible problem solving, and effective stress management facilitate good parenting (see Hess & Brinson, 1999; Otto, Buffington-Vollum, & Edens, 2003). Conversely, parents who exercise poor judgment, make decisions carelessly, deal with problems in an inflexible manner, and become unduly upset in managing stressful situations are likely to perform relatively poorly as parents. Among Rorschach variables that provide clues to a respondent's skill levels in these respects are the *X-%* (the higher the value, the more likely the person is to exercise poor judgment, and conversely), the *Zd* score (large negative values indicate a propensity for hasty and careless decision making, positive values the opposite), the *a:p* ratio (an imbalance is typically associated with cognitive rigidity and inflexibility, a balance with adequate ability to change set), and the *D* and *AdjD* scores (with minus scores identifying limited stress tolerance and zero or plus scores indicating good stress tolerance).

As for interpersonal accessibility, the quality of care that children receive is usually enhanced when their parents are nurturant, caring, and empathic individuals who are genuinely interested in people, comfortable in interpersonal relationship, and sensitive to the needs and concerns of others. Parental effectiveness is likely to suffer, on the other hand, when parents are detached, self-absorbed, and insensitive persons with limited interest in being around other people or tending to their welfare. In Rorschach terms, then, good parenting is likely to be associated with an adequate *SumH* (an index of interest in people), more *H* than *Hd + (H) + (Hd)* (an index of interpersonal comfort), a low Isolation Index (*ISOL*; an index of involvement with people), and the presence of Texture (*T*; an index of capacity to form attachments), Cooperative Movement (*COP*; an index of collaborative perspectives on interpersonal relationships), and accurate Human Movement responses (*M+*, *Mo*, *Mu*; an index of empathic capacity). Conversely, the interpersonal accessibility of parents who show a low *SumH*, fewer *H* than *Hd + (H) + (Hd)*, an elevated ISOL, *T = 0* (especially when *HVI* is positive), *COP = 0*, and numerous inaccurate *M* responses (*M−*) is likely to be limited.

In drawing such inferences about interpersonal accessibility, examiners should keep in mind that these Rorschach findings are suggestive as to how parents are likely to interact with their children but they are not conclusive. The test data identify probable parental strengths or limitations in interpersonal accessibility, but the actual expression of these personality characteristics must be determined from direct observation or dependable reports of how parents are in fact relating to their children. Similarly with respect to indications of adjustment level and coping skills, test findings may suggest or account for parental successes and shortcomings, and often prove useful on this basis, but they do not demonstrate either good or poor parenting unless affirmed by behavioral data.

Special Advantages

Special advantages of using the RIM in forensic applications include its cross-cultural applicability, its resistance to impression management, and the objectivity of a structural interpretive focus. With respect to the examination of minority group members in the United States, Rorschach assessors should keep in mind that 18% of the CS nonpatient reference sample are African-American, Hispanic-American, or Asian-American respondents. Such broad representation in a reference sample does not by itself rule out the possibility of cultural differences. However, the previously mentioned studies by Presley et al. (2001) and Meyer (2002) do show that the Rorschach structural summaries of minority groups in the United States are virtually identical to those produced by Caucasian respondents. In a review of relevant research findings gathered in many different countries around the world, Ritzler (2004) concluded even more broadly that "the Rorschach is a major, culture-free assessment method that is likely to yield similar results across a wide range of cultures" (pp. 580–581). The basic principles of Rorschach interpretation accordingly appear applicable to persons from many different backgrounds.

As for impression management, the RIM can be particularly helpful in forensic cases by virtue of its resistance to malingering and deception. This resistance derives from the direct relationship that usually exists between the face validity of a personality assessment measure and the ease with which it can be faked (see Bornstein, Rossner, Hill, & Stepanian, 1994). The limited face validity of indirect, relatively unstructured, and performance-based measures like the RIM makes them difficult to fake, and a proper Rorschach administration gives respondents little guidance on how they should proceed with their task and few clues to what their responses might signify.

Faced with such uncertainty, respondents who are attempting to feign disturbance or disability—which is a distinct possibility among criminal defendants and personal injury plaintiffs—tend to produce inconsistent patterns of responses that exaggerate certain aspects of disorder or incapacity. In particular, respondents who are attempting to "fake bad" on the RIM tend to produce dramatic records with strikingly pathological content elaborations but often without correspondingly deviant or unusual structural features. Such differences between dramatic Rorschach content and unremarkable or only moderately deviant Rorschach structure have been documented in research studies in which participants were given disorder-relevant information and instructed to simulate schizophrenia, depression, or posttraumatic stress disorder (Caine, Frueh, & Kinder, 1995; Frueh & Kinder, 1994; Netter & Viglione, 1994; Perry & Kinder, 1992). In a real-world study (not an analog study), Ganellen, Wasyliw, Haywood, and Grossman (1996) found similarly that the only Rorschach variable that differentiated groups of identified malingerers and honest responders was an ad hoc measure of dramatic content.

As for respondents who are attempting to deceive examiners by concealing their problems and thereby "looking good"—a test-taking attitude commonly encountered in child custody evaluations—these persons often give guarded records that reveal their effort to conceal but not much else about their personality characteristics. In the absence of guardedness, moreover, real-world research reported by Grossman, Wasyliw, Benn, and Gyoerkoe (2002) indicates that criminal defendants who have good reason to conceal psychological disturbance on the RIM are likely to have difficulty doing so. In the Grossman et al. study, 74 men charged with sex offenses and presumably motivated to make a good impression were identified on the basis of their MMPI validity scales as "minimizers" ($n = 53$) or "nonminimizers" ($n = 21$). The minimizers in this sample scored significantly lower than the nonminimizers on most of the MMPI clinical scales, but on the RIM they were not able to appear better adjusted than the nonminimizers. To the contrary, these would-be minimizers showed abnormal elevations on several Rorschach indices of psychological dysfunction and were unsuccessful in deflecting attention from various psychological problems they had.

Some malingering or deceptive respondents may have been "coached" on the kinds of Rorschach responses they should give, or they may have consulted manuals and Web sites that purport to give guidance on how to make a particular kind of Rorschach impression.

Because of the multifaceted nature of the RIM, however, and the multidimensional and interactive manner in which responses are interpreted, such coaching and guidance barely scratch the surface of the knowledge necessary to produce a convincingly malingered or deceptive Rorschach protocol. Even knowledgeable Rorschach clinicians are unlikely to succeed in giving a certain kind of record because of the difficulty they will encounter in keeping track of the summary score implications of their responses as they proceed through the 10 cards. Should knowledgeable clinicians take time to review and calculate in their heads how their summary scores are shaping up, their delayed answers will usually alert examiners that something is afoot other than a genuine and spontaneous set of Rorschach responses. The only certain way for an expert to mislead an examiner in some particular direction would be to write out a carefully designed set of responses in advance and then deliver these responses from memory.

With respect to interpretation in forensic cases, the advantage of a structural focus derives from some differences between the structural and thematic features of Rorschach data. The structural data are relatively objective and directly representative of what people are like or how they are likely to behave, whereas the thematic data for the most part are suggestive of what may be on a person's mind, with or without the person's conscious awareness. For example, inaccurate perception of the inkblots as measured by the X-% (structure) is an objective index of perceptual distortion in how one looks at the world, and a high frequency or percentage of inaccurate Rorschach percepts identifies a propensity to misperceive situations in the real world. By contrast, describing a percept of a human figure as "a fat person who eats too much" (thematic) suggests several alternative possibilities— for example, dissatisfaction with one's body size or shape, concerns about one's eating habits, disparaging attitudes toward people who are obese or appear undisciplined—but the imagery in the response is not conclusive for any of these possibilities.

Because of this difference, Rorschach inferences based on structural data can be explained more easily and defended more effectively than inferences derived from thematic imagery, with the latter being better suited for raising alternative possibilities than for formulating conclusions with reasonable certainty. This observation should not be taken to indicate a necessarily lesser role for thematic than for structural interpretations in applications of Rorschach assessment. To the contrary, in clinical work the underlying attitudes and concerns suggested by Rorschach imagery often illuminate more clearly than structural data the sources of patients' adjustment difficulties and the treatment approaches that will benefit them. In giving expert witness testimony, however, forensic examiners can improve their prospects for being helpful to the court and faring well on the witness stand it they confine their testimony to conclusions they can present with reasonable certainty.

Nevertheless, pervasive content themes may occasionally speak for themselves with some authority. As an example, numerous *MOR* responses involving recurrent images of bloody body parts constitute compelling evidence of preoccupying concerns about experiencing bodily harm, and testimony to this effect would be likely to have considerable impact if such responses were given by an accident or assault victim claiming stress disorder. With allowance for such exceptions, however, forensic examiners are well advised to base their Rorschach interpretations primarily on the structural data in a protocol.

CASE EXAMPLE

Mr. Clark (fictitious name) is a 27-year-old Caucasian man who was evaluated in the county jail following an incident that led to his being charged with burglary and criminal mischief. According to police reports, he had boarded a 34-foot sailing vessel docked at a seaside marina, ordered the owner of the boat ashore, and attempted without success to cast off. Called by the boat owner from his cell phone, the police arrived on scene and took Mr. Clark into custody. The Public Defender's Office, representing Mr. Clark and believing there was basis in his case for an insanity plea, requested a psychological evaluation.

When interviewed, Mr. Clark appeared to be in good spirits and talked freely about himself and his life. According to his report, his father was a disturbed man who lived an erratic lifestyle and had been hospitalized for manic-depressive disorder. About himself, he said that he had done poorly in school as a child and had been held back a few years. Nevertheless, he stated, he had eventually graduated from high school in an arts program with "the highest grade-point average ever recorded there." Asked about his employment history, he described working at some semiskilled jobs before getting into "security work," and he added that "breaking codes is my specialty." He then volunteered the information that he had suffered a "mental breakdown" 5 years earlier, been diagnosed as manic-depressive, and spent the next 2 years in and out of hospitals. Subsequent to his hospitalizations, he said, he was not able to convince any employers to hire him, "because my reputation had been ruined by being diagnosed mentally ill." For the last 3 years, he has for the most part been a homeless person subsisting on welfare.

Mr. Clark has never married, but he is preoccupied with Gretchen (fictitious name), whom he identifies as his girlfriend and says he plans to marry. When asked further about his relationship with Gretchen, however, he said that he has spent very little time with her since meeting her 3 years ago, around the time of his hospital discharge, and that he was not sure where she is. Immediately after giving this information, he expressed a firm conviction that the CIA and "special police" in Germany have been conspiring to keep him and Gretchen apart, and he then explained that he was attempting to take the boat because "she must be in Germany, and I was going to sail there and find her."

Mr. Clark was pleasant and personable while being interviewed and said that he appreciated an opportunity to "tell my story." His speech was pressured as he did so, and his flow of ideas was frequently dissociated and circumstantial. He rarely kept focused on a topic for more than a few moments before wandering off into irrelevant, tangential, and sometimes seemingly delusional asides. When presented with a battery of psychological tests, he cooperated fully with the procedures and showed considerable interest in being examined. His Rorschach Sequence of Scores and Structural Summary are shown in Tables 7.1 and 7.2. Consistent with the previously mentioned guidelines for forensic interpretation of Rorschach data, the following discussion of Mr. Clark's protocol centers on structural features of the data that illustrate the use of the RIM in differential diagnosis and may have a bearing on his insanity defense.

The Structural Summary indicates a valid Rorschach record with an above-average response total ($R = 29$) and indications of openness ($Lambda = .61$). In accord with the interpretive search strategies developed for the CS (see Exner, 2003a, chap. 13; Weiner, 2003a, chap. 3), the opening key variable is the presence of reflection responses, which identifies Mr. Clark's attitudes toward himself and other people as the most salient aspects of his current personality functioning. The relevant data in this regard suggest that he is a self-centered person who is inclined to overestimate his attributes and accomplishments, deny problems and shortcomings, externalize responsibility for difficulties, and feel a sense of entitlement ($Fr + rF = 3$, $3r + 2/R = .76$). Persons with these personality characteristics commonly show features of narcissism, psychopathy, or hypomania, with the last of these alternatives seeming most consistent with Mr. Clark's case history and interview behavior.

TABLE 7.1

Sequence of Scores for Mr. Clark

Card	Resp. No	Location and DQ	Loc. No.	Determinant(s) and Form Quality	(2)	Content(s)	Pop	Z Score	Special Scores
I	1	D+	1	Mpo	2	H,Cg,Ay		4.0	GHR
	2	Do	2	Fo	2	(A)			
II	3	Do	3	Mp.FC'.CF−		Ad			AG, ALOG, INC, PHR
	4	D+	6	Mao	2	H		3.0	COP, GHR
III	5	D+	9	Mp.FC'.Fr+		H,Cg	P	3.0	GHR
	6	W+	1	FCu	2	Cg,Id		5.5	AB
	7	D+	9	Mpo	2	H,Id	P	3.0	GHR
	8	DdS+	99	Mpo	2	H,An		4.5	FAB2, PHR
IV	9	W+	1	Mp.FDo		(H),Bt	P	4.0	DV, GHR
	10	Ddo	30	mpu		Hd,Sx			PHR
	11	Wo	1	Fu		(A),Ay		2.0	
V	12	Wo	1	Fo		A	P	1.0	PSV, DV
	13	Wo	1	Fo		A		1.0	
VI	14	Wo	1	Fo		Ad	P	2.5	MOR, DV
	15	Ddo	24	F−	2	H			PSV, DR2, PHR
	16	Ddo	31	Fu	2	Hd,Sx			DV, PHR
VII	17	Do	3	Mpu	2	(Hd)			AG, PHR
	18	W+	1	FC'−		H,Cg		2.5	DV, PHR
	19	DSo	7	Fo		Cl			
	20	D+	1	Mp+	2	Hd,Cg	P	3.0	GHR
VIII	21	W+	1	FMp.CF.Fro		A,Ls	P	4.5	INC
IX	22	Ddo	99	F−	2	Ad		5.5	
	23	Wv/+	1	CF.Fro		Na		5.5	AB, PHR
	24	W+	1	Ma.CF.mp−		H,Cg,Id		5.5	AB, PHR
X	25	DdSo	99	FC−		Hd			PHR
	26	D+	11	Mau	2	A,Id		4.0	FAB, PHR
	27	Do	7	Fo	2	A			
	28	Do	10	FMau		A			
	29	Do	13	F−		An			DV2

Table 7.2
Structural Summary for Mr. Clark

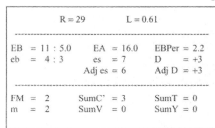
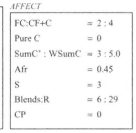
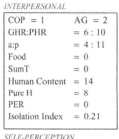

Location Features

Zf	=	17
ZSum	=	58.5
ZEst	=	56.0
W	=	10
(Wv	=	0)
D	=	13
W+D	=	23
Dd	=	6
S	=	3

DQ

			(FQ–)
+	=	12	(2)
o	=	16	(5)
v/+	=	1	(0)
v	=	0	(0)

Form Quality

		FQx	MQual	W+D
+	=	2	2	2
o	=	13	5	12
u	=	7	2	5
–	=	7	2	4
none	–	0	0	0

Determinants

Blends	Single	
M.FC'.CF	M	= 7
M.FC'.Fr	FM	= 1
M.FD	m	= 1
FM.CF.Fr	FC	= 2
CF.Fr	CF	= 0
M.CF.m	C	= 0
	Cn	= 0
	FC'	= 1
	C'F	= 0
	C'	= 0
	FT	= 0
	TF	= 0
	T	= 0
	FV	= 0
	VF	= 0
	V	= 0
	FY	= 0
	YF	= 0
	Y	= 0
	Fr	= 0
	rF	= 0
	FD	= 0
	F	= 11
	(2)	= 13

Contents

H	=	8
(H)	=	1
Hd	=	4
(Hd)	=	1
Hx	=	0
A	=	6
(A)	=	2
Ad	=	3
(Ad)	=	0
An	=	2
Art	=	0
Ay	=	2
Bl	=	0
Bt	=	1
Cg	=	6
Cl	=	1
Ex	=	0
Fd	=	0
Fi	=	0
Ge	=	0
Hh	=	0
Ls	=	1
Na	=	1
Sc	=	0
Sx	=	2
Xy	=	0
Idio	=	4

S-Constellation

☐	FV+VF+V+FD > 2
☑	Col-Shd Blends > 0
☑	Ego < .31 or > .44
☐	MOR > 3
☐	Zd > ±3.5
☐	es > EA
☑	CF + C > FC
☑	X+% < .70
☐	S > 3
☐	P < 3 or > 8
☐	Pure H < 2
☐	R < 17
4	Total

Special Scores

		Lvl-1	Lvl-2
DV	=	5 ×1	1 ×2
INC	=	2 ×2	0 ×4
DR	=	0 ×3	1 ×6
FAB	=	1 ×4	1 ×7
ALOG	=	1 ×5	
CON	=	0 ×7	
	Raw Sum6	=	**12**
	Wgtd Sum6	=	**33**

AB	= 2		GHR	= 6
AG	= 2		PHR	= 10
COP	= 1		MOR	= 1
CP	= 0		PER	= 0
			PSV	= 2

Ratios, Percentages, and Derivations

R = 29   L = 0.61

EB = 11 : 5.0   EA = 16.0   EBPer = 2.2
eb = 4 : 3   es = 7   D = +3
                Adj es = 6 Adj D = +3

FM = 2   SumC' = 3   SumT = 0
m = 2   SumV = 0   SumY = 0

AFFECT

FC:CF+C	= 2 : 4
Pure C	= 0
SumC' : WSumC	= 3 : 5.0
Afr	= 0.45
S	= 3
Blends:R	= 6 : 29
CP	= 0

INTERPERSONAL

COP	= 1	AG = 2
GHR:PHR		= 6 : 10
a:p		= 4 : 11
Food		= 0
SumT		= 0
Human Content		= 14
Pure H		= 8
PER		= 0
Isolation Index		= 0.21

IDEATION

a:p	= 4 : 11	Sum6	= 12
Ma:Mp	= 3 : 8	Lvl-2	= 3
2AB+(Art+Ay)	= 6	WSum6	= 33
MOR	= 1	M-	= 2
		M none	= 0

MEDIATION

XA%	= 0.76
WDA%	= 0.83
X-%	= 0.24
S–	= 1
P	= 7
X+%	= 0.52
Xu%	= 0.24

PROCESSING

Zf	= 17
W:D:Dd	= 10:13:6
W : M	= 10 : 11
Zd	= +2.5
PSV	= 2
DQ+	= 12
DQv	= 0

SELF-PERCEPTION

3r+(2)/R	= 0.76
Fr+rF	= 3
SumV	= 0
FD	= 1
An+Xy	= 2
MOR	= 1
H:(H)+Hd+(Hd)	= 8 : 6

PTI = 3	☑ DEPI = 5	☐ CDI = 2	S-CON = 4	☑ HVI = Yes	☐ OBS = No

Along with a hypomanic person's typical social expansiveness and quest for an appreciative audience, however, this man also gives evidence of being suspicious and mistrustful in his relationships with people and consequently intent on maintaining his privacy and keeping his distance from others (positive Hypervigilance Index [*HVI*]). This finding is consistent with, and helps to confirm, the paranoid quality of his presentational style and thought content. Hence the two main themes to pursue in Mr. Clark's record are his apparent hypomania and paranoia.

To elaborate first on Mr. Clark's moods, he seems inclined to express affect in a more intense and dramatic way than most adults ($FC:CF + F = 2:4$), which is consistent with hypomania. However, there are also indications in the record of dysphoria ($C' > 2$; *Col-Shd Blds* > 0), withdrawal from emotionally arousing situations ($Afr < .46$), and limited interest in collaborative interactions with others ($COP < 2$), which are depressive phenomena. Considered together with his hypomania, these findings suggest the possibility of a bipolar or cyclothymic disorder.

Further consideration of the paranoid elements in Mr. Clark's record brings to light some additional features of his condition. Of particular note are two findings commonly associated with delusion formation. First, he gives substantial evidence of having a thought disorder, with a predilection for dissociated ideation and illogical reasoning concerning relationships between events ($WSum 6 = 33$, with *Lvl-2* $= 3$). Second, he shows a prominent tendency to resort excessively to fantasy as a way of dealing with problems, that is, by imagining or daydreaming about how they will be solved ($Ma:Mp = 3:8$). Also noteworthy is the fact that Mr. Clark is an introversive person with a strong preference for dealing with his experience in an ideational and contemplative manner rather than by expressing feelings or taking action ($EB = 11:5.0$). Although being introversive does not preclude the possibility of bipolar disorder, manic-depressive individuals are typically more emotional than ideational in dealing with experience and thereby likely to show an extratensive *EB*. Hence, to the extent that inferring a *DSM* diagnosis may become relevant or required (which often is the case in expert witness testimony), the combination of Mr. Clark's thinking disorder and affective instability may indicate a schizoaffective disorder.

Although Mr. Clark's affective instability and paranoia are the cornerstones of his clearly demonstrated psychological disturbance, the presence of these conditions, as noted earlier, is not sufficient in a court of law to support an insanity defense. With respect to being able to tell right from wrong, the critical psychodiagnostic question is whether the defendant was capable of distinguishing between reality and fantasy when the alleged offense occurred. The perceptual and attentional variables in the Structural Summary indicate that Mr. Clark was able when he was examined to recognize conventional modes of response ($P = 7$) but had some limitations in his reality testing ($X-\% = .24$). This level of reality testing is not in the psychotic range, but it does indicate a propensity on his part to misperceive events, show poor judgment, and fail to anticipate the consequences of his actions. Although insufficient to document impaired reality testing at the time of his offense, these findings were consistent with observers' reports of his strange behavior on that day and with the account he gave of his irrational basis for attempting to commandeer the vessel.

Significantly, however, Mr. Clark's *WDA%* is .83, with six *Dd* locations and four of his seven inaccurate percepts (*FQ−*) occurring in these *Dd* responses. This finding indicates that his reality testing is within normal limits when he keeps his attention focused on the central and obvious details of his experience, which would account for his being able much of the time to present himself as a reasonably "sane" person. On the other hand, when he becomes distracted by peripheral details and focuses on irrelevant aspects of situations—which he is more likely than most people to do—he tends to lose touch with reality and form distorted impressions of what is happening around him. Instances of such loss of reality sense could explain why at times he could break the law without appreciating the wrongfulness of his conduct.

However warranted this conclusion about Mr. Clark's susceptibility to episodes of legal insanity may be, it does not yet speak to his mental state at the time of the particular offense with which he is presently charged. To identify another finding that could be relevant in this regard, note that the Structural Summary data identify not only emotional instability but also a probability that Mr. Clark's disturbance is chronic rather than acute in nature. The pertinent indications of chronicity are the D and $AdjD$ scores of $+3$. D and $AdjD$ scores in the plus range usually signify that the personality characteristics suggested by a Rorschach protocol are stable and well entrenched, for better or worse, and likely to have been present at previous points in an adult person's life. Hence, these particular Rorschach findings give reason to believe the susceptibility to episodic loss of reality sense shown by Mr. Clark when he was tested was likely to have been present as well when he committed the offense with which he is charged.

SUMMARY

As elaborated in this chapter, the Rorschach Inkblot Method (RIM) is a psychometrically sound personality assessment procedure that can facilitate decision making whenever personality characteristics participate in shaping conclusions and recommendations concerning people. In clinical practice, Rorschach findings help to identify the presence and nature of psychological disorder and a person's need for, amenability to, and progress in treatment of various kinds. In forensic work, Rorschach assessors can assist the court by identifying personality characteristics that are pertinent to resolving psycholegal issues in criminal, personal injury, and child custody cases. Also of value in forensic evaluations are the incremental validity of the RIM, which can add useful information to self-report and interview findings, and its sensitivity to malingering and deception. Forensic consultants should nevertheless be well schooled in the limitations as well as the utility of Rorschach assessment

REFERENCES

Acklin, M.W., McDowell, C.J., Verschell, M.S., & Chan, D. (2000). Interobserver agreement, intraobserver agreement, and the Rorschach Comprehensive System. *Journal of Personality Assessment, 74,* 15–57.

Armstrong, J. (1991). The psychological organization of multiple personality disordered patients as revealed in psychological testing. *Psychiatric Clinics of North America, 14,* 533–546.

Armstrong, J. (2002). Deciphering the broken narrative of trauma: Signs of traumatic dissociation on the Rorschach. *Rorschachiana, 25,* 11–27.

Armstrong, J., & Kaser-Boyd, N. (2004). Projective assessment of psychological trauma. In M. Hersen (series Ed.) & M. Hilsenroth & D. Segal (vol. Eds.), *Comprehensive handbook of psychological assessment: Vol. 2. Objective and projective assessment of personality* (pp. 500–512). Hoboken, NJ: Wiley.

Ball, J.D., Archer, R.P., & Imhof, E.A. (1994). Time requirements of psychological testing: A survey of practitioners. *Journal of Personality Assessment, 63,* 239–249.

Blais, M.A., Hilsenroth, M.J., Castlebury, F., Fowler, J.C., & Baity, M.R. (2001). Predicting DSM-IV Cluster B personality disorder criteria from MMPI-2 and Rorschach data: A test of incremental validity. *Journal of Personality Assessment, 76,* 150–168.

Beck, S.J., Beck, A.G., Levitt, E.E., & Molish, H.B. (1961). *Rorschach's test: I. Basic processes* (3rd ed.). New York: Grune & Stratton.

Beutler, L.E., & Groth-Marnat, G. (2003). *Integrative assessment of adult personality* (2nd ed.). New York: Guilford Press.

Beutler, L.E., Harwood, T.M., & Holaway, R. (2002). How to assess clients in pretreatment planning. In J.N. Butcher (Ed.), *Clinical personality assessment* (2nd ed., pp. 76–95). New York: Oxford University Press.

Blatt, S.J., & Ford, R.Q. (1994). *Therapeutic change.* New York: Plenum.

Bornstein, R.F., Rossner, S.C., Hill, E.L., & Stepanian, M.L. (1994). Face validity and fakability of objective and projective measures of dependency. *Journal of Personality Assessment, 63,* 363–386.

Caine, S.L., Frueh, B.C., & Kinder, B.N. (1995). Rorschach susceptibility to malingered depressive disorders in adult females. In J.N. Butcher & C.D. Spielberger (Eds.), *Advances in personality assessment* (Vol. 10, pp. 165–173). Hillsdale, NJ: Lawrence Erlbaum Associates.

Clarkin, J.F., & Levy, K.N. (2004). The influence of client variables on psychotherapy. In Lambert, M.J. (Ed.), *Bergin and Garfield's handbook of psychotherapy and behavior change* (5th ed., pp. 194–226). Hoboken, NJ: Wiley.

Craig, R.J. (2005). *Personality-guided forensic psychology.* Washington, DC: American Psychological Association.

Ellenberger, H.F. (1954). The life and work of Hermann Rorschach (1884–1922). *Bulletin of the Menninger Clinic, 18,* 173–219.

Exner, J.E., Jr. (1974). *The Rorschach: A comprehensive system.* New York: Wiley.

Exner, J.E., Jr. (2001). *A Rorschach workbook for the Comprehensive System.* Asheville, NC: Rorschach Workshops.

Exner, J.E., Jr. (2002). A new nonpatient data sample for the Rorschach Comprehensive System: A progress report. *Journal of Personality Assessment, 78,* 391–404.

Exner, J.E., Jr. (2003a). *The Rorschach: A comprehensive system: Vol. 1. Basic foundations and principles of interpretation* (4th ed.). Hoboken, NJ: Wiley.

Exner, J.E., Jr. (2003b, March). An update on the new non-patient sample for the Rorschach Comprehensive System. Paper presented at the meeting of the Society for Personality Assessment, San Francisco.

Exner, J.E., Jr., & Andronikof-Sanglade, A. (1992). Rorschach changes following brief and short-term therapy. *Journal of Personality Assessment, 59,* 59–71.

Exner, J.E., Jr., Thomas, E.A., & Mason, B. (1985). Children's Rorschachs: Description and prediction. *Journal of Personality Assessment, 49,* 13–20.

Fowler, J.C., Ackerman, S., Speanberg, S., Bailey, A., Blagys, M., & Conklin, A. (2004). Personality and symptom change in treatment-refractory inpatients: Evaluation of the phase model of change using Rorschach, TAT, and DSM-IV Axis V. *Journal of Personality Assessment, 76,* 333–351.

Fowler, J.C., Piers, C., Hilsenroth, M.J., Holdwick, D.J., Jr., & Padawer, J.R. (2001). The Rorschach Suicide Constellation: Assessing various degrees of lethality. *Journal of Personality Assessment, 76,* 333–351.

Frueh, B.C., & Kinder, B.N. (1994). The susceptibility of the Rorschach inkblot test to malingering of combat-related PTSD. *Journal of Personality Assessment, 62,* 280–298.

Ganellen, R.J., Wasyliw, O.E., Haywood, T.W., & Grossman, L.S. (1996). Can psychosis be malingered on the Rorschach? An empirical study. *Journal of Personality Assessment, 66,* 65–80.

Garb, H.N. (1999). Call for a moratorium on the use of the Rorschach Inkblot Test in clinical and forensic settings. *Assessment, 6,* 311–318.

Garb, H.N., Wood, J.M., Nezworski, M., Grove, W.M., & Stejskal, W.J. (2001). Towards a resolution of the Rorschach controversy. *Psychological Assessment, 13,* 433–448.

Golding, S.L., Skeem, J.L., Roesch, R., & Zapf, P.A. (1999). The assessment of criminal responsibility. In A.K. Hess & I.B. Weiner (Eds.), *Handbook of forensic psychology* (pp. 379–408). New York: Wiley.

Goldstein, A.M., Morse, S.J., & Shapiro, D.L. (2003). Evaluation of criminal responsibility. In I.B. Weiner (series Ed.) & A.M. Goldstein (vol. Ed.), *Handbook of psychology: Vol. 11. Forensic psychology* (pp. 381–406). Hoboken, NJ: Wiley.

Greenberg, S.A. (2003). Personal injury examinations in torts for emotional distress. In I.B. Weiner (series Ed.) & A.M. Goldstein (vol. Ed.), *Handbook of psychology: Vol. 11. Forensic psychology* Hoboken, NJ: Wiley.

Greenberg, S.A., & Brodsky, S. (2001). *The practice of civil forensic psychology.* Washington, DC: American Psychological Association.

Gronnerod, C. (2003). Temporal stability in the Rorschach method: A meta-analytic review. *Journal of Personality Assessment, 80*, 272–293.

Gronnerod, C. (2004). Rorschach assessment of changes following psychotherapy: A meta-analytic review. *Journal of Personality Assessment, 83*, 256–276.

Grossman, L.S., Wasyliw, O.E., Benn, A.F., & Gyoerkoe, K.L. (2002). Can sex offenders who minimize on the MMPI conceal psychopathology on the Rorschach? *Journal of Personality Assessment, 78*, 484–501.

Grove, W.M., & Barden, R.C. (1999). Protecting the integrity of the legal system: The admissibility of testimony from mental health experts under Daubert/Kumho analyses. *Psychology, Public Policy, and Law, 5*, 224–242.

Hess, A.K., Zachar, P., & Kramer, J. (2001). Rorschach. In B.S. Plake & J.S. Impara (Eds.), *Fourteenth mental measurements yearbook* (pp. 1033–1038). Lincoln: University of Nebraska Press.

Hess, K.D., & Brinson, P. (1999). Mediating domestic law issues. In A. K. Hess & I.B. Weiner (Eds.), *Handbook of forensic psychology* (2nd ed., pp. 63–104). New York: Wiley.

Hiller, J.B., Rosenthal, R., Bornstein, R.F., Berry, D.T.R., & Brunner-Neuleib, S. (1999). A comparative meta-analysis of Rorschach validity. *Psychological Assessment, 11*, 278–296.

Hilsenroth, M.J., & Stricker, G. (2004). A consideration of challenges to psychological assessment instruments used in forensic settings: Rorschach as exemplar. *Journal of Personality Assessment, 83*, 141–152.

Holaday, M. (2000). Rorschach protocols from children and adolescents diagnosed with posttraumatic stress disorder. *Journal of Personality Assessment, 75*, 143–157.

Hunsley, J., & Bailey, J.M. (1999). The clinical utility of the Rorschach: Unfulfilled promises and an uncertain future. *Psychological Assessment, 11*, 266–277.

Janson, H., & Stattin, H. (2003). Predictions of adolescent and adult delinquency from childhood Rorschach ratings. *Journal of Personality Assessment, 81*, 51–63.

Klopfer, B., Ainsworth, M.D., Klopfer, W.G., & Holt, R.R.R. (1954). *Developments in the Rorschach technique: Vol. 1. Technique and theory.* Yonkers-on-Hudson, NY: World Book.

Kamphuis, J.H., Kugeares, S.L., & Finn, S.E. (2000). Rorschach correlates of sexual abuse: Trauma content and aggression indexes. *Journal of Personality Assessment, 75*, 212–224.

Lambert, M.J., & Ogles, B.M. (2004). The efficacy and effectiveness of psychotherapy. In M.J. Lambert (Ed.), *Bergin and Garfield's handbook of psychotherapy and behavior change* (5th ed., pp. 139–193). Hoboken, NJ: Wiley.

Lerner, P.M. (1991). *Psychoanalytic theory and the Rorschach.* Hillsdale, NJ: Analytic Press.

Lerner, P.M. (1998). *Psychoanalytic perspectives on the Rorschach.* Hillsdale, NJ: Analytic Press.

Lilienfeld, S.O., Wood, J.M., & Garb, H.N. (2000). The scientific status of projective techniques. *Psychological Science in the Public Interest, 1*, 27–66.

Lohr, J.M., Fowler, K.A., & Lilienfeld, S.O. (2002). The dissemination and promotion of pseudoscience in clinical psychology: The challenge to legitimate clinical science. *The Clinical Psychologist, 55*, 4–10.

Luxenberg, T., & Levin, P. (2004). The role of the Rorschach in the assessment of trauma. In J.P. Wilson & T.M. Keane (Eds.), *Assessing psychological trauma and PTSD* (2nd ed., pp. 190–225). New York: Guilford Press.

Mattlar, C.-E. (2004). The Rorschach Comprehensive System is reliable, valid, and cost-effective. *Rorschachiana, 26*, 158–186.

McCann, J.T. (1998). Defending the Rorschach in court: An analysis of admissibility using legal and professional standards. *Journal of Personality Assessment, 70*, 125–144.

McGrath, R.E. (2003). Enhancing accuracy in observational test scoring: The Comprehensive System as a case example. *Journal of Personality Assessment, 81*, 104–110.

McGrath, R.E., Pogge, D.L., Stokes, J.M., Cragnolino, A., Zaccario, M., Hayman, J., et al. (2005). Field reliability of Comprehensive System scoring in an adolescent inpatient sample. *Assessment, 12*, 199–209.

Meyer, G.J. (1997a). Assessing reliability: Critical corrections for a critical examination of the Rorschach Comprehensive System. *Psychological Assessment, 9*, 480–489.

Meyer, G.J. (1997b). Thinking clearly about reliability: More critical corrections regarding the Rorschach Comprehensive System. *Psychological Assessment, 9*, 495–498.

Meyer, G.J. (2002). Exploring possible ethnic differences and bias in the Rorschach Comprehensive System. *Journal of Personality Assessment, 78*, 104–129.

Meyer, G.J. (2004). The reliability and validity of the Rorschach and Thematic Apperception Test (TAT) compared to other psychological and medical procedures: An analysis of systematically gathered evidence. In M. Hersen (series Ed.) & M.J. Hilsenroth & D.L. Segal (vol. Eds.), *Personality assessment: Vol. 2. Comprehensive handbook of psychological assessment* (pp. 315–342). Hoboken, NJ: Wiley.

Meyer, G.J., & Archer, R.P. (2001). The hard science of Rorschach research: What do we know and where do we go. *Psychological Assessment, 13,* 486–502.

Meyer, G.J., & Handler, L. (1997). The ability of the Rorschach to predict subsequent outcome: Meta-analysis of the Rorschach Prognostic Rating Scale. *Journal of Personality Assessment, 69,* 1–38.

Meyer, G.J., & Handler, L. (2000). Incremental validity of the Rorschach Prognostic Rating Scale over the MMPI Ego Strength Scale and IQ. *Journal of Personality Assessment, 74,* 356–370.

Meyer, G.J., Hilsenroth, M.J., Baxter, D., Exner, J.E., Jr., Fowler, J.C., Piers, C.C., et al. (2002). An examination of the interrater reliability for scoring the Rorschach Comprehensive System in eight data sets. *Journal of Personality Assessment, 78,* 219–274.

Netter, B.E.C., & Viglione, D.J. (1994). An empirical study of malingering schizophrenia on the Rorschach. *Journal of Personality Assessment, 62,* 45–57.

Otto, R.K., Buffington-Vollum, J.K., & Edens, J.F. (2003). Child custody evaluation. In I.B. Weiner (series Ed.) & A.M. Goldstein (vol. Ed.), *Handbook of psychology: Vol. 11. Forensic psychology* (pp. 179–208). Hoboken, NJ: Wiley.

Perry, G.G., & Kinder, B.N. (1992). Susceptibility of the Rorschach to malingering: A schizophrenia analogue. In C.D. Spielberger & J.N. Butcher (Eds.), *Advances in personality assessment* (Vol. 9, pp. 127–140). Hillsdale, NJ: Lawrence Erlbaum Associates.

Perry, W. (2001). Incremental validity of the Ego Impairment Index: A reexamination of Dawes (1999). *Psychological Assessment, 13,* 403–407.

Presley, G., Smith, C., Hilsenroth, M., & Exner, J.E. (2001). Rorschach validity with African Americans. *Journal of Personality Assessment, 77,* 491–507.

Ritzler, B. (2004). Cultural applications of the Rorschach, apperception tests, and figure drawings. In M. Hersen (series Ed.) & M.J. Hilsenroth & D.L. Segal (vol. Eds.), *Comprehensive handbook of psychological assessment: Vol. 2. Personality assessment* (573–585). Hoboken, NJ: Wiley.

Ritzler, B., Erard, R., & Pettigrew, T. (2002). Protecting the integrity of Rorschach expert witnesses: A reply to Grove and Barden (1999) re: The admissibility of testimony under Daubert/Kumho analysis. *Psychology, Public Policy, and Law, 8,* 201–215.

Roesch, R., Zapf, P.A., Golding, S.L., & Skeem, J.L. (1999). Defining and assessing competency to stand trial. In A.K. Hess & I.B. Weiner (Eds.), *Handbook of forensic psychology* (2nd ed., pp. 327–349). New York: Wiley.

Rorschach, H. (1942). *Psychodiagnostics: A diagnostic test based on perception* (P. Lemkau & B. Kronenberg, Trans.). Berne, Switzerland: Hans Huber. (Original work published 1921)

Schafer, R. (1954). *Psychoanalytic interpretation in Rorschach testing.* New York: Grune & Stratton.

Schwarz, W. (1996). Hermann Rorschach, M.D.: His life and work. *Rorschachiana, 21,* 6–17.

Sloan, P., Arsenault, L., & Hilsenroth, M. (2002).Use of the Rorschach in the assessment of war-related stress in military personnel. *Rorschachiana, 25,* 86–122.

Sloan, P., Arsenault, L., Hilsenroth, M., Handler, L., & Harvill, L. (1996). Rorschach measures of posttraumatic stress in Persian Gulf War veterans: A three-year follow-up study. *Journal of Personality Assessment, 66,* 54–64.

Smith, B. (1994). Object relations theory and the integration of empirical and psychoanalytic approaches to Rorschach interpretation. *Rorschachiana, 19,* 61–77.

Stafford, K.P. (2003). Assessment of competence to stand trial. In I.B. Weiner (series Ed.) & A.M. Goldstein (vol. Ed.), *Handbook of psychology: Vol. 11. Forensic psychology* (pp. 359–380). Hoboken, NJ: Wiley.

Stokes, J., Pogge, D., Powell-Lunder, J., Ward, A., Bilginer, L., & DeLuca, V. (2003). The Rorschach Ego Impairment Index: Prediction of treatment outcome in a child psychiatric population. *Journal of Personality Assessment, 81,* 11–19.

Stricker, G., & Gold, J.R. (1999). The Rorschach: Toward a nomothetically based, idiographically applicable configurational model. *Psychological Assessment, 11,* 240–250.

Viglione, D.J. (1999). A review of recent research addressing the utility of the Rorschach. *Psychological Assessment, 11,* 251–265.

Viglione, D.J. (2002). *Rorschach coding solutions: A reference guide for the Comprehensive System.* San Diego, CA: Author.

Viglione, D.J., & Hilsenroth, M.J. (2001). The Rorschach: Facts, fictions, and future. *Psychological Assessment, 13*, 452–471.

Viglione, D.J., & Taylor, N. (2003). Empirical support for interrater reliability of Rorschach Comprehensive System coding. *Journal of Clinical Psychology, 59,* 111–121.

Weiner, I.B. (2000). Using the Rorschach properly in practice and research. *Journal of Clinical Psychology, 56,* 435–438.

Weiner, I.B. (2001). Advancing the science of psychological assessment: The Rorschach Inkblot Method as exemplar. *Psychological Assessment, 13,* 423–432.

Weiner, I.B. (2003a). *Principles of Rorschach interpretation* (2nd ed.). Mahwah, NJ: Lawrence Erlbaum Associates.

Weiner. I.B. (2003b). Prediction and postdiction in clinical decision making. *Clinical Psychology: Science and Practice, 10,* 335–338.

Weiner, I.B. (2004a). Rorschach assessment: Current status. In M. Hersen (series Ed.) & M.J. Hilsenroth & D.L. Segal (vol. Eds.), *Comprehensive handbook of psychological assessment: Vol. 2. Personality assessment* (pp. 343–355). Hoboken, NJ: Wiley.

Weiner, I.B. (2004b). Rorschach Inkblot Method. In M. Maruish (Ed.), *The use of psychological testing for treatment planning and outcome assessment* (3rd ed., Vol. 3, pp. 553–588). Mahwah, NJ: Lawrence Erlbaum Associates.

Weiner, I.B. (2005). Integrative personality assessment with self-report and performance-based measures. In S. Strack (Ed.), *Personality and psychopathology* (pp. 317–331). Hoboken, NJ: Wiley.

Weiner, I.B., & Exner, J.E., Jr. (1991). Rorschach changes in long-term and short-term psychotherapy. *Journal of Personality Assessment, 56,* 453–465.

Wolf, E.B. (2000). Herman Rorschach. In A.E. Kazdin (Ed.), *Encyclopedia of psychology* (pp. 115–117). Washington, DC: American Psychological Association.

Wood, J.M., & Lilienfeld, S.O. (1999). The Rorschach Inkblot Test: A case of overstatement. *Assessment, 6,* 341–349.

Wood, J.M., Nezworski, M.T., Garb, H., & Lilienfeld, S.O. (2001). The misperception of psychopathology: Problems with the norms of the Comprehensive System. *Clinical Psychology: Science and Practice, 8,* 350–373.

Wood, J.M., Nezworski, M.T., & Stejskal, W.J. (1996). The Comprehensive System for the Rorschach: A critical examination. *Psychological Science, 7,* 3–10.

8

NEUROPSYCHOLOGICAL ASSESSMENT IN THE FORENSIC SETTING

ERIC A. ZILLMER
HEATHER K. GREEN

DREXEL UNIVERSITY

American psychology has become increasingly characterized by the development of applied specialty areas. The emergence of neuropsychological assessment within the legal domain illustrates this current momentum (Heilbrun et al., 2003). Forensic psychology is a specialty area within psychology that has broadly influenced the disciplines of law and psychology. By comparison, neuropsychological assessment in the forensic setting represents a somewhat narrower approach to forensic psychology and is particularly concerned with the relationship between cognitive parameters, such as attention or decision making, and the law. Forensic neuropsychological assessment is one of the fastest growing areas within the field of clinical neuropsychology, with an increasing number of neuropsychologists presenting and/or evaluating the results of neuropsychological assessments in the courtroom setting. In fact, it has become common for neuropsychologists to eventually be confronted with some sort of forensic issue in their clinical work. What constitutes appropriate practice for the forensic neuropsychologists? When is there a conflict of interest? What are the limitations of forensic neuropsychology?

In traditional clinical practice, the foremost commitment is to the well-being of the client. In forensic neuropsychology, however, the attorney or insurance company hiring the neuropsychology expert becomes the client. In such cases, the role of the neuropsychologist may represent a distinct change from the traditional client-clinician relationship. For example, the expert's testimony may actually not benefit the "patient." In addition, neuropsychologists often work for attorneys or insurance companies who are not informed about the ethical standards of psychologists. As neuropsychologists have broadened their approach to the study of behavior, they have become more influential in offering consultation to the courts and attorneys on topics ranging from traumatic brain injury to the comprehension of Miranda rights. As a result, the expertise of neuropsychologists can be very valuable. However, neuropsychologists face substantial challenges in expanding their role to meet the dynamic and complex demands of the legal process.

This chapter examines the emerging trends and concepts that neuropsychologists may face when employing neuropsychological assessment practices in the forensic setting. There have been some excellent comprehensive summaries written on forensic psychological assessment (e.g., Heilbrun, 2001; Heilbrun, Goldstein, & Redding, 2005) as well as forensic neuropsychology (e.g., Heilbronner, 2005; Larabee, 2005; see also Zillmer, 2003a, 2005). This chapter is intended not to provide an inclusive summary of forensic assessment issues in neuropsychology but to examine emerging trends and topics in the field. Specifically, it discusses the principles of forensic neuropsychological assessment, concerns regarding test selection, and psychometric and scientific considerations. Symptom validity testing, emerging ethical challenges, and the limitations and future trends of forensic neuropsychological assessment are all addressed. The chapter concludes with brief case examples.

HISTORY AND BACKGROUND

Neuropsychological assessment is a method of examining the brain by studying its behavioral product. Similar to traditional psychological assessments, neuropsychological evaluations employ standardized tests that provide sensitive indices of brain-behavior relationships. Neuropsychological tests have been used on an empirical and clinical basis in various medical and psychiatric settings. They are responsive to the organic integrity of the cerebral hemispheres and can often pinpoint specific neurocognitive deficits (Zillmer, 2003b). As a result, the objective and quantitative nature of the neuropsychological assessment has become a valuable asset in the courtroom by presenting information to the jury or judge regarding the determination, effects, and prognosis of brain dysfunction. Since neuropsychology assessment batteries typically evaluate a wide range of behaviors, their multidimensional approach has proven to be very helpful in quantifying specific cognitive disabilities, such as those resulting from head trauma or toxic conditions. Neuropsychological evaluations can be critical for the comprehensive understanding of the cognitive, behavioral, and emotional sequelae of a variety of neurological conditions for purposes of legal documentation. Therefore, neuropsychologists are often in a position to deal with varied aspects of brain dysfunction and are increasingly asked to conduct forensic assessments in cases related to personal injury, disability determination, or workers' compensation. Indeed, forensic neuropsychology is a rapidly emerging subspecialty of neuropsychology.

Civil Versus Criminal Cases

The expertise of neuropsychologists in the assessment of brain-behavior relationships makes them valuable in both criminal cases and civil personal injury cases. However, both types of cases require significant training and experience with specific legal standards and how neuropsychological assessment criteria relate to those standards. One issue that differentiates the two types is the potential monetary rewards often associated with civil cases. Many civil cases involve a plaintiff claiming damages directly related to an incident.

Those that require an assessment of brain injury represent the bread and butter of forensic neuropsychology. Here, it is common for the plaintiff's lawyer to refer the plaintiff to a forensic neuropsychologist for an evaluation of the claims before agreeing to take on the case. The purpose behind the evaluation is to determine the merits of the case as well as the potential difficulties (Sageman, 2003).

In contrast, criminal cases often focus on assessing the competencies and capacities of the defendant as they relate to the crime in question (e.g., murder, robbery, sale of weapons). There are many types of criminal cases, which makes this area a particularly rich area for study. The most common competency issues are competency to stand trial, the comprehension of Miranda rights, and criminal responsibility (especially as it pertains to the insanity defense).

One issue that continues to generate increasing attention from neuropsychologists is a defendant's comprehension of Miranda rights and the defendant's ability to waive them "knowingly, intelligently and voluntarily" (*Miranda v. Arizona*, 1966). Given that confessions remain the most compelling type of evidence (Kassin & Neumann, 1997), determining whether a client validly waived his or her rights to silence and counsel before making self-incriminating statements becomes critically important. Individuals with brain dysfunction, learning disabilities, or low intelligence may have difficulty understanding "intelligently" the abstract purpose of the Miranda statement. Because of their intellectual and emotional immaturity, juveniles are especially at risk for poor comprehension and false confessions (i.e., admitting to crimes they did not commit; Oberlander, Goldstein, & Ho, 2001). Adolescent defendants and adults with brain dysfunction may not fully comprehend the effect of the waiver and thus may have difficulty meeting the "intelligent" requirement for a valid waiver. Neuropsychological paradigms can provide a profile of cognitive deficits and strengths that may assist in the assessment of an individual's ability to understand forensic issues (Zillmer, 2003a, 2005). Thus, from a neuropsychological perspective there are correlates in the cognitive domain to the Miranda concepts of "knowingly" and "intelligently" that should allow for promising research and appropriate clinical applications. Other emerging issues in the criminal domain of interest to neuropsychologists are in the area of assisting with sentencing options. Particularly in capital sentencing neuropsychologists can assist by providing a picture of the defendant's neuropsychological functioning.

PRINCIPLES OF FORENSIC NEUROPSYCHOLOGICAL ASSESSMENT

Heilbrun et al. (2003) suggest that one of the challenges in forensic neuropsychology is to avoid scientific and applied fragmentation. Such fragmentation occurs when common topics of interest are considered by distinct specialties as if they were not common. Forensic neuropsychological evaluations face this challenge. It is important for neuropsychologists not to assume that traditional neuropsychological assessment procedures are appropriate for and readily transferable to forensic neuropsychological evaluations.

Important differences between traditional clinical assessments and forensic neuropsychology evaluations warrant discussion. One such distinction is that neuropsychological examinations include sections that relate neuropsychological abilities to functional legal capacities. In some cases, the neuropsychologist may describe a causal relationship between neuropsychological deficits and functional legal capacities, whereas in others situations, such as in a brain injury evaluation, neuropsychological pre-and-post comparisons may be highlighted. Because of the complexity of neurocognitive brain functioning models and the high level of technical language present in neurosciences, it is always necessary for neuropsychological assessments to translate, define, and give examples of the implications of a forensic neuropsychological assessment. Furthermore, symptom validity testing emerges as particularly important in assessing cognitive malingering in personal injury forensic cases.

Although important differences exist between forensic psychological and neuropsychological assessments, they also share many commonalities, including their fundamental bases. Heilbrun et al. (2003) highlighted the overlap between forensic mental health assessment principles and those that apply to neuropsychological assessments in forensic settings. Common principles include selecting the most appropriate model for data gathering, using multiple sources of information (self-reports, test data, third-party testimony), employing data sources with demonstrated reliability and validity, describing the limitations of one's findings, and deliberately not answering the ultimate legal question directly.

PSYCHOMETRIC APPLICATIONS

First and foremost, forensic neuropsychologists must embrace the scientific process. In the forensic arena, neuropsychologists assist either a legal decision-maker or a litigant in addressing a particular legal issue or legal standard. These legal issues can be murky. As already mentioned, the evaluation is not necessarily in the best interest of the individual being evaluated, and the examinee may have situational-based incentives that strongly influence his or her response style. In short, forensic evaluations tend to be very complex. Thus, the legal arena typically requires using a higher standard of accuracy in the assessment process, which ultimately mandates scrupulous attention to ethical and scientific processes (Zillmer, 2003a).

The forensic neuropsychologist must be well informed of the different forms of reliability and validity that apply to the individual neuropsychological assessments they employ. In the last 10 years, the U.S. Supreme Court, *in Daubert v. Merrell Dow Pharmaceuticals, Inc.* (1993) and *Kumbo Tire Co. v. Carmichael* (1999), heightened the requirements for the reliability of the methods and procedures that mental health experts use to formulate their opinions regarding a defendant's mental state at the time of the offense. *Daubert* specified that in order for the testimony of the expert to be admissible, the methods and procedures used by the expert had to be reliable. The four criteria that *Daubert* imposed are as follows: the methods and procedures used have to be testable and to have been tested; the scientific claims have been subjected to peer review and publication; the known or potential error rate of the scientific claims or generalizations has been reported; and the relevant scientific community has recognized the methods employed as generally acceptable. *Kumho Tire* (1999) extended the *Daubert* standards to testimony based on "technical and specialized knowledge," meaning that mental health experts could no longer avoid being subject to the *Daubert* standards by claiming to be "nonscientific" (Slobogin, 2003). Today, *Daubert* applies to all federal courts and has been adopted by a majority of the states.

Given these legal standards for addressing validity and reliability, neuropsychologists should not underestimate their significance in choosing the assessment tools they employ. Thus, any neuropsychological procedure in the arsenal of the forensic neuropsychologist must have been tested and peer reviewed, must have established error rates, and must have gained acceptance in the field to which it applies. Neuropsychologists must also be prepared to address the status of any neuropsychological procedure in their evaluation in reference to these criteria. If the courts are serious about enforcing the precedents set by *Daubert*, forensic neuropsychologists will need to become familiar with them (Reed, 1999).

One concept related to the area of forensic neuropsychology is that of incremental validity. In forensic neuropsychology, incremental validity carries particular importance. All else being equal, one gains predictive accuracy as one adds valid assessment tools that deliver unique information as opposed to instruments that collect overlapping or redundant information. In contrast, one should not add weaker or questionable assessment procedures to a group of stronger and scientifically established variables or predictors (Faust, 2003). Therefore, one neuropsychological assessment tool with poor reliability and/or validity may place into question the entire assessment process. Given the standards set forth by *Daubert* and *Kumho Tire*, forensic neuropsychologists should avoid the use of instruments with less than adequate validity and reliability.

TEST SELECTION IN FORENSIC NEUROPSYCHOLOGY

The neuropsychological evaluation is an objective, comprehensive assessment of a wide range of cognitive and behavioral areas of functioning. Different instruments neuropsychologists employ test the functioning of various areas of the brain. In using such tests, clinical neuropsychologists are interested principally in identifying, quantifying, and describing changes in behavior that relate to the cognitive integrity of the brain.

There is, however, no single neuropsychological test that addresses all aspects of brain functioning or answers every referral question. Therefore, it is important to select on a case-by-case basis the appropriate combination of tests that examine the parts of the brain relevant to each referral question. The instruments included in neuropsychological assessment batteries vary accordingly. Most assessments include objective measures of intelligence; academic achievement; language functioning; memory; new problem solving; abstract reasoning; constructional ability; motor speed, strength, and coordination; and personality functioning (Zillmer & Spiers, 2001). One way to approach the construction of a forensic neuropsychology battery is to include at least one instrument that tests each of the different functional areas of the brain. These are listed here hierarchically. However, it is important to note that higher cognitive functions depend to a large degree on intact lower functions, which are mentioned first: orientation (arousal), sensation and perception, attention/concentration, motor skills, verbal functions/language, visuospatial organization, memory, judgment/problem solving, and adaptive functioning.

The rules governing test selection for forensic neuropsychology clients differ from those for clinical practice or rehabilitation clients. Rather than employing a standard battery of tests, neuropsychologists often select specific tests and procedures for each exam, using information available about the patient and the legal question. There is, however, a growing controversy regarding this issue, which is reminiscent of the discussions 20 years ago in the field of neuropsychology about standard versus modified battery approaches. Those who adhere to the standard battery approach (e.g., Halstead-Reitan Neuropsychological Battery, Reitan & Wolfson, 1993) suggest that the clinician administer the same tests to all patients in all legal contexts regardless of his or her impression of an individual patient or the referral question. However, the complexity of neuropsychology and the specific legal competencies required in forensics support the strategy of using more than one battery.

For example, consider the complex task of assessing attention. Because attention is critical for learning and remains vulnerable to different traumas of the brain, most neuropsychologists would evaluate the domain of attention within the forensic context. Some patients tested are incapable of attending to their environment, whereas others may be able to attend to a learning task but only for a limited amount of time. An additional group of clients may be able to attend to a task only if there are no distractions in the environment.

Consequently, neuropsychologists divide the concept of attention into separate categories such as sustained attention (paying attention to something over a prolonged period of time) and selective attention (paying attention to more than one thing at a time). Thus, it comes as no surprise that neuropsychologists use over 40 different neuropsychological procedures for assessing attention (see Rabin, Barr, & Burton, 2005). Most essential to forensic neuropsychologists, then, is to select the most appropriate, reliable, and valid instruments and to employ a systematic, replicable, and scientific assessment approach.

PREMORBID FUNCTIONING

Premorbid functioning is the cognitive and neuropsychological status of an individual before the development of disease or the occurrence of trauma. Understanding a client's premorbid functioning is critical to developing an accurate portrayal of the decline in functioning from disease or trauma. Forensic cases, particularly those that involve compensation, require utmost precision in the determination pre- and postmorbid functioning. In order to effectively accomplish this task, neuropsychologists often consider variables such as education, occupation, and socioeconomic status. A research scientist with a doctorate, for example, may have a premorbid level of cognitive ability in the high average to superior range. After a head injury, he may function in the average range. When compared to the "norm" without regard to premorbid status, he might appear unimpaired. However, he is clearly impaired if his postinjury performance is compared to his preinjury performance. In the past, test validation studies determined whether different skills necessary for certain occupations give some individuals clinically reliable advantages on certain tests. More recently, researchers attempted to estimate premorbid levels of functioning empirically, using mathematical regression models.

FORENSIC USES AND LIMITATIONS

Symptom Validity Testing in Forensic Neuropsychology

Unlike traditional therapy clients, examinees in a forensic setting, because of the potential monetary compensation associated with personal injury or insurance claims, may have an incentive to exaggerate or distort their symptoms. For example, individuals suffering from neuropsychological dysfunction as a result of trauma frequently complain of problems in attention and memory (Zillmer & Spiers, 2001). Therefore, neuropsychologists need to assess for response bias. Psychologists have had a long and rich history of evaluating deception (e.g., polygraph procedures, assessing feigning of somatic symptoms). Using their expertise in psychometrics and test theory, neuropsychologists have generated assessment procedures to measure symptom validity.

Although symptom validity tests are commonly referred to as malingering tests, malingering is just one possible cause of invalid or biased performance. The causes of test bias on the part of the client may range from outright malingering and conscious distortion of test performance to subtler causes, such as exaggeration. Thus, the forensic neuropsychologist must also be expert in evaluating the test-taking approach and motivation of each individual. In some instances, a person's biased test-taking approach actually stems from his or her neurologic symptoms. For example, patients with right parietal-occipital stroke often have limited insight into their condition (Zillmer & Spiers, 2001).

However, recent research suggests that a substantial proportion of response bias takes the form of malingering. In forensic neuropsychological cases, the malingering rates may be as high as 25%, requiring neuropsychologists to assist the courts in evaluating the authenticity of claimed impairments (Reynolds, 1998). More recently, Slick, Tan, Strauss, and Hultsch (2004) reported that "approximately 79% of the respondents [i.e., neuropsychologists] reported using at least one specialized technique for detecting malingering" (p. 465) when performing neuropsychological evaluations involving financial compensation claims. According to the *DSM–IV*, malingering is "the intentional production of false or grossly exaggerated physical or psychological symptoms, motivated by external incentives such as avoiding military duty, avoiding work, obtaining financial compensation, evading criminal prosecution, or obtaining drugs" (American Psychiatric Association, 1994, p. 683). Thus, it has become standard procedure for neuropsychologists to assess malingering when performing independent neuropsychological evaluations (Zillmer, 2004).

Because the detection of feigned cognitive impairments has become a growing area of research, specialized tests and scales of malingering have been developed for this purpose (Hom & Denny, 2002). Rogers (1998), in fact, suggested that many malingerers remain undetected unless specific measures of malingering are used. These include, among others (see Iverson, 2003), the Structured Interview of Reported Symptoms (SIRS; Rogers, 1992), which focuses on assessing psychotic symptoms; the Validity Indictor Profile (VIP; Frederick, 1997, 2003); and the Test of Memory Malingering (TOMM; Tombaugh, 1996). Some tests of personality have built-in "validity indicators," such as the MMPI–2 (e.g., scales *L, F, K, VRIN, TRIN, F-K, $F_{B'}$*, and *FBS*; Butcher, Dahlstrom, Graham, Tellegen, & Kaemmer 1989) and the MCMI–III (e.g., scales *X, Y,* and *Z*; Millon, Davis, & Millon, 1997).

In addition to administering tests of symptom validity, neuropsychologists should pay specific attention to consistency across test results and the examinee's self-report, cultural factors, the pattern of test results, and demand characteristics of the testing situation. Because self-report data remains inherently biased, this needs to be compared with the client's history and third-party information. Wherever inconsistencies arise, efforts need to be taken to determine the truth.

Although there are several assessment instruments for malingering, the TOMM is briefly reviewed here to show how such tests can be used (also see clinical case study at the end of this chapter). The TOMM is one of the most recognizable measures for assessing memory malingering (Delain, Stafford, & Ben-Porath, 2003). Comprising two learning trials, the TOMM is a 50-item recognition test. During each learning trial, 50 simple line drawings are presented to the subject for 3 seconds each, followed by a forced-choice task in which the individual must select the previously shown stimulus from a new line drawing. The TOMM is introduced as and appears to the test taker to be a test of memory, but it is in fact much easier than it seems (Tombaugh, 2003). Scores range from 0 to 50 for each trial.

The standard cutoff score for the TOMM is 44 or below on Trial 2. Such a score should raise the suspicion of malingering, and the probability of malingering increases if the score falls below the average scores of various clinical samples. Rees, Tombaugh, & Boulay (2001) reported the results of a series of studies on the utility of the TOMM, demonstrating its exceptional performance and high levels of sensitivity and specificity. For example, in a recent study published by Teichner and Wagner (2004), the average Trial 2 TOMM score of cognitively intact elderly subjects was 49.7 out of 50, and the average score of cognitively impaired elderly subjects was 48.6. Vallabhajosula and van Gorp (2001) indicated that the TOMM, based on a positive predictive power of greater than 0.8, meets the *Daubert* standard for admissibility in judicial proceedings. The literature also suggests that although the TOMM is sensitive to malingering, it is insensitive to cognitive and neurological impairments.

Three important theoretical issues in the assessment of malingering are receiving research attention. First and foremost, malingering claims need to be validated by more than one measure of symptom validity. Multiple measures should be used and integrated with personal history information, test data, and behavioral observations. Second, it must be determined whether an individual examinee's malingering, on a memory test, for example, is limited to a specific cognitive domain or if it is found in other neuropsychology domains. In their reports, neuropsychologists should refrain from careful in generalizing malingering from one test to another. A third important issue in the field of symptom validity testing is related to whether the constructs of malingering or symptom exaggeration in the cognitive domain (e.g., memory malingering) transfer to the domain of personality testing (e.g., faking bad psychiatrically). Preliminary research with the MMPI–2 (Greiffenstein, Baker, Gola, Donders, & Miller, 2002; Larrabee, 2003; McCaffrey, O'Bryant, Ashendorf, & Fisher, 2003) and with the MCMI–III (Ruocco, 2005) suggests that the two domains do not represent one unitary construct of dissimulation. Thus, it is difficult to predict cognitive malingering from psychiatric malingering and vice versa. This lack of convergence of psychological and neuropsychological tests has also been shown on performance tests (Zillmer & Perry, 1996) and supports the practice of using different measures for assessing neuropsychological and psychiatric malingering.

Iverson (2003) offered the following practical suggestions to clinicians assessing negative response bias: Proactively "evaluate for biased responding with the same or greater effort as you evaluate for memory problems," "use a combination of approaches," and "intersperse validity indicators throughout the evaluation" (p. 168). For the interested reader, Slick, Sherman, and Iverson (1999) provide an excellent framework for classifying the malingering of neurocognitive symptoms. Furthermore, a position paper on symptom validity has recently been authored by the Policy and Planning Committee of the National Academy of Neuropsychology (2005). It reviews important neuropsychological principles of symptom validity testing and cautions that when the potential for secondary gain exists,

> neuropsychologists can, and must, utilize symptom validity tests and procedures to assist in the determination of the validity of the information and test data obtained. Determination of how to best assess the validity of the information and data obtained during neuropsychological evaluation, like all other domains assessed, rests with the examiner. (p. 426)

Ethical Issues in Forensic Neuropsychology

In principal, the ethical guidelines governing the practice of clinical psychology apply to neuropsychology as well (these are set forth in the Ethical Principles of Psychologists and Code of Conduct, American Psychological Association, 2002). For example, ethical principles that apply to traditional psychology practice and should be followed by forensic neuropsychologists include accepting referrals only within one's area of expertise and declining a referral when there is reason to believe that one would not be impartial.

However, during the rapid growth of forensic neuropsychology over the last decade, a number of unique and complex ethical issues have emerged. Although a number of special ethical guidelines for forensic psychology have been developed (these are contained in the Specialty Guidelines for Forensic Psychologists, Committee on Ethical Guidelines for Forensic Psychologists, 1991), ethical guidelines that apply specifically to forensic neuropsychological assessments are only now being formulated. As a consequence, many forensic neuropsychologists may be operating without a "magnetic north." This is particularly alarming given that the forensic process is full of pitfalls and loopholes. Clinicians who are not prepared to practice in the forensic context may be especially at risk for ethical misconduct (Morgan & Bush, 2005).

Therefore, neuropsychologists conducting forensic evaluations need to acquire the specific skills necessary to successfully navigate the ethical dilemmas that commonly arise. The ethical issues in forensic neuropsychology are dynamic and evolving and include conflict of interest or dual roles, third-party observation during a forensic neuropsychological evaluation, and releasing raw data resulting from a forensic neuropsychological exam. In order to be prepared, forensic neuropsychologists need to acquire specialty education in the practice of forensic neuropsychology as well as learn the relevant court processes and governing law. In addition, forensic neuropsychologists must abandon the advocacy role they otherwise might have held in traditional practice and adopt a neutral role by letting the evidence collected through testing speak for itself as much as is possible.

Dual Roles

In forensic neuropsychology, it is important to be absolutely clear on what role the forensic neuropsychologist will have in each case. Specifically, the forensic neuropsychologist should enter the business relationship fully understanding whether he or she will serve as a consultant, an attorney-requested evaluator (i.e., expert), or a court-appointed evaluator. The process of seeking specialized help typically is initiated when a lawyer is confronted with a scientific or clinical issue that is outside of his or her expertise (Sageman, 2003). Taking the role of an expert, a neuropsychologist would evaluate the client in order to form an opinion about a mental health matter, such as the causative relationship between a brain injury and the individual's cognitive functioning. The forensic neuropsychologist's role here is to seek the truth rather than be an advocate for the client. Alternatively, forensic neuropsychologists might serve as consultants. Here the practicing neuropsychologist may offer strategic advise to the hiring lawyer on a legal case. In these scenarios, the neuropsychology consultant may never see the plaintiff. As a consultant, a neuropsychologist may be asked to testify about a previous but theoretically related clinical case in order to highlight a specific point relevant to the case at hand. If this was the situation, the neuropsychologist would be able to respond only as a fact witness, not as an expert who grants opinion testimony. The wearing of two hats as a fact witness and expert witness, for example, or as a consultant and expert, is ethically problematic and clinically imprudent. Thus, forensic neuropsychologists must avoid assuming more than one role.

Often the roles assumed by a forensic neuropsychologist become blurred and come into conflict with each other. This is why it is best to clarify with the attorney from the start what role the forensic neuropsychologist is being hired to play. Furthermore, the forensic neuropsychologist needs to remember that it is the attorney's role to pursue the legal matter with bias toward the client. It is important to let the attorney do his or her work and understand that there is always the potential to be in conflict with the attorney's conceptualization of the case.

Neuropsychologists practicing in the forensic area must also be aware of the differences between a clinical and a forensic evaluation. Neuropsychologists venturing into the legal arena are simply guests in someone else's house (Sageman, 2003). The attorneys and courts operate on established rules and use the contributions of neuropsychologists as these rules dictate. Within the overall scope of a legal case, the neuropsychologist plays only a small (but potentially important) role in the process of litigation. It is necessary to remember that neuropsychologists never win or lose cases; lawyers do.

Crown, Fingerhut, and Lowenthal (2003) offer five comments that might help a neuro-psychologist "avoid conflict of interest that may lead to rather unanticipated and unpleasant results" (p. 420). First, courts almost never disqualify experts that have been retained by legal counsel. Second, "experts enjoy a unique independence and objectivity in the American legal system" (p. 388). What this means is that the forensic neuropsychology expert does not owe the attorney any loyalty. The forensic neuropsychologist is being asked to assist the trier of fact to understand the evidence or to determine a fact at issue. The pressure to "find" supporting evidence is on the lawyer, not the forensic neuropsychologist. Third, clinical treatment or assessment of a client "transforms the expert into a veritable eyewitness, of sorts." Fourth, the expert must be able to offer an independent opinion, which may be favorable, unfavorable, or neither, regarding a legal matter. Attorneys must use this information to the best of their ability to find a realistic solution to the case. And fifth, privileged communications in the expert-client relationship are diminished.

Third-Party Observation

Third-party observation, which includes being videotaped or audiotaped during a foren-sic neuropsychology evaluation or having an observer present, has been a cause of concern for many clinicians. Usually, opposing attorneys request the third-party observation. Most clinicians feel uncomfortable with the idea of being observed, as the observation period could last many hours and every move could be scrutinized. Most importantly, there are now a significant number of empirical findings indicating that third-party observation can have a detrimental effect on the performance of the examinee. In addition, as forensic neuropsychologists are quick to point out, the testing procedures were not normed with observers present.

The area of social facilitation has recently earned notable attention. Social facilitation research demonstrates that an observer (video camera, audio recorder, or third person) improves performance on easy or well-learned tasks and negatively affects performance on complex or novel tasks (Lynch, 2004). In addition, McCaffrey (2004) points out that although forensic neuropsychologists highlight the potentially detrimental impact of a third party on an examiner, the actual effect of having a third party present has not been studied. In any case, despite the opposition of neuropsychologists to third-party observation, legal literature provided by some state courts indicates that requests for such observation are typically granted.

Interestingly, some neuropsychologists do not object to the presence of an observer dur-ing the clinical interview and even the administration of neuropsychological procedures. On the other hand, others will flat out refuse to have any type of third-party observers present during the examination and risk losing the forensic referral for the evaluation. This has led to some confusion in the legal profession as to the willingness of neuropsy-chologists to be observed.

The case made for observation is almost always related to a forensic examination. In a clinical evaluation, there is a doctor-patient relationship, and inherent in this relationship are concerns about the welfare of the patient and a need for confidentiality. For example, it would be found unacceptable to have an examinee's spouse or therapist present during a clinical neuropsychological evaluation. In a forensic assessment, however, the person being evaluated does not benefit from the existence of a doctor-patient relationship, and the neuropsychologist is typically being hired by an attorney or another third party (e.g., an insurance company). Consequently, the neuropsychologist is required to disclose to the examinee the difference in confidentiality between a forensic and a clinical evaluation (Blase, 2003).

Recently, attention has been paid to the distinction between the presence of a trained observer (e.g., a supervisor or neuropsychology trainee) and the presence of an untrained one. Most neuropsychologists agree that the presence of a trained third-party observer during a forensic evaluation is acceptable and appropriate (Sewick, Blase, & Besecker, 1998). Some suggest that the presence of a trained third-party observer may improve the examinee's performance (Blase, 2003). Here arises an ethical dilemma regarding the appropriate conditions for performing a forensic neuropsychological examination. It is likely that this will continue to be an ethical dilemma for the profession. A further complication is that the neuropsychologist has an obligation to provide opposing counsel with basic information and documentation in anticipation that the findings of the examination will be challenged.

Releasing Test Data

The release of test data continues to be a complicated ethical issue in forensic neuropsychology and mystifies many clinicians and attorneys alike. Requests for raw data may come in the form of a subpoena, court order, a request by an attorney, or a request by another neuropsychologist. In short, neuropsychologists are under pressure to turn over raw data, including tests scores, forms, documents, and test materials, to a third party. Most neuropsychologists are aware that such information should only be made available to another licensed clinical neuropsychologist unless they are court-ordered to release it to someone else. Licensed colleagues represent an exception, as they must follow the guidelines of confidentiality proposed under HIPPA and the APA ethics code. The APA ethics code (9.04, Release of Test Data, 2002) indicates that psychologists must make reasonable efforts to maintain the integrity and security of test materials and other assessment techniques consistent with law and contractual obligations and in a manner that permits adherence to the ethics code. However, given the adversarial nature of the forensic arena and the fact that the documentation would be scrutinized by the opposing expert, many neuropsychologists remain apprehensive about turning over raw data. (National Academy of Neuropsychology, 2003).

Rapp and Ferber (2003) describe how, as part of the discovery process, attorneys require neuropsychologist to turn over everything they used relating to the evaluation and all other materials used to form their opinions (p. 339). But it makes most sense, from an ethical perspective, to turn the data over only to another licensed psychologist rather than leave the information in the attorney's files. Ethical principles attempt to balance the rights of the individual (in this case the right to privacy) against the rights of a group or other individuals to have access to legal documents that may be used against that person in court. Once the data are turned over to an attorney, the forensic neuropsychologist has essentially lost control of the data and any means of maintaining their security, normally a major professional concern. Thus, it would be ethically prudent for forensic neuropsychologists to resist the often-tempting requests by lawyers to have the raw data forwarded to a legal party (for the sake of "expediency"). As Rapp and Farber state, "What we have is a major failure of communication between two professions having very different procedures, ethical codes, codes of conduct, and rules of practice" (p. 341). In a nutshell, the ethical dilemma lies between the legal culture, which allows for full disclosure, and neuropsychology, which is concerned with the protection of privacy. In addition, test publishers and psychologists have an interest in preventing the public from gaining general access to specific test forms and questions that rely on their novelty for their effectiveness.

Most attorneys are not aware of the specific ethical guidelines that psychologists use and are often surprised to learn about them. In forensic neuropsychological practice, the best advice is to inform attorneys up front about the restrictions on disseminating raw data to opposing experts and legal counsel (National Academy of Neuropsychology, 2000). When approached from that perspective, these issues do not become an obstacle to the expert-lawyer relationship.

In summary, ethics in forensic neuropsychology is an important and expanding field. Developing a sensitivity to the ethical issues and difficult ethical situations in forensic neuropsychology, in addition to applying the established ethical codes to the forensic neuropsychological process, is a necessary first step (Bush & Drexler, 2002).

CASE EXAMPLES

Three brief cases are here presented. They are intended to illuminate different aspects of forensic neuropsychology. They represent an attempt to provide the clinician with contextual information as well as examples of how to use neuropsychological procedures. They are not, however, meant to be viewed as a comprehensive treatment of the topic. (*Note:* They are written from the point of view of the examining neuropsychologist, in each case E.A. Zillmer.)

Case 1: Malingering

Ms. A. was a 61-year-old woman who had been hospitalized for a viral infection of the brain 4 years prior to the evaluation. Since that time she has complained of various cognitive problems, including poor concentration, poor memory, fatigue, and "difficulties reading English." Her medical records report that she was making "an excellent recovery." A neurologist at the hospital wrote that Ms. A.'s "prognosis is quite good and the elements of cognitive impairment are largely resolved." A recent EEG revealed a normal recording. Similarly, her recent MRI was "unremarkable."

Ms. A. claimed a disability related to her illness and insisted that she has been unable to work for the last 2 years. She complained that her "level of concentration" has diminished, that she "can't concentrate"and is "getting older," and that she "has declined" in terms of her cognitive abilities. Ms. A. reported that her cognitive problems coincided with her medical diagnosis.

Throughout the exam, Ms. A. stated that she was not excited about being evaluated by an "expert." When asked to clarify, she responded that, because she worked in the medical field as a nurse supervisor, she was suspicious of any Independent Medical Evaluation (IME). I tried to reassure her that I was providing an independent opinion and that I routinely conduct similar types of evaluations. Nevertheless, she was rather uptight about the procedures and generally needed encouragement.

Because of the potential for secondary gain, several measures of test response style/symptom validity were administered. Ms. A.'s score on Trial 2 of the TOMM was 26 out of the 50 possible, significantly lower than the cutoff and, in fact, near chance (i.e., about "fifty-fifty"). This suggested that the patient may have actively selected against the correct responses, providing deceptive, nonoptimal answers. In fact, her test score was lower than those of cognitively intact elderly adults, cognitively impaired adults, and adults with mild dementia. In light of this result, I decided that Ms. A.'s performance on this measure was related to nonoptimal performance or malingering. This was also consistent with an additional brief measure of test validity, the Memorization of 15 Items Test. On this test, Ms. A. copied only 8 of 15 simple items from memory. She performed similarly poorly on the VIP, and she demonstrated an inconsistent pattern of performance on neuropsychological tests. The plaintiff's neuropsychology expert neglected to administer any tests of symptom validity.

The results of Ms. A.'s tests indicated the presence of malingering, poor effort, and a response bias on some of the tests that were administered. I believed that these behaviors were not psychiatric in nature (e.g., related to conversion disorder or factitious disorder) but were under Ms. A.'s volitional control and possibly related to a desire for secondary gain. Slick et al. (1999) provided a framework for classifying the malingering of neurocognitive symptoms. According to the Slick et al. model, Ms. A.'s presentation was most consistent with Definite Malingering Neurocognitive Dysfunction, as the data met the following criteria: (a) There existed a substantial external incentive (i.e., a disability pension); (b) the findings included a definite negative response bias (i.e., a positive test performance on a well-validated psychometric test of malingering consistent with feigning), a discrepancy between test data and known patterns of brain functioning, and a discrepancy between tests data and observed behavior; and (c) her behaviors were not fully accounted for by psychiatric, neurological, or developmental factors.

Case 2: Head Injury

Mr. B. was a 43-year-old man who had been struck by a moving vehicle. He reported, "We were driving home in the evening returning from friends. My wife was approaching a T-intersection. Out of nowhere a small car appeared at a high speed blowing through a stoplight." Mr. B., who was a restrained front-seat passenger, suffered a whiplash trauma resulting in a head injury and cervical sprain. The patient reported "snapping my head" but remembers little of what happened to him after the accident. He described his mental status after the accident as "groggy." The impact was substantial enough to have caused the automobile's air bag to be deployed. Mr. B.'s car was "totaled" as a result of this accident. Mr. B. reported having been bruised from the air bag. An MRI of the cervical spine revealed "a hemangioma in the C7 vertebral body" and "mild central disc bulge of C 3/4 and C 4/5." An MRI of the brain revealed no significant abnormality. Prior to the accident, Mr. B. was employed as a senior designer at a large engineering consulting firm and was primarily responsible for restoration projects that required structural engineering.

Mr. B. reported several problems regarding his inability to function cognitively, including fatigue, memory troubles, and concentration problems. "I always had this wonderful ability to focus on what I am doing and ignore everything else." Achieving sustained attention as well as selective attention was "harder to do." Emotionally, Mr. B. felt as if he had "a whole new personality." Mrs. B. shared with me that it was not easy to live with him anymore. She indicated that since the accident her husband snapped at everything, had become more impulsive, and at times was unbearable. Before the accident, her husband never was "one to get too depressed about things" and "was very even-keeled." After the accident, he had become a different type of person than the one she had married.

Furthermore, Mr. B. complained of experiencing changes in his sleep patterns. He reported, "I used to sleep like a dead man" and "I would fall asleep in seconds. When I woke up, I was so refreshed." Since the accident, he has been evaluated by a sleep specialist and has spent 2 nights in a sleep disorder laboratory. Subsequently, he was diagnosed with obstructive sleep apnea.

Mr. B.'s performance on neuropsychological testing was variable, with scores ranging from low average to very superior. The areas of reduced cognitive capacity included immediate memory functioning, working memory, and sustained and selective attention.

The results indicated a decreased degree of efficiency in managing his work duties. Because Mr. B. functioned at a high level in the past, still maintained a high degree of functioning in areas that require visual-perceptual processing, and exhibited above-average compensation skills, he attempted to use his cognitive strengths to circumvent his newly developed weaknesses. His strength's included the ability to navigate tasks that mandated working with multiple information sources, the ability to work with facts in his head, and the ability to deal with time constraints. Nevertheless, on tasks that required complex problem solving, he encountered difficulties, including cognitive slowing.

Overall, Mr. B.'s presentation on this neuropsychological evaluation demonstrated a pattern of performance consistent with a decline from a previously higher level of cognitive functioning. This type of test score profile has often been found in individuals who suffered from a head injury. The crystallized areas of neurocognitive functioning were essentially intact (i.e., those that are overlearned and resistant to traumatic brain injury), but decreases occurred in the areas of fluid intelligence (i.e., those dependent on new learning), which remain more susceptible to brain trauma. Because of Mr. B.'s average verbal skills and his good perceptual organization abilities, he was perceived to be functioning at a higher level than he really was.

After the accident, Mr. B. was diagnosed with severe sleep apnea. He and Mrs. B. indicated that his sleep problems were only apparent after the accident. Mr. B. received CPAP (nasal continuous positive airway pressure) treatment, which involves use of a mask that "forces" air through the nose or mouth during sleep. As typically found, his disordered breathing during sleep was related to the brain failing to send the necessary signals to the brain. This reflected abnormalities in the brain stem that manifested themselves only during sleep. A serious disorder, sleep apnea is caused by a complex interaction of physiological and anatomical factors and is associated with severe O_2 desaturation. There has been little research suggesting that a motor vehicle accident resulting in a closed head injury can directly induce sleep apnea. Therefore, it was difficult to assess the onset of sleep apnea in this case. In addition, many patients suffering from sleep apnea report memory and concentration difficulties, including significant changes in adaptive functioning (Barth, Findley, Zillmer, Gideon, & Surrat, 1993). Since the cognitive deficits of sleep apnea and those of a concussion are very similar, it was difficult to establish whether the accident or the apnea was the cause of Mr. B.'s overall cognitive decline.

Case 3: Somatization Disorder

Ms. C. is a 26-year-old female who was a restrained driver in a two-vehicle automobile accident. Ms. C. reported that she was struck by another automobile on the passenger side while passing through an intersection. After the accident, Ms. C. went to work and completed the workday but took herself to the emergency room that evening. Her CT scan, multiple MRI scans, and an angiogram of the neck vessels were all normal. A brainstem auditory evoked potential evaluation was "normal," and "visual evoked potentials absolute values appear normal." There was no loss of consciousness, no evidence of posttraumatic amnesia, and no evidence of lesions on CT, MRI, or angiography of the brain.

Ms. C.'s medical history included a gallbladder removal for recurrent "bouts [of] ... abdominal pain." She complained of nausea, a concussion, and dilated eyes. She was on several medications at the time of testing, including Effexor, Trazadone, Neurontin, and an unspecified medication that she reported taking for insomnia. She also complained of vestibular problems that manifested themselves as a feeling of dizziness; back pain; problems with her right foot, which, she reported, "turns inward"; and a feeling of "electricity" and burning pain in her extremities. She arrived with a cane and reported having to rely on it. She also complained of being unable to handle crowds and attempted to avoid places that have many people. Ms. C. also reported that she was in counseling but that she did not have the financial resources to pay for the weekly sessions.

Overall, Ms. C. performed within the average to low average range on the majority of the cognitive tests. Her testing profile was consistent with a normal ability to engage in concentration and attention, perceptual organization, and verbal reasoning. She demonstrated low average ability on tasks involving brief attention to auditory verbal information and tests requiring complex new problem solving. Her premorbid functioning, including her job history and school history, were entirely consistent with someone who has performed in the average to low average range of cognitive functioning.

The Minnesota Multiphasic Personality Inventory (MMPI–2) was administered to Ms. C. on three different occasions. Although the MMPI is not used in the diagnosis of brain damage per se, approximately 60% of neuropsychologists use the MMPI as part of a neuropsychological evaluation, often to see if other psychological factors are contributing to the patient's presentation.

The three MMPI profiles obtained were almost identical, but I limited my interpretations to the most recent one obtained, since it was the closest in proximity to her actual adaptive psychological functioning when I examined her. Ms. C. obtained a valid profile. Several of the clinical scales were elevated to degrees that suggest the presence of psychopathology and a chronic maladjustment to life. For example, Ms. C.'s highest clinical elevation was on scale 3 (Hysteria), which was at $T = 104$. In addition, her MMPI profile revealed that two other scales were markedly elevated, scale 2 (Depression, $T = 96$) and scale 1 (Hypochondriasis, $T = 82$). Typically, patients with elevations on these scales tend to develop physical complaints under stress. In these patients, little if any medical cause can be found to account for their somatic complaints. In addition, similar patients tend to have poor pain tolerance and frequently report a variety of physical complaints, including headaches and chest pain. Often the presentation of such physical complaints is quite dramatic. These patients have an increased desire for attention and emotional support, which leads them to visit the doctor frequently ("doctor shopping" or ER visits) and even receive medical procedures (e.g., X-rays or even unnecessary surgery). The tendency to worry excessively about one's health is known as a histrionic style, which in Ms. C.'s case appeared so ingrained that she was not entirely aware of it.

Ms. C's psychological test data, medical history, and clinical presentation indicated a constellation of symptoms all of which were of clinical significance. They were consistent with a psychological disorder known as "somatization disorder" (*DSM–IV* Code 300.81), which falls under a group of psychiatric disorders known as "somatoform disorders." Turmoil, dissatisfaction, and a general inability to function in life are characteristic of such a disorder. These disorders are thought to be chronic in nature. Thus it was my clinical opinion that Ms. C. fit the diagnosis of somatization disorder, which begins before age 30 and is characterized by a combination of pain and pseudoneurological symptoms. Impaired coordination and problems with balance are common pseudoneurological symptoms. In addition, Ms. C. complained of symptoms—including burning in her extremities, foot inversion, back pain, vertigo, palpitations, acne, difficulty swallowing, and difficulty walking—that are not commonly seen in subjects who have had a concussion. Impairment in social and occupational functioning is a likely result of a concussion but cannot be completely explained by a general medical condition. The complaints of individuals with somatization disorder often lead to frequent radiological examination (i.e., X-ray and MRI) and can even result in "abdominal surgery that in retrospect was unnecessary" (American Psychiatric Association, 1994, p. 446). The diagnostic criteria also include a pseudoneurological presentation and may include, as in Ms. C's case, conversion symptoms such as impaired coordination or balance. On videotape surveillance, Ms. C appeared to be able to ambulate just fine.

Several physicians had been puzzled by her medical presentation and had considered anxiety or a functional etiology as a possible explanation. For example, Dr. X. was mystified by Ms. C.'s presentation of multiple and vague medical complaints: "I am in a dilemma as to the etiology for her symptoms. When one tries to put together all of her symptoms into one diagnosis, I am not able to so. It seems to me that they were on a functional basis." Dr. Y.'s records revealed that the attending physician indicated that there was "no one injury that could explain her picture." And according to Dr. Z., Ms. C. complained to him that a flare of acne might have been related to the automobile accident, something he previously dismissed. A report from the Department of Otorhinolaryngology concluded, "No indications supportive of either direct peripheral or central vestibular system involvement [are] noted. Most probably her ongoing complaints are a combination of migraine, related disequilibrium, and phobic avoidance/anxiety with panic."

Thus, it was my opinion that her consistent presentation of vague and specific physical symptoms, which she attributed to a head injury, were related to a psychological condition known as "somatization disorder". Given her preoccupation with medical complaints prior to the accident, it was likely that this condition preexisted the accident.

CONCLUSION

As a scientist-practitioner, the forensic expert must keep abreast of new scientific techniques and research in the field of neuropsychology. Research in forensic neuropsychology remains important because it provides the practicing clinician with scientific data as well as with a scientific process that allows the clinician to pursue his or her work with increased precision. Future trends in forensic neuropsychology will include the development of specialized forensic neuropsychological assessment procedures, allowing forensic neuropsychologists not to have to rely on tests developed for clinical purposes. In addition, neurocognitive models that account for the cognitive characteristics of criminal offenders, including perspective taking and impulsivity, continue to emerge on the horizon. Research into forensic neuropsychology has the potential to influence policy on specific aspects of the law (e.g., the role of mental retardation in sentencing) and to provide refined approaches to treating offenders. Finally, the area of ethics in forensic neuropsychology and the scientific and professional integrity of practitioners will undoubtedly shape the future practice of forensic neuropsychology.

Forensic neuropsychological assessment is an emerging clinical and research field in which psychological expertise can be extremely valuable. As a result, clinical neuropsychologists have become increasingly involved in this field. Each legal case is different and has a circumscribed beginning and an end. The hours are good, as is the compensation. And it seems that in the forensic arena, neuropsychology matters. Indeed, this surely accounts for the growing sophistication of forensic neuropsychology.

REFERENCES

American Psychiatric Association. (1994). *Diagnostic and statistical manual of mental disorders* (4th ed.). Washington, DC: Author.

American Psychological Association. (2002). Ethical principles of psychologists and codes of conduct. *American Psychologist, 52,* 1060–1073.

Barth, J.T., Findley, L.J., Zillmer, E.A., Gideon, D.A., & Surrat, P.M. (1993). Obstructive sleep apnea, hypoxemia, and personality functioning: Implications for medical psychotherapy assessment. *Advances in Medical Psychotherapy, 6,* 29–36.

Blase, J.J. (2003). Third-part presence during evaluations. In A. M. Horton & L.C. Hartlage (Eds.) *Handbook of forensic neuropsychology.* New York: Springer.

Bush, S.S., & Drexler, M.L. (2002). *Ethical issues in clinical neuropsychology.* Lisse, NetherLands: Swets & Zeitlinger.

Butcher, J., Dahlstrom, W., Graham, J., Tellegen, A., & Kaemmer, B. (1989). *MMPI-2: Manual for administration and scoring.* Minneapolis: University of Minnesota Press.

Committee on Ethical Guidelines for Forensic Psychologists (1991). Specialty guidelines for forensic psychologists. *Law and Human Behavior, 15,* 655–665.

Crown, B.M., Fingerhut, H.S., & Lowenthal, S.J. (2003). Conflicts of interest and other pitfalls for the expert witness. In A.M. Horton & L.C. Hartlage (Eds.) *Handbook of forensic neuropsychology.* New York: Springer.

Daubert v Merrell Dow Pharmaceuticals, Inc., 509 U.S. 579 (1993).

Delain, S.L., Stafford, K.P., & Ben-Porath, Y.S. (2003). Use of the TOMM in a criminal court forensic assessment setting. *Assessment, 10,* 370–382.

Faust, D. (2003). Holistic thinking is not the whole story: Alternative or adjunct approaches for increasing the accuracy of legal evaluation. *Assessment, 10,* 428–441.

Frederick, R. (1997). *Validity Indictor Profile manual.* Minnetonka, MN:NSC Assessments.

Frederick, R.I. (2003). Review of the Validity Indicator Profile. *Journal of Forensic Neuropsychology, 2(3-4),* 125–146.

Greiffenstein, M.F., Baker, W.J., Gola, T., Donders, J., & Miller, L. (2002). The fake bad scale in atypical and severe closed head injury litigants. *Journal of Clinical Psychology, 58,* 1591–1600.

Heilbronner, R.L. (2005). *Forensic neuropsychology casebook.* New York: Guilford Press.

Heilbrun, K. (2001). *Principles of forensic mental health assessment.* New York: Plenum.

Heilbrun, K., Goldstein, N.E.S., & Redding, R.E. (2005). *Juvenile delinquency: Prevention, assessment, and intervention.* Oxford: Oxford University Press.

Heilbrun, K., Marczyk, G., DeMatteo, D., Zillmer, E., Harris, J., & Jennings, T. (2003). Principles of forensic mental health assessment: Implications for neuropsychological assessment in forensic contexts. *Assessment, 10,* 329–343.

Hom, J., & Denney, R. (Eds.). (2002). Detection of response bias in forensic neuropsychology. Binghamton, NY: Haworth Medical Press.

Iverson, G.I. (2003). Detecting malingering in civil forensic evaluations. In A.M. Horton & L.C. Hartlage (Eds.) *Handbook of forensic neuropsychology.* New York: Springer.

Kassin, S., & Neumann, K. (1997). On the power of confession evidence: An experimental test of the fundamental difference hypothesis. *Law and Human Behavior, 21,* 469–484.

Kumho Tire Co. v. Carmichael, 526 U.S. 137 (1999).

Larabee, G.J. (2005). *Forensic neuropsychology: A scientific approach.* New York: Oxford University Press.

Larrabee, G.J. (2003). Detection of malingering using atypical performance patterns on standard neuropsychological tests. *The Clinical Neuropsychologist, 17,* 410–425.

Lynch, J.K. (2004). Effect of a third party observer on neuropsychological test performance following closed head injury. *Journal of Forensic Neuropsychology, 4(2),* 17–25.

McCaffrey, R.J. (2004). Some final thoughts and comments regarding the issues of third party observers. *Journal of Forensic Neuropsychology, 4(2),* 83–91.

McCaffrey, R.J., O'Bryant, S.E., Ashendorf, L., & Fisher, J.M. (2003). Correlations among the TOMM, Rey-15, and MMPI-2 validity scales in a sample of TBI litigants. *Journal of Forensic Neuropsychology, 3(3),* 45–54.

Millon, T., Davis, R., & Millon, C. (1997). *Manual for the MCMI-III* (2nd ed.). Minneapolis, MN: National Computer Systems.

Miranda v. Arizona, 384 U.S. 436 (1966).

Morgan, J.E., & Bush, S.S. (2005). Anticipating forensic involvement: Ethical consideration for clinical neuro-psychologists. *Journal of Forensic Neuropsychology, 4*(3), 11–20.

National Academy of Neuropsychology. (2000). Presence of third party observers during neuropsychological testing [official statement]. *Archives of Clinical Neuropsychology, 15(5),* 379–380.

National Academy of Neuropsychology. (2003). Test security [Position paper]. *Archives of Clinical Neuropsychology, 15,* 383–386.

National Academy of Neuropsychology. (2005). Symptom validity assessment: Practice issues and medical necessity [Position paper]. *Archives of Clinical Neuropsychology, 20,* 419–426.

Oberlander, L.B., Goldstein, N.E., & Ho, C.N. (2001). Preadolescent adjudicative competence: Methodological considerations and recommendations for practice standards. *Behavioral Sciences and the Law, 19,* 545–563.

Rabin, L.A., Barr, W.B., & Burton, L.A. (2005). Assessment practices of clinical neuropsychologists in the United States and Canada: A survey of INS, NAN, and APA Division 40 members. *Archives of Clinical Neuropsychology, 20,* 33–65.

Rapp, D.L., & Ferber, P.S. (2003). To release, or not to release raw test data, that is the question. In A.M. Horton & L.C. Hartlage (Eds.), *Handbook of forensic neuropsychology.* New York: Springer.

Reed, J. (1999). Current status of the admissibility of expert testimony after *Daubert* and *Joiner. Journal of Forensic Neuropsychology, 1*(1), 49–69.

Rees, L.M., Tombaugh, T.N., & Boulay, L. (2001). Depression and the Test of Memory Malingering. *Archives of Clinical Neuropsychology, 16,* 501–506.

Reitan, R.M., & Wolfson, D. (1993). *The Halstead-Reitan neuropsychological test battery: Theory and clinical interpretation* (2nd ed.). Tucson, AZ: Neuropsychology Press.

Reynolds, C. (1998). *Detection of malingering during head injury litigation.* New York: Plenum Press.

Rogers, R. (1992). *Structured Interview of Reported Symptoms.* Odessa, FL: Psychological Assessment Resources.

Rogers, R. (1998). Assessment of malingering on psychological measures. In G.P. Koocher, J.C. Norcross, & S.S. Hill III (Eds.), *Psychologists' desk reference,* (pp. 53–57). New York: Oxford University Press.

Ruocco, A.C. (2005). *Neuropsychological and psychiatric malingering: One and the same?* Unpublished master's thesis, Drexel University, philadelphia.

Sageman, M. (2003). Three types of skills for effective forensic psychological assessments. *Assessment, 10,* 321–328.

Sewick, B.G., Blase, J.J., & Besecker, T. (1999, November). *Third-part observers in neuropsychological testing: A 1999 survey of NAN members.* Paper presented at the 19th Annual Meeting of the National Academy of Neuropsychology, San Antonio, TX.

Slick, D.J., Sherman, E.M.S., & Iverson, G.L. (1999). Diagnostic criteria for malingering neurocognitive dysfunction: Proposed standards for clinical practice and research. *The Clinical Neuropsychologist, 13,* 545–561.

Slick, D.J., Tan, J.E., Strauss, E.H., & Hultsch, D.F. (2004). Detecting malingering: A survey of experts' practices. *Archives of Clinical Neuropsychology, 19,* 465–473.

Slobogin, C. (2003). Pragmatic forensic psychology: A means of "scientizing" expert testimony from mental health professionals? *Psychology, Public Policy, and Law, 9,* 275–300.

Teichner, G., & Wagner, M.T. (2004). The Test of Memory Malingering (TOMM): Normative data from cogni-tively intact, cognitively impaired, and elderly patients with dementia. *Archives of Clinical Neuropsychology, 19*(3), 455–464.

Tombaugh, T.N. (1996). *Test of Memory Malingering (TOMM)* New York: Multi-Health Systems.

Tombaugh, T. (2003). The Test of Memory Malingering (TOMM) in forensic psychology. *Journal of Forensic Neuropsychology, 2*(3-4), 69–96.

Vallabhajosula, B., & van Gorp, W.G. (2001). Post-*Daubert* admissibility of scientific evidence on malingering of cognitive deficits. *Journal of the American Academy of Psychiatry and the Law, 29,* 207–215.

Zillmer, E.A. (2003a). Introduction to special issue on psychological and neuropsychological assessment in the forensic arena: Art or science? *Assessment, 10,* 318–320.

Zillmer, E.A. (2003b). Sports-related concussions. *Applied Neuropsychology, 10*(1), 1–3.

Zillmer, E.A. (2004). National Academy of Neuropsychology: President's address: The future of neuro-psychology. *Archives of Clinical Neuropsychology, 19,* 713–724.

Zillmer, E.A. (2005). *[Review of Handbook of forensic neuropsychology]. Journal of Forensic Neuropsychology, 4*(3).

Zillmer, E.A., & Perry, W. (1996). Cognitive-neuropsychological abilities and related psychological distur-bance: A factor model of neuropsychological, Rorschach, and MMPI indices. *Assessment, 3,* 209–224.

Zillmer, E.A., & Spiers, M.V. (2001). *Principles of neuropsychology.* Belmont, CA: Wadsworth.

The Achenbach System of Empirically Based Assessment

Thomas M. Achenbach

University of Vermont

Leslie A. Rescorla

Bryn Mawr College

BASIC DESCRIPTION

The Achenbach System of Empirically Based Assessment (ASEBA) includes standardized instruments for assessing behavioral, emotional, and social problems and adaptive functioning from the age of $1\frac{1}{2}$ to 90+ years. The purpose of the instruments is to assess a broad spectrum of problems and adaptive functioning, as seen from multiple perspectives, including self-reports and reports by people who know the person being assessed, designated as "collaterals." The instruments include quantified items that are scored on scales for empirically based syndromes and on *DSM*-oriented scales. In addition to quantified items and scales, the instruments also obtain clinically useful, individualized qualitative information.

If it is suspected that a respondent may have difficulty completing a form because of poor reading skills or for other reasons, the form can be administered orally by an interviewer who need not be a trained clinician. In such cases, the following procedure is recommended in order to maintain standardization: The interviewer hands the respondent a copy of the form while keeping a second copy. The interviewer then says, "I'll read you the questions on this form and I'll write down your answers." Respondents whose reading skills are adequate typically start answering the questions without waiting for them to be read. However, even for respondents who need to have the questions read by the

Please print CHILD BEHAVIOR CHECKLIST FOR AGES 6-18

For office use only
ID #

CHILD'S FULL NAME — First: **Wayne** Middle: **Andrew** Last: **Webster**

CHILD'S GENDER: ☒ Boy ☐ Girl CHILD'S AGE: **15** CHILD'S ETHNIC GROUP OR RACE: **African Amer. + white**

PARENTS' USUAL TYPE OF WORK, even if not working now. (Please be specific — for example, auto mechanic, high school teacher, homemaker, laborer, lathe operator, shoe salesman, army sergeant.)

FATHER'S TYPE OF WORK: **computer consultant**
MOTHER'S TYPE OF WORK: **computer programmer**

TODAY'S DATE: Mo. **04** Date **04** Yr. **01**   CHILD'S BIRTHDATE: Mo. **03** Date **23** Yr. **86**

THIS FORM FILLED OUT BY: (print your full name) **Alice N. Webster**

GRADE IN SCHOOL: **9**   NOT ATTENDING SCHOOL ☐

Please fill out this form to reflect *your* view of the child's behavior even if other people might not agree. Feel free to print additional comments beside each item and in the space provided on page 2. *Be sure to answer all items.*

Your gender: ☐ Male ☒ Female
Your relation to the child:
☒ Biological Parent ☐ Step Parent ☐ Grandparent
☐ Adoptive Parent ☐ Foster Parent ☐ Other (specify)

I. Please list the sports your child most likes to take part in. For example: swimming, baseball, skating, skate boarding, bike riding, fishing, etc.
☐ None

	Compared to others of the same age, about how much time does he/she spend in each?				Compared to others of the same age, how well does he/she do each one?			
	Less Than Average	Average	More Than Average	Don't Know	Below Average	Average	Above Average	Don't Know
a. **Basketball**	☐	☒	☐	☐	☐	☒	☐	☐
b. _____	☐	☐	☐	☐	☐	☐	☐	☐
c. _____	☐	☐	☐	☐	☐	☐	☐	☐

II. Please list your child's favorite hobbies, activities, and games, other than sports. For example: stamps, dolls, books, piano, crafts, cars, computers, singing, etc. (Do *not* include listening to radio or TV.)
☐ None

	Compared to others of the same age, about how much time does he/she spend in each?				Compared to others of the same age, how well does he/she do each one?			
	Less Than Average	Average	More Than Average	Don't Know	Below Average	Average	Above Average	Don't Know
a. **computers**	☐	☐	☒	☐	☐	☐	☒	☐
b. _____	☐	☐	☐	☐	☐	☐	☐	☐
c. _____	☐	☐	☐	☐	☐	☐	☐	☐

III. Please list any organizations, clubs, teams, or groups your child belongs to.
☒ None

	Compared to others of the same age, how active is he/she in each?			
	Less Active	Average	More Active	Don't Know
a. _____	☐	☐	☐	☐
b. _____	☐	☐	☐	☐
c. _____	☐	☐	☐	☐

IV. Please list any jobs or chores your child has. For example: paper route, babysitting, making bed, working in store, etc. (Include both paid and unpaid jobs and chores.)
☐ None

	Compared to others of the same age, how well does he/she carry them out?			
	Below Average	Average	Above Average	Don't Know
a. **cutting lawn**	☐	☒	☐	☐
b. _____	☐	☐	☐	☐
c. _____	☐	☐	☐	☐

Be sure you answered all items. Then see other side.

Copyright 2001 T. Achenbach
ASEBA, University of Vermont
1 South Prospect St., Burlington, VT 05401-3456
www.ASEBA.org

UNAUTHORIZED COPYING IS ILLEGAL

PAGE 1

6-1-01 Edition - 201

FIG. 9.1. Pages 1 and 2 of the Child Behavior Checklist completed for Wayne Webster by his mother (from Achenbach & Rescorla, 2001).

interviewer, seeing the form helps them follow along. For respondents who cannot read English but can read another language, translations are available in over 70 languages (Bérubé & Achenbach, 2005).

ASEBA Forms

The ASEBA self-report and collateral report instruments take about 10 to 20 minutes to complete. They are available as paper-and-pencil forms and also via *Web-Link*, a

Please print. Be sure to answer all items.

V. 1. About how many close friends does your child have? (Do not include brothers & sisters)

☐ None ☒ 1 ☐ 2 or 3 ☐ 4 or more

2. About how many times a week does your child do things with any friends outside of regular school hours?

(Do not include brothers & sisters) ☐ Less than 1 ☒ 1 or 2 ☐ 3 or more

VI. Compared to others of his/her age, how well does your child:

	Worse	Average	Better	
a. Get along with his/her brothers & sisters?	☒	☐	☐	☐ Has no brothers or sisters
b. Get along with other kids?	☒	☐	☐	
c. Behave with his/her parents?	☒	☐	☐	
d. Play and work alone?	☐	☒	☐	

VII. 1. Performance in academic subjects. ☐ Does not attend school because _____

Check a box for each subject that child takes	Failing	Below Average	Average	Above Average
a. Reading, English, or Language Arts	☒	☐	☐	☐
b. History or Social Studies	☐	☐	☒	☐
c. Arithmetic or Math	☐	☐	☐	☒
d. Science	☐	☒	☐	☐
e. Computer course	☐	☐	☐	☒
f. _____	☐	☐	☐	☐
g. _____	☐	☐	☐	☐

Other academic subjects—for example computer courses, foreign language, business. Do not include gym, shop, driver's ed. or other nonacademic subjects

2. Does your child receive special education or remedial services or attend a special class or special school?

☒ No ☐ Yes—kind of services, class, or school: _____

3. Has your child repeated any grades? ☐ No ☒ Yes—grades and reasons: 2nd grade Was immature

4. Has your child had any academic or other problems in school? ☐ No ☒ Yes—please describe: Seems to have lost interest in some subjects, Failing English, problems with anger

When did these problems start? 6 months ago

Have these problems ended? ☒ No ☐ Yes—when?

Does your child have any illness or disability (either physical or mental)? ☒ No ☐ Yes—please describe: _____

What concerns you most about your child? Loss of interest in school, falling grades, anger, conflicts with family, bad attitude

Please describe the best things about your child. Very bright, talent for computers. Can be very friendly sometimes

PAGE 3 Be sure you answered all items.

FIG. 9.1. (Continued)

Web-based application that enables respondents to interactively complete the forms on any Web-connected computer. In addition to enabling interactive entry on a computer, Web-Link also enables users to have paper forms printed by any Web-connected computer.

Machine-readable versions are available for parent-completed and teacher-completed forms for ages 6 to 18 and for self-report forms for ages 11 to 18. The machine-readable versions include Teleform® and optical mark read (OMR) forms. Both kinds of machine-readable forms are processed by the same ASEBA scanning software module.

One of the most widely used ASEBA forms is the *Child Behavior Checklist for Ages 6 to 18* (CBCL/6–18; Achenbach & Rescorla, 2001). The CBCL/6–18 is completed by parents and parent surrogates and allows them to describe and rate children's competencies and problems. Figure 9.1 displays the competencies reported for 15-year-old Wayne Webster on the CBCL/6–18 completed by his mother (all personal details in this chapter are fictitious). By looking at Fig. 9.1, you can see that the CBCL/6–18 first requests demographic information about the child, plus information about the person completing the form. Thereafter, it requests information about the child's involvement in sports, other kinds of activities, organizations, jobs and chores, and friendships. It also asks about the child's relationships with significant other people, how well the child plays and works alone, and the child's functioning in school, or if not attending school, the reason for not attending. Open-ended items request information about disabilities and illnesses, what concerns the respondent most about the child, and the best things about the child.

Figure 9.2 displays page 3 of the CBCL/6–18, which is a page on which parents and surrogates rate children's problems. Several items request descriptive information as well as quantitative ratings. The problem items are continued on page 4 of the CBCL/6-18 (not shown).

Table 9.1 summarizes the ASEBA self-report and collateral report forms, the age ranges for these forms, who completes them, and the types of scales on each form.

In addition to self-report and collateral report forms, the ASEBA includes the *Semistructured Clinical Interview for Children and Adolescents* (SCICA; McConaughy & Achenbach, 2001), which is administered by trained interviewers to obtain a wealth of standardized and individualized observational and self-report data from 6- to 18-year-olds. ASEBA instruments for obtaining observational data in other contexts include the *Direct Observation Form* (DOF; Achenbach & Rescorla, 2001), which is completed by paraprofessionals to document child and adolescent behavior in group settings, and the *Test Observation Form* (TOF; McConaughy & Achenbach, 2004), which is completed by psychological examiners to document problems observed during the administration of ability and achievement tests.

Profiles for Scoring the ASEBA Forms

The data obtained with each ASEBA form can be scored by clerical workers in about 10 minutes on hand-scored profiles or in 2 to 5 minutes using ASEBA computer software, which is called the "Assessment Data Manager" (ADM). Hand-scoring and computer-scoring procedures produce scores that are displayed on profiles of adaptive functioning and problem scales. The total score for each scale is obtained by summing the scores of all the items on the scale. The profiles display the scale scores in relation to norms for large samples of people of the same gender and age range as the person who is being assessed.

ASEBA Competence Profiles

Figure 9.3 shows a hand-scored profile of competence scales scored from pages 1 and 2 of the CBCL/6–18 completed for Wayne Webster by his mother.

By looking at Figure 9.3, you can see two broken lines printed across the graphic display. Scale scores above the top broken line are in the normal range, because they are high enough to be in the upper 93% of scores obtained by a nationally representative normative sample

Please print. Be sure to answer all items.

Below is a list of items that describe children and youths. For each item that describes your child *now or within the past 6 months*, please circle the *2* if the item is *very true or often true* of your child. Circle the *1* if the item is *somewhat or sometimes true* of your child. If the item is *not true* of your child, circle the *0*. Please answer all items as well as you can, even if some do not seem to apply to your child.

0 = Not True (as far as you know)   1 = Somewhat or Sometimes True   2 = Very True or Often True

0 1 **2** 1. Acts too young for his/her age	0 1 **2** 32. Feels he/she has to be perfect
0 **1** 2 a2. Drinks alcohol without parents' approval	0 1 **2** 33. Feels or complains that no one loves him/her
(describe): **3x**	0 1 **2** 34. Feels others are out to get him/her
	0 1 **2** 35. Feels worthless or inferior
0 1 **2** 3. Argues a lot	
0 1 **2** a4. Fails to finish things he/she starts	**0** 1 2 36. Gets hurt a lot, accident-prone
	0 **1** 2 37. Gets in many fights
0 1 **2** a5. There is very little he/she enjoys	
0 1 2 6. Bowel movements outside toilet	**0** 1 2 38. Gets teased a lot
	0 1 2 39. Hangs around with others who get in trouble
0 1 2 7. Bragging, boasting	
0 1 **2** 8. Can't concentrate, can't pay attention for long	**0** 1 2 40. Hears sound or voices that aren't there
0 1 **2** 9. Can't get his/her mind off certain thoughts;	(describe): _____
obsessions (describe): **computers;**	
people who cross him	0 **1** 2 41. Impulsive or acts without thinking
0 1 2 10. Can't sit still, restless, or hyperactive	0 **1** 2 42. Would rather be alone than with others
	0 1 2 43. Lying or cheating
0 1 2 11. Clings to adults or too dependent	
0 1 **2** 12. Complains of loneliness	**0** 1 2 44. Bites fingernails
	0 1 **2** 45. Nervous, highstrung, or tense
0 1 **2** 13. Confused or seems to be in a fog	
0 1 2 14. Cries a lot	**0** 1 2 46. Nervous movements or twitching (describe): ____
0 1 2 15. Cruel to animals	_____
0 1 **2** 16. Cruelty, bullying, or meanness to others	
	0 1 2 47. Nightmares
0 1 **2** 17. Daydreams or gets lost in his/her thoughts	**0** 1 2 48. Not liked by other kids
0 1 2 18. Deliberately harms self or attempts suicide	**0** 1 2 49. Constipated, doesn't move bowels
0 1 2 19. Demands a lot of attention	**0** 1 2 50. Too fearful or anxious
0 1 2 20. Destroys his/her own things	**0** 1 2 51. Feels dizzy or lightheaded
0 1 2 21. Destroys things belonging to his/her family or	**0** 1 2 52. Feels too guilty
others	**0** 1 2 53. Overeating
0 1 **2** 22. Disobedient at home	**0** 1 2 54. Overtired without good reason
0 1 2 23. Disobedient at school	**0** 1 2 55. Overweight
0 **1** 2 24. Doesn't eat well	56. Physical problems *without known medical*
0 1 **2** 25. Doesn't get along with other kids	*cause:*
0 **1** 2 26. Doesn't seem to feel guilty after misbehaving	**0** 1 2 a. Aches or pains (*not* stomach or headaches)
0 1 **2** 27. Easily jealous	0 1 **2** b. Headaches
0 **1** 2 a28. Breaks rules at home, school, or elsewhere	**0** 1 2 c. Nausea, feels sick
0 1 2 29. Fears certain animals, situations, or places,	**0** 1 2 d. Problems with eyes (*not* if corrected by glasses)
other than school (describe): _____	(describe): _____
_____	**0** 1 2 e. Rashes or other skin problems
0 **1** 2 30. Fears going to school	**0** 1 2 f. Stomachaches
0 1 2 31. Fears he/she might think or do something bad	**0** 1 2 g. Vomiting, throwing up
	0 1 2 h. Other (describe): _____

PAGE 3   *Be sure you answered all items. Then see other side.*

FIG. 9.2. Page 3 of the Child Behavior Checklist completed for Wayne Webster (from Achenbach & Rescorla, 2001).

of youths who had not received mental health or drug abuse services in the preceding 12 months. Scores below the bottom broken line are below the 3rd percentile, which is considered to be in the clinical range because it reflects very low levels of competence. And scores between the two broken lines are between the 3rd and 7th percentiles, which represent the borderline clinical range. Scale scores in the borderline clinical range are low

TABLE 9.1
ASEBA Self-Report and Collateral Report Forms

Forms	Ages	Completed by	Types of Scales[a]
Self-report forms			
Youth Self-Report (YSR)[b]	11–18	Youths	Competence, Syndromes, DSM-oriented
Adult Self-Report (ASR)[c]	18–59	Emancipated youths, adults	Adaptive, Syndromes, DSM-oriented
Older Adult Self-Report (OASR)[d]	60–90+	Older adults	Adaptive, Syndromes, DSM-oriented
Collateral report forms			
Child Behavior Checklist/1½–5 (CBCL/1½–5)[e]	1½–5	Parent figures	Language, Syndromes, DSM-oriented
Child Behavior Checklist/6–18 (CBCL/6–18)[b]	6–18	Parent figures, residential staff	Competence, Syndromes, DSM-oriented
Caregiver-Teacher Report Form (C-TRF)[e]	1½–5	Teachers, day-care staff	Syndromes, DSM-oriented
Teacher's Report Form (TRF)[b]	6–18	Educational personnel	Academic, Adaptive, Syndromes, DSM-oriented
Adult Behavior Checklist (ABCL)[c]	18–59	People who know the subject	Adaptive, Syndromes, DSM-oriented
Older Adult Behavior Checklist (OABCL)[d]	60–90+	People who know the subject	Adaptive, Syndromes, DSM-oriented

[a]Forms also include Total Problems, Internalizing, and Externalizing scales (except the OASR and OABCL). "Internalizing" refers to problems that are mainly within the self, such as anxiety, depression, and physical complaints without apparent medical cause. "Externalizing" refers to problems that involve conflicts with other people and with social mores, such as fighting, stealing, and lying.
[b]Achenbach & Rescorla, 2001.
[c]Achenbach & Rescorla, 2003.
[d]Achenbach, Newhouse, & Rescorla, 2004.
[e]Achenbach & Rescorla, 2000.
Note: Footnotes cite references for details of the forms, including their applications, reliability, validity, and norms.

enough to be of concern but not so low as to be clinically deviant in the area represented by the scale.

Figure 9.3 shows that Wayne's CBCL scores indicate a borderline clinical level of competence on the Activities scale, a clinically low level of competence on the Social scale, and a low-normal level of competence on the School scale, compared to a national normative sample of adolescent boys. Scores for these three scales are summed to provide a total competence score, for which Wayne's T-score was 26, as indicated to the right of the profile.

ASEBA Profiles of Empirically Based Syndromes

Ratings of problem items (Fig. 9.2) provide scores for empirically based syndrome scales. These scales reflect actual patterns of co-occurring problem items identified by factor analyzing parent ratings, teacher ratings, and self-ratings on over 12,000 ASEBA forms (Achenbach & Rescorla, 2001). By looking at Fig. 9.4, you can see a computer-scored profile of Wayne's scores on the eight syndromes derived by factor analyzing parent

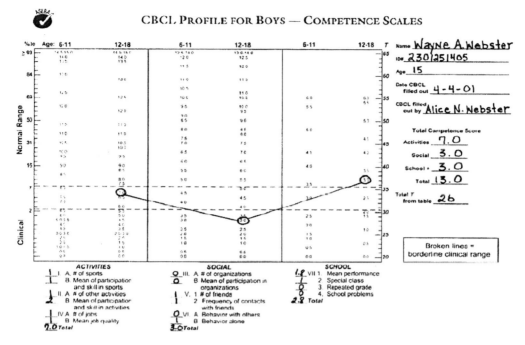

FIG. 9.3. Hand-scored competence profile for Wayne Webster's Child Behavior Checklist (from Achenbach & Rescorla, 2001).

ratings, teacher ratings, and self-ratings. The profile in Figure 9.4 was scored from Wayne's self-ratings on the *Youth Self-Report* (YSR; Achenbach & Rescorla, 2001). Note that, for the syndromes, scores *above the top* broken line are in the *clinical range*, because they are higher than the problem scores obtained by 97% of the normative sample. Scores *between* the two broken lines are in the *borderline clinical range* (93rd to 97th percentiles). And scores *below the bottom* broken line are in the *normal range*.

ASEBA Profiles of DSM-Oriented Scales

In addition to being scored on empirically based syndrome scales, ASEBA problem items are scored on *DSM*-oriented scales. The *DSM*-oriented scales consist of problem items identified by experts from 16 cultures as being very consistent with particular diagnostic categories of the American Psychiatric Association's (1994) *Diagnostic and Statistical Manual of Mental Disorders*, fourth edition (*DSM–IV*). Like the competence and syndrome scales, the *DSM*-oriented scales are scored on profiles in relation to age-, gender-, and informant-specific norms.

Figure 9.5 shows a profile of *DSM*-oriented scales scored by hand from the *Teacher's Report Form* (TRF; Achenbach & Rescorla, 2001) completed by one of Wayne Webster's teachers. Table 9.2 summarizes the scales scored from the ASEBA self-report and collateral report forms.

Cross-Informant Comparisons

ASEBA forms that are completed by different people to assess the same individual enable users to quickly and economically compare multiple reports about the individual. Documentation of cross-informant comparisons is especially valuable for assessment in a

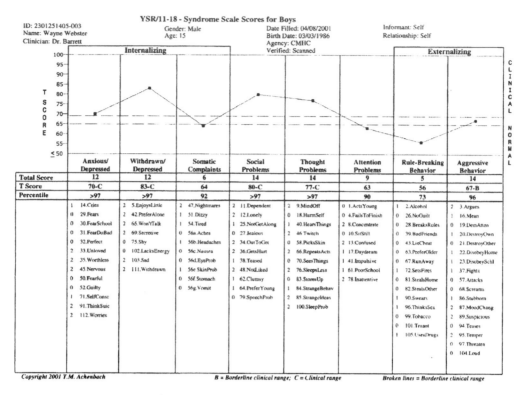

FIG. 9.4. Computer-scored syndrome profile for the Youth Self-Report completed by Wayne Webster (from Achenbach & Rescorla, 2001).

forensic setting, as different parties to a case are apt to have conflicting views and motivations. In child custody cases, for example, a mother and father may genuinely see their child differently as well as being forensic adversaries. It is therefore important to have each parent complete a separate CBCL/6–18 (or CBCL/1½ – 5 for a preschool child) and to have others who know the child complete the relevant forms, such as the TRF or the *Caregiver-Teacher Report Form for Ages 1½ to 5* (C-TRF; Achenbach & Rescorla, 2000). A clinical interviewer can also administer the SCICA (McConaughy & Achenbach, 2001). Adolescents should complete the YSR.

The ADM software prints side-by-side comparisons of the scores obtained from different respondents. These comparisons enable users to quickly see where informants agree and disagree on particular items and scales. The cross-informant comparisons are also useful for forensic evaluations of adolescents who may be adjudicated. For example, Fig. 9.6 shows bar graphs of syndrome scale scores obtained by Wayne Webster from CBCL ratings by his mother and father, YSR ratings by Wayne, and TRF ratings by three teachers. By looking at Figure 9.6, you can see that most or all informants reported borderline or clinical elevations of problems on the Anxious/Depressed, Withdrawn/Depressed, Social Problems, and Aggressive Behavior syndromes. By contrast, all informants' ratings were in the normal range for the Somatic Complaints and Rule-Breaking Behavior syndromes (the picture was more mixed for the Attention Problems syndrome). As illustrated in the case example at the end of this chapter, marked differences between the reports of one or two informants and the reports of the other informants can provide insight into particular characteristics of the informants and how they portray the individual being assessed.

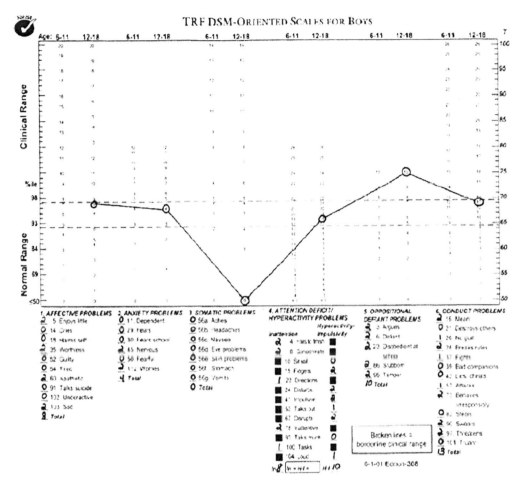

FIG. 9.5. Hand-scored *DSM*-oriented profile scored from the Teacher's Report Form completed by one of Wayne Webster's teachers (from Achenbach & Rescorla, 2001).

Because ASEBA forms are available for assessing adults as well as children, it is useful to have the adult parties to custody cases complete self-report forms and forms describing their spouse or partner. When possible, it is also helpful to have adult collaterals complete collateral report forms to describe each parent. The results can be viewed in terms of profiles and bar graphs of scale scores like those shown for Wayne Webster in Fig. 9.3 through 9.6.

Narrative Reports and Critical Items

In addition to displaying profiles and side-by-side comparisons of item and scale scores, the ADM software also prints narrative reports of the results obtained from each ASEBA form. As an example, Fig. 9.7 displays a narrative report of the results obtained from the YSR completed by Wayne Webster. At the bottom of the narrative report is a box in which Wayne's self-ratings of critical items are displayed. These are items that clinicians have identified as potentially presenting particular risks and challenges for management. The

TABLE 9.2
Scales Scored From ASEBA Self-Report and Collateral Report Forms

Forms	Competence and Adaptive	Syndromes	DSM-Oriented Scales
Ages 1½–5			
CBCL, C-TRF	Language Development Survey[a]	Emotionally Reactive	Affective Problems
	Length of Phrases[a]	Anxious/Depressed	Anxiety Problems
	Vocabulary[a]	Somatic Complaints	Pervasive Developmental Problems
		Withdrawn	Attention Deficit/Hyperactivity Problems
		Sleep Problems[a]	Oppositional Defiant Problems
		Attention Problems	
		Aggressive Behavior	
Ages 6–18			
CBCL, TRF, YSR	Activities[b]	Anxious/Depressed	Affective Problems
	Social[b]	Withdrawn/Depressed	Anxiety Problems
	School[b]	Somatic Complaints	Somatic Problems
	Total Competence[b]	Social Problems	Attention Deficit/Hyperactivity Problems[d]
	Academic[c]	Thought Problems	Oppositional Defiant Problems
	Adaptive Functioning[c]	Attention Problems[d]	Conduct Problems
		Rule-Breaking Behavior	
		Aggressive Behavior	
Ages 18–59[f]			
ASR, ABCL	Friends	Anxious/Depressed	Depressive Problems
	Spouse/Partner	Withdrawn	Anxiety Problems
	Family[e]	Somatic Complaints	Somatic Problems
	Job[e]	Thought Problems	Avoidant Personality Problems
	Education[e]	Attention Problems	Attention Deficit/Hyperactivity Problems[d]
	Mean Adaptive[e]	Aggressive Behavior	Antisocial Personality Problems
		Rule-Breaking Behavior	
		Intrusive	
Ages 60–90+			
OASR, OABCL	Friends	Anxious/Depressed	Depressive Problems
	Family[e]	Functional Impairment	Anxiety Problems
	Spouse/Partner	Irritable/Disinhibited	Somatic Problems
		Memory/Cognition Problems	Dementia Problems
		Somatic Complaints	Psychotic Problems
		Thought Problems	Antisocial Personality Problems
		Worries	

[a]CBCL/1½–5 only.

[b]CBCL/6–18 and YSR, only (on YSR, mean score for academic performance substitutes for the CBCL/6–18 School scale).

[c]TRF only.

[d]TRF, ASR, and ABCL scales have subscales for Inattention and Hyperactivity-Impulsivity.

[e]Self-report forms only.

[f]Tobacco, Alcohol, Drugs, and mean Substance Use sales are scored from ASR and ABCL. Substance use is assessed by specific items but not by normed scales on CBCL/6–18, TRF, YSR, OASR, and OABCL.

Note: Table 9.1 provides full names of forms. All forms are also scored for Total Problems and all, except the OASR and OABCL, are scored for Internalizing and Externalizing. Critical Items scales are scored from forms for ages 18–90+.

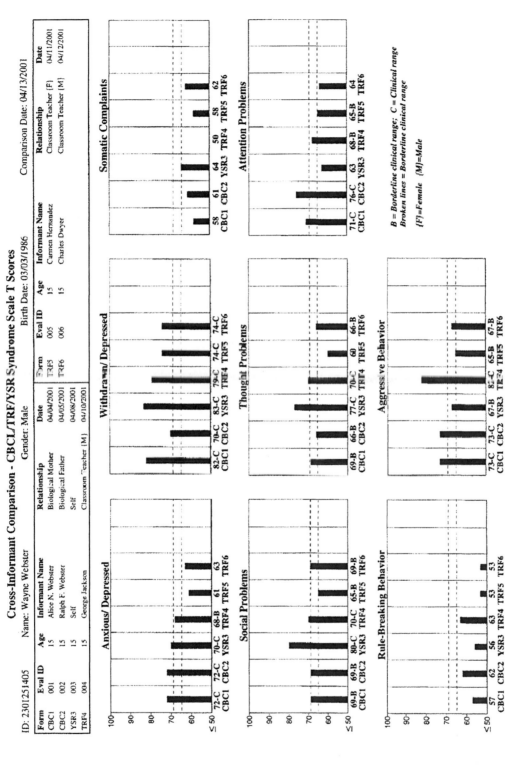

FIG. 9.6. Cross-informant comparison of syndrome scores obtained from forms completed by Wayne Webster, his mother, his father, and three teachers (from Achenbach & Rescorla, 2001).

YSR/11-18 - Narrative Report & Critical Items

ID: 2301251405-003   Birth Date: 03/03/1986   Date Filled: 04/08/2001
Name: Wayne Webster   Gender: Male   Informant: Self
Age: 15   Clinician: Dr. Barrett

The Youth Self-Report (YSR) was completed by Wayne to obtain his perceptions of his competencies and problems. Wayne reported that he participates in one sport and that he has interests in one hobby. He belongs to no social organizations, teams or clubs. Wayne reported that he has one job or chore. Wayne's responses indicate that he has one close friend and that he sees friends three or more times a week outside of regular school hours. Wayne rated his school performance as failing in language arts, below average in social studies, above average in math, and below average in science. He rated his performance in one additional subject as above average.

Wayne's Total Competence score was in the clinical range below the 10th percentile for self-reports by boys aged 11 to 18. His score on the Activities scale was in the borderline clinical range (3rd to 7th percentiles), and his score on the Social scale was in the clinical range below the 3rd percentile.

On the YSR problem scales, Wayne's Total Problems and Internalizing scores were both in the clinical range above the 90th percentile for boys aged 11 to 18. His Externalizing score was in the borderline clinical range (84th to 90th percentiles). His scores on the Somatic Complaints, Attention Problems, and Rule-Breaking Behavior syndromes were in the normal range. His scores on the Anxious/Depressed, Withdrawn/Depressed, Social Problems, and Thought Problems syndromes were in the clinical range above the 97th percentile. His score on the Aggressive Behavior syndrome was in the borderline clinical range (93rd to 97th percentiles). These results indicate that Wayne reported more problems than are typically reported by boys aged 11 to 18, particularly problems of anxiety or depression, withdrawn or depressed behavior, problems in social relationships, thought problems, and problems of an aggressive nature.

On the DSM-oriented scales, Wayne's scores on the Somatic Problems, Attention Deficit/Hyperactivity Problems, and Conduct Problems scales were in the normal range. His scores on the Affective Problems and Oppositional Defiant Problems scales were in the clinical range (above the 97th percentile). His score on the Anxiety Problems scale was in the borderline clinical range (93rd to 97th percentiles). These results suggest that the DSM should be consulted to determine whether Wayne meets diagnostic criteria for affective disorders and Oppositional Defiant Disorder. Wayne's score in the borderline clinical range suggests that the DSM should be consulted to determine whether Wayne might meet diagnostic criteria for disorders characterized by problems included on that scale.

Critical Items

In addition to the scale scores, it is important to consider scores on individual problem items. Because they may raise particular challenges for management, it is especially important to note the problems listed below that were reported with scores of 1 or 2. Look at comments made by the informant on the form in relation to these problems to obtain more information about risks associated with the problems and the contexts in which the problems occur.

Score	Problem Item	Score	Problem Item
0	18. HarmSelf	0	70. SeesThings
1	40. HearsThings	1	72. SetsFires
0	57. Attacks	2	91. ThinkSuic
0	67. RunAway	1	105. UsesDrugs

FIG. 9.7. Narrative report summarizing YSR results for Wayne Webster (from Achenbach & Rescorla, 2001).

designations for the critical items listed in the box are abbreviated versions of the items actually printed on the YSR. For example, the complete version of item 40 on the YSR is "I hear sounds or voices that other people think aren't there (describe)." Wayne gave item 40 a rating of 1, which means "somewhat or sometimes true," and he wrote, "Sometimes I think I hear people talking about me."

The ADM software also generates narrative reports and critical item scores from ASEBA forms completed by other respondents, such as parents, teachers, and interviewers.

HISTORY OF THE ASEBA

The development of the ASEBA can be summarized by organizing the main events into several stages extending over four decades.

Analyses of Psychiatric Case Records

The ASEBA originated in the 1960s with efforts to determine whether children's problems formed more differentiated patterns than were implied by the only two diagnostic categories for childhood disorders provided by the psychiatric nosology of that time (*DSM–I*; American Psychiatric Association, 1952). The two categories were Adjustment Reaction of Childhood and Schizophrenic Reaction, Childhood Type. By factor analyzing problems reported in child psychiatric case records, Achenbach (1966) found many more syndromes than were implied by the two *DSM–I* categories. The term "syndrome" is used here to designate empirically identified patterns of co-occurring problems without implying assumptions about whether the etiologies are biological, environmental, or a mixture of both.

In addition to the numerous syndromes, the factor analyses identified two broad groupings of problems for which Achenbach (1966) coined the terms "Internalizing" and "Externalizing." Internalizing problems are those that are primarily within the self, such as anxiety, depression, withdrawal, and somatic complaints without apparent physical cause. Externalizing problems are those that primarily involve conflict with other people and with social mores, such as aggressive behavior and delinquent behavior (now called "rule-breaking behavior"; Achenbach & Rescorla, 2001).

Normed Scales Derived From Parent, Teacher, Youth, and Observer Reports

Although numerous syndromes were derived from factor analyses of case record data, case records are compiled by mental health professionals who may not be fully aware of the problems and adaptive functioning that could be reported by various informants or by the individual being assessed. To systematically obtain informants' reports and self-reports, the CBCL, TRF, and YSR were developed to be completed by parents, teachers, and youths, respectively. Successive pilot editions of the CBCL, TRF, and YSR were tested and refined via data and feedback obtained from large samples of parents, teachers, and youths. The DOF was developed to enable paraprofessionals, such as teacher aides, to record observations of behavior in group settings such as classrooms and recreational activities.

Data for large samples of clinically referred children were factor analyzed to derive syndromes and Internalizing-Externalizing groupings of problems separately for different age groups of each gender on each form. In addition, data for large samples of nonreferred children were used to construct norms for each problem scale as well as for scales assessing competencies and adaptive functioning (Achenbach & Edelbrock, 1983, 1986, 1987). Hand-scored profiles and computer software were developed to facilitate the use of the ASEBA in forensic, clinical, educational, research, and other contexts.

Cross-Informant Syndromes

To test whether similar syndromes could be identified in parent ratings, teacher ratings, and self-ratings and to advance the coordination of assessment across multiple informants, new analyses of much larger and more diverse clinical and normative samples were conducted (Achenbach, 1991). Eight syndromes were identified as having clear enough counterparts in factor analyses of parent ratings, teacher ratings, and self-ratings to provide a basis for *cross-informant syndrome constructs*. Hand-scored and computer-scored profiles were constructed for displaying these eight syndromes in relation to gender- and age-specific norms separately for the CBCL, TRF, and YSR. In addition, to facilitate cross-informant comparisons, procedures like those illustrated earlier were developed to display item and scale scores obtained from multiple informants' reports regarding the individual being assessed (Achenbach, 1991). Thereafter, ASEBA assessment forms, syndromes, and scoring profiles were published for parents' reports on 2- and 3-year-olds (Achenbach, 1992), for caregivers' and teachers' reports on 2- to 5-year-olds (Achenbach, 1997a), and for self-reports and collateral reports for individuals aged 18 to 30 (Achenbach, 1997b).

Revised Forms, Profiles, and *DSM*-Oriented Scales for Ages 1½ to 18

In 2000 and 2001, slightly revised versions of the forms for ages 1½ to 18 were published. The revisions were undertaken for the following reasons: (a) to capitalize on experience accumulated with the previous editions, (b) to take advantage of advances in multivariate statistics and in Windows® software, (c) to incorporate norms from new national probability samples, and (d) to add *DSM*-oriented scales. The revisions involved replacing a few problem items with more effective items and improving the wording of a few other items. Large new clinical and normative samples were factor analyzed using cutting-edge combinations of exploratory factor analysis (EFA) and confirmatory factor analysis (CFA). For the CBCL/6–18, TRF, and YSR, the eight syndromes and Internalizing-Externalizing groupings published in 1991 were replicated with minor changes. Correlations between scores on the 1991 syndromes and their 2001 counterparts ranged from .87 to 1.00 (Achenbach & Rescorla, 2001). The 2001 counterpart of the 1991 Delinquent Behavior syndrome was named the "Rule-Breaking Behavior syndrome" because some of its constituent behavior problems would not necessarily be cause for adjudication and could be manifested by children too young to be adjudicated. The 2001 counterpart of the 1991 Withdrawn syndrome was designated "Withdrawn/Depressed" because certain problems indicative of depression were found to load on the same factor as problems of withdrawal. Other problems indicative of depression were found to load on the same factor as problems of anxiety, as embodied in the syndrome designated "Anxious/Depressed."

A major innovation of the 21st-century ASEBA instruments is the inclusion of the *DSM*-oriented scales described earlier. By using the judgments of international panels of experts to construct *DSM*-oriented scales from the same pool of items as the syndromes derived by factor analyses, we combined the "top-down" expert judgment approach with the "bottom-up" empirically based approach in the same instruments. Users can thus view reported problems in terms of both top-down *DSM*-oriented scales and bottom-up syndrome scales.

Forms for Ages 18 to 59 and 60 to 90+

As mentioned earlier, ASEBA young adult forms for ages 18 to 30 were published in 1997 (Achenbach, 1997b). To extend the assessment of adults through age 59, the young adult forms were substantially revised, tested through several pilot editions with many 18- to 59-year-olds, and used to assess thousands of clinically referred adults as well as a national probability sample of adults assessed in home interviews. Following procedures like those used for the age $1\frac{1}{2}$ to 18 forms, combinations of EFA and CFA were used to derive empirically based syndromes from the *Adult Self-Report* (ASR) and *Adult Behavior Checklist* (ABCL; Achenbach & Rescorla, 2003). In addition, *DSM*-oriented scales were constructed by having international experts in adult mental health identify ASR and ABCL items that they judged to be very consistent with particular *DSM–IV* diagnostic categories.

In response to the need for broad-spectrum, empirically based, and *DSM*-oriented assessment of the elderly, a geriatric psychiatrist, Professor Paul Newhouse, collaborated with the authors of this chapter to develop the *Older Adult Self-Report* (OASR) and *Older Adult Behavior Checklist* (ABCL; Achenbach, Newhouse, & Rescorla, 2004). The OASR and OABCL are scored in terms of empirically based syndromes and *DSM*-oriented scales developed according to the procedures used for the adult forms. Norms for the scales are based on large samples of 60- to 90-year-olds, but the research for deriving and testing the scales included participants as old as 102 years.

Multicultural Versions of ASEBA Instruments

As the United States and other countries become increasingly multicultural, psychologists must be prepared to assess people from cultures different from their own. Many immigrant children and adults become involved with the courts for many reasons. ASEBA instruments are used in diverse cultures, with translations in over 70 languages and over 6,000 published studies from 64 cultures. If respondents do not read or understand English but can read languages for which ASEBA translations are available, they can complete the translated ASEBA forms. Because the item numbers and scoring are the same for the translated forms, clerical workers need not know each language in order to score the translated forms via English language hand-scored or computer-scored profiles.

Confirmatory factor analyses have shown that CBCL problem item scores for over 56,000 children from 30 cultures met criteria for good fit to the eight-syndrome model derived from U.S. data on the CBCL/6–18, TRF, and YSR (Ivanova et al., 2006). The 30 cultures were very diverse, as the countries involved included Australia, China, Ethiopia, Greece, Iceland, Iran, Israel, Jamaica, Japan, Korea, Lithuania, Romania, Russia, Thailand, Turkey, and several western European countries.

Distributions of CBCL/6–18, TRF, and YSR scale scores showed modest effects of culture (Rescorla et al., 2006). The differences that were found are taken into account by multicultural versions of ASEBA software that enable users to compare individuals' scores with norms based on a variety of cultures.

PSYCHOMETRIC CHARACTERISTICS

The manuals for the ASEBA forms provide extensive details of the norming procedures, norms, and psychometric characteristics, which are summarized in the following sections.

Norming Procedures and Norms

The norms for the self-report and collateral report forms for ages $1^1/_2$ to 90+ were constructed primarily from data obtained in the National Survey of Children, Youths, and Adults (Achenbach & Rescorla, 2000, 2001, 2003). Conducted in 1999 and 2000, the National Survey was carried out by having interviewers visit homes selected by multistage probability sampling in 40 states and the District of Columbia. The homes were selected to be representative of the continental United States with respect to geographical region, socioeconomic status, ethnicity, and urbanization.

To obtain data on children and youths, the interviewers initially administered the CBCL/$1^1/_2$–5 or CBCL/6–18 to parents or surrogates. For $1^1/_2$- to 5-year-olds who attended school or day care, the parents' consent was requested to permit interviewers to send the C-TRF to the teacher or day-care provider who knew the child best. For 6- to 18-year-olds who attended school, the parents' consent was requested to permit interviewers to send the TRF to the teacher who knew the child best. For 11- to 18-year-olds, consent was requested from the parent and youth to have the youth complete the YSR. To obtain data on adults, the interviewers initially administered the ASR or OASR. They then requested consent to visit an informant who knew the adult participant well. If the participant and informant both consented, the interviewers administered the ABCL or OABCL to the informant.

Completion rates for the initial assessments ranged from 89.7% for ages 60 to 90+ to 94.4% for ages $1^1/_2$ to 5. In order to base norms on what epidemiologists call "healthy samples," we excluded from the normative samples people who had received mental health or substance abuse services in the preceding 12 months. Table 9.3 displays the size and demographic characteristics of the normative samples for the ASEBA self-report and collateral report forms. To include older adults who would not be represented in probability samples of private dwellings, the normative samples for ages 60 to 90+ included people drawn from senior centers and living facilities for the elderly as well as random probability samples from private dwellings.

TABLE 9.3
National Normative Samples for ASEBA Self-Report and Collateral Report Forms[a]

Forms	N	Male (%)	Non-Latino White (%)	African American (%)	Latino (%)	Mixed, Other (%)
CBCL/$1^1/_2$–5	700	52	56	21	13	10
C-TRF/$1^1/_2$–5	1,192	49	48	36	8	9
CBCL/6–18	1,753	52	60	20	9	12
TRF/6–18	2,319	48	72	14	7	7
YSR/11–18	1,057	52	60	20	8	11
ABCL/18–59	1,435	41	69	17	10	4
ASR/18–59	1,767	42	63	20	11	6
OABCL/60–90+[b]	822	42	79	13	5	3
OASR/60–90+[b]	1,397	37	79	14	5	2

[a]The normative samples are random samples drawn from people living in private dwellings, excluding people who had received mental health or substance abuse services in the preceding 12 months, as detailed by Achenbach and Rescorla (2000, 2001, 2003) and Achenbach, Newhouse, and Rescorla (2004).
[b]Includes people drawn from senior centers and living facilities for the elderly as well as people living in private dwellings.

Percentiles and *T*-Scores

The distributions of scale scores in the normative samples provided the data for determining percentiles and normalized *T*-scores for each raw score. The percentiles and *T*-scores were assigned to each gender separately within particular age ranges for each type of form. Thus, for example, percentiles and *T*-scores for the CBCL/6–18 scales were based on the distributions of scores obtained by boys and girls aged 6 to 11 and 12 to 18. Similarly, percentiles and *T*-scores for the TRF were based on the distributions of scores obtained on the TRF by boys and girls aged 6 to 11 and 12 to 18. And the percentiles and *T*-scores for the YSR were based on the distributions of scores obtained by boys and girls on the YSR. The profiles, percentiles, and *T*-scores shown in Figures 9.3 through 9.6 thus indicate how a child's scores compare with scores for normative samples of peers of the same gender and age range as assessed by a particular kind of informant.

Reliability of ASEBA Scales

The ASEBA manuals present extensive data on the test-retest correlations (*r*s) and Cronbach alpha coefficients for each scale of each instrument. For brevity, Table 9.4 summarizes the mean test-retest *r*s and alphas for each type of scale from the self-report and collateral report instruments for ages $1\frac{1}{2}$ to 90+. The *Bibliography of Published Studies Using the ASEBA* (Bérubé & Achenbach, 2006) lists dozens of additional studies that report on the reliability of ASEBA scales.

TABLE 9.4
Psychometric Characteristics of ASEBA Scales

Scales[a]	CBCL/$1\frac{1}{2}$–5	C-TRF	CBCL/6–18	TRF	YSR	ABCL	ASR	OABCL	OASR
Competence, Adaptive									
Test-retest *r*	.99	NA	.90	.90	.88	.83	.79	.94	.89
Alpha	.99	NA	.70	.90	.66	.72	.65	.77	.73
Syndromes									
Test-retest *r*	.82	.80	.89	.83	.79	.84	.85	.94	.86
Alpha	.76	.78	.83	.85	.79	.82	.78	.84	.82
DSM-oriented									
Test-retest *r*	.82	.76	.88	.78	.78	.85	.83	.93	.88
Alpha	.75	.82	.82	.84	.76	.79	.78	.82	.76
Internalizing									
Test-retest *r*	.90	.77	.91	.86	.80	.80	.89	NA	NA
Alpha	.89	.89	.90	.90	.90	.92	.93	NA	NA
Externalizing									
Test-retest *r*	.87	.89	.92	.89	.89	.92	.91	NA	NA
Alpha	.92	.96	.94	.95	.90	.93	.89	NA	NA
Total Problems									
Test-retest *r*	.90	.88	.94	.95	.87	.92	.94	.95	.95
Alpha	.95	.97	.97	.97	.95	.97	.97	.97	.96
Substance Use									
Test-retest *r*	NA	NA	NA	NA	NA	.91	.93	NA	NA
Alpha	NA	NA	NA	NA	NA	NA	NA	NA	NA

[a]Mean *r* or alpha for relevant scales. Test-retest *r* for 7- to 16-day intervals. For psychometric characteristics of individual scales, see Achenbach and Rescorla (2000, 2001, 2003) and Achenbach et al. (2004).

Validity of ASEBA Items and Scales

The ASEBA manuals report validity data for all ASEBA items in terms of significant discrimination between demographically similar clinically referred and nonreferred samples, significant loadings on syndromes derived from factor analyses, and/or identification by international panels of experts as being very consistent with *DSM–IV* diagnostic categories (Achenbach et al., 2004; Achenbach & Rescorla, 2000, 2001, 2003; McConaughy & Achenbach, 2001, 2004). In addition, criterion-related validity for the ASEBA scale scores has been demonstrated by their ability to discriminate significantly between clinically referred and nonreferred samples, with the effects of demographic characteristics partialed out. The validity of the clinical and borderline clinical T-score cutpoints on the ASEBA scales has been demonstrated by their significant discrimination between clinical and nonclinical samples in odds ratios and chi squares.

Many kinds of evidence for construct validity have been reported in the ASEBA manuals and in thousands of studies by thousands of authors, as listed in the *Bibliography of Published Studies Using the ASEBA* (Bérubé & Achenbach, 2006). Examples include significant associations with *DSM* diagnoses (e.g., Achenbach & Rescorla, 2001; Edelbrock & Costello, 1988; Kasius, Ferdinand, van den Berg, & Verhulst, 1997; Kazdin & Heidish, 1984; Weinstein, Noam, Grimes, Stone, & Schwab-Stone, 1990). As summarized by Achenbach and Rescorla (2000, 2001, 2003) and Achenbach et al. (2004), additional examples include significant correlations with other assessment instruments, such as the following: Beck Anxiety Inventory and Beck Depression Inventory (Beck & Steer, 1990); Conners' (1997) parent and teacher rating scales; the Behavior Assessment System for Children (BASC; Reynolds & Kamphaus, 1992); the Infant-Toddler Social and Emotional Assessment (ITSEA; Briggs-Gowan & Carter, 1998); the Mini-Mental State Exam (MMSE; Folstein, Folstein, & McHugh, 1975); the Minnesota Multiphasic Personality Inventory–Second Edition (MMPI-2; Butcher, Dahlstrom, Graham, Tellegen, & Kaemmer, 1989); the Neuropsychiatric Inventory (NPI; Cummings et al., 1994); the Richman Behavior Checklist (BCL; Richman, Stevenson, & Graham, 1982); the SCL–90–R (Derogatis, 1994); and the Toddler Behavior Screening Inventory (TBSI; Mouton-Simien, McCain, & Kelley, 1997).

Other kinds of validity evidence include longitudinal findings of significant predictions of outcomes, including substance abuse, trouble with the law, referral for mental health services, suicidal behavior, and psychiatric diagnoses over periods as long as 14 years (Achenbach, Howell, McConaughy, & Stanger, 1995, 1998; Ferdinand, Blüm, & Verhulst, 2001; Ferdinand et al., 2003; Ferdinand & Verhulst, 1994, 1995a, 1995b; Hofstra, van der Ende, & Verhulst, 2000, 2001, 2002a, 2002b). Table 9.5 summarizes validity data for ASEBA self-report and collateral report forms.

Psychometric Strengths and Limitations

The psychometric strengths of ASEBA instruments, in terms of reliability, internal consistency, and multiple kinds of validity, have been well documented in hundreds of studies (Bérubé & Achenbach, 2006). Some might regard the low to moderate correlations between scores typically obtained from different kinds of informants as a psychometric limitation. These cross-informant correlations are sometimes incorrectly equated with "interrater reliability." However, the cross-informant correlations reflect agreement (and disagreement) between informants whose roles differ vis-à-vis the person being assessed, who interact differently with the person being assessed, and whose knowledge of the person's

TABLE 9.5

Validity Data for ASEBA Self-Report and Collateral-Report Forms

Forms	Validity Data
CBCL/1½–5	All scales discriminate between referred and nonreferred at $p < .01$.
	Significant correlations with Behavior Checklist (Richman, 1977), Toddler Behavior Screening Inventory (Mouton-Simien et al., 1997), Infant-Toddler Social and Emotional Assessment (Briggs-Gowan & Carter, 1998), and *DSM* criteria (Arend et al., 1996; Keenan & Wakschlag, 2000).
C-TRF	All scales discriminate between referred and nonreferred at $p < .01$.
CBCL/6–18	All scales discriminate between referred and nonreferred at $p < .01$.
	Significant correlations with Conners (1997) and BASC (Reynold & Kamphaus, 1992) parent rating scales, plus concurrent and predictive associations with many other variables (Bérubé & Achenbach, 2006).
TRF	All scales discriminate between referred and nonreferred at $p < .01$.
	Significant correlations with Conners (1997) and BASC (Reynolds & Kamphaus, 1992) teacher rating scales, plus concurrent and predictive associations with many other variables (Bérubé & Achenbach, 2006).
YSR	All scales discriminate between referred and nonreferred at $p < .01$.
	Over periods of 3, 4, and 10 years, YSR scores predicted adult ASEBA scores, signs of disturbance, and *DSM* diagnoses (Achenbach et al., 1995, 1998; Ferdinand et al., 1995; Hofstra et al., 2001), plus they had concurrent and predictive associations with many other variables (Bérubé & Achenbach, 2006).
ASR	All scales discriminate between referred and nonreferred at $p < .01$.
	Significant correlations with SCL–90–R, MMPI–2, Beck Depression Inventory, and Beck Anxiety Inventory (Beck & Steer, 1990); discriminated between referred and nonreferred Dutch adults significantly better than General Health Questionnaire (Goldberg, 1992) and nonsignificantly better than the SCL–90–R; significantly predicted *DSM–IV* diagnoses over 6 years; significant correlations with GAF in American and Dutch samples; significantly predicted signs of disturbance over 2 years, including referral for mental health services, police contacts, alcohol abuse, and suicidal behavior and ideation.
ABCL	All scales discriminate between referred and nonreferred at $p < .01$ except Intrusive.
	Significant associations with diagnoses of major depressive disorder made 3 years earlier; significant prediction by scores on the corresponding CBCL scales obtained 8 years earlier in American clinical sample and 10.5 years earlier in Dutch clinical sample.
OASR	All problem scales discriminate between referred and nonreferred at $p < .01$.
	Significant associations with diagnoses, Mini Mental State Exam, cognitive measures, and the Neuropsychiatric Inventory.
OABCL	All problem scales discriminate between referred and nonreferred at $p < .01$.
	Significant associations with diagnoses, Mini Mental State Exam, cognitive measures, and the Neuropsychiatric Inventory.

Note: Many other validity data are presented in the manual for each instrument and in thousands of studies listed in the *Bibliography of Published Studies Using ASEBA Instruments* (Bérubé & Achenbach, 2006).

functioning differs. By contrast, interrater reliability concerns the level of agreement between trained raters who observe the same samples of behavior.

For the DOF, which uses trained nonparticipant observers to assess specific samples of behavior, the interrater reliability rs have averaged .90 for Total Problems scores and .84 for on-task scores across several studies (Achenbach & Edelbrock, 1983; McConaughy, Achenbach, & Gent, 1988; McConaughy, Kay, & Fitzgerald, 1998, 1999; Reed & Edelbrock, 1983). However, cross-informant correlations for reports and ratings of psychopathology have averaged from .21 between TRF and YSR ratings to .75 between mothers' and fathers' CBCL/6–18 ratings (Achenbach et al., 2004; Achenbach & Rescorla, 2000, 2001, 2003). Although the TRF × YSR correlation of .21 may seem very small, meta-analyses have shown that it is typical of correlations between teachers' ratings of students and the students' self-ratings (Achenbach, McConaughy, & Howell, 1987). Correlations between other combinations of informants, such as parents × their children, teachers × teachers, adults × collaterals, and clinicians × clients, are generally small to medium, as shown by meta-analyses of cross-informant correlations for adults (Achenbach, Krukowski, Dumenci, & Ivanova, 2005) as well as for children (Achenbach et al., 1987).

Because different informants have different knowledge of the person being assessed and also bring different perspectives, motives, memories, and interpretations to assessment tasks, it is simply a fact of life that their reports often differ. Some instruments include "validity," "social desirability," and "lie" scales that are intended to detect informant biases. However, research has shown that use of these scales to "correct" scores on substantive scales actually reduced the validity of the substantive scale scores (Piedmont, McCrae, Riemann, & Angleitner, 2000). In fact, Piedmont et al. concluded that "the best evidence on protocol validity, and the best alternative to the use of validity scales, comes from the comparison of self-report scores with independent assessments, on a case-by-case basis" (p. 590). Thus, as Meyer (2002) has argued, rather than viewing differences among reports by different informants as a psychometric weakness, psychologists should make use of the differences to improve assessment over what can be obtained with data from single sources. ASEBA instruments explicitly document both the similarities and differences between reports by different informants.

CLINICAL USES AND LIMITATIONS

ASEBA instruments are designed to be used in diverse mental health, medical, educational, counseling, forensic, foster care, training, and research contexts. Because the self-report and collateral report forms are completed by the people being assessed and by those who know them, no specific training is needed to obtain the assessment data. Even when ASEBA forms are read to respondents who cannot complete them independently, the person who reads the form and records the answers need not have clinical training, because no clinical probing or interpretation is involved. However, the SCICA does require interviewers who are trained to conduct clinical interviews with children. The TOF requires that the person administering the ability or achievement tests be trained to do so. And the DOF requires that the observers, who may be paraprofessionals, be trained to use it. Proper interpretation of ASEBA profiles and integration with other data require training in standardized assessment of at least the master's degree level in psychology or equivalent levels of training in other fields.

For decades, ASEBA instruments have been used routinely to assess children and adolescents in many mental health, education, forensic, medical, training, and research contexts. Since the publication of instruments for ages 18 to 30 in 1997 (Achenbach, 1997b), their extension to age 59 (Achenbach & Rescorla, 2003), and the addition of instruments for ages 60 to 90+ (Achenbach et al., 2004), ASEBA instruments have been increasingly used to assess adults as well. Their use with adults includes assessment of parents of children who are assessed for clinical and forensic purposes.

When the ASEBA is used routinely in mental health and medical settings, parents and foster parents of child clients are typically asked to complete the CBCL/1$^1/_2$–5 or CBCL/6–18 as part of the intake process. Other adults who are involved in the care of the child, such as grandparents, other relatives, and nonparental partners, may also be asked to complete the CBCL to provide their perspectives on the child's functioning. If the child attends school or daycare, teachers and/or daycare providers should complete the C-TRF or TRF, with parental permission. In the case of a youth aged 11 to 18, parental permission for the youth to complete the YSR is typically requested, unless the youth is being evaluated in a context where parental permission is not required, such as some forensic settings.

To make it easy to obtain data without requiring respondents to come to providers' offices or requiring forms to be mailed back and forth, a Web-based application (*Web-Link*) that enables users to send forms electronically to any Web-connected computer has been developed. The form can be printed at the remote computer or can be displayed on the monitor to enable respondents to key in their responses. The data can then be electronically transmitted back to the user's computer for scoring and cross-informant comparisons. The user can also transmit scored profiles and cross-informant comparisons electronically to other Web-connected computers.

In school settings, teachers may complete TRFs as part of referral and evaluation procedures for special education or accommodation. School psychologists often use TRF data to decide whether and what further assessments are needed, such as CBCLs completed by parents, YSRs completed by students, TOFs and SCICAs completed by school psychologists, DOFs completed by school psychologists or by paraprofessionals such as teacher aides, and other procedures. The ASEBA data can be used to support decisions about whether students meet criteria for particular services or whether other remedies, such as changes in teachers, are warranted.

Strengths and Limitations for Clinical Use

ASEBA instruments are employed in very diverse settings for very diverse purposes by diverse users without specialized training in any particular theory or profession. Consequently, they provide a common data language for communication among people of very different backgrounds. For record compliance purposes, the profiles can be used to concisely and concretely document functioning at intake and subsequent time points. If practitioners deem it appropriate, the profiles and cross-informant comparisons can be shown to parents, teachers, and others involved in a case.

When an individual is initially evaluated in a particular setting, the profiles scored from ASEBA forms provide baseline measures of functioning at that point. Thereafter, ASEBA forms can be completed periodically to monitor the course and outcome of problems and adaptive functioning. After termination of services, the forms can be completed again to provide follow-up data. By comparing scores and profiles from one administration to another, users can identify areas in which functioning improves, remains stable, or worsens.

If the person who is assessed needs to be evaluated in other settings, the profiles obtained in the first setting can be sent, with appropriate permissions, to practitioners in the other settings. If they elect to do so, these practitioners can request that the ASEBA forms be completed again. The resulting profiles can then be compared with the previous profiles to identify areas of stability and change as seen by each respondent.

Numerous published studies have reported the use of ASEBA instruments for the assignment of cases to particular treatments, for identifying problems qualifying for particular educational services, and for the evaluation of outcomes. The *Bibliography of Published Studies Using the ASEBA* (Bérubé & Achenbach, 2006) lists over 410 publications related to treatment and over 430 related to outcomes.

Although the ASEBA is designed to assess diverse aspects of functioning under diverse conditions, additional assessment procedures are often needed. These include standardized tests of ability and achievement; medical and neuropsychological assessment procedures, when indicated; and histories of development, illness, medications, and past functioning. Customized assessment procedures may also be needed to answer the specific questions arising in particular cases. Not only the ASEBA instruments but other assessment procedures can be employed according to empirically based principles, as documented in a special section of the *Journal of Clinical Child and Adolescent Psychology* organized by Mash and Hunsley (2005).

FORENSIC USES AND LIMITATIONS

Many individuals who are assessed for forensic purposes are also assessed for other purposes, either prior to forensic assessment or subsequent to forensic assessment. For example, in child abuse and child custody cases, the children in question may have been previously assessed by medical, mental health, and/or education professionals. In some cases, findings from these assessments may lead to litigation. The results of such assessments may be employed by one or more parties in litigation. The professionals who did the assessments may be called upon to consult, to serve as witnesses, and to perform further assessments. Depending on the disposition of the cases, the same or different professionals may be asked to do additional assessments as a basis for helping the children and for monitoring their progress. In child abuse and child custody cases, assessment of parents and other adults may also be needed.

When juveniles are arrested, previous psychological assessments are often considered in determining dispositions. If no previous assessments are available or if arrested juveniles appear to have significant psychological problems, assessments are likely to be warranted. In reviewing studies of psychopathology among incarcerated juveniles, Grisso (2005) concluded that 60% to 70% of youths in detention centers and correction facilities have diagnosable mental disorders. Furthermore, "at least 15,000 youths annually are incarcerated upon arrest not because they are especially dangerous, but because of their acute mental disorders. They are locked up in juvenile detention centers until someone can find psychiatric or community mental health resources to provide them treatment" (Grisso, Vincent, & Seagrave, 2005, p. xi).

Serious mental disorders should receive extensive evaluation and treatment. However, the realities of juvenile justice systems dictate that, for mental health assessments to be done at all, they must typically begin with brief, standardized, structured procedures that can be administered at low cost by people who do not have advanced degrees in any of the mental health professions (Grisso, 2005). Even if mental health specialists eventually perform more extensive evaluations in the most severe cases, subsequent reassessments of youths who remain in the justice system are likely to require brief, inexpensive procedures that can be used by less specialized personnel.

In adult criminal cases, psychological assessments are also most likely to be done if minimally trained personnel can use procedures that are inexpensive, brief, standardized, and structured. Although some adults in the criminal justice system may be subsequently evaluated by mental health specialists, initial decisions can seldom wait for such evaluations. Furthermore, assessment instruments that can be applied at low cost to many adults in the system can help to determine which ones will receive more extensive evaluations and can provide baseline data for comparison with findings from subsequent assessments.

In other kinds of adult forensic cases, including those requiring evaluations of the competence of elderly or infirm individuals, it is also valuable to have brief, standardized, structured procedures that can be routinely applied at low cost by people without advanced mental health training. As is true for other forensic applications, such assessments of the elderly and infirm can help to determine when more extensive evaluations should be done and can provide baseline data for comparison with subsequent assessments.

Applications of ASEBA Instruments in Forensic Contexts

As noted, ASEBA instruments are used in many contexts by people from diverse disciplines. Consequently, ASEBA instruments often provide exceptional continuity between assessments done in different contexts for different purposes. Because assessments done for forensic purposes often involve duress, it is especially helpful to be able to compare the results of such assessments with assessments done with the same instruments under conditions involving less duress. The fact that ASEBA forms are self-administered in 10 to 20 minutes and can be scored by clerical workers by hand or computer means that they can be routinely applied quickly, at low cost, and by individuals who are not mental health specialists. For respondents who cannot complete forms independently, ASEBA forms can be read aloud and the answers can be recorded by anyone who is familiar with the forms. Forensic personnel can easily learn to identify deviant scale scores and can use the single-page narrative reports to quickly identify strengths, deviance, and critical items reported for the person being assessed.

The parallel ASEBA forms completed by different informants and the systematic cross-informant comparisons provided by ASEBA software make it easy to identify similarities and differences between reports by different informants. This is especially valuable in forensic contexts, where conflicting perceptions and motives often lead to very different reports of problems and strengths. Because validity, social desirability, and lie scales cannot resolve such discrepancies (Piedmont et al., 2000), it is necessary to explicitly document consistencies and inconsistencies between reports by the person being evaluated and by various people who know that person.

As an example, suppose that ASEBA forms completed by several informants yield high scores on scales such as Rule-Breaking Behavior, Aggressive Behavior, Conduct Problems, and Antisocial Personality Problems, but an ASEBA self-report form yields low scores on these scales. This would be evidence that the person being assessed is not being candid or is unaware of his or her problem behaviors. On the other hand, if a very deviant Somatic Complaints syndrome score is obtained from a self-report form but not from any collateral report forms, this would suggest possible malingering

As another example, if a CBCL completed by a parent whose parental rights are in question yields scores that are very different from scores yielded by ASEBA forms completed by others who know the child, this would be evidence that the parent's report is not an accurate picture of the child's overall functioning.

Because ASEBA forms have been available for children and adolescents much longer than for adults, most of the published studies pertain to children and adolescents. As of this writing, the published studies include at least 177 on physical and sexual abuse, 145 on substance abuse, 128 on antisocial conduct, 109 on delinquent behavior, 77 on divorce, 57 on foster care, and 21 on custody (Bérubé & Achenbach, 2006). Because ASEBA forms are used for so many purposes in so many contexts, the data obtained with them can be relevant to many facets and stages of forensic assessment, as outlined earlier. The availability of forms for ages 18 to 59 and 60 to 90+ as well as for ages $1\frac{1}{2}$ to 18 enables users to do multigenerational assessments when indicated. For forensic cases involving abuse and custody issues, this means that ASEBA forms can be used to assess the relevant adults as well as the children from multiple perspectives. In cases of divorce, custody disputes, and foster care, ASEBA forms may also be used to periodically reassess children and the relevant adults in order to monitor their functioning after initial decisions are made.

As an example, if a child has been provisionally placed with one parent, a relative, or foster parents, it is often important to assess the child's progress after several months. Such assessments should include data from multiple informants, such as the adults with whom the child is placed, family members, teachers, daycare providers, and the child. As with initial assessments, informants' reports should be compared to identify similarities and differences as a basis for determining whether certain problems are limited to particular personal relationships or to particular situations such as school. If significant problems are reported by only one informant, then that informant's relationship with the child should be examined to determine the degree to which the informant's perceptions of the child or behaviors toward the child or contexts of their interactions contribute to reports of elevated problem levels. If multiple informants report especially high or low levels of problems in a particular situation, such as school or daycare, then that situation should be examined to determine why the child is seen as behaving worse or better in that situation than elsewhere. Professionals who conduct continuing and follow-up evaluations of this sort may be especially able to promote the best interests of the child by identifying and helping to ameliorate adverse dynamics among the relevant parties.

Examples of Relevant Research

Because the relevant research is so vast and diverse, it cannot be succinctly summarized. Instead, we illustrate some relevant research applications.

Maltreatment of children and placement of children in the custody of child protection agencies raise a host of forensic issues. In addition, children who are maltreated and those in the custody of protective agencies may be at especially high risk for subsequent problems in adolescence and adulthood, including delinquency, criminal behavior, and psychopathology. McGee, Wolfe, and Wilson (1997) tested associations between different kinds of maltreatment and subsequent problems in 11- to 17-year-old wards of a child protection agency. To assess current problems, the youths completed the YSR, and their primary caretakers completed the CBCL. The complex associations between kinds and degrees of maltreatment, gender of the youths, sources of data, and types of problems were illustrated by significant interactions such as the following:

- For both genders, YSR scores for Internalizing problems increased with the severity of physical maltreatment experienced by the youths. However, there was a strong interaction with gender such that, among youths who had not experienced physical maltreatment, girls reported fewer Internalizing problems than boys, but the opposite gender difference was found for youths who had experienced moderate to severe physical maltreatment.

- For youths whose case records were rated as indicating severe psychological maltreatment, YSR scores for Internalizing problems were much higher among those who self-reported moderate to severe psychological maltreatment than among those who self-reported none to mild psychological maltreatment. However, for youths whose case records were rated as indicating no psychological maltreatment, YSR Internalizing scores were slightly lower among those who self-reported moderate to severe psychological maltreatment than among those who self-reported none to mild maltreatment.

- For youths whose case records were rated as indicating severe sexual abuse, caretakers' CBCL ratings of Externalizing problems were higher for those who self-reported none to mild sexual abuse than for those who self-reported moderate to severe sexual abuse. However, for youths whose case records were rated as indicating no sexual abuse, caretakers' CBCL ratings of Externalizing problems were lower for those who self-reported none to mild abuse than for those who reported moderate to severe abuse.

As with so many aspects of forensic research and practice, these findings indicate important variations between reports by different sources, such as youths, caretakers, and agencies. To advance knowledge and practice, it is therefore necessary to use multiple data sources and to respect the complexity that they may reveal.

In a study of adjudicated delinquents, the YSR and CBCL were used to test the hypothesis that females would be more deviant than males with respect to psychological symptoms (McCabe, Lansing, Garland, & Hough, 2002). Using T-scores based on the age-, gender-, and informant-specific national normative samples for the YSR and CBCL, McCabe et al. found higher T-scores for delinquent girls than boys on both the YSR and CBCL Total Problems, Internalizing, and Externalizing scales. However, on both instruments, the gender differences were statistically significant for Total Problems and for Externalizing but not for Internalizing. This indicated that, compared to delinquent boys, delinquent girls were especially deviant with respect to Externalizing Problems, which, in turn, contributed to their significantly higher Total Problems T-scores.

Multicultural Aspects of Assessment

People who are assessed for forensic purposes are often of different ethnic and cultural backgrounds than the people who assess them. For example, it may easily happen that the people being assessed are from native-born minority groups or are immigrants or refugees from other cultures whereas the people doing the assessment are from native-born majority groups. In these and other cases where cultural issues may arise, it is important to use assessment instruments whose multicultural applications are well supported by research. As indicated earlier, translations of ASEBA forms are available in over 70 languages. Furthermore, confirmatory factor analyses have shown that patterns of problems reported for children in 30 cultures fit the ASEBA syndromes (Ivanova et al., 2006). The ASEBA scores for the sample from a particular culture can thus be used to contextualize scores obtained by immigrants and refugees who are members of that culture. In addition, analyses of ASEBA scores have shown that differences among native-born ethnic groups did not exceed chance expectations when controlling for socioeconomic status in U.S. national and clinical samples (Achenbach et al., 2004; Achenbach & Rescorla, 2000, 2001, 2003). These findings and the findings from 67 published studies of ethnicity and 1,590 published cross-cultural studies (Bérubé & Achenbach, 2006) support multicultural applications of ASEBA instruments.

Administrative and Interpretive Adjustments for Forensic Use

Because ASEBA self-report and collateral report forms are brief, standardized, structured, and self-administered, forensic use does not typically require special administrative adjustments. However, as detailed earlier, ASEBA forms can also be read aloud by interviewers who write down the respondents' answers. ASEBA forms can be completed by individuals at remote sites via Web-Link, which was described earlier. Self-report and collateral report forms can also be completed by respondents via ASEBA client-entry software in users' offices. For large-volume users, machine-readable Teleform® and optical mark read (OMR) versions of ASEBA forms are available.

Most people who do forensic assessments are accustomed to the stressful and adversarial aspects. They also understand that the people being assessed may not be candid or mentally competent. Because stress, conflict, lack of candor, and mental incompetence are common in forensic assessment, the need for reports by as many informants as possible is even more compelling than in assessment for nonforensic purposes. Depending on the goal of a particular forensic assessment, the consistencies and inconsistencies between reports by different informants contribute evidence regarding such questions as veracity, distortion, reality testing, fitness for parenting, and candidacy for restrictive settings such as incarceration, residential treatment, or nursing homes. Although systematic comparison of reports by multiple informants is a key ingredient of appropriate assessment, the specific findings should be tested against other sources of data, such as interviews, observations, and documents, before final conclusions are drawn.

Strengths and Limitations for Forensic Use

As outlined in the preceding sections, ASEBA instruments have the advantage of being applicable to very diverse cases and under very diverse conditions. ASEBA forms can be completed by a variety of respondents for comparison with national norms for ages $1\frac{1}{2}$ to 90+ years. ASEBA software provides systematic comparisons between data obtained from self-reports and multiple collateral reports. Thousands of published studies report findings for people of many backgrounds from many cultures. Because they can be self-administered or administered by nonclinician interviewers in 10 to 20 minutes, ASEBA forms can be quickly applied at low cost. They can also be readministered periodically, and the results obtained in nonforensic and forensic assessment contexts can be compared. With appropriate consents and protection of confidentiality, ASEBA profiles, cross-informant comparisons, and narrative reports can be presented as evidence in forensic cases.

No single approach can be expected to provide everything that is needed for comprehensive forensic evaluations. Although ASEBA instruments obtain data on diverse aspects of functioning from diverse perspectives, comprehensive evaluation involves comparison and supplementation of findings with data from interviews and histories as well as from reports regarding the forensic issues. Cognitive, neuropsychological, and personality tests may also be needed to assess aspects of functioning not assessed by ASEBA instruments.

CASE EXAMPLE

Custody Evaluation for Lisa Gordon, Age 4

Dr. Lorraine Mercer was hired to conduct a custody evaluation for 4-year-old Lisa Gordon in the divorce case of her parents, David and Cynthia Gordon, age 26 and 22, respectively. Two years prior to the custody evaluation, the Gordons had separated, David had taken a job about 3 hours drive away, and Cynthia had moved with their 2-year-old daughter Lisa back to her mother's home. Under the separation agreement, Lisa had been spending alternate weekends with her father.

As David became increasingly concerned about Cynthia's parenting of Lisa, he decided to sue for physical custody as part of the divorce proceedings. Because Cynthia also wished to have custody of Lisa, the family court recruited Dr. Mercer to evaluate Lisa and her parents in order to render an opinion on what custody arrangements would be in the child's best interests. Dr. Mercer made appointments to see Lisa and her parents and sent each parent several forms to complete: a developmental/family history form, an ASR, two ABCLs (for a relative or friend to complete about David and Cynthia), and a CBCL/1½–5 to complete about Lisa. Dr. Mercer also obtained consent from both parents to send C-TRFs to two teachers at Lisa's daycare center.

ASEBA Findings for Lisa

As can be seen in Table 9.6, the C-TRF completed by one of Lisa's daycare teachers yielded scores in the clinical range on Total Problems, Internalizing, Externalizing, the Emotionally Reactive and Anxious/Depressed syndromes, and the *DSM*-oriented Affective, Anxiety, and Oppositional Defiant Problems scales. Scores on the Withdrawn and Aggressive Behavior syndromes were in the borderline clinical range. The C–TRF completed

TABLE 9.6
T-Scores for Lisa Based on Ratings by Four Informants

Scale	Teacher 1	Teacher 2	Father	Mother
Emotionally Reactive	72 – C[a]	70 – C	66 – B	54
Anxious/Depressed	71 – C	68 – B	70 – C	53
Somatic Complaints	53	52	51	51
Withdrawn	67 – B[b]	64	60	57
Sleep Problems	NA	NA	66 – B	59
Attention Problems	55	56	52	54
Aggressive Behavior	66 – B	65 – B	53	67 – B
Internalizing	71 – C	68 – C	64 – B	51
Externalizing	72 – C	70 – C	58	53
Total Problems	72 – C	70 – C	67 – C	54
DSM Affective Problems	72 – C	68 – B	66 – B	52
DSM Anxiety Problems	71 – C	67 – B	65 – B	51
DSM PDD Problems	53	52	50	50
DSM ADH Problems	54	55	51	50
DSM ODD Problems	74 – C	71 – C	66 – B	68 – B

[a]C = clinical range ($T \geq 70$ for syndromes and *DSM* scales, $T \geq 64$ for I, E, and TP).
[b]B = borderline range ($T \geq 65$ for syndromes and *DSM* scales, $T \geq 60$ for I, E, and TP).

by Lisa's other teacher yielded scores in the borderline or clinical range on most of these same scales.

The CBCL completed by David showed above-average cross-informant correlations with the both teachers' C-TRFs. As shown in Table 9.6, David's CBCL yielded scores in the borderline or clinical range on most of the same scales as the C-TRFs did, with the exception of Aggressive Behavior, on which David scored Lisa in the normal range. David's CBCL also yielded a score in the borderline clinical range on the Sleep Problems syndrome, which is not scored from the C-TRF. In contrast, as seen in Table 9.6, Cynthia's CBCL yielded scores in the normal range on all scales with the exception of borderline clinical range scores on the Aggressive Behavior syndrome and the Oppositional Defiant Problems scale. Her CBCL had below-average cross-informant correlations with the forms completed by Lisa's teachers and by David.

In response to the C-TRF's open-ended questions, Lisa's teachers wrote that Lisa was often angry or withdrawn. They reported that Lisa often cried at morning drop-off but then sometimes refused to leave at evening pickup. They noted that Lisa was not fully toilet trained; some days she came to school in underpants and other days she wore pull-ups. They also wrote that she sometimes arrived at daycare without having eaten breakfast, in inappropriate or soiled clothing, or with uncombed hair. On the C-TRF item regarding the best things about the child, Lisa's teachers noted that she was a bright and verbal little girl with good imaginative play skills who could be lively and engaging when in a good mood.

Cynthia's responses to the open-ended questions on the CBCL indicated that Lisa was very demanding and stubborn and was a picky eater. She added that Lisa resisted going to sleep and staying in her own bed, using the potty, and having her hair washed and brushed. However, on the CBCL item regarding the best things about the child, Cynthia listed that Lisa was smart, pretty, funny, and good at singing, dancing, and drawing.

In response to the CBCL question about what concerned him most about Lisa, David expressed concern that Cynthia's erratic practices with regard to meals, bedtime, hygiene, and toilet training were putting Lisa at risk and preventing her from developing important skills. He added that although Cynthia could be affectionate toward and responsive to Lisa at times, she was often either overindulgent, neglectful, or angry. In response to the CBCL question regarding the best things about Lisa, he wrote that she was a smart, charming, pretty little girl who could be very loving and cooperative when she was in a good mood.

ASEBA Findings for David Gordon, Age 26

Based on David's self-reports on the ASR, his scores were in the clinical range on the Spouse/Partner scale, in the borderline clinical range on the Friends scale, and in the normal range on the Family, Job, and Education scales. He obtained scores in the borderline range on the Somatic Complaints syndrome and the *DSM*-oriented Anxiety Problems scale. David described himself as performing adequately in his job as an assistant computer systems manager in a health insurance company. He wrote that he lived near both his parents and his older sister, that he saw them frequently, and that they provided emotional support. However, he wrote that he was preoccupied about his custody battle, was not sleeping well or exercising enough, and was having trouble concentrating at work. On the ASR questions about substance use, David reported that he typically had two beers at night. He also reported that he had occasional headaches and stomach pain.

David asked his mother and older sister to complete the ABCLs sent by Dr. Mercer. Ratings by his mother yielded scores in the borderline clinical range on the Anxious/Depressed syndrome and on the *DSM*-oriented Anxiety Problems and Avoidant Personality Problems scales. His mother's responses to open-ended questions on the ABCL indicated that she admired her son for his struggle to manage his job, take care of his daughter, and deal with his divorce. In response to the ABCL question about her greatest concerns about her son, she listed his agitated and depressed state of mind.

The ABCL completed by David's sister Amanda yielded scores in the normal range on all scales except borderline clinical range scores on the Anxious/Depressed syndrome and on the *DSM*-oriented Anxiety Problems scale. On the ABCL item regarding the best things about her brother, Amanda wrote that she was impressed with how hard he was trying to be a good father to Lisa. Amanda also wrote that David regularly brought Lisa over to play with her two children and would often ask her for tips about how to handle Lisa or things to do with her. Amanda added that she provided home-based child care services for several young children and that Lisa sometimes joined this group when David was at work.

ASEBA Findings for Cynthia Gordon, Age 22

Cynthia's self-report on the ASR yielded scores in the normal range on all scales. The only problems she endorsed as very true were worrying, headaches, and sleep problems. Items she endorsed as somewhat or sometimes true included being nervous, forgetful, disorganized, poor at details, late, argumentative, stubborn, impatient, easily bored, and jealous. In response to the ASR open-ended item regarding her greatest concerns about herself, Cynthia wrote that she felt dissatisfied with her life, worried about her future, and concerned about losing custody of Lisa. On the ASR item regarding the best things about herself, she wrote that she was enthusiastic, fun-loving, generous, and attractive.

The ABCL completed by Cynthia's mother also yielded scores in the normal range on all scales. Cynthia's mother rated as very true some of the problems Cynthia rated as somewhat true, such as arguing with others, getting along badly with family members, rushing into things, and being disorganized, poor at details, forgetful, and stubborn. In response to the ABCL question regarding what concerned her most about Cynthia, Cynthia's mother listed her dropping out of college when she became pregnant, her frustration with her job, her quick temper, and her disorganization. On the ABCL item regarding the best things about Cynthia, her mother wrote that she was warm-hearted, fun to be with, lively, and generous. She added that Cynthia loved Lisa and did many nice things with her.

Cynthia also asked her Aunt Rosalie to complete an ABCL. Rosalie's ABCL yielded scores in the clinical range for Cynthia on the Spouse/Partner scale and on the Externalizing scale and in the borderline clinical range on the Attention Problems, Aggressive Behavior, and Rule-Breaking Behavior syndromes and the Total Problems, Friends, and Alcohol scales. In response to the ABCL item about what concerned her most about her niece, Rosalie listed Cynthia's immaturity, lack of independence, quick temper, and impulsivity. She added that Cynthia seemed to be struggling in her attempt to work, care for her daughter, and have some life of her own. Her comments about her niece's best qualities included that she was pretty, friendly, artistic, and creative.

Information Obtained from Clinical Interviews

Dr. Mercer interviewed David and Cynthia Gordon separately as well as together. She observed Lisa at home, at school, and in the office with both parents. She also spoke by phone with David's mother and sister and with Cynthia's mother and aunt in order to follow up on information they had provided on the ABCL.

Based on these contacts, Dr. Mercer learned that David and Cynthia had met at a fraternity party when he was a senior and she was a freshman. They had only been dating a few months when Cynthia became pregnant with Lisa, despite having told David she was taking birth control pills. Although the couple initially agreed that an abortion was the best option, Cynthia kept missing appointments for the procedure until it became too late to have it. At this point, David proposed that they get married. Cynthia completed her freshman year, and then dropped out to care for their daughter, and David started work in the computer center at the university where he had obtained his degree.

Dr. Mercer learned that the couple soon started arguing about money, housework, child care, and use of leisure time. David was dissatisfied with his job and critical of his wife's management of the apartment, their daughter, and finances. David was especially concerned with how angry Cynthia became at Lisa, and he worried that she might lose control and harm their daughter. On the other hand, Cynthia felt isolated staying home all day with Lisa, complained that David never liked to have fun anymore, and accused him of being unsympathetic.

After the couple separated and Cynthia returned to her mother's, her mother insisted that she find a job so that she could help with expenses. Cynthia found a job as a receptionist in a local doctor's office and enrolled Lisa in a daycare center. Cynthia's mother reported that having Cynthia back home was challenging at times but that she liked having contact with her little granddaughter. She reported that she sometimes babysat for Lisa when Cynthia went out with friends but that she often worked evenings and weekends.

Dr. Mercer learned that David and Cynthia had many conflicts about how to parent Lisa and that disagreement about basic issues such as diet, bedtime, toileting, medical care, discipline, and visitation were frequent. David said that Lisa had told him twice that Cynthia had slapped and scratched her. He also reported that Cynthia made it difficult for him to talk to his daughter on the phone, which he tried to do every night before she went to bed. Cynthia complained that David lectured her and made what she considered to be unreasonable demands. She added that David did not realize how infuriating Lisa could be because he was not with her all the time.

Custody Recommendations

Dr. Mercer interpreted the ASEBA results as indicating that David's perceptions of Lisa and of his own functioning were more realistic than Cynthia's perceptions of Lisa and her own functioning. She observed that Lisa's attachment to her mother was strong but conflicted, whereas her attachment to her father was less intense but also less ambivalent. Dr. Mercer noted that David appeared to understand what was developmentally appropriate for Lisa and knew when to ask for advice, whereas Cynthia did not appear knowledgeable about Lisa's needs. Dr. Mercer suspected that Cynthia might use excessive physical force with Lisa at times, although her evaluation did not substantiate any physical abuse.

Dr. Mercer also interpreted the ASEBA results as indicating that Lisa behaved more age-appropriately when in her father's care. She was less volatile and oppositional, and she cooperated more with eating, bathing, hygiene, and sleep routines. Lisa also appeared to be less demanding and bossy when with her father than when with her mother.

Citing ASEBA findings and her own observations, Dr. Mercer reported that David displayed more maturity in balancing his work, leisure time, and care of Lisa than did

Cynthia, who seemed resentful of child care responsibilities and frustrated that she could not have more free time. Dr. Mercer noted that both parents had full-time jobs and thus required child care for Lisa during the work day. Although both David and Cynthia had family nearby, Dr. Mercer concluded that David's parents and sister would be more likely to provide helpful backup and support for Lisa's care than Cynthia's mother and aunt.

Dr. Mercer concluded that David could provide a more stable, predictable, and wholesome environment for Lisa than Cynthia could. Dr. Mercer also expressed concern about Cynthia's lack of insight into her own issues, her impulsive lifestyle, and her volatile temper. Dr. Mercer therefore recommended that David have physical custody and that Cynthia have visitation privileges on alternate weekends, for half of the year's major holidays, and for 2 weeks during the summer.

SUMMARY

This chapter presented the ASEBA and its applications in forensic contexts. The ASEBA comprises a family of self-report and collateral report forms for assessing adaptive and maladaptive functioning for ages $1\frac{1}{2}$ to 90+ years. It also includes forms for completion by clinical interviewers, psychological examiners, and observers of behavior in group settings. The forms are scored on scales that include adaptive functioning, empirically based syndromes, *DSM*-oriented scales, and Internalizing, Externalizing, and Total Problems scales. Scores are displayed on profiles in relation to age, gender, and informant-specific norms. ASEBA software prints profiles, cross-informant comparisons, and narrative reports. ASEBA forms are available in over 70 languages, and findings have been reported in over 6,000 publications from 64 cultures.

Psychometric data, evidence of validity, strengths, and limitations were presented. Forensic applications were illustrated in a case example in which a child, her mother, and her father were each assessed by means of ASEBA forms completed by multiple informants. Because ASEBA forms can be self-administered in 10 to 20 minutes under diverse conditions and can be quickly scored by clerical workers, they can be routinely used not only for clinical assessment but for initial forensic assessment and for follow-up assessment after forensic decisions have been made.

REFERENCES

Achenbach, T.M. (1966). The classification of children's psychiatric symptoms: A factor-analytic study. *Psychological Monographs, 80* (No. 615).

Achenbach, T.M. (1991). *Integrative guide for the 1991 CBCL/4–18, YSR, and TRF profiles.* Burlington: University of Vermont, Department of Psychiatry.

Achenbach, T.M. (1992). *Manual for the Child Behavior Checklist/2–3 and 1992 Profile.* Burlington: University of Vermont, Department of Psychiatry.

Achenbach, T.M. (1997a). *Guide for the Caregiver-Teacher Report Form for Ages 2–5.* Burlington: University of Vermont, Department of Psychiatry.

Achenbach, T.M. (1997b). *Manual for the Young Adult Self-Report and Young Adult Behavior Checklist.* Burlington: University of Vermont, Department of Psychiatry.

Achenbach, T.M., & Edelbrock, C. (1983). *Manual for the Child Behavior Checklist and Revised Child Behavior Profile.* Burlington: University of Vermont, Department of Psychiatry.

Achenbach, T.M., & Edelbrock, C. (1986). *Manual for the Teacher's Report Form and Teacher Version of the Child Behavior Profile.* Burlington: University of Vermont, Department of Psychiatry.

Achenbach, T.M., & Edelbrock, C. (1987). *Manual for the Youth Self-Report and Profile*. Burlington: University of Vermont, Department of Psychiatry.

Achenbach, T.M., Howell, C.T., McConaughy, S.H., & Stanger, C. (1995). Six-year predictors of problems in a national sample: III. Transitions to young adult syndromes. *Journal of the American Academy of Child and Adolescent Psychiatry, 34*, 658–669.

Achenbach, T.M., Howell, C.T., McConaughy, S.H., & Stanger, C. (1998). Six-year predictors of problems in a national sample: IV. Young adult signs of disturbance. *Journal of the American Academy of Child and Adolescent Psychiatry, 37*, 718–727.

Achenbach, T.M., Krukowski, R.A., Dumenci, L., & Ivanova, M.Y. (2005). Assessment of adult psychopathology: Meta-analyses and implications of cross-informant correlations. *Psychological Bulletin, 131*, 361–382.

Achenbach, T.M., McConaughy, S.H., & Howell, C.T. (1987). Child/adolescent behavioral and emotional problems: Implications of cross-informant correlations for situational specificity. *Psychological Bulletin, 101*, 213–232.

Achenbach, T.M., Newhouse, P.A. & Rescorla, L.A. (2004). *Manual for the ASEBA Older Adult Forms and Profiles*. Burlington: University of Vermont, Research Center for Children, Youth, and Families.

Achenbach, T.M., & Rescorla, L.A. (2000). *Manual for the ASEBA Preschool Forms and Profiles*. Burlington: University of Vermont, Department of Psychiatry.

Achenbach, T.M., & Rescorla, L.A. (2001). *Manual for the ASEBA School-Age Forms and Profiles*. Burlington: University of Vermont, Research Center for Children, Youth, and Families.

Achenbach, T.M., & Rescorla, L.A. (2003). *Manual for the ASEBA Adult Forms and Profiles*. Burlington: University of Vermont, Research Center for Children, Youth, and Families.

American Psychiatric Association. (1952). *Diagnostic and statistical manual of mental disorders*. Washington, DC: Author.

American Psychiatric Association. (1994). *Diagnostic and statistic manual of mental disorders* (4th ed.). Washington, DC: Author.

Arend, R., Lavigne, J.V., Rosenbaum, D., Binns, H.J., & Christoffel, K.K. (1996). Relation between taxonomic and quantitative diagnostic systems in preschool children: Emphasis on disruptive disorders. *Journal of Clinical Child Psychology, 25*, 388–397.

Beck, A.T., & Steer, R.A. (1990). *Beck Anxiety Inventory manual*. San Antonio, TX: The Psychological Corporation.

Bérubé, R.L., & Achenbach, T.M. (2006). *Bibliography of published studies using the Achenbach System of Empirically Based Assessment (ASEBA): 2006 edition*. Burlington: University of Vermont, Research Center for Children, Youth, and Families.

Briggs-Gowan, M.J., & Carter, A.S. (1998). Preliminary acceptability and psychometrics of the Infant-Toddler Social and Emotional Assessment (ITSEA): A new adult-report questionnaire. *Infant Mental Health Journal, 19*, 422–445.

Butcher, J.N., Dahlstrom, W.G., Graham, J.R., Tellegen, A., & Kaemmer, B. (1989). *Minnesota Multiphasic Personality Inventory (MMPI-2): Manual for administration and scoring*. Minneapolis: University of Minnesota Press.

Conners, C.K. (1997). *Conners' Rating Scales–Revised technical manual*. North Tonawanda, NY: Multi-Health Systems.

Cummings, J.L., Mega, M., Gray, K., Rosenberg-Thompson, S., Carusi, D.A., & Gornbein, J. (1994). The Neuropsychiatric Inventory: Comprehensive assessment of psychopathology in dementia. *Neurology, 44*, 2308–2314.

Derogatis, L.R. (1994). *SCL-90-R: Administration scoring and procedures manual*. Minneapolis, MN: National Computer Systems.

Edelbrock, C., & Costello, A.J. (1988). Structured psychiatric interviews for children. In M. Rutter, A.H. Tuma, & I.S. Lann (Eds.), *Assessment and diagnosis in child psychopathology* (pp. 87–112). New York: Guilford Press.

Ferdinand, R.F., Blüm, M., & Verhulst, F.C. (2001). Psychopathology in adolescence predicts substance use in young adulthood. *Addiction, 96*, 861–870.

Ferdinand, R.F., Hoogerheide, K.N., van der Ende, J., Heijmens Visser, J.H., Koot, H.M., Kasius, M.C., et al. (2003). The role of the clinician: Three-year predictive value of parents', teachers', and clinicians' judgment of childhood psychopathology. *Journal of Child Psychology and Psychiatry, 44*, 867–876.

Ferdinand, R.F., & Verhulst, F.C. (1994). The prediction of poor outcome in young adults: Comparison of the Young Adult Self-Report, the General Health Questionnaire, and the Symptom Checklist. *Acta Psychiatrica Scandinavica, 89*, 405–410.

Ferdinand, R.F., & Verhulst, F.C. (1995a). Psychopathology from adolescence into young adulthood: An 8-year follow-up study. *American Journal of Psychiatry, 152*, 1586–1594.

Ferdinand, R.F., & Verhulst, F.C. (1995b). Psychopathology in Dutch young adults: Enduring or changeable? *Social Psychiatry and Psychiatric Epidemiology, 30*, 60–64.

Ferdinand, R.F., Verhulst, F.C., & Wiznitzer, M. (1995). Continuity and change of self-reported problem behaviors from adolescence into young adulthood. *Journal of the American Academy of Child and Adolescent Psychiatry, 34*, 680–690.

Folstein, M.F., Folstein, S.E., & McHugh, P.R. (1975). "Mini-mental state": A practical method for grading the cognitive state of patients for the clinican. *Journal of Psychiatry Research, 12*, 189–198.

Goldberg, D.P. (1992). *The detection of psychiatric illness by questionnaire*. London: Oxford University Press.

Grisso, T. (2005). Why we need mental health screening and assessment in juvenile justice programs. In T. Grisso, G. Vincent, & D. Seagrave (Eds.), *Mental health screening and assessment in juvenile justice* (pp. 3–21). New York: Guilford Press.

Grisso, T., Vincent, G., & Seagrave, D. (2005). *Mental health screening and assessment in juvenile justice*. New York: Guilford Press.

Hofstra, M.B., van der Ende, J., & Verhulst, F.C. (2000). Continuity and change of psychopathology from childhood into adulthood: A 14-year follow-up study. *Journal of the American Academy of Child and Adolescent Psychiatry, 39*, 850–858.

Hofstra, M.B., van der Ende, J., & Verhulst, F.C. (2001). Adolescents' self-reported problems as predictors of psychopathology in adulthood: 10-year follow-up study. *British Journal of Psychiatry, 179*, 203–209.

Hofstra, M.B., van der Ende, J., & Verhulst, F.C. (2002a). Child and adolescent problems predict *DSM*-IV disorders in adulthood: A 14-year follow-up of a Dutch epidemiological sample. *Journal of the American Academy of Child and Adolescent Psychiatry, 41*, 182–189.

Hofstra, M.B., van der Ende, J., & Verhulst, F.C. (2002b). Pathways of self-reported problem behaviors from adolescence into adulthood. *American Journal of Psychiatry, 159*, 401–407.

Ivanova, M.Y., Achenbach, T.M., Dumenci, L., Rescorla, L.A., Almqvist, F., Bilenberg, N., et al. (2006). Configural invariance of the Child Behavior Checklist syndromes in 30 cultures. Manuscript submitted for publication.

Kasius, M.C., Ferdinand, R.F., van den Berg, H., & Verhulst, F.C. (1997). Associations between different diagnostic approaches for child and adolescent psychopathology. *Journal of Child Psychology and Psychiatry, 38*, 625–632.

Kazdin, A.E., & Heidish, I.E. (1984). Convergence of clinically derived diagnoses and parent checklists among inpatient children. *Journal of Abnormal Child Psychology, 12*, 421–435.

Keenan, K., & Wakschlag, L.S. (2000). More than the terrible twos: The nature and severity of behavior problems in clinic-referred preschool children. *Journal of Abnormal Child Psychology, 28*, 33–46.

Mash, E.J., & Hunsley, J. (2005). Evidence-based assessment of child and adolescent disorders: Issues and challenges. *Journal of Clinical Child and Adolescent Psychology, 34*, 362–379.

McCabe, K.M., Lansing, A.E., Garland, A., & Hough, R. (2002). Gender differences in psychopathology, functional impairment, and familial risk factors among adjudicated delinquents. *Journal of the American Academy of Child and Adolescent Psychiatry, 41*, 860–867.

McConaughy, S.H., & Achenbach, T.M. (2001). *Manual for the Semistructured Clinical Interview for Children and Adolescents* (2nd ed.). Burlington: University of Vermont, Research Center for Children, Youth, and Families.

McConaughy, S.H., & Achenbach, T.M. (2004). *Manual for the Test Observation Form for Ages 2–18*. Burlington: University of Vermont, Research Center for Children, Youth, and Families.

McConaughy, S.H., Achenbach, T.M., & Gent, C.L. (1988). Multiaxial empirically based assessment: Parent, teacher, observational, cognitive, and personality correlates of Child Behavior Profiles for 6–to-11-year-old boys. *Journal of Abnormal Child Psychology, 16*, 485–509.

McConaughy, S.H., Kay, P.J., & Fitzgerald, M. (1998). Preventing SED through parent-teacher action: Research and social skills instruction: First-year outcomes. *Journal of Emotional and Behavioral Disorders, 6,* 81–93.

McConaughy, S.H., Kay, P.J., & Fitzgerald, M. (1999). The Achieving Behaving Caring Project for preventing ED: Two-year outcomes. *Journal of Emotional and Behavioral Disorders, 7,* 224–239.

McGee, R.A., Wolfe, D.A., & Wilson, S.K. (1997). Multiple maltreatment experiences and adolescent behavior problems: Adolescents' perspectives. *Development and Psychopathology, 9,* 131–149.

Meyer, G.J. (2002). Implications of information gathering methods for a refined taxonomy of psychopathology. In L.E. Beutler & M.L. Malik (Eds.), *Rethinking the DSM*: A psychological perspective (pp. 69–105). Washington, DC: American Psychological Association.

Mouton-Simien, P., McCain, A.P., & Kelley, M.L. (1997). The development of the Toddler Behavior Screening Inventory. *Journal of Abnormal Child Psychology, 25,* 59–64.

Piedmont, R.L., McCrae, R.R., Riemann, R., & Angleitner, A. (2000). On the invalidity of validity scales: Evidence from self-report and observer ratings in volunteer samples. *Journal of Personality and Social Psychology, 78,* 582–593.

Reed, M.L., & Edelbrock, C. (1983). Reliability and validity of the Direct Observation Form of the Child Behavior Checklist. *Journal of Abnormal Child Psychology, 11,* 521–530.

Rescorla, L.A., Achenbach, T.M., Ivanova, M.Y., Dumenci, L., Bilenberg, N., Bird, H., et al. (2006). Problems reported by parents of children ages 6 to 16 in 31 cultures. Manuscript submitted for publication.

Reynolds, C.R., & Kamphaus, R.W. (1992). *Behavior Assessment System for Children.* Circle Pines, MN: American Guidance Service.

Richman, N., Stevenson, J., & Graham, P.J. (1982). *Pre-school to school: A behavioural study.* London and New York: Academic Press.

Weinstein, S.R., Noam, G.G., Grimes, K., Stone, K., & Schwab-Stone, M. (1990). Convergence of DSM-III diagnoses and self-reported symptoms in child and adolescent inpatients. *Journal of the American Academy of Child and Adolescent Psychiatry, 29,* 627–634.

The Personality Inventory for Youth, the Personality Inventory for Children, Second Edition, and the Student Behavior Survey

David Lachar

UNIVERSITY OF TEXAS–HOUSTON MEDICAL SCHOOL

Byron A. Hammer

JEFFERSON PARISH HUMAN SERVICES AUTHORITY

Jill Hayes Hammer

LOUISIANA STATE UNIVERSITY HEALTH SCIENCE CENTER

BASIC DESCRIPTION

This chapter introduces a family of measures used in the evaluation of youths in a variety of settings, including court-ordered evaluations conducted in mental health settings and classification activities completed at juvenile justice facilities. The measures are the Personality Inventory for Youth (PIY), the Personality Inventory for Children, Second Edition (PIC–2), and the Student Behavior Survey (SBS). Each of these evaluates multiple dimensions of problem behavior (undercontrolled, overcontrolled, social adjustment, family-related, academic, and cognitive). Each collects observations either from youths (PIY), their parents (PIC–2), or their teachers (SBS) and provides standard scores derived from contemporary national samples. These measures are available from Western Psychological Services (12031 Wilshire Boulevard, Los Angels, CA 90025).

The use of multiple informants to obtain concurrent assessments of multiple dimensions of problem behavior is both efficient and meaningful. Salient dimensions of adjustment are assessed using a consistent format and are interpreted using the same or comparable standardization samples. Employment of multidimensional assessment assumes that the pattern of symptom presence and problem absence makes a meaningful diagnostic contribution. A multidimensional approach to assessment also recognizes that youths who present for psychological assessment often demonstrate a pattern of significant clinical problems rather than the externalizing symptoms that usually precipitate the referrals. Such patterns of problems or diagnoses are usually designated as "comorbid" and reflect the general process of youth referral in a variety of diagnostic and rehabilitative systems, in that the probability of such referrals is determined by the combined likelihood of referral for separate disorders or problem dimensions (Caron & Rutter, 1991). For example, the internalizing problem dimensions of anxiety and depression are often comorbid (Brady & Kendall, 1992; King, Ollendick, & Gullone, 1991; Lonigan, Carey, & Finch, 1994). Similarly, a variety of externalizing problem dimensions have been found to be comorbid with the diagnosis of attention deficit hyperactivity disorder (ADHD; Jensen, Martin, & Cantwell, 1997; Pliszka, 1998). It is often understood that the recognition and treatment of comorbid conditions are as important as the assessment and treatment of the primary presenting problem (see Cantwell, 1996).

Collection of observations from multiple informants has become the contemporary model for the psychological evaluation of youths and reflects the utility of parent and teacher observation (see LaGreca, Kuttler, & Stone, 2001). Unlike in the evaluation of adjustment in adults, which usually relies solely on self-report, such self-description by itself is usually less than optimal in the evaluation of youths. Indeed, the context of assessment is fundamentally different in that children and adolescents in all systems are highly unlikely to refer themselves for evaluation and treatment and may not possess the academic, cognitive, or motivational competence to complete many comprehensive self-report instruments. Another consideration is that youths are most often referred for evaluation because they are either noncompliant with the requests of the significant adults in their lives or exhibit problems in academic achievement, often presenting with inadequate reading skills. It is therefore not unusual for the completion of a self-report inventory of several hundred items to present a substantial assessment challenge, even for a high school student. Parents and teachers not only refer youths for assessment, they are also sources of useful systematic observational information. Certainly adults are the most direct informants who can report on the noncompliance of a child to their own requests. Parents are the only consistently available source for information on early childhood development and child behavior in the home. Teachers offer the most accurate observations of the age-appropriateness of a child's adjustment in the classroom and academic achievement as well as the attentional, motivational, and social phenomena unique to the classroom and to the school. Youth self-description, regardless of the problems that have been documented (Greenbaum, Dedrick, Prange, & Friedman, 1994; Jensen et al., 1996), is a direct and accurate source of information about personal thoughts and feelings—once the potentially distorting effects of response sets have been identified. Indeed, a youth may endorse symptoms or problems on a self-report measure that he or she may not feel comfortable expressing directly in a face-to-face interview.

The availability of two or three independent sets of descriptions of a youth provides a compelling opportunity for comparison across informants. Achenbach, McConaughy, and Howell (1987) conducted a comprehensive literature review and found very limited concordance in general between the descriptions of parent, teacher, and youth, although relatively greater between-source agreement was obtained for scales representing externalizing behaviors. A review of similar studies that evaluated the responses to parallel objective interviews of parent and child concluded that greater agreement was obtained for visible behaviors and in cases where the child was older (Lachar & Gruber, 1993).

Although one reasonable approach to the interpretation of differences between parent, teacher, and youth would be to assign such differences to situation-specific variation (e.g., the child is only oppositional at home, not in the classroom), other explanations are equally plausible. Cross-informant variance may reflect the fact that scales with similar names may contain significantly different content. The PIY, PIC–2, and SBS attempt in their structure and content to provide the opportunity both to compare similar scale content across informants and to measure phenomena that may be uniquely obtained from only one informant.

Along with dissimilar scale content, another source of limited cross-informant agreement may be the substantial effect of response sets on the accuracy of one source of information found to be discrepant when compared to the observations of other informants. The youth being assessed may not adequately comply with questionnaire instructions because of inadequate language comprehension, limited reading skills, and/or lack of sufficient motivation for the task. It is as likely that a youth may wish to hide a personal history of maladaptive behavior and current internal discomfort from mental health or corrections professionals, although a negative presentation of parent adjustment and home conflict may be more readily provided. At times, youths may also be motivated in an assessment context to admit to problems and symptoms that are not present. In forensic settings, expression of psychopathology may be seen as a means to escape responsibility for antisocial behaviors or to receive mental health services or placement, which may be seen as more desirable. Similar motivations and conditions may also influence parent reports. The PIY and PIC–2 incorporate validity scales to identify the effect of such response sets. These scales are designed to measure random or inadequate responses to statement content, defensive denial of existing problems, as well as admission of symptoms that are unlikely to be present or are the exaggeration of actual difficulties (Wrobel et al., 1999).

Clinicians may have different views about whether discordant data should be considered. At one extreme, a clinician might consider as valid any evidence of symptom presence from any informant source. At the other extreme, a clinician's focus on symptoms may exclude the interpretation of all scale dimensions not indicated as being within the clinical range by at least two, or all three, informant sources. Although best practice standards for the integrative interpretation of multi-informant questionnaires have not been established (which is not to say that the opinions of mental health professionals and parents have not been studied; Loeber, Green, & Lahey, 1990; Phares, 1997), there is a distinct pragmatic advantage in using an assessment system with instruments that can be completed by youth, parent, or teacher. Unfortunately, conditions regularly occur in conducting forensic psychological evaluations that make it difficult or impossible to obtain a valid completed PIC–2, SBS, or PIY. Although the youth will always be available, and when incarcerated may be the only available source of such psychological information, he or she may be uncooperative or language impaired, and the PIY values may be compromised. The youth may have not attended school for a considerable time, or the most recent classroom setting may not allow adequate comparison to normative youths in a typical classroom, making assessment with the SBS problematic. Indeed, a youth first referred to a court diagnostic unit may have already been administratively placed in a special school setting (i.e., "alternative school") with similarly behaviorally maladjusted youths, in which case behavioral options, including opportunities for inappropriate behavior, may have been restricted by an effective system of behavioral contingencies. That is, optimal description of the youth by a teacher (i.e., in the context of a regular education classroom in which initial noncompliant or otherwise disruptive behaviors were first observed) may no longer be possible. Parents may no longer have custody of the youth, and the current custodian may not know the child well (e.g., foster parent, group home, state custody). Many youths who are incarcerated at the time of evaluation may be placed far from their homes, making parent reports logistically difficult to obtain. In these common circumstances, use of a set of comprehensive parent-, teacher-, and self-report measures that can be applied independently of each other provides an element of flexibility to support a forensic assessment. Optimally, in the forensic context, all self-report, parent, and teacher data should be corroborated, if possible, with records (e.g., school, medical, or psychological records), clinical and collateral interview data, and other psychological assessment measures.

Personality Inventory for Children, Second Edition

The PIC–2 (Lachar & Gruber, 2001) administration booklet is designed to be completed by a parent or parent surrogate to describe school-aged children (K–12; a preschool version is under development). This booklet contains 275 statements that are written at a low to mid fourth-grade reading level and require a response of either "True" or "False" (see Table 10.1 for examples of PIC–2 items). Completion of the questionnaire, which takes about 40 minutes, allows the generation of a profile of gender-specific linear T-scores for three validity scales (Inconsistency, Dissimulation, and Defensiveness) and nine essentially nonoverlapping adjustment scales (Cognitive Impairment, Impulsivity and Distractibility, Delinquency, Family Dysfunction, Reality Distortion, Somatic Concern, Psychological Discomfort, Social Withdrawal, and Social Skill Deficits). Each scale is further divided into two or three nonoverlapping subscales that represent greater content homogeneity (see Table 10.1 and also Figure 10.2 in the "Case Example" section at the end of the chapter). A second profile of eight shortened 12-item scales and four scale composites (Externalizing, Internalizing, Social Adjustment, Total Score) may be derived from the first 96 booklet items or from a separate form, each of which can be completed in less than 15 minutes. This PIC–2 Behavioral Summary provides a shortened assessment when required and also allows the repeated measurement of youth behavior to assess the effects of rehabilitation efforts (see Figure 10.3 in the "Case Example" section). The PIC–2 standard format and behavioral summary formats may be scored by hand, or may be scored and/or interpreted by software provided by the publisher.

Personality Inventory for Youth

The PIY (Lachar & Gruber, 1995a, 1995b) is designed to evaluate youths from fourth grade through high school. The majority of the 270 items on the PIY were derived from rewriting statements from the 1982 PIC–R administration booklet into a first-person format (see Table 10.2 for examples of PIY items). The items were written at a low to mid third-grade reading level, and the entire inventory can be completed by responding either "True" or "False" to each descriptive statement in 30 to 60 minutes. The nine PIY clinical scales were constructed using a uniform methodology and represent the same dimensions as the PIC–2 scales. Each of 231 items that appear on these nine scales was assigned to only one adjustment scale, and each scale is characterized by a high degree of content saturation and homogeneity. As with the PIC–2, each of these scales has been further divided into two or three nonoverlapping subscales that represent factor-guided dimensions of even greater content homogeneity. The PIY answer sheet can be scored by hand, responses can

TABLE 10.1
PIC–2 Adjustment Scales and Subscales and Selected Psychometric Performance

SCALE or Subscale (Abbreviation)	Items	α	r_t	Subscale Representative Item
	STANDARD FORMAT PROFILE			
COGNITIVE IMPAIRMENT (COG)	39	.87	.94	
Inadequate Abilities (COG1)	13	.77	.95	My child seems to understand everything that is said.
Poor Achievement (COG2)	13	.77	.91	Reading has been a problem for my child.
Developmental Delay (COG3)	13	.79	.82	My child could ride a tricycle by age five years.
IMPULSIVITY & DISTRACTIBILITY (ADH)	27	.92	.88	
Disruptive Behavior (ADH1)	21	.91	.87	My child cannot keep attention on anything.
Fearlessness (ADH2)	6	.69	.86	My child will do anything on a dare.
DELINQUENCY (DLQ)	47	.95	.90	
Antisocial Behavior (DLQ1)	13	.88	.83	My child has run away from home.
Dyscontrol (DLQ2)	17	.91	.51	When my child gets mad, watch out!
Noncompliance (DLQ3)	17	.92	.87	My child often breaks the rules.
FAMILY DYSFUNCTION (FAM)	25	.87	.90	
Conflict Among Members (FAM1)	15	.83	.90	There is a lot of tension in our home.
Parent Maladjustment (FAM2)	10	.77	.51	One of the child's parents drinks too much alcohol.
REALITY DISTORTION (RLT)	29	.89	.92	
Developmental Deviation (RLT1)	14	.84	.87	My child needs protection from everyday dangers.
Hallucinations & Delusions (RLT2)	15	.81	.79	My child thinks others are plotting against him/her.
SOMATIC CONCERN (SOM)	28	.84	.91	
Psychosomatic Preoccupation (SOM1)	17	.80	.90	My child is worried about disease.
Muscular Tension & Anxiety (SOM2)	11	.68	.88	My child often has back pains.
PSYCHOLOGICAL DISCOMFORT (DIS)	39	.90	.90	
Fear & Worry (DIS1)	13	.72	.76	My child will worry a lot before starting something new.
Depression (DIS2)	18	.87	.91	My child hardly ever smiles.
Sleep Disturbance/				
Preoccupation With Death (DIS3)	8	.76	.86	My child thinks about ways to kill himself/herself.

(Continued)

267

TABLE 10.1
(Continued)

SCALE or Subscale (Abbreviation)	Items	α	r_{tt}	Subscale Representative Item
SOCIAL WITHDRAWAL (WDL)	19	.81	.89	
Social Introversion (WDL1)	11	.78	.90	Shyness is my child's biggest problem
Isolation (WDL2)	8	.68	.88	My child often stays in his/her room for hours.
SOCIAL SKILL DEFICITS (SSK)	28	.91	.92	
Limited Peer Status (SSK1)	13	.84	.92	My child is very popular with other children.
Conflict With Peers (SSK2)	15	.88	.87	Other children make fun of my child's ideas.
BEHAVIORAL SUMMARY PROFILE				
SHORT ADJUSTMENT SCALES				
Impulsivity & Distractibility–Short (ADH–S)	12	.88	.87	
Delinquency–Short (DLQ–S)	12	.89	.85	
Family Dysfunction–Short (FAM–S)	12	.82	.86	
Reality Distortion–Short (RLT–S)	12	.82	.87	
Somatic Concern–Short (SOM–S)	12	.73	.85	
Psychological Discomfort–Short (DIS–S)	12	.81	.87	
Social Withdrawal–Short (WDL–S)	12	.76	.88	
Social Skill Deficits–Short (SSK–S)	12	.82	.89	
COMPOSITE SCALES				
Externalizing (EXT–C)	24	.94	.89	
Internalizing (INT–C)	36	.89	.89	
Social Adjustment (SOC–C)	24	.86	.89	
Total Score (TOT–C)	96	.95	.89	

TABLE 10.2

PIY Clinical Scales and Subscales and Selected Psychometric Performance

SCALE or Subscale (Abbreviation)	Items	α	r_{tt}	Subscale Representative Item
COGNITIVE IMPAIRMENT (COG)	20	.74	.80	
Poor Achievement & Memory (COG1)	8	.65	.70	School has been easy for me.
Inadequate Abilities (COG2)	8	.67	.67	I think I am stupid or dumb.
Learning Problems (COG3)	4	.44	.76	I have been held back a year in school.
IMPULSIVITY & DISTRACTIBILITY (ADH)	17	.77	.84	
Brashness (ADH1)	4	.54	.70	I often nag and bother other people.
Distractibility & Overactivity (ADH2)	8	.61	.71	I cannot wait for things like other kids can.
Impulsivity (ADH3)	5	.54	.58	I often act without thinking.
DELINQUENCY (DLQ)	42	.92	.91	
Antisocial Behavior (DLQ1)	15	.83	.88	I sometimes skip school.
Dyscontrol (DLQ2)	16	.84	.88	I lose friends because of my temper.
Noncompliance (DLQ3)	11	.83	.80	Punishment does not change how I act.
FAMILY DYSFUNCTION (FAM)	29	.87	.83	
Parent-Child Conflict (FAM1)	9	.82	.73	My parent(s) are too strict with me.
Parent Maladjustment (FAM2)	13	.74	.76	My parents often argue.
Marital Discord (FAM3)	7	.70	.73	My parents' marriage has been solid and happy.
REALITY DISTORTION (RLT)	22	.83	.84	
Feelings of Alienation (RLT1)	11	.77	.74	I do strange or unusual things.
Hallucinations & Delusions (RLT2)	11	.71	.78	People secretly control my thoughts.

(Continued)

269

TABLE 10.2
(Continued)

SCALE or Subscale (Abbreviation)	Items	α	r_{tt}	Subscale Representative Item
SOMATIC CONCERN (SOM)	27	.85	.76	
Psychosomatic Syndrome (SOM1)	9	.73	.63	I often get very tired.
Muscular Tension & Anxiety (SOM2)	10	.74	.72	At times I have trouble breathing.
Preoccupation with Disease (SOM3)	8	.60	.59	I often talk about sickness.
PSYCHOLOGICAL DISCOMFORT (DIS)	32	.86	.77	
Fear & Worry (DIS1)	15	.78	.75	Small problems do not bother me.
Depression (DIS2)	11	.73	.69	I am often in a good mood.
Sleep Disturbance (DIS3)	6	.70	.71	I often think about death.
SOCIAL WITHDRAWAL (WDL)	18	.80	.82	
Social Introversion (WDL1)	10	.78	.77	Talking to others makes me nervous.
Isolation (WDL2)	8	.59	.77	I almost always play alone.
SOCIAL SKILL DEFICITS (SSK)	24	.86	.79	
Limited Peer Status (SSK1)	13	.79	.76	Other kids look up to me as a leader.
Conflict With Peers (SSK2)	11	.80	.72	I wish that I were more able to make and keep friends.

be entered into scoring and/or interpretive software, or special sheets can be processed by the test publisher. The pattern of scale and subscale elevations (i.e., the profile) is the major focus of the PIY and PIC–2 interpretive process. The PIY also provides four validity scales: Inconsistency, Dissimulation, and Defensiveness (also present in the PIC–2) and a fourth scale that consists of six unique items specifically written to reflect highly improbable behaviors or beliefs in both regular education and clinically referred populations (see Table 10.2 and Figure 10.1).

Student Behavior Survey

The SBS (Lachar, Wingenfeld, Kline, & Gruber, 2000) is designed to collect information from teachers on students from kindergarten through the 12th grade of high school. The SBS teacher rating results are profiled onto 14 scales that assess a student's academic status, work habits, and social skills; the parents' participation in the educational process, and a variety of problems such as aggressive or atypical behavior and emotional stress. The 102 SBS items and their rating options are arrayed on both sides of one sheet of paper, and the survey can be completed by a teacher in less than 15 minutes. These items are sorted into content-meaningful dimensions and are placed under 11 scale headings to enhance the clarity of item meaning rather than being presented in a random order. The SBS consists of three sections. In the first section of 8 items, the teacher selects one of five rating options (Deficient, Below Average, Average, Above Average, and Superior) to describe eight areas of achievement, such as Reading Comprehension and Mathematics; the scores are then summed to provide an estimate of current Academic Performance (AP). The remaining 94 items are rated on a 4-point frequency scale: Never, Seldom, Sometimes, and Usually.

The second SBS section (Academic Resources) contains positively worded statements divided into three scales. The first two of these scales consist of descriptions of positive behaviors that can be used to indicate the student's adaptive behaviors: Academic Habits (AH) and Social Skills (SS). The third scale consists of descriptions of parents that are very school specific. In Parent Participation (PP), the teacher is asked to judge the degree to which the parents support the student's educational program.

The third SBS section, Problems in Adjustment, provides seven scales composed of negatively worded items: Health Concerns (HC), Emotional Distress (ED), Unusual Behavior (UB), Social Problems (SP), Verbal Aggression (VA), Physical Aggression (PA), and Behavior Problems (BP).

An additional SBS component consists of three additional 16-item nonoverlapping scales (Pisecco et al., 1999). These scales incorporate SBS items drawn from several content dimensions that were consensually nominated as representing characteristics that would be associated with youths who obtain one of three disruptive behavior *DSM–IV* diagnoses: Attention Deficit Hyperactivity Disorder combined type (9 items from AH, 4 items from BP, and 1 each from SS, UB, and SP), Oppositional Defiant Disorder (4 items each from ED and VA, 3 items each from SS and BP, and 2 items from SP), and Conduct Disorder (8 items from BP, 5 items from PA, and 3 items from VA). These three SBS Disruptive Behavior scales have been named "Attention-Deficit/Hyperactivity" (ADH), "Oppositional Defiant" (OPD), and "Conduct Problems" (CNP). The SBS form is self-scoring; alternatively, SBS items can be processed by entering the items into scoring software. Examples of SBS items are provided in Table 10.3, and a SBS profile is presented in the "Case Example" section (Fig. 10.4).

SBS Scales. Their Psychometric Characteristics, and Sample Items

Scale Name (Abbreviation)	Items	α	r_{tt}	$r_{1.2}$	Example of Scale Item
Academic Performance (AP)	8	.89	.78	.84	Reading comprehension
Academic Habits (AH)	13	.93	.87	.76	Completes class assignments
Social Skills (SS)	8	.89	.88	.73	Participates in class activities
Parent Participation (PP)	6	.88	.83	.68	Parent(s) encourage achievement
Health Concerns (HC)	6	.85	.79	.58	Complains of headaches
Emotional Distress (ED)	15	.91	.90	.73	Worries about little things
Unusual Behavior (UB)	7	.88	.76	.62	Says strange or bizarre things
Social Problems (SP)	12	.87	.90	.72	Teased by other students
Verbal Aggression (VA)	7	.92	.88	.79	Argues and wants the last word
Physical Aggression (PA)	5	.90	.86	.63	Destroys property when angry
Behavior Problems (BP)	15	.93	.92	.82	Disobeys class or school rules
Attention-Deficit/ Hyperactivity (ADH)	16	.94	.91	.83	Waits for his/her turn
Oppositional Defiant (OPD)	16	.95	.94	.86	Mood changes without reason
Conduct Problems (CNP)	16	.94	.90	.69	Steals from others

Note: Scale alpha (α) values based on a referred sample $n = 1.315$. Retest correlation (r_{tt}) 5- to 11-year-old student sample ($n = 52$) with average rating interval of 1.7 weeks. Interrater agreement ($r_{1.2}$) sample $n = 60$ fourth- and fifth-grade team-taught or special-education students. Selected material from the SBS copyright © 2000 by Western Psychological Services. This table and individual SBS items placed within this chapter reprinted by permission of the publisher. Western Psychological Services. 12031 Wilshire Boulevard. Los Angeles, California. 90025. U.S.A.. www.wpspublish.com. Not to be reprinted in whole or in part for any additional purpose without the expressed. written permission of the publisher. All rights reserved.

HISTORY OF TEST DEVELOPMENT

PIC and PIY

Almost 50 years ago, two University of Minnesota psychologists began the development of a new inventory approach for youth assessment. They assembled a 600-statement administration booklet and entitled it the "Personality Inventory for Children. For use with children from six through adolescence." The directions stated that each item was to be answered "True" or "False" by the child's mother in order to describe both the child and family relationships. Professors Wirt and Broen accumulated administration booklet descriptive statements following a general outline. To ensure comprehensive coverage of child behavior and adjustment, 50 statements were written for 11 content areas: Aggression, Anxiety, Asocial Behavior, Excitement, Family Relations, Intellectual Development, Physical Development, Reality Distortion, Social Skills, Somatic Concern, and Withdrawal. To these 550 potential scale items, 50 items were added in an effort to strengthen or clarify the meaning of certain areas of concern. Although responses to all inventory statements were to be provided by a parent, statement format varied: Some statements described historical fact ("My child has failed a grade [repeated a year] in school"), other statements reported the observation of others ("School teachers complain that my child cannot sit still"), and still others involved direct parental report. These direct statements described behaviors ("My child sometimes swears at me") as well as emotional states ("My child worries some"). This original item format had been found to require a sixth- to seventh-grade reading level (Harrington & Follett, 1984). Following many of the general procedures employed in the development of the Minnesota Multiphasic Personality Inventory, PIC scales were constructed from these potential items over a span of 20 years.

The initial 1977 published profile consisted of a visual display of the linear T- scores of three validity scales, a general adjustment screening scale, and 12 measures of child ability and adjustment and family function developed through either empirical item-selection techniques or through iterative content-validity procedures. In 1981, the administration booklet was revised to form the PIC–R; these administration booklet statements were sorted into one of four parts. Completion of part I (items 1–131) allowed the scoring of four additional broadband factor-derived scales (Lachar, Gdowski, & Snyder, 1982); completion of parts II and I (items 1–280) generated the entire clinical profile with "shortened scales" (Lachar, 1982); and completion of parts III, II, and I (items 1–420) allowed the scoring of the original-length scales. The last 180 items of this booklet were eventually excluded because they did not appear on any of the standard full-length profile scales.

Because of research conducted before its first publication in 1977 and over the subsequent two decades, the interpretation of PIC scales and profile assigned little importance to item content (except for the construction of a Critical Items list). Instead, an integrated program of research established external correlatives and interpretive guidelines for individual profile scales (Lachar & Gdowski, 1979) and replicated profile patterns (Gdowski, Lachar, & Kline, 1985; Kline, Lachar, & Gdowski, 1987; Lachar, Kline, Green, & Gruber, 1996; LaCombe, Kline, Lachar, Butkus, & Hillman, 1991). A profile interpretive procedure in which similarity coefficients are calculated between the individual profile to be interpreted and the mean profiles of students receiving specific special education services has also been incorporated into profile scoring and interpretation software (Kline, Lachar, Gruber, & Boersma, 1994). Special effort has also focused on demonstrating that PIC scale validity is not affected by a child's age, gender, or ethnicity (Kline & Lachar, 1992; Kline, Lachar, & Sprague, 1985). Lachar and Kline (1994) provide a comprehensive review of this version of the PIC. In addition, a bibliography of over 350 relevant publications is presented in the 2001 PIC–2 manual.

The most recent test revision efforts began in 1989 with the rewriting of the first 280 items of the PIC–R booklet into a self-report format for the PIY (Lachar & Gruber, 1993, 1995a, 1995b). Development of the PIY facilitated concurrent critical review of the structure and content of the PIC–R scales and profile. Revision efforts have been sensitive to the need to maintain continuity with PIC interpretation principles established over the past 20 years as well as to introduce psychometric changes that improve its efficiency. A research edition administration booklet that allowed both the scoring of the PIC–R profile and the collection of data on revised and new inventory items facilitated test revision. Over 1,000 of these clinical protocols were subjected to considerable statistical analysis, and as a result the PIC–R (now the PIC–2) and the PIY are closely similar, facilitating the comparison of parent description and self-description. Their similarity includes a comparable subscale-within-clinical- scale structure and specific item revisions that have improved comprehension and application. For example, almost all negatively worded statements to which "True" (vs. the natural response of "False") represents the unscored response (e.g., "My child has never had cramps in the legs"), have been removed, and "parent(s)" is now the designation for either mother or father (or parent surrogates) in family descriptions.

Each of these nine clinical scales was constructed using a uniform iterative process (Lachar & Gruber, 2001). Initial scale composition was based on either previous PIC or PIY item placement or substantive item content. Item-to-scale correlation matrices generated from an initial sample of 950 clinical protocols were then inspected to establish the accuracy of these initial item placements. Each inventory statement retained on a final clinical scale demonstrated a significant and substantial correlation to that scale. In almost all cases, when an item obtained a significant correlation to more than one clinical scale it was placed on the scale to which it had the highest correlation.

In this manner, 94% of the 264 PIC–2 statements that make up the nine adjustment scales were placed on only one scale. The 16 items that were placed on two of the final scales obtained substantial correlations to both and represented substantive content consistent with the descriptive intent of both. For example, "Others often say that my child is moody" has been placed on both the *DIS2*: Depression ($r = .63$) and *DLQ2*: Dyscontrol ($r = .61$) subscales, as "moody" may signify both dysphoria and anger. The relatively unique item composition of the nine PIC–2 clinical scale dimensions is in contrast to the previous PIC–R structure. For example, in the PIC–R, 68% of Anxiety scale items also appeared on the Depression scale. In addition, considerable between-scale overlap occurred among the three PIC–R cognitive scales: Achievement (56%), Intellectual Screening (37%), and Development (84%).

The items of each of the nine PIC–2 adjustment scales have also been partitioned into two or three subscales. Application of principal component factor analysis with varimax rotation guided the identification of two or three relatively homogeneous item subsets for each adjustment scale. PIC–2 subscales average 13 items in length (range 6 to 21 items), with only 3 of 21 subscales incorporating less than 10 items. PIY self-report scales and subscales were constructed in the same manner as PIC–2 scales (Lachar & Gruber, 1993, 1995a, 1995b).

PIY and PIC–2 Validity Scales

Forensic assessment of emotional and behavioral adjustment relies on the assumption that psychometric evaluation improves upon the accuracy of subjective assessments, such as unstructured interviews. One advantage of the PIY and PIC–2 is the substantial effort applied in the development of validity scales. Although a variety of threats to scale validity are not unique to forensic assessments, these threats are often heightened. For example, regarding youth performance a consistent concern is to judge the adequacy of motivation and the competence of questionnaire response. In the juvenile justice system, there are many problem readers who are also not convinced that serious participation in completion of a diagnostic questionnaire will be to their benefit. Concern is often raised as to the competence of parent report. The PIY and PIC–2 Inconsistency (*INC*) scales and the PIY Validity (*VAL*) scale address these concerns.

Although assessment of the mental health of juveniles is necessary for the development of a comprehensive understanding of youths in the justice system and also necessary to support its mission of rehabilitation, youths and parents may view the portrayal of poor adjustment as a way to avoid the more punitive aspects of forensic placements. It is therefore useful not only to measure various aspects of adjustment but to also consider the accuracy of these estimates. The PIY and PIC–2 Dissimulation (*FB*) scales assess the accuracy of report of poor adjustment. Similarly, the denial of problematic behaviors, such as antisocial or especially aggressive or destructive behaviors, may be more likely from these youths and their parents due to their concern that additional revelations may increase the likelihood of negative administrative consequences. The PIY and PIC–2 Defensiveness (*DEF*) scales evaluate the degree to which informants are open and honest regarding these descriptions.

Both PIY and PIC–2 profiles incorporate validity scales. The first of these on the profile, INC, evaluates the likelihood that responses to items are random or reflect in some manner inadequate comprehension of inventory statement content or compliance with test instructions. FB identifies profiles that may result from either exaggeration of current problems or a malingered pattern of atypical or infrequent symptoms. The third validity scale, *DEF*, identifies profiles likely to demonstrate the effect of minimization or denial of current problems. The PIY also provides a fourth unique validity measure that consists of six items written so that a "True" or a "False" response would be highly improbable, such as a "False" response to "I sometimes talk on the telephone." These six items, although also highly infrequent in the form of parent description, were omitted from the PIC–2, as they contributed no additional information beyond that provided by the other three validity scales.

PIY and PIC–2 Inconsistency (INC) scales measure semantic inconsistency (Tellegen, 1988) through the classification of responses to 35 pairs of highly correlated items drawn from all nine clinical scales (e.g., "I have many friends/I have very few friends," "My child has a lot of talent/My child has no special talents"). For each item pair, two response combinations are consistent (True/True and False/False) and two are inconsistent (True/False and False/True). Each inconsistent pair identified in a given protocol contributes one point to the INC raw score. Application of a cutting raw score of less than 13 resulted in correct identification of 90% to 95% of clinical protocols and a score of greater than 12 correctly identified 92% to 96% of random protocols.

The PIY and PIC–2 Dissimulation scales (abbreviation *FB* for "fake bad") were empirically constructed through item analyses that compared clinical protocols and two sets of protocols completed by nonreferred regular education students or their mothers. The PIY or PIC–2 was first completed with directions to provide an accurate or valid description. The same student or mother then completed a second questionnaire in which the student was now described as in need of mental health counseling or psychiatric hospitalization. Selected *FB* items in the scored direction were found on average to be very infrequent in valid normal protocols (PIY, 11%; PIC–2, 4%) and valid clinical protocols (PIY, 18%; PIC–2, 15%), while these responses were found on average to be very frequent (PIY, 83%; PIC–2, 55%) in the "fake bad" or dissimulated protocols. *FB* items reflect "erroneous stereotype" in that they reflect face valid content by naïve informants, but demonstrate no empirical validity (Lanyon, 1997). Examples of the 42 PIY *FB* items include "People are out to get me" and "I do not care about having fun." Examples of the 35 PIC–2 *FB* items include "My child is not as strong as most children" and "My child often talks about sickness." Application of one *FB* cutting score to PIY data correctly identified 99% of accurate, 98% of fake bad, and 96% of clinical protocols. Application of two potential cutting scores to similar PIC–2 protocols revealed that both correctly classified 97% to 100% of accurate regular education student descriptions. A cutting score of greater than 8 ($>69T$) resulted in correct classification of 92% of dissimulated protocols and 78% of clinical protocols (possible dissimulation), whereas a cutting score of greater than 14 ($>89T$) resulted in correct classification of 70% of dissimulated protocols and 95% of clinical protocols (probable dissimulation). The pattern of *FB* and *INC* scale elevations facilitates the differentiation of inadequate from inaccurate response. A deliberate exaggerated response (or for that matter an accurate description of a severe or atypical psychopathological adjustment) would generate an elevated *FB* score and an unelevated INC score. Protocols completed without adequate statement comprehension, in contrast, exhibit raw *INC* and *FB* scores approximating 50% of each scale's length; in these protocols, both scales would be clinically elevated (see Figures 11 and 12 in Lachar & Gruber, 1995b).

The PIY and PIC–2 Defensiveness (*DEF*) scales are expanded versions of the original PIC Lie scale. *DEF* items represent either the denial of common problems ("Sometimes I put off doing a chore" [False], "My child almost never argues" [True]) or attributions of improbable positive adjustment ("My child always does his/her homework on time" [True], "I am almost always on time and remember what I am supposed to do" [True]). Such items represent inaccurate knowledge in the form of overendorsement (Lanyon, 1997). *DEF* elevations above 59*T*, even in hospitalized patients, result in profiles that either minimize current problems or consistently deny the presence of most or all problems in adjustment. A secondary interpretation of an elevated PIY *DEF* scale has more general implications for youth response. Youths who respond with denial to administration booklet items are most likely to respond in a similar manner during a diagnostic interview. The *INC-FB-DEF* pattern readily identifies profiles that must be interpreted cautiously. Fricker and Smith (2001) obtained a moderate correlation ($r = .48$) between the PIY *DEF* scale and the Underresponse scale of the Trauma Symptom Checklist for Children.

PIC–2 and PIY Screening and Short Forms

The PIY and PIC–2 each incorporate a screening or shortened assessment procedure. The first 80 items of the PIY include a 32-item screening scale (*CLASS*) that accurately identifies regular education students who, when administered the full PIY, produce clinically significant results. These items also include three "scan items" for each clinical scale. Scan items were selected in such a manner that students who endorse two or more of each set of three items would be those with a high probability of scoring greater than 59*T* on the corresponding clinical scale. Shortened versions of three validity scales can also be derived from these items. *CLASS* has demonstrated its effectiveness with nonreferred elementary school children (Wrobel & Lachar, 1998) as well as nonreferred adolescents attending high school (Ziegenhorn, Tzelepis, Lachar, & Schubiner, 1994). In the former study, *CLASS* predicted elevations on PIY adjustment scales and problem descriptions from parents. In the latter study, *CLASS* significantly correlated with 16 of 18 potential indicators of maladjustment or behavioral risk.

The PIC–2 provides a short form, the Behavioral Summary, designed to measure change in clinical status associated with therapeutic intervention. Although PIC and PIC–R scales have demonstrated sensitivity to change (see the example of treatment-related PIC–R and PIY change in Lachar & Kline, 1994), the Behavioral Summary was constructed specifically for this purpose. The items that were candidates for selection were written in the present tense, were frequently endorsed in the context of clinical assessment, and described clinical phenomena often the focus of short-term intervention. Using these guidelines, the 12 most favorable items from each of eight PIC–2 clinical scales were chosen. (See the bottom of Table 10.1 for the psychometric characteristics of the PIC–2 Behavioral Summary measures.) Comparable items were not selected from the Cognitive Impairment scale because the majority of *COG* items either have historical content or demonstrate a lack of appropriate associated therapeutic focus due to the global or stable nature of the descriptions. The 96 inventory statements of the Behavior Summary have been placed at the beginning of the 275-item PIC–2 administration booklet to serve as both a short form and a method of efficient reevaluation of a child following short-term intervention. These 96 items are also available as a separate form with a self-scoring format. The scale scores and four scale composites may be graphed on the same profile at baseline and at appropriate interim and posttreatment intervals to demonstrate both dimensions of change and dimensions of stability. The Externalization composite is the sum of the *ADH* and *DLQ* shortened scales, the Internalization composite is the sum of the *RLT*, *SOM*, and *DIS* shortened scales, the Social Adjustment composite is the sum of the *WDL* and *SSK* shortened scales, and all eight scales (representing the response to all

96 items) are combined into a Total Score that is placed at the end of the profile. Current efforts are underway to develop a parallel 96-item Behavioral Summary form for the PIY.

Student Behavior Survey (SBS)

The development of the Student Behavior Survey (SBS; Lachar, Wingenfeld, Kline, & Gruber, 2000) consisted of several iterations of a process in which the test authors reviewed established teacher rating scales and wrote new rating statements focused on content appropriate to teacher observation. SBS items are not derived from the PIY or PIC–2. Unlike measures that provide separate parent and teacher norms for the same questionnaire items (see. e.g., the Devereux Scales of Mental Disorders; Naglieri, LeBuffe, & Pfeiffer, 1994), the SBS items exhibit a specific school focus. Review of the SBS reveals that 58 out of its 102 items specifically refer to in-class or in-school behaviors and judgments that can only be made by school staff (Wingenfeld, Lachar, Gruber, & Kline, 1998).

PSYCHOMETRIC CHARACTERISTICS

PIC–2

The PIC–2 gender-specific T-score values are derived from a contemporary national sample of parent descriptions of youths 5 to 18 years of age (kindergarten through 12th grade; $N = 2,306$); a large sample of referred youths was analyzed to provide evidence of instrument validity ($N = 1,551$). Current efforts are focused on the development of a PIC for preschool children (ages 3 to 5). Standardization data were collected in urban, suburban, and rural areas and included a spectrum of socioeconomic conditions as well as a solid representation of the major ethnic groups. Parents participating in this survey of regular education students came from 23 schools in 12 states drawn from all four major U.S. census regions. Over 40% came from lower socioeconomic groups, and over 25% from minority groups. One third of this sample consisted of either single-parent families or families with a stepparent, and 18% of the surveys were completed by fathers or guardians other than mothers. The influence of gender and age on standardization scores and the effects of referral status are discussed in detail in the PIC–2 manual. In summary, the influence of gender was most prominent on scales COG and ADH, with boys more likely to be described as having cognitive and externalizing problems and girls as having internalizing problems. Such differences justify the development of same-gender norms, but meaningful age effects were only evident for one subscale (COG3) and then only for children 5 or 6 years of age. In contrast, referral status had a substantial effect on the majority of PIC–2 scores. Indeed, on just one subscale (WDL1) did it have only a small effect. This dimension, social introversion, although clinically meaningful, represents a normally distributed personality dimension that was not expected to be associated with referral status. As presented in Table 10.1, these scales demonstrate substantial internal consistency and short-term temporal stability. PIC–2 clinical scales average 31 items in length (range 19 to 47 items) and obtained a median coefficient alpha of .89 (range .81 to .95). These scales obtained a median 1-week test-retest reliability of .90 (range .88 to .94) and median interrater reliability (mother/father) of .73 (range .67 to .80) in clinical samples. The similarity of the PIC–2 clinical scales to the PIC-R and PIY clinical scales was measured by percentage item overlap as well as correlation between PIC–2 scales and comparable PIC/PIY scales. PIC–2 scales on average have a 66% overlap with PIC-R scales (range 33% to 96%) and a substantial median correlation of .93 (range .81 to .99) with the PIC-R equivalent. As would be expected, PIC–2 clinical scales have a substantial item overlap with PIY scales similarly named (average 79%, range 51% to 100%). In spite of this substantial scale similarity, the difference in informants (parent vs. youth) resulted in only moderate concordance estimates (median correlation = .43, range .28 to .53). Appendix D of the PIC–2 manual provides considerable evidence of validity for a Spanish translation of the PIC–2 administration booklet (Lachar & Gruber, 2001, pp. 183–193).

Table 10.1 provides coefficient alpha values for subscales and lists a representative item for each subscale. The majority of subscales demonstrate psychometric characteristics comparable to those of scales on shorter published questionnaires. In all instances, the division of scales into subscales facilitates the interpretation process. For example, the actuarial interpretation of the PIC-R Delinquency scale (Lachar & Gdowski, 1979) identified *T*-score ranges associated with the dimensions of noncompliance, poorly controlled anger, and antisocial behaviors. These dimensions are each represented by a specific PIC–2 *DLQ* subscale; the pattern of *DLQ* subscale elevations represents the dominant endorsed content of this adjustment scale. (Note the comparable subscales on the PIY Delinquency scale.)

Correlations between PIC–2 scale scores and clinician, teacher, and youth descriptions readily provide actuarial interpretive guidelines for these nine dimensions. These interpretive guidelines are detailed in the PIC–2 manual, which also provides 13 case studies that often incorporate PIY and SBS assessments:

Cognitive Impairment (COG)

The statements that reflect limited general intellectual ability (*COG1*), problems in achieving in school (*COG2*), and a history of developmental delay or deficit (*COG3*) have been placed on this scale. *COG2* elevation has been found to be associated with a broad range of inadequate academic habits and poor achievement in the classroom. Both teacher and clinician ratings demonstrate a strong relation between *COG3* elevation and language deficits.

Impulsivity and Distractibility (ADH)

The majority of these items (21 of 27) appear on the first dimension. *ADH1* (Disruptive Behavior) receives substantial support from teacher ratings. Elevation on this subscale is associated with poor behavioral control in the classroom that disrupts the classroom process, and clinicians report impulsive, hyperactive, and restless behaviors associated with excessive attention-seeking. The second dimension (*ADH2*, Fearlessness) appears to measure an aspect of bravado that may best be classified as a personality dimension.

Delinquency (DLQ)

DLQ1 (Antisocial Behavior) elevation is associated with behaviors readily associated with the total scale name and consistently appears as a dominant elevation in forensic samples. *DLQ1* subscale elevation predicts admission by both clinician and youth of a variety of unacceptable behaviors: truancy, alcohol and drug misuse, theft, running away from home, deceit, and association with other youths who are similarly troubled. *DLQ2* (Dyscontrol) elevation suggests the presence of disruptive behavior associated with poorly modulated anger. Teachers note fighting, and youths admit to similar problems ("I lose friends because of my temper"). Clinicians rate these children as assaultive, defiant, argumentative, irritable, destructive, and manipulative. Their lack of emotional control often results in behaviors that demonstrate poor judgment. *DLQ3* (Noncompliance) elevation reflects disobedience to parents and teachers, ineffectiveness of discipline, and a tendency to blame others for problems. Youth agreement with this perception of adults is demonstrated by a variety of PIY item correlates, including "I give my parent(s) a lot of trouble."

Family Dysfunction (FAM)

This scale is divided into two meaningful dimensions. *FAM1* (Conflict Among Members) reflects conflict within the family ("There is a lot of tension in our home," "My parents do not agree on how to raise me"). Clinicians note conflict between the child's guardians and concern regarding the emotional or physical abuse of the child. The second *FAM* dimension more directly measures parent adjustment. Youth-report correlates of *FAM2* (Parent Maladjustment) include "One of my parents sometimes gets drunk and mean" as well as "My parents are now divorced or living apart."

Reality Distortion (RLT)

This content valid scale is considerably different from the empirically keyed PIC–R Psychosis scale, but it has substantial overlap with the PIY *RLT* scale (*RLT1*, 57%; *RLT2*, 80%). *RLT1* (Developmental Deviation) elevation indicates a level of intellectual, emotional, and social functioning usually associated with substantial developmental retardation or regression. *RLT2* (Hallucinations and Delusions) describes symptoms and behaviors often associated with a psychotic adjustment. Rorschach measures of maladaptive thought and adjustment have been found to covary with comparable PIC–R dimensions (Stokes, Pogge, Grosso, & Zaccario, 2001) and the comparable PIY scale and subscales (Smith, Baity, Knowles, & Hilsenroth, 2001).

Somatic Concern (SOM)

The first dimension of *SOM* measures a variety of health complaints often associated with poor psychological adjustment. *SOM1* (Psychosomatic Preoccupation) elevation is often associated with the self-report of similar complaints ("I feel tired most of the time," "I often have headaches," "I often have an upset stomach"). The second *SOM* dimension (*SOM2*, Muscular Tension and Anxiety) appears to measure the somatic components of internalization.

Psychological Discomfort (DIS)

This relatively long scale of 39 items is best described as a measure of negative affectivity, divided, as in the PIY, into three meaningful dimensions. The first dimension (*DIS1*) measures fearfulness and worry and is associated with clinician description of anxiety, fear, and tearfulness as well as self-report of fear and emotional upset. The second dimension (*DIS2*) is a general measure of depression that shows considerable correlation with parent, teacher, and youth description. Teachers see students with an elevated *DIS2* subscale score as sad or unhappy, moody and serious, and not having fun. Clinicians note many of the classical symptoms of depression, including feelings of helplessness, hopelessness, and worthlessness. Demonstrating inadequate self-esteem, such children are overly self-critical and usually expect rejection. The third *DIS* subscale is similar to the PIY *DIS3* dimension, combining the report of problematic sleep and a preoccupation with death. Elevation of *DIS3* correlates with clinician concern regarding suicide potential and a wide variety of self-report descriptions, including sleep disturbance, dysphoria, and thoughts about suicide.

Social Withdrawal (WDL)

This is the shortest PIC–2 adjustment scale (19 items). The two *WDL* dimensions parallel those of the PIY: The first *WDL* subscale (*WDL1*: Social Introversion) measures the personality dimension social introversion. Most items reflect psychological discomfort in social interactions. Clinician observation and youth self-report describe shyness and an unwillingness to talk with others. The second *WDL* dimension (*WDL2*: Isolation) is a brief subscale of eight items that measures intentional lack of contact with others.

Social Skill Deficits (SSK)

This scale consists of two dimensions. Both dimensions receive considerable support from self-report correlates in the form of PIY statements. The first *SSK* subscale reflects limited social influence. Elevation of *SSK1* (Limited Peer Status) relates to self-report of few friends, lack of popularity with peers, and little social influence. Teachers note avoidance of peers and lack of awareness of the feelings of others. Elevation of *SSK2* (Conflict with Peers), in contrast, measures problematic relations with peers. Self-report correlates document these conflicts, while clinicians observe poor social skills and a problematic social adjustment.

Insight into the empirical foundations of PIC–2 interpretation (as well as PIY and SBS interpretation) is provided by an example organized into Table 10.4. (Also see the expanded detail provided in appendix C and chapter 4 of the PIC–2 manual.) The concurrent validity of PIC–2 shortened scales was established through the correlation of scale scores with clinician ratings, teacher descriptions, and self-report descriptions. These correlations were drawn from the data generated from a clinical project in which PIC–2, PIY, and SBS scores; clinician ratings; diagnoses; and the results of individually administered cognitive ability and academic achievement tests were collected to some degree in over 1,500 assessments. In Table 10.4, each obtained scale descriptor was classified with only the one shortened scale with which it received the largest correlation, all being at least significant at $p < .01$. The table summarizes the number of external ratings identified in this manner from each source (clinician, teacher, and student) and provides up to two examples from each rating source for each of these eight scales. Correlations between these shortened scales and their full-length versions are also presented.

Table 10.4 documents that these 12-item scales correlate substantially with their full-length versions ($r = .92$ to .96) and obtain independent correlates from nonparent observers that match expressed scale content and diagnostic intent. Clinician ratings provided the greatest support for *ADH, DLQ,* and *DIS,* focusing on problems of disruptive and noncompliant behavior and intense and dysphoric affect that often form the basis of clinical referral. These analyses also demonstrate that *ADH,* as previously demonstrated for the PIC Hyperactivity scale (Lachar & Gdowski, 1979), assesses those behaviors most related to problems in classroom adjustment. In addition, observations obtained directly from the student being evaluated provide those internal and subjective judgments that demonstrate the clinical value of PIC–2 dimensions that do not receive robust correlates from clinicians or teachers.

PIY

Gender-specific linear *T*-scores have been derived from a national normative sample of 2,327 regular education students in grades 4 through 12, while a variety of analyses have been conducted using a large sample of clinically referred students ($N = 1,178$).

TABLE 10.4
Correlates of PIC–2 Short Adjustment Scales

	r	Rule	Performance
IMPULSIVITY & DISTRACTIBILITY (ADH-S: .96*)			
Clinician Ratings: total = 27			
Impulsive behavior	.43	>59T	27%/75%
Defiant	.45	> 69T	24%/63%
Teacher Ratings: total = 26			
Disobeys class or school rules	.45	>59T	28%/67%
Disrupts class by misbehaving	.41	>59T	25%/65%
Self-Report Ratings: total = 3			
Recently my school has sent notes home about			
my bad behavior	.29	>59T	17%/41%
Teachers complain that I can't sit still	.32	>69T	28%/53%
DELINQUENCY (DLQ-S: .93)			
Clinician Ratings: total = 48			
Poorly modulated anger	.57	>59T	19%/74%
Disobedient to teachers	.47	>69T	22%/64%
Teacher Ratings: total = total = 23			
Angers other students	.32	>59T	26%/69%
Complains about the requests of adults	.31	> 59T	28%/69%
Self-Report Ratings: total = 28			
Sometimes I lie to get out of trouble	.27	>59T	48%/73%
Several times I have said that I would run away	.29	>69T	37%/64%
FAMILY DYSFUNCTION (FAM-S: .93)			
Clinician Ratings: total = 3			
Conflict between parents/guardians	.35	>59T	15%/43%
Emotionally abused	.31	>69T	12%/32%
Teacher Ratings: total = 0			
Self-Report Ratings: total = 8			
There is a lot of tension in our home	.30	>59T	31%/57%
There is a lot of swearing (cursing) at our house	.27	>69T	31%/57%
REALITY DISTORTION (RLT-S: .94)			
Clinician Ratings: total = 5			
Auditory hallucinations	.30	>79T	5%/21%
Inappropriate emotion (affect)	.25	>69T	9%/24%
Teacher Ratings: total = 0			
Self-Report Ratings: total = 2			
I need a lot of help from others	.26	>59T	18%/43%
I hear voices that no one else can hear or understand	.21	>79T	21%/38%
SOMATIC CONCERN (SOM-S: .93)			
Clinician Ratings: total = 3			
Somatic response to stress	.26	>79T	7%/28%
Continually tired (listless)	.19	>79T	10%/28%
Teacher Ratings: total = 0			
Self-Report Ratings: total = 11			
I often get very tired	.27	>59T	38%/61%
I often have headaches	.22	>59T	38%/58%

(*Continued*)

TABLE 10.4
(Continued)

	r	Rule	Performance
PSYCHOLOGICAL DISCOMFORT (DIS-S: .92)			
Clinician Ratings: total = 23			
Depressed, sad, unhappy	.48	>69T	27%/71%
Inadequate self-esteem	.42	>69T	27%/61%
Teacher Ratings: total = 2			
Appears sad or unhappy	.33	>59T	31%/59%
Becomes upset for little or no reason	.31	>59T	28%/54%
Self-Report Ratings: total = 3			
I tend to feel sorry for myself	.23	>69T	34%/52%
I am often afraid of little things	.23	>79T	17%/43%
SOCIAL WITHDRAWAL (WDL-S: .96)			
Clinician Ratings: total = 1			
Withdrawn	.32	>59T	15%/37%
Teacher Ratings: total = 0			
Self-Report Ratings: total = 1			
Shyness is my biggest problem	.25	>69T	19%/49%
SOCIAL SKILL DEFICITS (SSK-S: .95)			
Clinician Ratings: total = 3			
Poor social skills	.46	>59T	21%/63%
Isolated (few or no friends)	.41	>69T	22%/56%
Teacher Ratings: total = 0			
Self-Report Ratings: total = 13			
Other kids make fun of my ideas	.25	>59T	16%/33%
Other kids are often angry with me	.24	>69T	20%/58%

Note: * indicates correlation between standard form and behavioral summary version of PIC–2 adjustment scale in a sample of referred students; r = correlation between scale and external rating; Rule = minimum value of clinical range; Performance = endorsement rate below/above interpretive rule. Selected material from the PIC–2 copyright © 2001 by Western Psychological Services. Reprinted by permission of the publisher, Western Psychological Services, 12031 Wilshire Boulevard, Los Angeles, California, 90025, U.S.A., www.wpspublish. com. Not to be reprinted in whole or in part for any additional purpose without the expressed, written permission of the publisher. All rights reserved.

Normative data were collected in urban, suburban, and rural areas and included a spectrum of socioeconomic conditions from poor through blue-collar and middle-class to upper socioeconomic status areas as well as a solid representation of the major ethnic groups. Thirteen school districts in five states (California, Illinois, Michigan, South Dakota, and Texas) participated in this regular education classroom survey. Analysis of gender effects reported in the PIY manual supported the development of gender-specific norms, whereas age effects were limited to two scales (*DLQ* and *FAM*) and two age groups, 10 years and under 11 years. As regards the use of the PIY for forensic assessment,

> The stability of the norms for ages 12 to 18 years deserves special note. The results of this study demonstrate that there is virtually no difference in the overall self-report rate for a variety of dimensions of behavioral difficulties among nonreferred youth throughout adolescence. This

stability suggests that all youth, essentially regardless of chronological age in these pre-adult years, can be accurately assessed with the PIY. (Lachar & Gruber, 1995b, p. 68)

Although family composition was found to influence only *FAM*, differences between regular education and referred samples suggested that in general scale elevations above 59T and subscale elevations above 64T should receive special consideration. PIY clinical scales average 26 items in length (range 17 to 42 items), and the median coefficient alpha in referred protocols was .85 (range .74 to .92). The 24 subscales average 10 items in length (range 4 to 16 items, with 5 subscales less than 8 items in length), and the mean coefficient alpha in referred protocols was .73 (range .44 to .84, with 8 of 24 subscales less than .70). The PIY administration and interpretation guide (Lachar & Gruber, 1995a) provides empirically derived interpretive guidelines for scales and subscales as well as 15 case studies. Considerable effort has gone into the development of a Spanish translation of the PIY (Negy, Lachar, & Gruber, 1998; Negy, Lachar, Gruber, & Garza, 2001).

Differences between the character of self-report and parent report are demonstrated when PIY scale and subscale content is compared to the content of PIC–2 equivalents. The PIY Cognitive Impairment scale includes only half of the items of the comparable PIC–2 scale. This difference reflects the exclusion of developmental or historical items in the self-report format (children are not accurate reporters of developmental delay) as well as the reality that fewer inventory statements correlated with this dimension of youth self-report. The PIY Impulsivity and Distractibility scale also incorporated fewer scale items (17) than its PIC–2 equivalent (27 items). Perhaps the report of ADH disruptive behavior is more likely to come from an adult informant, who probably finds such behavior distressful, than from a student, who may not find it disturbing. Such results suggest that the PIC–2 *COG* and *ADH* scales will demonstrate superior diagnostic performance in comparison with these PIY scales. In contrast, the other seven PIY clinical scales are very similar in content and length to their PIC–2 equivalents. In a novel application of peer ratings from fourth-grade to eighth-grade students of the dimensions Withdrawn, Disruptive, and Sociable, evidence of the interpretive meaning of PIY dimensions was demonstrated. Subscales made a relatively greater contribution to the prediction of peer ratings, and the dimensions *SSK* and *DLQ* played a prominent role (Wrobel, Lachar, & Wrobel, 2005).

SBS

Norms that generate linear T-scores are gender specific and are divided into two age groups: 5 to 11 ($n = 1{,}309$) and 12 to 19 years ($n = 1{,}303$). Ratings of regular education students were obtained from teachers in 22 schools from 22 states. In terms of gender, age, ethnic background, and parents' education, the standardization sample was representative of the relevant population as reflected by contemporary census figures. Table 10.3 provides examples of SBS scale items, scale length, temporal stability, interrater reliability, and co-efficient alpha based on protocols from students either obtained in clinical evaluation or receiving special education services in grades K–12. Initial item and scale analysis showed that 99 of 102 items statistically separated the clinical and special education protocols from the protocols of regular education students. In addition, age-related differences tended to be smaller than gender-related differences, although these latter differences were generally small. The scale differences between regular education and referred students were generally larger than those differences obtained for demographic effects and usually represented a moderate or large effect. Comparison of intellectually impaired, emotionally impaired, and learning disabled students revealed that intellectually impaired students were rated with the poorest academic performance, poorer academic habits and social skills, and more social problems and physical aggression than learning disabled students, whereas emotionally impaired students were described as more emotionally distressed, physically aggressive, verbally aggressive, and behaviorally disturbed than either the intellectually impaired or learning disabled students (Wingenfeld et al., 1998). It was found that each item had been placed on the scale with which it had the largest correlation. The scale scores of special education and referred students obtained meaningful three-factor solutions: externalizing symptoms, internalizing symptoms, and academic performance. The correlation between the Conners' Hyperactivity Index and SBS dimensions was greatest for the Disruptive Behavior scale *ADH* ($r = .86$) in a sample of 226 learning disabled students (Lachar et al., 2000). A substantial degree of criterion validity is demonstrated when SBS scales are correlated with PIC–2 scales and subscales (see Lachar & Gruber, 2001, Tables 32 and 33, pp. 142–143).

CLINICAL USES AND LIMITATIONS

The PIC has been in use as a diagnostic tool for approximately 3 decades. The 2001 revision assesses the same basic dimensions, provides actuarial interpretive guidelines, and has improved validity scale performance. New features include consistency in scale development, a subscale-within-scale structure, and two companion instruments, the PIY and the SBS. Although subscales improve interpretive options, additional assessment dimensions and two additional inventories represent increased complexity and a major challenge for the novice. Several easy guidelines simplify this challenge: First question the informant who introduces the possibility that the youth has problems of adjustment. Often this informant is obvious: the teacher who discusses the difficult student with the school psychologist, the parent who makes the appointment for an initial evaluation of her angry son, and the adolescent who raises personal concerns with his high school counselor. At other times, such as in administrative evaluations, the only informant is the youth because of ease of availability. In such cases, the effectiveness of the PIY may be contingent upon the degree to which the psychologist can convince the adolescent that providing a competent self-appraisal is in the adolescent's best interest.

The PIC–2 manual provides guidelines that group PIC–2, PIY, and SBS dimensions into five categories: Academic and Cognitive Status, Undercontrolled Behavior, Family and Parent Status, Overcontrolled Behavior, and Social Adjustment. Consistencies (clinical or normative elevations) within categories across informants should be noted and applied, and inconsistencies are often best understood when validity scale elevations are taken into account. Of greatest importance are the actuarial interpretive guidelines detailed in each manual and summarized in the first dozen pages of chapter 5 of the PIC–2 manual. Recent presentations provide additional case studies and examples of the use of validity scales in the interpretive process (Lachar, 2003, 2004a, 2004b; Lachar & Gruber, 2003).

The PIY, PIC–2, and SBS together or individually are often combined with parent and youth interviews to provide assessments in a variety of settings in which problems in youth adjustment are to be ruled out or studied in detail. In some settings, ideographic measures such as storytelling or sentence completion techniques will also be employed. These measures are often applied in clinical, school, medical, and forensic settings.

FORENSIC USES AND LIMITATIONS

The PIC–2, PIY, and SBS have been designed as general diagnostic aids to support the assessment of youth adjustment, not as measures for a specific forensic or juvenile justice purpose. The value of each instrument will depend on the availability of parents or teachers as informants or observers. Parents will provide optimal observation when the youth is resident in their household or has only recently been transferred to a diagnostic or treatment facility. Likewise, teachers are most likely to provide meaningful observation when youths are observed in their regular education classroom placements rather than in the classrooms of "alternative" schools that have been designed to restrict disruptive behaviors and reward compliance with authority figures. It should be noted that, except for application to a case study, the SBS has not been studied in forensic samples (Lachar & Boyd, 2005). Because the PIY was developed with considerable attention to statement simplicity and parsimony, the standardization sample was able to incorporate youths as young as fourth and fifth graders. This measure therefore provides some advantage over questionnaires that require well-developed reading skills and language comprehension and contain more than 270 statements. Considerable effort has been applied in the development of validity scales that provide reasonable estimates of scale accuracy and suggest behavioral factors that require caution in test data application: problem behavior denial or minimization, inadequate attention to or comprehension of statement content, and exaggeration of problems.

Review of concurrent validity evidence for PIC–2 scales *ADH* and *DLQ* and their five subscales as presented in chapter 7 of the PIC–2 manual (Lachar & Gruber, 2001), "Test Construction and Validation," suggests measure effectiveness in forensic applications. A sample of almost 900 youths were rated by clinicians. Six dimensions were formed through factor analysis from 110 descriptors: the first two rating dimensions, Disruptive Behavior (e.g., argues, complains, disobedient, impulsive, labile, etc.) and Antisocial Behavior (e.g., alcohol abuse, vandalism, expelled, lies, police involvement, runs away, steals, etc.), assist in the understanding of *ADH* and *DLQ*. *ADH* (*ADH1*), *DLQ* (*DLQ2, DLQ3*), their two shortened scales, and the composite Externalization all obtained correlations between .63 and .66 with Disruptive Behavior. In contrast, Antisocial Behavior obtained a correlation of .75 with *DLQ1*, whereas all other ADH and DLQ dimensions had correlations in the .36 to .51 range with this distinctly forensic-relevant behavior dimension. Also of note, in a sample of 588 youths, the greatest agreement between PIC–2 and PIY was obtained for *DLQ1* ($r = .68$). Chapter 7 also contrasts PIC–2 performance to the *DSM–IV* diagnostic category of Conduct or Other Disruptive Behavior disorder ($n = 83$). As expected, *DLQ1* obtained both the highest scale elevation ($T = 92.0$) and was the profile that differenticited this group element from all other diagnosis ($d = 3.13$). *DLQ2* and *ADH2* were also elevated with this diagnosis but these elevations were in common with youths who obtained a diagnosis of Oppositional Defiant disorder.

Comparison of PIY profiles obtained from psychiatric inpatients provides some evidence of utility in forensic practice. For example, matched samples of adolescents with discharge diagnoses of either Conduct Disorder or Major Depression were correctly classified by PIY subscales in 83% of these cases (Lachar, Harper, Green, Morgan, & Wheeler, 1996). The PIY has recently been applied to the evaluation of samples of youths from a variety of juvenile justice settings and to protocols that have been selected from the case files of facilities that routinely administer the PIY. In looking at the results obtained, it is important to consider the typical prior experiences of youths evaluated in a specific setting in order to consider the diagnostic and classification issues that would be typical in each setting. How heterogeneous is the population served? Have the issues of diagnosis of and response to educational and mental health problems been previously addressed? Have specific behavioral criteria already been applied in the placement of each youth in a specific juvenile justice setting?

For example, Negy et al. (2001) collected PIY protocols from 52 of 82 Mexican-American adolescents who volunteered for the study, identified themselves as bilingual, and were incarcerated in a southern Texas facility of the Texas Youth Commission. In this study, which was designed to compare language of administration (English, Spanish), gender, and juvenile justice status (versus regular education), gender accounted for less than 1% of the variance, and language no more than 3% of the variance, in scale and subscale scores (with scores in Spanish receiving lower values), whereas juvenile justice status accounted for 13% of both scale and subscale variance. The average language difference was only $1.4T$ points lower for the scales and $1.1T$ points lower for the subscales of the Spanish translation. In contrast, the average PIY values obtained by the incarcerated male adolescents were 8.6 and $7.5T$ points higher for the scales and subscales than the values obtained by regular education male adolescents. Inspection of the frequency of scale and subscale scores showing at least a minimal clinical elevation identified five scales (COG, ADH, DLQ, RLT, SOM) and nine subscales (COG2, COG3, ADH2, DLQ1, DLQ2, DLQ3, RLT1, SOM2, SSK2) on which the incarcerated adolescents obtained a statistically significant greater proportion of clinical elevations than the regular education adolescents. It is useful to note that no protocol was discarded because of informant defensiveness (DEF < 60T) and that these youths probably had participated in previous assessments as part of treatment and rehabilitation efforts, given that this facility represented an ultimate placement within the juvenile, justice system.

Tyndall (2002), in contrast, evaluated 90 PIY protocols randomly selected from the records of the Cook County Juvenile Court, Forensic Clinical Services. All participants were male and African American, were between 12 and 18 years of age, and were referred to the court for charges that varied from theft and damage to property to aggravated assault, possession of a controlled substance, and discharge of a firearm. It is useful to note that validity scales were not applied to disqualify case selection and that youth outcome was associated with test results. In this study, only the DLQ scale and its subscale were studied, and there was no indication whether problems in adjustment could have been documented by other scales and subscales. Only 34% of DLQ values were elevated (>59T), and inspection of subscale elevations (>64T) showed that these elevations mainly reflected the admission of illegal behaviors (DLQ1, 37%; DLQ2, 12%; DLQ3, 4%). Although Tyndall did not provide the distribution of DEF T-scores, she did demonstrate that there was a substantial correlation between DEF and DLQ values in these 90 PIY protocols (DLQ, $r = -.51$; DLQ1, $r = -.30$; DLQ2, $r = -.43$; DLQ3, $r = -.57$. Tyndall also demonstrated that even though DLQ1 in this sample was associated with a defensive response set, this dimension did significantly correlate with the number of court referrals. It is hoped that a more comprehensive study of the PIY will be conducted in this forensic setting.

Two additional studies suggest that PIY reports obtained from incarcerated youths have some diagnostic value. Aikman and Snyder (2005) examined valid PIY protocols routinely administered in the assessment of 107 adolescent girls 13 to 18 years of age (68% African American, 30% Caucasian) whose offenses ranged from ungovernable behavior to murder and aggravated assault and whose correctional sentences ranged from 4 months to 7 years. Although the predictors were limited to PIY scales (subscales were not considered), the weighted number of disciplinary infractions documented during the first 3 months of incarceration were predicted by elevations on both DLQ and ADH, the primary measures of disruptive behavior on the PIY profile. Marsh (2002) examined the ability of PIY scales (apart from the traditional predictors of demographic information, offense history, and DSM–IV diagnoses) to predict the number of moderate and major offenses committed during the first 6 months of incarceration. PIY values were obtained from the routine assessment of 193 juvenile offenders incarcerated at one of two juvenile justice facilities in Virginia for at least 6 months. The majority of these youths were minorities (57%) and male (78%), and all were between 12 and 18 years of age. In this restricted sample, relatively heterogeneous self-report dimensions made an unique contribution beyond other established nontest measures to the prediction of disruptive behaviors during incarceration. *DLQ* made an unique contribution to the prediction of both moderate and major offenses, SSK made an unique contribution to the prediction of moderate offenses, and *COG* elevation was associated with the commission of fewer major offenses.

Other studies with juvenile justice samples have compared the PIY to the Millon Adolescent Clinical Inventory (MACI). Blumentritt and Van Voorhis (2004) demonstrated a degree of consistency between MACI Personality Scales and selected PIY subscales. Depression (*DIS2*) obtained the highest correlation with Inhibited ($r = .44$), Dyscontrol (*DLQ2*) and Noncompliance (*DLQ3*) with Oppositional ($r = .60$), and Limited Peer Status (*SSK1*) with Inhibited ($r = .40$). Branson and Cornell (2005) likewise examined this relationship for 105 incarcerated juvenile offenders and obtained statistically significant correlations for 191 (79%) of 243 comparisons, although the diagnostic correspondence between these two quite dissimilar instruments was characterized as only modest, with kappa coefficients for five pairs of conceptually similar scales ranging from .04 to .56.

The original PIC *DLQ* scale was constructed through item comparisons of samples of normative and adjudicated delinquents (Lachar, Abato, & Wirt, 1975, cited in Wirt, Lachar, Klinedinst, & Seat, 1977) and subsequently obtained numerous correlations with other clinical ratings in a large child guidance/child psychiatry sample (Lachar & Gdowski, 1979). McAuliffe and Handal (1984) demonstrated that *DLQ* could identify antisocial acting-out tendencies in high school students. Rothermel (1985) demonstrated the diagnostic potential of the PIC, especially *DLQ*, when compared to a self-report questionnaire in a large sample of adolescents recruited from a juvenile court population. In a similar manner, *DLQ* of the PIC–2 has demonstrated construct and predictive validity in forensic settings.

Although there is value in the demonstration of a relation between an admission PIY score and subsequent noncompliance in a juvenile justice facility, the PIY, PIC–2, and SBS can be applied in a broad range of forensic contexts, including clinical and diagnostic contacts that precede incarceration or help to avoid it. Because of the juvenile justice system's emphasis on rehabilitation, the real value of PIY, PIC–2, and SBS profiles should be in defining indicators of need for treatment, not documenting antisocial behavior. Additional effort will be necessary to establish the contribution of these instruments to general forensic practice.

CASE EXAMPLE

"Roberta" was a 16-year-old daughter of a Hispanic family newly referred by the juvenile court in a major metropolitan area to a court-administered and -funded intensive treatment program because of her chronic behavior problems, her substance use, and a possible mood disorder. She was initially examined by herself, but later her mother participated in the evaluation. The PIY, PIC–2, and SBS were administered in the context of gathering intake diagnostic information on this young woman, who had a considerable history of contact with the juvenile justice system.

Roberta described a history of conflict with authority figures and repeated noncompliance with probation guidelines and previous treatment programs. When she was 12 years old, she began associating with a new peer group and getting into trouble for arguing with teachers and fighting with other female students. Roberta recalled several school suspensions for fighting and for disrespectful behavior toward teachers that year. At the same time, her relationship with her father deteriorated. She claimed that he became more strict and demanding and that they argued to the point that she harbored homicidal thoughts toward him. Due to her emotional outbursts and destructive behaviors, Roberta was incarcerated on several occasions. At age 15, she was hospitalized on a psychiatric unit because of severe suicidal and homicidal threats.

Roberta's juvenile justice history began when she was 12 and was arrested for stealing from a department store. She was placed into a diversion program for 6 months but was arrested 6 more times over the next 3 years for stealing, fighting, and disturbing the peace. She was finally given a 2-year sentence, which was suspended while she was placed in an intensive probation program. During this time, she began smoking marijuana and was eventually arrested for contempt when she screened positive for marijuana.

After years of maladjustment, Roberta was referred for psychiatric consultation and was placed on antidepressant medication but without concurrent psychotherapy. Soon after starting her medication, she again became noncompliant, providing another focus for conflict with her father. Roberta began spending more time away from home with her older boyfriend and became pregnant at age 15. Although her mother provided childcare so that her daughter could return to school, Roberta again began to skip classes and smoke marijuana.

Her behavior and return to substance use led the court to place her in the intensive treatment program for nonviolent recidivist substance abusers mentioned at the beginning. As stated, Roberta completed the PIY as part of the initial psychiatric evaluation (see Fig. 10.1). The evaluating psychiatrist noted a variety of symptoms of depression, including decreased energy, irritability, feelings of hopelessness, crying spells, and talk of suicide. The scores obtained on the PIY validity scales were within normal limits. PIY subscale elevations in the clinical range suggested current problems in adjustment, reflecting poor behavioral and emotional control, specifically violation of societal rules (DLQ1) and maladjustment due to poorly modulated anger (DLQ2). Roberta described her family of origin as problematic. She admitted to conflict with a family member or members (FAM1), who were also described as poorly adjusted (FAM2). In addition, Roberta obtained a considerable elevation on DIS2, suggesting a problematic depression that required some form of intervention. A secondary elevation of WDL2 suggested social withdrawal, which often accompanies a clinical degree of depression. Critical item endorsements of particular interest included these:

> Several times I have said I wanted to kill myself.
>
> I often stay in my room for hours.
>
> I spend time with friends who often get into trouble.
>
> I have threatened to kill others more than once.
>
> I have been in trouble with the police.
>
> I have been in trouble for stealing more than once.
>
> I have been expelled from school.
>
> I have run away from home.
>
> My parents disagree a lot about how to raise me.

Note that Roberta denied the primary behavior that has kept her assigned to court, substance abuse, answering "False" to "I have problems because I use drugs or take pills."

Roberta's mother independently provided a description of an angry and irritable young woman who has considerable difficulty with authority figures, especially her father. Following an interview with Roberta's treating psychiatrist, she was given the PIC–2 to complete (see Fig. 10.2). Although the standard form profile includes an Inconsistency scale

Youth Name: Roberta H.
Birthdate: 2-10-1988
Age: 16
Date Administered: 02/10/05

Gender: Female
Grade: Not Entered
Date Processed: 02/14/05

Youth ID: Not Entered
Ethnicity: Hispanic

Administered By: B Hammer

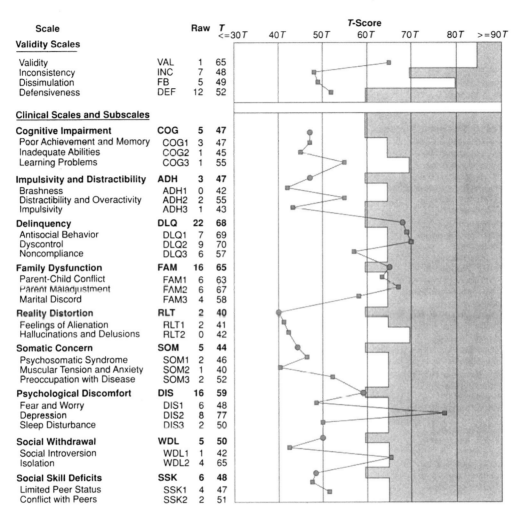

Scale		Raw	T
Validity Scales			
Validity	VAL	1	65
Inconsistency	INC	7	48
Dissimulation	FB	5	49
Defensiveness	DEF	12	52
Clinical Scales and Subscales			
Cognitive Impairment	COG	5	47
Poor Achievement and Memory	COG1	3	47
Inadequate Abilities	COG2	1	45
Learning Problems	COG3	1	55
Impulsivity and Distractibility	ADH	3	47
Brashness	ADH1	0	42
Distractibility and Overactivity	ADH2	2	55
Impulsivity	ADH3	1	43
Delinquency	DLQ	22	68
Antisocial Behavior	DLQ1	7	69
Dyscontrol	DLQ2	9	70
Noncompliance	DLQ3	6	57
Family Dysfunction	FAM	16	65
Parent-Child Conflict	FAM1	6	63
Parent Maladjustment	FAM2	6	67
Marital Discord	FAM3	4	58
Reality Distortion	RLT	2	40
Feelings of Alienation	RLT1	2	41
Hallucinations and Delusions	RLT2	0	42
Somatic Concern	SOM	5	44
Psychosomatic Syndrome	SOM1	2	46
Muscular Tension and Anxiety	SOM2	1	40
Preoccupation with Disease	SOM3	2	52
Psychological Discomfort	DIS	16	59
Fear and Worry	DIS1	6	48
Depression	DIS2	8	77
Sleep Disturbance	DIS3	2	50
Social Withdrawal	WDL	5	50
Social Introversion	WDL1	1	42
Isolation	WDL2	4	65
Social Skill Deficits	SSK	6	48
Limited Peer Status	SSK1	4	47
Conflict with Peers	SSK2	2	51

FIG. 10.1.   Personality Inventory for Youth (PIY) Profile generated from youth response for the case study of "Roberta." The PIY Profile copyright © 1994, 1997, 2003 by Western Psychological Services. Reprinted by permission of the publisher, Western Psychological Services, 12031 Wilshire Boulevard, Los Angeles, California, 90025, U.S.A., www.wpspublish.com. Not to be reprinted in whole or in part for any additional purpose without the expressed, written permission of the publisher. All rights reserved.
Note: Actuarial interpretive guidelines for PIY scales may be found on pages 14–21 of the 1995 PIY administration and interpretation guide.

elevation that raises the possibility of inadequate understanding of some statement content ($T = 72$), the pattern of scale and subscale elevations were both consistent with Roberta's PIY profile and a variety of elements provided in her history. Of primary note were elevations indicating violations of rules (*DLQ1*), problems associated with poorly controlled anger (*DLQ2*), a lack of respect and compliance with authority figures (*DLQ3*), and conflict among family members (*FAM1*). Other elements of this PIC–2 profile suggest that

Child Name: Roberta H.   **Child ID:** Not Entered
Birthdate: 2-10-1988   **Gender:** Female   **Ethnicity:** Hispanic
Age: 16   **Grade:** Not Entered
Respondent: Maria H.   **Relationship to Child:** Mother
Date Administered: 02/17/05 **Date Processed:** 02/21/05 **Administered By:** B Hammer

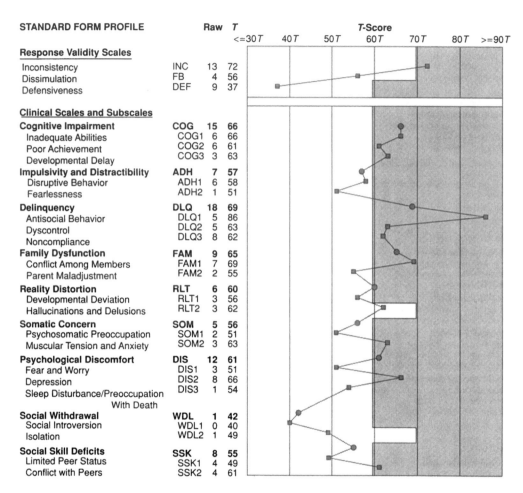

FIG. 10.2. Personality Inventory for Children Second Edition (PIC–2) Standard Form Profile
generated from maternal response for the case study of "Roberta." The PIC–2 Standard Form
Profile copyright © 2001, 2003 by Western Psychological Services. Reprinted by permission of the
publisher, Western Psychological Services, 12031 Wilshire Boulevard, Los Angeles, California,
90025, U.S.A., www.wpspublish.com. Not to be reprinted in whole or in part for any additional
purpose without the expressed, written permission of the publisher. All rights reserved.
Note: Actuarial interpretive guidelines for the scales of the PIC–2 Standard Form Profile are
highlighted in chapter 3 (pp. 19–53) of the 2001 PIC–2 manual.

Roberta's behavior has been associated with poor school adjustment (*COG1, COG2*), and
a review of records identified repetition of the seventh grade, subsequent poor classroom
performance, and a series of school expulsions. In addition, Roberta's mother noted the
presence of depression (*DIS2*), somatic components of tension and anger (*SOM2*), and
social adjustment that may include conflict with peers (*SSK2*). The PIC–2 Critical Item
endorsements also indicate problems with oppositional behavior and family conflict, although Roberta's mother denied her daughter's substance abuse:

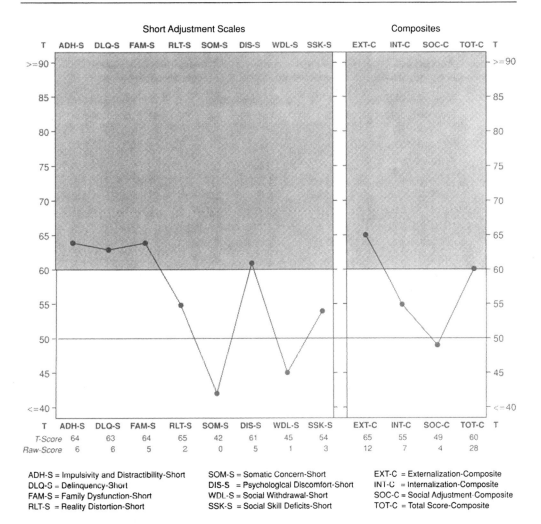

T	ADH-S	DLQ-S	FAM-S	RLT-S	SOM-S	DIS-S	WDL-S	SSK-S	EXT-C	INT-C	SOC-C	TOT-C	T
T-Score	64	63	64	65	42	61	45	54	65	55	49	60	
Raw-Score	6	6	5	2	0	5	1	3	12	7	4	28	

ADH-S = Impulsivity and Distractibility-Short
DLQ-S = Delinquency-Short
FAM-S = Family Dysfunction-Short
RLT-S = Reality Distortion-Short

SOM-S = Somatic Concern-Short
DIS-S = Psychological Discomfort-Short
WDL-S = Social Withdrawal-Short
SSK-S = Social Skill Deficits-Short

EXT-C = Externalization-Composite
INT-C = Internalization-Composite
SOC-C = Social Adjustment-Composite
TOT-C = Total Score-Composite

FIG. 10.3. **Personality Inventory for Children Second Edition (PIC–2) Behavioral Summary Profile generated from maternal response for the case study of "Roberta." The PIC–2 Behavioral Summary Profile copyright © 2001, 2003 by Western Psychological Services. Reprinted by permission of the publisher, Western Psychological Services, 12031 Wilshire Boulevard, Los Angeles, California, 90025, U.S.A., www.wpspublish.com. Not to be reprinted in whole or in part for any additional purpose without the expressed, written permission of the publisher. All rights reserved.**
Note: Actuarial interpretive guidelines for the scales of the PIC–2 Behavioral Summary Profile are highlighted in chapter 4 (pp. 55–66) of the 2001 PIC–2 manual.

My child often acts without thinking.

My child does not learn from her mistakes.

My child often complains that others do not understand her.

Other children often get mad at my child.

My child has been in trouble for attacking others.

My child belongs to a gang.

One of the child's parents often gets very angry with the child.

My child feels that her punishment has been too strict or extreme.

Student Name: Roberta H.   Student ID: Not Entered
Birthdate: 2-10-1988   Gender: Female   Ethnicity: Hispanic
Age: 16   Grade: Not Entered
Rater: GED Classroom   Role of Rater: Teacher   Months Observing Child: 3
Date Administered: 03/24/05   Date Processed: 03/28/05   Administered By: B Hammer

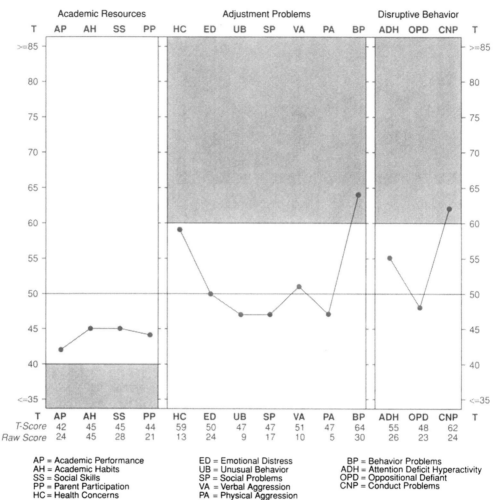

AP = Academic Performance   ED = Emotional Distress   BP = Behavior Problems
AH = Academic Habits   UB = Unusual Behavior   ADH = Attention Deficit Hyperactivity
SS = Social Skills   SP = Social Problems   OPD = Oppositional Defiant
PP = Parent Participation   VA = Verbal Aggression   CNP = Conduct Problems
HC = Health Concerns   PA = Physical Aggression

FIG. 10.4.   Student Behavior Survey (SBS) Profile generated from teacher response for the case
study of "Roberta." The SBS Profile copyright © 2000, 2003 by Western Psychological Services.
Reprinted by permission of the publisher, Western Psychological Services, 12031 Wilshire
Boulevard, Los Angeles, California, 90025, U.S.A., www.wpspublish.com. Not to be reprinted in
whole or in part for any additional purpose without the expressed, written permission of the
publisher. All rights reserved.
Note: Actuarial interpretive guidelines for SBS scales may be found on pages 13–17 of the 2000
SBS manual.

The Behavioral Summary profile of the PIC–2 was also scored in order to identify areas in
which treatment should be considered and to provide a baseline for subsequent assessments
(see Fig. 10.3). Four of eight brief scales fell within the clinical range, as did the composite
Externalization. This profile suggests the need to modify inadequately controlled behavior
(*ADH-S, DLQ-S*), family relations (*FAM-S*), and the role that psychological distress might
play in the development or maintenance of poor adjustment and current problems (*DIS-S*).

After another altercation with her father, Roberta was again arrested for assault and evaluated in the juvenile detention facility. Following an unsuccessful return to home, Roberta was again hospitalized and was started on antidepressant medication and psychotherapy. A decision was made to place her with another relative and to make arrangements for her to attend an alternative school with the goal of obtaining a general education diploma (GED). Continued intensive therapy has led to improved behavioral control, although a few curfew violations have been noted at her new placement. Two months into this mandated 9-month program, Roberta continues with therapy, antidepressant medication, and GED class attendance. Although collection of a SBS rating from a regular education teacher would have contributed the most to an understanding of Roberta when her problems first surfaced at age 12, an SBS was obtained from her current teacher for the sake of completeness (see Fig. 10.4). Considering that alternative schools usually have effective procedures to inhibit problem behaviors, and GED classes have a primary focus of preparation for an exam rather than academic skills acquisition, it is fairly remarkable that this profile has any scale elevations at all. For example, all eight dimensions of Academic Performance had been rated "3" (Average), most likely reflecting an absence of knowledge to the contrary and most certainly inconsistent with Roberta's academic history and her mother's PIC–2 description (e.g., her response of "False" to the statement "My child does fairly well in math (arithmetic) classes"). In addition, the SBS statements describing the response to homework assignments were intentionally left blank, suggesting that no structured after-class effort was expected. At any rate, the SBS profile shows significant elevations on Behavior Problems and Conduct Problems. Reference to the 2000 SBS manual (Lachar et al., 2000) suggests the applicability of the following two interpretive paragraphs:

BP 60-69T. Teachers often describe similar students as disobeying class or school rules and as requiring close supervision. Their misbehavior disrupts class activities, and teachers often describe them as impulsive, overactive, or given to talking excessively. Such students frequently blame others for their problems and may associate with students who are also in trouble. These students are frequently described by their parents as in need of effective discipline; they are unlikely to complete their homework and are usually described as underachieving in school. Parents often report that these children lie to get out of trouble, take unfair advantage of others, and are bossy to other children. Clinicians note that these students are likely to be angry, inattentive, argumentative, frequently frustrated, and easily upset. These students often describe themselves as easily angered and unresponsive to discipline.

CNP 60-69T. Teachers often describe similar students as associating with children who are in trouble, and as being sent to the school office due to misbehavior. They may lie to adults, threaten, hit, or push peers, start fights, and destroy property when angry. Their parents also report misbehavior at home and the need for effective discipline. These children are often described as impulsive, bored with school, and as taking unfair advantage of others. Clinicians usually note behavior suggesting problematic anger, irritability, defiance, poor judgment, and an irresponsible attitude. They are likely to blame others for their problems and to demonstrate poor social skills. These students often admit to being disobedient and to behaving with inadequate emotionally control.[1]

The PIY, PIC–2, and SBS facilitate the rapid accumulation of comprehensive adjustment information to determine the need for mental health services and to identify specific areas in need of intervention. This assessment and subsequent observation over time demonstrated the need for therapeutic intervention in the areas of poorly controlled behavior, family conflict, and problematic depression. Current intervention efforts appear to have stabilized Roberta, and her short-term response to customized intensive treatment suggests these improvements may continue.

REFERENCES

Achenbach, T.M., McConaughy, S.H., & Howell, C.T. (1987). Child/adolescent behavioral and emotional problems: Implications of cross-informant correlations for situational specificity. *Psychological Bulletin, 101*, 213–232.

Aikman, G.G., & Snyder, D.K. (2005). *Predicting disruptive behavior in female adolescents confined to correctional facilities.* Manuscript submitted for publication.

Blumentritt, T.L., & Van Voorhis, C.R.W. (2004). The Millon Adolescent Clinical Inventory: Is it valid and reliable for Mexican American youth? *Journal of Personality Assessment, 83*, 64–74.

Brady, E.U., & Kendall, P.C. (1992). Comorbidity of anxiety and depression in children and adolescents. *Psychological Bulletin, 111*, 244–255.

Branson, C.E., & Cornell, D.G. (2005). *Correspondence of the MACI and the PIY in juvenile offenders.* Manuscript submitted for publication.

Cantwell, D.P. (1996). Attention deficit disorder: A review of the past 10 years. *Journal of the American Academy of Child and Adolescent Psychiatry, 35*, 978–987.

Caron, C., & Rutter, M. (1991). Comorbidity in child psychopathology: Concepts, issues, and research strategies. *Journal of Child Psychology and Psychiatry, 32*, 1063–1080.

Fricker, A.E., & Smith, D.W. (2001). Trauma specific versus generic measurement of distress and the validity of self-reported symptoms in sexually abused children. *Journal of Child Sexual Abuse, 10*, 51–66.

Gdowski, C.L., Lachar, D., & Kline, R.B. (1985). A PIC profile typology of children and adolescents: I. An empirically-derived alternative to traditional diagnosis. *Journal of Abnormal Psychology, 94*, 346–361.

Greenbaum, P.E., Dedrick, R.F., Prange, M.E., & Friedman, R.M. (1994). Parent, teacher, and child ratings of problem behaviors of youngsters with serious emotional disturbances. *Psychological Assessment, 6*, 141–148.

Harrington, R.G., & Follett, G.M. (1984). The readability of child personality assessment instruments. *Journal of Psychoeducational Assessment, 2*, 37–48.

Jensen, P.S., Martin, D., & Cantwell, D.P. (1997). Comorbidity in ADHD: Implications for research, practice, and *DSM-IV. Journal of the American Academy of Child and Adolescent Psychiatry, 36*, 1065–1079.

Jensen, P.S., Watanabe, H.K., Richters, J.E., Roper, M., Hibbs, E.D., Salzberg, A.D., et al. (1996). Scales, diagnoses, and child psychopathology: II. Comparing the CBCL and the DISC against external validators. *Journal of Abnormal Child Psychology, 24*, 151–168.

King, N.J., Ollendick, T.H., & Gullone, E. (1991). Negative affectivity in children and adolescents: Relations between anxiety and depression. *Clinical Psychology Review, 11*, 441–459.

Kline, R.B., & Lachar, D. (1992). Evaluation of age, sex, and race bias in the Personality Inventory for Children (PIC). *Psychological Assessment, 4*, 333–339.

Kline, R.B., Lachar, D., & Gdowski, C.L. (1987). A PIC typology of children and adolescents: II. Classification rules and specific behavior correlates. *Journal of Clinical Child Psychology, 16*, 225–234.

Kline, R.B., Lachar, D., Gruber, C.P., & Boersma, D.C. (1994). Identification of special education needs with the Personality Inventory for Children (PIC): A profile-matching strategy. *Assessment, 1*, 301–313.

Kline, R.B., Lachar, D., & Sprague, D.J. (1985). The Personality Inventory for Children (PIC): An unbiased predictor of cognitive and academic status. *Journal of Pediatric Psychology, 10*, 461–477.

Lachar, D. (1982). *Personality Inventory for Children (PIC) revised format manual supplement.* Los Angeles: Western Psychological Services.

Lachar, D. (2003). Psychological assessment in child mental health settings. In I.B. Weiner (Series Ed.) & J.R. Graham & J.A. Naglieri (Vol. Eds.), *Handbook of psychology: Vol. 10. Assessment psychology* (pp. 235–260). New York: Wiley.

Lachar, D. (2004a). The Personality Inventory for Children, Second Edition (PIC-2), Personality Inventory for Youth (PIY), and Student Behavior Survey (SBS). In M. Hersen (Series Ed.) & M.J. Hilsenroth & D.L. Segal (Vol. Eds.), *Comprehensive handbook of psychological assessment: Vol 2. Personality assessment* (pp. 192–212). New York: Wiley.

Lachar, D. (2004b). The Personality Inventory for Children, Second Edition (PIC-2), Personality Inventory for Youth (PIY), and Student Behavior Survey (SBS). In M. Maruish (Ed.), *The use of psychological testing for treatment planning and outcome assessment* (3rd ed.): *Vol. 2. Instruments for children and adolescents* (pp. 141–178). Mahwah, NJ: Lawrence Erlbaum Associates.

Lachar, D., & Boyd, J. (2005). Personality Inventory for Children, Second Edition; Personality Inventory for Youth; and Student Behavior Survey. In T. Grisso, G. Vincent, & D. Seagrave (Eds.), *Mental health screening and assessment in juvenile justice* (pp. 205–223). New York: Guilford Press.

Lachar, D., & Gdowski, C.L. (1979). *Actuarial assessment of child and adolescent personality: An interpretive guide for the Personality Inventory for Children profile*. Los Angeles: Western Psychological Services.

Lachar, D., Gdowski, C.L., & Snyder, D.K. (1982). Broad-band dimensions of psychopathology: Factor scales for the Personality Inventory for Children. *Journal of Consulting and Clinical Psychology, 50*, 634–642.

Lachar, D., & Gruber, C.P. (1993). Development of the Personality Inventory for Youth: A self-report companion to the Personality Inventory for Children. *Journal of Personality Assessment, 61*, 81–98.

Lachar, D., & Gruber, C.P. (1995a). *Personality Inventory for Youth (PIY) manual: Administration and interpretation guide*. Los Angeles: Western Psychological Services.

Lachar, D., & Gruber, C.P. (1995b). *Personality Inventory for Youth (PIY) manual: Technical guide*. Los Angeles: Western Psychological Services.

Lachar, D., & Gruber, C.P. (2001). *Personality Inventory for Children, Second Edition (PIC-2) Standard Form and Behavioral Summary manual*. Los Angeles: Western Psychological Services.

Lachar, D., & Gruber, C.P. (2003). Multisource and multidimensional objective assessment of adjustment: The Personality Inventory for Children, Second Edition; Personality Inventory for Youth; and Student Behavior Survey. In C.R. Reynolds & R.W. Kamphaus (Eds.), *Handbook of psychological and educational assessment of children: Personality, behavior, and context* (2nd ed., pp. 337–367). New York: Guilford Press.

Lachar, D., Harper, R.A., Green, B.A., Morgan, S.T., & Wheeler, A.C. (1996, August). *The Personality Inventory for Youth: Contribution to diagnosis*. Paper presented at the 104th Annual Convention of the American Psychological Association, Toronto, Canada.

Lachar, D., & Kline, R.B. (1994). The Personality Inventory for Children (PIC) and the Personality Inventory for Youth (PIY). In M. Maruish (Ed.), *Use of psychological testing for treatment planning and outcome assessment* (pp. 479–516). Hillsdale NJ: Lawrence Erlbaum Associates.

Lachar, D., Kline, R.B., Green, B.A., & Gruber, C.P. (1996, August). *Contribution of self-report to PIC profile type interpretation*. Paper presented at the 104th Annual Convention, American Psychological Association, Toronto, Canada.

Lachar, D., Wingenfeld, S.A., Kline, R.B., & Gruber, C.P. (2000). *Student Behavior Survey (SBS) manual*. Los Angeles: Western Psychological Services.

LaCombe, J.A., Kline, R.B., Lachar, D., Butkus, M., & Hillman, S.B. (1991). Case history correlates of a Personality Inventory for Children (PIC) profile typology. *Psychological Assessment, 13*, 1–14.

LaGreca, A.M., Kuttler, A.F., & Stone, W.L. (2001). Assessing children through interviews and behavioral observations. In C.E. Walker & M.C. Roberts (Eds.), *Handbook of clinical child psychology* (3rd ed., pp. 90–110). New York: Wiley.

Lanyon, R.I. (1997). Detecting deception: Current models and directions. *Clinical Psychology: Science and Practice, 4*, 377–387.

Loeber, R., Green, S.M., & Lahey, B.B. (1990). Mental health professionals' perception of the utility of children, mothers, and teachers as informants on childhood psychopathology. *Journal of Clinical Child Psychology, 19*, 136–143.

Lonigan, C.J., Carey, M.P., & Finch, A.J., Jr. (1994). Anxiety and depression in children and adolescents: Negative affectivity and the utility of self-reports. *Journal of Consulting and Clinical Psychology, 62,* 1000–10008.

Marsh, T.Y. (2002). Prediction of institutional misbehavior among juvenile offenders with the Personality Inventory for Youth. *Dissertation Abstracts International, 63*(03), 1568B. (UMI No. 3044902)

McAuliffe, T.M., & Handal, P.J. (1984). PIC Delinquency scale: Validity in relation to self-reported delinquent acts and a socialization scale. *Criminal Justice and Behavior, 11,* 35–46.

Naglieri, J.A., LeBuffe, P.A., & Pfeiffer, S.I. (1994). *Devereux Scales of Mental Disorders manual.* San Antonio TX: The Psychological Corporation.

Negy, C., Lachar, D., & Gruber, C.P. (1998). The Personality Inventory for Youth (PIY): Spanish version: Reliability and equivalence to the English version. *Hispanic Journal of Behavioral Sciences, 20,* 391–404.

Negy, C., Lachar, D., Gruber, C.P., & Garza, N.D. (2001). The Personality Inventory for Youth (PIY): Validity and comparability of English and Spanish versions for regular education and juvenile justice samples. *Journal of Personality Assessment, 76,* 250–263.

Phares, V. (1997). Accuracy of informants: Do parents think that mother knows best? *Journal of Abnormal Child Psychology, 25,* 165–171.

Pisecco, S., Lachar, D., Gruber, C.P., Gallen, R.T., Kline, R.B. & Huzinec, C. (1999). Development and validation of disruptive behavior scales for the Student Behavior Survey (SBS). *Journal of Psychoeducational Assessment, 17,* 314–331.

Pliszka, S.R. (1998). Comorbidity of attention-deficit/hyperactivity disorder with psychiatric disorder: An overview. *Journal of Clinical Psychiatry, 59*(Suppl. 7), 50–58.

Rothermel, R.D., Jr. (1985). A comparison of the utility of the Personality Inventory for Children and the Jesness Inventory in assessing juvenile delinquents. *Dissertation Abstracts International, 46*(5), 1740B.

Smith, S.R., Baity, M.R., Knowles, E.S., & Hilsenroth, M.J. (2001). Assessment of disordered thinking in children and adolescents: The Rorschach Perceptual-Thinking Index. *Journal of Personality Assessment, 77,* 447–463.

Stokes, J.M., Pogge, D.L., Grosso, C., & Zaccario, M. (2001). The relationship of the Rorschach Schizophrenia Index to psychotic features in a child psychiatric sample. *Journal of Personality Assessment, 76,* 209–228.

Tellegen, A. (1988). The analysis of consistency in personality assessment. *Journal of Personality, 56,* 621–663.

Tyndall, M.L. (2002). Validation of the Personality Inventory for Youth (PIY) on a juvenile delinquent population. *Dissertation Abstracts International, 63*(04), 2106B. (UMI No. 3049750)

Wingenfeld, S.A., Lachar, D., Gruber, C.P., & Kline, R.B. (1998). Development of the teacher-informant Student Behavior Survey. *Journal of Psychoeducational Assessment, 16,* 226–249.

Wirt, R.D., Lachar, D., Klinedinst, J.K., & Seat, P.D. (1977). *Multidimensional description of child personality: A manual for the Personality Inventory for Children.* Los Angeles: Western Psychological Services.

Wrobel, N.H., & Lachar, D. (1998). Validity of self- and parent-report scales in screening students for behavioral and emotional problems in elementary school. *Psychology in the Schools, 35,* 17–27.

Wrobel, N.H., Lachar, D., & Wrobel, T.A. (2005). Self-report problem scales and subscales and behavioral ratings provided by peers: Unique evidence of test validity. *Assessment, 12,* 255–269.

Wrobel, T.A., Lachar, D., Wrobel, N.H., Morgan, S.T., Gruber, C.P., & Neher, J.A. (1999). Performance of the Personality Inventory for Youth validity scales. *Assessment, 6,* 367–376.

Ziegenhorn, L., Tzelepis, A., Lachar, D., & Schubiner, H. (1994, August). *Personality Inventory for Youth: Screening for high-risk adolescents.* Paper presented at the 102nd Annual Convention of the American Psychological Association, Los Angeles.

11

THE PARENTING STRESS INDEX

RICHARD ABIDIN

UNIVERSITY OF VIRGINIA, CURRY SCHOOL

JAMES R. FLENS

CHILD CUSTODY CONSULTANTS

WILLIAM G. AUSTIN

CONSULTING FORENSIC PRACTICE

INTRODUCTION

The Parenting Stress Index (PSI) was not designed for forensic purposes, but increasingly it is being used in forensic contexts. The author of the PSI (Abidin, 1998) has acknowledged that he is not a forensic psychologist and that he never envisioned that the PSI would be used for forensic purposes. Nevertheless, the PSI, like other psychological measures, has had its utility extended through the research and clinical efforts of others. The purpose of this chapter is to provide information about the nature of the PSI, the types of information it generates, its core reliability and validity, and its possible uses in forensic work. The writing of it represents a collaboration between the PSI's developer and two forensic experts with extensive experience using the PSI. The goal of the authors is give potential users of the PSI a better understanding of its utility and validity and its limitations.

Basic Description of the Parenting Stress Index

The purpose of the PSI is to identify parents in need of guidance and support, identify potential dysfunctional parent-child relationships, and identify children at risk for emotional and behavioral developmental problems. Over time, the PSI has been found to be also useful as a treatment planning tool and as a means of evaluating both individual and group interventions. The treatment planning function involves identifying problem areas using the domain and subscale scores and focusing interventions in those areas that are most stressful for the parent.

The 101 items of the PSI focus on two domains: Child Characteristics and Parent Characteristics (or family context). There is also an optional 19-item life events stress scale designed to provide an overview of the context of the parent-child relationship. The Child Characteristics domain consists of six subscales generated from 47 items. Four of these subscales address child characteristics that are related to both temperament and learned behaviors. These child characteristics are recognized as ones that make parenting more challenging. The other two child characteristic subscales relate to the parents' cognitive/affective responses to their child. The Child Characteristic domain subscales are as follows:

Adaptability: difficulties adjusting to changes, inflexible.

Distractibility/Hyper: ADHD-type behaviors.

Demandingness: demands requiring accommodation or attention.

Mood: moodiness, crying, displays of unhappiness.

Acceptability: behaviors that do not match parent's expectations or hopes for child.

Reinforces Parent: parent does not experience positive reinforcement from interactions with the child.

The Parent Characteristics domain consists of a Total Domain score and seven subscales derived from 54 items. The seven subscales cover characteristics of the parents and their perception of their social support for parenting. The Parent Characteristics domain subscales are as follows:

Competence: sense of competence in the parenting role.

Isolation: lack of social support for his or her role as parent.

Attachment: assesses parent's sense of attachment to the child.

Health: the impact of physical health on parenting.

Role Restriction: impact of the restrictions parenting places on parent's choices and freedom.

Depression: impact of depression and feelings of guilt on parenting behavior.

Spouse: help and emotional support from the child's other parent.

It is important to note that although some of the PSI subscale names are similar to concepts measured by other instruments, the items relate to the impact of each concept on the individual's perception of his or her ability to parent and the distress he or she experiences in the parenting role. This is an important distinction, as it relates to the PSI score's validity in relation to parenting. For example, whereas a general measure of depression will likely have a stronger association with the diagnosis of clinical depression in a parent, the PSI Depression subscale has a stronger association with parental behavior. The PSI Depression subscale has correlations with general measures of depression ranging from .40 to .76. This issue of the relation of the PSI subscales to important clinical variables is addressed more fully in the section on the PSI's validity.

The PSI is a self-report measure that may be completed by a parent or parent surrogate in relation to a specific child between the ages of 3 months and 12 years. The items are responded to using a 5-point Likert scale with anchor points ranging from "strongly agree" to "strongly disagree." The PSI requires approximately 20 minutes to complete and requires a fourth- to fifth-grade reading level. The PSI may be administered using either a test booklet and a self-scoring answer sheet or a computer program that administers, scores, and writes an interpretive report. The computer program not only interprets the results but provides recommendations, at-risk-for diagnoses, profile comparisons to known clinical samples, and a topically arranged research reference list of validity studies. There is also an upward extension of the PSI called the Stress Index for Parents of Adolescents (SIPA; Sheras, Abidin, & Konold, 1998) for use with adolescents aged 11 to 19. The SIPA is a separate measure and is mentioned for information purposes; but is not covered in this presentation.

There are at present official translations of the PSI into 28 languages, and these are available from the publisher, Psychological Assessment Resources, Inc. In some instances there are norms for the non-English speaking respondents and a professional manual in their language.

Development of the PSI

The Parenting Stress Index was originally designed for use as a screening and triage tool to be used in pediatric medical practices by psychologists and pediatricians. In 1965 Dr. Abidin was working at Wilford Hall USAF Hospital, San Antonio, Texas, and consulting with pediatricians, parents, and teaching pediatric residents in an elective course of "behavioral pediatrics." A recurrent problem for the pediatricians was the limited time they had to devote to parents for anticipatory guidance and/or the management of minor behavioral problems. The pediatric staff and residents expressed the need for a valid system that would identify situations requiring a referral without consuming much of their time. They expressed the challenge thus: "Can you give us 3 or 4 questions that we can ask parents and that would help us distinguish those in need of additional attention from those parents who are okay?" The PSI was developed in response to that question. The key task was to find a way to efficiently and validly identify parent-child systems that are either currently dysfunctional or at risk for dysfunction or situations in which the child's development has gone awry and the parents need support and consultation.

It quickly became apparent that the 3- or 4-item solution would not work and that some sort of framework or theoretical model would be needed to guide the effort to create an early identification screening tool that was empirically based and informed by the research and theorizing of others. One primary source of data consisted of interactions with parents and the clinicians who worked with them on parenting issues in the Pediatric Center of Wilford Hall USAF Hospital and the Parenting Clinic of Pediatric Associates of Charlottesville, VA. The observations gained through these interactions were considered in the context of the work of the leaders in the field of human stress at the time (Ellis, 1973; Lazarus, 1966; Selye 1952, 1974). The result of these deliberations was the creation of a theoretical model that helped guide the development of the PSI (Fig. 11.1).

PSI Model Assumptions

The PSI model is based on these assumptions:

- All stresses in the parenting system, regardless of source, are multidimensional and summative.

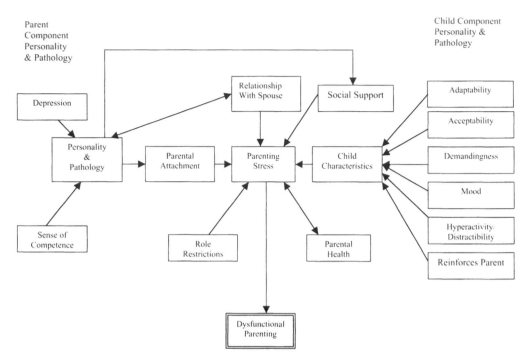

FIG. 11.1. Theoretical model for the development of the PSI (Abidin & Burke 1978).

- Stress results from important transactions between parent and child and the parent's social environment.

- All these transactions are cognitively appraised by the parent and given either a positive or negative stress value.

- Life events provide a context that may add to the stress load of a parent.

- Parents generally act as buffers for their children, and the most proximal sources of parenting stress will have the greatest impact on the parenting behavior exhibited.

- The total level of parenting stress is the best predictor of dysfunctional parenting and that portion of the child's development that is linked to parent-child transactions.

The PSI items were developed by using four sources of information: (a) Abidin's and other clinicians' experience working with parents in pediatric contexts and parent education groups; (b) reviews of parents' daily stress logs regarding interactions with their child and their performance in the parenting role; (c) interviews with 25 prominent clinical child, developmental psychologists, and child psychiatrists regarding what they perceived to be the primary sources of parenting stress; and (d) a wide-ranging review of the research literature regarding child and parent characteristics associated with parenting stress, dysfunctional parenting, and negative child outcomes. The information gathered using these methods was then used to guide the writing of each questionnaire item. The general strategy in constructing the questions was to ask about a child or parent characteristic, an event, or the parenting context so that there would be a specific referent to be connected to the level of distress the parent was experienceing. For example: "My child is so active that it exhausts me," "I often feel my child's needs control my life," "Since having my child, my spouse (male/female friend) has not given me as much help and support as I expected."

The initial question item pool was administered to a series of samples of parents and subjected to revision using item analyses, criteria for inclusion, alpha reliability estimates, and exploratory and confirmatory factor analyses. The current edition of the PSI is the sixth version (Burke, 1978; Hauenstein, Scarr, & Abidin, 1987; Solis & Abidin, 1991).

PSI Short Form (PSI–SF)

In the early 1990s, researches and some clinicians began inquiring about and asking for an abbreviated version of the PSI, and the "3 or 4 questions" idea arose again. Abidin resisted the idea of a short form until it became apparent that users in a variety of ways were shortening the PSI and calling their version the PSI. Questions about the validity of these PSI variants and of the published works using the variants, as well as reported clinical experiences with the different short forms, required a response. The response chosen was the creation of the PSI–SF. All of the items of the PSI–SF came from the 101 items of the PSI parent and child domains of the regular PSI. The decision was made to subject the original PSI item data pool to a three-factor solution.

The rational for this decision was that some researchers reported that when they exposed their PSI data sets to exploratory factor analysis, a third weak factor could be justified based on the eigen values of the factor analysis. Examination of the items' loadings on the three factors suggested that if the 12 strongest items were retained, a three-factor solution would result, with factor loadings of .40 or greater for all items and with only 2 of the 36 items having a double loading with another factor. The newly created PSI–SF was then submitted to a replication using confirmatory factors analysis with a new sample. The replication produced the same factor structure (with two double loadings) and very similar factor loading weights. Independent replications of the factors suggest that the three-factor solution is stable, although some researchers suggest that there are higher order factors imbedded in the subscales that could be used for more refined data interpretation (Reitman, Currier, & Stickle, 2002).

Based on the item content, the three factors were labeled Difficult Child, Parental Distress, and Parent-Child Dysfunctional Interaction. The first two are reflections of the Child Characteristics and Parent Characteristics domains of the full PSI, and scores on these should be interpreted as one would the scores on those domains. The interpretation of the score on the third factor relates to parents' perceptions of their transactions with and expectations of their child and thus addresses the quality of the parent-child relationship.

PSYCHOMETRIC CHARACTERISTICS

Norms and Generalization

The 2,633 mothers in the norm group were recruited primarily (41%) from well-child pediatric clinics inn central Virginia. The remainder were from public day care in Virginia (20%), health maintenance programs in Massachusetts (10%), pediatric clinics in New York city, (12%), clinics in North Carolina (7%), and public schools in Georgia (6%) and Wisconsin (4%). The ethnic composition was as follows: 76% Caucasian of western European descent, 11% African American, 10% Hispanic, and 2% Asian. The sample was not random or stratified and primarily represents an opportunistic approach to data gathering.

One important consideration in the use of the PSI (and all other evaluation measures and procedures) is its applicability to different populations. One crude method of addressing this issue is to use a sampling procedure that is designed to match all segments of society, for example, men versus women, various racial and ethnic groups, various income and educational levels, and various geographic groups. The problem is that the endless subdivisions would require samples in the hundreds of thousands, and even if a particular group was included in the sample, that fact would not indicate the validity of the measure for that group. The most powerful test of the robustness of a measure and its likely utility and validity is its construct integrity and predictive validity when it is applied to populations that are vastly different than the original normative sample. The research literature on the transcultural use of the PSI and other studies of diverse U.S. populations that are vastly different from the original normative sample indicate that the PSI is a robust and valid measure for use with diverse populations both inside and outside of the United States. These studies required the PSI to hold its construct and predictive validity after surviving a language translation and application to a different racial and cultural group. The following is a sampling of studies that address the issue of generalizability of the PSI. All the studies referenced in this section contain normative data for the specified population.

Supplemental Norm Samples From the United States

Hutcheson and Black (1996) examined the psychometric properties of the PSI in a sample of 191 low-income, urban (Baltimore, MD) African-American mothers of infants and toddlers. They reported that

> despite differences from the normative sample in ethnicity, socioeconomic class, family structure, and child age, internal consistency coefficients ranged from acceptable to excellent and were similar in magnitude to those reported for both Hispanic (Solis and Abidin, 1991) and Caucasian samples (Abidin, 1990).... Parenting Stress Index, Manual Charlottosville, VA, Pediatric Psychology Press. The results of the confirmatory factor analysis were consistent with Abidin's (1983) original child and parent domains. (p. 396)

Solis and Abidin (1991) conducted a psychometric study of the Spanish version of the PSI based on a sample of 223 urban (New York City) Hispanic mothers. They reported alpha reliabilities comparable to those reported for the original normative sample. Confirmatory factor analysis of the subscales supported the original two-factor solution; nevertheless, Solis and Abidin suggested that a three-factor solution based on the subscale factor analysis may facilitate interpretation of the PSI for Hispanic parents.

Innocenti, Huh, and Boyce (1992) reported on a PSI data set of 725 families collected across the United States as a normative study for parents of children with disabilities. The children in the sample had a wide array of disabilities, they ranged in age from 4 to 60 months, and 76% were Caucasian. Family income and parental education approximated the national statistics. Innocenti et al. reported 1-year test-retest reliabilities between .67 and .76, which is in the range reported in the PSI manual. Mean comparisons by age between the norms in the PSI manual and the current sample confirmed statements in the manual that parents of disabled children have significantly more stress related to the children's characteristics and that no significant differences occur in the parent domain. A norm table at the domain level is presented to facilitate interpretations with parents of preschool-aged disabled children.

International Cross-Validation Norm Studies

Bigras, LaFreniere, and Abidin (1996) described the translation and norming of the PSI on a sample of 377 French-speaking parents from Quebec, Canada. The results obtained from a confirmatory factor analysis closely approximated the results of the original factor analysis report by Abidin (1995), and in fact the subscale loadings were generally higher than those reported by Abidin. The alpha reliabilities for the total and domain scores were essentially identical with those reported by Abidin. At the subscale level, however, the reliabilities were lower, clustering around .75. The norms generated for the French Canadian sample closely approximated those for the U.S. population, with the exception of two child domain subscales, Adaptability and Mood, which were slightly higher for the French Canadian sample. Based on the norms and the French Canadian validity studies reported, Bigras et al. recommend the use of the same cutoff scores for interpretation of the French Canadian parents scores as those reported in the PSI manual for the U.S. population. They also report that high PSI scores were predictive of eight known risk factors in their sample. These findings suggest that the PSI is robust enough to survive translation and maintain its validity in application to a population markedly different from the original norming group.

Abidin and Santos (2003) reported a factor analytic and normative study ($N = 600$) conducted in Lisbon, Portugal, using a Portuguese translation (Santos, 1992). The results confirm the U.S. norm group's two-factor solution, with stress levels in the child and parent domains comparable to those of the U.S. normative sample.

The sample used in a study by Tam, Chan, and Wong (1994) entitled "The Validation of the Parenting Stress Index Among Chinese Mothers in Hong Kong" is probably as different from the original PSI norm group as any group one could find in the United States. In a sample of 248 mothers, Tam et al. reported a factor structure that duplicated that of the U.S. sample. To validate the PSI, they used interviews, self-reports about parenting difficulties, mothers' social service status, and independently created high- and low-stress parent groups of 34 and 96 parents, respectively. Univariate analysis of the PSI domain and subscale scores found that 14 of the 16 scores significantly discriminated between groups at $p < .001$, and scores for the other two, Mood and Parent Attachment, at $p < .01$. The data were subsequently submitted to a discriminant analysis, which resulted in a 93.1% correct classification. Only 4 of the 34 high-stress group members were classified as low stress, and only 5 of the 96 low-stress parents were classified as high stress.

Limitation of the Original PSI Norms

One limitation of the PSI is that the normative sample ($N = 2,633$) consists only of mothers. Data from a sample of 200 fathers are presented in the manual. These data suggest that, from a normative perspective, fathers of young children aged 6 months to 6 years report less stress than mothers and possibly experience less stress, indicating that the clinical cutoff for the total score recommended for fathers should be 15 to 20 raw score points lower than that recommended for mothers. The manual does not provide data suggesting whether stress levels differ between mothers and fathers for children above 6 years of age. For information relevant to the differential interpretation of mothers' and fathers' PSI scores, users need to be familiar with the research literature regarding mothers' and fathers' responses to the PSI. Some brief abstracts of a sampling of relevant studies follow.

Parental Gender Differences on the PSI

Deater-Deckard and Scarr (1996), using the standard PSI short form in a study of 589 married couples, examined the relation of parenting stress to parental gender. Their sample was predominately college educated and Caucasian (90%), with, 2.6 years as the mean age for the children. Gender differences were described as "negligible"; the Parental Distress score for the mothers was statistically significantly higher than for the fathers at $p < .05$ but not clinically significant given that the mean was only "one tenth of a standard deviation" higher. There was no difference in the Parent-Child Dysfunctional Interaction subscale and the Difficult Child score. No ethnic group or child gender differences were found. Using LISREL modeling, the relation of PSI scores to parental discipline and child behavior was examined, and no gender differences in the overall model were found. In more fine grained analyses, differences in the size of the associations of a few of the PSI scores to criteria were found between mothers and fathers.

In a study of 121 families of toddlers with disabilities, M.W. Krauss (1993) examined the similarities and differences in the parenting stress reported by mothers and fathers. No difference was found for the Parent Domain; however, for the Child Domain, fathers reported higher stress (mean score = 106) than mothers (101). The source of the difference was that fathers were more distressed as shown by the elevation of the Adaptability, Mood, and Reinforces Parent subscales on the Child Domain. At the subscale level of the Parent Domain, fathers showed significantly more stress on Attachment, whereas mothers showed significantly more stress on Restriction of Role, Relation with Spouse, and Health. These differences appear related to the parenting roles traditionally performed by mothers and fathers.

In a study of 54 families, Beckman (1991) examined the effect of young child disabilities on the stress experienced by the mothers and fathers. In both, the disabled and nondisabled samples, the mothers reported higher levels of stress than fathers on Parenting Domain and Total Score. The differences were approximately 0.05 standard deviations higher. At the subscale level for the disabled sample, mothers showed greater stress on Child Demandingness, Parental Depression, Restriction of Role, Sense of Competence, and Health. Fathers reported greater stress associated with the Child Domain and in relation to their attachment to their child. Social support was significantly associated with parent stress for both mothers ($r = .65$) and fathers ($r = .47$).

In an exploratory study, Barker (1994) examined the level of parenting stress of 20 married couples with a child diagnosed as having ADHD (child mean age = 9 years). Mothers reported significantly more stress in the Child Domain but not in the Parent Domain or the Total Score. As regards of the 13 subscales, the only significant difference ($p < .05$) was that fathers reported feeling less attached to their child.

Frank et al. (1991) explored the relation of child illness and the quality of the parenting alliance to mothers' and fathers' perceptions of parenting stress. The sample consisted of 56 couples who were parents of 3- or 4-year-old children and of middle-class socioeconomic status; 86% were Caucasian. Gender differences were noted for both the parenting alliance and the level of parenting stress. Child illness was linked to mothers' but not fathers' experience of parenting stress. Fathers' experience of parent stress was associated with the strength of their parenting alliance with their spouse for both the Child Domain and Parent Domain of the PSI and all their subscales. Mothers' perceptions of the quality of their parenting alliance were not associated with the Parent Domain but were associated with the Child Domain and showed the strongest association with the Acceptability of Child scores. No interaction (buffering) effects were found for the quality of parenting alliance and child illness in predicting maternal stress. However, the quality of the parenting alliance does seem to buffer fathers from the stresses of parenting a sick child.

Webster-Stratton (1988) compared the PSI responses of 85 mother-and-father couples in a study of children (mean age = 4.4 years) with conduct problems. Fathers reported significantly less stress on the Child Domain ($p < .001$, 10 raw score points) and less stress on the Parent Domain ($p < .01$, 9 raw score points). The only subscale on which fathers reported significantly more stress than mothers was Attachment, which relates to the fathers' feeling less connected to their child. Both mothers' and fathers' PSI scores were found to be significantly correlated to their perception of the child's adjustment as measured by the CBCL and the Eyberg Child Behavior Inventory. The magnitude of these associations varied between parents. The most interesting difference was that the CBCL Hyperactivity scale was correlated .60 with the PSI Parent Domain ($p < .001$) for mothers but was not significantly correlated ($r = .17$) for fathers.

PSI Interpretation: Cautions and Supporting Data

Users of the PSI are cautioned to remember that the interpretation of the PSI proceeds from the global to the specific. For the Total Score, the alpha reliability is .95; for the Child Domain, it is .90; and for the Parent Domain, it is .93. These measures of internal consistency suggest that these components of the PSI may be interpreted as coherent. However, when the user proceeds to the interpretation of specific subscales, more caution may be needed. In this regard, the alpha reliabilities of the PSI subscales range from .70 for the shortest Health subscale (five items) to .84 for Depression. Care should also be taken not to overinterpret the PSI clinical profiles presented in the manual, because their sample sizes are generally small. These profiles need to be considered as starting points for relating a particular case to the profiles presented and to the research on the population in question. For example, although the manual provides three profiles of samples that related to child abuse, familiarity with the abuse research literature, such as that presented later, is necessary for the proper interpretation.

Another limitation of the PSI manual (Abidin, 1995) is the absence of standard errors of measurement and confidence intervals; this lack is corrected by the addition of Table 11.1, page 316 of this chapter. This information is provided to facilitate the precision of the PSI interpretative process.

One question that has been raised about the PSI norms is why norms are not reported by the age of the child and the child's gender. Normative information relative to the PSI Total Score and domain scores are reported in an appendix of the test manual in terms of the child's age in 1-year intervals from 1 year to 8 years of age and for a 9+ years group. The results of an ANOVA across the groups indicated that a statistically significant age effect was present across the groups. The detection of a difference occurred as a result of the large sample size and the statistical power. The amount of variance accounted for, however, based on between-group differences, was insignificant. The omega statistic indicated that the percentage of variance was 1.6%. When an ANOVA was run based on 3-year age groupings (1–3, 4–6, 7–9+), no significant differences were detected despite the large sample size. No significant differences were found based on the gender of the child. Based on these analyses, the decision was made not to report age or gender norms.

Although the PSI professional manual describes the test norms and procedures used to develop the PSI, it needs to be recognized that a number of different reference samples or norms have been developed by researchers both in the United States and other countries: Portuguese (Abidin & Santos, 2003); African-American (Hutcheson & Black, 1996); French (Lacharite, Ethier, & Piche, 1992); Chinese, Hong Kong (Chan, 1994); Chinese, Formosa (Tam, et al., 1994); PSI–SF Head Start (Reitman, Currier, & Stickle, 2002); Dutch (DeBock, Vermulist, Gerris, & Abidin, 1992). This body of research indicates that the PSI's factor structure, construct, and predictive validity is very robust, since it has been replicated internationally and survived language translations and cultural differences from the original norm groups. Given this evidence, it is highly likely that the PSI would be valid for the broad spectrum of parents in the United States.

One caution is that the PSI does not have a large normative sample supporting its use with fathers. There are, however, a significant number of research studies indicating that the PSI is as valid a predictor of dysfunctional parenting in fathers as it is with mothers. Unfortunately, this circumstance requires the forensic user to be familiar with a literature that is published in a wide array of journals (Bagner & Eyberg, 2003; Burbach, Fox, & Nicholson, 2004; Calzada, Eyberg, Rich, & Querido, 2004; Deater-Deckard & Scarr, 1996; Judge, 2003; McBride, 1989; Schiller, 2003; Webster-Stratton, 1988). Recent work with the PSI–SF also suggests that there are not distinct gender differences in perceived parenting stress for the three subscales of the PSI–SF Baker et al., 2003; (Schiller, 2003).

CLINICAL USES AND LIMITATIONS

The PSI and the PSI–SF have both been used clinically in three primary ways: (a) for screening and triage of large populations, (b) as a first-gate intake measure, and (c) as part of an individual clinical assessment.

Screening and Triage (Predictive Validity Research)

As a screening and triage measure, it is most commonly used in pediatric practices, public health outreach programs, and preventative programs such as Head Start. When it is used in this manner, the objective is to help identify parent-child systems that are under sufficient stress to lead to dysfunctional parenting and to problems in child development. Given that there are never sufficient resources to provide guidance, consultation, and treatment to all parents in any given population, the PSI helps to identify those in the greatest distress and in need of services and is predictive of future child adjustment (Abidin, Jenkins, & McGaughey, 1992; Endriga, Jordan, & Speltz, 2003; Florsheim, et al., 2003; Goldberg, et al., 1997; Saylor, Boyce, & Price, 2003).

Two examples of such uses follow. First, the PSI is used as a component of a screening battery that is periodically given to mothers on the island nation of Bermuda as a part of National Health screening. The battery typically identifies 10% to 15% of parents, who are referred to the Child Development Center for services. Second, the PSI and PSI–SF have also been used by a number of Head Start programs to identify parents who would benefit from supportive guidance and consultation (Grossman & Shigaki, 1994; Reitman, et al., 2002; Seo, 2004). Critical evaluations of the use of the PSI and the PSI–SF with such low-income, minority, and single parents have indicated that these instruments are useful and valid predictors of parental dysfunction and problem child behaviors (Bendell, Stone, Field, & Goldstein, 1989; Bhavnagri, 1999; Hutcheson & Black, 1996; Kelley, 1998; Moss, Cyr, & Dubois-Comtois, 2004; LeCuyer-Maus, 2003; Reitman, et al., 2002). Studies have replicated both the factor structure and the construct validity of the PSI and PSI–SF, in low socioeconomic status, minority populations (Breen & Barkley, 1988; Cuccaro, Holmes, & Wright, 1993; Reitman, et al., 2002; Wakschlag & Keenan, 2001).

First-Gate Intake Measure

The use of the PSI as a first-gate intake measure involves administering it as the first psychometric measure in a clinical assessment. This is typically handled in one of two ways.

First, the PSI can be sent to the parent along with other forms to be completed and returned prior to the first face-to-face contact. This allows the clinician to score and interpret the results and thus be able to better structure, and focus the interview and select other appropriate psychometric instruments to include in the assessment. The PSI subscales cover the major child characteristics, parent characteristics, and situational variables that relate to parenting difficulties. These subscales are not diagnoses oriented but rather identify issues and areas in need of intervention or further examination. Second, the parent can take the PSI by computer administration immediately prior to the initial interview. The PSI report is then reviewed by the clinician prior to the clinical interview and can even be used as part of the assessment interaction with the parent.

Routine Clinical Assessment

The PSI and PSI–SF are often used as a part of the assessment of a parents child or family system. Their purpose is to help the clinician determine the level and sources of parenting stress. The PSI scores are related to a number of critical diagnostic and intervention issues. They are associated with parental compliance with treatment expectations and continuation in treatment. High PSI total scores have been found to be associated with premature termination of treatment and noncompliance (Calam, Bolton, & Roberts, 2002; Gerson, Farth, New, & Fivisch, 2004; Hipke, Wolchik, Sandler, & Braver, 2002; Kazdin, 1990, 1995; Kazdin, Mazurick, & Bass, 1993; Mellins, Kang, Leu, Havens, & Chesney, 2003). There is also evidence that high Stress scores are linked to excessive and inappropriate medical services utilization (Abidin & Wilfong, 1989; Waisbren et. al., 2003).

The PSI scores are also associated with insecure attachment relationships (Jarvis & Creasey, 1991; Teti, Nakagawa, Das, & Wirth, 1991), which are related to the quality of the parent's perception of and cognitions about the child and the quality of parent-child interactions (Adamakos, Ryan, Ullman, & Pasese, 1986; Barkley, Anastopoulos, Guevremont, & Fletcher, 1992; Beck, Young, & Tarnowski, 1990; Bigras & LaFreniere, 1994; Diener, Nievar, & Wright, 2003; Hitchcock, 2003; Jarvis & Creasey, 1991; Laganiere, Tessier, & Nadeau, 2003; Levendosky & Grahambermann, 1998). PSI scores are also associated with harsh punishment (Burbach, et al., 2004; Florsheim et al., 2003; Jackson, et al., 1998), and they typically have the strongest correlations of all the family variables examined. High levels of parenting stress is in general a predictor of harsh punishment, and especially when the PSI subscales of Child Adaptability, Reinforces Parent, Parental Competence, and Parental Attachment are elevated (Coyle, Roggman, & Newland, 2002; Lyons-Ruth, Lyubchik, Wolfe, & Bronfman, 2002; Repetti & Wood, 1997).

Depression, a variable that has been linked to dysfunctional parenting behavior, is highly related to stress in the Parent Domain of the PSI and to the subscale Depression (Anastopoulos, Guevremont, Shelton, & DuPaul, 1992; Frankel & Harmon, 1996; Gelfand, Teti, & Fox, 1992; Milgrom & McCloud, 1996; Willner & Goldstein, 2001). The PSI Depression subscale has items that more directly relate to parenting behavior and has been shown to be a better predictor of dysfunctional parenting behavior and problems in child adjustment than the more common broadband measures of depression (Breen & Barkley, 1988; Donenberg & Baker, 1993; Kazdin, et al., 1993; Webster-Stratton, 1988). High levels of total parenting stress and elevation of the Depression, Social Isolation, and Attachment scores are related to a variety of mental health problems in both mothers and fathers (LeCuyer-Maus, 2003; Wong, Lam, & Kwoak, 2003).

The PSI Child Domain and its various subscales have in other studies been found to be predictive of children's current level of psychosocial adjustment. The pattern of subscales provides the clinician with an indication of likely types of problematic behavior (Anastopoulos, Shelton, DuPaul, & Guevremont, 1993; Bagley & Mallick, 1997; Bigras, LaFreniere, & Dumas, 1996; Breen & Barkley, 1988; Ethier & LaFreniere, 1993; Irvin, Carter, & Briggs-Gowan, 2002; Karp, Serbin, Stack, Schwartzman, 2004; Murphy & Barkley, 1996; Tomanik, Harris, & Hawkins, 2004; Weiss, Sullivan, & Diamond, 2003). PSI scores have been used as outcome measures to document changes resulting from treatments that target children's behavior problems (Barkley, Edwards, Laneri, Fletcher, & Metevia, 2001; Kazdin & Wassell, 1999, 2000; Sanders & McFarland, 2000).

Children's academic success in school is moderated by the quality of their home environment, in particular, by the support and direction they receive from their parents. Parenting Stress Index scores relate to those parenting behaviors and are predictive of a child's problem-solving skills (Hughes, Brestan, Christens, Klinger, & Valle, 2004) and of their achievement scores, particularly in the early years of school (Bramlett, Hall, Barnett, & Rowell, 1995; Bramlett, Rowell, & Mandenberg, 2000).

Martial conflict and the quality of the parenting alliance are major variables impacting the quality of parenting in a family and a child's adjustment. The Parent Domain score of the PSI and the Relationship with Spouse subscales have been shown to have a significant association with child adjustment (Frank et al., 1991; Ha, Oh, & Kim, 1999; Kazui, Muto, & Sonoda, 1996). Likewise, social support as measured by the social isolation subscale is linked to the level of parenting stress and both the quality of parenting and child adjustment (Chan, 1994; Feldman, Varghese, Ramsay, & Rajska, 2002; Jackson, Gyamfi, Brooksgunn, & Blake, 1998; Trute, 2003).

The level of parenting stress as measured by the PSI total score, and the Parent Domain subscales have been shown to be predictive of a wide variety of observed inappropriate and dysfunctional parenting behaviors (Bigras et al., 1996; Calkins, Hungerford, & Dedmon, 2004; Degroat, 2003; Diener et al., 2003; Feinfield & Baker, 2004; Hall & Marteau, 2003; LeCuyer-Maus, 2003; Moran, Pederson, Pettit, & Krupka, 1992; Onufrak, Saylor, Taylor, Eyberg, & Boyce, 1995; Rodriquez & Green, 1997; Teti et al., 1991; Wilfong, Saylor, & Elksnin, 1991).

THE FORENSIC APPLICATION OF THE PSI

When issues arise as part of a legal proceeding that require a mental health professional to address specific behavioral questions, a forensic mental health evaluation (FMHE) may be requested by an attorney or ordered by the court (Heilbrun, 2001). Such an evaluation generally utilizes a multimethod and multisource approach to collecting information. The methods and sources chosen are those seen as likely to produce the data that are necessary and sufficient to answer the questions before the court (Austin & Kirkpatrick, 2004; Gould, 1999). Sometimes a private party through an attorney will contract for a mental health professional's services, and in other instances a professional will be appointed by the court to conduct the evaluation. In either case, the evaluator's obligation is to conduct an evaluation and (usually) prepare a report that will answer the questions before the court to the extent that the data allow. The court ultimately is the consumer of the FMHE (Heilbrun, 2001).

Psychological testing is one frequently employed methodology and source of data for the FMHE. It is easy for psychologists to overemphasize its importance in forensic evaluations (Brodzinsky, 1993; Otto & Collins, 1995) for reasons that will be discussed later. In many forensic contexts, testing data will have a vital role to play, but in any competently conducted FMHE, they will always be part of a larger package and often secondary to forensic interview data in importance. Testing can be a valuable source of hypotheses about the functioning of the parties being evaluated. Testing can also provide valuable information about how the litigants approached the evaluation (i.e., response style). The response style provides valuable information regarding the amount of confidence the evaluator can place in data self-reported by the litigants. When a litigant is honest and open, the evaluator can place more confidence in data obtained from interviewing and testing. On the other hand, when a litigant has attempted to present an overly positive picture of him-or-herself, less confidence can be placed in data obtained from self-report formats, necessitating reliance on other sources of data, such as third-part interviews and records.

The PSI yields data on potential sources of stress in the family system by examining a parent's perceptions of his or her functioning in the parental role, issues in the parent-child relationship, child developmental issues, life stress, and degree of support from the other parent. As one reviewer indicated, "The potential uses of the PSI are wide and varied. The PSI will be helpful for anyone interested in the evaluation or assessment of children and parents within a systems context" (Allison, 1998, p. 3). It would appear that the PSI could be used as a screening tool and as a complement to other data sources in forensic contexts in which parent-child relationships and the impact of psychosocial stressors in the family system need to be examined.

In this section we focus on child custody evaluations as one forensic area where the potential application of the PSI is readily apparent. One other potential application would be in cases of suspected child maltreatment. Stress in the family system and issues of parenting capacity are often the focus of social service and mental health evaluations in dependency and neglect cases. Two texts on parental capacity evaluations for cases involving child maltreatment and legal proceedings for the termination of parental rights both mention the PSI as a potentially useful source of data (Condie, 2003; Dyer, 1999). One of the authors of this chapter has found the PSI useful in dozens of such "termination" cases.

Child Custody Evaluations

These forensic evaluations deal with issues of child custody, physical custodial arrangements, parenting time, visitation, access, parenting plans, and parental responsibility and decision making. They occur in the context of child custody and parenting time litigation following marital separation and pending dissolution. With increasing frequency, evaluators are called on to examine the needs of children whose parents never married but are in conflict over a parenting plan (Insabella, Williams, & Pruett, 2003). Evaluations also may be requested when one party files a motion for modification of an existing parenting plan or petitions the court to relocate with the child (or children). In many states, the parents, through their attorneys, will agree to or stipulate the choice of a mental health professional to conduct an evaluation to help with the resolution of the dispute, either through settlement or a court hearing. This stipulation then may be incorporated into a court order. In other states, the court will directly appoint the evaluator to conduct an evaluation after one of the parties filed a motion for a parenting evaluation. The attorneys frequently nominate one or more evaluators. Often, the evaluators are private practitioners; in some states, there are public, court-based programs for providing evaluations. States often allow for a second evaluation when one party is dissatisfied with the results of the first evaluation, but almost always both parties will need to agree on the choice of the second evaluator, and sometimes the court will appoint the evaluator. The practice of one party unilaterally hiring his or her own evaluator is almost universally disapproved of.

Although there have been vocal critics of the practice, and even the concept, of child custody evaluations to assist the courts in the difficult task of creating parenting plans for the children of divorcing parents, the practice is accepted in all of the states and in many is codified by statute (e.g., Dissolution of Marriage, Parental Responsibilities, Colorado Revised Statutes, Sect. 14-10-124[1.5]) or court rules (e.g., California Rules of Court, Rule 5.222, Court-ordered Child Custody Evalution; Florida Family Law Rules of Procedure, Rule 12.363, Evaluation of Minor Child). Critics have asserted there is not a sufficient scientific basis for a family study methodology that could assist in making accurate pre- dictions about a child's future welfare (Melton, Petrila, Poythress, & Slobogin, 1997; O'Donahue & Bradley, 1999; Gould & Martindale, 2005; see also Tippins & Wittman, 2005). Others have suggested the legal concept of the "best interests of the child" is too broad, has not been specifically defined by mental health professionals, and therefore can- not be operationalized in the context of a child custody evaluation (Shuman, 2002, see also Ackerman & Ackerman, 1997; Jameson, Ehrenberg, & Hunter, 1997; D.A. Krauss & Sales, 2000).

Forensic theorists and practitioners have more recently attempted to systematically describe the scientific basis for child custody evaluations (Galatzer-Levy & Kraus, 1999; Gould, 1998; Martindale & Gould, 2004) and presented research-based forensic evaluation models for topics that may surface in parenting evaluations, such as child maltreatment (Kuehnle, Coulter, & Firestone, 2000), partner violence (Austin, 2001), child sexual abuse (Kuehnle, 1996, 1998), and relocation of parent with a child (Austin, 2000a, 2000b).

The child custody evaluator usually will interview parents, interview children if they are old enough, observe the children both alone and together with the parents, conduct psychological testing with all relevant parties, interview a diversity of third parties, and review relevant documents and records (Austin, 2002; Austin & Kirkpatrick, 2004; Heil- brun, 2001). The evaluator strives for a diverse and thorough database in order to achieve an understanding of the family system and dynamics and to address the questions in the case effectively. In some cases, the evaluator is asked to make recommendations about the distribution of parenting time and decision making between two fit and very capable parents who simply cannot reach agreement on a parenting plan. More often, there will be considerable conflict between the parents, including allegations made by each that call into question the parenting effectiveness of the other parent and even the potential for harm to the children if the other parent is given custody. There may allegations of past partner violence, child maltreatment, or child sexual abuse. Alcohol or substance abuse is not an infrequent issue. One parent may be seeking to relocate with the child to a different state. The case confronting the evaluator is generally quite complex and characterized by conflicts of interest. Child custody evaluations are likely to be the most complicated and time-consuming of all forensic evaluations (Flens, 2004; Otto, Edens, & Barcus, 2000).

The Forensic Approach to Parenting Evaluations

The evaluator needs to acknowledge that there are factors that the court may deem relevant to a custody determination but that lie outside of the competence of an evaluator or are not appropriate for consideration by an evaluator, such as which parent is most likely to provide the opportunity for religious training; which environment will be most conducive to the child's moral upbringing; and which parent, if either, is morally fit. For this reason, the evaluator needs to provide an analysis of the child's *psychological* best interests (American Psychological Association [APA], 1994, Jameson et al., 1997; D.A. Krauss & Sales, 2000).

Forensic theorists and practitioners have described an emerging evaluation paradigm for child custody, variously referred to as the "forensic method" (Martindale & Gould, 2004) or the "forensic scientist-practitioner approach" (Austin & Kirkpatrick, 2004; Kuehnle, 1998). This approach proposes the universal use of multiple methods of data collection and the need for utilizing multiple sources of information about the parents and children. The goal is to create a comprehensive and diverse data set. It is acknowledged that each parent will be motivated to provide positively biased data about him- or herself and negatively biased data about the other parent, and because evaluators possess no special skills at deciphering the truth (Ekman & O'Sullivan, 1991; Meissner & Kassen, 2002), collateral interview data and documentary data are a necessary part of the FMHE in parenting cases (Austin, 2002; Austin & Kirkpatrick, 2004; Heilbrun, Warren, & Picarello, 2003). The evaluator structures the evaluation around alternative hypotheses on each salient issue, and the data collection and analysis then become a process of ruling out rival hypotheses (Heilbrun, 2001). Testing data are useful in generating hypotheses relevant to parenting and the child's development. The evaluator looks for support for hypotheses from multiple sources so as to achieve convergent validity (Austin, 2002). This process of data interpretation often requires careful investigation by the evaluator in order to obtain critical data and go well beyond the superficial data that may be presented by the parents or their representatives (Austin & Kirkpatrick, 2004). The evaluator in the end will usually make specific recommendations to the court on custodial parental arrangements and parenting time (Gould, 1998), but there may be instances where the evaluator needs to stop short of addressing these ultimate issues because only the court can know the pertinent "threshold of harm" (Austin, 2000b). Some critics suggest the evaluator should never address the ultimate issues for the court (Gould & Martindale, 2005; Melton et al., 1997; Tippins & Wittman, 2005). Finally, the evaluator needs to be cognizant of issues of admissibility of expert testimony. Although child custody experts have largely been exempted from application of the increasingly higher standards required for showing reliability and helpfulness to the trier of fact (D.A. Krauss & Sales, 2000; Shuman, 2002), it is to be expected this will change (Ramsey & Kelley, 2004). In the case of testimony about psychological testing data, it has been proposed there should be a higher standard for reliability in the forensic context (Goodman-Delahunty, 1997).

The reliability and validity data on the PSI, its publication in peer-reviewed journals, and the known error rate of the instrument in different contexts suggest it would meet recent standards for admissibility as a scientific instrument (as set by *Daubert v. Merrell Dow Pharmaceuticals*, 1993). Limitations of the instrument that make it vulnerable to attack in this regard are (a) the difference between the clinical sample and the referent forensic population and (b) the lack of males in the clinical normative sample (addressed to some degree by the inclusion in the manual of a sample of 200 men and by the published literature on gender differences).

Population of Custody Litigants

The population of child custody litigants represents a statistically extreme group. It is estimated that about 90% of all custody cases reach a settlement and do not require formal litigation and that about 90% of the remaining cases do not go to trial (Ash & Guyer, 1986). So, it is fairly unusual for a custody case to require an evaluator, and even more rarely does such a case go to trial after the completion of an evaluation. Later in the chapter, we present the first normative data to be available on the PSI for the population of child custody litigants. A more complete presentation of the data will be available in a future publication.

It is important to understand that the litigants in a custody case are seen by the custody evaluator as the result of a court order. Rarely do these individuals participate voluntarily.

By the time the litigants are seen by an evaluator, each has levied multiple allegations against the other, who responds by upping the ante and responding with even more allegations. The litigants will likely respond to the varied allegations at some point during the evaluation.

It is a common practice for the evaluator to use psychological testing as part of a multimethod forensic assessment (Ackerman & Ackerman, 1997; Bow & Quinnell, 2001, Gould, 1998, 1999; Heilbrun, 2001; Keilin & Bloom, 1986). The situational and contextual variables must be taken into account when the psychological tests are interpreted. The PSI has unique potential to contribute to the psychological testing data in a parenting evaluation because the variables being measured are similar to several statutory factors that most states require to be considered in these evaluations: the child's developmental status, the parents' psychological health, and the relationship between all the parties

A review of the content of many of the common psychological tests used in custody cases will quickly show how transparent the items really are. Because of their transparency, it is possible to identify when parents are trying to present themselves in the best possible light. Many tests have response style indicators that will identify the approach used by the litigant to answer the questions. The *defensive* individual is likely to approach psychological tests by developing a response style consisting of two interwoven elements: (a) the assertion of mentally healthy attributes that are inaccurate and (b) the denial of characteristics that are accurate but less than desirable. Nichols and Greene (1997), for example, noted the defensive test taker "may endorse items not merely to conceal symptoms and maladjustment, but to assert a degree of soundness, virtue, prudence, strength and well-being that is, if anything, superior to 'normal' levels" (p. 254). More specifically, these authors added, "In child custody, the evaluator is likely to see underreporting by a mix of trying to conceal any indication of psychological distress (dissimulation) and trying to assert superior adjustment (simulation). The defensive individual will use a combination of dissimulation—"concealing what one believes to be true"—and simulation—"displaying what one believes to be false" (p. 252). Exner, McDowell, Pabst, Stackman, and Kirk (1963) noted more than 40 years ago that psychological tests rely heavily on the test taker's willingness to answer the items honestly:

> Thus the total usefulness of the device as a diagnostic instrument, particularly when used for screening or in situations where social desirability is an important element, seems to be dependent largely upon the honesty of the subject or on the ability of the interpreter to detect willful attempts at dishonest responding. (p. 91)

Between the contextual variables in a child custody evaluation and the item content of the tests, it is not surprising that several common profiles emerge on the commonly used tests. Discussing the contextual variables associated with child custody evaluation allows the evaluator to understand the mindset of the parent who responds to the items on any given test battery. The following sequence of events is frequently seen in child custody evaluations:

1. Parents in a stressful divorce challenge each other for custody of their child (or children).
2. The contextual variables (described earlier) generate defensive postures in the parents.
3. The parents are forced to take tests with "loaded" item content.
4. The evaluator is faced with prototypical defensive test profiles.

Given this sequence, the typical rules of test interpretation simply may not apply. The American Psychological Association's Ethics Code addresses the issue of situational and contextual variables as a threat to the reliability of test data and interpretations:

9.06 Interpreting Assessment Results

When interpreting assessment results, including automated interpretations, psychologists take into account the purpose of the assessment as well as the various test factors, test-taking abilities, and other characteristics of the person being assessed, such as situational, personal, linguistic, and cultural differences, that might affect psychologists' judgments or reduce the accuracy of their interpretations. They indicate any significant limitations of their interpretations. (American Psychological Association, 2002, p. 24. See also Standards 2.01b and 2.01c, Boundaries of Competence, and 3.01, Unfair Discrimination.)

Here is where it is important to have a thorough understanding of the psychometric properties of the tests. It is also essential to be aware of the effects that a defensive response style can have on test data. Defensive test-taking attitudes impact each test differently. It is the responsibility of the prudent evaluator to understand and consider these effects when interpreting results in the child custody context.

Goodness of Fit Between the PSI and the Child Custody Context

Variables that are measured by evaluators in a child custody case generally revolve around family relationship factors, which makes it logical to use the PSI as part of the assessment. Competently conducted evaluations will assess the child's development, each parent's parenting effectiveness, each parent's psychological health, the parent-child relationships, and interparental conflict. Some variations of these factors are often found in state statutes that have incorporated the *Uniform Marriage and Divorce Act* (1979) criteria. PSI data are relevant to this combination of factors.

Researchers have examined the role of stress and parental coping ability in studying the adjustment of children to separation and divorce. The majority of children show adequate or normal development and functioning as adults (Emery & Forehand, 1994), but a significant percentage, perhaps 25%, do not. Divorce stands as a general developmental risk factor for children. Evaluators need to uncover risk factors for adjustment problems as well as strengths and resources available to the children that would increase the likelihood of their successful coping with the stress of divorce and finding a normal developmental course. Evaluators need to follow the lead of researchers on issues of risk and resiliency facing children (Kelly & Emery, 2003).

Research has shown that the long-term stresses the result from divorce cause the affected children on average to be poorer students, have a poorer self-concept, and have higher rates of psychological maladjustment than children who did not experience parental separation and divorce (Amato, 2001). Children who grow up with single mothers after divorce show higher high school dropout rates, poorer academic achievement, and higher rates of teen pregnancy (McLanahan & Sandefur, 1994). School-age children and adolescents from divorced families show a higher frequency of problematic behaviors and often appear not to be on a normal developmental track in terms well-being, social interactions, and academic achievement (Amato, 2001; Guidubaldi, Perry, & Nastasi, 1987; McLanahan & Teitler, 1999). The effects of divorce on very young children have been less extensively studied (M.K. Pruett, Williams, Insabella, & Little, 2003), but studies have shown lower academic achievement among primary school children (Amato, 2001), lower cognitive ability scores

(Clarke-Stewart, Vandell, McCartney, Owen, & Booth, 2000), and insecurities about attachment relationships with both parents and physical and emotional safety (K.D. Pruett & Pruett, 1999).

Research has shown parental dysfunction and interparental conflict place children at risk following divorce by the mere presence of the high levels of stress reported by divorced and separated parents compared with married adults (Kitson & Morgan, 1991). When dysfunctional parental emotional states diminish warm and authoritative parenting, children show more externalizing and internalizing symptoms (DeGarmo & Forgatch, 1999; Kelly, 2000).

Parental depression and anxiety interfere with parenting capacity and are correlated with more negative child adjustment (Pett, Wampold, Turner, & Vaughan-Cole, 1999). Numerous studies have established a link between parental distress and diminished well-being and adjustment problems experienced by the children (Hetherington, Bridges, & Insabella, 1998). This link is strongest at the time of a marital separation and the subsequent 2 years (Hetherington & Kelly, 2002), a period when the parents are most likely to be participating in a custody evaluation. One of the most reliable empirical findings in the research on divorce is that children's adjustment is negatively correlated with greater levels of inter parental conflict (Lamb, 2002), and families experiencing such conflict are more likely to litigate, which means that more child adjustment problems might be expected to be observed and reported in the context of custody evaluations.

The state legal standards for child custody determinations are variants of a "best Interests of the child" standard (BIS). When the issue of harm or detriment surfaces, it is treated as another dimension of BIS issues (*In re Marriage of Martin*, 2002), and parenting time arrangements may be discussed in terms of the least detrimental alternative (LDA) residential parenting plan. LDA is the conceptual obverse of BIS (Austin, 2000b). The role of the evaluator is to operationalize these general legal concepts in behavioral terms and gather meaningful data so that helpful recommendations can be made to the court on what parenting arrangements will be most likely to maximize the child's positive developmental outcomes and insulate the child from harm. The PSI holds potential for identifying sources of stress in the family system that raise concerns about potential harm to the child. In custody cases where there are issues of partner violence, child maltreatment, child alienation, and major parental dysfunction, such as with a major mental illness or substance abuse, test data may help ferret out the potential effects on the child and parent-child relationship.

A Mindful Approach to Psychological Testing in the Forensic Context

Hypothesis Generation

Commentators have not been kind in their appraisal of how psychological testing is generally used of custody evaluations (Brodzinsky, 1993; Melton et al., 1997; Otto & Collins, 1995). The main criticism is that testing data are often used to evaluate an individual directly rather than in conjunction with other sources of data (Clark & Clark, 1991; Heilbrun, 1992). It is strongly urged that testing data only be used as a source for hypotheses (Brodzinsky, 1993) and not as confirmatory of any hypotheses. When data from several tests and other methods are consistent, then there may be a basis for hypothesis confirmation (Heilbrun, 2001). Unfortunately, when reviewing the forensic work of evaluators, it is not uncommon to find one-to-one interpretations of a parent's psychological functioning based on psychological testing, sometimes with verbatim quotes from a computer-generated report (Bow, Flens, Gould, & Greenhut, in press).

The rationale for not employing test data as confirmatory or treating results as isomorphic with an individual's psychological functioning is that the interpretation of a test profile is made by the profile scores to group average scores, or aggregate data. To then make the reductionistic interpretative leap to the individual is to commit what statisticians call the "ecological fallacy" (Ostroff, 1993; Robinson, 1950). That is, the individual data cannot be explained by the aggregate data norms and need to be supported by other sources of data specific to the individual.

Emphasis on Function

Grisso (1986) expresses a caution regarding the use of psychological testing in the custody context largely on the grounds that the instruments were not designed specifically to measure aspects of parental capacity or the legal competencies before the court. Grisso's warning should alert evaluators to be sensitive to what the test is measuring in what context and to translate the testing data into functional capacities. In the custody context, this means the evaluator needs to uncover to what extent the instruments are tapping elements of parenting effectiveness, parent-child relationships, and child development.

Response Bias and Impression Management

Evaluators routinely need to be sensitive to response bias, defensiveness, and impression management in an individual's approach to test taking when interpreting the data. As noted, a general rule of thumb is that parties will be somewhat defensive when taking a psychological test and will try to create a favorable impression in the custody context. On *preliminary* normative data on the PSI, we found male and female custody litigants to have essentially the same scores on the domains, subscales, and total scores (using $p > .001$ significance levels; see Table 11.1). Interestingly, only the Defensive Indicator scores showed a statistical—and clinical—difference between the male and female caregivers ($p = .0002$). As noted in Table 11.1, the average Defensive Indicator score was 27.3 ($SD = 6.7$). Both male and female caregivers obtained scores in the nondefensive range. Female caregivers obtained defensive scores of 28.9 ($SD = 7.0$), and males obtained scores of 25.6 ($SD = 6.1$). This suggests that male caregivers in the custody sample were slightly more defensive than female caregivers.

Normative Comparisons and Extrapolation

When comparing test data gathered in a forensic context with the normative data in a test manual, one needs to be cautious because of differences between the original normative sample and the population represented by the forensic examinee. Researchers have gathered normative data on special populations who are tested in forensic setting using various instruments, especially the MMPI–2. Norms for custody litigants are available for the MMPI–2 (Bathurst, Gottfried, & Gottfried, 1997) and the MCMI–III (McCann et al., 2001). Authorities have recommended utilizing such norms as a way of providing enhanced contextual interpretation and as a supplement to the normal profile interpretation using the original normative sample for the instrument (Otto, 2002). Preliminary norms for custody litigants taking the PSI are presented below.

Descriptive Data and Item Analysis

Psychological tests with a high degree of "face validity," such as the PSI, allow for content analysis that is relevant to the working hypotheses for the case. Individual test item responses may overlap and supplement answers to questions asked during the forensic

TABLE 11.1
Preliminary Descriptive Data for the PSI in the Child Custody Context

Scales and Subscales	Mean[a]	SD	SEM	±68%	±95%
				Confidence Intervals	
Total Stress Score	185.5	33.2	8.2	±8.2	±16.1
Child Domain	87.4	17.5	6.0	±6.0	±11.8
Distractibility	20.9	4.6	2.0	±2.0	±3.9
Adaptability	23.2	5.2	2.8	±2.8	±5.5
Reinforces Parent	7.9	2.5	1.2	±1.2	±2.4
Demandingness	15.4	4.3	2.4	±2.4	±4.7
Mood	8.8	2.7	1.6	±1.6	±3.1
Acceptability	11.2	3.7	1.6	±1.6	±3.1
Parent Domain	98.1	19.2	6.5	±6.5	±12.7
Competence	21.2	5.1	2.5	±2.5	±4.9
Isolation	10.2	3.0	1.6	±1.6	±3.1
Attachment	10.1	2.6	1.6	±1.6	±3.1
Health	10.0	3.0	1.9	±1.9	±3.7
Role Restriction	14.1	3.7	2.4	±2.4	±4.7
Depression	15.1	4.1	2.2	±2.2	±4.3
Spouse	17.5	5.3	2.2	±2.2	±4.3
Life Stress	16.8	10.2	—	—	—
Defensive Indicator	27.3	6.7	3.4	±3.4	±6.7

[a]Total sample of custody litigants = 214 (male = 107, female = 107).

interviews. The evaluator may want to follow up test responses with specific interview questions for clarification. Using this type of "critical item analysis," a better understanding of the parent's perceptions can be achieved. Other measures that may lack proven predictive validity, such as the Parenting Alliance Measure (Abidin & Konold, 1999) and the Parenting Satisfaction Survey (Guidubaldi & Cleminshaw, 1994), can be similarly used as a source of descriptive data.

Interpretation of PSI Data in a Custody Evaluation

A few preliminary comments are in order. First, when using the PSI (or any other test), it is essential to read the accompanying test manual thoroughly, including the psychometric characteristics of the test. This may seem like a given, but the authors have reviewed cases where the evaluator had little actual knowledge of the content of the manual or did not even own current version of the manual or any earlier version. It is also important to know the literature regarding the test. A good source of information consists of reviews contained in *Buros Mental Measurements Yearbook*. In addition, it is often prudent to read both supportive and critical literature regarding the test (Flens, 2004). Learning about published criticisms of the test on the witness stand could be an unpleasant experience for the unprepared evaluator.

It is important to use the standardized instructions when administering the PSI. This allows the evaluator to rely on the standardization sample to make interpretive comparisons. One slight modification may be in order when using the PSI in a custody setting. The Spouse subscale contains questions regarding the test taker's partner. Since many custody evaluations involve modification of existing custody, visitation arrangements, or relocation issues, the test taker may have a new partner, possibly someone more supportive of the test taker's parenting of the child at issue. In such cases, it may be appropriate to ask the test taker to have the former partner (spouse) in mind those when answering questions that address issues associated with other parent of the child. On theoretical grounds, this appears to be an appropriate alteration of the standardized instructions. Currently, however, no data exist regarding this issue. Should the evaluator chose to use this altered instruction, a caveat should be included in the report, which is consistent with the Ethics Code of the American Psychological Association (see e.g., 9.06 Interpreting Assessment Results; APA, 2002).

The author of the PSI now recommends taking into account the context of the test administration when giving instructions on how to answer the items referring to the "spouse." In the context of a custody evaluation, the other spouse should refer to the other parent of the child. When a remarried or repartnered parent is completing the PSI in a nonforensic setting, then "spouse" should be interpreted as referring to the current spouse or partner. This limitation of the PSI in custody evaluations concerns the Spouse subscale. An examination of the seven items shows that some of them are worded in a manner that assumes the parents are still together, as in this example: "Since having my child, my spouse and I don't do as many things together." Therefore, the theoretical basis of using this subscale seems weak, and evaluators who interpret it must specify what construct is being measured. Items on measures such as the Parenting Alliance Measure have more face validity as regards the process of supporting the other parent child relationship and the test taker's view of the other parent's parenting ability.

Interpretation of the PSI in a custody case begins with a review of the response style the caregiver used when responding to the test items. Both Heilbrun (1992) and Otto et al. (2000) recommended using tests in forensic evaluations that contain response style indicators. The PSI includes the Defensive Responding indicator, which consists of 15 items scattered throughout the Parenting Domain subscales. The breakdown of items is as follows: Isolation (4 items), Depression (4 items), Role Restriction (3 items), Spouse (3 items), and Competence (1 item). The Attachment and Health subscales do not contain any items on the Defensive Responding indicator. A PSI profile is considered "defensive" when the Defensive Responding score is 24. Roughly one third of the profiles in the preliminary data were considered "defensive" (see Table 11.1). Lower scores on the Parent Domain may indicate a defensive profile, since all the Defensive Responding items are on the Parent Domain scales. As would be expected, a defensive profile should be interpreted with caution—an important caveat mentioned in the PSI manual.

Research on the issue of response styles has indicated that two different factors account for the "fake good" presentation (Bagby & Marshall, 2004; Friedman, Lewak, Nichols, & Webb, 2001; Lanyon, 2004; Strong, Green, Hoppe, Johnston, & Olesen, 1999; Strong, Greene, & Kordinak, 2002). The first, impression management, involves a conscious and deliberate attempt to present a favorable impression. As noted, this can include affirming favorable but inaccurate characteristics and denying unfavorable but accurate characteristics. The parent in this case is trying to fool the evaluator into believing he or she is more virtuous and mentally healthy than may actually be the case. The second factor, self-deceptive enhancement, involves a tendency toward overconfidence in one's own strengths and abilities. In cases where the responses are influenced by self-deceptive enhancement, the individual actually believes he or she embodies the favorable image presented. It could be said that the individual is actually fooling him- or herself. A parent who presents with self-deceptive enhancement can be described as having a lack of insight and narcissistic qualities and may be easily angered when confronted. The parent believes that his or her responses are accurate and justified. A preliminary analysis of PSI data suggests that the defensive responding is strongly related to the second factor, self-deceptive enhancement, and is almost completely unrelated to the first factor, impression management. This would suggest that caregivers who score in the defensive range have a narcissistic overconfidence in their abilities, have a lack of insight into their own behavior, and are easily angered when confronted (*e.g.*, see Paulhus, 1998).

The prudent evaluator would do well to make affirmative statements regarding the response style issues and how they affect the psychological confidence and certainty that can be placed in the PSI interpretation. This is also consistent with the Ethics Codes of the American Psychological Association (see, e.g., 9.06 Interpreting Assessment Results; APA, 2002). Finally, after addressing the response style issues, the evaluator can address any domain and subscale elevations. To aid in the interpretation, the caregivers' profiles can be plotted on the same profile form, allowing comparison of the various domains and subscales. It may also be appropriate to compare the resultant profiles with the context-specific normative data presented in Table 11.1. A cautionary statement is appropriate at this point. The context-specific normative data do not supplant the standardization data presented in the PSI manual. These data simply allow for a comparison with other care-givers going through similar evaluation contexts. The manual states that the standardization sample contained only female caregivers. Data from 200 male caregivers are available in the test manual, but these are not used to profile the results. In other words, PSI percentiles are based solely on the more than 2,600 female caregivers in the normative sample. This appears to be one of the only major weaknesses of the PSI (see, e.g., Allison, 1998). A footnote, however, indicates that male caregivers typically score lower than female care-givers. This is consistent with the results of the context-specific normative data found in Table 11.1.

From this point on, interpretation of the individual domains and subscales is straight-forward. A domain or subscale is considered elevated at or above the 85th percentile. The manual describes the issues and hypotheses associated with the individual domains and subscales. As noted, interpretations from the PSI should be used as hypotheses to be corroborated or refuted by other sources of data. It is important that the evaluator consider elevations on the domains and subscales not as stand-alone data but rather as hypotheses to be confirmed (or not) by other forensically relevant data collection methods (i.e., interview, observation, testing, collateral interview, and record review). As the appropriate focus of a custody evaluation is the parent-child match, the PSI is a particularly useful instrument because of its emphasis on attributes of the child and parent that may lead to dysfunctional parenting (Abidin, 1995).

CASE STUDY: "THE FATHER WHO COULDN'T SIT STILL"

The parents lived in a very rural area of northern Colorado, where the mother's family owned a large cattle ranch. Two children were born, a 6-year-old daughter and an 8-year-old son. The parents agreed to separate after the mother became disillusioned with the father because of his financial irresponsibility and his hiding debts from her. The parents signed a separation agreement but continued to live together for another 6 months. The parents prepared the children for the pending split-up. Interviews with the parents indicated that they had worked reasonably well together. Although their parenting styles appeared to complement each other, they both appeared to utilize an authoritative parenting style. Both parents worked many hours, and often one parent would handle all responsibilities while the other was working. The mother was a nurse practitioner, the father was an auto mechanic who had his own custom body repair business. The father had stepped in when the mother went to graduate school in nursing and was gone 1 weekend a month. When the mother worked 2 weekends a month at a hospital obstetrics unit, the father was the sole available parent.

The mother had agreed to divide parenting time almost equally when the decision to end the marriage was made. The father intended to stay in the home community and had arranged to get his own residence; the mother and children would stay in the family residence on the ranch. This was the expectation of the children. The father had a job driving a propane gas truck after his auto business failed. About a week after the separation, the father aburptly decided to relocate to a town in eastern Wyoming about 4 hours away from the children to work for an auto dealership. He told the children that he needed to make more money to support them, but his new job did not pay any more money. He apparently could not stand the idea of continuing to live in the same community as the mother and had some shame issues related to his financial failures.

The son had a "difficult temperament," with oppositional traits, and had trouble getting along with other children. He had been evaluated during his kindergarten year for these problems. ADHD was ruled out, but he had traits of this disorder, exhibited oppositional behaviors, and was often difficult to deal with. Not surprisingly, he did not cope well with his parents' separation and his dad's relocation. He acted out considerably. The school sent a letter of concern about incidents on the bus and at school. The child was difficult to control, and there was an incident of stealing from his grandfather. His poor coping with divorce is consistent with research showing that children with difficult temperaments manifest externalizing behaviors, adjust poorly to the negative transition of divorce, and are not resilient (Hetherington, 1989). Five months later, the father relocated a second time, to Texas, where he took a job managing an auto repair shop. The father minimized the likely effect his moving away would have on the children. He again asserted that he needed to make more money, but the data showed that his salary did not increase.

Collateral data were gathered on the children's functioning. The children's teachers and the principal of the school were interviewed. The parents completed behavior rating forms on the children. The school collateral data on the son depicted a child who had struggled greatly with behavioral control and caused other children to reject him. The mother's PSI data on the son showed an elevation on the *DE* scale (85th percentile), which reflected the child's demanding nature and conduct problems. Item analysis showed that the mother felt the son did things that were really bothersome and that she had become more concerned he would do things that would cause him to get in trouble or hurt. Another subscale (*MO*) approached significance (75th percentile), suggesting the mother perceived the child as frequently unhappy and perhaps depressed. The item analysis on the PSI was helpful in understanding the scale elevation, as the items are practical and have high face validity. During her interview, it was apparent that the mother was concerned because the father's relocation had greatly affected the boy; he was hurt, sad, and depressed. Convergent validation of the PSI data came from behavioral rating form responses. The data showed the mother thought the following were extreme problems for her son:

> Disruptive and annoying others.
> Stealing.
> Withdraws from others; not liked by peers.
> Uncooperative in a group setting.
> Argumentative; oppositional.
> Impulsive; impatient.
> Teases others.

The PSI and behavioral ratings taken together showed that the mother had a realistic appraisal of her son's problems and needs. There were some marginal elevations on Parent Domain subscales indicating that the mother was also concerned about her relationship with this child. For example, she had to travel a substantial distance to her nursing work and sometimes stay overnight, thus needing to depend on her extended family to help provide child care. She was frustrated by the father's move away from the area and felt she was going it alone as a parent. She had planned on the father helping out with parenting after the separation because of her work schedule. The marginal elevation on the *IS* subscale showed that she felt somewhat isolated and was experiencing considerable stress. The marginal elevation on *HE* reinforced this interpretation, along with the elevation on the *LS* (Life Stress; 97th percentile). The evaluator had to do a careful assessment of the mother's coping ability, because of these data, and collateral data showed she was functioning at a high level at both work and home. Table 11.1 shows that it is normal to find a high life stress score among this population (90th percentile). The mother's level of stress reflected the divorce transition, the ongoing litigation, dealing with a child with a difficult temperament as a single mom, and having to depend on others to help out with child care.

The father's profile showed an absence of elevations that would have indicated developmental concerns about his son. There also were no elevations or marginal elevations in the Parent Domain. He was communicating that he had no concerns about his son, his comfort with parenting, or his relationship with the children. Convergent data were obtained from the behavior rating form. Out of 89 items on behavioral symptoms, only 2 indicated any degree of concern. The father's approach to the PSI was not defensive ($DR = 35$), and he apparently believed his ratings were accurate (see the earlier discussion of defensive-responding). The PSI data were part of the data set that confirmed the hypothesis that the father was out of touch with his son's developmental problems and needs and that he was minimizing the effect of his relocation on his children. The evaluator had sufficient data to support the hypothesis that the father was not sensitive to his son's developmental needs and so would have a difficult time coparenting with the mother and engaging in joint decision making. The information was also relevant to the issue of working out a long-distance parenting plan. The father thought the children should be able to spend the entire summer with him in Texas. He dismissed the importance of their summer rodeo activities, which were highly important to the children. He minimized any adjustment problems the children might have in response to such an extended summer visitation schedule. In this case, the PSI data blended nicely with other sources of data to help confirm and disconfirm hypotheses on how well the parents could respond to the special needs created by the son's temperamental difficulties and exacerbated by the stress caused by the parents' divorce and the father's relocation.

REFERENCES

Abidin, R.R. (1983) *Parenting Stress Index manual*. Charlottesville VA: Pediatric Psychology Press.
Abidin, R.R. (1995). *Parenting Stress Index: Professional manual* (3rd ed.). Odessa, FL: Psychological Assessment Resources.
Abidin, R.R. (1998). Parenting Stress Index: Its empirical validation. In *Symposium on Child Custody*. Symposium conducted at the APA Annual Conference, San Francisco.
Abidin, R.R., & Burke, W.T. (1978). *Parenting Stress Index-Draft Manual*. Unpublished manuscript. Dept. of Foundations of Education, University of Virginia, p. 6.
Abidin, R.R., Jenkins, C.L. & McGaughey, M.C. (1992). The relationship of early family variables to children's subsequent behavior adjustment. *Journal of Clinical Child Psychology, 21*, 60–69.

Abidin, R.R., & Konold, T.R. (1999). *Parenting Alliance Measure: Professional manual*. Sarasota, FL: Psychological Assessment Resources.

Abidin, R.R., & Santos, S.V. (2003). *Indice de Stress Parental Portuguese*. Lisbon, Portugal: CEGOC-TEA, Lda.

Abidin, R.R. & Wilfong, E. (1989). Parenting stress and its relationship to child health care. *Children's Health Care, 18*, 114–117.

Ackerman, M.J., & Ackerman, M.C. (1997). Child custody evaluation practices: A survey of experienced professionals (revised). *Professional Psychology: Research and Practice, 28*, 137–145.

Adamakos, H., Kathleen, R.G., Ullman, D.G., & John, P. (1986). Maternal social support as a predictor of mother child stress and stimulation. *Child Abuse and Neglect, 10*, 463–470.

Allison, J.A. (1998). Parenting Stress Index, third edition. In J. C. Impara & B. S. Plake (Eds.), *The thirteenth mental measurements yearbook* (pp. 1–8). Lincoln, NE: Buros Institute of Mental Measurements.

Amato, P.R. (2001). Children and divorce in the 1990s: An update of the Amato and Keith (1991) meta-analysis. *Journal of Family Psychology, 15*, 355–370.

American Psychological Association. (1994). Guidelines for child custody evaluation in divorce proceedings. *American Psychologist, 49*, 677–680.

American Psychological Association. (2002). Ethical principles of psychologists and code of conduct. *American Psychologist, 57*, 1060–1073.

Anastopoulos, A.D., Guevremont, D.C., Shelton T.L., & DuPaul, G.J. (1992). Parenting stress among families of children with attention deficit hyperactivity disorder. *Journal of Abnormal Child Psychology, 20*, 503–520.

Anastopoulos, A.D., Shelton, T.L., DuPaul, G.J., & Guevremont, D.C. (1993). Parent training for attention-deficit hyperactivity disorder: Its impact on parent functioning. *Journal of Abnormal Child Psychology, 21*, 503–521.

Ash, P., & Guyer, M. (1986). Psychiatry and the law: The functions of psychiatric evaluation in contested custody and visitation cases. *Journal of the American Academy of Child Psychiatry, 25*, 554–561.

Austin, W.G. (2000a). A forensic psychology model of risk assessment for child custody relocation law. *Family and Conciliation Courts Review, 38*, 186–201.

Austin, W.G. (2000b). Relocation law and the threshold of harm: Integrating legal and behavioral perspectives. *Family Law Quarterly, 34*, 63–82.

Austin, W.G. (2001). Partner violence and risk assessment in child custody evaluations. *Family Court Review, 39*, 483–496.

Austin, W.G. (2002). Guidelines for utilizing collateral sources of information in child custody evaluations. *Family Court Review, 40*, 177–184.

Austin, W.G., & Kirkpatrick, H.D. (2004). The investigation component in forensic mental health evaluations: Considerations in the case of parenting time evaluations. *Journal of Child Custody, 1*, 23–43.

Bagby, R.M., & Marshall, M.B. (2004). Assessing underreporting response bias on the MMP-2. *Assessment, 11*, 115–126.

Bagley, C., & Mallick, K. (1997). Temperament, CNS problems and maternal stressors: Interactive predictors of conduct disorder in 9-yr-olds. *Perceptual and Motor Skills, 84*, 617–618.

Bagner, D.M., & Eyberg, S.M. (2003). Father involvement in parent training: When does it matter? *Journal of Clinical Child and Adolescent Psychology, 32*, 599–605.

Baker, B.L., McIntyre, L.D., Blacher, J., Crnic, K., Edelbrock, C., & Low, C. (2003). Pre-school children with and without developmental delay: Behavior problems and parenting stress over time. *Journal of Intellectual Disability Research, 47*, 217–230.

Barker, D.A. (1994). Parenting stress and ADHD: A comparison of mothers and fathers. *Journal of Emotional and Behavior Disorders, 2*, 46–50.

Barkley, R.A., Anastopoulos, A., Guevremont, D.C., & Fletcher, K.E. (1992). Adolescents with attention deficit hyperactivity disorder: Mother adolescent interactions, family beliefs and conflicts, and maternal psychopathology. *Journal of Abnormal Child Psychology, 20*, 263–288.

Barkley, R.A., Edwards, G., Laneri, M., Fletcher, K., & Metevia, L. (2001). The efficacy of problem-solving communicationtraining alone, behavior management training alone, and their combination for parent-adolescent conflict in teenagers with ADHD and ODD. *Journal of Consulting and Clinical Psychology, 69*, 926–941.

Bathurst, K., Gottfried, A., & Gottfried, A. (1997). Normative data for the MMPI-2 in child custody litigation. *Psychological Assessment, 9*, 205–211.

Beck, S.J., Young, G.H., & Tarnowski, K.J. (1990). Maternal characteristics and perceptions of pervasive and situational hyperactives and normal controls. *Journal of the American Academy of Child and Adolescent Psychiatry, 29*, 558–565.

Beckman, P.J. (1991). Comparison of mothers' and fathers' perceptions of the effect of young children with and without disability. *American Journal of Mental Retardation, 95*, 585–595.

Bendell, R.D., Stone, W.L., Field, T.M., & Goldstein, S. (1989). Children's effects on parenting stress in a low income, minority population. *Topics in Early Childhood Special Education, 8*, 58–71.

Bhavnagri, N.P. (1999). Low income African-American mothers' parenting stress and instructional strategies to promote peer relationships in preschool children. *Early Education and Development, 10*, 551–571.

Bigras, M., & LaFreniere, P.J. (1994). Influence of psychosocial risk, marital conflicts and parental stress on the quality of mother-son and mother-daughter interactions. *Canadian Journal of Behavioral Science Vol. 26*(2) 280–297.

Bigras, M., LaFreniere, P., & Dumas, J. (1996). Discriminant validity of the parent and child scales of the Parenting Stress Index. *Early Education and Development, 7*, 167–178.

Bow, J.N., Flens, J.R., Gould, J.W., & Greenhut, D. (in press). An analysis of administration, scoring, and interpretation of the MMPI-2 and MCMI-III in child custody evaluations. *Journal of Child Custody*.

Bow, J.N., & Quinnell, F.A. (2001). Psychologists' current practices and procedures in child custody evaluations: Five years after American Psychological Association guidelines. *Professional Psychology: Research and Practice, 32*, 261–268.

Bramlett, R.K., Hall, J.D., Barnett D.W., & Rowell, K. (1995). Child developmental/educational status in kindergarten and family coping as predictors of parenting stress: Issues for parent consultation. *Journal of Psychoeducational Assessment, 13*, 157–166.

Bramlett, R.K., Rowell R.K., & Mandenberg, K. (2000). Predicting first grade achievement from kindergarten screening measures: A comparison of child and family predictors. *Research in the Schools, 7*(1), 1–9.

Breen, M.J., & Barkley, R.A. (1988). Child psychopathology and parenting stress in girls and boys having attention deficit disorder with hyperactivity. *Journal of Pediatric Psychology, 13*, 265–280.

Brodzinsky, D.M. (1993). On the use and misuse of psychological testing in child custody evaluations. *Professional Psychology: Research and Practice, 24*, 213–219.

Burbach, A.D., Fox, R.A., & Nicholson, B.C. (2004) Challenging behaviors in young children: The father's role. *Journal of Genetic Psychology, 165*(2), 169–183.

Burke, (1978). *Parenting stress*. Unpublished doctoral dissertation, University of Virginia, Charlottesville.

Calam, R., Bolton, C., & Roberts, J. (2002). Maternal expressed emotion, attributions and depression and entry into therapy for children with behavioral problems. *British Journal of Clinical Psychology, 41*, 213–216.

Calkins, S.D., Hungerford, A., & Dedmon, S.E. (2004). Mothers' interactions with temperamentally frustrated infants. *Infant Mental Health Journal, 25*, 219–239.

Calzada, E.J., Eyberg, S.M., Rich B., & Querido, J.G. (2004). Parenting disruptive preschoolers: Experiences of mothers and fathers. *Journal of Abnormal Child Psychology, 32*, 203–213.

Canadian Journal of Behavioral Science, 26(2), 280–297.

Chan, Y.C. (1994). Parenting stress and social support of mothers who physically abuse their children in Hong Kong. *Child Abuse and Neglect, 18*, 261–269.

Clark, B.K., & Clark, C.R. (1991). Psychological testing in child forensic evaluations. In D. Schetsky & E. Benedek (Eds.), *Clinical handbook of child psychiatry and the law* (pp. 34–52). Baltimore: Williams & Wilkins.

Clarke-Stewart, K.A., Vandell, D.L., McCartney, K., Owen, M.T., & Booth, C. (2000). Effects of parental separation and divorce on very young children. *Journal of Family Psychology, 14*, 304–326.

Condie, L.O. (2003). *Parenting evaluations for the court: Care and protection matters*. New York: Kluwer Academic/Plenum.

Coyle, D.D., Roggman, L.A., & Newland, L.A. (2002). Stress, maternal depression, and negative mother-infant interactions in relation to infant attachment. *Infant Mental Health Journal, 23*, 145–163.

Cuccaro, M.L., Holmes, G.R., & Wright, H.H. (1993). Behavior problems in preschool children: A pilot study. *Psychological Reports, 72*, 121–122.

Daubert v. Merrell Dow Pharmaceuticals, Inc., 509 U.S. 579 (1993).

Deater-Deckard, K., & Scarr, S. (1996). Parenting stress among dual-earner mothers and fathers: Are there gender differences? *Journal of Family Psychology, 10*, 45–59.

de Brock, A.J., Vermulist, A.A., Gerris, J.R., Abidin, R.R. (1992). *Nijmeese Ouderlijke Stress Index*, Lisse, Netherlands, Swets en Zertlinger. b.v.

DeGarmo, D.S., & Forgatch, M.S. (1999). Contexts as predictors of changing maternal parenting practices in diverse family structures: A social interactional perspective of risk and resilience. In E.M. Hetherington (Ed.), *Coping with divorce, single parenting, and remarriage* (pp. 227–252). Mahwah, NJ: Lawrence Erlbaum Associates.

Degroat, J.S. (2003). Parental stress and emotion attributions as correlates of maternal positive affect and sensitivity during interaction with young children. *Dissertation Abstracts International: B. The Sciences and Engineering, 64*(5-B), 2383.

Diener, M.L., Nievar, M.A., & Wright, C. (2003). Attachment security among mothers and their young children living in poverty: Associates with maternal, child and contextual characteristics. *Merrill-Palmer Quarterly, 49*, 154–182.

Donenberg, G., & Baker, B.L. (1993). The impact of young-children with Externalizing behaviors on their families. *Journal of Abnormal Child Psychology, 21*, 179–198.

Dyer, F.J. (1999). *Psychological consultation in parental rights cases.* New York: Guilford Press.

Ekman, P., & O'Sullivan, M. (1991). A few can catch a liar. *American Psychologist, 46*, 913–920.

Ellis, A. (1973). Humanistic psychology: The rational-emotive approach. New York: McGraw-Hill.

Emery, R.E., & Forehand, R. (1994). Parental divorce and children's well being: A focus on resilience. In R.J. Haggerty, L.R. Sherrod, N. Garmezy, & M. Rutter (Eds.), *Stress, risk, and resiliency in children and adolescents* (pp. 64–99). Cambridge: Cambridge University Press.

Endriga, M.C., Jordan, J.R., & Speltz, M.L. (2003). Emotion self-regulation in preschool-aged children with and without orofacial clefts. *Journal of Developmental and Behavioral Pediatrics, 24*, 336–344.

Ethier, L.S., & LaFreniere, P.J. (1993). Le stress des meres monoparentales en relation avec l'agressivite de l'enfant d'age prescolair. *Journal Interanational de Psychologie, 28*, 273–289.

Exner, J.E., McDowell, E., Pabst, J., Stackman, W., & Kirk, L. (1963). On the detection of willful falsifications in the MMPI. *Journal of Consulting Psychology, 27*, 91–94.

Feinfield, K.A., & Baker, B.L. (2004). Empirical support for a treatment program for families of young children with externalizing problems. *Journal of Clinical Child & Adolescent Psychology, 33*, 182–195.

Feldman, M.A., Varghese, J., Ramsay, J., & Rajska, D. (2002). Relationships between social support, stress and mother-child interactions in mothers with intellectual disabilities. *Journal of Applied Research in Intellectual Disabilities, 15*(4), 314–323.

Flens, J.R. (2004, October). *Advanced Institute: Psychological testing in child custody.* Paper presented at the 6th International Symposium on Child Custody Evaluations, Nashville, TN.

Florsheim, P., Sumida, E., McCann, C., Winstanley, M., Fukui, R., Seefeldt, T., et al. (2003). The transition to parenthood among African-American and Latino couples: Relational predictors of risk for dysfunction. *Journal of Family Psychology, 17*, 65–79.

Frank, S.J., Olmsted, C.L., Wagner, A.E., Lamb, C.C., Freeark, K., Breitzer, G.M., et al. (1991). Child illness, the parenting alliance, and parenting stress. *Journal of Pediatric Psychology, 16*, 361–371.

Frankel, K.K., & Harmon, R.J. (1996). Depressed mothers: They don't always look as bad as they feel. *Journal of the American Academy of Child and Adolescent Psychiatry, 35*, 289–298.

Friedman, A.F., Lewak, R., Nichols, D.S., & Webb, J.T. (2001). *Psychological assessment with the MMPI-2.* Mahwah, NJ: Lawrence Erlbaum Associates.

Galatzer-Levy, R.M., & Kraus, L. (Eds.). (1999). *The scientific basis of child custody decisions.* New York: Wiley.

Gelfand, D.M., Teti D.M., & Fox, C.E. (1992). Sources of parenting stress for depressed and nondepressed mothers of infants. *Journal of Clinical Child Psychology, 21*, 262–272.

General Electric v. Joiner, 522 U.S. 136 (1997).

Gerson, A.D., Farth, S.L., New, A.M., & Fivisch, B.A. (2004) Assessing associations between medication adherence and potentially modifiable psychosocial variables in pediatric kidney transplant recipients and their families. *Pediatric Transplant, 8*, 543–550.

Goldberg, S., Janus, M., Washington, J., Simmons, R.J., MacLusky I., & Fowler, R.S. (1997). Prediction of preschool behavioral problems in healthy and pediatric samples. *Journal of Developmental and Behavioral Pediatrics, 18*, 304–313.

Goodman-Delahunty, J. (1997). Forensic expertise in the wake of Daubert. *Law and Human Behavior, 21*, 121–140.

Gould, J.W. (1998). *Conducting scientifically crafted child custody evaluations*. Thousand Oaks, CA: Sage.

Gould, J.W. (1999). Scientifically crafted child custody evaluations: II. A paradigm for forensic evaluation of child custody determination. *Family and Conciliation Courts Review, 37*, 159–178.

Gould, J.W., & Martindale, D.A. (2005). A second call for clinical humility and judicial vigilance. *Family Court Review, 43*, 246–252.

Grisso, T. (1986). *Evaluating competencies: Forensic assessments and instruments*. New York: Plenum.

Grossman, J., & Shigaki, I.S. (1994). Investigation of familial and school-based risk-factors for Hispanic Head-Start children. *American Journal of Orthopsychiatry, 64*, 456–467.

Guidubaldi, J., & Cleminshaw, H.K. (1994). *Parenting Satisfaction Scale*. San Antonio, TX: The Psychological Corporation.

Guidubaldi, J., Perry, J.D., & Nastasi, B.K. (1987). Growing up in a divorced family: Initial and long-term perspective on children's adjustment. *Annual Review of Applied Social Psychology, 7*, 202–237.

Ha, E.H., Oh, K.J., & Kim, E.J. (1999). Depressive symptoms and family relationship of married women: Focused on parenting stress and marital dissatisfaction. *Korean Journal of Clinical Psychology, 18*(1), 79–93.

Hall, S., & Marteau, T.M. (2003). Causal attributions and blame: Associations with mothers' adjustment to the birth of a child with Down syndrome. *Psychology, Health and Medicine, 8*, 415–423.

Hauenstein, E., Scarr, S., & Abidin, R.R. (1987). Detecting children at-risk for developmental delay: Efficacy of the Parenting Stress Index in a non-American culture. Unpublished manuscript, University of Virginia, Charlottesville.

Heilbrun, K. (1992). The role of psychological testing in forensic assessment. *Law and Human Behavior, 16*, 257–272.

Heilbrun, K. (2001). *Principles of forensic mental health assessment*. New York: Kluwer Academic/Plenum.

Heilbrun, K., Warren, J., & Picarello, K. (2003). Third party information in forensic assessment. In A. Goldstein (Ed.), *Handbook of psychology: Vol. 11. Forensic psychology* (pp. 69–86). Hoboken, NJ: Wiley.

Hetherington, E.M. (1989). Coping with family transitions: Winners, losers, and survivors. *Child Development, 60*, 1–14.

Hetherington, E.M., Bridges, M., & Insabella, G.M. (1998). What matters? What does not? Five perspectives on the association between marital transitions and children's adjustment. *American Psychologist, 53*, 167–184.

Hetherington, E.M., & Kelly, J. (2002). *Divorce reconsidered: For better or for worse*. New York: Norton.

Hipke, K.N., Wolchik, S.A., Sandler, I.N., & Braver, S.L. (2002). Predictors of children's intervention-induced resilience in a parenting program for divorced mothers. *Family Relations, 51*, 121–129.

Hitchcock, D.L. (2003). A construct validity study of the Marschank Interaction Method Rating System with adolescent mother-child dyads. *Dissertation Abstracts International: B. The Sciences and Engineering, 64*(6-B), 2977.

Hughes, J.D., Brestan, E.V., Christens, B.D., Klinger, L.J., & Valle, L.A. (2004). Problem-solving interactions between mothers and children. Child and *Family Behavior Therapy, 26*(1), 1–16.

Hutcheson, J.J., & Black, M.M. (1996). Psychometric properties of Parenting Stress Index in a sample of low-income African-American mothers of infants and toddlers. *Early Education and Development, 7*, 381–400.

Innocenti, M.S., Huh, K., & Boyce, G.C. (1992). Families of children with disabilities: Normative data and other considerations of parenting stress. *Topics in Early Childhood Special Education, 12*, 403–427.

Insabella, G.M., Williams, T., & Pruett, M.K. (2003). Individual and coparenting differences between divorcing and unmarried fathers: Implications for family court services. *Family Court Review, 41*, 290–306.

Irvin, J.R., Carter, A.S., & Briggs-Gowan, M.J. (2002) The social-emotional development of "late-talking" toddlers. *Journal of the American Academy of Child and Adolescent Psychiatry, 41*, 1324–1332.

Jackson, A.P., Gyamfi, P., Brooksgunn, J., & Blake, M. (1998). Employment status, psychological well being, social support, and physical discipline practices of single Black mothers. *Journal of Marriage and the Family, 60*, 894–902.

Jameson, B.J., Ehrenberg, M.F., & Hunter, M.A. (1997). Psychologists' ratings of the best-interests-of-the-child custody and access criterion: A family systems assessment model. *Professional Psychology: Research and Practice, 28*, 253–262.

Jarvis, P.A., & Creasey, G.L. (1991). Parental stress, coping, and attachment in families with an 18-month-old infant. *Infant Behavior and Development, 14*, 383–395.

Judge, S. (2003). Determinants or parental stress in families adopting children from Eastern Europe. *Family Relations, 52*, 241–248.

Karp, J., Serbin, L.A., Stack, D.M., & Schwartzman, A.E. (2004). An observational measure of children's behavioral style: Evidence supporting a multi-method approach to studying temperament. *Infant and Child Development, 13*, 135–158.

Kazdin, A. (1990). Premature termination from treatment among children referred for antisocial behavior. *Journal of Child Psychology and Psychiatry and Allied Disciplines, 31*, 415–425.

Kazdin, A. (1995). Child, parent and family dysfunction as predictors of outcome in cognitive-behavioral treatment of anti-social children. *Behavior Research and Therapy, 33*, 271–281.

Kazdin, A.E., Mazurick, J.L., & Bass, D. (1993). Risk for attrition in treatment of antisocial children and families. *Journal of Clinical Child Psychology, 22*, 2–16.

Kazdin, A.E., & Wassell, G. (1999). Barriers to treatment participation and therapeutic change among children referred for conduct disorder. *Journal of Clinical Child Psychology, 38*, 1051–1062.

Kazdin, A.E., & Wassell, G. (2000). Therapeutic changes in children, parents and families resulting from treatment of children with conduct problems. *Journal of American Academy of Child and Adolescent Psychiatry, 39*(4), 414–420.

Kazui, M., Muto, T., & Sonoda, N. (1996). The roles of marital quality and parenting stress in mother-preschooler relationships [in Japanese]. *Japanese Journal of Developmental Psychology, 7*(1), 31–40.

Keilin, W.G., & Bloom, L.J. (1986). Child custody evaluation practices: A survey of experienced professionals. *Professional Psychology: Research and Practice, 17*, 338–346.

Kelly, J. B. (2000). Children's adjustment in conflicted marriage and divorce: A decade of review of research. *Journal of the American Academy of Child and Adolescent Psychiatry, 39*, 963–973.

Kelly, J.B. & Emery, R. (2003). Children's adjustment following divorce: Risk and resilience perspectives. *Family Relations, 52*, 352–362.

Kitson, G.C., & Morgan, L.A. (1991). The multiple consequences of divorce: A decade review. *Journal of Marriage and the Family, 52*, 913–924.

Krauss, D.A., & Sales, B.D. (2000). Legal standards, expertise, and experts in the resolution of contested child custody cases. *Psychology, Public Policy and Law, 6*, 843–879.

Krauss, M.W. (1993). Child-related and parenting stress: Similarities and differences between mothers and fathers of children with disabilities. *American Journal of Mental Retardation, 97*, 393–404.

Kuehnle, K. (1996). *Assessing allegations of child sexual abuse.* Sarasota, FL: Professional Resources Press.

Kuehnle, K. (1998). Child sexual abuse evaluations: The scientist-practitioner model. *Behavioral Sciences and the Law, 16*, 5–20.

Kuehnle, K., Coulter, M., & Firestone, G. (2000). Child protection evaluations: The forensic stepchild. *Family and Conciliation Courts Review, 38*, 368–391.

Kumho Tire Company, Ltd v. Carmichael, 526 U.S. 137 (1999).

Lacharite, C., Ethier, L., & Piche, C. (1992) Le stress parental chez les meres d'enfants d'age prescolaire: Validation et norms quebecoises pour l'inventaire de stress parental. *Sante Mentale au Quebec, 17*(2), 183–203.

Laganiere, J., Tessier, R., & Nadeau, L. (2003). Mother-infant attachment and prematurity: A link mediatized by maternal perceptions. *Enfance, 55*(2), 101–117.

Lamb, M.E. (2002). Placing children's interests first. *Virginia Journal of Social Policy and the Law, 10*, 98–119.

Lanyon, R.I. (2004). Favorable self-presentation on psychological inventories: An analysis. *American Journal of Forensic Psychology, 22*, 53–65.

Lazarus, R. (1966). *Psychological stress and the coping process.* New York: McGraw-Hill.

LeCuyer-Maus, E.A. (2003). Stress and coping in high-risk mothers: Difficult life circumstances, psychiatric-mental health symptoms, education and experiences in their families of origin. *Public Health Nursing, 20*, 132–145.

Levendosky, A.A., & Grahambermann, S.A. (1998). The moderating effects of parenting stress on children's adjustment in woman-abusing families. *Journal of Interpersonal Violence, 13*, 383–397.

Lyons-Ruth, K., Lyubchik, A., Wolfe, R., & Bronfman, E. (2002). Parental depression and child attachment: Hostile and helpless profiles or parent and child behavior among families at risk. In S. Goodman & I. Gotlib (Eds.), *Children of depressed parents: Mechanisms of risk and implications for treatment* (pp. 89–120). Washington, DC: American Psychological Association.

Martin, In re the Marriage of, 42 P.3d 75 (Colo.App. 2002).

Martindale, D.A., & Gould, J.W. (2004). The forensic model: Ethics and scientific methodology applied to custody evaluations. *Journal of Child Custody, 1*, 1–22.

McBride, B. (1989). Stress and fathers' parental competence: Implications for family life and parent educators. *Family Relations, 38*, 385–389.

McCann, J.T., Flens, J.R., Campagna, V., Collman, P., Lazzaro, T., & Connor, E. (2001). The MCMI-III in child custody evaluations: A normative study. *Journal of Forensic Psychology Practice, 1*, 27–44.

McLanahan, S., & Sandefur, G. (1994). *Growing up with a single parent: What hurts, what helps.* Cambridge, MA: Harvard University Press.

McLanahan, S., & Teitler, J. (1999). The consequences of father absence. In M.E. Lamb (Ed.), *Parenting and child development in nontraditional families* (pp. 83–102). Mahwah, NJ: Lawrence Erlbaum Associates.

Meissner, C.A., & Kassen, S.M. (2002). "He's guilty!": Investigator bias in judgments of truth and deception. *Law and Human Behavior, 26*, 469–480.

Mellins, C.A., Kang, E., Leu, C.S., Havens, J.F., & Chesney, M.A. (2003). Longitudinal study of mental health and psychosocial predictors of medical treatment adherence in mothers living with HIV disease. *Aids Patients Case Study, 7*, 407–416.

Melton, G.B., Petrila, J., Poythress, N.G., & Slobogin, C. (1997). *Psychological evaluations for the courts* (2nd ed.). New York: Guilford Press.

Milgrom, J., & McCloud, P. (1996). Parenting stress and postnatal depression. *Stress Medicine, 12*(3), 177–186.

Moran, G., Pederson, D.R., Pettit, P., & Krupka, A. (1992). Maternal sensitivity and infant mother attachment in a developmentally delayed sample. *Infant Behavior and Development, 15*, 427–442.

Moss, E., Cyr, C., & Dubois-Comtois, K. (2004). Attachment at early school age and developmental risk. *Developmental Psychology, 40*, 519–532.

Murphy, K.R., & Barkley, R.A. (1996). Parents of Children with attention-deficit hyperactivity disorder: Psychological and attentional impairment. *American Journal of Orthopsychiatry, 66*, 93–102.

Nichols, D.S., & Greene, R.L. (1997). Dimensions of deception in personality assessment: The example of the MMPI-2. *Journal of Personality Assessment, 68*, 251–266.

O'Donohue, W., & Bradley, A.R. (1999). Conceptual and empirical issues in child custody evaluations. *Clinical Psychology: Science and Practice, 6*, 310–322.

Onufrak, B., Saylor, C.F., Taylor, M.J., Eyberg, S.M., & Boyce, G.C. (1995). Determinants of responsiveness in mothers of children with intraventricular hemorrhage. *Journal of Pediatric Psychology, 20*, 587–99.

Ostroff, C. (1993). Comparing correlations based on individual-level and aggregate data. *Journal of Applied Psychology, 78*, 569–582.

Otto, R. K. (2002). Use of the MMPI-2 in forensic settings. *Journal of Forensic Psychology Practice, 2*, 71–91.

Otto, R.K., & Collins, R.P. (1995). Use of the MMPI-2/MMPI-A in child custody evaluations. In Y. S. Ben-Porath, J. R. Graham, G. C. N. Hall, R. Hirschman, & M.S. Zaragoza (Eds.), *Forensic applications of the MMPI-2* (pp. 222–252). Thousand Oaks, CA: Sage.

Otto, R.K., Edens, J.F., & Barcus, E.H. (2000). The use of psychological testing in child custody evaluations. *Family and Conciliation Courts Review, 38*, 312–340.

Paulhus, D.L. (1998). *Paulhus Deception Scales (PDS): The Balanced Inventory of Desirable Responding–7*. North Tonawanda, NY: Multi-Helth Systems.

Pett, M.A., Wampold, B.E., Turner, C.W., & Vaughan-Cole, B. (1999). Paths of influence of divorce and preschool children's psychosocial adjustment. *Journal of Family Psychology, 13*, 145–164.

Pruett, K.D., & Pruett, M.K. (1999). "Only God decides": Young children's perceptions of divorce and the legal system. *Journal of the American Academy of Child and Adolescent Psychiatry, 38*, 1544–1550.

Pruett, M.K., Williams, T.Y., Insabella, G., & Little, T.D. (2003). Family and legal indicators of child adjustment to divorce among families with young children. *Journal of Family Psychology, 17*, 169–180.

Ramsey, S.H., & Kelley, R.F. (2004). Social science knowledge in family law cases: Judicial gate-keeping in the *Daubert* era. *University of Miami Law Review, 59*, 1–81.

Reitman, D., Currier, O.R., & Stickle, T.R. (2002). A critical evaluation of the Parenting Stress Index–Short Form (SPSI-SF) in a Head Start population. *Journal of Clinical Child and Adolescent Psychology, 31*, 384–392.

Repetti, R.L., & Wood, J. (1997) Families accommodating to chronic stress: Unintended and unnoticed processes. In B.H. Gottlieb (Ed.), *Coping with chronic stress* (pp. 191–220). New York: Plenum.

Robinson, W.S. (1950). Ecological correlations and the behavior of individuals. *American Sociological Review, 15*, 351–357.

Rodriquez, C.M., & Green, A.J. (1997). Parenting stress and anger expression as predictor of child abuse potential. *Child Abuse and Neglect, 21*, 367–377.

Sanders, M.R., & McFarland, M. (2000). Treatment of depressed mothers with disruptive children: A controlled evaluation of cognitive behavioral family intervention. *Behavior Therapy, 31*, 89–112.

Santos, S. (1992). Adaptacao Portuguesa, Para Criances Em Idade Escolar, Do Parenting Stress Index (PSI): Resultados Preliminares. *Revista Portuguesa de Psicologia, 28*, 115–132.

Saylor, C.F., Boyce G.C., & Price, C. (2003). Early predictions of school-age behavior problems and social skills in children with intraventricular hemorrhage (IVH). *Child Psychiatry and Human Development, 33*, 175–192.

Schiller, E.W. (2003). Gender differences in coping and stress among parents of children with complex congenital heart disease (CHD). *Dissertation Abstracts International: B: The Sciences and Engineering, 64*(5-B), 2404.

Selye, H. (1952). *The story of adaptation syndrome*. Montreal, Quebec, Canada: Acto.

Selye, H. (1974). *Stress without distress*. Philadelphia: J.P. Lippincott.

Seo, S. (2003). Maternal self-efficacy, quality of parenting, and child development outcome among mothers with young children from Early Head Start. Michigan State University PhD. 2003. (UMI) Publication Number AAT 3100497 ISBN 0-496-48088-: Dissertation Abstracts International (DAI-A 64/08, p. 2774, Feb 2004).

Sheras, P.L., Abidin, R.R. & Konold, T.R. (1998). *Stress Index for Parents of Adolescents: Professional manual*. Lutz, FL: Psychological Assessment Resources.

Shuman, D.W. (2002). The role of mental health experts in custody decisions: Science, psychological tests, and clinical judgment. *Family Law Quarterly, 36*, 135–162.

Solis, M.L., & Abidin, R.R. (1991). The Spanish version Parenting Stress Index: A psychometric study. *Journal of Clinical Child Psychology, 20*, 372–378.

Strong, D.R., Greene, R.L., Hoppe, C., Johnston, T., & Olesen, N. (1999). Taxometric analysis of impression management and self-deception on the MMPI-2 in child-custody litigation. *Journal of Personality Assessment, 73*, 1–18.

Strong, D.R., Greene, R.L., & Kordinak, S.T. (2002). Taxometric analysis of impression management and self-deception in college student and personnel evaluation settings. *Journal of Personality Assessment, 78*, 161–175.

Tam, K.-K., Chan, Y.-C., & Wong, C.-K., M. (1994). Validation of the Parenting Stress Index among Chinese mothers in Hong Kong. *Journal of Community Psychology, 22*(3), 211–223.

Teti, D.M., Nakagawa, M., Das, R., & Wirth, O. (1991). Security of attachment between preschoolers and their mothers: Relations among social interaction, parenting stress, and mother's sorts of the Attachment Q-Set. *Developmental Psychology, 27*, 440–447.

Tippins, T., & Wittman, J. (2005). Empirical and ethical problems with custody recommendations. *Family Court Review, 43,* 193–222.

Tomanik, S., Harris, G.E., & Hawkins, J. (2004). The relationship between behaviors exhibited by children with autism and maternal stress. *Journal of Intellectual and Developmental Disability, 29,* 16–26.

Trute, B. (2003). Grandparents of children with developmental disabilities: Intergenerational support and family well-being. *Families in Society, 84,* 119–126.

Waisbren, S.E., Albers, S., Amato, S., Ampola, M., Brewster, T.G., Demmer, L., et al. (2003). Effect of expanded newborn screening for biochemical genetic disorders on child outcomes and parental stress. *Journal of the American Medical Association, 290,* 2564–2572.

Wakschlag, L.S., & Keenan, K. (2001). Clinical significance and correlates of disruptive behavior in environmentally at-risk preschoolers. *Journal of Clinical Child Psychology. 30,* 262–275.

Webster-Stratton, C. (1988). Mothers' and fathers' perceptions of child deviance: Roles as parent and child behaviors and parent adjustment. *Journal of Consulting and Clinical Psychology, 56,* 909–915.

Weiss, J.A., Sullivan, A., & Diamond, T. (2003). Parent stress and adaptive functioning of individuals with developmental disabilities. *Journal on Developmental Disabilities, 10*(1), 129–135.

Wilfong, E.W., Saylor, C., & Elksnin, N. (1991). Influences on responsiveness: Interactions between mothers and their premature infants. *Infant Mental Health Journal, 12,* 31–40.

Willner, P., & Goldstein, R.C. (2001). Mediation of depression by perceptions of defeat and entrapment in high-stress mothers. *British Journal of Medical Psychology, 74,* 473–485.

Wong, D.F., Lam, D.O., & Kwoak, S.Y. (2003). Stresses and mental health of fathers with younger children in Hong Kong: Implications for social work practices. *International Social Work, 46,* 103–119.

Note: To obtain a more complete topically arranged PSI research reference list, readers are encouraged to access the home page of the first author at http://www.people.virginia.edu/~rra/.

Author Index

A

Abidin, R.R., 15, *16*, 297, 299, 300, 301, 302, 303, 305, 306, 307, 316, 318, *320, 321, 323, 324, 327*
Abracen, J., 157, *176*
Achenbach, T.M., 15, *16*, 78, *83*, 234, 236, 241, 242, 243, 244, 245, 246, 247, 248, 249, 254, *259, 260, 261, 262*, 264, *294*
Ackerman, M.C., 10, *16, 83*, 133, *139*, 310, 312, *321*
Ackerman, M.J., 10, *16, 83*, 133, *139*, 310, 312, *321*
Ackerman, R.J., 133, *144*
Ackerman, S., 191, *204*
Acklin, M.W., 186, *203*
Adamakos, H., 307, *321*
Adams, N., 33, *52*
Ahlmeyer, S., 133, *139*
Aiduk, R., 25, 26, *48, 49*
Aikman, G.G., 286, *294*
Ainsworth, M.D., 183, *205*
Akerlind, I., 27, *48*
Albaugh, B., 32–33, *51, 54*
Albers, S., 307, *328*
Alexander, P.C., 132, *139*
Allain, N., 28, *55*
Allan, A., 29, *53*
Allan, M.M., 29, *53*
Allen, J.G., 132, *139*
Allison, J.A., 309, 318, *321*
Almagor, M., 22, 25, *49, 52*
Almqvist, F., 243, 253, *261*
Alnaes, R., 130, *144*
Alperin, J.J., 64, 69, *83*
Alterman, A.I., 95, 102, 108, *116*, 153, 154, *177*
Amato, P.R., 313, *321*
Amato, S., 307, *328*
Amos, N.L., 156, *178*

B

Ampola, M., 307, *328*
Anastasi, A., 153, *172*
Anastopoulos, A.D., 307, 308, *321*
Andershed, H., 169, *176*
Andershed, H.A., 165, *172*
Anderson, C.L., 132, *139*
Anderson, G.L., 64, *83*
Anderson, R.W., 27, *51*
Andrews, B.P., 156, *176*
Andronikof-Sanglade, A., 190, *204*
Angleitner, A., 248, 251, *262*
Angold, A., 72, *83*
Anthony, C., 158, *174*
Appelbaum, P.S., 153, *178*
Arbisi, P.A., 20, 21, 24, 25, 26, 27, 30, 31, 32, 47, *48, 50, 55*, 65, *83*
Archer, R.P., 1, 10, *16*, 19, 25, 26, *48, 49, 50*, 57, 59, 60, 61, 63, 64, 65, 68, 69, 70, 71, 72, 73, 74, 75, 76, 77, 79, 81, *83, 84, 85, 86*, 182, 188, *203, 206*
Arend, R., 247, *260*
Armstrong, J., 194, *203*
Arnett, J.J., 169, 170, *172*
Arsenault, L., 194, *206*
Arvey, R.D., 27, *53*
Ash, P., 311, *321*
Ashendorf, L., 216, *225*
Atlis, M.M., 31, *50*
Auble, P.M., 97, 104, *117*
Austin, W.G., 297, 308, 310, 311, 314, *321*
Avery, R.D., 27, *49*

B

Babiak, P., 25, 31, 153, *172*
Bacchiochi, J.R., 98, 99, *116*
Baer, R.A., 20, 25, 31, 37, *49, 55*, 65, *84*

SUBJECT INDEX

Page references followed by *f* indicate a figure and *t* indicate a table.

A